NEW ENGLAND
CAMPING

NEW ENGLAND
CAMPING

The Complete Guide to More Than
800 Tent and RV Campgrounds

Fourth Edition

Carol Cambo & Stephen Gorman

AVALON
TRAVEL

FOGHORN OUTDOORS NEW ENGLAND CAMPING

Fourth Edition

Carol Cambo & Stephen Gorman

Text © 2005 by Carol Cambo and Stephen Gorman.
All rights reserved.
Maps © 2005 by Avalon Travel Publishing.
All rights reserved.

Printing History
1st edition—1997
Fourth edition—March 2005
5 4 3 2 1

 Avalon Travel Publishing
An Imprint of
AVALON Avalon Publishing Group, Inc.
publishing group incorporated

ISBN: 1-56691-603-8
ISSN: 1093-2739

Editor: Christopher Jones
Series Manager: Grace Fujimoto
Acquisitions Editor: Rebecca Browning
Copy Editor: Donna Leverenz
Graphics Coordinator: Justin Marler
Production Coordinator: Tabitha Lahr
Cover and Interior Designer: Darren Alessi
Map Editor: Kevin Anglin, Olivia Solís
Cartographers: Kat Kalamaras, Kat Smith, Mike Morgenfeld
Indexer: Christopher Jones
Illustrator: Bob Race

Front cover photo: © Stephen Gorman

Printed in the United States of America by Worzalla

About the Author

Stephen Gorman's work has taken him to the Lewis and Clark Trail in Montana's rugged Missouri Breaks, remote Inupiat Eskimo villages in arctic Alaska, and the World War II airfields and turquoise lagoons of Midway Atoll.

Always an active participant in his areas of interest, Stephen has worked as a cowboy on a ranch in Wyoming, an exploration geologist in Alaska and Nevada, and an Outward Bound wilderness instructor throughout the U.S. and Canada.

Stephen holds a Master's Degree in Environmental Studies from Yale and a Bachelor's Degree in American Studies from Wesleyan. Throughout his career, he has worked on assignment for magazines such as *Men's Journal, National Geographic, Sports Illustrated, Boston Globe Magazine, Sierra, Outside,* and *Yankee.*

Stephen has a lifelong interest in history, conservation, and land-use issues. Prior to devoting himself to writing and photography, he conducted National Wild and Scenic River studies for the National Park Service. He and his wife Mary live in Norwich, Vermont, where they enjoy easy access to the mountains, forests, rivers, and lakes of northern New England.

About the Author

Upon graduating college in 1988, Carol Cambo repeatedly fielded the dreaded question: "What's next for you?"

How *would* she be using her magna cum laude degree to its fullest potential? Her parents were less than thrilled with her answer: Carol and her boyfriend had mapped out a grand Kerouac-ian plan to save up their summer earnings and travel across the country, living out of a van. She may even have been so bold as to call it a "graduate level course in real life." As every traveler knows, some of the best lessons are learned outside of a classroom, and from those four months on the road, from seeing America's parks and city slums up close to camping on mountainsides and behind truck stops, she learned that she had a yen for leading the less-showered life.

This masochistic yearning led her to spend two summers in a tent on the banks of the Yukon River in Alaska in the early '90s. She helped raise 50 Huskies–sled-dogs-in-training–and fed them salmon that she had fished for herself. Always with a notebook and camera by her side, fueled by the dream of the writer's life, she waitressed her way through her frugal freelancing years. Eventually she began writing columns for newspapers and branched out into magazine work. In the mid-'90s, *Yankee* magazine made a mainstream woman out of her, hiring her as a writer and editor and paying her enough to afford indoor plumbing.

Her parents were thrilled to learn that when she married and moved to Massachusetts, she would finally be going back to school, if only as the editor of the UMass Amherst alumni magazine. Despite having a cushy state job, camping is never far from her mind.

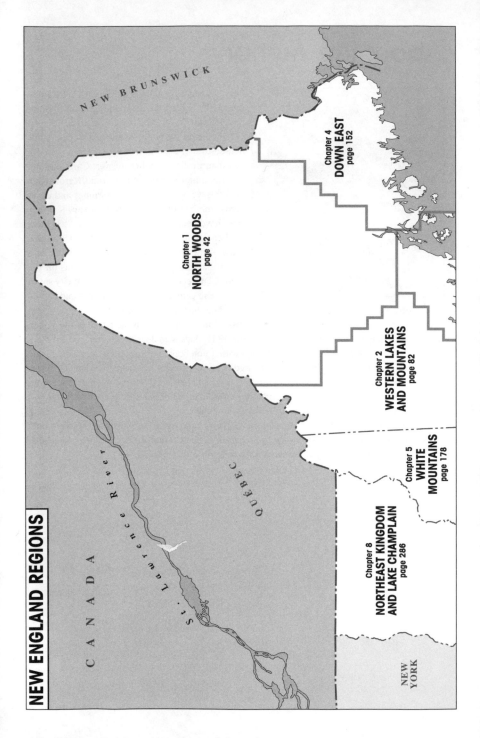

NEW ENGLAND REGIONS

NEW BRUNSWICK

CANADA

St. Lawrence River

QUEBEC

NEW YORK

Chapter 1
NORTH WOODS
page 42

Chapter 4
DOWN EAST
page 152

Chapter 2
WESTERN LAKES
AND MOUNTAINS
page 82

Chapter 5
WHITE
MOUNTAINS
page 178

Chapter 8
NORTHEAST KINGDOM
AND LAKE CHAMPLAIN
page 286

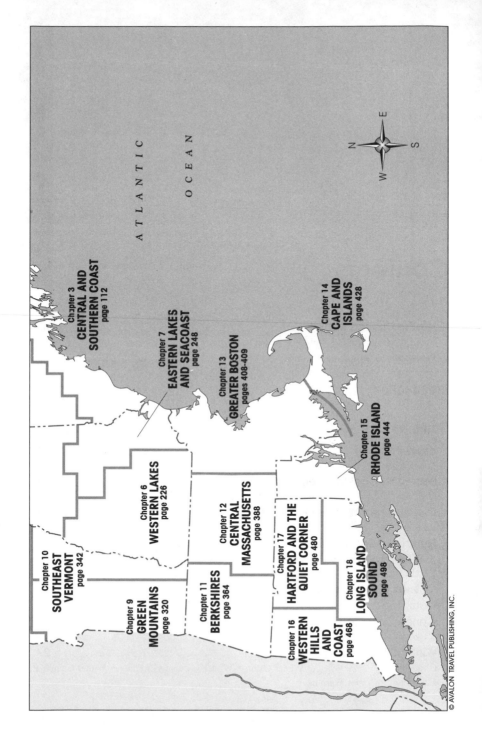

N E S W

ATLANTIC OCEAN

Chapter 3
CENTRAL AND
SOUTHERN COAST
page 112

Chapter 7
EASTERN LAKES
AND SEACOAST
page 248

Chapter 13
GREATER BOSTON
pages 408–409

Chapter 14
CAPE AND
ISLANDS
page 428

Chapter 15
RHODE ISLAND
page 444

Chapter 6
WESTERN LAKES
page 226

Chapter 10
SOUTHEAST
VERMONT
page 342

Chapter 12
CENTRAL
MASSACHUSETTS
page 388

Chapter 17
HARTFORD AND THE
QUIET CORNER
page 480

Chapter 9
GREEN
MOUNTAINS
page 320

Chapter 11
BERKSHIRES
page 364

Chapter 18
LONG ISLAND
SOUND
page 498

Chapter 16
WESTERN
HILLS AND
COAST
page 468

© AVALON TRAVEL PUBLISHING, INC.

Contents

Special Topics

Plan Ahead 3 • Campground Ethics 5 • Campfires 7 • The Dangers of Dehydration 9 • Sanitation 10 • Travel Lightly 11 • Camp with Care 16 • Keep the Wilderness Wild 19 • Respect Other Users 23 • Winter Gear Checklist 24 • Camping Gear Checklist 26

Best Campgrounds

MAINE

Including:
- Allagash River
- Aroostook River
- Attean Pond
- Bangor
- Baxter State Park
- Chesuncook Lake
- Cold Stream Pond
- Eagle Lake
- East Grand Lake
- Echo Lake
- First Roach Pond
- Flagstaff Lake
- Frost Pond
- Greenville
- Jackman
- Kennebec River
- Lake Moxie
- Lake Parlin

- Long Pond
- Medway
- Millinocket
- Moose River
- Moosehead Lake
- Mount Katahdin
- Newport
- Penobscot River
- Pleasant Lake
- Presque Isle
- Pushaw Lake
- Ripogenus Lake
- Sebasticook Lake
- Sebec Lake
- St. Froid Lake
- Wassataquoik Stream
- Wesserunsett Lake
- Wood Pond

Including:
- Androscoggin
- Androscoggin Lake
- Annabessacook Lake
- Appalachian Mountains
- Aziscohos Lake
- Bay of Naples
- Bear Pond

- Belgrade Lakes
- Bethel
- Brownfield
- Crescent Lake
- Cupsuptic Lake
- Dead River
- Flagstaff Lake
- Fryeburg

NEW HAMPSHIRE

- Echo Lake
- Franconia Notch State Park
- Iona Lake
- Jacobs Brook
- Lake Francis
- Lost River
- Meadow Brook
- Moore Reservoir
- Moores Pond
- Ossipee Lake
- Patch Brook

- Pemigewasset River
- Saco River
- Swain Brook
- Swift River
- Twin Mountain
- Umbagog Lake
- Walker Brook
- White Lake
- White Lake State Park
- White Mountain National Forest
- Wild River

Including:
- Beaver Pond
- Canaan Street Lake
- Cass Pond
- Cheshire Pond
- Contoocook Lake
- Henniker
- Hillsborough
- Lake Massasecum
- Mascoma Lake

- Mount Monadnock
- New Boston
- Norway Pond
- Otter Lake
- Pontanipo Pond
- Rand Pond
- Sip Pond
- Sugar River
- Surry Mountain Lake
- Swanzey Lake

Including:
- Angle Pond
- Ayers Lake
- Baxter Lake
- Country Pond
- Dead Pond
- Epsom Four Corners
- Exeter River
- Great Bay
- Great East Lake
- Gunstock Mountain
- Hampton Beach
- Island Pond
- Lake Ivanhoe
- Lake Wentworth
- Lake Winnipesaukee
- Little Squam Lake
- Massabesic Lake
- Milton Pond

- Moultonborough Neck
- North Pond
- Ossipee
- Paugus Bay
- Pawtuckaway Lake
- Pemigewasset Lake
- Pemigewasset River
- Province Lake
- Rochester Reservoir
- Seabrook Beach
- Shaw Brook
- Silver Lake
- Swains Lake
- Tuxbury Pond
- Wash Pond
- Weirs Beach
- Wheelright Pond
- Winnisquam Lake

VERMONT

MASSACHUSETTS

RHODE ISLAND

CONNECTICUT

Our Commitment

We are committed to making *Foghorn Outdoors New England Camping* the most accurate, thorough, and enjoyable camping guide to the region. With this fourth edition you can rest assured that every campground in this book has been carefully reviewed and accompanied by the most up-to-date information. Be aware that with the passing of time some of the fees listed herein may have changed, and campgrounds may have closed unexpectedly. If you have a specific need or concern, it's best to call the location ahead of time.

If you would like to comment on the book, whether it's to suggest a campground we overlooked, or to let us know about any noteworthy experience—good or bad—that occurred while using *Foghorn Outdoors New England Camping* as your guide, we would appreciate hearing from you. Please address correspondence to:

Foghorn Outdoors New England Camping, fourth edition
Avalon Travel Publishing
1400 65th Street, Suite 250
Emeryville, CA 94608

email: atpfeedback@avalonpub.com
If you send us an email, please put "New England Camping" in the subject line.

How to Use This Book

Foghorn Outdoors New England Camping is divided into six sections, one for each state: Maine, New Hampshire, Vermont, Massachusetts, Rhode Island, and Connecticut. Each state, with the exception of Rhode Island, is then broken down into smaller chapters based on regional divisions. Maps at each chapter's beginning show where all the campgrounds in that region are located.

For **Maine** campgrounds see:
North Woods, pages 39–77
Western Lakes and Mountains, pages 79–107
Central and Southern Coast, pages 109–148
Down East, pages 157–180

For **New Hampshire** campgrounds see:
White Mountains, pages 175–221
Western Lakes, pages 223–243
Eastern Lakes and Seacoast, pages 245–280

For **Vermont** campgrounds see:
Northeast Kingdom and Lake Champlain, pages 283–316
Green Mountains, pages 317–337
Southeast Vermont, pages 339–357

For **Massachusetts** campgrounds see:
Berkshires, pages 361–383
Central Massachusetts, pages 385–403
Greater Boston, pages 405–423
Cape and Islands, pages 425–441

For **Rhode Island** campgrounds see: pages 445–462

For **Connecticut** campgrounds see:
Western Hills and Coast, pages 465–475
Hartford and the Quiet Corner, pages 477–493
Long Island Sound, pages 495–514

You can search for the ideal campsite in two ways:
1. If you know the name of the specific campground where you'd like to stay, or the name of the surrounding geographical area or nearby feature (town, national or state park or forest, mountain, lake, river, etc.), look it up in the index.
2. If you know the general area you want to visit, turn to the New England map and map list on the preceding pages. Find the state or region in which your destination lies, and turn to that map at the beginning of that chapter. You can then determine which campsites are in or near your destination by their corresponding numbers. Opposite the map will be a chapter table of contents listing each campsite in the chapter by map number and the page number it's profiled on. Then turn to the corresponding page for the campground you're interested in.

About the Campground Profiles

Each campground in this book is listed in a consistent, easy-to-read format to help you choose the ideal camping spot. From a general overview of the setting to detailed driving directions, the profile will provide all the information you need. Here is an example:

Map number and campground name ➤

1 SOMEWHERE USA CAMPGROUND

🏃 🚴 🏊 🏕 🐕 ⛹ ♿ 🚐 ⛰

◄ Icons noting activities and facilities at or nearby the campground

General location of the campground named by its proximity to the nearest major town or landmark ➤

Rating: 10 ◄ Rating, on a scale of 1–10

South of Somewhere USA Lake

Symbol indicating that the campground is listed among the top author's picks ➤

Each campground in this book begins with a brief overview of its setting. The description typically covers ambience, information about the attractions, and activities popular at the campground.

Campsites, facilities: This section provides the number of campsites for both tents and RVs and whether hookups are available. Facilities such as restrooms, picnic areas, recreation areas, laundry, and dump stations will be addressed, as well as the availability of piped water, showers, playground, stores, and others amenities. The campground's pet policy is also mentioned here.

Reservations, fees: This section notes whether reservations are accepted, and the rates for tent sites and RV sites. If there are additional fees for parking or pets, or discounted weekly or seasonal rates, those will also be noted here.

Directions: This section provides mile-by-mile driving directions to the campground from the nearest major town.

Contact: This section provides an address, phone number, and Internet address, if available, for each campground.

About the Icons

The icons in this book are designed to provide at-a-glance information on activities, facilities, and services provided that are available on-site or within walking distance of each campground. The icons are not meant to represent every activity or service, but rather those that are most significant.

 — Hiking trails are available.

— Biking trails or routes are available. This usually refers to mountain biking, although it may represent road cycling as well. Refer to the text for that campground for details.

— Swimming opportunities are available.

— Fishing opportunities are available.

— Boating opportunities are available. Various types of vessels apply under this umbrella activity, including motorboats and personal watercrafts (Jet Skis). Refer to the text for that campground for more details, including mph restrictions and boat ramp availability.

 — Canoeing and/or kayaking opportunities are available. Typically, canoeing is available on inland lakes and rivers, whereas kayaking is available along the coast. Refer to the text for that campground for more details.

— Winter sports are available. This general category may include activities such as downhill skiing, cross-country skiing, snowshoeing, snowmobiling, snowboarding, and ice skating. Refer to the text for that campground for more details on which sports are available.

— Pets are permitted. Campgrounds that allow pets may require an additional fee or that pets be leashed. Campgrounds may also restrict pet size or behavior. Refer to the text for that campground for specific instructions or call in advance.

— A playground is available. A campground with a playground can be desirable for campers traveling with children.

— Wheelchair access is provided, as advertised by campground managers. However, concerned persons are advised to call the contact number of a campground to be certain that their specific needs will be met.

— The campground is in a remote location or may be difficult to reach. The icon represents the 5% of American vacationers who actively seek to escape the crowds and to discover California's hidden gems.

— RV sites are provided.

— Tent sites are provided.

— Hunting is permitted. Campers need to be aware of hunting season in a particular state, and that they may be near hunters when camping in some state parks or in the backcountry. Hunting is a popular sport throughout New England; the season varies from state to state, but generally extends from fall into early winter. Call the state departments of Fish and Game or park and forest offices to find out actual dates.

About the Maps

This book is divided into chapters based on regions; an overview map of these regions precedes the table of contents and is printed on the inside of the back cover. At the start of each chapter, you'll find a map of the entire region, enhanced by a grid that divides the region into smaller sections. These sections are then enlarged into individual detail maps. Campgrounds are noted on the detail maps by number.

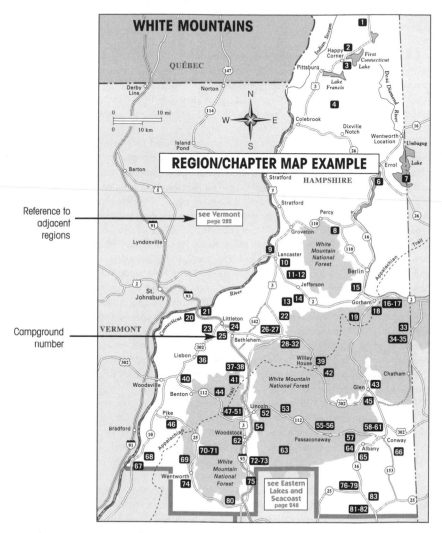

Reference to adjacent regions

Campground number

Preface

New England is the birthplace of America. Whether you set up camp near the bricks and mortar of American history, or beside a rippleless pond at sunset, you'll find the roots of freedom here, and much more in between.

New England has been called the nation's attic, tucked away up here in the eaves atop all the other states. And like any good attic, New England holds a wealth of cherished memories and treasured antiques—family heirlooms, if you will—reminders of who we are and where we come from.

Poke around a bit and you turn up the Pilgrims and the first Thanksgiving, Paul Revere's midnight ride, the Battle of Bunker Hill. Look around a little more and you come across the first flourishes of our nation's literature, the founding of American education, the flowering of American art and music. Before long you discover curious artifacts scattered about, like the House of the Seven Gables, Plymouth Rock, the Old North Church, covered bridges, and the tall ships of the Yankee whaling fleet.

In many parts of New England, life goes on much as it used to: Maine lobstermen still set their traps in the frothy swells; Vermont farmers still harvest a bumper crop of rocks in the fall (the raw material for all those stone walls snaking through the woods); students still sit reading under the oaks in Harvard Yard in Cambridge. But New England has changed too, even since the first edition of this book was published. Like many places in the country, development and new housing is changing the landscape faster than it can be preserved. As we updated campgrounds, we noted a handful of small campgrounds that didn't survive, and just as many new ones that look less like campgrounds than theme parks. As society has shifted, so have campers' demands: Many campground owners know that to stay in business they must offer cable TV and Internet access for at least some of their guests. Many have begun building cabins to supplement campsites, since some folks simply don't want to pitch a tent anymore.

Still, nature is truly in charge here, and no matter where you go in New England, you are never far from the outdoors. This is an uncompromising landscape—an Old Testament kind of place: mostly harsh and demanding, sometimes benevolent, always stern. Whether in downtown Boston or in the high White Mountains, nature touches everyone's lives, as she has for many generations. As a result, most Yankees feel a closeness to the land born of familiarity and respect. Perhaps more than any other region, nature has molded the New England character, dictating who the people are, what they do, and when they do it.

Though it seems winter lasts forever in New England ("nine months of snow and three months of damn poor sleddin'" is a phrase commonly heard in the north), nature furnishes a medley of seasons. Autumn, though glorious in its extravagant hues, is a time of hurried preparation for the fierce winter to come. Winter is actually four or five months of ice, cold, and snow. Spring is an explosion of rebirth. And, though short, summer is a sunny reward for making it through another year.

Not only does New England have well-defined seasons, it has a rich palette of landscapes as well. From the Arctic tundra of the high mountain summits, through the heavily forested uplands, to the gleaming granite islands off the Maine coast and the sandy shores of Cape Cod, New England packs the greatest variety into the smallest package. Though New England is a small geographic area (the entire region is only one-third the size of California, for example), it looms large in the national consciousness. Nowhere else will you find the marvelous array of cultural and natural amenities within easy reach of each other.

© MAINE OFFICE OF TOURISM/JEFF GREENBERG

Introduction

A man may stand here and put all America behind him.
—Henry David Thoreau, *Cape Cod*

Diversity is the hallmark of New England camping. Though this little collection of six states in the upper right-hand corner of the map is but a small portion of the entire country, it offers the traveler an unparalleled variety of rich and memorable experiences.

New England is blessed with one of the most beautiful landscapes imaginable, and camping is perhaps the best way to get out there and enjoy it. Camping in New England means: sharing a crackling fire with friends as the haunting cry of the loon echoes across a vast wilderness lake; watching the brightest stars you've ever seen pulse brightly in the inky night sky; climbing high rocky mountain summits; rafting down wild and rapid rivers; catching your limit of big game fish in both saltwater and fresh.

And though the New England outdoors holds a special allure, camping in New England is also about: visiting historic battlefields where our nation's story begins; spending leisurely days poking around picture-perfect small villages where life goes on much as it used to; enjoying an evening out on the town in historic Boston; savoring a lobster pulled fresh from the sea; sailing a three-masted schooner along the bold rocky coast.

If you decide to give New England camping a try, come prepared for four seasons of wide-ranging activities and adventures. Whether you want to go backpacking or mountain biking, canoe camping or fly-fishing, white-water rafting or sea kayaking, rock climbing or merely apple picking or walking down a peaceful country lane, you'll find ample opportunities to do it here. No other part of the country offers such a rich and eclectic menu of things to see and do.

The campgrounds in New England are as varied as the landscape, the seasons, and the activities. If you are looking for large motor-home parks near the city or the beach, you'll have your choice of locations catering to your every whim. And if you are searching for a remote campsite in the wildest country outside of Alaska, you'll find that here too. New England camping is about having it all.

Camping Tips

Keep It Simple

The first sound I heard when I shut off the engine was the flutelike song of the wood thrush. Then I caught a whiff of sunshine and soil wafting through the open window. I shut my eyes for a moment and breathed deeply. Still jittery from a harried drive, I got out and cinched my pack with trembling hands (too much coffee? too many close encounters with tractor-trailers?), then I shut and locked the car door. Casting a quick glance at my companions, I thought they looked a bit tense too. But soon, I knew, our careworn expressions would brighten as Vermont's Green Mountains worked their magic on us.

We left the trailhead parking lot, turned toward the forest, and confronted a dense canopy, an impenetrable green thicket as mysterious as any Amazonian jungle. I thought about machetes—the vegetation was that thick. But probing the foliage was a slight opening leading in and then disappearing around a bend: the Long Trail. Our trail. That rough footpath to Canada was all the invitation we needed. We strode through the slim gap into the obscure half-light of the north woods and slipped from view.

The track lured us upward through a cool understory of hobblebush and moosewood. The worries I had carried from home vanished around the time I noticed scrolls of peeling birch bark unfurling like banners in the soft breeze. Among the birches stood silver beech trees with smooth trunks scarred by the claws of foraging bears. Through gaps in the canopy I caught glimpses of a long blue gash in the valley below: Lake Champlain. Beyond the lake the high peaks of the Adirondack Mountains in New York state scratched the sky. Barely half an hour on the trail and I had shed most of my early 21st-century, information-age anxieties, trading them for the peace and tranquillity I can only find outdoors.

(F) Plan Ahead

Everything you do before you hit the trail makes your time out there less hectic and much more enjoyable. Here's a checklist to help speed you on your way. Copy it and post it on your refrigerator, on your closet door, in the garage, or wherever it will be most helpful.
- Learn about the regulations and issues that apply to the area you're visiting.
- Obtain maps, permits, and emergency contact numbers.
- Plan your route. Tell a friend where you are going and when you will be back.
- Prepare your menu and purchase camping food during the week when you do your regular shopping.
- Top off your car's gas tank the night before you depart.
- Run any errands, such as using an ATM machine, the night before.
- Check gear and clothing to be sure it's in good repair.
- Make a personal gear, group gear, clothing, and food checklist. Post it wherever you store your equipment and check off items as you pack.
- Pack the evening before you plan to depart. Make sure everything fits comfortably inside your car or backpack.

Our greatest escape artist, Henry David Thoreau, wrote, "I think I cannot preserve my health and spirits, unless I spend four hours a day at least—and it is commonly more than that—sauntering through the woods and over the hills and fields, absolutely free from all worldly engagements." Modern saunterers, we practice what he preached, seeking the simple pleasures offered by the woods and hills. These outings restore us; they provide a necessary counterbalance to the pressures of daily life.

For me, replenishing mind and body after a hard week means spending at least a night, and preferably two, on the trail. I find the trick is to get out there as quickly as possible. But getting away for more than a day introduces the problem of toting adequate food and shelter. The answer: "Simplify," said Thoreau.

In a lifetime of wilderness wandering, I've concluded that the Master was quite correct. The simpler the outfit, the faster we can get out and leave our worries behind. John Muir was reportedly a genius at this: leaving all the heavy gear behind, he stuffed his pockets full of bread crumbs and hopped the back fence. Muir was on to something.

Personally, I'd rather lose myself in the color of the sunset than focus on my aching shoulders. And if I don't have to expend precious energy microtuning some equipment "design breakthrough" of dubious merit, I am happiest. I value my outfit most if I am utterly unaware of it. The gear is a means to an end, and the end is to get out there as quickly and easily as possible.

Travel Light

The joys of traveling light are many. For starters, it's easier on your back. It's also a lot easier on your wallet. And it's easier to hit the trail when there's less to organize. But the key to intelligent paring away isn't to do without; it's to do without excess. Your needs are shaped by where you travel. Climate and terrain aren't constant, so a Vermonter would be foolish to mimic a Californian's load. And vice versa.

Think about where you're going and then take a look at your gear. Can you go with the light sleeping bag if you wear extra clothes to sleep? Will a mug do double duty as a bowl? Will a light tarp serve instead of a tent?

Lighten up and the effect amplifies: Leave the heavy wafflestompers behind and hike in comfortable lightweight boots. Then you can ditch the comfy camp shoes as well!

Some load paring is done for us by the gear manufacturers, who consistently turn out new, lightweight materials weighing a fraction of what their bloated ancestors did. As an added bonus, these new materials are often stronger and perform better. By being a smart shopper who buys well-made, lightweight designs—especially those that serve more than one purpose—and little else, you will reduce your load and still bring everything you need.

Food and Cooking Gear

All the wisdom I have gained during my lifetime has funneled down into a simple understanding. There is one chief human desire driving our existence on the planet: humans live to eat. This is never more true than when outdoors and camping. Our bodies need the right fuel at the right time to keep operating smoothly. And food really does seem to taste better when eaten outdoors or after a long day on the trail.

With some forethought and an open mind, you will be a well-fed, and therefore happy, camper. Vittles are vital to our emotional well-being. Time spent in the planning reduces your food-related chores in the field and lets you concentrate on what's really important—the Great Outdoors.

Four of us once skied out of the wintry wilderness after a seven-day hut tour in a northeast mountain range with smug, slightly self-righteous grins. We had planned our food needs so closely that

Ⓕ Keep It Wild: A Guide to Campground Ethics

As America's cities and towns become increasingly crowded, a growing number of people are turning to the outdoors for serenity, simplicity, and solitude. That's the good news. The bad news is that as urban centers become increasingly crowded, a growing number of people are bringing their bad habits—primarily thoughtlessness toward fellow campers and a disrespect for the land—into the backcountry. Even folks who have the best intentions sometimes unwittingly go awry, taking the "great" out of the Great Outdoors for others.

Use common sense and consideration while camping. Common sense in a campground means keeping quiet; noise is the most common breach of campground ethics. It arrives in a variety of amplitudes, from the laughter of children sitting at a campfire roasting marshmallows at midnight to an all-out brawl between drinking buddies at the next campsite in the wee hours. A gas-powered electrical generator that can't be heard inside a well-insulated RV is torture for tent campers up to six sites away. A group that breaks up camp the moment the sun rises—rattling pots and pans, shouting orders, and running the car (or, worse, motorcycle) engine—can wake up everyone in the campground.

Other ways in which disrespect is manifested in the Great Outdoors are through carelessness with litter, spur-of-the-moment vandalism, and destruction of the natural environment. Litter—from trash left on a picnic table or strewn around a campsite to aluminum foil, beer cans, and glass tossed into a campfire pit—can be unsightly and annoying. It can also be a health hazard: have you ever been greeted by sewage left by an RVer who was too lazy to dispose of it at a dump station?

Vandalism and malicious destruction are increasing in the backcountry, too. Vandalism is immediately identifiable: graffiti; picnic tables and tree trunks carved with knives; and signs, garbage cans, and outhouses shot up for target practice. Considering recent and looming cuts in the budgets of the state and federal government agencies that oversee public lands, vandalized facilities may never be repaired or replaced. Worse, if picnic tables are smashed or cut up for firewood, toilets are removed from privies, and water pumps are knocked over by vehicles, the campground itself may be in danger of being closed permanently.

To promote responsible camping, we repeat: "Enjoy America's country and leave no trace." That's the motto of the Leave No Trace program, and we strongly support it. Promoting responsible outdoor recreation through education, research, and partnerships is its mission. Look for the **Keep It Wild Tips,** developed from the policies of Leave No Trace, sprinkled throughout the Camping Tips section.

For a free pocket-sized, weatherproof card printed with these policies, as well as information that details how to minimize human impact on wild areas, contact Leave No Trace at P.O. Box 997, Boulder CO, 80306, 800/332-4100, website: www.lnt.org.

---

between us there remained a small sack of cheese, a few packets of oatmeal, some dried milk, and tea. In the course of our tour we encountered below-zero wind chills, whipping winds, blistering sun, relentless snow, and meddlesome rain. We covered nearly 60 miles of mountainous terrain on telemark skis carrying full backpacks. Starting out, we shouldered four days' worth of food and met up with our second installment at a mountaintop hut on the fourth night. How did we achieve such a near-perfect ratio of food consumption to food carried? Careful, pre-trip meal-by-meal planning.

Of course, there is a universal law of "out there" grubbing that allowed us to achieve this noshing nirvana—if it is edible, a hungry camper will eat it. Along the way, we helped ourselves to food other campers had left behind in the huts—instant mashed potatoes, mixed nuts, pasta—but we had enough to be comfortable without these bonus calories. Granted, we all agreed we could have carried a few more candy bars, tequila, and popcorn, but space and weight were so essential given our mode of travel that we pared down our meals to the essentials.

Planning your camp food this successfully is not rocket science. There is no mystery other than planning ahead and anticipating your needs. Food and cooking gear vary given your style of camping. There are big differences in what's needed for car camping, backpacking, and camping in extreme conditions. Start out with a basic mess kit you can adapt to every situation and make a meal-by-meal plan.

A basic cooking kit should consist of the following: a pair of nesting pots (they should be sizable but not so large that they dwarf your stove), coffeepot, frying pan (all of light-gauge aluminum), metal pot-grabber, plastic bowls, insulated cups, matches, lighter, knife, and spoons. A word about the pots: there are some excellent designs out there nowadays made out of lightweight aluminum with nonstick surfaces and grooved bottoms to prevent topples. Hurray for technology. Another advance is in insulating thermoses. Invest in the most lightweight model you can find—hot drinks on the trail are equally useful for reviving flagging spirits and chilled bodies.

Stoves

The most important piece of cooking gear is your stove. Drive-in sites will likely have a fire pit or ring or permanent hibachi for cooking over an

Stoves are available in many styles and burn a variety of fuels. These are three typical examples. Top: **White gas stoves** are the most popular because they are inexpensive and easy to find; they do require priming and can be explosive. Middle: **Gas canister stoves** burn propane, butane, isobutane, and mixtures of the three. These are the easiest to use but have two disadvantages: 1) Because the fuel is bottled, determining how much fuel is left can be difficult. 2) The fuel is limited to above-freezing conditions. Bottom: **Liquid fuel stoves** burn Coleman fuel, denatured alcohol, kerosene, and even gasoline; these fuels are economical and have a high heat output, but most must be primed.

open flame. There is nothing like a grilled dinner under the stars in the shadow of a mountain or by a lake, but even during the most favorable conditions, a stove is always a better way to cook anything in a pot and to boil water. More on water later.

Gasoline stoves are the most evolved species available. They are reliable in bad weather, and gasoline has the highest heat output of all stove fuels. Generally, gasoline stoves take white gas or Coleman fuel—it's not safe to burn leaded gas in them. It's safer to use additive-free white gas than unleaded gas that you can get at any drive-up pump, as white gas is less volatile. You'll have to make a trip to your nearest sporting goods store to get white gas, but if you camp with any kind of frequency, it's worth it.

If you are purchasing a stove, there's no reason to get anything other than a gasoline-burning rig. But if you are borrowing someone else's equipment, here are a few words about lesser fuels: Kerosene burns as hot as gas and is much less volatile. But it smells, and stoves that use it must be primed with alcohol or gasoline. Watch out if your fuel spills or leaks, too—you won't be able to get rid of the odor anytime soon. Propane is inexpensive, but the heavy steel cylinders it comes in are too cumbersome for anything but a four-wheeled outfit. Butane simply stops working at freezing temperatures, but stoves that take it need no pumping, priming, or filling—just attach a new cylinder.

There are a few other considerations when choosing a stove:

Stability: Take the stove out of the box and give it a tip test. I ruined a breakfast of perfectly delicious buckwheat pancakes with just-gathered wild red raspberries because of a precariously balanced stove. The unfortunate incident cast a cloud over the whole day.

Startability: Get a stove with a built-in fuel pump. They start faster and put out more heat.

Simmerability: Try to buy a model that offers some kind of flame adjustability so you don't end up with burnt crud in the bottom of all your pans.

Old Man Wind: Some stoves come with wind protection—usually a metal guard that surrounds the stove—or you can buy windstops à la carte (thin aluminum works best), and these also help to conserve fuel on trips where that's a concern.

Allow your salesperson to demonstrate how particular stoves work if they are willing. If not, read all the directions and try your stove outside in the relatively innocuous location of your backyard, not once, but several times. Get to know your stove.

Water Treatment

Lots of campgrounds have safe drinking water readily available from nearby spigots. However, in the winter and when backcountry camping, you'll have to find sources for water to cook and clean. You can pack in drinking water or become a backcountry chemist and treat the wild stuff. If you choose the latter, make sure there is water where you are camping! Consulting maps is sometimes not enough—try to talk to a ranger or a local. In the heat of summer, certain streambeds might dry up.

The two readily available treatments used by most campers to eliminate the health threats posed by microorganisms lurking in most streambeds are iodine tablets (funny tasting) or pump filters (awkward, not foolproof). Option three is to boil all your drinking and cooking water for at least one minute. This kills *Giardia* and any other vile critters waiting to make you sick. Then fill your water bottles, cap them tightly, set them in the stream and voilà!—cold, delicious, safe drinking water. In case of stove failure, always pack a bottle of iodine tablets for backup.

Planning Meals

If you're camping with a group, it's wise to invite along that friend who likes nothing better than to linger in camp all day cooking up a feast to regale his or her fellow campers with upon their return from the hinterlands. But most of us are out there for a reason—to get away from convention, to subsist without all the hindrances of our workaday lives. Domestically inclined campers are somewhat of an oxymoron. Thus, ideal meal planning results in hearty, good tasting meals without a lot of fuss. I like to start off the day with a hot drink and some oatmeal or granola, munch a cold lunch on the trail, and put the bulk of my culinary efforts into dinner.

Water filters are a wise investment since all wilderness water should be considered contaminated. Make sure the filter can be easily cleaned or has a replaceable cartridge. The filter pores must be 0.4 microns or less to remove bacteria.

Breakfast

Except for the dog days of summer, a hot drink in the morning, whether tea, coffee, or hot chocolate, seems to hit the spot. Cereals are lightweight and can be packaged in plastic bags with powdered milk already added. Just add water and you've got breakfast in your bowl. If it's going to be a scorcher, you might make your tea the night before and set it out to cool for a refreshing drink in the morning.

Dehydration doesn't just mean that your body is in need of water. It also means that you're in danger of a rising body temperature, nausea, and, in hot weather, suffering from heat-related illness. The solution? Replace your body fluids by drinking lots of water, 8–10 cups per day, and up to a gallon if the weather is warm or if you're really active.

If you're feeling thirsty, you are mildly dehydrated. But if you're experiencing headaches and dry mouth—and your urine output is under two cups over 24 hours—chances are your case is serious. Replace electrolytes (salt, potassium, and bicarbonate) by drinking fruit juice or an energy drink such as Gatorade. If these drinks or purified water are not available, drink whatever liquid is at hand. That's right, even if the water may be contaminated, avoiding or treating serious cases is worth the risk.

Although physicians once recommended that hikers take salt pills, they now believe that regular diets, including dehydrated foods that campers often consume, provide enough salts without supplements.

Lunch

Hopefully, your lunch will be taken on a lake, atop a mountain, beside a clear stream, or while you're docked on an island off the coast. Flat "mountain breads" are a smart lunch choice—they hold up well and can be filled and rolled (to minimize napkin use) with anything from peanut butter and jelly to pepperoni and cheese to smoked salmon and capers. Personally, lunch is when my sweet tooth gets ornery, so I like to have cookies or some kind of chocolate midday. Hard crackers and cured meats make for excellent luncheon foods, too. Make tea or coffee at breakfast and fill your thermos. Hot or cold, that extra boost will fuel you through the afternoon. Dried or fresh fruit, cookies, energy bars, nuts, and the like make smart snacks to boost energy between meals.

Dinner

Back at camp, with the bugs at bay and the long light of day giving into the blue-black of night, it's time for dinner. Time to replenish all those calories expended cavorting outdoors all day. If you've converted the trunk of your car into a food pantry, home cooking is in order. When you are a little deeper into the woods, you've got to get a little more creative. Certainly, if you're willing to shell out the bucks, a fine array of prepared freeze-dried meals are available at sporting goods stores. But many inexpensive choices exist on the shelves of your local market.

Macaroni and cheese, couscous, chili, and rice dishes are lightweight choices. Check the diet-food section of the market for just-add-water soups and stews, and the gravy aisle for packets of powdered sauces. Embellishing is encouraged. Dried meats and vegetables go a long way toward dressing up a meal. Health-food stores carry a variety of alternative grains including quinoa, bulgur, millet, and barley, which also carry well into the woods. Be careful to note cooking times and water needs for anything you buy in bulk.

Don't be afraid to pack a little extra treat or two. My favorite sin food to sneak along is a tin of smoked oysters.

It may seem like overkill, but spread out your food and package it meal by meal, day by day. Discard all packaging and mix up your ingredients ahead of time in plastic bags. Double-bagging is strongly encouraged anytime the food will go some distance. Be sure to compress and remove

Keep It Wild Tip: Sanitation

- Keep restroom facilities clean. Tidy up messes you make when brushing your teeth, shaving, or using toiletries.
- Do not put any kind of garbage in vault toilets. Trash—such as plastic bags, sanitary napkins, and diapers—cannot be pumped and have to be picked out, piece by piece, by some unfortunate soul.
- If showers are available, bathe quickly so others can use the facilities.
- Use biodegradable soap for washing dishes and cleaning up. Scatter dishwater after all food particles have been removed.
- Scour your campsites for even the tiniest piece of trash and any other evidence of your stay. Pack out all the trash you can, even if it's not yours. Finding cigarette butts, for instance, provides special irritation for most campers. Pick them up and discard them properly.
- Never litter. Never. Or you become the enemy of all others.
  If no refuse facility is available:
- Deposit human waste in "cat holes" dug six to eight inches deep. Cover and disguise the cat hole when finished. Make sure this is done at least 75 paces (200 feet) from any water source or camp.
- Use toilet paper sparingly. When finished, carefully burn it in the cat hole, then bury it. If no appropriate burial locations are available, such as in popular wilderness camps above tree line in granite settings, then all human refuse should be double-bagged and packed out.

air if you are using Ziploc bags. Remember to include instructions and label the meal with an indelible marker to avoid confusion.

Pack a stuffsack or a large Ziploc each with breakfasts, lunches, dinners, and snacks, or pack one day's worth in a sack. That way you won't have to tear through all your food just to find that one item.

Clothing and Weather Protection

Did anyone ever stop to think that Adam and Eve, those intrepid, foraging, biblical campers, may well have wanted to wear clothes? They take all the blame for our agony over having to cover up our bodies, but who would really want to be doing all that gardening in Eden unprotected, especially in blackfly season? They might have been darn relieved when they got dressed.

Camping in the wilderness sometimes provides ideal opportunities to bare all. The thrill of midnight skinny-dipping, the wild abandon of hiking without a top on, feeling the wind at every part of your back, sweat drying instantly in a cool breeze—these are some of the moments campers live for. They bring us closer to our untamed selves. But wind, water, snow, cold, and sun are forces to be reckoned with. New England is notorious for its sudden and vast changes in weather; when it's 80 degrees and sunny at the base of a mountain, it could be stormy and freezing by the time you reach the top. Likewise, the temperature on the beach is usually much warmer than out on the water. The good news is that having the right apparel in most cases makes you equal to the challenge of the elements.

There are several rules of thumb to dress by: Wear layers, dress for comfort, and carry a spare set of dry clothes in case you land in the drink or get caught in a downpour. Cotton garments are only appropriate in warm weather or when you have something dry to change into. Know the weather forecast before you go into the backcountry, whether for a day or for a week.

Contrary to the cliché, I rarely call my women friends to inquire what they are wearing to a certain event. Outdoor pursuits are the exception. My friend Mary and I were headed up to Mount Moosilauke in New Hampshire for a spring telemark ski. I called her to confer about her outfit. The day was sunny and warm, and we thought we'd be fine in Lycra pants, but decided to pack our waterproof gear just in case. We would be skinning up on our skis—adhering a mole-skin strip to the base of the boards allows telemarkers to ascend a slope as if on snowshoes. Once at the top, we would remove our skins and make turns all the way back down. Our climb would put us well above 4,000 feet, and the area had just received a fresh foot or so of powder.

It was so warm out we could have worn short-sleeved shirts on the way up, the most exerting part of our trek. But once we got above tree line, the wind turned the temperatures to frigid. We had to don full wind gear—waterproof pants and jackets, fleece vests, and our warmest hats and gloves to make it to the summit. It was so cold we stayed there only a few minutes. We both wore polypropylene shirts, which kept us dry underneath our jackets. Then, five minutes after we began our descent, we were shedding the same gear, back to spring skiing mode.

The point is, no matter where you are in New England, no matter what season, plan to be surprised. This doesn't mean you need to spend a fortune on clothing and weather gear. But you will need a few essentials to be comfortable and to prevent hypothermia.

Hypothermia

Hypothermia is the lowering of the body's core temperature, usually below 95 degrees Fahrenheit. Most frequently, this affliction occurs when a camper gets wet—either by rainfall or falling into cold water. The first symptom of hypothermia is uncontrollable shivering. Then your speech thickens and you become disoriented. If these signs are ignored, your body will give in about an hour later. Shivering stops, muscles become stiff, and skin turns puffy white. If you don't warm up, death is just around the corner. To treat mild hypothermia, the victim needs to dress in warm, dry clothing, exercise to stimulate blood flow, and drink hot liquids. More advanced cases may require being wrapped in blankets soaked in hot water. @3:The Art of Layering @$:When suiting up for any length outing, think layers. What you wear closest to your skin and the exterior layer braving the elements are the most important. What comes in between is subject to endless personal preference and experience.

Keep It Wild Tip: Travel Lightly

- Visit the backcountry in small groups.
- Below tree line, always stay on designated trails.
- Don't cut across switchbacks.
- When traveling cross-country where no trails are available, follow animal trails or spread out with your group so no new routes are created.
- Read your map and orient yourself with landmarks, a compass, and an altimeter. Avoid marking trails with rock cairns, tree scars, or ribbons.

In the doggiest days of summer, you won't want much more than a pair of roomy shorts, a tank top or bathing suit, and a supply of bug repellent to be comfortable during the daytime. But even when it's hot out, if you're in the water, especially the ocean, bring dry clothes along. At night, even in the summertime, New England can get quite chilly. Always bring long pants and long-sleeved shirts.

Polypropylene, capilene, and several other fancy names are the best outdoor-garb fabrics invented to date in terms of undergarments, aka long underwear or long johns. This lightweight, synthetic material wicks moisture away from the skin, keeping your epidermis dry and comfortable. It's available in a variety of weights, colors, and styles. You'll find it incomparable for dry warmth during outdoor winter activities and useful as pajamas in all seasons. This miracle fabric does have one significant drawback, however. While wicking away all that dampness, it also soaks up body odor. After a few very active days, your polypropylene becomes an odiferous nightmare. Some blends are less smelly than others, but the comfort of this fabric, believe it or not, far outweighs its aromatic inconvenience. I have found that polypropylene actually reaches a stasis point; once it gets to a certain ripeness, you can continue wearing it without increasing its stench. What a bonus.

You know your favorite jeans—the ones that get worn first right out of the dryer? You'll probably want to bring these camping, but more for hanging around the fire at night than for daytime romping. In good weather, loose cotton/canvas blend pants or Lycra/cotton blend stretch pants will be far more comfortable and have another distinct advantage over jeans: when they get wet, they'll dry fairly quickly. Dungarees hang on to every last bit of moisture as long as possible. Not a fun state of affairs in the event of an unanticipated soaking. On top, you'll be most comfortable with a cotton or cotton/wool blend shirt over your interior garments, with additional layers added according to the temperature and your activity.

Another miracle fabric now widely available is Polartec fleece. This environmentally correct stuff (it's often made from recycled plastic bottles) is warm and fuzzy—and pervasive. It is sewn into coat liners, crafted into natty long-tailed caps, and made into mittens, scarves, vests, pullovers, jackets, pants, socks, jog bras, shorts, and skirts. Different weaves and weights and a host of colorful patterns make this a versatile, funky fabric. If you are wearing a wicking material underneath, it won't get wet from the inside. In the event of moisture, fleece can still provide some insulation like wool. My most-used fleece item is a vest. It provides that extra little layer of warmth on top. I also favor a thick pair of fleece gloves under mitten shells for skiing or snowshoeing on cold days. Fleece is an alternative to the traditional insulating fabric—wool. Both will retain heat when wet, but fleece weighs much less than wool in this compromised state. I find fleece garments have a lot more give than wool and they are also machine washable and dryable.

Cotton is made out to be the bad guy of outdoor garb. True enough—it actually takes heat away from your body when it gets wet. In summertime, cotton is comfy in the hot sun. When it gets wet from perspiration, it actually helps your body cool down. In extreme winter conditions, I always wear polypropylene when active, but like to carry a cotton turtleneck for nighttime.

Rain

In all seasons, a camper's biggest foe is water. A freezing downpour is not only a pain in the neck for the ill-prepared, it's dangerous. Ideally, your camping trip will be sunny, clear, and dry. But even if the forecast doesn't call for a drop of precipitation, pack your rain gear anyway. The hills of New England sometimes have weather patterns all their own.

If you can afford them, GoreTex (lightweight, breathable waterproof fabric) pants and jacket shells will serve you well in most rainy situations. If caught in a freezing, sleety April shower that could last for days, you can layer underneath a roomy shell system. If the August sky unleashes a hellish thunder and lightning drencher, you can stay dry for the brief but fierce duration by donning your shells. GoreTex doesn't have to be out of your price range if you are willing to bargain shop. February is a good time to check the sales racks for GoreTex items. You might not find a matching set, but you can often find excellent quality separates for half the price, about $100 and up apiece.

If you're strictly a summer camper, any coated nylon rain gear will suffice. Nylon is only troublesome below about 20 degrees when it becomes brittle and stiff. Another lower-priced alternative is a rubber pants-and-jacket set. These are fine for short periods of time or longer periods of inactivity, but they don't breathe at all and you'll be clammy and uncomfortable if you work up any kind of sweat.

Other Gear

When packing your clothing, don't forget to bring a hat. Wind can cause the air temperature to plummet and a cold, unrelenting gust can bring about an "ice-cream headache" lickety-split. Covered skin is also less prone to windburn and frostbite. Hats with visors provide good sun protection, but you'll want to pack sunglasses. Sunscreen is another necessity except during fall and the early winter months. Late winter, spring, and summer sun will burn your skin to a crisp if given the chance.

When the snow flies and the rivers freeze, you're going to have to add some extra insulation to your get-up. Down garments—vests and parkas—offer the best quality heat retention for the weight and space. But don't bother with down unless you're willing to make the commitment to quality rain gear. If down gets wet, it's useless. Less serious campers will be comfortable with synthetic filled versions—they cost less and can still provide insulation when soggy.

Sleeping Bags and Tents

My parents gave me my first sleeping bag when I was eight. It was pink cotton, soft and fluffy, decorated with pictures of little girls in bonnets picking flowers. It came with a matching suitcase. This special set served me perfectly for years of sleep-over parties. Hot fudge and popcorn butter came out in the wash.

When I turned 13, my parents presented me with a Coleman mummy bag. That worked pretty well for tenting in the summer and fall. Its heyday was during a four-day excursion with my eighth-grade class to Mount Cardigan in New Hampshire. Our group of 25 was caught in a torrential downpour, so we had to hike several extra miles to sleep in a cabin for the night. Many of my campmates hadn't adequately wrapped their bags in plastic, so we had to share. I shared my dry Coleman with Matt Avery, the cutest

Even with the warmest sleeping bag in the world, if you just lay it down on the ground and try to sleep, you will likely get as cold as a winter cucumber. That is because the cold ground will suck the warmth right out of your body. The solution? A sleeping pad.

boy in our school. I was only willing to make such a sacrifice because his survival depended on it, of course.

Once I became an avid backpacker and
winter camper, I had to retire the Coleman
and find something warmer and lighter.
Sleeping bags are as individual as the
people who use them and the environments in which they find
themselves. The first stop on the
road to successful snoozing is assessing
your own personal slumberology. Take a good look at yourself. Are you shivering to death while your companion dozes dreamily in a similar bag? Do you constantly find
yourself hanging five out the zippered side to cool down even when the mercury dips below
freezing?

Next, consider your typical destination. For sea kayaking on the Maine coast, you'll need a
different bag than you would when RVing on Cape Cod. In the first case, a warm, lightweight,
quick-drying, compressible bag is essential. In the latter, almost any bag will do. Certain sleeping environments demand a more specialized tool than others.

Remember, though, that the bag itself does not provide warmth, rather it's an insulator. When
all the fish have been caught, all the miles have been hiked, and all the rapids have been run, it's
your own body heat that keeps you warm. To choose the proper insulation for your body, you've
got to consider the shape, size, fill, and temperature rating of sleeping bags, always keeping in
mind your intended usage.

Bag Shapes and Sizes

A bag that's too roomy will be cooler than a tailored one because less interior space needs to
be warmed up. On the other hand, if the bag's shape is too tight for your frame, you'll compress
the insulation and sleep colder.

Mummy bags are narrow at the foot, wider at the shoulders, and tapered to an insulated hood.
Their snug fit makes them the efficient favorite of wilderness travelers in all regions and cli-
mates. But this shape is also the most restrictive. There is little room to roll over, toss, and turn.
If you're a nocturnal pugilist, you might feel like you are in a straitjacket.

Rectangular bags offer plenty of room for the to and fro of sleeping. But this luxury has a
cost: Heat escapes from the head and shoulder area and there is more dead space for your body
to keep warm. And generally, these bags are too bulky and heavy for travelers who need to
be weight and space conscious, such as backpackers and bicyclists. Rectangular bags are
suited to car camping and RVs.

In between these two extremes are shapes, styles, and
accessories enough to suit individual needs. One aid
for sleeping in colder climes is a liner bag or overbag.
These protect and prolong the life span of your
traveling boudoir and increase insulation.
Both interior and exterior liners can add
about 20 degrees of warmth to your
bag's temperature rating.

Extreme campers should consider a bivy sack. This uninsulated waterproof envelope fits over your regular bag and acts like a mini-tent, warding off most of the big, bad elements. A bivy sack won't keep you totally dry in an extended heavy downpour, but it will allow you to forgo a tent in less than terrible conditions. Insist on factory-sealed seams for best weather resistance.

Most bags come in a couple of lengths; some are sized almost as closely as shoes. Look for enough length to stretch out your frame without too much extra airspace inside to warm up. Go ahead and zip yourself into the bag right there on the showroom floor.

Experienced cold-weather campers prefer a larger bag for storing water bottles or boots in the foot area to keep them from freezing overnight. The extra room leaves space for a liner bag or added clothing layers to extend the bag's range.

Temperature ratings are like speed limits—they sometimes seem arbitrary. That's because there is no industry standard, so you will have little luck when comparing these ratings across manufacturer lines. Only one thing about them is universal: the lower the temperature rating, the higher the price of the bag.

For most purposes, the best all-around backpacking bag for spring/summer/fall in New England is a roomy mummy in the 20-degree range. You'll be cursing your "summer bag" rated at 40 or 50 degrees on those cool late August nights in the Green Mountains. Only winter camping diehards headed for northern New England need bother with 20-below bags or even warmer "maximum mummies," which are simply too hot to sleep in above freezing. For car campers, or those who plan to rent an RV or cabin, the flannel-lined rectangular bags are the next best thing to bringing your real bed. They're plump, cozy, and roomy.

The Anatomy of Sleeping Gear

Sleeping bags aren't hard to dissect. Remember the worm from biology lab? There's the outer shell and the filling. Unless you are willing to shell out the dough for a bag with a GoreTex or other waterproof/breathable exterior, plan on taking some measures to keep your bag dry. All fillings lose at least some of their insulation ability when they get wet, but the synthetic fills can still keep you warm when soggy.

Down fill is light, cozy, warm, and ultimately packable. It requires careful cleaning and storage, but a well-kept down bag retains its loft about three times longer than most synthetic creations. When wet, down is about as warm and comfy as a damp paper towel. Down also dries painfully slowly. Keep it dry with a waterproof stuffsack, bivy bag, and/or waterproof shell.

Efforts to counterfeit down still haven't quite matched the

A-frame style **tents** have gone the way of the dinosaur. With the world going high-tech, tents of today vary greatly in complexity, size, price, and put-up time. And they wouldn't be fit for this new millennium without offering options such as moon roofs, rain flies, and tent wings. Be sure to buy the one that's right for your needs.

warmth, loft, and space-efficiency of lightweight natural feathers, but several new-generation synthetics have narrowed the gap. Synthetic fills retain most of their insulating value when wet, dry quickly, and are relatively inexpensive. They are also, unfortunately, bulkier, heavier, and lose their loft more quickly than down. Synthetic bags excel for cool, wet climes like northern New England's. Canoeists and kayakers should have solid personal reasons for not choosing synthetics when camping around watery environs.

When getting outfitted with your perfect bedroll, consider where it will be unfurled. If you are tenting, you'll need a sleeping pad or the ground will suck out all your body heat. When in a motor home, consider the proximity of your neighbors. Some RV parks are little more than parking lots with shade where you'll be camping "wheel to wheel." You might want to pull the shades or wear earplugs if you don't sleep soundly. If you've made a dozing den out of your pickup truck, you'll want to line the bed with something to prevent the cold metal from cutting short your zzzzs.

Tent Shopping

Choosing a good tent and using it correctly presents more challenges for the New England camper. Sporting goods manufacturers are more than ready to peg you into a certain niche: there are summer/screen tents, three-season tents, all-season tents, and mountaineering tents. Pyramids, domes, hoops, A-frames, and freestanding are just some of the available shapes and styles on the market.

When choosing a tent, consider some of the following issues: First, find out the tent's ability to keep you dry. Make sure the rain fly is long enough to cover the bottom sidewalls of the tent. Seal the seams to prevent leakage. To do this properly, pitch the tent, put the rain fly on upside down (sealer bonds best to the coated side), and run a bead of sealer down every line of stitching. Apply several thin coats instead of a single goopy one. You can also treat the outer surface of the fly for extra protection, but be aware that sealer may discolor dark fabrics. It's also wise to seal both sides of the floor seams as well as all reinforcement areas (corners, pole tabs, etc.). Let the sealer dry overnight.

You'll want to choose a tent that's easily assembled even in low light. When possible, opt for aluminum poles. Fiberglass poles are heavier and easier to break. You can usually spot better-quality, tempered aluminum poles by their bright anodized finish.

Another factor to consider is what size tent you'll need. Sleeping capacity ratings are an inexact guideline only; a "two-person" tent does not allow space for two people and their gear, nor room to cook when seeking refuge from a storm. For cooking under cover you'll need a vestibule. For ample gear storage or winter expeditions, try a tent capacity rated one person be-

Keep It Wild Tip: Camp with Care

- Choose an existing, legal site. Restrict activities to areas where vegetation is compacted or absent.
- Camp at least 75 steps (200 feet) from lakes, streams, and trails.
- Always choose sites that won't be damaged by your stay.
- Preserve the feeling of solitude by selecting camps that are out of view when possible.
- Don't dig trenches or build structures or furniture.

yond your intended number; plan on about 20 square feet per person and their gear.

Finally, check the weight of your pop-up home. If you're traveling long distances on foot, every pound makes a difference. Think about how much it will weigh if it gets wet.

Finding a Good Campsite

Armed with the right bag and tent, all that's left is scouting out a good site. Pick a level spot facing west to catch the sunset or east to greet dawn's light. Just remember that cold air settles into valley floors, so in winter be sure to pitch camp partway up a slope or ridge. Try not to pitch your tent in a low-lying area or in a runoff drainage; seek higher, well-drained ground instead. Look for signs of prevailing wind directions by checking for bent trees, scoured ground around rocks, or snowdrifts. In nasty weather, seek out windbreaks—a boulder, clump of trees, or big bush—and place the tent close, but not so close that the fly will be scraped if the wind blows. Finally, look up and check that there are no broken branches waiting to fall on you.

A ground cloth absorbs the wear and tear of rocky, rough campsites so your tent won't have to. Use a lightweight nylon tarp or sheet of polyethylene. The groundsheet should be slightly smaller than the floor of your tent. Place your tent directly over the groundsheet. Groundsheets that stick out will catch water and funnel it directly under the tent, where it will inevitably soak your sleeping bag and you.

Many New England campgrounds offer rental RVs or cabins in addition to traditional tent and RV sites. Amenities differ from place to place, but if you rent an RV, linen rentals are often included in the price so you don't need to bring your own. On the other hand, cabins are not usually equipped with bed linens. Again, each place is different—just remember to find out before you arrive.

Of Bugs and Beasts

Canoeing Maine's Allagash Wilderness Waterway one gorgeous June day, my friend Dan and I soaked up the bright sunshine as we paddled under a flawless blue sky. Effortlessly, we put miles of sparkling water behind us as a gentle tailwind eased us down Eagle Lake.

In late afternoon, just as we were beginning to think about camping, the most exquisite site came into view. Situated on a grassy point jutting into the water, the campsite offered sumptuous views for miles up and down the lake. There were beautiful beaches, great swimming spots, and good fishing off the point. Not only that, but the site promised the luxury of both late afternoon and early morning light. Perfect.

Still congratulating ourselves on our good fortune, we had barely finished setting up the tent when the wind died. It was then that our perfect day came crashing to an end as we were instantly enveloped in a storm of blackflies. We literally dove into the tent and watched in horror through the bug netting as the bloodthirsty beasts swirled around our little sanctuary like a black cyclone.

We were stuck inside for hours—to go out would have been madness. As the sun went down, the blackflies retired, only to be replaced by their equally fiendish cousins, the North Woods mosquitoes.

Insect Repellent

Your first line of defense is to use your head. Remember, mosquitoes and no-see-ums enjoy things cool, damp, and shady, so stay away from these areas as much as possible. Make sure to have all outside camp chores done before sunset. Recall that wind helps keep the blackflies down, so look for open, sunny, breezy areas where your chances of being relatively bug free are best.

Your next strategy is to adopt the garb of the traditional Maine Guide. Not only will this apparel protect you from bugs, sun, and chilly weather, but you're going to look authentic. Here's what you need to wear, plus a couple of extra items: • A broad-brimmed hat • A tightly woven long-sleeved cotton or light wool shirt • Light cotton twill or wool pants • A brightly colored bandanna worn around the neck • Rubber-bottomed, leather-topped boots of the sort made famous by native son L. L. Bean, high enough to tuck your pant leg into (keeps bugs from biting your ankles and legs) • A bug headnet for those times when you just can't take it anymore • Earplugs, for those nights when the whiiinnniiinnnggg of the skeeters keeps you from falling asleep

A word about bug dope. Cover up with appropriate clothing that bugs can't bite through instead and only use the stuff (it's poison, after all) in situations of extreme discomfort. You can reduce direct contact with the toxins in effective repellents by dabbing a little dope on your bandanna, on your shirt and pant cuffs, and on the brim of your hat.

Your final refuge, your last bastion against an all-out bug assault, is your trusty tent. I once worked for an internationally known outdoor education program that for some crackpot reason decided not to issue tents for its summer programs in Maine. It's hard to know what the directors were thinking—I guess their goal was to make sure none of the students would ever go camping again as long as they lived.

The best tents for bug season in northern New England are the inexpensive, extremely lightweight, easy-to-use "bug shelters" offered by various tent manufacturers. These ultralight havens are essentially domes of fire-resistant no-see-um netting suspended over collapsible alloy poles. You can set them up in less than a minute and relax inside, laughing at the little winged fiends as they fly their insane traffic patterns around your neighborhood.

Nice features offered by the bug shelters include lots of ventilation, good headroom, feather weight (less than a pound and a half for a two-person model), and a view of the stars at night. And what about rain, you ask? During inclement weather simply place the shelter under a lightweight tarp.

Flies

There are billions and billions of reasons why much of northern New England has never been settled, and they hatch every year around the end of May. Biting flies are the main reason Native Americans migrated to the seashore in the summer, there to dine on lobster and clams on breezy beaches and rocky points, far from the madding swarms of voracious forest insects.

Mosquitoes

Mosquitoes and no-see-ums, those infinitesimally tiny winged horrors that rise in vaporous clouds in the night and whose bite feels like a burning ember, multiply in stagnant pools and low-lying swampy areas. They like humidity and are most active on damp days and in the evening, as the relative humidity increases. The blackfly breeding cycle takes place not in swamps, but in swiftly running streams and rapids. Blackflies prefer hot, dry, sunny days and they vanish when the sun goes down. Fortunately, because of their different preferences, you almost never have to deal with mosquitoes and blackflies at the same time. Unfortunately, the changing of the guard at sundown takes place with such efficiency, you may only have a few minutes of blessed peace.

Northern New England, and especially Maine, has plenty of both flat and quick water. That's

ⓕ Keep It Wild Tip: Keep the Wilderness Wild

- Let nature's sound prevail. Avoid loud voices and noises; leave radios and tape players at home.
- Treat natural heritage with respect. Leave plants, rocks, and historical artifacts where you find them. Do not cut down limbs or branches or remove leaves from trees.
- Respect the animals that inhabit the area. Don't feed or harass animals that visit your campground. Animals need to stick to their natural diets or else they may become ill. Keep your camp area clean, especially if you're in or near bear country, so you don't tempt any animals to visit your site.
- Control pets at all times or leave them with a sitter at home.

what makes it such an exceptional place to canoe camp. But as a prolific breeding ground for bugs, it's hard to beat. What can you do?

Well, you can go to the beach, lie in the sand, and read trashy romance novels. Or you can stay out of the woods and waters until the height of the bug season is over and the little devils start thinning out—most years around the end of July. Or you can cop an attitude, arm yourself with a little knowledge, and beat the pests at their own game.

Ticks

Unlike some other parts of the country, New England is comparatively free of creatures that doubtless serve a noble purpose in the grand scheme of things, but are nonetheless grouped by humans in a category called "pests." This company includes, but isn't limited to, scorpions, gila monsters, kissing bugs, black widows, tarantulas, coral snakes, cottonmouths, pygmy rattlers, and many other reasons to shake out your boots in the morning. Still, even up here there are a few critters to keep in mind when exploring the back of beyond. After all, Lyme disease, carried by the tiny deer tick, is named for its place of origin, Lyme, Connecticut. For the most part, however, most dangers are far more imagined than real.

Lyme disease, a bacterial infection transmitted by a deer tick's bite, is certainly a reason to be vigilant. On a recent hour-long walk in the Connecticut woods, I picked up a half dozen deer ticks while my dog managed to acquire another five or six. As a precaution, wear the same outfit that helps ward off the mosquitoes and blackflies—long sleeves and pants, a hat, and sturdy boots. Avoid pants with upturned cuffs that provide a hiding place for ticks. Brush off your clothing before entering your tent or RV, and be sure to thoroughly check yourself and your pet.

Snakes

Poisonous snakes are extremely rare in northern New England and are totally absent from Maine, northern New Hampshire, and northern Vermont. Elsewhere in New England, they are so rare many people who spend most of their lives outdoors never see one, so you might consider yourself lucky if you do.

The northern copperhead is native to southwest New England and is usually associated with deciduous forests, rocky ledges, areas with damp leaf litter, rotting woodpiles, boulder fields, in short, anywhere and everywhere. In the summer, the snakes sometimes frequent the vicinity of swamps, ponds, and streams.

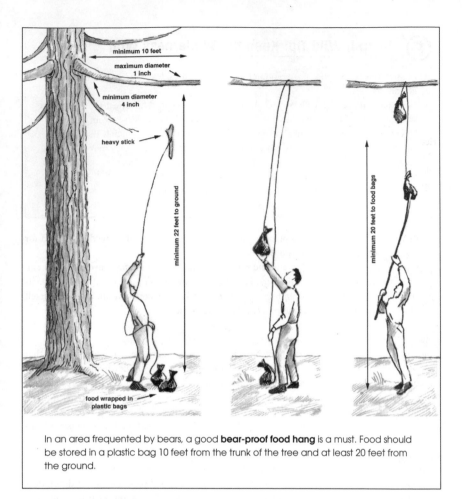

minimum 10 feet

maximum diameter 1 inch

minimum diameter 4 inch

heavy stick

minimum 22 feet to ground

minimum 20 feet to food bags

food wrapped in plastic bags

In an area frequented by bears, a good **bear-proof food hang** is a must. Food should be stored in a plastic bag 10 feet from the trunk of the tree and at least 20 feet from the ground.

The eastern timber rattlesnake is a bit more widespread (but no more common), reaching up into southern New Hampshire and Vermont, and seems to prefer the same environments as the copperhead. The timber rattler is also associated with a few other habitats, such as old stone walls and cellar holes. Both the copperhead and the timber rattler avoid contact with humans and will flee if given the chance. They are active at night during the summer, a hunting strategy that further reduces the chance of encounters with humans.

Bears

No chapter on bugs and beasts would be complete without a mention of bears. Yes, there are bears in New England, lots of them, especially in Vermont, New Hampshire, and Maine. These are black bears—there are no grizzlies here—and for the most part they are shy, secretive forest dwellers, wary of humans and aspiring to solitude. If you are fortunate enough, you might see a flash of black fur crashing off through the brush away from you at warp speed.

But let's not overgeneralize bear behavior. They are, after all, highly evolved and intelligent creatures, and like people each bear is an individual. So, while their natural tendency may be toward flight at the first sign of humans, some bears have been trained by sloppy campers (the most dangerous animals in the forest) that people can provide them with food in the form of garbage or poorly stored supplies.

Unfortunately, slob campers may lose their food and sometimes equipment when a bear taught to rob camps tears through their gear. But it's usually the bear that ends up paying the heavy price by being relocated or destroyed.

Your best protection in bear country is to keep a spotless camp. When RV or car camping, make sure all coolers, containers, equipment, and utensils that come in contact with food are properly stored and put away for the night inside your vehicle. When backpacking or canoeing, make sure all dishes, pots, pans, and cooking gear are washed and stored in your food bags. Burn all leftover food or store it in plastic bags with the rest of your food supplies. Hang your food from a tree, suspended at least 15 feet off the ground and 10 feet away from any tree trunks or extending branches. An easy way to do this is to tie a rock to a rope, then toss the rock over an appropriate branch. Untie the rock, tie on your food bag, then hoist the bag up into the air. When the food bag is hanging out of reach, tie off the loose end of the rope to a nearby tree.

One of the best parts about camping is the chance to spend time in the company of fellow creatures. Most often these shared moments in the wild are delightful the cow and calf moose we saw feeding in midstream, or the hawk soaring overhead. Some interactions are somewhat less pleasant, but no less memorable—the skeeters buzzing in my ear, or the time old Shep came back to camp with a half dozen ticks. It's really up to us. By learning about wildlands, and the habits of the creatures who live there, we can make sure more of these encounters are of the pleasant kind.

Camping with Kids

Camping is a terrific way to introduce a child to the world of nature. Everything—playing, eating, sleeping, learning –is done under the sun and the clouds and the moon and the stars. More than a fun vacation (although it should be that, too), it's a chance to learn lifelong skills and experience nature outside of the everyday routine.

In addition, camping is one of the more affordable trips families can take. Sleeping in campgrounds is much less expensive than staying at a motel or hotel, and activities such as hiking, fishing, and exploring nature are not as pricey as amusement-park admission fees. And since you're cooking your meals at the campsite, the high cost of eating in a restaurant is avoided.

When planning a camping trip with the kids, remember a few simple rules: tailor the trip to their capabilities, focus on their interests, and adjust to their limitations, which are generally defined by their age and development level.

Babies can be great campers, as long as you're prepared to limit your outdoor activities and can address their special requirements (crib, stroller, formula, diapers, etc.). Toddlers especially appreciate exploring a new environment. They love to get dirty and wet, collect leaves and rocks, and watch wildlife and insects.

Elementary school–age children are typically enthusiastic campers, anxious to learn about the outdoors, help with the chores, and participate in all camping activities. They like to swim, hike, build fires, and roast hot dogs. And they can't resist hearing a good ghost story or tall tale about falling stars or wild animals.

Teenagers? Well, you're on your own there. Some teens like to camp, especially if it's an annual family vacation routine. Others consider it a drag and will take every opportunity to remind you of it. Try to involve teens in every aspect of the trip: deciding where to go, what to take, what to eat, what to do. Let them bring a friend and give them a little more freedom than they get at home. They'll be much better company during group activities and meals if they know they'll be able to go off and hike, fish, or swim on their own later.

Here are some tips on how to ensure that a fun, rewarding vacation is had by all:

• Expect short attention spans. By staying a step or two ahead of the kids in the planned activities department, you can keep them from getting bored or into trouble. Unlike adults, the kids need action on a vacation. Plan activities and games to keep them occupied. That means staying prepared by knowing what the next fun event will be—an activity that will inspire or distract a restless child.

• Bring the right gear and games. What you pack partly depends on where you'll be camping and what your children like to do. Are you camping at a sandy lake with toddlers? Then buckets, shovels, sieves, toy trucks, and plastic molds are in order. Will you be sleeping on top of a mountain? Then binoculars, a telescope and star chart, a magnifying glass, and an altimeter are ideal. Will there be a river nearby? Then bring along a fishing rod. No matter where you go, pack along a ball, a Frisbee, a pack of cards, pens and paper, or crayons and coloring pads for younger kids.

• Have a still or video camera ready to capture the moment. Photographs or videos of your family in the outdoors—hiking up a mountain, catching a fish, taking down the tent—will go a long way toward helping your kids hang on to memories of the last trip and build up a head of steam for the next.

• Let your kids help with the practical stuff. When you're camping, there are essential campground tasks that must be done—such as setting up camp, building a fire, cooking dinner—and kids would rather be involved than just watch you do everything. Show them how to help put up the tent, collect sticks for the campfire, add water and stir the pancake mix, read a compass.

• Help your children learn, but also let them play. Spending time outdoors provides the opportunity to teach them outdoor skills and safety, campground ethics, even some lessons about life. While teaching them to pick up after themselves (and others) and to respect the outdoors is very important, remember that taking your children to the woods, mountains, or desert doesn't have to be strictly an educational experience. This is first and foremost a vacation—and kids need to relax, too.

• Let them have a say in the agenda. It's everybody's trip. Listen to what the kids want to do and don't want to do. If a hike is planned and they want to spend the day swimming or tossing a Frisbee instead, let the majority rule. Follow their lead sometimes, go with their flow, let the adventure happen.

• Set rules for acceptable behavior. Giving the youngsters a say in the agenda doesn't mean letting them run wild. Rules and limits are essential to ensure kids' safety and their consideration for other campers. Let them know what behavior is acceptable around a campfire, how close they can come to a cliff or wildlife, and why it's important to stay within sight.

• Prepare kids for the ups and the downs. Enthusiasm is a key ingredient for a successful camping trip, but letting children become excessively excited can backfire when things don't go their way. If it rains or is unseasonably cold, if the fish aren't biting, or if one of them twists an ankle or catches a cold, it could ruin the whole experience for them. Tell them about the possible negative as well as the positive aspects of the trip—that way they'll be better prepared for whatever little disasters or disappointments come their way.

Canoe Camping

In western Maine, hard against the mountainous Quebec border, a clear little river comes tumbling down from the high country and meanders through a thick dark forest of spruce and fir. Along the way, the river splashes over a series of rapids, plunges down a magnificent 40-foot waterfall, and eventually empties into a beautiful, island-studded lake at the base of a high mountain ridgeline.

This is the Moose River, and it's a classic canoe trip, one of many in the region. The lakes here are lovely, with beautiful beaches and campsites offering striking vistas down the waterway. The rapids are thrilling but not dangerous. And even the portage around the cascade is neither excessively long nor rugged, but rather more of a chance to stretch your legs.

For knocking around in the New England wilds, you really can't beat canoe travel. Light, simple, elegant, and strong enough to carry heavy loads, the canoe is the vehicle of choice for exploring a region laced by countless rivers and streams.

In fact, the canoe was invented here in the northeastern woodlands by Algonquin craftsmen, who built the nimble little vessels out of birch bark. Small wonder European explorers adopted the canoe when they set out to explore the continent; their heavy rowboats were useless on inland waters, and the swift Indian canoes paddled circles around them. Not only that, but the natives could see where they were going. The Old World took a bow to superior technology.

Today, the best camping canoes are 17 to 18 feet long and are made of strong synthetic material such as ABS Royalex, fiberglass, or Kevlar. These boats are designed to carry two people plus their gear. Experienced paddlers may choose to paddle their own, smaller canoes.

The secret to the canoe's beauty, grace, and ability to whisk you to the heart of the wild is its simplicity. The long, tapered lines ending in a gentle upsweep at bow and stern are a classic marriage of form and function. It's wonderful: you get in one end, your partner gets in the other, and you keep the boat roughly parallel to the shoreline (it helps to know the basic strokes). Soon, a deep sense of well-being blossoms as you drift along. You settle into a soothing rhythm of wilderness travel. Deadlines and commitments fade into irrelevance. This is the real world. You're on river time now.

A canoe trip in the New England wilds is a chance for viewing wildlife. Seeing a moose is a highlight of many trips here, especially in Maine, but the forest is home to other creatures as well.

Winter Gear Checklist

Clothing
Ski boots or insulated pacs
Gaiters
Several pairs of wool socks
Liner socks
Wool or synthetic long underwear
Wool or synthetic pants
Wool or synthetic shirt or sweater
Synthetic pile jacket
Down parka with hood
Wind- and waterproof pants and jacket
Wool or synthetic hat
Glove liners
Wool or synthetic pile mittens
Wind- and waterproof mitten shells

Equipment
Backpack
Skis/snowshoes
Ski poles (for skiing and snowshoeing)
Sleeping bag
Foam pad
Tent
Stove, fuel, and repair kit
Two pots with lids and pot scrubber
Snow shovel (grain scoops work well)
Maps
Compass
Water bottles (wide-mouthed)
Matches/lighter
Bowl, cup, spoon
Flashlight and extra batteries
First-aid kit

Personal Items
Camera and film
Sunglasses and sunscreen
Moleskin (for blisters)
Duct tape (for general repairs)
Reading material and journal

Deer are plentiful, as are bear, bobcat, beaver, raccoon, and porcupine. In the north, sharp-eyed paddlers may see a rare Canada lynx or a pine marten. Sometime in your travels you are likely to be serenaded by coyotes. The haunting sound of the loon is the voice of this northern wilderness.

Besides loons, canoe campers also have an excellent chance of seeing terns, gulls, kingfishers, great blue herons, ruffed grouse, ospreys, bald eagles, and a rich assortment of ducks and song-birds. Canoe parties that move quietly, especially at dawn and dusk, stand the best chance of encountering wildlife.

In northern Maine, especially, the fishing is superb, and unlike most other parts of the country, the fish populations are wild, not stocked. Clearly, canoe-camping parties are well positioned to take advantage of the angling opportunities. Brook trout, known locally as "squaretails," are found in nearly all the lakes, rivers, and streams. Lake trout, called "togue," inhabit the cold, deep waters of the larger lakes.

Canoeing Equipment

Here's what to bring: In the clothing department, place the emphasis on covering up from the sun, bugs, and brush while staying cool and comfortable. A broad-brimmed hat and lightweight cotton clothing are great for blue-sky days. Bring along the polypropylene, wool, and pile for cool days and cold nights, and be sure to pack the rain gear. As in most outdoor pursuits, layering is the key to comfort.

For footwear on warm-weather trips where you don't plan to do any portaging or lining, river sandals or some mesh-topped slippers are fine. Rubber-bottomed, leather-topped boots are your best bet elsewhere.

Most any backpacking tent will suffice, but take advantage of the canoe's cargo capacity and feel free to bring a larger version and leave the ultralight sensory deprivation chamber at home. Also, a 10-by-12-foot tarp for cooking and lounging under on rainy days is a luxury that quickly becomes a necessity.

Bring a sleeping bag, sleeping pad, and a folding camp chair for relaxing by the fire or camp stove. And speaking of stoves, you can bring your lightweight backpacking stove or again take advantage of the canoe's capacity and pack a larger, two-burner stove. That way, you can keep the hot drinks coming while you cook your dinner—a nice option on a wet, windy day. And while you're at it, why not bring along a gas lantern for when the sun goes down? As for fires, dry driftwood is usually plentiful, as are dry fallen trees and branches in the surrounding forest.

Pack your clothing and equipment in heavy-duty, waterproof, rubber gear bags or traditional canvas Duluth-style packs waterproofed with heavy-duty plastic liners. Traditional rigid ash pack baskets are excellent for transporting hard-edged or fragile items. Small rubber dry bags are very useful for keeping little items handy; stash your sunscreen, shades, and bug repellent in a day pack. The day pack will come in handy if you take time off from paddling to do any day hiking.

Your gear should be packed low and in the center of the canoe, below the gunwales. There it will stay dry and won't catch the wind.

On most of the big rivers and lakes in northern Maine, the water is pure and drinkable, and locals keep a cup handy for dipping while they paddle—one of the last places in the continental United States you can experience the pleasure of drinking directly from a natural source. However, if you aren't sure about the water quality, treat it with iodine or a water purifier.

Sometimes, as on the Connecticut River or most waterways in southern New England, you have to bring water with you. Haul your own in new, unused, and clearly marked five-gallon plastic gasoline jugs.

⒡ Camping Gear Checklist

Sleeping Gear
Extra blankets
Ground cloth
Pillow
Sleeping bag
Sleeping pad
Tent

Cooking Utensils
Aluminum foil
Can opener
Charcoal
Coffee
Cooking kit
Cooler
Cups
Forks, knives, and spoons
Fuel
Grill
Hot chocolate
Matches
Plates
Salt and pepper
Spatula
Stove
Water jugs

Packing and Cleaning Supplies
Cloth towels
Dish soap
Paper towels
Plastic bags (large and small)
Sponge

First Aid
Acetaminophen, ibuprofen, or aspirin, for pain relief
Adhesive tape
Aloe vera–based burn ointment
Antibiotic ointment, for minor cuts and scrapes
Band-Aids, for minor cuts and scrapes
Betadine solution, for disinfection
Elastic bandages, to wrap sprains
Extractor, for snake venom

Gauze pads (extra thick and at least four inches square) or sanitary napkins, to reduce blood flow from major wounds
Insect repellent
Moleskin, to treat blisters
Notebook and pencil, to record the details of any accident or injury that might be needed by a physician
Sunscreen (at least SPF 15), to prevent sunburn
Syringe (10 cc to 50 cc), to flush wounds
Thermometer
Tweezers

Recreational Gear
Binoculars
Books and magazines
Camera and film
Car games for kids
Deck of cards
Field guides
Fishing rod, reel, and tackle box
Journal
Portable stereo and tapes

Miscellaneous
Camp chairs
Compass
Day pack
Extra batteries
Firewood
Flashlight
Lantern
Maps
Mosquito-net tent
Portable table
Propane heater

Don't forget your life jacket, one extra paddle per boat, and a large sponge to swab the decks. And last, bring along a camera, film, binoculars, fishing gear, and a well-worn paperback copy of *Deliverance.* Happy paddling!

Winter Camping

Old-timers call it "termination dust." Wake up on a crisp fall morning and there it is, sprinkled sugar on the mountaintops: the first snow of the season. Another summer gone. Another camping season coming to a close.

In the mountains of northern New England, the first snows dust the high peaks anytime after mid-September. By Thanksgiving, the ski season is well under way, rivers and lakes are freezing solid, and warm-weather campers have stored their gear for the winter. The land and people are settling in for the long dark silence.

For many folks up here, winter is a time to reflect on past camping adventures, to sit around the stove reliving shared moments in the outdoors, to anticipate the return of the sun. But other folks have a different, some might say peculiar, attitude toward winter. When the days grow short, when the cold winds blow and the snow piles high, these people spring into action. The fact that the mercury is curling into a tight little ball at the bottom of the thermometer doesn't faze them. These zealots think winter is the best time of all to head outdoors.

And why not? After all, in northern New England especially, winter lasts half the year or longer. And hidden under the snowy forest canopy, locked beneath frozen lakes, and tucked away in the hollows of fallen trees, life goes on despite winter's cold. Nature can't afford to wait for the big spring thaw: there's too much to do.

The same goes for us humans. Days spent traversing crystalline landscapes renew us in hardy ways unknown to the fair-weather crowds of summer. Learn the techniques for coming to terms with the cold and snow and you'll discover a whole new bright shining world of camping adventure.

Choosing Where and When to Winter Camp

If you are planning your first trip, the best time to go is after the brutally cold days of December and January. A midwinter trip can be cruelly cold. By February and March, the days are longer, the temperatures are more moderate, and snow and sunshine are plentiful. Gain some experience before you tackle an early-season trip.

Fortunately, New England is blessed with a variety of terrain perfect for winter camping. We have it all here—the snowy summits of Acadia National Park overlooking the Atlantic Ocean, the elegant forests of the interior, the frosty crags of Mounts Washington and Katahdin—perhaps no other region offers so many diverse experiences to the winter adventurer. Don't overlook favorite hiking areas, which can be great places for winter camping. Becoming familiar with a small wilderness is sometimes as satisfying as trekking across a vast, expansive tract.

Spreading out maps and choosing a route is part of the fun. Most veteran winter campers can daydream for hours, linking trails and connecting routes they would love to explore. A primitive urge to go takes hold: a longing to see what lies beyond the next ridge.

Next, gather information on the area you wish to explore. Maps, guidebooks, and advice from experienced travelers will help you prepare and add to your enjoyment. The more you know about an area, the more you can seek out its rewards—the best views, camping spots, and trails—and avoid its hazards—dangerous stream crossings, impassable trails, or unwanted human intrusion such as roads or new development.

How far to go will depend upon many factors, such as the terrain's steepness, the weather, your pack's weight, and the pace of your slowest companion. If the snow is either slush or deep powder, you can expect tough going. If the snow has settled or is firm and wind-packed, you will be able to pick up the pace. In New Hampshire's White Mountains, covering five miles might make for an exhausting day. In a valley or on a lake or river, you may well cover that distance in a couple of hours. Beginners should start with short trips over easy terrain.

Winter Camping Clothing

Because you will heat up while climbing and cool down while descending or when standing in camp, adjusting your clothing to suit the needs of the moment will be critical. The key to comfort is a system of layers you can add to or subtract from quickly.

A wool hat, wool or synthetic long underwear, wool pants, a wool shirt or sweater, a pile jacket, a down parka with hood, and a waterproof shell are the essential components of a layer system. When in camp on a cold night, you may need to wear all of these items to stay warm. While active you will probably leave the heavy insulating layers in the pack. Keep these layers accessible—when you stop for lunch along the trail, put them on before you start to cool down.

The layer system applies to hands and feet, too. A warm-hand combination includes thin liner gloves worn under wool mittens with waterproof shells. If your hands are too hot, just hike along with the liners until you stop and then add more layers.

Winter Camping Equipment

Depending upon your method of travel, you will probably be wearing ski boots or insulated shoepacs. Regardless, cold feet are no fun on a winter trip, so make sure that you can fit a liner sock and a thick wool sock comfortably in your boot. Tight boots are iceboxes: they constrict the blood flow to your feet, making it impossible for them to warm up. For a real treat for your feet, bring along a soft pair of Polarguard booties to slip into when you get to camp. Never underestimate the simple pleasures.

Whether to ski or snowshoe is really a matter of personal preference. Skis are faster, but snowshoes may be more versatile when the going gets rugged. Unless you are an expert skier able to handle steep descents through the woods while wearing a pack, snowshoes are probably a better choice for most trips in New England.

For overnights, you will want a sturdy tent. Domes and pyramids offer the best designs and most efficient use of space, but any summer backpacking tent will do. Some people prefer tarps, which are lighter and easier to carry, but do not offer the warmth and protection of tents.

A sleeping bag with plenty of loft will ensure a good night's sleep. A mummy bag is the best for winter use. Make sure the bag is roomy enough for you to sleep in several layers of clothing, and long enough to keep your boots warm inside (but not on your feet) at the bottom of the bag.

All sleeping bags come with a temperature rating, but use this only as a guideline. While a friend sleeps soundly in a bag rated at 10 degrees Fahrenheit, you may shiver the night away in an identical bag. A hefty three-season bag may suffice if you wear plenty of clothing to bed. If you aren't sure, go with a thicker bag. The extra warmth won't hurt. Always put a thick pad of closed-cell foam under your sleeping bag or the cold ground will suck the warmth right out of you. Keep some food handy to nibble on at night.

Changing into dry, long underwear will help you stay warm in the evenings and so will eating well. On a winter camping trip, you'll need to consume some 5,000 calories to keep you going all day. Food is fuel, so eat plenty of fats and carbohydrates. Keep your meal preparation simple— one-pot meals are easiest and fastest. Add cheese, nuts, butter, and raisins to your meals for a fuel boost, and don't forget to bring spices for adding a little zip to your creations.

You can cook your meals over a fire or a stove. While you will most likely have a fire for warmth and cheer, bring along a reliable backpacking stove in case of rain or thaw. Become familiar with the stove's use before you leave on your trip. Starting stoves in cold weather can be tricky. Be sure not to bring a butane stove on a winter trip. Below 32 degrees Fahrenheit, butane is simply not reliable.

Winter Warnings

As important as eating lots of food, drinking plenty of water is critical in winter. Despite the presence of snow, the winter environment is extremely dry, and breathing the cold, dry air can cause you to become dehydrated much faster than in more moderate temperatures. Also, you lose heat through perspiration, and even breathing. In order to maintain a comfortable body temperature and avoid dehydration, you must constantly replace this lost moisture. Drink plenty of water every time you stop for a short rest.

Planning a trip takes careful preparation, but for many campers, the winter wilderness is irresistible. There is a quality to the silence, the fresh, trackless snow, and the sense of solitude and space that more than makes up for any hardships.

But winter can be a hard master, and there is no avoiding an apprenticeship as you learn winter's ways. Hopefully, you won't repeat my first experience, huddled around a campfire on a January Wyoming night in a place literally named the Freeze-Out Range, dressed in cowboy boots and blue jeans, waiting for the sun to show. That wasn't fun, but something about the frozen moonlight on the peaks and snowy plains, the yipping coyotes filling the night with song, and the simple fact that I was out there, doing it, kept luring me back. I know it will bring you back, too.

Best Campgrounds in New England

Can't decide where to camp this weekend? Here are our picks for the best campgrounds in New England in five categories:

ⓕ Top 10 Lakeside Campgrounds

Burton Island State Park, Northeast Kingdom and Lake Champlain, Vt., page 295. Set on 253-acre Burton Island in the northern end of Lake Champlain, the campground accommodates boats for overnight stays at its full-service marina and also offers tent and lean-to sites along the mostly open northern shore.

Frost Pond Camps, North Woods, Maine, page 56. Staying here in these rustic wilderness cabins and tent sites is like stepping back in time to another, more peaceful era."

Lake Waramaug State Park, Western Hills and Coast, Conn., page 471. You'll be rubbing elbows with well-heeled weekenders on this lake studded with grand summer homes.

Lily Bay State Park, North Woods, Maine, page 65. Overlooking the vast expanses of 40-mile-long Moosehead Lake, it's a short and easy paddle to dozens of islands from the campground.

Loon Echo Campground, North Woods, Maine, page 63. When you stay here be sure to listen to the haunting cry of the loons, soak in the beauty of the undeveloped lakeshore, and be sure to take a fly-casting lesson from owner Bill Erven.

Mattawamkeag Wilderness Park Campground, North Woods, Maine, page 69. Not only does this campground offer plenty of opportunities for water sports, there are fifteen miles of maintained hiking trails.

Nickerson State Park, Cape and Islands, Mass., page 435. Most folks go to the Cape for sand and surf, but more than a dozen freshwater kettle ponds at Nickerson offer swimming, powerboating, and fishing.

Stillwater State Park, Northeast Kingdom and Lake Champlain, Vt., page 312. Sites are on or near the shore of Lake Groton, a north country gem flanked by mountains. The lake is open to swimming and all types of boating.

Umbagog Lake State Park, White Mountains, N.H., page 181. Nearly 8,000 acres of water are available for wildlife viewing, canoeing, boating, fishing, and swimming; some campsites are accessible only via boat.

Whispering Pines Campground, Down East, Maine, page 155. Situated under giant white pines and hemlocks by the shores of a wild lake, the setting is the very essence of serenity.

ⓕ Top 10 Beachfront Campgrounds

Cobscook Bay State Park, Down East, Maine, page 166. Situated on one of the wildest stretches of the Maine Coast, it's hard to imagine a better location for sea kayak explorations.

Ellacoya State RV Park, Eastern Lakes and Seacoast, N.H., page 260. The view over the island-dotted expanse of Lake Winnespesaukee towards the Ossipee and Sandwich Ranges of the white Mountains is breathtaking.

Horseneck Beach State Reservation, Greater Boston, Mass., page 423. Spread across 600 acres of barrier beach and salt marsh, always-breezy Horseneck is a favorite with windsurfers and campers who want a break from summer heat.

Lamoine State Park, Down East, Maine, page 158. If you are looking for a splendid campground with easy access to the water, this is the place. Acadia National Park and Bar Harbor are less than an hour away by car.

Mainayr Campground, Down East, Maine, page 165. This is a great place to hop in your canoe or kayak and explore the tidal cove emptying into the wild Atlantic Ocean.

Ocean Wood Campground, Down East, Maine, page 169. Many of the spacious sites here are situated directly on the shoreline of Schoodic Point, a wild peninsula jutting out into the Atlantic Ocean.

Paine's Campground, Cape and Islands, Mass., page 431. Cape Cod National Seashore beaches are a short, sandy hike from these campsites.

Rocky Neck State Park, Long Island Sound, Conn., page 514. A half-mile-long crescent-shaped beach is the focal point here; a bike path leads to it from the campground.

Sunset Point Trailer Park, Down East, Maine, page 170. It's just a short drive to Quoddy Head State park, the easternmost point in the United States and the first place in the country to be struck by the sun's rays every morning.

William F. Miller Campground in Hammonasset Beach State Park, Long Island Sound, Conn., page 513. Located at the mouth of the Hammonasset River, the campsites overlook both beaches as well as marshlands that are home to herons and various waterfowl.

ⓕ Top 10 Campgrounds for Canoeing

Abol Bridge Campground, North Woods, Maine, page 57. From the sandy waterfront the view is of the mile-high ramparts of Mount Katahdin rising above the West Branch of the Penobscot River.

Allagash Wilderness Waterway, North Woods, Maine, page 43. The Allagash is simply one of the finest multi-day canoeing trips in the country.

Barton Cove, Berkshires, Mass., page 371. Lovely, natural campsites are set along a wooded peninsula on the Connecticut River.

Connecticut River Canoe Sites, White Mountains, N.H., page 188, and Southeast Vt., page 357. Mostly primitive campsites are sprinkled along the 410-mile-long river, an easy-to-moderate paddle the whole way.

Housatonic Meadows State Park, Western Hills and Coast, Conn., page 470. Canoeists will find Class I, II, and III white water on a 12-mile stretch of the river north of the campground.

Jackman Landing Campground, North Woods, Maine, page 62. From the campground it's just a short paddle to the Moose River, an excellent two-to-three day canoeing adventure.

Lake Carmi State Park, Northeast Kingdom and Lake Champlain, Vt., page 288. Sites along the shoreline of the state's fourth largest lake are a good jumping-off point for canoe exploration of the Missisquoi River just to the south of the campground.

River Run Canoe and Camping, Western Lakes and Mountains, Maine, page 99. The sites are situated directly on the banks of the Saco River, a cold clear stream flowing down from the White Mountains off to the west.

Saco River Camping Area, White Mountains, N.H., page 209. The Saco offers easy to moderate paddling for day trips, overnights, and extended canoe camping if you paddle into Maine.

South Arm Campground, Western Lakes and Mountains, Maine, page 87. Paddle out to your own private island and enjoy the opportunity to explore one of the country's premier wilderness lake regions.

✆ Top 10 Campgrounds for Hiking

Appalachian Trail, page 89. All along the Appalachian Trail's route through Connecticut, Vermont, New Hampshire and Maine are a variety of campgrounds, from backcountry primitive sites to shelters and huts.

Green Mountain Camping Area, Vt., page 321. The Green Mountains are the spine of Vermont, criss-crossed with hiking trails; the Long Trail spans the length of the state.

Greenleaf Hut, White Mountains, N.H., page 203. The most popular route to this Appalachian Mountain Club cabin the Old Bridle Path (2.9 miles) from Lafayette Place Campground in Franconia Notch; from the hut you can continue on the Greenleaf trail (1.1) miles to the summit of Lafayette. From there, the Franconia Ridge trail, part of the Appalachian Trail, runs along the ridgetop above the hut.

Macedonia Brook State Park, Western Hills and Coast, Conn., page 471. The Appalachian Trail passes through the park; try the Blue Trail, which crosses Cobble Mountain and other peaks, affording good views of the Catskill and Taconic mountains.

Monadnock State Park, Western Lakes, N.H., page 239. One of the most-hiked mountains in the world is a short but steeply-pitched ascent and rewarding views from its treeless summit.

Mount Greylock State Reservation, Berkshires, Mass., page 368. From the campground, take the Money Brook Trail to the Hopper, a protected region of old-growth forest with trees as old as 150 years. There are 45 miles of trails in all.

Nahmakanta Management Unit Maine, page 58. Located throughout the state, the Public Reserve lands offer a variety of hiking experiences, from rugged mountain peaks to rocky coastline trails. Encompassing more than 43,000 acres, this is the largest management unit in the state's public lands system

South Branch Pond Campground, North Woods, Maine, pages 48. Spectacular hiking trails heading into the forest, the mountains, and alongside the rivers and lakes are located near all of the campgrounds in Baxter State Park, including this one.

Underhill State Park, Northeast Kingdom and Lake Champlain, Vt., page 303. Underhill is part of the 34,000-acre Mount Mansfield State Forest and four popular trails lead from the campground to the summit ridge of Mount Mansfield, Vermont's tallest peak at 4,393 feet. The Sunset Ridge Trail is the most popular and scenic, offering views for much of the way.

Waterville Campground, White Mountains, N.H., page 211. A scenic bowl formed by Mounts Tecumseh, Osceola, Kancamagus, Tripyramid, and Sandwich Dome offer miles of hiking trails traversing the Sandwich Range Wilderness.

Ⓕ Top 10 Campgrounds near Historic Sites

Bissellville, Berkshires, Mass., page 375. Down every road it seems is another piece of history, from historic estates, such as Edith Wharton's home, to museums, like Hancock Shaker Village.

Blackwoods Campground, Down East, Maine, page 169. The Acadia region is the scene of some of America's earliest episodes, from Champlain's voyages of discovery to the earliest conflicts in the French and Indian Wars.

Boston Harbor Islands State Park, Greater Boston, Mass., page 414. From remains of military forts to old homesteads, these 34 islands hold much history.

Coolidge State Park, Southeast Vt., page 348. Nearby is the birthplace of Calvin Coolidge, the 30th president of the United States and the man for whom the park was named. Learn about him at the Calvin Coolidge Homestead historical museum.

Ellis Haven Family Campground, Greater Boston, Mass., page 419. Get a sense of what life was like for those early, intrepid campers, the Pilgrims, on a stroll around nearby Plimoth Plantation, a living history museum re- creating life in 1627.

Flying Dutchman, Down East, Maine, page 154. Just upstream is Fort Knox, an impressive stone fort built during the Civil War era to defend Penobscot Bay and the Penobscot River from Confederate Raiders.

Fort Getty Recreation Area, R.I., page 461. During the Revolutionary War the waters around

Jamestown and Newport were controlled first by the British, then by the French. In the early 1900s, the gun batteries at Fort Getty stood ready to defend Narragansett Bay's West Passage against invading fleets. Some of the gun batteries and concrete foundations are visible today.

Melville Pond Campground, R.I., page 462. It's just a short distance to the site of Butts Hill Fort, where the men of the First Rhode Island Regiment, composed mainly of African-American soldiers, fought the British in 1778.

Minuteman KOA, Greater Boston, Mass., page 413. Every April, locals reenact the Battle Lexington on the town green. Learn about America's revolutionary history at area museums.

Seaport Campgrounds, Long Island Sound, Conn., page 512. This is the campground closes to Mystic Seaport, a world-famous indoor/outdoor maritime museum that tells America's seaside story.

Maine

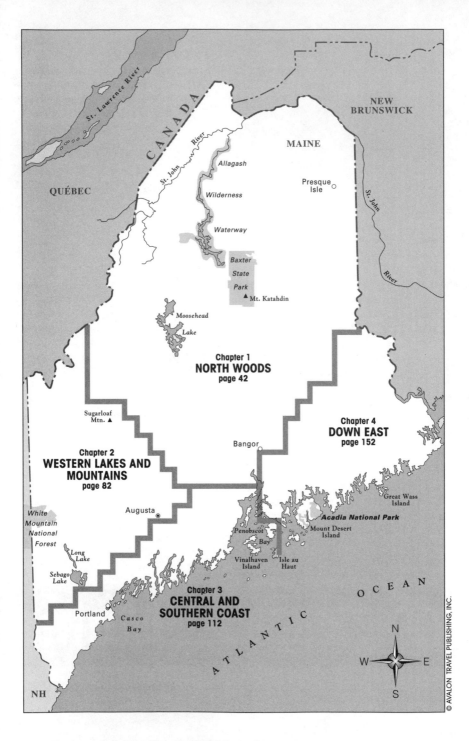

Chapter 1

© MAINE OFFICE OF TOURISM/JEFF GREENBERG

North Woods

North Woods

Remote and undeveloped, Maine's North Woods is home to moose and bear, loons and eagles, salmon and brook trout, but not many people. An expansive region of forests, mountains, rivers, and lakes, this is one of the last truly wild places left in the United States.

These millions of forested acres along the Canadian border are blessed with spectacular natural features, including two major wilderness rivers, the Allagash and the St. John. The 40-mile-long Moosehead Lake, ringed by woods and mountains, offers plenty of fishing and boating opportunities. And overlooking all are the high rocky mountains jutting above the landscape in Baxter State Park.

This corner of New England is a four-season wonderland. Ever since Henry David Thoreau paddled the Penobscot River and climbed mile-high Mount Katahdin while writing the journals that became *The*

Maine Woods, outdoors enthusiasts have traveled here in search of adventure. The North Woods is one of the country's premier destinations to canoe, hike, hunt, fish, snowmobile, dogsled, and just plain get away from it all.

Up here you'll find plenty of solitude. Except for a few small frontier towns on its fringes, the North Woods is virtually uninhabited. Paved roads and visitor services are few, so be prepared to rough it a bit. An indispensable travel aid to trip planning in the North Woods is the *DeLorme Maine Atlas & Gazetteer* (website: www.delorme.com). It's chock-full of topographic maps, contact numbers and addresses, and loads of recreational information. Even locals make sure to bring it with them before heading out on the ever-changing network of logging roads that crisscross this vast region.

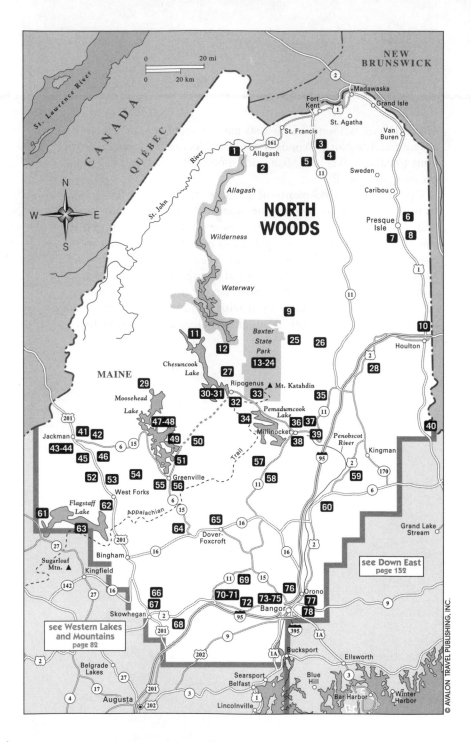

1 ALLAGASH WILDERNESS WATERWAY

Rating: 10

Along the Allagash River

Northern Maine is a canoe camper's paradise, and the Allagash Wilderness Waterway flows right through the heart of it. With miles of undeveloped wildlands and several enormous wilderness lakes to paddle through, canoe tripping just doesn't get any better than this. The St. John River and the watershed of the Allagash River are the largest uninhabited regions in the lower 48 states, so if you are looking for solitude, you've found the right spot. Taking a side trip up Allagash Stream to mountain-rimmed Allagash Lake is highly recommended. And there's a wonderful nine-mile stretch of moderate white water below the ranger station at Churchill Dam. Cast a line for togue in the bigger lakes or go fly-fishing for trout along the riverbank, always keeping your eyes open for moose. In the winter, a few hardy wilderness travelers who don't mind deep snow and fierce cold venture out to these parts. No matter when you come to explore the Allagash Wilderness Waterway, remember to plan ahead, as supplies and services are unavailable.

Campsites, facilities: There are 80 primitive tent sites along this section of the waterway. Each site has a pit toilet, a fire ring and grate, and a picnic table. Pets are allowed.

Reservations, fees: Sites are available on a first-come, first-served basis. The fee is $5 a night per person for Maine residents, $6 a night per person for out-of-staters.

Open: Year-round.

Directions: The 100-mile-long Allagash Wilderness Waterway flows from Telos Lake in the south to near Allagash Village in the north.

Contact: Maine Bureau of Parks and Lands, 22 State House Station, Augusta, ME 04333, 207/287-3821, website: www.state.me.us/doc/parks.

2 DEBOULLIE MANAGEMENT UNIT

Rating: 10

South of St. Francis

This remote slice of Maine is extraordinarily beautiful, a land graced with forests, lakes, and rolling hills. Unsullied and little-visited, the Deboullie Management Unit is a fine example of what the heart of the Maine Woods can offer those intrepid souls willing to venture far off the beaten path. The rewards, in terms of solitude and superior wilderness recreation, are many. With access to lakes and streams, campers can paddle around in a canoe or boat, or take a refreshing dip. And for anglers looking for a place to cast out a line, the native brook trout fishery is exceptional. To gain some perspective on the land, hit the hiking trail that leads to the fire tower atop Deboullie Mountain.

Campsites, facilities: There are 13 primitive tent sites located on the lakes and streams encompassed by the management unit. Picnic tables, fire rings, and pit toilets are provided. Several of the lakes have boat ramps. Pets are allowed.

Reservations, fees: Sites are available on a first-come, first-served basis. There is no fee.

Open: Year-round.

Directions: From Fort Kent on the northern border of Maine, drive west on Highway 161 to St. Francis. At the paper company checkpoint, head south on one of the logging roads for approximately 10 miles to access the management unit.

Contact: Maine Bureau of Parks and Lands, 22 State House Station, Augusta, ME 04333, 207/287-3821, website: www.state.me.us/doc/parks.

3 BIRCH HAVEN CAMPGROUND

Rating: 7

On Eagle Lake, south of the hamlet of Soldier Pond

Life at Birch Haven Campground—located on the long, narrow, and largely undeveloped Eagle

Lake—revolves around the waterfront, making this a good choice for campers who enjoy swimming, fishing, and boating. The lake empties into the Fish River, which meanders north to Fort Kent and then joins the St. John River before flowing into Canada. The fishing here is excellent, as these waters are teeming with trout, salmon, smelt, and togue, and you'll certainly find many spots where you can try your luck.

Campsites, facilities: There are 80 sites for tents and RVs, many with full hookups and the remainder with water and electric hookups. Facilities include picnic tables, fireplaces, flush toilets, hot showers, a general store, laundry facilites, and a dump station. For recreation, there's a swimming beach, boat dock, canoe and paddleboat rentals, basketball court, horseshoe pit, sports field, volleyball, arcade, and a pool table. Leashed pets are permitted.

Reservations, fees: Reservations are accepted. Sites are $18–25 a night.

Open: Memorial Day–Labor Day.

Directions: From Fort Kent on the northern border of Maine, drive south on Highway 11 and turn left at the hamlet of Soldier Pond. After crossing the Fish River, turn right on Sly Brook Road and travel approximately five miles south to the campground.

Contact: Ron and Jacky Roy, Birch Haven Campground, Sly Brook Road, Soldier Pond, ME 04781, 207/444-5102.

4 EAGLE LAKE MANAGEMENT UNIT

🏊 🛶 🚗 🎣 ❄ 🐕 ⛺

Rating: 8

Near the small town of Eagle Lake

The Eagle Lake Management Unit encompasses some 23,000 acres of northern woods and waters, including most of Eagle Lake. In addition, the land abuts Square Lake, another large freshwater pond connected to Eagle Lake by a small stream, or thoroughfare, as such connecting waterways are commonly called

in Maine. As is the case with most of the state's management units, Eagle Lake is used primarily by hunters and anglers during the spring and autumn months.

Campsites, facilities: There are nine primitive tent sites set along the shores of Eagle Lake and nearby Square Lake. Picnic tables, fire rings, and pit toilets are provided. Pets are allowed.

Reservations, fees: Sites are available on a first-come, first-served basis. There is no fee.

Open: Year-round.

Directions: From Fort Kent on the northern border of Maine, drive south on Highway 11 and turn left at the hamlet of Soldier Pond. After crossing the Fish River, turn right on Sly Brook Road and travel approximately six miles south to the management unit. You can also access the area by boat from the hamlet of Eagle Lake.

Contact: Maine Bureau of Parks and Lands, 22 State House Station, Augusta, ME 04333, 207/287-3821, website: www.state.me.us/doc/parks.

5 WINTERVILLE LAKEVIEW CAMPS

🏊 🛶 🚗 🎣 ❄ 🐕 🛶 🚐

Rating: 8

On St. Froid Lake in Winterville

Set alongside St. Froid Lake, the Winterville campground caters to the outdoorsmen and women who flock to this part of northern Maine to fish for trout, salmon, and togue in the summer; hunt deer, bear, moose, and grouse in the fall; and go snowmobiling, snowshoeing, cross-country skiing, or ice fishing in the winter. The lake itself is crystal clear, with many sheltered coves and inlets, and is surrounded by hundreds of square miles of woodlands for hiking.

Campsites, facilities: There are 16 sites for tents and RVs with partial hookups. Facilities include a boat dock, playground, and horseshoe pit. Pets are allowed.

Reservations, fees: Reservations are not necessary. Sites are $15–18 a night.

Open: Year-round.

Directions: From Fort Kent, drive south on Highway 11 to the hamlet of Eagle Lake and then continue south for another 2.5 miles. At the campground sign, turn right onto a private dirt road and travel .5 mile west.

Contact: The Hagenmillers, Winterville Lakeview Camps, Highway 11, P.O. Box 397, Eagle Lake, ME 04739, 207/444-4581.

6 ARNDT'S AROOSTOOK RIVER LODGE AND CAMPGROUND

Rating: 7

On the Aroostook River near the town of Presque Isle

From your campsite at Arndt's River Lodge and Campground, you are perched on a hill side overlooking the pretty Aroostook River. The campground provides good access to the water for swimming, fishing, and canoeing enthusiasts. And for mountain bikers, the Vicious Cycle bike shop in Presque Isle rents mountain bikes for use on local trails and logging roads, as well as on the biking and hiking trail system on the property.

Arndt's is located just outside of downtown Presque Isle and pretty close to the Maine–New Brunswick border. For more information on the surrounding area, see the following listing for Aroostook State Park.

Campsites, facilities: There are 65 sites for RVs and 20 tent sites. Facilities include a store, laundry machines, flush toilets, free hot showers, and a dump station. You will also find a recreation room, swimming pool, canoe and bike rentals, basketball and badminton courts, a sports field, and hiking and mountain biking trails on the property. Leashed pets are permitted.

Reservations, fees: Reservations are recommended. To reserve, you must stay at least two nights and make a deposit of up to 50 percent of the list rate. Sites are $18–25 a night.

Open: May 15–October 15.

Directions: From the junction of Highway 167 and U.S. 1 in Presque Isle, drive three miles east on Highway 167 to the intersection with Highway 205. Turn left (north) on Highway 205 and drive less than a mile to the campground.

Contact: Clare and Ken Arndt, Arndt's Aroostook River Lodge and Campground, 95 Parkhurst Siding Road, Highway 205, Presque Isle, ME 04769, 207/764-8677, website: www.arndtscamp.com.

7 AROOSTOOK STATE PARK

Rating: 7

On Echo Lake south of Presque Isle

The quiet, wooded campground at Aroostook State Park is nestled at the base of a small mountain range in Maine's northernmost county, which also happens to be the largest county east of the Mississippi River. Aroostook County is the heart of the state's potato-growing region, in addition to being a heavily forested area. Sparsely populated, the county retains a strong frontier flavor. It was settled largely by French Canadians, and the French influence is still pervasive: conversations in local establishments are as likely to be spoken in French as in English. Campers at the state park may spend time swimming or fishing in Echo Lake, or hiking the trail to the nearby Quaggy Joe Mountain summit. The campground also puts you close to Presque Isle, the largest community in the county, and just minutes from the New Brunswick border.

Campsites, facilities: There are 30 sites for tents or RVs up to 24 feet in length. Nonflush toilets, fire grills, and picnic tables are provided. On the waterfront, you will find a boat ramp, canoe rentals, and a swimming area with a lifeguard on duty. Leashed pets are permitted.

Reservations, fees: Reservations are accepted, although the State of Maine does allocate some sites on a first-come, first-served basis. Contact the Maine Bureau of Parks and Lands at the number below. Sites are $8 a night for

Maine residents and $10 a night for nonresidents.

Open: May 15–October 15.

Directions: From the junction of Highway 163 and U.S. 1 in Presque Isle, drive 3.75 miles south on U.S. 1, then turn right on Spragueville Road, and drive two miles west to the park entrance.

Contact: Aroostook State Park Ranger, 207/768-8341; Maine Bureau of Parks and Lands, 22 State House Station, Augusta, ME 04333, 207/287-3821, website: www.state.me.us/doc/parks.

8 NEIL E. MICHAUD CAMPGROUND

Rating: 6

On the southern outskirts of Presque Isle

Located just outside the town of Presque Isle, this campground puts you within minutes of plenty of places where you can fish, swim, canoe, and boat. A popular hike to the nearby Quaggy Joe Mountain summit leaves from nearby Aroostook State Park. In the fall, make this your base camp for hunting excursions, as you try to bag bear, moose, deer, duck, and grouse. In the winter, the area is crisscrossed with hundreds of miles of snowmobile trails. Cross-country skiing and snowshoeing are other popular pursuits. For more information on the area, see the previous listing for Aroostook State Park.

Campsites, facilities: There are 45 sites for tents and RVs, eight with full hookups, and 37 with water and electric hookups. Flush toilets, hot showers, picnic tables, fireplaces, laundry facilities, a dump station, store, recreation room, basketball and volleyball courts, and a playground are provided. Leashed pets are permitted.

Reservations, fees: Reservations are not necessary. Sites are $15–20 a night.

Open: May 1–October 15.

Directions: From Presque Isle, drive south on U.S. 1 for 2.5 miles to the campground on the left (east) side of the road.

Contact: Bob and Barb Kinney, Neil E. Michaud Campground, 164 Houlton Road, Presque Isle, ME 04769, 207/769-1951.

9 SCRAGGLY LAKE MANAGEMENT UNIT

Rating: 10

Northeast of Baxter State Park

Scraggly Lake is the centerpiece of this 10,000-acre public landholding in the North Woods. Characterized by rolling hills, heavily forested terrain, and numerous lakes, ponds, brooks, and bogs, the area provides excellent habitat for more than 200 species of wildlife, while the lakes and ponds are home to healthy populations of trout and salmon. This is a very remote region, so be sure to bring adequate supplies of food, gasoline, spare tires, and emergency equipment, especially in winter. No supplies are available in the vicinity.

Campsites, facilities: There are five primitive tent sites along the shore of Scraggly Lake. Each site has a picnic table, fire ring, and pit toilet. There's also a boat ramp. Pets are permitted.

Reservations, fees: Reservations are not accepted, and the sites are available on a first-come, first-served basis. There is no fee.

Open: Year-round.

Directions: From Patten, drive 10 miles northwest on Highway 159 to Shin Pond and then continue about 18 miles north of Shin Pond on logging roads to access the unit.

Contact: Maine Bureau of Parks and Lands, 22 State House Station, Augusta, ME 04333, 207/287-3821, website: www.state.me.us/doc/parks.

10 MY BROTHER'S PLACE

Rating: 6

In Houlton near the New Brunswick border

My Brother's Place is a small, quiet retreat set

on open, well-maintained fields just off the county's major north-south highway. Although the campground is not a resort in its own right, and there are few activities available at the campground, you have access to a small pond where you can toss out a fishing line, swim, or paddle around in a canoe. This is a good place to stay if you are on your way to or from Canada, as the line separating us from our northern neighbor is only four miles away.

Campsites, facilities: There are 100 sites for tents and RVs, 40 with full hookups, 40 with water and electric hookups, and 20 with no hookups. Flush toilets, hot showers, picnic tables, fireplaces, laundry facilities, and a dump station are provided. Amenities also include a pond for swimming, boating, and fishing; recreation room and playground; and basketball, volleyball, and horseshoes. Leashed pets are permitted.

Reservations, fees: Reservations are recommended. Sites are $16–20 a night.
Open: May 1–October 31.
Directions: From Houlton, drive two miles north on U.S. 1 to the campground on the right (east) side of the road.
Contact: Art and Sally Nickel, My Brother's Place, RR 3, Box 650, Houlton, ME 04730, 207/532-6739, website: www.mainerec.com/mybro.

11 GERO ISLAND MANAGEMENT UNIT
☀ 🚣 🎿 🏕 ❄ 🐕 ⛰

Rating: 10
West of Baxter State Park
on Chesuncook Lake

Gero Island is a 3,100-acre island at the northern tip of Chesuncook Lake, a large and undeveloped body of water in the heart of the Maine Woods. The land is used primarily by fishers, hunters, and canoeists retracing Henry David Thoreau's canoe journey down the West Branch of the Penobscot River. Most of the historic logging village of Chesuncook, on the mainland, is incorporated into this unit as well.

Campsites, facilities: Six primitive campsites are located along the shore of the island and are accessible by canoe. Picnic tables, fire rings, and pit toilets are provided. Pets are permitted.
Reservations, fees: Reservations are not accepted; the sites are available on a first-come, first-served basis. The fee is $4 a night per person.
Open: Year-round.
Directions: Access to the unit is gained via water highways connecting Chesuncook Lake, the West Branch of the Penobscot River, and the Allagash Wilderness Waterway. The nearest launch sites are at Chesuncook Dam at the lake's southern end and at the North Maine Woods campsite on Umbazooksus Stream.
Contact: Maine Bureau of Parks and Lands, 22 State House Station, Augusta, ME 04333, 207/287-3821, website: www.state.me.us/doc/ parks.

12 TELOS MANAGEMENT UNIT
☀ 🚣 🎿 🏕 ❄ 🐕 ⛰

Rating: 8
Northwest of Baxter State Park

A remote region of lakes, forests, and gently rolling hills is home to the Telos Management Unit, where intrepid campers find a few primitive tent sites and a bounty of recreational offerings, from paddling a canoe on a lazy summer day to strapping on the snowshoes and exploring the surrounding terrain in the winter. Telos and Chamberlain Lakes are outstanding fisheries for togue and brook trout. Telos Lake is the most popular starting point for canoeists who plan to travel the Allagash Wilderness Waterway (see listing earlier in this chapter).

Campsites, facilities: There are three primitive tent sites, each with a picnic table, fire ring, and pit toilet. Pets are permitted.
Reservations, fees: Reservations are not accepted; sites are available on a first-come, first-served basis. The fee is $4 a night per person.
Open: Year-round.
Directions: To access the unit, drive 30 miles west from Millinocket on the Golden Road to

Ripogenus Dam, then bear right on the Telos Road and head 16 miles north.

Contact: Maine Bureau of Parks and Lands, 22 State House Station, Augusta, ME 04333, 207/287-3821, website: www.state.me.us/doc/parks.

13 TROUT BROOK FARM CAMPGROUND

🏃 ≋ 🛶 🚤 🎿 ❄ ⛺

Rating: 8

In Baxter State Park

The park's northernmost campground is situated, not surprisingly, along Trout Brook, a lovely stream that flows into Grand Lake Matagamon, where anglers can try to catch brook trout, togue, and salmon. Behind the campground looms Trout Brook Mountain. The Freezeout Trail, a beautiful long-distance hiking route, leaves from the campground. For more information on Baxter State Park, see Abol Campground in this chapter.

Campsites, facilities: This group camping area holds 18 tent sites. Picnic tables, fire rings, and pit toilets are provided. No vehicle larger than nine feet high, seven feet wide, and 22 feet long may enter Baxter State Park. Pets are not allowed in the park.

Reservations, fees: Reservations are strongly recommended and may be made either by mail or in person. The full fee must accompany reservations made by mail. Sites are $9 a night per person, with a minimum fee of $18 per site.

Open: May 15–October 15 and December 1–April 1.

Directions: From the intersection of Highways 11 and 159 in Patten, travel northwest on Highway 159 for 24 miles to the Matagamon Gatehouse. Continue approximately two miles west on Perimeter Road to the campground. There is an $8 road-use fee for out-of-state vehicles.

Contact: Baxter State Park, 64 Balsam Drive, Millinocket, ME 04462-2190, 207/723-5140, website: www.state.me.us.

14 SOUTH BRANCH POND CAMPGROUND

🏃 ≋ 🛶 🚤 🎿 ❄ ⛺

Rating: 10

In Baxter State Park

Ⓕ South Branch Pond is a large campground situated at the tip of a long, narrow lake nestled in a cleft between high mountains. The scenery is absolutely sensational. Trails to the surrounding heights fan out in all directions from the campground. If you paddle, you can rent a canoe right here. For more information on Baxter State Park, see Abol Campground in this chapter.

Campsites, facilities: There are 12 lean-tos, each of which can accommodate up to four people, a bunkhouse with a six-person capacity, and 21 tent sites. Picnic tables, fire rings, and pit toilets are provided. No vehicle larger than nine feet high, seven feet wide, and 22 feet long may enter Baxter State Park. Pets are not allowed in the park.

Reservations, fees: Reservations are strongly recommended and may be made either by mail or in person. The full fee must accompany reservations made by mail. Tent sites and lean-tos are $9 a night per person, with a minimum fee of $18 per site. The bunkhouse costs $10 per person.

Open: May 15–October 15 and December 1–April 1.

Directions: From the intersection of Highways 11 and 159 in Patten, travel northwest on Highway 159 for 24 miles to the Matagamon Gatehouse. Continue nine miles west on Perimeter Road. There is an $8 road-use fee for out-of-state vehicles.

Contact: Baxter State Park, 64 Balsam Drive, Millinocket, ME 04462-2190, 207/723-5140, website: www.state.me.us.

15 RUSSELL POND CAMPGROUND

Rating: 10

In Baxter State Park

In the very heart of Baxter State Park, there's a hike-in campground at Russell Pond, a worthy destination for the adventurous traveler seeking an off-the-beaten-path experience. North of the highest peaks surrounding Katahdin, Russell Pond sits nestled among low mountains. Trails that ascend the surrounding heights radiate in all directions from the campground. For more information on Baxter State Park, see Abol Campground in this chapter.

Campsites, facilities: There are two lean-tos for up to four people each, one lean-to with a six-person capacity, one lean-to with an eight-person capacity, a bunkhouse for up to 13 people, and four tent sites. Picnic tables, fire rings, and pit toilets are provided. No vehicle larger than nine feet high, seven feet wide, and 22 feet long may enter Baxter State Park. Pets are not allowed.

Reservations, fees: Reservations are strongly recommended and may be made either by mail or in person. The full fee must accompany reservations made by mail. Tent sites and lean-tos are $9 a night per person, with a minimum fee of $18 per site. The bunkhouse costs $10 per person.

Open: May 15–October 15 and December 1–April 1.

Directions: From the junction of Highway 11/157 and the Baxter State Park Road in Millinocket, drive 18 miles west on the Baxter State Park Road to the Togue Pond Gatehouse. Continue approximately eight miles north on the Roaring Brook Road to the parking lot at Roaring Brook Campground and then hike seven miles north on the Russell Pond Trail to the campground. There is an $8 road-use fee for out-of-state vehicles.

Contact: Baxter State Park, 64 Balsam Drive, Millinocket, ME 04462-2190, 207/723-5140, website: www.state.me.us.

16 NESOWADNEHUNK FIELD CAMPGROUND

Rating: 8

In Baxter State Park

Nesowadnehunk, pronounced by locals as *Sow-Dee-Hunk,* is a site where large groups can camp in a grassy, open area surrounded by strikingly beautiful scenery. Especially noteworthy are the views to the east toward Katahdin. Campers can swim and fish in Nesowadnehunk Stream, as well as in nearby lakes, ponds, and rivers. A trail leads south from the campground to the Doubletop Mountain summit. For more information on Baxter State Park, see Abol Campground in this chapter.

Campsites, facilities: There are 10 lean-tos that can accommodate up to four people each, one lean-to with a three-person capacity, and 12 tent sites. Picnic tables, fire rings, and pit toilets are provided. No vehicle larger than nine feet high, seven feet wide, and 22 feet long may enter Baxter State Park. Pets are not allowed in the park.

Reservations, fees: Reservations are strongly recommended and may be made either by mail or in person. The full fee must accompany reservations made by mail. Tent sites and lean-tos are $9 a night per person, with a minimum fee of $18 per site.

Open: May 15–October 15 and December 1–April 1.

Directions: From the junction of Highway 11/157 and the Baxter State Park Road in Millinocket, drive 18 miles west on the Baxter State Park Road to the Togue Pond Gatehouse. Continue about 17 miles west of the park entrance on the Perimeter Road to the campground. There is an $8 road-use fee for out-of-state vehicles.

Contact: Baxter State Park, 64 Balsam Drive, Millinocket, ME 04462-2190, 207/723-5140, website: www.state.me.us.

17 CHIMNEY POND CAMPGROUND

Rating: 10

In Baxter State Park

Chimney Pond is a glacial tarn set amid some of the most spectacular high-mountain scenery in the United States. On all sides of the campground, jagged rocky summits swoop toward the sky. Mountain adventure beckons in all directions, and hikers will find myriad trails that leave from here. For more information on Baxter State Park, see Abol Campground in this chapter.

Campsites, facilities: There are nine lean-tos that can accommodate up to four people each and one bunkhouse with a 12-person capacity; there are no tent sites. Pit toilets are provided. No vehicle larger than nine feet high, seven feet wide, and 22 feet long may enter Baxter State Park. Pets are not allowed in the park.

Reservations, fees: Reservations are strongly recommended and may be made either by mail or in person. The full fee must accompany reservations made by mail. Lean-tos are $9 a night per person, with a minimum fee of $18 per site. The bunkhouse costs $10 per person.

Open: May 15–October 15 and December 1–April 1.

Directions: From the junction of Highway 11/157 and the Baxter State Park Road in Millinocket, drive 18 miles west on the Baxter State Park Road to the Togue Pond Gatehouse. Continue approximately eight miles north on the Roaring Brook Road to the parking lot at Roaring Brook Campground and then hike 3.3 miles to Chimney Pond Campground. There is an $8 road-use fee for out-of-state vehicles.

Contact: Baxter State Park, 64 Balsam Drive, Millinocket, ME 04462-2190, 207/723-5140, website: www.state.me.us.

18 ROARING BROOK CAMPGROUND

Rating: 8

In Baxter State Park

Perched above a tumbling, boulder-filled mountain stream, Roaring Brook is a good spot for hikers who want to get an early start on Katahdin's infamous Knife Edge Trail, a walk along a sharp spine of rock with precipitous drops on either side. This is also a good camp for skiers heading to Chimney Pond from the park entrance. For more information on Baxter State Park, see Abol Campground in this chapter.

Campsites, facilities: There are seven lean-tos that can accommodate four people each, three lean-tos with a three-person capacity, two lean-tos with a six-person capacity, and 10 tent sites. A bunkhouse can hold 12 people. Picnic tables, fire rings, and pit toilets are provided. No vehicle larger than nine feet high, seven feet wide, and 22 feet long may enter Baxter State Park. Pets are not allowed in the park.

Reservations, fees: Reservations are strongly recommended and may be made either by mail or in person. The full fee must accompany reservations made by mail. Tent sites and lean-tos are $9 a night per person, with a minimum fee of $18 per site. The bunkhouse costs $10 per person.

Open: May 15–October 15 and December 1–April 1.

Directions: From the junction of Highway 11/157 and the Baxter State Park Road in Millinocket, drive 18 miles west on the Baxter State Park Road to the Togue Pond Gatehouse. Continue approximately eight miles north of the park entrance on the Roaring Brook Road to the campground. There is an $8 road-use fee for out-of-state vehicles.

Contact: Baxter State Park, 64 Balsam Drive, Millinocket, ME 04462-2190, 207/723-5140, website: www.state.me.us.

19 AVALANCHE FIELD CAMPGROUND

Rating: 8

In Baxter State Park

This small campsite lies on the eastern side of the Katahdin massif. It's a great place to spend the night before hiking the infamous Knife Edge Trail, a strenuous trek that traces the precipitous rim of Katahdin—not for those who suffer from a fear of heights. For more information on Baxter State Park, see Abol Campground in this chapter.

Campsites, facilities: There are two lean-tos, each with a four-person capacity, and nine tent sites. Picnic tables, fire rings, and pit toilets are provided. No vehicle larger than nine feet high, seven feet wide, and 22 feet long may enter Baxter State Park. Pets are not allowed in the park.

Reservations, fees: Reservations are strongly recommended and may be made either by mail or in person. The full fee must accompany reservations made by mail. Tent sites and lean-tos are $9 a night per person, with a minimum fee of $18 per site.

Open: May 15–October 15 and December 1–April 1.

Directions: From the junction of Highway 11/157 and the Baxter State Park Road in Millinocket, drive 18 miles west on the Baxter State Park Road to the Togue Pond Gatehouse. Continue approximately six miles north of the park entrance on the Roaring Brook Road. There is an $8 road-use fee for out-of-state vehicles.

Contact: Baxter State Park, 64 Balsam Drive, Millinocket, ME 04462-2190, 207/723-5140, website: www.state.me.us.

20 FOSTER FIELD CAMPGROUND

Rating: 8

In Baxter State Park

The group tenting area known as Foster Field is well situated for those who want to embark on hikes to some of the less-visited peaks near Katahdin. Try following the O-J-I Trail to the Mount O-J-I summit, or continue on a loop that includes Mount Coe and the Brothers. For more information on Baxter State Park, see Abol Campground in this chapter.

Campsites, facilities: There are five group tent sites. Picnic tables, fire rings, and pit toilets are provided. No vehicle larger than nine feet high, seven feet wide, and 22 feet long may enter Baxter State Park. Pets are not allowed in the park.

Reservations, fees: Reservations are strongly recommended and may be made either by mail or in person. The full fee must accompany reservations made by mail. Tent sites are $9 a night per person, with a minimum fee of $18 per site.

Open: May 15–October 15 and December 1–April 1.

Directions: From the junction of Highway 11/157 and the Baxter State Park Road in Millinocket, drive 18 miles west on the Baxter State Park Road to the Togue Pond Gatehouse. Continue approximately 12 miles west of the park entrance on the Perimeter Road until you reach the campground. There is an $8 road-use fee for out-of-state vehicles.

Contact: Baxter State Park, 64 Balsam Drive, Millinocket, ME 04462-2190, 207/723-5140, website: www.state.me.us.

21 KIDNEY POND CAMPGROUND

Rating: 10

In Baxter State Park

Cabins at this old-style North Woods fishing resort overlook Kidney Pond and, in the distance, mile-high Katahdin. A spectacularly pretty, peaceful spot, it combines the best elements of the park: woods, waters, mountains, and wildlife. For more information on Baxter State Park, see Abol Campground in this chapter.

Campsites, facilities: There are five cabins with

a two-person capacity, four cabins with a four-person capacity, and two cabins with a three-person capacity. Pit toilets are provided. No vehicle larger than nine feet high, seven feet wide, and 22 feet long may enter Baxter State Park. Pets are not allowed in the park.

Reservations, fees: Reservations are strongly recommended and may be made either by mail or in person. The full fee must accompany reservations made by mail. Fees start at $25 a night per person in a small cabin, to $75 a night at a larger cabin.

Open: May 15–October 15 and December 1–April 1.

Directions: From the junction of Highway 11/157 and the Baxter State Park Road in Millinocket, drive 18 miles west on the Baxter State Park Road to the Togue Pond Gatehouse. Continue approximately 13 miles west of the park entrance. There is an $8 road-use fee for out-of-state vehicles.

Contact: Baxter State Park, 64 Balsam Drive, Millinocket, ME 04462-2190, 207/723-5140, website: www.state.me.us.

22 KATAHDIN STREAM CAMPGROUND

🏕 🏊 🎣 ✖ ❄ 🚐 ⛺

Rating: 8

In Baxter State Park

Katahdin Stream is a popular campground with a prime location alongside its namesake stream where the water pours down the mountainside and through the woods before joining the Penobscot River. Here the final stretch of the Appalachian Trail—called the Hunt Trail at this point—begins to ascend the Katahdin summit. For more information on Baxter State Park, see Abol Campground in this chapter.

Campsites, facilities: There are five lean-tos that can accommodate up to four people each, four lean-tos with a five-person capacity, three lean-tos with a three-person capacity, and 10 tent sites. A bunkhouse holds six people. Picnic tables, fire rings, and pit toilets are provided. No

vehicle larger than nine feet high, seven feet wide, and 22 feet long may enter Baxter State Park. Pets are not allowed in the park.

Reservations, fees: Reservations are strongly recommended and may be made either by mail or in person. The full fee must accompany reservations made by mail. Tent sites and lean-tos are $9 a night per person, with a minimum fee of $18 per site. The bunkhouse costs $10 per person.

Open: May 15–October 15 and December 1–April 1.

Directions: From the junction of Highway 11/157 and the Baxter State Park Road in Millinocket, drive 18 miles west on the Baxter State Park Road to the Togue Pond Gatehouse. Continue approximately eight miles west of the park entrance on the Perimeter Road until you reach the campground. There is an $8 road-use fee for out-of-state vehicles.

Contact: Baxter State Park, 64 Balsam Drive, Millinocket, ME 04462-2190, 207/723-5140, website: www.state.me.us.

23 DAICEY POND CAMPGROUND

🏕 🏊 🎣 ✖ ❄ 🚐

Rating: 10

In Baxter State Park

Before Baxter State Park assumed control, these cabins at Daicey Pond were part of a fishing resort, and they still maintain that rustic North Woods camp flavor that so many outdoors lovers have come to appreciate in this part of Maine. While staying in one of the cabins, you enjoy views over the spruce- and fir-rimmed lake to the mile-high Katahdin summit. The park rents canoes at Daicey Pond, and a day spent on these waters fishing for togue under the shadow of the Katahdin massif is not soon forgotten. For more information on Baxter State Park, see the following listing for Abol Campground.

Campsites, facilities: There are two lean-tos for Appalachian Trail hikers, five cabins with a four-person capacity, four cabins with a two-person capacity, and one cabin with a three-person capacity. Pit toilets are provided. No vehicle larger than nine feet high, seven feet wide, and 22 feet long may enter Baxter State Park. Pets are not allowed in the park.

Reservations, fees: Reservations are strongly recommended and may be made either by mail or in person. The full fee must accompany any reservation made by mail. Tent sites and lean-tos are $9 a night per person, with a minimum fee of $18 per site.

Open: May 15–October 15 and December 1–April 1.

Directions: From the junction of Highway 11/157 and the Baxter State Park Road in Millinocket, drive 18 miles west on the Baxter State Park Road to the Togue Pond Gatehouse. Continue approximately 11 miles west to the campground turnoff, then turn left and drive about one mile to Daicey Pond. There is an $8 road-use fee for out-of-state vehicles.

Contact: Baxter State Park, 64 Balsam Drive, Millinocket, ME 04462-2190, 207/723-5140, website: www.state.me.us.

24 ABOL CAMPGROUND

Rating: 9

In Baxter State Park

For many people who venture into the interior of Maine, Baxter State Park is the focal point of their travels. Established in 1931, the park is surrounded by timber company landholdings that extend to the Canadian border. The views in any direction from the 5,267-foot summit of Katahdin, Maine's highest peak, are of unbroken forest, rivers, and lakes. More than 170 trail miles have been blazed throughout the park, allowing visitors to take short day hikes or more extended backpacking trips in the interior. For many Mainers, a trek up the Katahdin summit is almost a right of passage. Hiking the Knife Edge on Katahdin is not for the faint of heart: this narrow ridge—in places less than one yard wide—is flanked on each side by 2,000-foot

precipices. (If you plan to day hike in the park, be sure to pick up the "Day Use Hiking Guide" at park headquarters.) For those who prefer water-based activity, there are numerous lakes, rivers, and streams within park boundaries as well as plentiful opportunities for boating and fishing just outside the park.

This popular campground is located at the southern edge of the park. Some of the sites have lean-tos, while others offer simply a place to pitch your tent.

Campsites, facilities: There are 12 lean-tos that can accommodate up to four people each, plus nine tent sites. Picnic tables, fire rings, and pit toilets are provided. No vehicle larger than nine feet high, seven feet wide, and 22 feet long may enter Baxter State Park. Pets are not allowed in the park.

Reservations, fees: Reservations are strongly recommended and may be made either by mail or in person. The full fee must accompany reservations made by mail. Tent sites and lean-tos are $9 a night per person, with a minimum fee of $18 per site.

Open: May 15–October 15 and December 1–April 1.

Directions: From the junction of Highway 11/157 and the Baxter State Park Road in Millinocket, drive 18 miles west on the Baxter State Park Road to the Togue Pond Gatehouse. The campground is approximately six miles west of the park entrance. There is an $8 road-use fee for out-of-state vehicles.

Contact: Baxter State Park, 64 Balsam Drive, Millinocket, ME 04462-2190, 207/723-5140, website: www.state.me.us.

25 MATAGAMON WILDERNESS CAMPGROUND

Rating: 10

Northwest of Patten

These remote, wooded sites offer campers a sense of privacy. Situated on the East Branch of the Penobscot River just outside the Baxter State Park northern entrance, and immediately south of Grand Lake Matagamon, the campground is ideally located for anyone who loves the outdoors. From here, summer visitors have easy access to river and lake water for fishing, canoeing, and swimming. Other local activities include hiking in the remote northern portion of Baxter State Park and exploring the miles of waterways accessible from the campground by canoe. In the fall, this is a popular spot for deer, bear, grouse, and moose hunters. And in the winter, more than 100 miles of groomed trails for snowmobilers and cross-country skiers await hardy souls. If you are feeling more sedentary, go ice fishing in one of the nearby lakes.

Campsites, facilities: There are 36 sites for tents and RVs, all without hookups. Pit toilets, hot showers, picnic tables, fire rings, a dump station, boat ramp, and a store are provided. Motorboats and canoes may be rented. Heated cabins are also available. Leashed pets are permitted.

Reservations, fees: Reservations are recommended. Payment in full is required for one or two nights; for stays of three or more nights, a $20 deposit is required. Sites are $13 a night.

Open: Year-round; fully operational May 1–November 1.

Directions: From the junction of Highways 11 and 159 in Patten, travel northwest on Highway 159 for 24 miles to the campground.

Contact: Matagamon Wilderness Campground, Box 220, Patten, ME 04765, 207/528-2448, website: www.campmaine.com/matagamon.

26 SHIN POND VILLAGE

Rating: 10

North of Patten

Shin Pond Village is an ideal getaway for folks seeking a choice of accommodations. You can pitch a tent or pull up in an RV at one of the large and uncrowded campsites, rent an 80-

year-old log cabin with modern furnishings, or bed down in a guest room at the lodge. Both Upper and Lower Shin Ponds offer excellent trout and salmon fishing, and Baxter State Park—home to many other lakes, rivers, and streams—is only minutes away. Like numerous other camps in northern New England, Shin Pond caters to hunters in search of deer, moose, bear, and grouse in the fall, and lures ice fishers, skiers, and snowmobilers in the winter. Hundreds of miles of groomed snowmobile trails leave from the campground.

Campsites, facilities: There are 41 sites for tents and RVs. Flush toilets, hot showers, picnic tables, fireplaces, a dump station, and laundry facilities are provided. You will also find a playground, TV room, and a store with a snack bar. Canoes are available for rent. Leashed pets are permitted.

Reservations, fees: Reservations are accepted and require a 50 percent deposit. Sites are $23 a night.

Open: Year-round.

Directions: From Patten, drive west on Highway 159 for 10 miles to the campground.

Contact: Craig and Terry Hill, Shin Pond Village, RR 1, Box 280, Patten, ME 04765, 207/528-2900, website: www.shinpond.com.

27 ALLAGASH GATEWAY CAMPSITE

Rating: 10

On Ripogenus Lake northwest of Millinocket

The campground is located on spectacular Ripogenus Lake, which is actually a long arm of even larger Chesuncook Lake. This is the heart of the Maine woods, and the campground is surrounded by hundreds of square miles of lake and forest wildlands. If you are looking for a campground as a base for canoeing, fishing, hunting, and moose watching, this is a great spot.

Campsites, facilities: There are 30 sites for tents and RVs. Flush toilets, hot showers, picnic tables, fire rings, a dump station, and a store are provided. Cabin rentals are available. Pets are permitted.

Reservations, fees: Reservations are recommended. Tent sites are $12–15 a night.

Open: May 1–November 30.

Directions: From Millinocket, drive 33 miles northwest on the Golden Road to the campground. Be prepared to encounter logging trucks carrying tree-length logs along the way.

Contact: Bill and Janet Reeves, Allagash Gateway Campsite, Star Route 76, Box 675, Greenville, ME 04441, 207/723-9215, website: www.allagashgateway.com.

28 BIRCH POINT CAMPGROUND

Rating: 7

On Pleasant Lake, north of the town of Island Falls

Sites at Birch Point line the shore of Pleasant Lake, a large, undeveloped body of water rimmed by forest. The campground waterfront is the park's most attractive feature, and the view over the lake to the woods along the far shore is expansive. Fishing, boating, canoeing, and swimming are the main activities enjoyed by summer campers. In the fall, the campground is open for bear, deer, moose, duck, and grouse hunting.

Campsites, facilities: There are 65 sites for tents and RVs, some with full hookups including cable TV and the rest with water and electric hookups. Eight housekeeping cottages equipped with hot showers, kitchenettes, and cable TV are also available. Facilities include laundry, hot showers, flush toilets, a store, and a dump station. A boat ramp, recreation room, and volleyball, basketball, and horseshoe courts are on the property as well. Canoes, paddleboats, and motorboats are available for rent. Leashed pets are permitted.

Reservations, fees: Reservations are recommended and require a 50 percent deposit. Sites are $22–24 a night, plus $1 per pet.

Open: May 1–October 31, but cottages can be rented year-round.

Directions: From Island Falls, drive east on Highway 159 for .5 mile and then go three miles northeast on U.S. 2. Turn right on Pleasant Lake Road and travel 1.5 miles east to the campground.

Contact: Steve and Joey Edwards, Birch Point Campground, P.O. Box 120, Pleasant Lake, Island Falls, ME 04747, 207/463-2515, website: www.mainerec.com/birch.

29 SEBOOMOOK WILDERNESS CAMPGROUND

Rating: 10

On Moosehead Lake

Seboomook Wilderness Campground is tucked away at the northwest end of Moosehead Lake, a remote and peaceful setting in the heart of the Maine woods. The place is a bit off the beaten path, as it's accessible by logging road, by boat from Greenville or Rockwood, or by seaplane from either of those towns. Sites are strewn along the waterfront and offer sweeping views over the lake and the surrounding mountains. Bring your fishing gear; the angling for salmon, brook trout—or squaretail, as they are called here—and togue is renowned. In autumn, pack your rifle and warm clothing and stalk the wildlands around you for deer, bear, and grouse. In winter, the campground keeps several heated cabins open and available for snowmobilers, snowshoers, cross-country skiers, and ice fishers.

Campsites, facilities: There are 84 sites for tents and RVs with full, partial, and no hookups. Flush toilets, hot showers, picnic tables, fireplaces, a dump station, and a store are provided. Recreational facilities include a boat launch and dock, sand beach, canoe and motorboat rentals, playing field, volleyball, badminton, and horseshoes. Leashed pets are permitted.

Reservations, fees: Reservations are accepted. Sites are $12–16 a night.

Open: Year-round.

Directions: From Jackman, travel east on Highway 6/15 to Rockwood. At the Moose River bridge in Rockwood, turn left and head north for approximately 28 miles on logging roads to the campground. You can also boat or take a seaplane from either Rockwood or Greenville.

Contact: Seboomook Wilderness Campground, HC 85, Box 560, Rockwood, ME 04478, 207/534-8824. website: www.maineoutdoors.com.

30 FROST POND CAMPS

🏕️ 🏊 🎣 🚣 ✈️ 🐕 🏔️ 🚐 ⛺

Rating: 10

On Frost Pond near Ripogenus Lake

Frost Pond Camps is located on a beautiful, remote pond surrounded by hundreds of square miles of uninhabited wildlands. This rustic retreat, featuring isolated sites and classic backcountry cabins, is a classic hunting and fishing camp in the heart of the Maine North Woods. Fish for brook trout in Frost Pond or venture to Chesuncook Lake, the West Branch of the Penobscot River, or any of the numerous nearby rivers and streams to catch salmon, bass, and other species. The Appalachian Trail is a mere five miles away, and Baxter State Park lies within a 50-minute drive. For more information on the area, see the next listing, Allagash Gateway Campsite.

Note: Bicycles, motorcycles, and all-terrain vehicles are not permitted on paper company lands and must be left at the gate.

Campsites, facilities: There are 10 sites for tents and RVs, all without hookups. Eight rustic cabins are also available. Each site has a pit toilet, and some have Adirondack-style shelters. Hot showers, picnic tables, fireplaces, a playground for small children, a boat launch, and short hiking trails are provided. Canoes, motorboats, and rowboats are rented out. The maximum RV length is 18 feet. Leashed pets are permitted.

Reservations, fees: Reservations are recommended. A deposit of one night's fee is required. The Bowater/Great Northern Paper Company requires a special permit for single or combined vehicles measuring 44 feet or longer; for a permit, call 207/723-2106 with registration numbers of all vehicles, as well as arrival and departure dates. Sites are $18 a night.

Open: May 1–November 30.

Directions: From the junction of Highway 11/157 and the Baxter State Park Road in Millinocket, drive 9.75 miles northwest on the Baxter State Park Road. At the junction with the Golden Road/Bowater/Great Northern Paper Company Road, drive north on the Golden Road. After passing Ripogenus Dam, bear to the right, following signs to Frost Pond Camps, and drive three miles to the campground. Please remember that you are on a private logging road where heavily laden logging trucks have the right-of-way. Be prepared to stop and pull over for trucks.

Contact: Rick and Judy Given, Frost Pond Camps, Box 620, Star Highway 76, Greenville, ME 04441, 207/695-2821 (radio phone at Folsom's seaplane base in Greenville; leave a message between 8:15 A.M. and 5 P.M.). Off-season: Rick and Judy Given, 36 Minuteman Drive, Millinocket, ME 04462, 207/723-6622, website: www.maineguide.com/Katahdin/frostpond.

31 ALLAGASH GATEWAY CAMPSITE

🏕️ 🏊 🎣 🍴 🚣 🏔️ 🚐 ⛺

Rating: 10

On the shores of Ripogenus Lake

Few campgrounds offer as much for the outdoor enthusiast as Allagash Gateway. Ripogenus Lake connects with 30-mile-long Chesuncook Lake, as well as Black Pond, the West Branch of the Penobscot River, and numerous other rivers and streams. Fish these waters for salmon, trout, and perch. Or take a boat ride to Chesuncook Village, now home to four permanent residents, but once a bustling logging town until the log drives were halted in the early 1970s. Canoe on the lakes and rivers, or arrange a shuttle for an extended journey. Hike on the

Appalachian Trail and venture into nearby Baxter State Park. Take a guided rafting trip down the Cribworks, Big Ambejackmockamus Falls, and other rapids on the West Branch of the Penobscot. In the fall, hunt for moose, deer, and bear.

Note: Bicycles, motorcycles, and all-terrain vehicles are not permitted on paper company lands and must be left at the gate.

Campsites, facilities: There are 30 sites for tents and RVs, some with electric hookups. Flush toilets, hot showers, picnic tables, fireplaces, a playground, boat ramp, and docks are provided. Canoes are available for rent, and canoe shuttle service can be arranged. No pets are allowed.

Reservations, fees: Reservations are recommended. A $5 deposit is required. The Bowater/Great Northern Paper Company requires a special permit for single or combined vehicles measuring 44 feet or longer; for a permit, call 207/723-2106 with registration numbers of all vehicles, as well as arrival and departure dates. Sites are $10–12 a night.

Open: Ice-out (around mid-May)–November 30.

Directions: There are two routes to Allagash Gateway Campsite. From Greenville, travel north on the Lily Bay Road through Lily Bay and Kokadjo for about 44 miles to the campground, which is right before the Ripogenus Dam. Or, from the junction of Highway 11/157 and the Baxter State Park Road in Millinocket, travel 9.75 miles northwest on the Baxter State Park Road. At the junction with the Golden Road/Bowater/Great Northern Paper Company Road, travel north on the Golden Road for 23.5 miles. Please remember that you are on a private logging road where heavily laden logging trucks have the right-of-way. Be prepared to stop and pull over for trucks.

Contact: Bill and Jan Reeves, Allagash Gateway Campsite, Star Highway 76, Box 675, Greenville, ME 04441; no telephone. Off-season: Bill and Jan Reeves, Allagash Gateway Campsite, Box 396, Millinocket, ME 04462, 207/723-9215.

32 CHEWONKI'S BIG EDDY CAMPGROUND

Rating: 10

On the Penobscot River northwest of Millinocket

The campground is situated on the banks of the West Branch of the Penobscot River, one of the finest whitewater rivers in the country flowing just outside the boundaries of Baxter State Park at the base of Mount Katahdin. The campsite is perfectly situated to take advantage of the abundance of opportunities for outdoor recreation here in the heart of the Maine woods. From hiking in Baxter State park, to whitewater rafting and kayaking, to fly fishing for salmon and trout, this is an outdoorsmen's and outdoorswomen's paradise.

Campsites, facilities: There are 62 sites for tents and RVs, some with electrical hookups. Flush toilets, hot showers, picnic tables, and fireplaces are provided.

Reservations/fees: Reservations are strongly suggested. Sites are $8.50–9 per person per night.

Open: May 1–October 15.

Directions: From Millinocket, drive 28 miles northwest on the Golden Road to the campground.

Contact: Greg Shute, Chewonki's Big Eddy Campground, P.O. Box 238, Millinocket, ME 04462, 207/350-1599, website: www.bigeddy.org.

33 ABOL BRIDGE CAMPGROUND

Rating: 9

West of Millinocket near Baxter State Park

Abol Bridge Campground is located at the confluence of Abol Stream and the West Branch of the Penobscot River, making this an ideal destination for those who enjoy swimming, fishing, and canoeing. Additionally, the views of mile-high Katahdin—Maine's tallest peak—are simply breathtaking. This area is a haven for outdoorspeople. Nearby Baxter State Park offers hiking, rock climbing, fishing, and canoeing. More hiking terrain is available on the 2,158-mile-long Appalachian Trail, which you can access south of Baxter State Park. Note: Bicycles, motorcycles, and all-terrain vehicles are not permitted on paper company lands and must be left at the gate.

Campsites, facilities: There are 36 sites for tents and RVs, all without hookups. Flush toilets, hot showers, picnic tables, fire rings, and a limited store are provided. Campers have access to a beach and rental canoes. The use of generators is permitted between noon and 5 P.M. daily. Leashed pets are permitted.

Reservations, fees: Reservations are recommended and require a deposit of one night's fee. The Bowater/Great Northern Paper Company requires a special permit for single or combined vehicles measuring 44 feet or longer; for a permit, call 207/723-2106 with registration numbers of all vehicles as well as arrival and departure dates. There is a $4 fee to enter the paper company's woodlands, where the campground is located. Sites are $18 a night.

Open: May 15–September 30.

Directions: From the junction of Highway 11/157 and the Baxter State Park Road in Millinocket, travel 9.75 miles northwest on the Baxter State Park Road. At the junction with the Golden Road/Bowater/Great Northern Paper Company Road, travel north on the Golden Road for 8.2 miles. Please remember that you are on a private logging road where heavily laden logging trucks have the right-of-way. Be prepared to stop and pull over for trucks.

Contact: Art and Linda Belmont, Abol Bridge Campground, P.O. Box 536, Millinocket, ME 04462-0536; no phone.

34 NAHMAKANTA MANAGEMENT UNIT

South of Baxter State Park

Rating: 10

Encompassing more than 43,000 acres, this is the largest management unit in the state's public lands system. It is crossed by the Appalachian Trail, which hugs the south shore of Nahmakanta Lake. Some 56 lakes and ponds also lie within the unit, many of which support native populations of trout and salmon. Nahmakanta and the nearby Debsconeag Lakes area provide a wonderful challenge for experienced backpackers, cross-country skiers, and snowshoers.

Campsites, facilities: There are nine primitive tent sites and one Appalachian Trail lean-to. Each site has a pit toilet and a fire ring. Pets are permitted.

Reservations, fees: Reservations are not accepted; the sites are available on a first-come, first-served basis. There is no fee.

Open: Year-round.

Directions: From Millinocket, drive south on Highway 11 for about 15 miles. Turn right on the Jo-Mary Road, a logging road, and continue northwest to access the unit. Or, you can enter by hiking in on the Appalachian Trail.

Contact: Maine Bureau of Parks and Lands, 22 State House Station, Augusta, ME 04333, 207/287-3821, website: www.state.me.us/doc/ parks.

35 WASSATAQUOIK MANAGEMENT UNIT

Along Wassataquoik Stream

Rating: 8

This small preserve incorporates several miles of scenic shoreline along the splendid East Branch of the Penobscot River as well as Wassataquoik Stream, which flows through the forest down from the heights along the Baxter State Park's eastern border. Though there's no formal trail system here, the woods are a lovely place to walk.

Campsites, facilities: There are two primitive campsites with pit toilets. Pets are permitted.

Reservations, fees: Reservations are not accepted; the sites are available on a first-come, first-served basis. There is no fee.

Open: Year-round.

Directions: From Patten, drive south on Highway 11 to Stacyville. Continue approximately six miles west on logging roads to the management unit.

Contact: Maine Bureau of Parks and Lands, 22 State House Station, Augusta, ME 04333, 207/287-3821, website: www.state.me.us/doc/ parks.

36 BIG MOOSE INN, CABINS & CAMPGROUND

Rating: 8

Between two large lakes near the base of Mount Katahdin northwest of Millinocket

Big Moose Inn, Cabins & Campground offers access to two large undeveloped lakes in the heart of the Maine woods. If you are looking for a base for North Woods adventure, this is an excellent choice. The campground is situated close to World class Whitewater Rafting on the class V Penobscot River; to hiking and climbing on Maine's tallest Mountain, Mount Katahdin; to wildlife viewing and hiking in Baxter State Park; and to long-distance hiking on the Appalachian Trail. There are also the two lakes out the front door for swimming, boating, and fishing.

Campsites, facilities: There are 40 sites for tents and RVs, as well as six lean-tos. Rental cabins are available, call for prices. Flush toilets, hot showers, picnic tables, fireplaces, a dump station, and a store are provided. Recreational facilities include two white-water rafting companies based on the premises, and guided hiking, canoeing, hunting, and fishing excursions.

Reservations, fees: Reservations are recom-

mended. Campsites are $10 per person per night. Lean-tos are $13 per person per night.

Open: May 15–Columbus Day.

Directions: From Millinocket, drive eight miles northwest on the Golden Road to the campground.

Contact: Laurie Cormier, Big Moose Inn, Cabins & Campground, P.O. Box 98, Baxter Park Road, Millinocket, ME 04462, 207/723-8391, website: www.bigmoosecabins.com.

37 PINE GROVE CAMPGROUND AND COTTAGES

Rating: 5

In East Millinocket

Situated in low, swampy lands along the East Branch of the Penobscot River, Pine Grove is a moist and shady spot, the kind of place where mosquitoes thrive. On the plus side, the river flowing through here is quite beautiful, and the swimming, canoeing, and fishing (for smallmouth bass) is excellent. Also, Pine Grove is just 20 miles or so from the Baxter State Park southern entrance gate and is within a short drive of dozens of lakes, rivers, and streams.

Campsites, facilities: There are 43 sites for tents and RVs, four with with full hookups, 23 with water and electric hookups, and 16 with none. Flush toilets, hot showers, picnic tables, fire rings, a dump station, laundry facilities, a playground, a recreation hall, horseshoe pits, basketball, hiking trails, and a store are provided. Canoes and cabins are available for rent. Leashed pets are permitted.

Reservations, fees: Reservations are recommended. A deposit of 50 percent of the total amount due is required. Sites are $16–20 a night.

Open: May 15–Columbus Day.

Directions: From I-95 in Medway, take Exit 56 and travel west on Highway 157 for a mile. Turn right on Highway 11 and travel north for four miles.

Contact: Judy and Charlie Theriault, Pine Grove Campground and Cottages, H.C.R. 86, Box 107B, Medway, ME 04460, 207/746-5172. Off-season: Judy and Charlie Theriault, 40 Pine Street B, East Millinocket, ME 04430, 207/746-5105, website: www.mainerec.com/pinegrove.

38 HIDDEN SPRINGS CAMPGROUND

Rating: 6

In Millinocket

The Millinocket area is the gateway to Mount Katahdin, the north Maine woods, the East and West Branches of the Penobscot River, and numerous large lakes where visitors can enjoy boating, fishing, swimming, and canoeing. Nearby Baxter State Park is a 300-square-mile mountainous preserve crowned by Mount Katahdin, Maine's highest peak. The area also offers a Lumberman's museum, dozens of clear lakes, and a spectacular gorge nicknamed the "Grand Canyon of the East" that has eight miles of rugged hiking trails that meet up with the Appalachian Trail.

Campsites, facilities: There are 103 sites for tents and RVs, some with water and electric hookups. Flush toilets, hot showers, picnic tables, fireplaces, a dump station, store, laundry facilities, and a swimming pool are provided. Pets are welcome.

Reservations/rates: Reservations are accepted. Sites are $18–21 a night. ·

Open: May 15–October 1.

Directions: From the junction of Highway 11/157 and the Baxter State Park Road in Millinocket, drive 2.25 miles northwest on Baxter State Park Road to the campground.

Contact: Michael and Gail Seile, Hidden Springs Campground, 224 Central Street, Millinocket, ME 04462, 207/723-6337, website: www.hiddenspring.com.

39 KATAHDIN SHADOWS CAMPGROUND

Rating: 5

In Medway

Providing good access to the Maine Woods, this large, popular campground is set right off the interstate on the road to Millinocket. Baxter State Park is fewer than 15 miles away, and many of the lakes and rivers that characterize the region are within an easy drive. One distinguishing feature of this campground is the plethora of rabbits. Domestic rabbits are everywhere—hopping along the roads, through the woods, and in the campsites. If you don't like rabbits, head elsewhere.

Campsites, facilities: There are 115 sites for tents and RVs. Group tenting areas are available. Wheelchair-accessible restrooms with flush toilets, free hot showers, picnic tables, fireplaces, a dump station, laundry facilities, and a store are provided. Recreational facilities include a playground, recreation room, fields, heated pool, hiking trails, volleyball, basketball, canoe rentals, guided fishing trips, and float trips. Ice and firewood are available. Leashed pets are permitted.

Reservations, fees: Reservations are not necessary. Sites are $22–24 a night.

Open: Memorial Day–Labor Day.

Directions: From I-95 in Medway, take Exit 56 and travel west on Highway 11/157 for 1.7 miles to the campground.

Contact: Rick LeVasseur, Katahdin Shadows Campground, Highway 157, P.O. Box H, Medway, ME 04460, 207/746-5267 or 800/794-5267, website: www.katahdinshadows.com.

40 GREENLAND COVE CAMPGROUND

Rating: 9

On East Grand Lake near the town of Danforth

Many sites at Greenland Cove are on the shore of a large, remote lake, while others are perched on a wooded hillside directly overlooking the water. Be sure to bring your rod and reel, for East Grand Lake is one of the best fisheries for landlocked salmon in Maine. Anglers also find it's an excellent place to try for bass, perch, and togue. As part of the international boundary, the lake provides an unusual opportunity to fish in both American and Canadian waters, and international bass and salmon tournaments are conducted here throughout the season. If you would rather not cast a line, there is a sandy beach for swimming.

Campsites, facilities: There are 40 sites for tents and RVs with water and electric hookups. Flush toilets, hot showers, a dump station, picnic tables, fire rings, a playground, recreation hall, canoe and paddleboat rentals, boat ramp, horseshoe pits, volleyball, basketball, and a store are provided. Leashed pets are permitted.

Reservations, fees: Reservations are recommended. A deposit of $15 for one night or $30 for two or more nights is required. Sites are $22 a night.

Open: Ice-out (usually around mid-May)–October 1.

Directions: From the intersection of Highway 169 and U.S. 1 in Danforth, drive south on U.S. 1 for 2.3 miles. Turn left on Campground Road and drive 2.5 miles east to the campground.

Contact: Roger and Brenda Habrie, Greenland Cove Campground, Danforth, ME 04424, 207/448-2863, website: www.mainerec.com/gcc.

41 MOOSE RIVER CAMPGROUND

Rating: 8

In Jackman

The clean and well-kept Moose River Campground is a great little spot near a tiny border town in a wild corner of the state. It adjoins hundreds of miles of wilderness trails open to camping vehicles in the summer and snow mobiles in the winter. The woods and woodland streams here offer tremendous opportunities for hunting and fishing, and hikers can tackle the trails of nearby Sally and Bald Mountains. For more information on the Jackman area, see the Holeb Preserve Management Unit in this chapter.

Campsites, facilities: There are 52 sites for tents and RVs, 11 with full hookups, 26 with water and electric hookups, two with electric hookups only, and 13 with none. Flush toilets, hot showers, picnic tables, fireplaces, a dump station, laundry facilities, and a store with a restaurant are provided. A swimming pool, trout ponds, canoe rentals, a playground, volleyball, badminton, and horseshoes are among the recreational offerings. Leashed pets are permitted.

Reservations, fees: Reservations are accepted. Sites are $20–22 a night.

Open: May 15–November 1.

Directions: From the junction of U.S. 201 and Highway 6/15 in Jackman, drive two miles north on U.S. 201 to Nichols Road, then turn right and drive 1.5 miles east to the campground.

Contact: Francis and Carmen Cousineau, Moose River Campground, P.O. Box 98, Jackman, ME 04945, 207/668-3341.

42 THE LAST RESORT CAMPGROUND AND CABINS

Rating: 10

On Long Pond near Jackman

The Last Resort is a very rustic, remote fishing camp, a private getaway in the Maine Woods. Tent sites are situated along the lakeshore and are spaced far enough apart to allow for maximum privacy. However, if you've ever dreamed of having your own little log cabin beside a wilderness lake in the North Woods, this is the place for you. Each cabin is constructed of hand-hewn logs and is nestled among 70 acres of spruce, cedar, pine, and birch trees along the shores of Long Pond, a narrow lake that stretches for 12 miles. Each cabin has a front porch overlooking the lake, with a spectacular view of the mountains across the water.

Campsites, facilities: There are four tent sites and eight rental cabins. Tent sites have picnic tables, fireplaces with grills, and pit toilets, and the resort provides centrally located hot showers. Cabins are fully equipped with gas ranges and refrigerators, wood stoves, kerosene and gas lamps, and the necessary cooking, eating, and bedding supplies. A rustic fishing lodge has board games, books, and videos. Leashed pets are permitted.

Reservations, fees: Reservations are accepted. Cabins are $275–400 a week. Tent sites are $12 a night per person.

Open: Year-round.

Directions: From the center of Jackman, drive six miles east on Moose River Road (four-wheel-drive vehicles are recommended) to the campground.

Contact: Tim and Ellen Casey, The Last Resort Campground and Cabins, P.O. Box 777, Jackman, ME 04945, 207/668-5091, website: www.connectmaine.com/lastresort.

43 JOHN'S FOUR SEASON ACCOMMODATIONS

Rating: 8

In Jackman

The main attraction at John's isn't the campground itself, which is very nondescript. Rather, it's the sense of being at the very edge of civilization that draws people here. This is an outpost in the true sense of the word, an establishment that caters to those who come to the Jackman region for an unsurpassed wilderness adventure. For more information on the Jackman area, see the Holeb Preserve Management Unit in this chapter.

Campsites, facilities: There are 14 sites for tents and RVs, two with full hookups, six with electric hookups, and six with none. Flush toilets, hot showers, picnic tables, a dump station, recreation room, and laundry facilities are provided. Leashed pets are permitted.

Reservations, fees: Reservations are not necessary. Tent sites are $13 a night, and RV sites are $ 20 a night.

Open: Year-round.

Directions: From the junction of U.S. 201 and Highway 6/15 in Jackman, drive half a mile north on U.S. 201 to the campground.

Contact: John Baillargeon, John's Four Season Accommodations, Star Highway 64, Box 132, Jackman, ME 04945, 207/668-7683, website: www.johnsfourseasons.com.

44 JACKMAN LANDING CAMPGROUND

Rating: 8

On Wood Pond in the town of Jackman

Jackman Landing is a great little campground on beautiful Wood Pond, a clean and cold lake that's part of the Moose River system. The campground is located right in the tiny frontier town of Jackman, very close to the Quebec border, and the general store and post office are within convenient walking distance. Don't be surprised to hear French spoken as often as English, for in this border country, families who live on both sides of the line are related. For additional information on the Jackman area, see the next listing for the Holeb Preserve Management Unit.

Campsites, facilities: There are 25 sites for tents and RVs, 16 with water and electric hookups and nine with none. Flush toilets, hot showers, picnic tables, fireplaces, a dump station, laundry facilities, and cable TV are provided. For recreation, there is a boat launch and dock, canoe rentals, and canoe shuttle service. A floatplane on-site takes campers for rides over the Maine Woods. Leashed pets are permitted.

Reservations, fees: Reservations are accepted. Sites are $12–15 a night.

Open: Year-round.

Directions: From the junction of U.S. 201 and Highway 6/15 in Jackman, drive north on U.S. 201 for approximately 1.5 miles to the campground.

Contact: Stephen Coleman, Jackman Landing Campground, P.O. Box 567, Main Street, Jackman, ME 04945, 207/668-3301.

45 HOLEB PRESERVE MANAGEMENT UNIT

Rating: 10

On the Moose River and Attean Pond near Jackman

The preserve incorporates the popular Moose River, one of the best streams for multiday canoe trips in the state. Put your paddle to these waters and you float through a region of wild rivers, expansive lakes, dense forests, and rugged mountains. Fishing, swimming, and hiking are popular summer activities, while in winter, the area lures snowmobilers, cross-country skiers, snowshoers, and ice-fishing enthusiasts. Be very careful when driving on U.S. 201 at night; this road is known as Moose Alley,

and many an unfortunate driver has collided with one of the 1,000-pound beasts.

Campsites, facilities: There are about 26 primitive campsites in this unit and on neighboring lands. All are waterfront sites set along the shores of Attean Pond and the Moose River, and are accessible only by water. The typical site includes a picnic table, fire ring, and pit toilet. Pets are permitted.

Reservations, fees: Registration is not required, and sites are available on a first-come, first-served basis. There is no fee.

Open: Year-round.

Directions: From the junction of U.S. 201 and Highway 6/15 in Jackman, drive west on Attean Pond Road for two miles to the boat launch.

Contact: Maine Bureau of Parks and Lands, 22 State House Station, Augusta, ME 04333, 207/287-3821, website: www.state.me.us/doc/ parks.

46 LOON ECHO CAMPGROUND

Rating: 9

South of Jackman on Lake Parlin

Loon Echo is a very peaceful, quiet campground with spectacular shoreline sites overlooking a large North Woods lake surrounded by hundreds of square miles of uninhabited woodlands; the kind of place where you want to settle in for a while. Campers have access to 900 feet of waterfront on Lake Parlin. While you're here, take advantage of Bill Erven's expertise with the fly rod; he offers instruction right on the premises. For more information about the Jackman area, see the previous listing for the Holeb Preserve Management Unit.

Campsites, facilities: There are 15 tent sites without hookups. Flush toilets, hot showers, picnic tables, fireplaces, and a dump station are provided. For recreation, you will find a small boat ramp, canoe and fly-fishing equipment rentals, and a playing field. White-water rafting trips in the Kennebec River Gorge can be arranged. Leashed pets are permitted.

Reservations, fees: Reservations are recommended. A 50 percent deposit is required. Sites are $17 a night.
Open: May 1–October 15.
Directions: From Jackman, drive 12 miles south on U.S. 201 to the campground.
Contact: Bill and Holly Erven, Loon Echo Campground, P.O. Box 711, Jackman, ME 04945, 207/668-4829, website: www.campmaine.com/loonecho.

47 MOOSEHEAD LAKE MANAGEMENT UNIT

Rating: 10

On Moosehead Lake

At 40 miles long and up to 10 miles wide, Moosehead Lake is the largest lake set entirely within in New England. The public landholding incorporates two large islands and extensive acreage on the lake's eastern shore. There are numerous boat-in campsites, as well as trails that ascend the 1,806-foot Mount Kineo summit, where a fire tower rewards hikers with spectacular views over the sprawling lake. For more information on the Moosehead Lake area, see Lily Bay State Park in this chapter.

Campsites, facilities: There are 26 primitive tent sites on the shore of Moosehead Lake. Each site has a pit toilet, picnic table, and fire ring. Pets are permitted.

Reservations, fees: Reservations are not accepted; the sites are available on a first-come, first-served basis. There is no fee.

Open: Year-round.

Directions: Access to the unit is gained via boat, canoe, foot, cross-country ski, or snowmobile over the lake's surface. Good points of departure are the towns of Greenville and Rockwood, and Lily Bay State Park. You could also drive in on a labyrinth of logging roads, which would require a detailed map.

Contact: Maine Bureau of Parks and Lands, 22 State House Station, Augusta, ME 04333, 207/287-3821, website: www.state.me.us/doc/ parks.

48 OLD MILL CAMPGROUND

Rating: 8

On Moosehead Lake in Rockwood

Located on the western side of Moosehead Lake, Old Mill Campground offers a spectacular waterfront setting with many sites right on the shoreline. Surrounded by hundreds of square miles of unpeopled woodlands, this campground is well situated for hunters who venture this way to try for deer, bear, moose, and grouse in the fall months. For more information on the Moosehead Lake area, see Lily Bay State Park in this chapter.

Campsites, facilities: There are 50 sites for tents and RVs with full and partial hookups. Flush toilets, hot showers, picnic tables, fire rings, a dump station, laundry facilities, a playground, recreation room, boat ramp, horseshoe pits, volleyball, badminton, and a store are provided. Cabins are available. The campground also rents motorboats, paddleboats, and canoes, and can arrange the services of a fishing guide. Leashed pets are permitted.

Reservations, fees: Reservations are recommended. A deposit of one night's fee is required for stays of less than one week; for stays of a week or more, a deposit of 25 percent is required. Sites are $18–22 a night for two people, plus $2 for each additional person.

Open: Mid-May–Columbus Day; the cabins are open from May–November.

Directions: From Greenville, travel 18 miles north on Highway 6/15 to the campground entrance.

Contact: Kay and Rick Annunziato, Old Mill Campground, Highway 15, Rockwood, ME 04478, 207/534-7333, website: www.old millcampground.com.

49 CASEY'S SPENCER BAY CAMPS

Rating: 10

On Moosehead Lake

Casey's Spencer Bay Camps enjoys a great location on a narrow peninsula jutting into Moose-head Lake, the largest lake entirely within New England and an outdoors lover's paradise since Henry David Thoreau passed through here in the mid-19th century. The fishing in the lake is superb, and miles of secluded coves and unde-veloped wooded shoreline are perfect for canoe outings. Views over the water to distant peaks only enhance the scenic beauty of this spot. The campground is reached via several miles of log-ging roads and is well off the traveled path. Campers can swim and fish right from their site, paddle a canoe around for a few hours, or maybe explore on a bike. If that's not enough, Baxter State Park, with its more than 200,000 acres of woods, waters, and mountains, is nearby. For more information on the Moosehead Lake area, see Lily Bay State Park in this chapter.

Campsites, facilities: There are 50 sites for tents and RVs. Flush toilets, hot showers, picnic ta-bles, fireplaces, laundry facilities, a dump sta-tion, and a store are provided. Recreational facilities include canoe and motorboat rentals, bike rentals, hiking trails, and horseshoes. Leashed pets are permitted.

Reservations, fees: Reservations are accepted. Sites are $23 a night.

Open: Mid-May–mid-October.

Directions: From the intersection of Highway 6/15 and the Lily Bay Road in Greenville, drive 12 miles north on the Lily Bay Road, then turn left and travel six miles west on the campground road.

Contact: Casey's Spencer Bay Camps, P.O. Box 1161, Greenville, ME 04441, 207/695-2801, website: www.caseysspencerbaycamps.com.

50 NORTHERN PRIDE LODGE

Rating: 8

On First Roach Pond in Kokadjo

Located on First Roach Pond, Northern Pride Lodge is an upscale yet inexpensive place to spend your camping vacation. Just remember to bring the fishing gear. The pond is limited to

fly-fishing and spin casting, while the Roach River is limited to catch-and-release fly-fishing. Big brook trout—also known in these parts as squaretail—togue, and large salmon live in these waters in healthy numbers. Seaplane trips to more remote lakes can be arranged through the campground. Swimming, canoeing, and boat-ing on the pond and in the river are other pop-ular pursuits. In the fall, base yourself here for moose-, deer-, bear-, and bird-hunting excursions. And note that even though the campground does close for the winter, the lodge is open year-round for cross-country skiing, snowshoeing, and snow-mobiling. For additional information about the Moosehead Lake area, see Lily Bay State Park in this chapter.

Campsites, facilities: There are 24 sites for tents and RVs, all without hookups. Pit toilets, a central water supply, hot showers, picnic ta-bles, fire rings, a boat launch, and docks are provided. Mountain bikes, motorboats, canoes, paddleboats, and an 18-foot pontoon boat are available for rent. A lodge and a restaurant are on the premises. Leashed pets are permitted.

Reservations, fees: Reservations are not nec-essary. Sites are $20 a night for two people, plus $1 for each additional person. The fee for pets is $2 a night.

Open: May 1–November 1.

Directions: From Greenville, travel northeast on the Kokadjo Road for about 20 miles.

Contact: Jeff and Barbara Lucas, Northern Pride Lodge, HC 76, Box 588, Kokadjo, ME 04441, 207/695-2890.

51 LILY BAY STATE PARK

Rating: 10

North of Greenville on Moosehead Lake

Lily Bay State Park is tucked into a cove on the shores of giant Moosehead Lake and overlooks this very beautiful expanse of water dotted with dozens of islands. Campers can explore the 40-mile-long, 10-mile-wide lake by boat or canoe, while anglers will be thrilled by the superb fishing for salmon, perch, togue, and trout. From Greenville, known as the gateway town to the North Woods, campers can secure guide services, rent canoes or boats, arrange for a rafting trip on the West Branch of the Penobscot River, or embark on a scenic seaplane ride. A restored 1914 steamboat, the SS *Katahdin,* takes passengers on three-hour cruises around the lake. A six-hour cruise stops at Mount Kineo, a rocky cliff rising 750 feet above the lake. Paths lead to a fire tower atop the cliff, and a trail along the shore circles the peninsula. The Moosehead Marine Museum, home of the SS *Katahdin,* houses a display chronicling the history of steamboats on the lake since 1836.

Campsites, facilities: There are 91 sites for tents and RVs, all without hookups. Each site has a pit toilet, picnic table, and fireplace. A dump station, playground, boat launch, beach, and hiking trails are provided. Leashed pets are permitted.

Reservations, fees: Reservations are accepted, and the total amount due must accompany your request. Contact the Maine Bureau of Parks and Lands at the number below. The State of Maine allocates some sites on a first-come, first-served basis. Sites are $14 a night for Maine residents and $19 for nonresidents.

Open: May 1–October 15.

Directions: From Greenville, drive north on the Lily Bay Road for nine miles to the park entrance and the campground.

Contact: Lily Bay State Park Ranger, 207/695-2700; Maine Bureau of Parks and Lands, 22 State House Station, Augusta, ME 04333, 207/287-3821, website: www.state.me.us/doc/parks.

52 MOXIE OUTDOOR ADVENTURES

🛶 🗙 🏊 🛶 🥾 🐕 🛖

Rating: 8

On the shores of Lake Moxie

Lake Moxie Camps is one of the oldest and most renowned sporting camps in New England. Located on the shores of beautiful Moxie Lake, the resort has hosted guests from around the world for over a century. In the early days, guests would take the train from New York, Hartford, and Boston for a summer holiday at Lake Moxie. Still known for its great hunting and fishing, the area is now a mecca for world-class white-water rafting, canoeing, kayaking, hiking, and mountain biking.

Campsites, facilities: There are 10 campsites for tents. Each site has a picnic table and a fire ring. Rental cabins are available. Hot showers, flush toilets, a store, laundry facilities, a recreation hall, wood-fired hot tub, and a volleyball court are provided. Rental canoes and kayaks are available.

Reservations/fees: Reservations are recommended. Tent sites are $10 per person per night.

Open: May 1–October 30.

Directions: From The Forks, drive north on U.S. Route 201 to Moxie Road. Turn east on Moxie Road and drive five miles to the campsite.

Contact: Moxie Outdoor Adventures, HC 63, Box 60, The Forks, ME 04985, 800/866-6943, website: www.moxierafting.com.

53 NORTHERN OUTDOORS

🛶 🗙 🏊 🛶 🥾 🐕 🚐 🛖 🤸

Rating: 8

On the banks of the Kennebec River

Northern Outdoors makes a reasonable claim to being New England's number-one outdoor adventure resort. Situated directly on the banks of the beautiful Kennebec River, Northern Outdoors is well-known as a white-water rafting, kayaking, and canoeing destination. In addition to white-water activities, the resort offers guided hiking, lake kayaking, rock climbing, hunting, and fishing excursions.

Campsites, facilities: There are 80 sites for tents and RVs, all without hookups. Rental cabins are available. Each site has a picnic table and fire ring. Facilities include hot showers, flush toilets, laundry facilities, a store, recreation

hall, swimming pool, platform tennis courts, a basketball court, volleyball court, and on-site day care.
Reservations/fees: Reservations are strongly recommended. Tent sites are $10 per person per night.
Open: May 1–October 31.
Directions: From Bingham, drive 18 miles north on U.S. Route 201 to the campground.
Contact: Jim Yearwood, Northern Outdoors, P.O. Box 100, Route 201, The Fork, ME 04985, 800/765-7238, website: www.northernoutdoors.com.

54 INDIAN POND CAMPGROUND

🚶 🏊 🛶 🚐 🎣 🐕 🚌 ⛺

Rating: 10

On the banks of the Kennebec River

Just downstream of giant Moosehead Lake on the Kennebec River is Indian Pond, a 3,600-acre lake with 35 miles of undeveloped shoreline surrounded by hundreds of square miles of uninhabited woodlands. The pond is known for offering a superlative smallmouth bass fishery, as well as for its healthy populations of trout and salmon. In the fall, the campground is open to hunters tracking down deer, bear, moose, and birds. This is an off-the-beaten-path destination for those in search of a North Woods adventure.
Location: On Indian Pond north of The Forks; see North Woods map.
Campsites, facilities: There are 27 sites, all without hookups; 22 are suitable for tents, trailers, and self-contained units, and five are tent platforms. A three-bedroom house is available year-round for rent. Flush toilets, hot showers, tables, fireplaces, a dump station, and laundry facilities are provided. There is also a boat launch, dock, and canoe rentals. Leashed pets are permitted.
Reservations, fees: Reservations are accepted. For stays of up to three days, payment in full is required, and for four or more days, a 50 percent deposit is requested. Refunds are given with seven days' notice. Sites are $18 a night.

Open: Mid-April–mid-October.
Directions: From U.S. 201 in The Forks, turn right and drive five miles east on Moxie Pond Road to Moxie Pond. Turn left on Harris Station Road and drive eight miles north to the Indian Pond Reception Center.
Contact: Indian Pond Campground, H.C.R. 63, Box 52, The Forks, ME 04985, 800/371-7774.

55 LITTLE SQUAW MANAGEMENT UNIT

🚶 🏊 🛶 🚐 🎣 🐕 �̇ ⛺

Rating: 10

Near Greenville

This is a spectacular 13,500-acre parcel of land overlooking the southern end of Moosehead Lake, the largest lake set entirely in New England. Within the area are five remote ponds that offer fishing, canoeing, and a few scenic campsites; the Little Squaw Mountains, with hiking trails and terrific views; and miles of forest open for hunting, fishing, cross-country skiing, and snowmobiling.
Campsites, facilities: There are five primitive campsites on Big Squaw Pond and Little Squaw Pond. Each site has a pit toilet. Pets are permitted.
Reservations, fees: Reservations are not accepted; the sites are available on a first-come, first-served basis. There is no fee.
Open: Year-round.
Directions: To access the unit, hike in from Highway 6/15 in Greenville.
Contact: Maine Bureau of Parks and Lands, 22 State House Station, Augusta, ME 04333, 207/287-3821, website: www.state.me.us/doc/parks.

56 MOOSEHEAD FAMILY CAMPGROUND

🏊 🛶 🚐 🐕 🚶 🚌 ⛺

Rating: 5

In Greenville

Just south of Greenville, this family campground puts you very close to Moosehead Lake,

Baxter State Park, and the numerous attractions of the Maine Woods. It's a no-frills place that serves as a launching pad for outdoor adventures throughout the region. For information on activities in the Moosehead Lake region, see Lily Bay State Park in this chapter. For more on Baxter State Park, see Abol Campground in this chapter.

Campsites, facilities: There are 35 sites for tents and RVs, 22 with water and electric and 13 with no hookups. Chemical toilets, hot showers, picnic tables, fire rings, a dump station, a playground, and a recreation room are provided. Leashed pets are permitted.

Reservations, fees: Reservations are not necessary. Sites are $22–24 a night.

Open: May 1–November 30.

Directions: From Greenville, travel a mile south on Highway 6/15 to the campground.

Contact: Bob and Lillian Weingart, Moosehead Family Campground, P.O. Box 1244, Greenville, ME 04441, 207/695-2210.

57 JO-MARY LAKE CAMPGROUND

Rating: 9

South of Millinocket

The Katahdin Iron Works/Jo-Mary Multiple Use Management Forest surrounds this campground on the south shore of Upper Jo-Mary Lake. Teeming with salmon, trout, togue, and white perch, the five-mile-long, two-mile-wide lake is a great spot for fishing as well as canoeing, boating, and swimming. For hikers, the Appalachian Trail is just five miles away. A hike to Gulf Hagas, known as the Grand Canyon of the East with its three-mile-long canyon and five major waterfalls, makes a good day outing. The campground is approximately 50 miles away from Baxter State Park.

Campsites, facilities: There are 60 sites for tents and RVs, all without hookups. Flush toilets, hot showers, picnic tables, fireplaces, a dump station, laundry facilities, a playground, recre-

ation room, and a store are provided. You will also find horseshoe pits, a basketball hoop, a sandy beach, and rental canoes, rowboats, and paddleboats. Leashed pets are permitted.

Reservations, fees: Reservations are recommended. A $10 deposit is required for weekend stays; for a full week a $20 deposit is required. There is a two-night minimum for reservations. Sites are $18 a night.

Open: Mid-May–October 1.

Directions: From Millinocket, travel south on Highway 11 for 15 miles. Turn right on a logging road and travel northwest for about five miles to the campground.

Contact: Jim and Lauretta Smith, Jo-Mary Lake Campground, P.O. Box 329, Millinocket, ME 04462, 207/723-8117 or 207/746-5512, website: www.campmaine.com/jo-mary.

58 SEBOEIS MANAGEMENT UNIT

Rating: 7

South of Millinocket

Several large lakes are contained within this 13,000-acre public land unit. The land around the shorelines was cut prior to the state acquiring ownership, thus the forest is in a stage of regrowth. Campers and day visitors can enjoy hunting, fishing, and savoring the impressive views of surrounding mountains, including Katahdin. In winter, snowmobilers pass through the unit while traveling between the villages of Milo and Medway. Ice fishing on Seboeis Lake is also popular at that time.

Campsites, facilities: There are four primitive campsites. RVers may be able to negotiate the entry roads, but no services are available. Each site has a picnic table, fire ring, and pit toilet. Pets are permitted.

Reservations, fees: Reservations are not accepted; the sites are available on a first-come, first-served basis. There is no fee.

Open: Year-round.

Directions: To access the unit, drive south from

Millinocket on Highway 11 for approximately 12 miles.

Contact: Maine Bureau of Parks and Lands, 22 State House Station, Augusta, ME 04333, 207/287-3821, website: www.state.me.us/doc/parks

59 MATTAWAMKEAG WILDERNESS PARK CAMPGROUND

Rating: 8

Near the town of Mattawamkeag

Mattawamkeag Wilderness Park offers superb outdoor recreation opportunities for just about everyone. Hikers can enjoy 15 miles of wilderness trails, anglers will discover good salmon and trout fishing along the Mattawamkeag River, and canoeists have some 60 miles of wilderness to paddle through, including several exciting stretches of white water. There's even a beach for swimmers. You'll have a rustic Maine camping experience in a splendid wilderness setting.

Campsites, facilities: There are 52 sites for tents and RVs, some with electric hookups, plus 11 lean-tos. Flush toilets, hot showers, picnic tables, fireplaces, a recreation building, and a limited store are provided. Pets are permitted.

Reservations, fees: Reservations are not necessary. Sites are $12–14 a night.

Open: Mid-May–mid-September.

Directions: From the junction of U.S. 2 and Highway 157 in Mattawamkeag, drive approximately half a mile south on U.S. 2. After crossing the Mattawamkeag River, drive about six miles east on a logging road to Mattawamkeag Wilderness Park.

Contact: Mattawamkeag Wilderness Park Campground, U.S. 2, Box 5, Mattawamkeag, ME 04459, 207/736-4881.

60 LAKESIDE CAMPING AREA

Rating: 5

On Cold Stream Pond in Enfield

Vehicles and tents are lined up in rows at this campground on the shore of Cold Stream Pond. The pond has a reputation for offering good fishing for togue, salmon, and trout. Additionally, the park is within a short drive of many other lakes and rivers where you can escape for a day of fishing, boating, and rafting. For nonanglers (or anglers needing a refreshing dip), the camp has a sandy beach, perfect for swimming. Canoes, paddleboats, and "splash" boats are available for rent.

Campsites, facilities: There are 32 sites for tents and RVs with full and partial hookups. Flush toilets, hot showers, picnic tables, fire rings, a dump station, playground, recreation room, and store are provided. Boat rentals are available. Leashed pets are permitted.

Reservations, fees: Reservations are not necessary. Sites are $18–20 a night.

Open: May 15–September 9.

Directions: From I-95 in Howland, take Exit 55 and drive east on Highway 155 for about five miles to the intersection with Highway 188 in Enfield. Continue north on Highway 155 for approximately 2.5 miles to the campground.

Contact: Gene and Candy Libby, Lakeside Camping Area, Enfield, ME 04433, 207/732-4241. Off-season: Gene and Candy Libby, P.O. Box 38, Lincoln, ME 04457, 207/732-4241.

61 CATHEDRAL PINES CAMPGROUND

Rating: 9

On the west shore of Flagstaff Lake in Eustis

Just 26 miles from the Canadian border, this campground is set in a magnificent 300-acre grove of towering red pines on the shore of giant Flagstaff Lake. It would be easy to mistake the place for a state or national park campground because the sites are so well spaced and the grounds are impeccably clean. Flagstaff Lake, nestled among some of the most spectacular mountain scenery in Maine, is renowned for supporting a high-quality freshwater sport fishery. Campers can cool off at the sandy beach or paddle their canoes around the lake. Hikers should not miss the opportunity to explore the mountains of the Bigelow Range looming over these waters. The Appalachian Trail crosses the range, providing access for day hikes as well as multiday treks. History buffs will be interested to know that the campground stands on the site of one of General Benedict Arnold's stops during his ill-fated march to Quebec in 1775; a monument at the entrance marks his visit.

Campsites, facilities: There are 115 sites, including two group sites, 98 with water and electric hookups and 17 with none. Flush toilets, hot showers, picnic tables, fireplaces, a dump station, and laundry facilities are provided. Recreational facilities include a boat ramp and docking facilities, canoe rentals, a playground, and a recreation room. Leashed pets are permitted.

Reservations, fees: Reservations are necessary. A deposit of one night's fee is required. Sites are $16–20 a night.

Open: May 15–October 1.

Directions: From the intersection of Highways 16 and 27 in Stratton, drive four miles north on Highway 27 to the campground.

Contact: Cathedral Pines Campground, HC 72, Box 80, Eustis, ME 04936, 207/246-3491.

62 DEAD RIVER MANAGEMENT UNIT

🧍🏊🛶🛥️✕🎣❄️🐕🏕️

Rating: 9
On the north shore of Flagstaff Lake

Remote campsites dot the wild and undeveloped shores of both the Dead River and Flagstaff Lake. These sites are spaced far apart, so you definitely don't feel crowded. Anglers should not leave their fishing rods at home, for this is a good place to cast a line. The Dead

River presents challenging terrain for kayaking and canoeing; just be sure to assess your skills well beforehand, as this is not a beginner's river. From the campground, you gain spectacular views across the lake to the Bigelow Mountains. On the way to or from the management unit, hikers should spend a day (or a week) hiking or traversing this range. For more information, see Bigelow Preserve Management Unit in this chapter.

Campsites, facilities: There are several primitive campsites on the north shore of Flagstaff Lake. While some of the sites on the lake are accessible only by water, other sites on the Dead River can be reached by vehicle. Each site has a picnic table, fire ring, and pit toilet. A boat ramp on the lake is located just south of Long Falls. Pets are permitted.

Reservations, fees: Reservations are not accepted; sites are available on a first-come, first-served basis. Camping is free of charge, but you must pay a paper company road fee (it varies, but is less than $10) to access the management unit.

Open: Year-round; contact the Maine Bureau of Parks and Lands in the winter to check on road conditions.

Directions: From the crossroads at North New Portland, drive north on the Long Falls Road for about 22 miles to the management unit.

Contact: Maine Bureau of Parks and Lands, 22 State House Station, Augusta, ME 04333, 207/287-3821, website: www.state.me.us/doc/parks.

63 BIGELOW PRESERVE MANAGEMENT UNIT

🧍🏊🛶🛥️✕🎣❄️🐕🏕️

Rating: 10
On and just south of Flagstaff Lake

The Bigelow Range and 20 miles of the Flagstaff Lake southern shore are part of this wilderness preserve that encompasses 35,000 acres. Hiking options include many one-day and multiday hikes on the 30 miles of Appalachian Trail that bisect the management unit. The Bigelow Range summits are above tree line and offer sweeping vistas of the surrounding forests, mountains, and lakes. Fishing, boating, canoeing, and swimming are popular pursuits on Flagstaff Lake. Given the wide range of habitat in the preserve, many of the wildlife species indigenous to the state are represented here. In the fall, the backcountry area is open to deer, bear, moose, and grouse hunting. In the winter, snowmobilers travel on more than 20 miles of trails within the preserve, while snowshoers and cross-country skiers head off on hiking trails and unplowed roads. A heated lodge is kept open in the winter as a warming station.

Campsites, facilities: There are about 16 primitive campsites. Sites for backpackers are located along the mountain range ridgeline and typically include a lean-to or tent platform, fire ring, and a pit toilet. Tent sites with fire rings and pit toilets are set at various points on the lakeshore and are accessed by water or by hiking trail. One group site on the lake can accommodate up to 30 people. Pets are permitted.

Reservations, fees: Registration is not required; sites are available on a first-come, first-served basis. There is no fee.

Open: Year-round.

Directions: To access the preserve, follow gravel roads off of Highway 16/27 in Carrabassett, or take Long Falls Dam Road north from North New Portland.

Contact: Maine Bureau of Parks and Lands, 22 State House Station, Augusta, ME 04333, 207/287-3821, website: www.state.me.us/doc/parks.

64 BALSAM WOODS CAMPGROUND

Rating: 6

In Abbot Village

Off-the-beaten-path Balsam Woods is a peaceful, comfortable campground that is also very well maintained. Close to Moosehead Lake, the Appalachian Trail, Baxter State Park, and white-water rafting on the West Branch of the

Penobscot River, the place is well situated for campers who want to venture out on day trips, yet is far enough from the region's attractions to virtually guarantee peace and quiet. If you don't feel like driving half an hour to Moosehead Lake, you'll find a public beach and boat ramp one mile down the road at Piper Pond.

Campsites, facilities: There are 50 sites for tents and RVs, 44 with water and electric hookups and six with none. Flush toilets, hot showers, picnic tables, fire rings, a dump station, laundry facilities, and a store with a snack bar are provided. The campground also offers a playground, recreation hall, pavilion, pool, horseshoe pits, basketball, badminton, volleyball, hiking trails, and movies. Leashed pets are permitted.

Reservations, fees: Reservations are recommended. For less than one week, a deposit of one night's fee is required; for a week or more, a deposit of 25 percent of the total cost is required. Sites are $25 a night.

Open: May 11-October 28.

Directions: From Dover-Foxcroft, drive west on Highway 6/15/16 to the junction with Highway 6/15 in Abbot Village. Drive north for one mile on Highway 15, then turn left on Piper Pond Road and drive three miles west to the campground.

Contact: Jay and Lynn Eberhard, Balsam Woods Campground, Piper Pond Road, Abbot Village, ME 04406, 207/876-2731, website: www.balsamwoods.com.

65 PEAKS-KENNY STATE PARK

Rating: 9

In Dover-Foxcroft on Sebec Lake

Park yourself here to spend some time fishing, boating, swimming, or just soaking up the North Woods beauty. For many, the Sebec Lake region is where the real Maine Woods of lore begin, for there are no paved roads between Sebec Lake and the Canadian border. The lake itself, undeveloped and with little road access, is nestled in the mountains. A public boat launch is available just down the road from the campground, and the surrounding mountains and woodlands await hikers.

From Sebec Lake, Moosehead Lake is just an hour away and Baxter State Park is 1.25 hours away.

Campsites, facilities: There are 56 sites for tents and RVs, all without hookups. Wheelchair-accessible restrooms, flush toilets, hot showers, picnic tables, fireplaces and grills, a playground, and a dump station are provided. Hiking trails and a lifeguarded beach are also available. Leashed pets are permitted.

Reservations, fees: Reservations are taken, and the total amount due must accompany your request. Contact the Maine Bureau of Parks and Lands at the number below. The State of Maine allocates some sites on a first-come, first-served basis. Sites are $15 a night for Maine residents and $20 for nonresidents.

Open: Year-round; fully operational May 15–September 30.

Directions: From Dover-Foxcroft, travel north on Highway 153 for six miles. Turn left at the end of the road and continue west for approximately three miles to the park.

Contact: Peaks-Kenny State Park Ranger, 207/564-2003; Maine Bureau of Parks and Lands, 22 State House Station, Augusta, ME 04333, 207/287-3821; website: www.state.me.us/doc/parks.

66 ABNAKI CAMPING CENTER

Rating: 4

On Wesserunsett Lake in Madison

This venerable old campground offers well-spaced sites set amid pine trees on the shores of Wesserunsett Lake. The pretty, sandy beach has no drop-off, making this a good place to swim with small children. Bring your fishing gear if you'd like to catch dinner while the others swim. Like many campgrounds in central Maine, Abnaki caters to locals, in this case the weekend crowd from Skowhegan.

Campsites, facilities: There are 96 sites for tents

and RVs with partial hookups. Flush toilets, hot showers, picnic tables, fireplaces, a dump station, and a store are provided. Recreational facilities include a sandy beach, playground, recreation room, volleyball, horseshoe pits, and canoe and bicycle rentals. Leashed pets are permitted.

Reservations, fees: Reservations are recommended. A deposit of 25 percent is required. Wooded sites are $18 a night, and waterfront sites are $22 a night.

Open: Memorial Day–Labor Day.

Directions: From the intersection of U.S. 201 and Madison Avenue in Skowhegan, drive six miles north on Madison Avenue.

Contact: Dot Labonte, Abnaki Camping Center, RR 2, Box 1500, Madison, ME 04950, 207/474-2070.

67 TWO RIVERS CAMPGROUND

Rating: 6

On the Kennebec River near Skowhegan

A peninsula at the confluence of the Kennebec River and Wesserunsett Stream is the site of this campground. Sites are either in open fields or under cool shade trees along the waterfront. The campground is spacious and well maintained, and there is ample access to the shore for fishing, boating, and swimming.

Campsites, facilities: There are 65 sites for tents and RVs, 40 with full hookups, 12 with water and electric hookups, and 13 with none. Flush toilets, hot showers, picnic tables, fireplaces, cable TV, a dump station, laundry facilities, and a store are provided. Recreational facilities include a playground, horseshoe pits, volleyball court, canoe rentals, and 1,300 feet of waterfront for swimming, fishing, and boating. A state-run boat ramp is nearby. Leashed pets are permitted.

Reservations, fees: Reservations are recommended. Sites are $18–22 a night.

Open: May 1–October 31.

Directions: From the intersection of U.S. 2 and U.S. 201 in Skowhegan, drive 2.5 miles east on U.S. 2 to the campground.
Contact: The Beauregard Family, Two Rivers Campground, H.C.R. 71, Box 14, Skowhegan, ME 04976, 207/474-6482.

68 SKOWHEGAN/ CANAAN KOA

Rating: 3

West of Skowhegan in Canaan

You find no surprises here, for every KOA looks pretty much the same whether it's in Kansas or Maine. This is a full-service campground with all the usual options. The Skowhegan/Canaan KOA is located on a grassy hillside above a major east-west highway.
Campsites, facilities: There are 120 sites for tents and RVs, 59 with full hookups, 43 with water and electric hookups, and 18 with none. Flush toilets, hot showers, picnic tables, fireplaces, a dump station, laundry facilities, an adult lounge, and cable TV are provided. Recreational facilities include a playground, video game room, swimming pool, volleyball, basketball, and badminton. LP gas is available. Leashed pets are permitted.
Reservations, fees: Reservations are accepted. Sites are $22–26 a night.
Open: May 1–December 1.
Directions: From I-95 near Fairfield, take Exit 36 and head north on U.S. 201 toward Skowhegan. Turn right onto Highway 23 and travel north for eight miles to Canaan. Turn right onto U.S. 2 and drive east for 1.5 miles to the campground.
Contact: The Kennedy Family, Skowhegan/Canaan KOA, P.O. Box 87, Highway 2, Canaan, ME 04924, 207/474-2858 or 800/291-3514.

69 STETSON SHORES CAMPGROUND

Rating: 4

On Pleasant Lake in Stetson

Rural and woodsy, this campground is set on 32 acres beside the shores of a large spring-fed lake known for its excellent bass, perch, and pickerel fishing. For campers, the main attraction is the lake. If you bring your own boat, you can use the on-site boat launch. Otherwise, rent a kayak, paddleboat, or canoe for a lazy day on the water. Sites are available in the woods, in an open field, or right on the lakefront. This is a no-frills kind of place, where improvements have been kept to a minimum.
Campsites, facilities: There are 43 sites for tents and RVs, 40 with water and electric hookups and three with none. Flush toilets, hot showers, picnic tables, fireplaces, laundry facilities, a dump station, and a store are available. Recreational facilities include volleyball, badminton, horseshoes, a boat launch, lake fishing, and canoe, kayak, and paddleboat rentals. Leashed pets are permitted.
Reservations, fees: Reservations are accepted. Sites are $20–22 a night.
Open: May 15–October 15.
Directions: From I-95 west of Hampden, take Exit 43 and drive six miles north on Highway 143 until you reach the campground entrance.
Contact: The Adams Family, Stetson Shores Campground, Highway 143, P.O. Box 86B, Stetson, ME 04488, 207/296-2041, website: www.campmaine.com/Stetson.

70 CHRISTIE'S CAMPGROUND

Rating: 7

On Sebasticook Lake in Newport

Offering quiet shorefront sites on Sebasticook Lake, Christie's Campground is a shady, comfortable facility with an established feel and a relaxed pace. This pleasant park is well situated for campers who want to take day trips to the mountains that lie to the north or the coast to the south. Bring your fishing tackle and frying pan, because Sebasticook Lake is renowned for its smallmouth bass, perch, and pickerel fishing. **Campsites, facilities:** There are 50 RV sites, 15 with full hookups, 20 with water and electric hookups, and 15 without hookups. Flush toilets, hot showers, picnic tables, fireplaces, a dump station, laundry facilities, and a store are provided. Recreational facilities include a boat launch, canoe and boat rentals, a beach, playground, recreation room, volleyball, basketball, badminton, and horseshoe pits. Leashed pets are permitted. **Reservations, fees:** Reservations are recommended. Sites are $20-22 a night. **Open:** May 1-October 30. **Directions:** From the junction of I-95 and U.S. 2 at Newport, drive three miles east on U.S. 2 to the campground. **Contact:** Bruce and Patti Newhall, Christie's Campground, Highway 2, Box 565, Newport, ME 04953, 207/368-4645 or 800/688-5141.

71 TENT VILLAGE TRAVEL TRAILER PARK

🏊 🎣 🚤 🐾 🚐 ⛺

Rating: 5

On Sebasticook Lake in Newport

Tent Village is a clean, well-maintained, and established campground on the shores of Sebasticook Lake. The 50 wooded or sunny sites are spread out over 50 acres, giving visitors a sense of open space and privacy. Though it is not near major attractions, the place does make you feel right at home. People looking for a lakeside camp, or those who are just passing through the area, will find it worthwhile to stop at Tent Village. **Campsites, facilities:** There are 50 sites for tents and RVs with full, partial, and no hookups. Flush toilets, hot showers, picnic tables with rooftops, fireplaces, metered LP gas, a dump station, and a store are provided. Recreational facilities include a swimming pool, recreation room, volleyball, basketball, badminton, horseshoes, a boat

launch, and canoe, paddleboat, and motorboat rentals. Leashed pets are permitted. **Reservations, fees:** Reservations are accepted and require a deposit of one night's fee. Sites are $18-22 a night. **Open:** May 15-October 15. **Directions:** From the junction of I-95 and U.S. 2 at Newport, drive two miles east on U.S. 2 until you reach the campground entrance. **Contact:** Vern and Joan Holyokes, Tent Village Travel Trailer Park, RR 2, Box 580, Newport, ME 04953, 207/368-5047 or 800/319-9333.

72 SHADY ACRES CAMPGROUND

🏊 🎣 🐾 🚐 ⛺

Rating: 4

In Carmel a few miles west of Bangor

Here is yet another small campground located close to Bangor. Although there are few attractions in the immediate area, you are not too far from the coast, the North Woods, and the Canadian border. As the name suggests, the campsites at Shady Acres are set amid trees, giving the park a peaceful, pretty quality and providing cooling shade in the summer. Best of all for anglers, the trout fishing in the pond is reputed to be excellent. **Campsites, facilities:** There are 50 sites for tents and RVs, 20 with full hookups and 30 with water and electric hookups. Flush toilets, hot showers, picnic tables, fireplaces, laundry facilities, a dump station, and a store are provided. Recreational facilities include a fishing pond, swimming pool, recreation room, volleyball, badminton, and horseshoes. Leashed pets are permitted. **Reservations, fees:** Reservations are accepted with a $5 deposit. Sites are $20 a night. **Open:** May 15-October 15. **Directions:** From the intersection of I-95 and Highway 69 south of Carmel, drive 2.5 miles west on Highway 69 to the campground. **Contact:** Mike and Elsie Hamel, Shady Acres Campground, RR 2, Box 7890, Carmel, ME 04419, 207/848-5515.

73 PLEASANT HILL CAMPGROUND

Rating: 5

In Bangor

The aptly named Pleasant Hill Campground is spread out over rolling, shaded hills that catch cooling breezes and make for a quiet, relaxing retreat. Someone obviously had children in mind when they designed this place: in addition to two playgrounds, a good-sized swimming pool, and a miniature golf course, the park boasts children's trout fishing in a private stocked pond and a private frog pond.

Located within the city limits of Bangor, the crossroads of the state, Pleasant Hill Campground is convenient to the downtown area, airport, and University of Maine, as well as within easy reach of Acadia National Park, Canadian Maritime Provinces, and wild regions of northern Maine.

Campsites, facilities: There are 105 sites for tents and RVs, 33 with full hookups, 52 with water and electric hookups, and 20 with none. Flush toilets, free hot showers, picnic tables, fireplaces, laundry facilities, a dump station, cable TV, and a store are provided. Recreational facilities include a heated swimming pool, miniature golf, recreation room, volleyball, basketball, badminton, and horseshoes. Leashed pets are permitted.

Reservations, fees: Reservations are recommended. For stays of up to three days, send a deposit of one night's fee; for four or more days, send a $40 deposit. Sites are $20–35 a night.

Open: May 1–Columbus Day.

Directions: From the intersection of I-95 and Highway 222 near Exit 47 in Bangor, drive five miles west on Highway 222 to the campground.

Contact: Bev and Frank Montford, Pleasant Hill Campground, R.F.D. 3, P.O. Box 180, Bangor, ME 04401, 207/848-5127, website: www.pleasanthillcampground.com.

74 WHEELER STREAM CAMPING AREA

Rating: 2

In Bangor

Wheeler Stream is a small, open campground in the middle of a residential/business section of Bangor and was not designed to be a vacation spot for visitors. Many of those who stay here are out-of-state contractors and construction workers who prefer to live at the campground in their own RVs instead of at a motel.

Campsites, facilities: There are 25 sites for tents and RVs, all with water and electric hookups. Flush toilets, free hot showers, picnic tables, fireplaces, laundry facilities, a dump station, and a whirlpool are provided. Leashed pets are permitted.

Reservations, fees: Reservations are recommended. Sites are $16–22 a night.

Open: May 15–October 15.

Directions: From I-95 at Bangor, take Exit 44 and drive 2.5 miles west on Cold Brook Road to the intersection with U.S. 2. The campground is 300 feet ahead on U.S. 2.

Contact: David and Marybeth Archdeacon, Wheeler Stream Camping Area, RR 2, Box 2800, Bangor, ME 04401, 207/848-3713.

75 PAUL BUNYAN CAMPGROUND

Rating: 5

Just off I-95 in Bangor

For a campground located within the limits of Bangor—one of Maine's largest cities—Paul Bunyan is surprisingly peaceful and relaxing. Nestled in rolling countryside near the middle of the state, this is an ideal place to stop for those traveling to Acadia National Park, Canadian Maritime Provinces, or the wild northern reaches of the state.

Campsites, facilities: There are 52 sites for tents and RVs, 12 with full hookups and 40 with water and electric hookups. Facilities include flush toilets, hot showers, picnic tables, fireplaces, a dump station, and a store. Recreational facilities include a heated swimming pool, recreation room, fishing pond, volleyball, basketball, badminton, and horseshoes. Leashed pets are permitted.

Reservations, fees: Reservations are recommended. For stays of up to three days, send one night's fee as a deposit; for four or more days, send a $40 deposit. Sites are $15–27 a night.

Open: Year-round.

Directions: From the intersection of I-95 and Highway 222 near Exit 47 in Bangor, drive 2.5 miles west on Highway 222 to the campground.

Contact: Dennis and Shirley Hachey, Paul Bunyan Campground, 1862 Union Street, Bangor, ME 04401, 207/941-1177, website: www.paulbunyancampground.com.

76 VILLA VAUGHN CAMPGROUND

Rating: 5

On Pushaw Lake near Orono

The sites at Villa Vaughn are set beneath shade trees and beside the shore of Pushaw Lake, a nine-mile-long body of water offering some excellent bass, perch, and pickerel fishing, and calm water for canoeing. It's an open, airy place with a shallow, sandy beach that's safe for swimming. Nearby Orono is home to the University of Maine.

Campsites, facilities: There are 75 sites for tents and RVs, some with full hookups and some with water and electric hookups. Flush toilets, hot showers, picnic tables, fireplaces, laundry facilities, a dump station, and a store are provided. Recreational facilities include a boat launch, canoe and rowboat rentals, a recreation room, and horseshoes. Leashed pets are permitted.

Reservations, fees: Reservations are required for lakefront sites. Sites are $16–20 a night.

Open: May 15–October 15.

Directions: From I-95 near Orono, take Exit 51 and drive one mile south on Stillwater Avenue. Turn right and go three miles west on Forest Avenue to the campground.

Contact: Villa Vaughn Campground, R.F.D. 5, Box 205, Bangor, ME 04401, 207/945-6796.

77 GREENWOOD ACRES

Rating: 2

Near Brewer

Greenwood Acres is situated just off busy Highway 178 on a 50-acre land parcel covered with pine trees and open fields very near the twin cities of Bangor and Brewer. Most of the activity here takes place at the on-site playground and swimming pool. The Penobscot River, which happens to be a very good stream for salmon fishing, is directly across the highway from the campground and within easy walking distance. If you want to bask in the natural beauty of Maine, this isn't your best choice. It is, however, a convenient stop on the way to or from the various highlights of the state.

Campsites, facilities: There are 50 sites for tents and RVs, six with full hookups, 28 with water and electric hookups, and 16 with none. Flush toilets, hot showers, picnic tables, fireplaces, a dump station, laundry facilities, and a store are provided. You will also find a swimming pool, playground, recreation room, volleyball, basketball, and horseshoe pits. Leashed pets are permitted.

Reservations, fees: Reservations are recommended. Sites are $15–22 a night.

Open: Year-round.

Directions: From the junction of U.S. 1A and Highway 9 in Brewer, drive 4.5 miles east on Highway 9 and then one mile north on Highway 178 to the campground.

Contact: Tom and Donna Foster, Greenwood Acres, R.F.D. 2, Box 210, Brewer, ME 04412, 207/989-8898.

78 RED BARN RV PARK

Rating: 3

In Holden

The campground is set in a grassy field just off a major highway. Convenient to downtown Bangor, known as the crossroads of Maine, this is a good place to stop if you are heading east to Canadian Maritime Provinces, south to the coast, or north to Maine Woods. Though not a destination campground for most vacationers, it does provide a clean, pleasant place to spend a day or two while traveling.

Campsites, facilities: There are 126 sites for RVs, 52 with full hookups, 49 with water and electric hookups, and 25 with none. Flush toilets, hot showers, picnic tables, fireplaces, laundry facilities, a dump station, and a store are provided. A swimming pool, recreation room, volleyball, basketball, badminton, and horseshoes are among the recreational offerings. Leashed pets are permitted.

Reservations, fees: Reservations are recommended July through Labor Day and require a $10 deposit. Sites are $16–28 a night.

Open: May 15–October 15.

Directions: From the intersection of I-395 and U.S. 1A near Bangor, drive three miles east on U.S. 1A to the campground.

Contact: Phil and Belinda Robinson, Red Barn RV Park, U.S. 1A, Holden, ME 04429, 207/843-6011, website: www.redbarnmaine.com.

Chapter 2

© MAINE OFFICE OF TOURISM/JEFF GREENBERG

Western Lakes and Mountains

Western Lakes and Mountains

While New Hampshire's tall and picturesque White Mountains get most of the attention, western Maine's rugged, glaciated ranges are spectacular in their own right. Though not as high as their relatives just to the west, the mountains at this northern end of the Appalachian chain are cut through by numerous wild rivers and pocked with high mountain lakes. The combination of mountain summits, northern forests, and wilderness lakes and streams is unique in the United States, and it offers outdoor recreationalists an unsurpassed variety of activities to enjoy.

From hiking and alpine skiing, to canoe tripping, to mountain biking, to white-water kayaking and rafting, the western lakes and mountains are a destination during any season. Winters are long, cold, and snowy, generally lasting from November to May with average temperatures in the low teens. But for those summer visitors seeking relief from the humid heat farther south, the clean, cool air up here is a delight. July and August temperatures are generally in the 70s, and at night things cool down noticeably, with the thermometer commonly registering temperatures in the 40s and 50s.

And while the water on the coastal beaches is comfortable for polar bears, the waters in Maine's myriad lakes are delightful swim spots for most humans. On the northern lakes in the Rangeley area, you'll find great fishing, spectacular mountain views, and refreshing waters. Farther to the south, travelers can enjoy the lakes and ponds and still zip off to the coast for a day trip. The adventurous might want to explore the more remote state management areas in the northern part of this region.

Autumn is an especially wonderful time to visit this area. For a brief period in late September and early October, the northern hardwoods ringing the lakes and cloaking the mountainsides turn incandescent with color. But no matter when you time your visit, the western mountains and lakes will enchant you with their beauty and diversity.

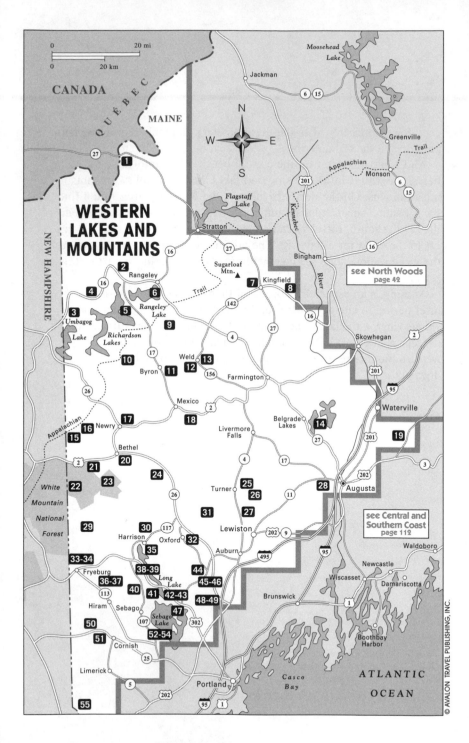

WESTERN LAKES AND MOUNTAINS

CANADA

QUÉBEC

MAINE

NEW HAMPSHIRE

Moosehead Lake

Jackman

6 15

Greenville Trail

Appalachian Trail

Monson

6 15

27

1

Flagstaff Lake

Stratton

Sugarloaf Mtn.

16

27

Kingfield

7

8

Bingham

201

Kennebec River

16

see North Woods
page 42

2

Rangeley

16

4

3

6

5

Umbagog Lake

Rangeley Lake

Richardson Lakes

9

Trail

142

4

27

16

Skowhegan

2

17

10

Byron

Weld

13

12

11

156

Farmington

201

95

Waterville

26

Appalachian

16

15

Newry

17

Mexico

18

2

Belgrade Lakes

14

27

201

19

3

Bethel

20

24

Livermore Falls

4

17

White Mountain National Forest

2

21

22

23

26

Turner

25

26

31

27

11

28

Augusta

202

29

30

117

Harrison

Oxford

35

32

Lewiston

202

9

495

Auburn

see Central and Southern Coast
page 112

Waldoboro

33-34

Fryeburg

36-37

38-39

40

113

Hiram

Sebago

41

Long Lake

44

45-46

42-43

48-49

47

302

Brunswick

95

Newcastle

Wiscasset

Damariscotta

1

50

51

Cornish

Sebago Lake

52-54

107

25

Limerick

5

202

Portland

95

1

Casco Bay

ATLANTIC OCEAN

Boothbay Harbor

© AVALON TRAVEL PUBLISHING, INC.

0   20 mi
0   20 km

N
W   E
S

1 CHAIN OF PONDS MANAGEMENT UNIT

≈ 🛶 🏕 🎣 ❄ 🐕 ⛰

Rating: 9

Along the Dead River northwest of Flagstaff Lake

Campers will feel as if they are miles away from civilization when they arrive at this remote retreat. Each secluded lakefront site is like a true backcountry spot. You can fetch drinking water from the ponds or rivers—just be sure to filter or treat it before consumption. The chain of ponds includes Nautis, Long, Bag, and Lower Ponds. These wilderness pools are connected by navigable sections of the Dead River, so bring a canoe and explore all the hidden coves and inlets. Anglers should not leave behind their fishing rods. If you have two cars and want to arrange a shuttle, the North Branch of the Dead River makes for an excellent flat-water canoe trip.

Campsites, facilities: Some primitive campsites are located on the shores of the ponds. Some are drive-up sites, while others are accessible by boat. Water is available from the rivers and ponds. Boat launches are provided nearby. Pets are permitted.

Reservations, fees: Reservations are not accepted; sites are available on a first-come, first-served basis. There is no fee.

Open: Year-round.

Directions: From Eustis, drive approximately 12 miles north on Highway 27 to the management unit.

Contact: Maine Bureau of Parks and Lands, 22 State House Station, Augusta, ME 04333, 207/287-3821, website: www.state.me.us/doc/parks.

2 CUPSUPTIC CAMPGROUND

🏕 ≈ 🚐 🎣 🎣 🐕 �- ⛰

Rating: 9

On the north end of Cupsuptic Lake near Rangeley

Secluded in a mature forest on Cupsuptic Lake's northern end, these sites provide welcome privacy for campers. And the setting, on a vast freshwater lake connected to several other enormous freshwater lakes—among them Mooselookmeguntic, Rangeley, and Upper and Lower Richardson—couldn't be more conducive to getting out and exploring. Miles of waterways await adventuresome souls. Bring a canoe, or rent one here for days of peaceful paddling. Meanwhile, fishing fans will be busy casting into these freshwater pools. This is wild country, with plenty of woods, water, and wildlife to satisfy hunters in search of deer, duck, moose, and grouse.

Campsites, facilities: There are 55 sites for tents and RVs. Flush toilets, hot showers, picnic tables, fireplaces, a dump station, and a store are provided. Recreational facilities include a boat launch, canoe rentals, recreation room, volleyball, badminton, and horseshoes. Leashed pets are permitted.

Reservations, fees: Reservations are accepted. Sites are $16–25 a night.

Open: May 1–December 1.

Directions: From the junction of Highways 4 and 16 in Oquossoc, drive 4.5 miles northwest on Highway 16 to the campground.

Contact: Cupsuptic Campground, Rangeley, ME 04970, 207/864-5249, website: www.cupsuptic campground.com.

3 AZISCOOS VALLEY CAMPING AREA

🏕 ≈ 🛶 🚐 🍴 🐕 🚴 🚐 ⛰

Rating: 8

On the banks of the Magalloway River northwest of Bethel

Situated on a well-maintained lawn that stretches downhill to the Magalloway River, the Aziscoos campground is especially clean and offers spacious sites. Jumping into the river for a dip is a popular activity here. The main attraction to the area, however, is the easy access it affords those who want to explore nearby waterways. From the campground, you can launch a canoe into the Magalloway River, which flows into Umbagog Lake and ultimately into the Androscoggin River. In addition to this waterway, campers can use the nearby public boat launches for trips on Aziscohos Lake and Richardson Lake. From these two launching points, a camper can access hundreds of miles of canoeing, boating, and fishing water. Hikers can hit the trails at Aziscohos Mountain, a 3,215-foot peak only a few miles from the campground.

Campsites, facilities: There are 31 sites for tents and RVs, 16 with water and electric hookups and 15 with none. Flush toilets, hot showers, picnic tables, fireplaces with grills, a dump station, laundry facilities, and a playground are provided. A large tepee is available for rent. Leashed pets are permitted.

Reservations, fees: Reservations are not necessary. Sites are $15–20 a night.

Open: May 15–October 30.

Directions: From Errol, New Hampshire, travel north on Highway 16 for 14 miles. The campground is on your left.

Contact: Muriel and Norman Littlehale, Aziscoos Valley Camping Area, H.C.R. 10, Box 302, Wilsons Mills, ME 03579, 207/486-3271, website: www.sundayriveron-line.com/Aziscoos-Valley-Camping-Area.htm.

4 BLACK BROOK COVE CAMPGROUND

🏃 🛶 🏊 ➔ 🎣 🐕 🚣 🚐 ⛺

Rating: 10

On Aziscohos Lake in Oquossoc, west of Rangeley

Though well maintained, this campground offers a wilderness setting. The sites on the east shore of the lake are spaced 75–100 feet apart, allowing for privacy and a greater sense of remoteness. Boat-in sites on Beaver Island are very popular, drawing some campers who return to the same spots each year. Aziscohos is a large, undeveloped lake surrounded by mountains. Evidently it has the best waters in the area for brook trout, but people also try their hand at catching landlocked salmon. If fishing isn't your passion, paddling or cruising around this peaceful lake is a great way to spend a few days. Fishing guides, seaplane, and a shuttle service are also available. If you get tired of the water, take a hike on the wooded trails or to the nearby Aziscohos Mountain summit.

Campsites, facilities: In the central camping area, there are 28 RV sites with water and electric hookups and six tent sites. It offers hot showers, flush toilets, a dump station, boat ramp, playground, beach, and store. On the east shore of the lake, there are 20 additional sites for small campers or tents. Finally, there are 16 remote sites on 20-acre Beaver Island, accessible by boat. Sites on the east shore and the island have outhouses. Picnic tables and fire rings are provided at all sites. Leashed pets are permitted.

Reservations, fees: Reservations are recommended and, on summer weekends, are necessary. A deposit of 50 percent is required. Sites are $18–20 a night.

Open: April 15–October 31.

Directions: From the junction of Highways 4 and 16 in Oquossoc, travel west on Highway 16 for 16 miles. Turn right on Aziscohos Road and drive .5 mile north.

Contact: Bob and Cecile Paradis, Black Brook Cove Campground, P.O. Box 319, Oquossoc, ME 04964, 207/864-2161 (radio phone; let it ring), website: www.blackbrookcove.com.

5 STEPHEN PHILLIPS MEMORIAL PRESERVE

🛶 🏊 ➔ 🐕 ⛺

Rating: 10

On Mooselookmeguntic Lake near Oquossoc

Stephen Phillips Memorial Preserve provides a wilderness camping experience for those who are looking for peace and solitude in a true Maine woods setting. Most of the sites are on islands or are scattered along the wooded shores of Mooselookmeguntic Lake, a large, wild body of water that stretches for many miles and is renowned as a high-quality freshwater sport fishery. These sites are reached by canoe or boat, while other sites are located on the mainland. The charitable trust that manages the preserve strives to maintain the land in its natural state. Come here for primitive camping in a spectacular mountain, forest, and lake setting.

Campsites, facilities: There are 60 tent sites with no hookups. Fireplaces, picnic tables, and nonflush toilets are provided. Leashed pets are permitted.

Reservations, fees: Reservations must be paid in full two weeks prior to arrival. Cancellations must be received a week before arrival for a full refund. Sites are $12 a night, plus $1 a night for dogs.

Open: May 1–September 15.

Directions: From the junction of Highway 4 and Bald Mountain Road in Oquossoc, drive south on Bald Mountain Road for four miles to the campground.

Contact: Jim and Olive Turner, Stephen Phillips Memorial Preserve, P.O. Box 21, Oquossoc, ME 04964, 207/864-2003.

6 RANGELEY LAKE STATE PARK

🏃 🏊 🎣 🚤 ❌ ❄️ 🐕 ⛹️ ♿ 🚐 ⛺

On Rangeley Lake

Rating: 8

A real gem, Rangeley Lake State Park is situated on a large lake nestled among the mountains of western Maine. Eight large lakes—Aziscohos, Upper and Lower Richardson, Cupsuptic, Mooselookmeguntic, Kennebago, Umbagog, and Rangeley—lie within a 20-mile radius of the village of Rangeley. There are also dozens of ponds and miles of wild streams and rivers, plus tall, fir-covered mountains, making this area one of Maine's prime vacation destinations. You can fish in the big lakes for trout and landlocked salmon or explore these waters by boat or canoe. Campers can secure guide services, rent canoes or boats,

hike trails to the nearby mountain summits, or find fine dining and shops in the village of Rangeley. In winter, this is paradise for cross-country and downhill skiers; the Saddleback Ski Resort is just north of town.

Campsites, facilities: There are 50 sites for tents and RVs, all without hookups. Wheelchair-accessible restrooms, hot showers, a dump station, a concrete boat launch ramp with floats, a group camping area, a playground, and a swimming area are provided. Leashed pets are permitted.

Reservations, fees: Reservations are accepted, and the total amount due must accompany your request. Contact the Maine Bureau of Parks and Lands for reservations at 207/287-3821. The State of Maine allocates some sites on a first-come, first-served basis. Fees are $15 a night for Maine residents and $20 for non-residents.

Open: Year-round; fully operational May 15–October 1.

Directions: From Rangeley, drive three miles south on Highway 4, then turn right on South Shore Road and go five miles west.

Contact: Rangeley Lake State Park Ranger, 207/864-3858; Maine Bureau of Parks and Lands, 22 State House Station, Augusta, ME 04333, 207/287-3821, website: www.state.me.us/doc/parks.

7 DEER FARM CAMPGROUND

🏃 🏊 🚐 🏕️ ⛹️ 🚐 ⛺

Near the Sugarloaf Resort in Kingfield

Rating: 2

A raw, well-used feeling marks this campground, where the roads and campsites, which are tucked into the woods, have become eroded. Campers can swim and canoe at a private beach across the street and about half a mile down a dirt road from here. The lake is adequate for a dip, but neither the beach nor the views entice you to remain for hours. While this is not the most appealing campground, the Carrabassett Valley is home to some great hiking routes. By not venturing far, hikers can head off for day trips or multiday treks to Sugarloaf Mountain, the Bigelow Range, or Mount Abraham.

Campsites, facilities: There are 47 sites for tents and RVs, 45 with water and electric hookups and two with no hookups. Flush toilets, hot showers, picnic tables, fireplaces, a standing barbecue grill, a dump station, laundry facilities, and a store are provided. Recreational facilities include a playground, recreation room, volleyball, basketball, and horseshoe pits. A private beach for campers is located nearby. Leashed pets are permitted.

Reservations, fees: Reservations are not necessary. Sites are $15–17 a night.

Open: Mid-May–Columbus Day.

Directions: From Kingfield, go about two miles north on Highway 27. Turn left on Tufts Farm Road and drive to the campground.

Contact: Brenda Finwick, Deer Farm Campground, Tufts Pond Road, Kingfield, ME 04947, 207/265-4599, website: www.deerfarmcamps.com.

8 HAPPY HORSESHOE CAMPGROUND

Rating: 5

In North New Portland

Very clean, nondescript, and unassuming, this campground caters almost exclusively to the local people living within a 50-mile radius who use it for weekend getaways in the summer.

Campsites, facilities: There are 91 sites for tents and RVs with water and electric hookups. Flush toilets, hot showers, picnic tables, fireplaces, a dump station, laundry facilities, and a store are provided. A playground, recreation room, volleyball, basketball, shuffleboard, badminton, and horseshoe pits are among the recreational facilities. Leashed pets are permitted.

Reservations, fees: Reservations are required on weekends, and you must make a deposit of one night's fee. Sites are $24 a night.

Open: Memorial Day–Labor Day.

Directions: From the junction of Highways 146 and 16 in North New Portland, drive east on Highway 16 for .5 mile and then head north on Long Falls Dam Road for 5.25 miles to the campground.

Contact: Judy and Buster Pinkham, Happy Horseshoe Campground, H.C.R. 68, Box 170, North New Portland, ME 04961, 207/628-3471.

9 FOUR PONDS MANAGEMENT UNIT

Rating: 8

Just east of Mooselookmeguntic Lake in the Rangeley area

This area is characterized by mountainous terrain, a thick spruce forest, and six ponds (not four as the name implies). Campers access the lean-to and campsite by hiking on the Appalachian Trail, which crosses the length of this 6,000-acre unit. With the highest elevation just under 3,000 feet, the area offers relatively easy backpacking. You find the lean-to nestled between Long and Sabbath Day Ponds, while the campsite lies some five miles farther down the trail on the smaller Little Swift River Pond. Fishing enthusiasts should be aware that all of the ponds contain brook trout. A population of Sunapee trout was introduced in Long Pond in 1977 and remains viable. In addition to trout, Beaver Mountain Lake holds salmon and smelt. After a day or even a few hours of hauling a backpack, you may want to take a dip in the fresh water, a truly inviting prospect. There are some private camps, accessed by private roads, on Beaver Mountain Lake.

Campsites, facilities: There is a campsite on Little Swift River Pond and a lean-to on Sabbath Day Pond. Fire rings and a pit toilet are provided, and campers can get water from the ponds. These backcountry sites are accessible by foot only.

Reservations, fees: Reservations are not accepted; sites are allocated on a first-come, first-served basis. There is no fee.

Open: Year-round.

Directions: From Houghton, drive north on Highway 17 for approximately seven miles to where the Appalachian Trail crosses the road. Park and start hiking northeast on the trail. You reach the shelter in about 3.5 miles; the campsite is about five miles farther up the trail.

Contact: Maine Bureau of Parks and Lands, 22 State House Station, Augusta, ME 04333, 207/287-3821, website: www.state.me.us/doc/parks.

10 SOUTH ARM CAMPGROUND

Rating: 10

On the Richardson Lakes near Andover

(F) One of the country's premier wilderness regions—a land graced with lakes, forests, and mountains—is home to South Arm Campground. From the main camping area, Upper and Lower Richardson Lakes stretch northward for 17 miles and connect with several other equally expansive and undeveloped lakes. Paddlers can put in for multiday wilderness canoe trips from here, and anglers can cast a line for landlocked salmon, trout, and togue in these waters, which are renowned for their excellent fishing. In this truly wild region, you can find that North Woods wilderness experience you've been seeking.

Campsites, facilities: There are 35 isolated wilderness tent sites on the shores of Upper and Lower Richardson Lakes and on several islands. The main campground at South Arm has an additional 70 wooded sites for tents and RVs, all with water and electric hookups. Most are situated along the waterfront, and each has a picnic table and fire ring. Hot showers, flush toilets, laundry facilities, a store and deli, motorboat and canoe rentals, a dump station, playing field, and boat launch are provided at the main campground. Leashed pets are permitted.

Reservations, fees: Reservations are required. There is a two-night minimum stay on weekends except for Memorial Day, July 4, and Labor Day, when you must reserve at least three nights. Deposits must be received within five days of making reservations by telephone. In the main camping area, beach sites are $23 a night, waterfront sites are $20, and off-water sites are $16. Wilderness tent sites are $17 a night.

Open: May 20–September 9.

Directions: From Andover, drive about 12 miles north on South Arm Road.

Contact: South Arm Campground, P.O. Box 310, Andover, ME 04216, 207/364-5155 or 207/784-3566, website: www.southarm.com.

11 COOS CANYON CAMPGROUND

Rating: 8

About halfway between Rumford and Oquossoc in the Coos Canyon of the Swift River

Quiet time is all the time at this peaceful spot. An off-the-beaten-path find, the simple, well-tended campground is located next to a dramatic gorge. Sites are nestled in the woods and allow for more privacy than you find at most campgrounds. A novel addition is the swinging wooden bench that hangs from a tree at each site. Whether you use the bench to read a book, enjoy a cup of tea, or chat with a loved one, you'll agree that every campground should add this special touch.

Coos Canyon is a gorge that was cut into bedrock by the flows of the Swift River, and you are surrounded by cliffs as high as 30 feet. Swimming and fishing in the clear water are popular pastimes, as are walking and biking the trails and dirt roads that pass by the canyon. The most unique activity here, however, is panning for gold. From the early years of the 18th century, gold panning has been a favorite pursuit in the Swift River. Lessons are available, and the campground rents or sells the necessary prospecting equipment.

Campsites, facilities: There are 20 primitive sites for tents, pop-ups, truck campers, and small trailers. Each site has a picnic table, a fireplace with grill, and a swinging bench. Water is provided at the entrance, outhouses are available near the campsites, and hot showers are centrally located. There's also a store selling limited supplies. Leashed pets are permitted.

Reservations, fees: Reservations are accepted. A deposit of the first night's fee is required. Sites are $15–20 a night.

Open: April 15–November 15.

Directions: From the town of Mexico, travel 13 miles northwest on Highway 17 to the campground.

Contact: Gerry and Rosey Perrier, Coos Canyon Campground, Highway 17, HC 62, Box 408, Byron, ME 04275, 207/364-3880.

12 DUMMER'S BEACH CAMPGROUND

🏃 🏊 🚣 🛶 🎣 🐕 🚐 ⛺

Rating: 8

Next to Webb Lake in the town of Weld

The half-mile-long natural sand beach on clearwater Webb Lake is no doubt the highlight of this campground. Swimming here is a popular activity with youngsters, as the water deepens gradually, while others can launch canoes and boats right from the campground. Hikers may want to trek to any of three nearby peaks: Mount Blue (elevation 3,187 feet), Tumbledown Mountain (3,035 feet), and Little Jackson Mountain (3,535 feet). Bring a fishing rod and frying pan if you choose to head to Tumbledown, for you'll discover a trout lake when you reach the summit. Back at Webb Lake, there is good fishing for trout, bass, pickerel, and white perch. For more information on the area, see the next listing, Mount Blue State Park.

Campsites, facilities: There are 200 sites for tents and RVs, nearly all with water and electric hookups. Flush toilets, hot showers, picnic tables, fireplaces, a dump station, laundry facilities, and a store are provided. Recreational facilities include a sandy beach, playground,

swings, recreation room, volleyball, basketball, and horseshoe pits. Leashed pets are permitted.

Reservations, fees: Reservations are welcome. Sites are $22–25 a night.

Open: Memorial Day–Labor Day.

Directions: From Weld, at the junction of Highways 142 and 156, follow Bypass Road for less than one mile to Fire Lane 9. Drive southwest on Fire Lane 9 to the camp.

Contact: Elizabeth Dummer Shreve, Dummer's Beach Campground, P.O. Box 82, Weld, ME 04285, 207/585-2200.

13 MOUNT BLUE STATE PARK

🏃 🚴 🚣 🛶 🎣 ❄ 🐕 🏃 🚐 ⛺

Rating: 10

In the western mountains near Weld

Mount Blue State Park is effectively split into two parts: the mountain section just north of the town of Weld and the section that lies along the western shore of beautiful Webb Lake. The mountains are laced with miles of hiking, cross-country skiing, mountain biking, and snowmobile trails. Webb Lake, on the other hand, offers superb swimming, fishing, and canoeing opportunities. The state park campground on the lakeshore is pleasant, spacious, well maintained, and affords expansive views over the water to the mountains beyond. Some trails lead through the forest and to the summits of surrounding peaks.

Campsites, facilities: There are 136 sites for tents and trailers, all without hookups. Fire rings, picnic tables, nonflush toilets, a dump station, playground, and boat ramp are provided. Canoe and rowboat rentals are available. Leashed pets are permitted.

Reservations, fees: Campsites may be reserved for stays between June 15 and Labor Day, but otherwise are available on a first-come, first-served basis. Fees are $15 a night for Maine residents and $20 for nonresidents.

Open: Year-round; fully operational May 15–October 15.

Directions: From Weld, drive two miles west

on Highway 142, then turn left in Weld Corner and drive approximately four miles south to the campground.

Contact: Mount Blue State Park Ranger, 207/585-2347 in the summer, or 207/585-2261 in the winter; Maine Bureau of Parks and Lands, 22 State House Station, Augusta, ME 04333, 207/287-3821, website: www.state.me.us/doc/parks.

14 GREAT POND CAMPGROUND

Rating: 6

On a lake near Belgrade Lakes

Great Pond Campground surrounds a large body of water in the Belgrade Lakes chain, a string of lakes renowned as great fishing spots for northern pike, landlocked salmon, bass, trout, perch, and pickerel. This lake covers 8,300 acres and is bordered by a sandy beach with boat docks. The nearby small town of Belgrade Lakes is an attractive village situated at the junction of two lakes. The campground is small and pleasant, but some sites are backed up too close to Highway 27 and are occasionally hit with traffic noise.

Campsites, facilities: There are 55 sites for tents and RVs, 34 with full hookups and 21 with water and electric hookups. Flush toilets, hot showers, picnic tables, fireplaces, a dump station, laundry facilities, and a store are provided. Seasonal campers can get cable TV. Recreational facilities include a playground, recreation room, swimming pool, sandy beach, boat launch and boathouse, and paddleboat, motorboat, and canoe rentals. Leashed pets are permitted.

Reservations, fees: Reservations are recommended. A deposit of 25 percent is required. Sites are $25 a night.

Open: May 1–September 30.

Directions: From the Belgrade Lakes town center, drive half a mile south on Highway 27 to the campground.

Contact: Doris Bilodeau, Great Pond Campground, R.F.D. 1, Box 913, Belgrade, ME 04917, 207/495-2116.

15 APPALACHIAN TRAIL

Rating: 10

Along the Appalachian Mountains

From Springer Mountain in Georgia to the summit of Katahdin in Maine, the Appalachian Trail traverses the Appalachian Mountain chain on a 2,158-mile continuous, marked footpath. The first 150 miles in Maine cross spectacular mountain ranges, including the Mahoosucs, the Baldpates, the Saddlebacks, and the Bemis. Views of the Rangeley Lakes and the major mountains of New Hampshire and western Maine are stunning. The Mahoosuc Notch, a deep cleft in the mountains filled with house-sized boulders, is considered the toughest stretch of the entire route. While most day hikers swarm to the nearby Presidential Range in New Hampshire, people who hike this section get to bask in the stunning views, remoteness, and an overall sense of quiet. The most popular hike in this region is the one that ascends 4,180-foot-high Old Speck Mountain. Try your luck at fishing (or just cool off by dunking) in one of the area's many streams, rivers, or ponds.

Moving eastward, the Bigelow Range traverse is among the finest long-distance, high-elevation hikes in Maine, crossing six major peaks and several lesser ones. From these ridge tops, views of the surrounding country—graced by forests and lakes—are expansive. The trail also wanders through the Carry Ponds country, a beautiful lake-filled region that was traversed by General Benedict Arnold and American army troops during a surprise attack on Quebec in 1775. Continuing on toward the Katahdin summit, a major portion of the trail's final 130 miles lies within the so-called 100-Mile Wilderness, an uninhabited stretch of forests, mountains, rivers, and lakes as wild as any region in the lower 48 states. If you plan to hike here, make sure you carry adequate supplies and are well prepared; of the entire 2,100-plus miles of the Appalachian Trail, this portion is the most untamed.

Campsites, facilities: There are 31 lean-tos, accommodating up to six people each, and six primitive tent campsites along this trail stretch. Some sites have fire rings and pit toilets. Pets are permitted.

Reservations, fees: Sites are first come, first served. There is no fee.

Open: Year-round.

Directions: Maine's portion of the Appalachian Trail enters the state at the Mount Carlo base in the Mahoosuc Range in the White Mountain National Forest, winds north to the Bigelow Range base, and continues to just east of Bald Mountain Pond. The final 130-mile section in the northern part of the state ascends the summit of mile-high Katahdin, Maine's tallest mountain and the trail's terminus.

Contact: Maine Appalachian Trail Club, P.O. Box 283, Augusta, ME 04330, website: www.matc.org; Appalachian Trail Conference, P.O. Box 807, Harpers Ferry, WV 25425, 304/535-6331, website: www.appalachiantrail.org.

16 MAHOOSUC MANAGEMENT UNIT

🏃 ≈ 🎣 📷 ❄ 🐕 🏠

Rating: 10

In the western mountains near Bethel

Natural wonders fill this rugged 27,000-acre section of the Mahoosuc Range. The Appalachian Trail traverses the spine of the mountain range, offering excellent hikes along the ridgeline, and it reaches some of the highest summits in the state, affording spectacular views of mountains, forests, and lakes in all directions. Features include the infamous Mahoosuc Notch— considered the toughest leg of the entire 2,158-mile-long Appalachian Trail—Cataract Gorge, and Speck Pond, a glacial lake perched high atop Old Speck Mountain. The unit extends on either side of Grafton Notch State Park.

Campsites, facilities: There are five hike-in lean-to shelters in or immediately adjacent to the unit boundaries. Each site has a fire ring and pit toilet. Leashed pets are permitted.

Reservations, fees: Registration is not required; the sites are available on a first-come, first-served basis. There is no fee.

Open: Year-round.

Directions: From Newry, drive approximately 12 miles west on Highway 26 to access the unit.

Contact: Maine Bureau of Parks and Lands, 22 State House Station, Augusta, ME 04333, 207/287-3821, website: www.state.me.us/doc/parks.

17 STONY BROOK RECREATION

🏃 ≈ 🎣 📷 ❄ 🐕 🏠 🚐 ⛺

Rating: 6

Near Hanover

Stony Brook is a small campground situated on 50 acres of woods and fields near the western mountains of Maine. The sites are well spaced and offer some privacy. Many natural attractions are close at hand, including the White Mountain National Forest, Appalachian Trail, Grafton Notch State Park, Umbagog Lake National Wildlife Refuge, and the Sunday River Ski Resort. From here, you can hike the Appalachian Trail, visit Screw Auger Falls in nearby Grafton Notch State Park, canoe on the Androscoggin River, or fish in nearby rivers and lakes.

Campsites, facilities: There are 30 sites for tents and RVs, six with full hookups, 16 with water and electric hookups, and eight with none. Flush toilets, hot showers, picnic tables, fireplaces, a dump station, laundry facilities, and a store are provided. Recreational facilities include a playground, recreation room, pool, miniature golf, volleyball, shuffleboard, basketball, and horseshoe pits. Leashed pets are permitted.

Reservations, fees: Reservations are not required. Sites are $20–22 a night.

Open: May 15–October 15.

Directions: From the intersection of U.S. 2 and Highway 26 in Newry, drive one mile east to the campground.

Contact: Bruce and Shirley Powell, Stony Brook Recreation, U.S. 2, H.C.R. 61, Box 130, Hanover, ME 04237, 207/824-2836, website: www.stonybrookrec.com.

18 HONEY RUN BEACH AND CAMPGROUND

Rating: 5

On Worthley Pond in Peru

The owners of this very well-maintained park pride themselves on offering leisurely family camping at spacious sites in open fields. Across the street from the campground is Worthley Pond, which boasts a sandy beach and a shallow, sloping shore—perfect for swimming with small children. The pond is about 2.5 miles long and is nestled among the woods and low mountains that are characteristic of the area. If you are a racing fan, be sure to head over to nearby South Paris to watch the race cars at the Oxford Plains Speedway.

Campsites, facilities: There are 70 sites for tents and RVs with full and partial hookups. Flush toilets, hot showers, picnic tables, fireplaces, a dump station, laundry facilities, and a store are provided. Recreational facilities include a beach area, playground, large field, and basketball court. Leashed pets are permitted.

Reservations, fees: Reservations are not necessary. Sites are $18–22 a night.

Open: Memorial Day–Columbus Day.

Directions: From Rumford, travel east on Highway 108 for 10 miles. Turn right at the sign for Worthley Pond and drive 3.5 miles south to the campground.

Contact: Dennis Thibodeau, Honey Run Beach and Campground, RR 1, Box 1230, Peru, ME 04290, 207/562-4913, website: www.honeyrun campground.com.

19 GREEN VALLEY CAMPGROUND

Rating: 6

On Webber Pond in Vassalboro

Green Valley is aptly named, for this is a very pleasant, quiet campground in a fertile, pastoral region of rolling hills and farms. Its centerpiece, the 1,254-acre Webber Pond, has warm water and a gently sloping, sandy bottom, making this a terrific choice for people who enjoy swimming and bass fishing.

Campsites, facilities: There are 90 sites for tents and RVs, half with full hookups, some with water and electric hookups, and nine with none. Flush toilets, hot showers, picnic tables, fireplaces, a dump station, laundry facilities, and a store are provided. Recreational facilities include a boat launch, large swimming float, canoe and boat rentals, a playground, recreation room, volleyball, bocce court, basketball, and horseshoes. Leashed pets are permitted.

Reservations, fees: Reservations are not necessary. Sites are $21–25 a night.

Open: May 1–September 30.

Directions: From the junction of U.S. 201 and Webber Pond Road north of Augusta, drive north on Webber Pond Road for 4.5 miles, following signs to the campground.

Contact: Sybil and Fred Saucier, Green Valley Campground, Vassalboro, ME 04989, 207/923-3000, website: www.greenvalleycampground.com.

20 BETHEL OUTDOOR ADVENTURE AND CAMPGROUND

Rating: 6

On the banks of the Androscoggin in Bethel

Situated directly on the Androscoggin River where it curves along the eastern edge of the White Mountains, the campground is in a great spot for outdoors enthusiasts looking for a true multi-activity location. Nearby are rivers, lakes, forests, and mountains perfect for canoeing, kayaking, hiking, biking, swimming, and skiing and snowshoeing in winter. The Sunday River Ski Resort is just five miles away.

Campsites, facilities: There are 25 sites for tents and RVs. Flush toilets, hot showers, picnic tables, fireplaces, a dump station, laundry facilities, and a store are provided. Recreational facilities include a recreation hall, a playground, and canoe and kayak rentals.

Reservations, fees: Reservations are accepted. Sites are $20–35 a night.

Open: Year-round.

Directions: From the center of Bethel, travel east for .5 mile on U.S. Route 2 to the campground.

Contact: Jeff and Patti Parsons, Bethel Outdoor Adventure and Campground; 121 Mayville Road/Route 2, Bethel, ME 04217, 800/533-3607, website: www.betheloutdooradventure.com.

21 PLEASANT RIVER CAMPGROUND

🏃 🏊 🎣 🔱 🐕 🚐 ⛺

Rating: 7

In West Bethel

Pleasant River Campground sits in the Androscoggin River Valley in the shadows of the Mahoosuc and Carter-Moriah Mountains near the White Mountain National Forest boundary. Here campers have access to a river where they can canoe and fish. Hiking trails radiate from the area in all directions, many of them ascending the summits of nearby peaks. Just to the east is the town of Bethel, which has been a summer and winter resort community since the mid-1800s, when the Portland-to-Montreal railroad began stopping here. Today, Bethel is primarily known as the home of the giant Sunday River Ski Resort. If you love the outdoors, this is a good place to spend some time.

Campsites, facilities: There are 45 sites for tents and RVs, four with full hookups, 28 with water and electric hookups, and 13 with none. Flush toilets, hot showers, picnic tables, fireplaces, laundry facilities, a dump station, and a swim-

ming pool are provided. Leashed pets are permitted.

Reservations, fees: Reservations are accepted. Sites are $16–22 a night.

Open: May 15–October 31.

Directions: From the junction of U.S. 2 and Highway 5 in Bethel, drive 4.5 miles west on U.S. 2 to the campground on the left.

Contact: Barbara Dumont, Pleasant River Campground, P.O. Box 27, Highway 2, West Bethel, ME 04286, 207/836-3575, website: www.sundayriveron-line.com/Pleasant-River-Campground.htm.

22 HASTINGS CAMPGROUND

🏃 🏊 🎣 🔱 ❄ 🐕 ♿ 🚐 ⛺

Rating: 9

In the White Mountain National Forest at Evans Notch

One of the most scenic yet least-visited corners of the White Mountain National Forest, this site is situated in a stately stand of white spruce trees that were planted by members of the Civilian Conservation Corps in the 1930s. The camping area is close to fishing in the Wild River and hiking in the surrounding mountains. Hikes up the western side of the Carter-Moriah Mountains to the west or in the Caribou–Speckled Mountain Wilderness to the east provide moderate challenges. The vistas from trails on both sides of Highway 113 encompass many miles of mountain scenery. Continue down that road into New Hampshire to find a bounty of hiking options in the Royce Mountains, the Baldfaces, and others.

Hunting in the fall for deer, grouse, moose, and bear is popular in season, while the trails and old logging roads are well used in the winter months by snowmobilers, cross-country skiers, and snowshoers. Hastings Campground is one of four U.S. Forest Service campgrounds on Highway 113 in this area. See the White Mountains chapter for information on the Wild River, Basin, and Cold River Campgrounds.

Campsites, facilities: There are 24 sites for tents and RVs, all without hookups. Wheelchair-accessible vault toilets, picnic tables, fire rings with grates, and a hand pump for drinking water are provided. Leashed pets are permitted.

Reservations, fees: Reservations are accepted for a maximum of 14 days; call 800/280-2267 or 800/879-4496. Sites are $14 a night.

Open: Mid-May–mid-October.

Directions: From Bethel, travel approximately nine miles west on U.S. 2 to the junction with Highway 113. Turn left and travel south on Highway 113 for about three miles to Hastings Campground.

Contact: White Mountain National Forest, Evans Notch Visitor Center, 18 Mayville Road, Bethel, ME 04217, 207/824-2134.

23 CROCKER POND CAMPGROUND

Rating: 9

South of Bethel in the White Mountain National Forest

Crocker Pond Campground is a gem tucked away in the mountains on the shore of a small lake. The sites, scattered among hemlock, pine, and hardwood trees, are secluded and peaceful. Hiking trails leave the parking lot and climb to the Albany Mountain summit. You can spend your days fishing or swimming in nearby Round Pond or Broken Bridge Pond, as well as in Crocker Pond; brook trout is the major game fish, and Crocker Pond also is home to horned pout. Not far away is the self-guided Patte Brook auto tour, which shows various aspects of forest management (signs are evident on the way in to the campground). Hunting is permitted in season for game that includes grouse, hare, deer, black bear, and migratory birds. Cross-country skiing, snowmobiling, and snowshoeing are popular wintertime pursuits.

Campsites, facilities: There are seven primitive sites. Three are suitable for RVs but have no hookups. Wheelchair-accessible vault toilets, a hand pump for water, picnic tables, and fire

rings with grates are provided. Leashed pets are permitted.

Reservations, fees: Reservations are not accepted; sites are allocated on a first-come, first-served basis. The fee is $14 a night except during winter, when they are free (for hardy souls!).

Open: Year-round, but the road to the campground may not be plowed in winter. Check with the ranger station.

Directions: From Bethel, travel south on Highway 5 for about five miles. Turn right on Forest Service Road 7 and continue west for approximately four miles, following signs to the campground.

Contact: White Mountain National Forest, Evans Notch Ranger District, RR 2, Box 2270, Bethel, ME 04217, 207/824-2134.

24 LITTLEFIELD BEACHES LAKESIDE CAMPGROUND

Rating: 6

In the town of Bryant Pond

Families will enjoy this pleasant campground in the foothills of the White Mountains in western Maine. In addition to the recreation opportunities of the Bethel area, such as hiking the White Mountains, canoeing the Androscoggin River, and mountain biking on miles of little-traveled back roads, campers can take advantage of the three connecting lakes that virtually surround the campground, providing miles of canoe routes awaiting exploration. Anglers should bring their gear, as these waters arc alive with togue and bass.

Campsites, facilities: There are 130 sites for tents and RVs, eight with full hookups, 117 with water and electric hookups, and five with none. Flush toilets, hot showers, picnic tables, fireplaces, a dump station, laundry facilities, and a store are provided. Recreational facilities include a natural sand beach, playground, recreation room, boat ramp, volleyball and basketball courts, and horseshoe pits. A golf course is six miles away in Bethel. Leashed pets are permitted.

Reservations, fees: Reservations are recommended, especially in July and August. A deposit of $20 is required. Sites are $18–25 a night, plus $1 for sewage hookups.
Open: Memorial Day–October 1.
Directions: From the intersection of U.S. 2 and Highway 26 in Bethel, drive six miles southeast on Highway 26 to the campground.
Contact: Sue Stevens, Littlefield Beaches Lakeside Campground, RR 2, Box 4300, Bryant Pond, ME 04219, 207/875-3290.

25 RIVERBEND CAMPGROUND

Rating: 6

Near Androscoggin Lake in Leeds

Riverbend is a pleasant campground situated on a slow-moving stream that flows into Androscoggin Lake, a large body of water renowned for its excellent bass fishing. Wildlife and nature enthusiasts will enjoy spending hours exploring the lake, the woods, and the quiet river.
Campsites, facilities: There are 80 sites for tents and RVs, 60 with water and electric hookups and 20 with none. Flush toilets, hot showers, picnic tables, fireplaces, a dump station, laundry facilities, and a store are provided. Recreational facilities include a playground, recreation room, horseshoe pits, swimming pool, 3,000 feet of river frontage, and canoe and motorboat rentals. Leashed pets are permitted.
Reservations, fees: Reservations are recommended. Sites are $22–25 a night.
Open: May 1–September 30.
Directions: From the intersection of U.S. 202 and Highway 106, drive 7.5 miles north on Highway 106 to the campground.
Contact: The Gomolkas, Riverbend Campground, H.C.R. 70, P.O. Box 50, Highway 106, Leeds, ME 04263, 207/524-5711, website: www.megalink.net/~riverbend.

26 BEAVER BROOK CAMPGROUND

Rating: 5

On Androscoggin Lake in North Monmouth

Set on the wooded shores of eight-square-mile Androscoggin Lake, which is renowned for its great bass fishing, is Beaver Brook, a family-oriented campground. For a large campground, this place offers some well-spaced sites. The lake hosts four bass tournaments each year, so bring the fishing tackle. Even if you don't fish, you will not run out of things to do here. With a full schedule of children's activities, live entertainment on Saturday nights, a miniature golf course, and a continuing array of other options, campers may never find a moment to rest. The state capital in Augusta is only half an hour away.
Campsites, facilities: There are 191 RV sites with water and electric hookups and five tent sites with no hookups. Flush toilets, hot showers, picnic tables, fireplaces, a dump station, laundry facilities, a snack bar, and a store are provided. You will also find a lake with a sandy beach, a swimming pool, canoe and rowboat rentals, a boat ramp, playground, recreation room, volleyball, basketball, shuffleboard, miniature golf, Frisbee golf, badminton, and horseshoe pits. Ice, firewood, and LP gas are available. Leashed pets are permitted.
Reservations, fees: Reservations are recommended. A 50 percent deposit is required. Sites are $18–20 a night.
Open: May 1–Columbus Day.
Directions: From Auburn, take U.S. 202 northeast to Monmouth. Turn left on Back Street and head north for three miles to the campground.
Contact: Jean Parent, Beaver Brook Campground, R.F.D. 1, Box 1835, North Monmouth, ME 04265, 207/933-2108 or 800/873-CAMP (800/873-2267), website: www.beaver-brook.com.

27 ALLEN POND CAMPGROUND

🏊 🚣 ⛴ 🍴 🐾 ⛳ 🚐 ⛺

Rating: 2

On a small pond outside of Lewiston-Auburn

Situated on the side of a hill overlooking Allen Pond, this campground is popular with the locals and attracts many seasonal campers. Swimming, boating, canoeing, and fishing at the waterfront are the main activities, though visitors also find an old miniature golf course and a worn-out playground. With its eroded land, low-maintenance landscaping, and dark woods setting, the campground has a tired appearance. Nearby are the twin cities of Lewiston-Auburn, which offer the usual assortment of restaurants, theaters, and shops.

Campsites, facilities: There are 65 sites for tents and RVs, 55 with water and electric hookups and 10 with none. Flush toilets, hot showers, picnic tables, fire rings, a dump station, and a limited store are provided. For recreation, the campground offers a playground, ball field, boat ramp, swimming area, basketball, and miniature golf. The maximum RV length is 20 feet. Leashed pets are permitted.

Reservations, fees: Reservations are recommended. Sites are $12–20 a night.

Open: Mid-May–September 30.

Directions: From Lewiston, travel north on U.S. 202 for about six miles. Turn left on Patten Road and then take the first right onto Quaker Ridge Road. Turn left at the first road, Allen Pond Road, and travel about two miles to the top of the lake. Turn left and follow signs to the campground.

Contact: Gary Yakawonis, Allen Pond Campground, R.F.D. 1, Box 2030, Greene, ME 04236, 207/946-7439.

28 AUGUSTA WEST LAKESIDE RESORT KAMPGROUND

🚶 🏊 🚣 ⛴ 🐾 🚐 ⛺

Rating: 3

On Annabessacook Lake in Winthrop

Augusta West is located in rolling, rural countryside just eight miles from the state capital in Augusta. A shallow, sandy beach here is perfect for swimming with young children, and the fishing in the lake for smallmouth bass, perch, and pickerel is great. Moreover, the campground offers an unsurpassed array of mechanized rides for all to enjoy. If riding in a seaplane, Jet Skiing, or waterskiing is your idea of summer fun, Augusta West won't disappoint, for plenty of very loud, gas-guzzling, motorized vehicles cover the surface of Annabessacook Lake.

Campsites, facilities: There are 81 sites for tents and RVs, some with partial hookups and others without hookups. Flush toilets, hot showers, picnic tables, fireplaces, a dump station, and a laundry facility are provided. Recreational facilities include badminton, volleyball, horseshoes, a boat launch and dock, swimming pool, a lake with a sandy beach, and canoe, paddleboat, and motorboat rentals. LP gas is available. Leashed pets are permitted.

Reservations, fees: Reservations are accepted. A 30 percent deposit is required. Sites are $17–35 a night.

Open: May 15–October 15.

Directions: From the intersection of U.S. 202 and Highway 41 in Winthrop, drive .75 mile east on U.S. 202. Turn right on Highland Avenue, drive one mile south, and then go .75 mile west to the campground.

Contact: Augusta West Lakeside Resort Kampground, Box 232, Winthrop, ME 04364, 207/468-6930.

29 KEZAR LAKE CAMPING AREA

🚶 🏊 🛶 🚤 ✖ ❄ 🐕 🚴 🚐 ⛺

Rating: 6

On Kezar Lake in Lovell

A large, popular family campground, the park is located on a crystal-clear lake in Maine's western hills. Kezar Lake offers a wide range of camping accommodations, including waterfront sites along the 400 feet of shoreline, wooded sites set back in the shade trees, and sunny spots in open fields. Anglers should bring their gear to try for land-locked salmon, trout, and largemouth and small-mouth bass. This is a great place for those who wish to take advantage of all the area's attractions, including hiking in the White Mountains, canoeing the Saco River, or shopping at outlets in nearby North Conway, New Hampshire.

Campsites, facilities: There are 110 sites for tents and RVs. Flush toilets, hot showers, picnic tables, fireplaces, a dump station, laundry facilities, and a store are provided. Recreational facilities include a playground, recreation room, boat ramp, canoe and paddleboat rentals, volleyball, basketball, and horseshoe pits. Leashed pets are permitted.

Reservations, fees: Reservations are welcome. A deposit of 50 percent is required. Sites are $20–35 a night.

Open: May 15–Columbus Day.

Directions: From the town of Lovell, drive 2.5 miles north on Highway 5. Turn left at the Kezar Lake Camping Area sign and drive three miles to the entrance on the right.

Contact: Tom Pierce, Kezar Lake Camping Area, RR 1, Box 246, Lovell, ME 04051, 207/925-1631, website: www.kezarlakecamping.com.

30 BEAR MOUNTAIN VILLAGE CABINS AND SITES

Rating: 6

North of Bridgton on Bear Pond

You will find Bear Mountain Village Cabins

and Sites a bit off the beaten path in the Sebago Lake region. It's situated on private Bear Pond, and the waterfront is the center of all the action. Campers can bring their own canoes or they can rent a canoe, rowboat, or even an aqua bike for the day. Many footpaths lead through the woods and near the lake at the 33-acre site. Only three miles to Long Lake and 30 miles to Sebago Lake, Bear Mountain Village is conveniently placed for those who want to take in all of the region's major attractions. For more information on the area, see Sebago Lake State Park in this chapter.

Campsites, facilities: There are 68 sites, all with water and electric hookups, and 20 housekeeping cabins. Flush toilets, hot showers, picnic tables, fireplaces, a dump station, laundry facilities, and a small store are provided. Recreational facilities include a playground, recreation room, volleyball, basketball, and horseshoe pits. Canoes, rowboats, and paddleboats may be rented. Leashed pets are permitted.

Reservations, fees: Reservations are recommended. A deposit of 50 percent is required. For holiday weekends, there is a minimum three-night stay and full payment must be received in advance. Sites are $20–30 a night.

Open: May 15–October 15.

Directions: From Bridgton, travel north on Highway 117. Bear left on Highway 37 in North Bridgton. After a few miles, bear left onto Bear Pond Road and continue to the campground.

Contact: Bear Mountain Village Cabins and Sites, RR 2, Box 745, Harrison, ME 04040, 207/583-2541. Off-season: 114 Bennett Avenue, Auburn, ME 04210, 207/782-2275.

31 HEBRON PINES CAMPGROUND

🚶 🚴 🏊 🎣 🐕 🚴 🚐 ⛺

Rating: 5

On Bog Brook in Hebron

Hebron Pines is situated on 400 acres in the southern interior portion of the state. There's plenty to do here, so come prepared for lots of activity. A must-do day trip is a hike to the nearby Streaked Mountain summit, where a fire tower awaits those who make it to the top. Mountain bikers enjoy hitting the network of dirt roads and wooded trails, while anglers should be sure to bring their gear, for this region is laced with small lakes and streams. Hebron Pines also prides itself on staging an impressive lineup of music festivals throughout the summer, good news for those who like to swing their partners to bluegrass tunes.

Campsites, facilities: There are 32 sites for tents and RVs, 20 with water and electric hookups, eight with electric hookups, and four with none. Flush toilets, hot showers, picnic tables, fireplaces, a dump station, and a limited store are provided. Recreational facilities include a pool, playground, recreation room, hiking and mountain biking trails, volleyball, basketball, badminton, and horseshoe pits. Leashed pets are permitted.

Reservations, fees: Reservations are not necessary. Sites are $16–18 a night.

Open: Memorial Day–Columbus Day.

Directions: From the junction of Highways 119 and 124 in West Minot, travel 2.5 miles north on Highway 124 to the campground.

Contact: Hebron Pines Campground, RR 1, Box 1955, East Hebron, ME 04238, 207/966-2179.

32 TWO LAKES CAMPGROUND

Rating: 5

In Oxford

There is good fishing for largemouth and smallmouth bass here in Hogan and Whitney Lakes. The campground also offers a full range of planned activities, such as a buffet breakfast every Sunday morning, a summer Halloween party, pool table tournaments, and paddleboat races. If you are a racing fan, you will enjoy the stock car races at the nearby Oxford Plains Speedway. An hour's drive takes you to the White Mountains to the west or the coast of Maine to the south.

Campsites, facilities: There are 119 sites for tents and RVs. Flush toilets, hot showers, picnic tables, fireplaces, a dump station, laundry facilities, and a store are provided. Recreational facilities include a playground, recreation room, volleyball, basketball, bocce court, shuffleboard, buggy rides, horseshoe pits, a boat ramp and dock, canoe rentals, and 600 feet of sandy beach. Leashed pets are permitted.

Reservations, fees: Reservations are recommended. Sites are $21–32 a night.

Open: May 1–October 1.

Directions: From the intersection of Highways 26 and 121 in Oxford, drive approximately one mile south on Highway 26 to the turnoff for the campground.

Contact: Barbara Varney, Two Lakes Campground, P.O. Box 206, Oxford, ME 04270, 207/539-4001, website: www.twolakescamping.com.

33 ZEN FARM RV RESORT

Rating: 7

Just north of Fryeburg

You will find the new campground known as Zen Farm just north of Fryeburg, a small village tucked away in the Saco River Valley at the base of the White Mountains. The surrounding countryside is sprinkled with large freshwater lakes known for their excellent bass and trout fishing. Hikers head to nearby White Mountain National Forest to hit the trails there, while skiers flock to the region in the winter to test their skills on the area's other trails and slopes. The Saco River is a popular summer destination for canoe trips, and there are several outfitters ready to rent you a canoe and shuttle you to and from the river. Finally, for the more sedentary camper, there is unsurpassed factory outlet shopping just across the state line in North Conway, New Hampshire.

Campsites, facilities: There are 68 sites for tents and RVs, 40 with water and electric hookups and 28 with none. Flush toilets, hot showers, picnic tables, fireplaces, a dump station, and a store are provided. Recreational facilities include a boat launch, swimming pool, canoe rentals, recreation room, volleyball, basketball, badminton, and horseshoe pits. Leashed pets are permitted.

Reservations, fees: Reservations are accepted. Sites are $20–30 a night.

Open: Year-round.

Directions: From the intersection of U.S. 302 and Highway 5 in Fryeburg, drive four miles north on Highway 5 and then turn left on Fish Street and travel 1.5 miles west to the campground.

Contact: Zen Farm RV Resort, RR 1, Box 97A, Fryeburg, ME 04037, 207/ 697-2702.

34 CANAL BRIDGE CAMPGROUND
🏊 🛶 ⛺ 🐕 🚶 🚐 ⛺

Rating: 6
On the Saco River in Fryeburg

Located on the shore of the Saco River in a floodplain forest, Canal Bridge has many waterfront sites to offer. For swimmers, there is a large, sandy beach, but the main attraction here is the canoeing. From Canal Bridge, paddlers can put in for day trips on the river. After trying out those cool waters, they can explore Bog Pond, the Hemlock Covered Bridge area, and Kezar Pond, all easy side trips off of the stream itself. Advanced paddling skills are not needed in this river section. While the water flows at a moderate pace for most of the way, paddlers encounter small rapids at Walker's Falls, seven miles from the campground. Note: You should arrange a shuttle before you begin.

Campsites, facilities: There are 50 sites for tents and RVs. Flush toilets, hot showers, picnic tables, fireplaces, a dump station, and a limited store are provided. Recreational facilities include a playground, boat ramp, a large sandy beach, volleyball, badminton, and horseshoe pits. Canoes are available for rent, and shuttle service may be arranged. Leashed pets are permitted.

Reservations, fees: Reservations are recom-

mended and are necessary for weekends. A deposit of 50 percent is required. Sites are $17–22 a night.

Open: May 18–October 8.

Directions: From the town of Fryeburg, travel north on Highway 5 for about four miles to the campground.

Contact: Dick and Anita Lamby, Canal Bridge Campground, P.O. Box 181, Fryeburg, ME 04037, 207/935-2286 or 508/744-2549.

35 LAKESIDE PINES CAMPGROUND
🏊 🛶 🚐 🐕 🚶 🚐 ⛺

Rating: 7
Near the Songo Locks in Bridgton

Lakeside Pines is located on Long Lake, a clear body of water connected to giant Sebago Lake via the Songo Locks. Campsites—situated on 50 acres of woods and streams—are strewn along the shore of the narrow, 15-mile-long lake. The campground is in a stand of tall virgin pine trees, and the terrain is varied, with a pleasant brook meandering through here. For more on the area, see Sebago Lake State Park in this chapter.

Campsites, facilities: There are 185 sites for tents and RVs, 140 with full hookups and 45 with water and electric hookups. Flush toilets, hot showers, picnic tables, fireplaces, a dump station, and laundry facilities are provided. Recreational facilities include a swimming beach, float and diving tower, a dock, playground, recreation room, basketball court, and horseshoe pits. Leashed pets are permitted.

Reservations, fees: Reservations are recommended and must be made for a minimum of one week in July and August. Sites are $24–32 a night.

Open: Memorial Day–September 15.

Directions: From the junction of U.S. 302 and Highway 117 in Bridgton, drive two miles north on Highway 117 to the campground.

Contact: The Doucettes, Lakeside Pines Campground, P.O. Box 182, North Bridgton, ME 04057, 207/647-3935, website: www.lakesidepines camping.com.

36 WOODLAND ACRES CAMP 'N' CANOE

Rating: 7

In Brownfield

Woodland Acres offers camping in a wooded setting in the White Mountains foothills, but the main draw is its accessibility to the Saco River, a great stream for swimming, canoeing, and fishing for trout and bass. This is a well-maintained, spacious campground with private sites situated directly on the waterfront. It makes an ideal base camp for those interested in paddling a canoe down the cool, clear waters of the Saco River with frequent stops on its sandy beaches.

Campsites, facilities: There are 108 sites for tents and RVs. Flush toilets, hot showers, picnic tables, fireplaces, a dump station, laundry facilities, and a store are provided. Recreational facilities include a playground, recreation room, volleyball, basketball, horseshoe pits, canoe rentals, and a sandy beach. Leashed pets are permitted.

Reservations, fees: Reservations are recommended. A deposit of 50 percent must be received within seven days of making a reservation. In July and August, riverfront sites are available for a minimum of seven nights. Sites are $25–36 a night.

Open: May 10–October 15.

Directions: From the intersection of Highways 160 and 5/113 in Brownfield, drive north on Highway 160 for one mile. The campground is on the left, just before you reach the bridge over the Saco River.

Contact: Woodland Acres Camp 'n' Canoe, Highway 160, RR 1, Box 445, Brownfield, ME 04010, 207/935-2529, website: www.woodland acres.com.

37 RIVER RUN CANOE AND CAMPING

Rating: 7

On the Saco River

A beautiful, primitive campground, River Run lies directly on the shore of the Saco River, a popular canoeing stream that flows down from the White Mountains to the west. Campsites are dispersed over 130 acres of woods, fields, and meadows, and afford a great deal of privacy. The campground maintains a fleet of 100 rental canoes and provides shuttle service to and from the river. Hikers can head to the nearby White Mountain National Forest for trails. If you are looking for a quiet facility to be a base camp for outdoor adventures in the Saco Valley, this is the place.

Campsites, facilities: There are 22 sites for tents and RVs, all without hookups. Nonflush toilets, picnic tables, and fireplaces are provided. There are group tenting areas, and many sites are situated directly on the Saco River. Well-behaved, leashed pets are permitted.

Reservations, fees: Reservations are accepted. Sites are $7 a night per person.

Open: Memorial Day–Labor Day.

Directions: From the intersection of Highways 160 and 5/113 in Brownfield, drive 1.25 miles north on Highway 160. Directly after crossing the bridge over the Saco River, turn right into the campground.

Contact: Joyce and Bob Parker, River Run Canoe and Camping, P.O. Box 90, Brownfield, ME 04010, 207/452-2500, website: www.riverrun canoe.com.

38 FOUR SEASONS CAMPING AREA

Rating: 7

On Long Lake in the Sebago–Long Lake region

Whether nestled under birch and pine trees, pitched on the hilly terrain, or set right on the shoreline, the sites in this popular campground are all well maintained. A long, sandy beach is the main attraction on most days. The gradually sloping bottom here makes swimming safe for young children, while the sundeck and float are popular destinations for more able swimmers. Many people bring their powerboats and rent a slip for the week. From the campground, more than 40 miles of lake water are accessible. For more peaceful exploration, bring or rent a canoe. The large field with barbecue grills provides a great gathering place for multifamily dinners and impromptu games. For more information on the area, see Sebago Lake State Park in this chapter.

Campsites, facilities: There are 115 sites for tents and RVs, most with water and electric hookups and a few with none. Groups may also pitch tents in a large field. Flush toilets, hot showers, picnic tables, fireplaces, a dump station, and a store are provided. Recreational facilities include a playground, recreation room, volleyball, basketball, and horseshoe pits. A field with barbecue grills is available for cookouts and gatherings. There is a sandy beach with a boat ramp and dock, and you can rent canoes, rowboats, paddleboats, or motorboats. Leashed pets are permitted.

Reservations, fees: Reservations are recommended and are accepted for a minimum of one week. Weekend reservations are not accepted. A deposit of $70 is required. Sites are $23–36 a night.

Open: Mid-May–Columbus Day.

Directions: From the junction of U.S. 302 and Highway 11 in Naples, travel 2.5 miles northwest on U.S. 302 to the campground.

Contact: Bob and Judith Van Dee Zee, Four Seasons Camping Area, P.O. Box 927, Naples, ME 04055, 207/693-6797.

39 COLONIAL MAST CAMPGROUND

Rating: 7

On Long Lake in Naples

Tucked into Mast Cove on Long Lake, this campground has a small sandy beach as well as a boat ramp that allows campers to access Long Lake and, through the Songo Locks, neighboring Sebago Lake. Especially popular are the waterfront sites, where you can head out for an early-morning or late-evening dip from your tiny, private beach. If you bring your own boat, be sure to reserve a slip at the campground, so you can easily access more than 40 miles of water for boating and fishing. The recreation room here resembles a rustic lodge, complete with pine floors and comfortable furniture. For more information on Sebago Lake, see Sebago Lake State Park in this chapter.

Campsites, facilities: There are 79 sites for tents and RVs, with either full or partial hookups. Wheelchair-accessible restrooms with flush toilets and hot showers, picnic tables, fireplaces, a dump station, laundry facilities, and a store selling limited supplies are provided. Recreational facilities include a sandy beach, a playground, recreation room, pavilion, boat ramp and docks, volleyball, basketball, horseshoe pits, and shuffleboard. A schedule of planned activities for children and teens is offered. Rowboats, paddleboats, and canoes are available for rent. Leashed pets are permitted.

Reservations, fees: Reservations are recommended. Sites are $32–35 a night.

Open: Year-round.

Directions: From Naples, travel north for three miles on U.S. 302. Turn right onto Kansas Road and continue .2 mile east to the campground.

Contact: Eileen and Peter Marucci, Colonial Mast Campground, Kansas Road, P.O. Box 95, Naples, ME 04055, 207/693-6652, website: www.colonialmast.com.

40 GRANGER POND CAMPING AREA

Rating: 3

Just outside the town of Denmark

Granger Pond does steady business with seasonal campers: about half of the sites have permanent residents. The campground is located in the forest on the rise above a small, quiet lake. Canoeing on this calm pond is a pleasant experience, as it's a bit small for many motorboats. From the rise, campers can look west and experience a colorful sunset on many nights. While the town of Denmark itself is small and unremarkable, from here campers can access Sebago Lake, the White Mountains, and the Maine coast in less than an hour.

Campsites, facilities: There are 45 sites for tents and RVs; all RV sites have water and electric hookups, and some come with additional sewer connections. Flush toilets, hot showers, picnic tables, fireplaces, and a dump station are provided. Recreational facilities include a beach and floating dock, playground, and a basketball hoop. Leashed pets are permitted.

Reservations, fees: Reservations are accepted. A deposit of $10 is required. Sites are $20–22 a night.

Open: June 30–Labor Day.

Directions: From Denmark, travel northeast on Highway 117. Take the first right onto Bush Row Road and continue 1.5 miles south to the campground.

Contact: Susan Cody, Granger Pond Camping Area, Bush Row Road, Denmark, ME 04022, 207/452-2342.

41 K'S FAMILY CIRCLE CAMPGROUND

Rating: 5

On Trickey Pond in Naples

Plenty of freshwater fish live in Trickey Pond, a clear spring-fed pool surrounded by a mature forest, and the waterfront at this classic family campground is always bustling with people fishing from docks, children swimming, and canoes and boats launching. In case you get your fill of all this water-based fun, the extensive activities program keeps you and your family busy. Although you may not want to leave this delightful pond, campers can easily travel from here to other nearby, bigger lakes—Sebago and Long.

Campsites, facilities: There are 125 sites for tents and RVs with water and electric hookups. Flush toilets, hot showers, picnic tables, fireplaces, a dump station, laundry facilities, and a store are provided. Recreational facilities include a playground, recreation room, volleyball, basketball, and horseshoe pits, in addition to a full activities program. On the waterfront, you find a sandy beach, boat launch and docks, and canoe and boat rentals. Ice and firewood are available. Leashed pets are permitted.

Reservations, fees: Reservations are recommended. Sites are $23–28 a night.

Open: May 15–September 15.

Directions: From Naples, travel south on U.S. 302 and then bear left onto Highway 114. The campground is on the left, a couple miles down the road.

Contact: K's Family Circle Campground, Highway 114, Box 557M, Naples, ME 04055, 207/693-6881.

42 BAY OF NAPLES FAMILY CAMPING

Rating: 7

In Naples on the Bay of Naples

This campground is located on the Bay of Naples, a small lake set between Long Lake and the Songo Locks, which lead to Sebago Lake. The sites here are spacious and well maintained. With a large sandy beach at the Bay of Naples, campers have good access to swimming, boating, and fishing right from the campground. The shallow beach is inviting to young bathers, and the older children often swim out to the floating dock. For an additional fee, motorboats can be docked in a waterfront slip. Adjacent to this campground is an 18-hole golf course. For more information on the area, see the next listing for Sebago Lake State Park.

Campsites, facilities: There are 150 sites for tents and RVs, 61 with full hookups, 60 with water and electric hookups, and 29 with none. Flush toilets, hot showers, picnic tables, fireplaces, a dump station, laundry facilities, and a store are provided. Recreational facilities include a playground, two recreation halls, volleyball, basketball, badminton, horseshoe pits, a sandy beach, and boat slips. Canoes and rowboats are available for rent. No pets are allowed.

Reservations, fees: Reservations are highly recommended. They may be made for a minimum of three days, and full payment must be received to guarantee the reservation. Sites are $22–28 a night.

Open: Memorial Day–Columbus Day.

Directions: From I-95 at Portland, take Exit 8 and travel north on U.S. 302 for 26 miles to the town of Naples. Turn left onto Highway 11/114 and travel another mile to the campground.

Contact: The Ruhlins, Bay of Naples Family Camping, Highway 114, Box 240, Naples, ME 04055, 207/693-6429 or 800/348-9750, website: www.bayofnaples.com.

43 SEBAGO LAKE STATE PARK

Rating: 8

On Sebago Lake

Sebago Lake is a spectacular body of water, some 11 miles long by eight miles wide. Ringed by wooded hills, this clear, cool lake is renowned as a high-quality freshwater sport fishery for landlocked salmon and togue. The campsites are sheltered in a mixed pine forest directly adjacent to the water and are bordered by long, sandy beaches. Campers can take advantage of an active interpretive program, amphitheater, and guided hikes. The lake bottom is sandy

and drops off at a gentle angle, perfect for swimming. Many visitors tour the lake on the *Songo River Queen,* a 90-foot-long stern-wheeler. Another way to see the lake is aboard the mail boat, a pontoon boat that travels on local waterways. If you'd like a bird's-eye view of the region, hike to the summit of Douglas Mountain, a Nature Conservancy preserve; it takes only about 20 minutes. More hikes are available at nearby Pleasant Mountain. Naples is the primary town in the Sebago Lake region.

Campsites, facilities: There are 250 sites for tents and RVs, all without hookups. Wheelchair-accessible restrooms, hot showers, a dump station, boat ramp, sandy beaches, bathhouses, lifeguards, and a group camping area are provided. The maximum RV length is 30 feet. No pets are allowed in the campground or on park beaches, but leashed pets are permitted in the picnic area.

Reservations, fees: Reservations are accepted, and the total amount due must accompany your request. Contact the Maine Bureau of Parks and Lands at the number below. The State of Maine allocates some sites on a first-come, first-served basis. Sites are $15 a night for Maine residents and $20 for nonresidents.

Open: Year-round for tenting; fully operational June 20–Labor Day.

Directions: From the intersection of U.S. 302 and Highway 11/114 in Naples, drive four miles east on U.S. 302 to the park entrance sign. Follow the entrance road for 2.5 miles to the gate.

Contact: June 20–Labor Day: Sebago Lake State Park Ranger, 207/693-6613. After Labor Day–June 19: Sebago Lake State Park Ranger, 207/693-6231. Maine Bureau of Parks and Lands, 22 State House Station, Augusta, ME 04333, 207/287-3821, website: www.state.me.us/doc/parks.

44 HEMLOCKS CAMPING AREA

Rating: 5

On Tripp Lake in West Poland

Tripp Lake offers good boating, fishing, and swimming. Filled with bass, brown trout, and pickerel, this three-mile-long lake keeps fishing enthusiasts busy. From West Poland, campers can take day trips to the Maine coast, Sebago Lake, and the White Mountains. Only a few miles from Lewiston-Auburn, the campground provides easy access to the various restaurants, shops, and theaters in these small cities.

Campsites, facilities: There are 74 sites for tents and RVs, some with full hookups and most with water and electric. Flush toilets, hot showers, picnic tables, fireplaces, a dump station, laundry facilities, and a store are provided. Recreational facilities include a sandy beach, swimming float, boat launch, playground, recreation room, and horseshoe pits. Canoes, rowboats, and paddleboats may be rented. Leashed pets are permitted.

Reservations, fees: Reservations are not necessary. Sites are $18–24 a night.

Open: Mid-May–October 1.

Directions: From Mechanic Falls, travel southwest on Highway 11 to the intersection with Highway 26 and Tenney Road. Turn right on Tenney Road, continue to the end, and turn left on Megouier Hill Road. Follow signs to the campground.

Contact: Leo and Cecile Bilodeau, Hemlock Camping Area, 161 Washington Street, Auburn, ME 04210, 207/998-2384, website: www.hemlocks campground.com.

45 POLAND SPRING CAMPGROUND

Rating: 6

In Poland Spring

Poland Spring Campground is located on Lower Range Pond, a lovely three-mile-long lake that is regularly stocked with brown and rainbow trout. The fishing for largemouth and smallmouth bass and pickerel is also excellent. Best of all, a 9.9 horsepower limit on boat motors ensures that loons and other resident waterfowl—not to mention anglers—are not disturbed, and helps preserve the peaceful setting. The pond has a sandy

beach and a gradually sloping sand bottom, perfect for swimming with small children.

Campsites, facilities: There are 132 sites for tents and RVs, 42 with full hookups, 65 with water and electric hookups, and 12 with none. Wheelchair-accessible flush toilets, metered hot showers, picnic tables, fire rings, a dump station, laundry facilities, and a store are provided. A playground, recreation room, volleyball, basketball, and horseshoe pits are among the recreational offerings. Leashed pets are permitted.

Reservations, fees: Reservations are recommended. Sites are $25–29 a night.

Open: May 1–October 15.

Directions: From the town of Gray, drive 12 miles north on Highway 26 to the campground. The entrance sign is .5 mile beyond the causeway between Middle and Lower Range Ponds.

Contact: The Wight Family, Poland Spring Campground, P.O. Box 409, Highway 26, Poland Spring, ME 04274, 207/998-2151, website: www.polandspringcamp.com.

46 RANGE POND CAMPGROUND

Rating: 6

In Poland

The campground is located directly next to Range Ponds State Park on Lower Range Pond. This is a family-oriented facility with planned activities such as horseshoe tournaments, karaoke, a Fourth of July Parade, and Christmas in July, as well as an arts-and-crafts program for children. The fishing is good in the nearby Range Ponds. Also in the area is the historic Sabbathday Lake Shaker Community and Museum, the last functioning Shaker community in the United States; it's well worth a visit.

Campsites, facilities: There are 80 sites for tents and RVs, 62 with full hookups, 13 with water and electric hookups, and five with none. Flush toilets, hot showers, picnic tables, fireplaces, a dump station, laundry facilities, and a store are provided. Recreational facilities include a playground, recreation room, volleyball court, badminton court, horseshoe pits, and a large swimming pool. Leashed pets are permitted.

Reservations, fees: Reservations are necessary. Payment in full for holidays is required. Sites are $18–22 a night.

Open: April 15–October 15.

Directions: From the junction of Highways 26 and 122 in Poland Spring, drive east on Highway 122 for 1.3 miles, then bear left and drive north on Empire Road for 1.3 miles. Bear left again on Plains Road and drive .5 mile to the campground.

Contact: Paul and Sheila Vaccaro, Range Pond Campground, RR 3, P.O. Box 635, Poland, ME 04273, 207/998-2624, website: www.rangepond camp.com.

47 POINT SEBAGO GOLF AND BEACH RV RESORT

🏕️ 🏊 🎣 🚗 🥾 🚐 ⛺

Rating: 8

On Sebago Lake

Point Sebago is a vacation resort destination that happens to be a campground rather than a hotel. Situated on 800 wooded acres on the northeastern shore of beautiful Sebago Lake, Point Sebago provides a host of amenities not normally found at campgrounds, such as a championship 18-hole golf course, marina, cruise boat, nightclub, and a staff of more than 400 people. Golfers are pampered with putting greens, sand trap and chip-shot area, driving range, and a learning center. For those hoping to include a little golf in their camping itinerary, this is the place to do it in style.

Campsites, facilities: There are 500 sites for tents and RVs, 244 with full hookups and 256 with water and electric. Vacation rental units are also available. Facilities include flush toilets, hot showers, picnic tables, fireplaces, a dump station, a laundry room, and a store. Recreational facilities include an 18-hole golf course; miniature golf; motorboat, sailboat, and canoe rentals; a playground; recreation

room; volleyball, tennis, and basketball courts; horseshoe pits; shuffleboard; and movies. No pets are allowed.

Reservations, fees: Reservations are recommended. A deposit of 50 percent is required within 10 days of making a reservation. Sites are $25–55 a night.

Open: May 1–November 1.

Directions: From I-95 at Portland, take Exit 8 and drive north on U.S. 302 for 22 miles to the gate.

Contact: Point Sebago Golf and Beach RV Resort, RR 1, Box 712B, Casco, ME 04015, 800/655-1232, website: www.pointsebago.com.

48 KOKATOSI CAMPGROUND

🏊 🎣 🚗 🥾 🐕 🥾 🚐 ⛺

Rating: 6

On Crescent Lake in Raymond

Families will enjoy Kokatosi's location on the shores of crystal-clear, five-mile-long Crescent Lake. Take a canoe and paddle a mile and a half on the Tenney River into Panther Pond, another five-mile-long lake with good fishing and plenty of hidden coves and inlets to explore. At Kokatosi's waterfront, enjoy the sandy beach, swimming, and boating. The campground also offers many planned activities, live bands, and special events. Kids will love taking a ride in the campground's restored fire engine.

Campsites, facilities: There are 162 sites for tents and RVs, 71 with full hookups, 82 with water and electric hookups, and nine with none. Flush toilets, hot showers, picnic tables, fireplaces, a dump station, laundry facilities, and a store are provided. Recreational facilities include a playground, recreation room, volleyball, basketball, horseshoe pits, a sandy beach, and canoe, paddleboat, and motorboat rentals. Ice, wood, and LP gas are available. Leashed pets are permitted.

Reservations, fees: Reservations are recommended. Sites are $28–36 a night.

Open: May 15–Columbus Day.

Directions: From the intersection of U.S. 302

and Highway 85 in Raymond, drive 6.5 miles north on Highway 85 to the campground.
Contact: Kokatosi Campground, 635 Highway 85, Raymond, ME 04071, 207/627-4642, website: www.maine.com/kokatosi.

49 TWIN BROOKS CAMPING AREA

Rating: 6

In Gray

Twin Brooks is a small campground located at the northern tip of Little Sebago Lake. The sites are spacious and secluded, and campers have access to a sandy beach for swimming. The campground is only 25 miles from Portland and the many attractions of the Maine coast.

Campsites, facilities: There are 43 sites for tents and RVs, 10 with full hookups, 28 with water and electric hookups, and five with none. Flush toilets, hot showers, picnic tables, fireplaces, and a dump station are provided. Recreational facilities include basketball, badminton, horseshoes, volleyball, canoe rentals, and a boat ramp. Leashed pets are permitted.

Reservations, fees: Reservations are accepted. Sites are $20–25 a night.

Open: Memorial Day–September 15.

Directions: From Highway 26 in Gray, drive one mile north on North Raymond Road to its intersection with Egypt Road. Turn left on Egypt Road and drive approximately one mile to the campground.

Contact: Geneva and Calvin Austin, Twin Brooks Camping Area, P.O. Box 194, Gray, ME 04039, 207/428-3832, website: www.campmaine. com/twinbrooks.

50 LOCKLIN CAMPING AREA

Rating: 5

On a small lake in Kezar Falls

A small, simple campground, Locklin is situated on a pretty lake in a rural area between giant Sebago Lake to the east, the White Mountains to the west, and the Portland area on the Maine coast to the south. Hike in the White Mountains, take a drive in the scenic Mount Washington Valley, or just relax at your site on the shore of Staley Pond. If you are feeling adventurous, there is good canoeing in the vicinity on the Ossipee River and on the Saco River.

Campsites, facilities: There are 50 sites for tents and RVs, some with water and electric hookups. Flush toilets, hot showers, picnic tables, fireplaces, and a dump station are provided. Recreational facilities include good lake swimming, rental canoes, a playing field, volleyball, badminton, softball, and horseshoe pits. Leashed pets are permitted.

Reservations, fees: Reservations are accepted. Sites are $18–22 a night.

Open: Memorial Day–Labor Day.

Directions: From the junction of Highways 25 and 160 in Kezar Falls, drive two miles north on Highway 160 to the campground.

Contact: Lionel Locklin, Locklin Camping Area, P.O. Box 197, Kezar Falls, ME 04047, 207/625-8622.

51 WINDSONG CAMPGROUND

Rating: 4

In Kezar Falls

Windsong is a small, out-of-the-way place. Situated in the woods in a semirural area, the campground is not near any attractions, but it is within 30 minutes of Sebago Lake, the White Mountain National Forest, and the Saco River. The campground itself is very quiet, and the sites are under tall shade trees. If you are looking for a place where there are very few distractions, this is a good choice for you.

Campsites, facilities: There are 35 sites for tents and RVs. Flush toilets, showers, tables, fireplaces, a dump station, laundry facilities, and a store are provided. There's a playground, recreation room, volleyball, basketball, horseshoes, a pool, and a kids' library. Leashed pets are permitted.

Reservations, fees: Reservations are not necessary. Sites are $14–22 a night.
Open: Year-round.
Directions: From Kezar Falls, drive south on Elm Street for 1.5 miles. Turn left on Banks Road, which becomes Pendexter Road, and continue one mile east.
Contact: Bruce Frantz, Windsong Campground, P.O. Box 547, Kezar Falls, ME 04047, 207/625-4389.

52 ACRES OF WILDLIFE

🚶 🚴 🏊 🎣 🏕 🐴 🎿 🚐 ⛺

Rating: 4

West of Sebago Lake in the town of Steep Falls

Surrounding two small lakes, this campground is an off-the-beaten-path choice in the Sebago Lake area. Rainbow Lake and Chub Pond are stocked with largemouth bass and rainbow trout. No license is required for anglers who want to try their luck in these waters. For walkers, five miles of trails extend from the campground into the surrounding woods. A daily activities schedule offers a multitude of options for campers including hayrides, scavenger hunts, and family sports challenges. Special themed weeks and weekends—such as Elvis in the Fifties, Halloween Week, and Down East Days—are planned. In addition to the many activities at the campground, there are plenty of options for day trips. It's a short distance to Sebago Lake, the ocean beaches are a half hour's drive away, and the city of Portland can be reached in 45 minutes.
Campsites, facilities: There are 200 sites for tents and RVs, 65 with full hookups, 102 with water and electric hookups, and 33 with none. In addition, trailers, cabins, houses, and rooms in a rustic inn may be rented. Hot showers, flush toilets, a dump station, laundry facilities, and a store are provided. Recreational facilities include a playground, ball field, volleyball, basketball, horseshoes, miniature golf, walking trails, and a daily activities schedule. Campers may rent canoes, kayaks, paddleboats,

rowboats, inner tubes, and bikes. Leashed pets are permitted.
Reservations, fees: Reservations are recommended and are accepted for no fewer than two nights. On holiday weekends, a three-night reservation is required. Reservations for less than one week in July and August are only accepted 30 or more days prior to arrival. Sites are $27–35 a night. There is also a $5 fee per dog per night on holiday weekends.
Open: May 1–Columbus Day.
Directions: From Gorham, travel west on Highway 25 for approximately six miles. Bear right onto Highway 113 and continue for six miles. Turn right on the campground road and travel another 2.5 miles.
Contact: The Wentworth Family, Acres of Wildlife, P.O. Box 2, Steep Falls, ME 04085, 207/675-3211, website: www.acresofwildlife.com.

53 SEBAGO LAKE RESORT AND CAMPGROUND

🏊 🎣 🏕 🐴 🎿 🚐 ⛺

Rating: 6

On Sebago Lake

Spacious, wooded sites on Sebago Lake—a huge and spectacular body of water within an hour of Portland and the Maine coast—are featured at this campground. For more information on the area, see Sebago Lake State Park in this chapter.
Campsites, facilities: There are 100 sites for RVs, 43 with full hookups and 57 with water and electric hookups, plus wilderness tent sites. Flush toilets, hot showers, cable TV, picnic tables, fireplaces with grills, a dump station, laundry facilities, a restaurant, and a store are provided. Recreational facilities include a playground, recreation room, volleyball, badminton, horseshoe pits, a private sandy beach, paddleboat and canoe rentals, and a boat dock. Leashed pets are permitted.
Reservations, fees: Reservations are recommended. You must send a deposit of 50 percent within seven days of reserving. Sites are $22–37 a night.

Open: Memorial Day–Columbus Day.

Directions: From the intersection of Highways 35 and 114 in Sebago Lake, drive seven miles north on Highway 114 to the campground.

Contact: Sebago Lake Resort and Campground, R.F.D. 1, Box 9360, Highway 114, Sebago Lake, ME 04075, 207/787-3671.

54 FAMILY-N-FRIENDS CAMPGROUND

Near Sebago Lake

Rating: 5

Just down the road from Sebago Lake, Family-N-Friends Campground offers all the amenities of a big campground in a smaller setting. The large, heated pool and the bubbling hot tub are the main attractions. An exhaustive activities schedule includes karaoke, live bands, children's events, and bonfires. A series of theme weekends begins in May and continues to the end of the season: pig roasts, adults-only weekends, and Yard Sale Weekend are among the special events. Only a few miles away is Sebago Lake with its full range of opportunities for boating, fishing, and lake swimming. For more information on the area, see Sebago Lake State Park in this chapter.

Campsites, facilities: There are 60 sites for tents and RVs. Flush toilets, hot showers, picnic tables, fireplaces, a dump station, laundry facilities, and a store are provided. Recreational facilities include a heated pool and hot tub, playground, recreation room, volleyball, basketball, and horseshoe pits. Also available are planned children's activities, dances, and theme weekends held throughout the season. Leashed pets are permitted.

Reservations, fees: Reservations are recommended. Sites are $28 a night.

Open: April 1–November 1.

Directions: From the intersection of Highways 114 and 35 in Sebago Lake, travel northwest on Highway 114 for .75 mile to the campground.

Contact: Dick and Sheri Huff, Family-N-Friends Campground, Highway 114, Box 9895, Sebago Lake, ME 04075, 207/642-2200, website: www.familynfriends.com.

55 APPLE VALLEY CAMPGROUND

Near Acton

Rating: 4

A lush valley near the foothills of the White Mountains is the setting for this campground. Most of the guests at Apple Valley are seasonal campers who use their RVs as summer vacation homes. Virtually every camper we saw here appeared to own a golf cart for getting around in, and this was the only place where we noticed that kind of traffic. In other words, it's a popular spot for retirees.

Campsites, facilities: There are 145 sites for RVs with full and partial hookups. Flush toilets, hot showers, picnic tables, fireplaces, a dump station, laundry facilities, and a store are provided. Recreational facilities include a pool, playground, recreation room, perfectly round artificially constructed pond for fishing, miniature golf course, volleyball, basketball, and horseshoe pits. Leashed pets are permitted.

Reservations, fees: Reservations are not necessary. Sites are $25 a night.

Open: May 15–October 15.

Directions: From the junction of Highways 11 and 109 in Emery Mills south of Acton, drive two miles north on Highway 109 to the campground.

Contact: Apple Valley Campground, P.O. Box 92, Highway 109, Acton, ME 04001, 207/636-2285.

Chapter 3

© MAINE OFFICE OF TOURISM/JEFF GREENBERG

Central and
Southern Coast

Central and
Southern Coast

The southern and central coast is the Maine that most people see. In a sense, this region is Maine in microcosm, for here are long, sandy beaches, rocky points and coves, deep harbors, granite islands, forested wildlife refuges, and meandering tidal rivers. But here too are tacky amusement parks, busy outlet malls, the state's largest city of Portland, and of course Freeport and L.L.Bean.

Don't expect to find much solitude in the southern and central coast region. It's a fact that Freeport sees more tourists on a single summer weekend than the entire state of North Dakota sees in a whole year. But if joining the throngs for lobster rolls, clam baskets, and ice-cream cones at a popular sandy beach is your idea of fun, then you've come to the right place.

But you can also find ways to get away from it all here in the southern and central coast. Turn off of the major highways, poke around a bit on the back roads, and you'll discover a region that is still largely rural and quite connected to the land and sea, a place where small farms, woodlots, and an armada of lobster boats still provide important local employment.

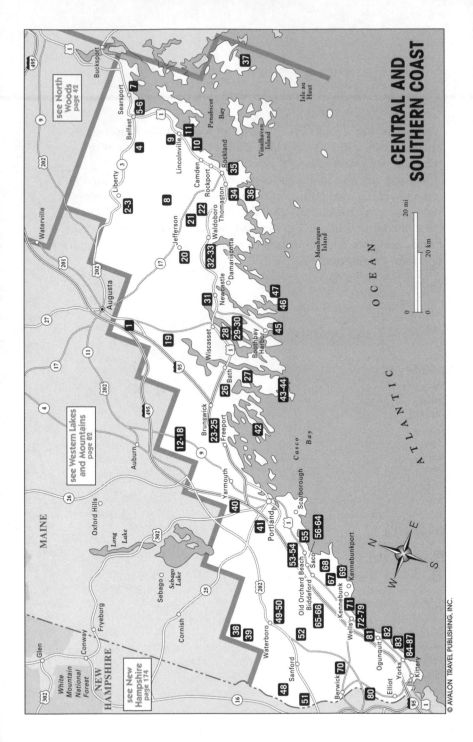

see North
Woods
page 42

see Western Lakes
and Mountains
page 82

see New
Hampshire
page 174

MAINE

NEW
HAMPSHIRE

White
Mountain
National
Forest

OCEAN

ATLANTIC

Casco
Bay

Penobscot
Bay

Isle au
Haut

Vinalhaven
Island

Monhegan
Island

20 mi

20 km

Bucksport

Searsport

Belfast

Liberty

Lincolnville

Camden

Rockport

Rockland

Thomaston

Waldoboro

Jefferson

Damariscotta

Newcastle

Wiscasset

Bath

Brunswick

Freeport

Yarmouth

Portland

Scarborough

Saco

Old Orchard Beach

Biddeford

Kennebunkport

Kennebunk

Wells

Ogunquit

Yorks

Kittery

Elliot

Berwick

Sanford

Waterboro

Cornish

Sebago

Sebago
Lake

Long
Lake

Oxford Hills

Auburn

Augusta

Waterville

Fryeburg

Conway

Glen

© AVALON TRAVEL PUBLISHING, INC.

◻1 AUGUSTA/GARDINER KOA

🏃 ⛵ 🎣 🚤 🦌 🚗 ⛺

In Richmond

Rating: 4

KOA is a national chain, so you find no surprises here. The campground is situated on Pleasant Pond, actually a wide part of Cobbosseecontee Stream. This part of Maine features pretty, rolling farm and forest country dotted with lakes, and lies within easy driving distance of the coast. The campground is just minutes from the state capital at Augusta and the historic Kennebec River town of Hallowell, where you find shops, restaurants, and a bustling 19th-century waterfront.

Campsites, facilities: There are 80 sites for tents and RVs, 28 with full hookups, 41 with water and electric hookups, and 11 with none. Flush toilets, hot showers, picnic tables, fireplaces, laundry facilities, a dump station, and a store are provided. Recreational facilities include a swimming pool, canoe and rowboat rentals, a recreation room, volleyball, basketball, badminton, and horseshoes. Leashed pets are permitted.

Reservations, fees: Reservations are accepted. Sites are $20–30 a night.

Open: May 20–October 15.

Directions: From I-95 near Gardiner, take Exit 27 and drive 2.25 miles south on U.S. 201 to the campground.

Contact: Augusta/Gardiner KOA, Highway 1, Box 2410, Richmond, ME 04357, 207/582-5086, website: www.koa.com/where/me.

◻2 LAKE ST. GEORGE STATE PARK

🏃 ⛵ 🎣 🚤 ❄ 🦌 🚣 🚗 ⛺

On Lake St. George in Liberty

Rating: 7

Midway between the state capital at Augusta and the coast at Belfast, Lake St. George State Park makes the perfect stopover point for travelers who want to cool off with a refreshing swim, as well as those searching for a great place to spend the night. The park incorporates part of the shoreline of a clear, spring-fed lake. There is a swimming area with lifeguards and a bathhouse, and boat and canoe rentals are available. For landlubbers, eight miles of hiking trails wind through the park. In winter, a snowmobile trail connecting the park with the Frye Mountain Game Management Area is maintained.

Campsites, facilities: There are 38 sites for tents and RVs, all without hookups. Facilities include hot showers, a dump station, boat rentals, a concrete boat ramp, group camping area, playground, and swimming area. Leashed pets are permitted.

Reservations, fees: Reservations are accepted, and the total amount due must accompany your request. Contact the Maine Bureau of Parks and Lands at 207/287-3821. The State of Maine allocates some sites on a first-come, first-served basis. Sites are $15 for Maine residents and $20 for nonresidents.

Open: Year-round; fully operational May 15–September 30.

Directions: From Belfast, drive west on Highway 3 to Liberty. Continue one mile east on Highway 3 to the park entrance.

Contact: Lake St. George State Park Ranger, 207/589-4255; Maine Bureau of Parks and Lands, 22 State House Station, Augusta, ME 04333, 207/287-3821, website: www.state.me.us/doc/parks.

◻3 PINE RIDGE CAMPGROUND AND COTTAGES

🏃 ⛵ 🎣 🚤 📆 ❄ 🦌 🚗 ⛺

Rating: 6

Near Lake St. George State Park in Liberty

Not only is Pine Ridge conveniently located between the state capital of Augusta and the coastal town of Belfast, it is close to Lake St. George State Park, a great destination for anglers and boaters. This campground is open year-round, with cozy cabins available for rent in the summer and winter. In addition, it's set along the International Trail System, so snowmobilers can ride from here all the way to Canada. For more information on the area, see previous listing for Lake St. George State Park.

Campsites, facilities: There are 35 sites for tents and RVs, nine with full hookups, eight with water and electric hookups, and 18 with none. Flush toilets, hot showers, picnic tables, fireplaces, laundry facilities, a dump station, and a store are provided. Recreational facilities include a heated swimming pool, canoe rentals, hiking trails, a recreation room, volleyball, badminton, and horseshoes. Leashed pets are permitted.

Reservations, fees: Reservations are accepted. Sites are $20–26 a night.

Open: Year-round.

Directions: From the intersection of Highway 3 and Highway 220 in the town of Liberty, drive 1.5 miles east on Highway 3 to the campground.

Contact: Randy and Rachel Gardner, Pine Ridge Campground and Cottages, P.O. Box 7, Liberty, ME 04949, 207/589-4352.

4 ALDUS SHORES LAKESIDE CAMPGROUND

Rating: 6

On Quantibacook Lake in Searsmont

You will find Aldus Shores in the rolling, rural countryside just inland from the coast and Penobscot Bay. The campground is situated on Quantibacook Lake, which offers excellent fishing for bass, perch, and pickerel. The spacious campsites are either directly on the lakeshore or set back under shade trees. This pleasant spot is within easy reach of midcoast Maine's plentiful attractions.

Campsites, facilities: There are 150 sites for tents and RVs, 148 with partial hookups and two with none. Facilities include flush toilets, hot showers, picnic tables, fireplaces, a laundry room, a dump station, and a store. Recreational facilities include a boat launch, canoe rentals, a recreation room, playing field, volleyball, badminton, and horseshoes. Leashed pets are permitted.

Reservations, fees: Reservations are recommended. Payment in full is required for stays of up to three nights; for four or more nights, a deposit of $30 is required. Sites are $20–23 a night for RVs; tent sites are $5 a night, plus $5 per person.

Open: May 15–October 15.

Directions: From the junction of Highway 3 and U.S. 1 in Belfast, drive six miles west on Highway 3. Turn left on Highway 131 and drive 2.5 miles south. Make a right turn at the campground sign and drive .5 mile west to the campground.

Contact: John and Phyllis McEvoy, Aldus Shores Lakeside Campground, Highway 131, P.O. Box 38, Searsmont, ME 04973, 207/342-5618.

5 THE MOORINGS OCEANFRONT CAMPGROUND

Rating: 7

On Penobscot Bay in Belfast

The Moorings lies directly off U.S. 1 where the highway parallels the ocean between the villages of Belfast and Searsport. All sites have ocean views over the wide expanse of Penobscot Bay, and campers enjoy easy access to saltwater fishing and swimming. The campground opened in 1993 and faces south, with great exposure to the sun and to cool ocean breezes. Both Belfast and Searsport are classic Maine villages where you will find shops, museums, restaurants, and boat-excursion operators.

Campsites, facilities: There are 39 sites for tents and RVs with water and electric hookups. Flush toilets, hot showers, picnic tables, fireplaces, laundry facilities, and a dump station are provided. You will also find a sandy beach, recreation room, volleyball, tetherball, badminton, and horseshoes. Leashed pets are permitted.

Reservations, fees: Reservations are recommended. A 25 percent deposit is required. Sites are $34–40 a night.

Open: May 15–October 15.

Directions: From the intersection of U.S. 1 and the Belfast Harbor Bridge, drive 2.1 miles north on U.S. 1 to the campground.

Contact: Ben Hill, The Moorings Oceanfront Campground, RR 1, P.O. Box 69, Searsport Avenue, Belfast, ME 04915, 207/338-6860, website: www.oceanfrontrvcamping.com.

6 NORTHPORT TRAVEL PARK CAMPGROUND

Rating: 6

North of Camden in Belfast

Both open and shaded sites are offered at Northport. Located just off busy U.S. 1, five miles south of Belfast and 10 miles north of Camden, the campground lies right across the highway from Penobscot Bay. From here, you have easy access to Camden Hills State Park, restaurants, shops, boat excursions, sea kayaking, and saltwater fishing, as well as the picturesque seacoast towns of Belfast, Searsport, and Camden. Sites are at the edge of a wooded area surrounding the stocked trout pond. Those desiring more privacy can request one of the secluded sites in the woods.

Campsites, facilities: There are 77 sites for tents and RVs, 38 with full hookups, 22 with water and electric hookups, and 17 with none. Flush toilets, hot showers, picnic tables, fireplaces, laundry facilities, a dump station, and a store are provided. Recreational facilities include a pool, stocked trout pond, hiking trails, recreation room, volleyball, badminton, and horseshoes. Leashed pets are permitted.

Reservations, fees: Reservations are recommended. Sites are $15–20 a night.

Open: May 15–October 15.

Directions: From the junction of U.S. 1 and Highway 3 in Belfast, drive six miles south on Highway 3 to the campground.

Contact: Charles Knight, Northport Travel Park Campground, U.S. 1, Northport, ME 04849, 207/338-2077.

7 SEARSPORT SHORES CAMPGROUND

Rating: 9

On Penobscot Bay in Searsport

This clean, attractive campground is located right on the Penobscot Bay shore. The spacious RV sites are scattered among shade trees, while the tent sites are separated by a small brook in a wild seaside setting. There are sandy beaches for swimmers and sunbathers, hiking trails, and plenty of places to launch a sea kayak. A unique touch is the fax and word-processing service available for those who want to mix a little work in with their play.

Campsites, facilities: There are 100 sites for tents and RVs, 80 with water and electric hookups and 20 with none. Chemical nonflush toilets, wheelchair-accessible restrooms, hot showers, picnic tables, fireplaces, laundry facilities, a dump station, and a store are provided. Recreational facilities include a playground, recreation room, hiking trails, volleyball, basketball, and horseshoes. A nearby town wharf can be used for boat launching. Leashed pets are permitted.

Reservations, fees: Reservations are accepted. Sites are $30–40 a night.

Open: May 15–Columbus Day.

Directions: From the center of Searsport, drive one mile south on U.S. 1 to the campground.

Contact: Asthig Koltookian Tangway, Searsport Shores Campground, 216 West Main Street, Searsport, ME 04974, 207/584-6059, website:www.campocean.com.

8 SENNEBEC LAKE CAMPGROUND

Rating: 8

On Sennebec Lake in Appleton

Sennebec Lake is actually the point where the St. George River widens to fill a scenic, rural valley between rolling, forested hills. Located just inland from the coast near Camden, Sennebec

Lake and environs feel like a place apart, a Currier and Ives vision of New England when, at the dawn of the 21st century, the 20th has yet to arrive. The campground is spacious, with several discreet areas and a long shorefront that holds some hidden coves. This is a relaxed, well-kept place near the coastal attractions of Camden and Rockport, yet with its own considerable attributes as well. Potluck dinners are held every Friday night, and there's live entertainment on Saturday night.

Campsites, facilities: There are 100 sites for tents and RVs, 11 with full hookups and 79 with water and electric hookups. Flush toilets, hot showers, tables, fireplaces, laundry facilities, a dump station, and a store are provided. Recreational facilities include a large freshwater lake with a beach, a boat launch and dock, canoe and rowboat rentals, a recreation room, volleyball, badminton, and horseshoes. Leashed pets are permitted.

Reservations, fees: Reservations are accepted. A deposit of one night's fee is required. Sites are $23–26 a night.

Open: Early May–mid-October.

Directions: From the junction of Highway 131 and Highway 17 in Union, drive three miles north on Highway 131 to the campground.

Contact: Pat and John Blennerhasset, Sennebec Lake Campground, Highway 31, Box 602, Appleton, ME 04862, 207/785-4250.

9 OLD MASSACHUSETTS HOMESTEAD CAMPGROUND

🏃 🏊 🚣 🚐 🍴 🐕 🚙 🔺

Rating: 8

North of Camden at Lincolnville Beach

When all is said and done, the Old Massachusetts Homestead emerges as one of our favorites. Perhaps we are won over by the location among great tall pines, or the clean, well-kept facilities, or the private, wooded sites tucked away in a mature forest. It might be due to the way the campground loops are laid out discreetly through the woods, or the fact that the

place has obviously been so well cared for over the years. Regardless, this little campground, whose main building dates back to 1718, is a special destination within easy access of the midcoast region's many attractions.

Campsites, facilities: There are 68 sites for tents and RVs, 10 with full hookups, 33 with water and electric hookups, and 25 with none. Flush toilets, hot showers, picnic tables, fireplaces, laundry facilities, a dump station, and a store selling limited supplies are provided. You'll also find a swimming pool, recreation room, volleyball, horseshoes, and hiking trails. Leashed pets are permitted.

Reservations, fees: Reservations are accepted with a credit card. Sites are $25–30 a night.

Open: May 1–November 1.

Directions: From the junction of U.S. 1 and Highway 173 in Lincolnville, drive two miles north on U.S. 1 to the campground entrance.

Contact: Dwight Wass, Old Massachusetts Homestead Campground, P.O. Box 5, Lincolnville, ME 04849, 207/789-5135 or 800/213-8142.

10 CAMDEN HILLS STATE PARK

🏃 🏊 🚣 🚐 🎣 🌼 🐕 🏃 ♿ 🚙 🔺

Rating: 10

Just north of the town of Camden

The coastal village of Camden is widely considered one of the prettiest in the entire country. With its quaint clapboard houses, white church steeples, and schooner-dotted harbor, it certainly appears to be the quintessential New England village. Camden Hills State Park is set amid all this splendid scenery, encompassing much of the Megunticook Mountain Range, which rises up directly behind the town in a stunning backdrop.

From the Mount Battie summit, the views of Camden, Camden Harbor, and Penobscot Bay are absolutely breathtaking. Similar to Acadia National Park, Camden Hills State Park has something to please almost everyone: mountains, ocean, forests, freshwater lakes, hiking trails, and easy access to the shops and restaurants in town. One trail near the campsites traces the shore of Penobscot Bay.

Campsites, facilities: There are 112 sites for tents and RVs, all without hookups. Facilities include wheelchair-accessible flush toilets, hot showers, a dump station, a group camping area, and a playground. The maximum RV length is 31 feet. Leashed pets are permitted.

Reservations, fees: Reservations are taken, and the total amount due must accompany your request. Contact the Maine Bureau of Parks and Lands at 207/287-3821. The State of Maine allocates some sites on a first-come, first-served basis. Sites are $15 for Maine residents and $20 for nonresidents.

Open: Year-round; fully operational May 15–October 15.

Directions: From the junction of Highway 105 and U.S. 1 in Camden, drive two miles north on U.S. 1 to the park entrance.

Contact: Camden Hills State Park Ranger, 207/236-3109; Maine Bureau of Parks and Lands, 22 State House Station, Augusta, ME 04333, 207/287-3821, website: www.state.me.us/doc/parks.

11 WARREN ISLAND STATE PARK

Rating: 10

On Warren Island in Lincolnville

This spruce-covered island lies just offshore from Lincolnville and adjacent to the much larger Islesboro Island in Penobscot Bay, considered by many to be the most beautiful body of water in the entire state of Maine. The park was designed to serve the needs of small-boat travelers and is accessible only by boat or sea kayak. There is no public transportation to the island. If you have the means to get here, camping on Warren Island is a great way to literally leave it all behind. You can spend time swimming, fishing, and relaxing.

Campsites, facilities: There are 10 tent sites and two Adirondack lean-tos with no hookups. Pit toilets, fire rings, drinking water, and dock-

ing and mooring facilities are provided on the property. Leashed pets are permitted.

Reservations, fees: Reservations are accepted, and the total amount due must accompany your request. Contact the Maine Bureau of Parks and Lands at 207/287-3821. The State of Maine allocates some sites on a first-come, first-served basis. Sites are $14 a night for Maine residents and $19 for nonresidents.

Open: May 1–October 15.

Directions: To reach these campsites on Warren Island, launch a boat at any of the public docks along the coast. Lincolnville is the closest.

Contact: Warren Island State Park, c/o Camden Hills State Park Ranger, 207/236-0849; Maine Bureau of Parks and Lands, 22 State House Station, Augusta, ME 04333, 207/287-3821, website: www.state.me.us/doc/parks.

12 DURHAM LEISURE CENTER AND CAMPGROUND

Rating: 5

In Durham

Bring your bathing suit and robe and get ready to relax, for the owners claim that this is Maine's only campground with an indoor heated pool and spa. The facility is located in a rural setting within minutes of Freeport, L.L.Bean, and the Maine coast.

Campsites, facilities: There are 38 sites for tents and RVs, several with full hookups. Flush toilets, hot showers, picnic tables, fireplaces, a dump station, laundry facilities, and a store are provided. You will also find an indoor heated pool and spa with private hot tubs and sauna, as well as a playground, basketball court, and horseshoe pits. Leashed pets are permitted.

Reservations, fees: Reservations are required for holiday weekends. Sites are $20–25 a night.

Open: Year-round.

Directions: From I-95 at Freeport, take Exit 20 and drive about 5.5 miles north on Highway 136 to the campground on the right.

Contact: Harold and Lorraine Cochrane,

Durham Leisure Center and Campground, Highway 136, Durham, ME 04222, 207/353-4353.

13 BRADBURY MOUNTAIN STATE PARK

Rating: 7

In Pownal

Bradbury Mountain is a lovely wooded ridge topped with a 460-foot peak that affords splendid views of Casco Bay, New Hampshire's White Mountains, and the surrounding countryside. The summit of the "mountain"—actually more of a low-lying ridge—is easily accessible via hiking trails that depart from the picnic area. Situated within six miles of downtown Freeport and the coast, the 297-acre parkland is within easy reach of midcoast Maine's many attractions.

Campsites, facilities: There are 41 sites for tents and trailers, all without hookups. Picnic tables, fireplaces, piped water, and pit toilets are provided. Hiking trails and a playing field are found within the park. Leashed pets are permitted.

Reservations, fees: Reservations are accepted, and the total amount due must accompany your request. Contact the Maine Bureau of Parks and Lands at the number below. Note that the State of Maine allocates some sites on a first-come, first-served basis. Sites are $11 a night for Maine residents and $14 for nonresidents.

Open: Year-round.

Directions: From the center of Pownal, drive one mile east on Highway 9 to the park. The campsites are located near the park entrance.

Contact: Bradbury Mountain State Park Ranger, 207/688-4712; Maine Bureau of Parks and Lands, 22 State House Station, Augusta, ME 04333, 207/287-3821, website: www.state.me.us/doc/parks.

14 BIG SKYE ACRES CAMPGROUND

Rating: 5

Near Bradbury Mountain State Park in Durham

Though it's just inland from the ocean and only minutes from the factory outlet stores in downtown Freeport, this campground feels as if it could be a hundred miles away from those popular tourist destinations and all their crowds. That's because it's surrounded by rural, rolling farm country. Nearby is Bradbury Mountain State Park, which provides visitors with views of the White Mountains that rise up to the west, and the ocean to the east. For more information on the area, see the previous listing for Bradbury Mountain State Park.

Campsites, facilities: There are 153 RV sites, 80 with full hookups and 73 with water and electric hookups. Facilities include flush toilets, hot showers, picnic tables, fireplaces, a laundry room, a dump station, and a store. Recreational facilities include a pavilion, swimming pool, recreation room, hiking trails, volleyball and badminton nets, and horseshoes. Leashed pets are permitted.

Reservations, fees: Reservations are accepted. Sites are $17–23 a night.

Open: May 15–October 15.

Directions: From I-95 at Freeport, take Exit 20 heading west toward Pownal Center and follow the signs to Bradbury Mountain State Park. When you reach the park entrance, drive 2.5 miles east on Highway 9 to the campground.

Contact: Big Skye Acres Campground, 1430 Hallowell Road, Durham, ME 04222, 207/688-4147.

15 BLUEBERRY POND CAMPGROUND

Rating: 5

West of Freeport in Pownal

Blueberry Pond is a small, peaceful campground situated in a rural, wooded setting within an easy drive of Portland, Freeport, and Maine's coastal beaches and islands. Each site covers half an acre, providing plenty of privacy. Nature trails for strolling and bird-watching wind through the property. For more serious hiking, head to nearby Bradbury Mountain State Park (see listing in this chapter).

Campsites, facilities: There are 38 sites for tents and RVs, 12 with full hookups, 10 with water and electric hookups, and 16 with none. Flush toilets, free hot showers, picnic tables, fireplaces, and a dump station are provided. Recreational facilities include a playground, hiking trails, swimming pool, and horseshoe pits. Leashed pets are permitted.

Reservations, fees: Reservations are accepted. Sites are $22–28 a night.

Open: May 15–October 15.

Directions: From I-95 at Freeport, take Exit 20 and drive 2.5 miles north on Highway 136 to Pownal Road. Turn left on Pownal Road and drive 1.5 miles west to the campground.

Contact: Donald and Patricia Searfoss, Blueberry Pond Campground, 218 Poland Range Road, Pownal, ME 04069, 207/688-4421, website: www.blueberrycampground.com.

16 CEDAR HAVEN CAMPGROUND

👫 🏊 🎣 🚍 🐕 🚗 ⛺

Rating: 4

In Freeport

Most sites at Cedar Haven are wooded, and the roads are wide enough to accommodate RVs of any length. There's also a separate tenting area with spacious sites. Just inland from the coast and island-speckled Casco Bay, the campground is within a short drive of many midcoast attractions, including downtown Freeport and the giant L.L.Bean store. To escape the crowds in Freeport, head to Wolf Neck Woods State Park, where trails wander through woods along a rocky shoreline. Another nearby option for a quiet walk is the Audubon Society of Maine's Mast Landing

Wildlife Sanctuary, where the hiking paths cross wooded ridges, fields, and orchards. Both are pleasant places to walk aimlessly and clear your head. For a swim, Popham Beach State Park is about 30 minutes away by car.

Campsites, facilities: There are 58 sites for tents and RVs, four with full hookups, 44 with water and electric hookups, and 10 with none. Facilities include flush toilets, free hot showers, picnic tables, fireplaces, a laundry room, a dump station and on-site service, and a store. A swimming pond, miniature golf, a recreation room, volleyball, basketball, badminton, and horseshoe pits are among the recreational offerings. Leashed pets are permitted.

Reservations, fees: Reservations are accepted. Sites are $20–28 a night. Group and senior discounts are available.

Open: May 1–October 26.

Directions: From I-95 in Freeport, take Exit 20, drive .5 mile north on Highway 125/136 and then go .5 mile north on Highway 125. Turn right and drive .25 mile northeast on Baker Road to the campground.

Contact: The Kirby Family, Cedar Haven Campground, 19 Baker Road, Freeport, ME 04032, 207/865-6254, website: www.campmaine.com/cedarhaven/.

17 FLORIDA LAKE CAMPGROUND

🏊 🎣 🚍 🐕 🚗 ⛺

Rating: 4

On a small lake in Freeport

The small campground at Florida Lake is within minutes of downtown Freeport, L.L.Bean, and more than 100 factory outlet stores. For more information on the Freeport area, see the previous listing for Cedar Haven Campground.

Campsites, facilities: There are 40 sites for tents and RVs, some with water and electric hookups. Facilities include flush toilets, hot showers, picnic tables, fireplaces, and a dump station. Recreational facilities include a playing field; a 30-acre lake for swimming, boating, and fishing; and a swimming pool. Canoe and paddleboat rentals are available. Leashed pets are permitted.

Reservations, fees: Reservations are recommended and require a deposit of $20 for weekend stays and $40 for weeklong reservations. Sites are $15–20 a night.

Open: May 15–October 15.

Directions: From I-95 at Freeport, take Exit 20 and drive three miles north on Highway 125 to the campground on the right.

Contact: Alan and Vera Rogers, Florida Lake Campground, 82 Wardtown Road, Freeport, ME 04032, 207/865-4874.

18 WHITE'S BEACH AND CAMPGROUND

🚶 🏊 🎣 🛶 🐕 🧍 🚐 ⛺

Rating: 4

In Brunswick

White's Beach is a tidy little campground set on a small freshwater lake. A spacious sandy beach with a lifeguard on duty, quiet wooded sites, and hiking trails that meander throughout the premises are featured here. An added attraction is that the campground is conveniently located near downtown Freeport, with its shops, restaurants, and the main attraction, L.L.Bean.

Campsites, facilities: There are 45 sites for tents and RVs, some with water and electric hookups. Flush toilets, hot showers, picnic tables, fireplaces, a dump station, and a store are provided. Recreational facilities include freshwater swimming, a playground, volleyball, basketball, and hiking trails. Leashed pets are permitted.

Reservations, fees: Reservations are accepted. Sites are $18–22 a night.

Open: May 15–October 15.

Directions: From the intersection of U.S. 1 and Durham Road in Brunswick, drive 2.2 miles north on Durham Road to the campground.

Contact: White's Beach and Campground, Durham Road, Brunswick, ME 04011, 207/729-0415.

19 DOWN EAST FAMILY CAMPING

🚶 🏊 🛶 🛶 🐕 🚐 ⛺

Rating: 7

In Wiscasset

Down East Family Camping is designed for tent campers. The sites are large, private, and wooded, and the campground boasts more than 6,000 feet of waterfront on a spring-fed lake. The swimming, boating, canoeing, and fishing are all great, and a feeling of peaceful relaxation pervades this wild setting.

Campsites, facilities: There are 40 sites for tents and RVs, two with water and electric hookups, six with electric hookups only, and 32 with none. Flush toilets, free hot showers, picnic tables, fireplaces, and a store are provided. Recreational facilities include a boat launch, canoe and rowboat rentals, a recreation room, volleyball, badminton, and horseshoes. Leashed pets are permitted.

Reservations, fees: Reservations are accepted. A deposit of one night's fee is required. Sites are $18–26 a night.

Open: May 25–September 15.

Directions: From the intersection of U.S. 1 and Highway 27 in Wiscasset, drive four miles north on Highway 27 to the campground.

Contact: Bob and B. J. Nesbitt, Down East Family Camping, RR 3, Box 223, Wiscasset, ME 04578, 207/882-5431.

20 TOWN LINE CAMPSITES

🚶 🏊 🛶 🛶 🐕 🚐 ⛺

Rating: 8

On Damariscotta Lake in North Nobleboro

Town Line Campsites offers 160 acres of shorefront on 14-mile-long Damariscotta Lake, which has a reputation for good salmon, trout, bass, pickerel, and perch fishing. The campground is tucked away in pine trees, surrounded by rural countryside and rolling hills, and is very quiet and peaceful. Town Line prides itself on its noncommercial atmosphere, so if you are looking for a place to kick back and relax, this may be the one.

Campsites, facilities: There are 55 sites for tents and RVs, some with partial hookups. Flush toilets, hot showers, picnic tables, fireplaces, laundry facilities, a dump station, and a store are provided. There are also two sandy beaches with floats, canoe and rowboat rentals, a recreation room, volleyball, basketball, badminton, and horseshoes. Leashed pets are permitted.

Reservations, fees: Reservations are accepted. Payment in full is required for reservations of one week or less; send one week's fee for stays lasting longer than a week. Sites are $20–30 a night.

Open: Memorial Day–Labor Day.

Directions: From the intersection of Highway 32 and East Pond Road in Jefferson, drive three miles south on East Pond Road to the campground.

Contact: Louise Newbert, Town Line Campsites, 483 East Pond Road, Jefferson, ME 04348, 207/832-7055.

21 MIC MAC COVE CAMPGROUND

On Crawford Pond in Union

Rating: 6

Located midway between the state capital at Augusta and the coastal towns of Camden and Rockport, Mic Mac Cove is a pleasant, spacious, shaded campground on a hillside that slopes down to the shores of Crawford Pond, a large spring-fed lake.

Campsites, facilities: There are 82 sites for tents and RVs, some with water and electric hookups. Flush toilets, hot showers, picnic tables, fireplaces, a dump station, and a store are provided. Recreational facilities include a boat launch, canoe and rowboat rentals, a sandy beach, recreation room, sauna, volleyball, and horseshoes. Leashed pets are permitted.

Reservations, fees: Reservations are accepted. A deposit of 50 percent is required. Sites are $17–19 a night.

Open: May 1–October 5.

Directions: From the intersection of Highway 17 and Highway 131 in Union, drive one mile east on Highway 17 to the campground.

Contact: Howard Brinckenhoff, Mic Mac Cove Campground, Highway 17, Union, ME 04862, 207/785-4100, website: www.coastlinememories.com/mic.mac.campground.html.

22 LOON'S CRY CAMPGROUND

Rating: 7

On North Pond in Warren

Loon's Cry offers large, spacious sites in open fields, woods, and along the shores of North Pond, a spring-fed freshwater lake. The campground owns 1,500 feet of shoreline with a boat launch and a sandy beach. Loon's Cry is a clean, attractive facility that's well situated in the heart of the midcoast region and within easy reach of the nearby villages and attractions of Camden, Rockland, Rockport, and Penobscot Bay.

Campsites, facilities: There are 45 sites for tents and RVs, four with full hookups, 15 with water and electric hookups, and 26 with none. Flush toilets, hot showers, picnic tables, fireplaces, laundry facilities, a dump station, and a store are provided. Recreational facilities include canoe and paddleboat rentals, a playground, hiking trails, and horseshoes. Leashed pets are permitted.

Reservations, fees: Reservations are accepted. A $10 deposit is required. Sites are $20–26 a night.

Open: May 1–October 15.

Directions: From the intersection of U.S. 1 and Highway 90, drive a mile south on U.S. 1 to the campground.

Contact: The Goff Family, Loon's Cry Campground, Highway 1, Warren, ME 04864,

207/273-2324 or 800/493-2324, website: www.midcoast.com/~loonscry.

23 DESERT OF MAINE CAMPGROUND

🚶 🏊 🛶 🚣 🐕 🚐 ⛺

Rating: 4

In Freeport

Offering a thought-provoking lesson on what can happen when people abuse land, the Desert of Maine is a 40-acre plot of sand that was once a prosperous farm. After being intensively cultivated, the land was heavily logged. Eventually, the topsoil blew away, leaving nothing but sand. Campers are given free admission to the Desert of Maine Visitor Center, where they find nature trails and narrated coach tours. The campground is within a short drive of downtown Freeport and its centerpiece attraction: the famous L.L.Bean store that never closes. From the campground, you can catch a shuttle to downtown Freeport. For more information on the Freeport area, see the Cedar Haven Campground listing in this chapter.

Campsites, facilities: There are 50 sites for tents and RVs, four with full hookups, 37 with water and electric hookups, and nine with none. Flush toilets, hot showers, picnic tables, fireplaces, a dump station, laundry facilities, and a store are provided. Leashed pets are permitted.

Reservations, fees: Reservations are recommended. Sites are $19–28 a night.

Open: May 5–October 15.

Directions: From I-95 in Freeport, take Exit 19 and drive two miles west on Desert Road to the campground.

Contact: The Dobson Family, Desert of Maine Campground, Desert Road, Freeport, ME 04032, 207/865-6962, website: www.desertof maine.com.

24 FLYING POINT CAMPGROUND

🏊 🛶 🚣 🛶 🐕 🚐 ⛺

Rating: 7

On Casco Bay in Freeport

Flying Point is a side of Freeport that most outlet shoppers never get a chance to explore, a beautiful neck of land jutting into island-strewn Casco Bay. The campsites here are situated directly on the oceanfront. This is the place for people who seek the beauty and tranquillity of the Maine coast, yet want to be near the attractions of downtown Freeport. For more information on the Freeport area, see the Cedar Haven Campground listing in this chapter.

Campsites, facilities: There are 46 sites for tents and RVs, 38 with water and electric hookups and eight with none. Facilities include flush toilets, hot showers, picnic tables, fireplaces, and a dump station. Recreational facilities include saltwater swimming, fishing, and boating; volleyball and badminton nets; and horseshoes. Leashed pets are permitted.

Reservations, fees: Reservations are recommended and require a deposit of $18 for a weekend or $30 for a week. Sites are $18–25 a night.

Open: May 1–October 15.

Directions: From I-95 north of Yarmouth, take Exit 19 and drive 1.5 miles south on U.S. 1 into Freeport. At the L.L.Bean store in the center of town, turn south onto Bow Street, which becomes Flying Point Road, and drive 3.75 miles to Lower Flying Point Road. Turn right and drive less than .25 mile to the campground.

Contact: Flying Point Campground, Lower Flying Point Road, Freeport, ME 04032, 207/865-4569.

25 RECOMPENSE SHORE CAMPGROUND

Rating: 8

On Casco Bay in Freeport

Recompense Shore is owned and operated by the University of Southern Maine, which employs the land as a demonstration of sustainable natural and recreational resource management. The campground claims a great location on the shore of island-filled Casco Bay, and sites are either situated on or near the shore, tucked away in and among towering pines, or bordering the fields of the campground's 600-acre farm. Next door is Wolf Neck Woods State Park, offering miles of hiking trails that meander through the woods and along the water. Also nearby is the Audubon Society of Maine's Mast Landing Wildlife Sanctuary. The lightly traveled roads in the area are great for biking. And for shoppers, the campground is only minutes from L.L.Bean in downtown Freeport. For more information on the Freeport area, see the Cedar Haven Campground listing in this chapter.

Campsites, facilities: There are 103 sites for tents and RVs, eight with partial hookups and 95 with none. Facilities include flush toilets, hot showers, picnic tables, fireplaces, a dump station, and a store. Recreational facilities include saltwater swimming, fishing, and boating; volleyball and badminton nets; and horseshoes. Leashed pets are permitted.

Reservations, fees: Reservations are accepted. Sites are $14–26 a night.

Open: Mid-May–mid-October.

Directions: From I-95 north of Yarmouth, take Exit 19 and drive 1.5 miles south on U.S. 1 into Freeport. At the L.L.Bean store in the center of town, turn south onto Bow Street, which becomes Flying Point Road, and drive 2.25 miles east. Turn south on Wolf Neck Road and go 2.4 miles to the campground.

Contact: Recompense Shore Campground, 10 Burnett Road, Freeport, ME 04032, 207/865-9307, website: www.freeportcamping.com.

26 THOMAS POINT BEACH AND CAMPGROUND

Rating: 4

On the shore in Brunswick

Thomas Point Beach is a popular waterfront gathering place for local people who use it as a town park for reunions, company picnics, and other functions. There are campsites situated in the tall pines near the shore, and the clean, sandy beach is watched over by a lifeguard. Note, however, that the campground is near a very busy intersection, consumption of alcohol is not allowed in the park, and pets are not permitted. Also be aware that this place has one of the earliest closing dates of any campground in the state.

Campsites, facilities: There are 75 sites for tents and RVs, 22 with electric hookups and 53 with none. Flush toilets, hot showers, picnic tables, fireplaces, a dump station, and a store are provided. Recreational facilities include a sandy beach, recreation room, ice-cream shop, and a playing field. Ice and firewood are available. No pets are allowed.

Reservations, fees: Reservations are accepted. Sites are $20–25 a night.

Open: Memorial Day–August 24.

Directions: From the intersection of U.S. 1 and Highway 24 at Cooks Corner, drive 100 yards south on Highway 24, then go approximately 2.5 miles east on Thomas Point Road to the campground.

Contact: Patricia Crooker, Thomas Point Beach and Campground, 29 Meadow Road, Brunswick, ME 04011, 207/725-6009, website: www.thomaspointbeach.com.

27 MEADOWBROOK CAMPING AREA

Rating: 7

On the road to Popham Beach in Bath

Like several others in this area, Meadowbrook Camping Area is set on an arm of the Atlantic

Ocean that reaches up into the Maine midcoast. This region is filled with islands and bays, wildlife-rich estuaries, and long peninsulas stretching out from the coast like fingers. The campground, with its large open and forested sites, is well situated to offer access to this unique part of the country. While you are here, enjoy a Meadowbrook specialty: the Down East lobster-and-clam bake. Staying here puts you close to Popham Beach State Park, Reid State Park, L.L.Bean, and the Maine Maritime Museum, where the state's seafaring legacy is brought to life.

Campsites, facilities: There are 125 sites for tents and RVs, 56 with water and electric hookups and 34 with none. Flush toilets, free hot showers, picnic tables, fireplaces, laundry facilities, a dump station, and a store are provided. Recreational facilities include a mile-long trail, nature preserve, swimming pool, miniature golf, recreation room, volleyball, basketball, badminton, and horseshoes. LP gas is available. Leashed pets are permitted.

Reservations, fees: Reservations are required in winter. Sites range from $20–28 a night.

Open: May 1–October 15 for vehicles requiring hookups; year-round for tents and self-contained RVs.

Directions: From the junction of U.S. 1 and Highway 209 in Bath, drive 2.5 miles south on Highway 209, then turn right and drive three miles southwest on Meadowbrook Road to the campground.

Contact: Cathy and Gary Bilodeau, Meadowbrook Camping Area, H.C.R. 32, Box 280B, Bath, ME 04530, 207/443-4967 or 800/370-CAMP (800/370-2267), website: www.meadowbrookme.com/.

28 CHEWONKI CAMPGROUNDS

Rating: 7

In Wiscasset

Wiscasset calls itself the "prettiest" village in Maine, and this seaport town where the Sheep-

scot River empties into the Atlantic Ocean is indeed picturesque. The campground is located on Chewonki Neck, one of numerous fingers of land jutting out into the ocean in this part of the state, and it has great access to the water, tidal rivers, salt marshes, and estuaries of the region. Be warned, however, that the Maine Yankee nuclear power plant shares this splendid natural setting with the campground.

Campsites, facilities: There are 48 sites for tents and RVs, nine with full hookups, 30 with water and electric hookups, and nine with none. Flush toilets, hot showers, picnic tables, fireplaces, a dump station, and a store are provided. Recreational facilities include a boat launch, swimming pool, tennis court, canoe rentals, recreation room, volleyball, basketball, badminton, and horseshoes. Leashed pets are permitted.

Reservations, fees: Reservations are accepted. For stays of three days or fewer, a $20 deposit is required; for four or more days, there is a $50 deposit. Sites are $22–32 a night.

Open: Mid-May–mid-October.

Directions: From the junction of U.S. 1 and Highway 144 in Wiscasset, drive .25 mile south on Highway 144 and then one mile southwest to the campground.

Contact: Pamela Brackett and Ann Brackett Beck, Chewonki Campgrounds, Box 261, Wiscasset, ME 04578, 207/882-7426 or 800/465-7747

29 SHORE HILLS CAMPGROUND

Rating: 8

On the Cross River near Boothbay Harbor

Shore Hills Campground is located on the Cross River, a pretty tidal stream that empties into the Atlantic Ocean. Waterfront sites, fishing rocks, and direct access to the water are just some of the perks. From here, it is a short distance to the shops and restaurants of Boothbay

Harbor. And the park is within very easy reach of other midcoast attractions, such as boating and deep-sea fishing excursions, sandy beaches, wildlife refuges, and picturesque seaside villages. A shuttle bus to Boothbay Harbor is provided. Note that Shore Hills has one of the earliest opening dates of any campground in Maine. So if you want to brave the last of winter's icy winds, come on up. Brrr.

Campsites, facilities: There are 150 sites for tents and RVs, 83 with full hookups, 52 with water and electric hookups, and 15 with none. Flush toilets, hot showers, picnic tables, fireplaces, laundry facilities, a dump station, and a store are provided. Recreational facilities include saltwater fishing and swimming, boating and sea kayaking, a recreation room, volleyball, basketball, badminton, and horseshoes. Leashed pets are permitted.

Reservations, fees: Reservations are recommended. A $15 deposit is required. Sites are $20–32 a night.

Open: April 19–Columbus Day.

Directions: From the junction of U.S. 1 and Highway 27 in Edgecomb, drive eight miles south on Highway 27 to the campground.

Contact: Milon and Peggy Fuller, Shore Hills Campground, Highway 27, Box 448, Boothbay, ME 04537, 207/633-4782, website: www.shorehills.com.

30 LITTLE PONDEROSA CAMPGROUND

Rating: 8

In Boothbay

Little Ponderosa is located on the Cross River, a tidal inlet in Maine's midcoast region. This is a spectacular land- and seascape of maritime spruce-fir forests, peninsulas jutting into the ocean, and mazes of interconnected waterways. The area is rich in natural beauty and wildlife, and you could easily spend months trying to see it all. Little Ponderosa would be a good place to start. The sites are nestled among tall pine trees, and 30 of them have been placed along the shore. Weekend activities are scheduled in July and August, including a gospel concert on Saturday night and mini-church services on Sunday. The campground provides a shuttle bus to Boothbay Harbor.

Campsites, facilities: There are 96 sites for tents and RVs, 37 with full hookups, 57 with water and electric hookups, and two with none. Wheelchair-accessible restroom facilities, flush toilets, hot showers, cable TV, picnic tables, fireplaces, laundry facilities, a dump station, and a store are provided. You'll find canoe and rowboat rentals, a recreation room, miniature golf, volleyball, basketball, badminton, and horseshoes. LP gas and RV supplies are available. Leashed pets are permitted.

Reservations, fees: Reservations are recommended. Sites are $20–27 a night.

Open: May 15–October 15.

Directions: From the junction of U.S. 1 and Highway 27 in Edgecomb, drive five miles south on Highway 27 to the campground.

Contact: The Roberts Family, Little Ponderosa Campground, Boothbay, ME 04537, 207/633-2700.

31 SHERMAN LAKE VIEW CAMPGROUND

Rating: 4

In North Edgecomb

Sherman Lake View does indeed afford a fine view over Sherman Lake from the top of a hill; however, the campground is situated directly across busy U.S. 1 from the lake. As a base camp from which to venture forth and explore the area, it's only minutes away from the towns of Bath, Wiscasset, and Damariscotta, as well as within easy reach of the ocean. This is a convenient place to spend the night if you are on your way to Down East Maine or to the Canadian Maritime Provinces.

Campsites, facilities: There are 30 sites for tents and RVs, eight with full hookups, 10 with water and electric hookups, and 12 with none. Flush toilets, hot showers, picnic tables, fireplaces, laundry facilities, a swimming pool, and a dump station are provided. Leashed pets are permitted.

Reservations, fees: Reservations are accepted. Sites are $20–25 a night.

Open: Memorial Day–Columbus Day.

Directions: From the intersection of U.S. 1 and Highway 27 in Edgecomb, drive approximately 3.5 miles north on U.S. 1 to the campground.

Contact: Norm and Ann Benner, Sherman Lake View Campground, RR 1, P.O. Box 1150, North Edgecomb, ME 04556, 207/563-3239.

32 DUCK PUDDLE CAMPGROUND

🏊 🛶 🚤 ✖ 🐕 🏠 🚐 ⛰️

Rating: 7

On Lake Pemaquid in Nobleboro

Duck Puddle is a family campground situated on a seven-mile-long freshwater lake. While all of the sites are well maintained, those on the waterfront have wonderful views of Lake Pemaquid. The open and wooded sites are spacious. Much of the activity takes place at the shore, where there is a small swimming beach and good trout, bass, and pickerel fishing. Families can rent canoes, paddleboats, and motorboats. If you bring your own boat, be sure to reserve a dock space. This is a clean, well-tended campground within easy reach of midcoast Maine's attractions.

Campsites, facilities: There are 95 sites for tents and RVs, 45 with full hookups, 45 with water and electric hookups, and five with none. Flush toilets, hot showers, picnic tables, fireplaces, laundry facilities, a dump station, and a store are provided. Recreational facilities include a swimming pool, recreation room, volleyball, basketball, badminton, horseshoes, a boat launch, and canoe, paddleboat, and motorboat rentals. Leashed pets are permitted.

Reservations, fees: Reservations are accepted. Sites are $20–30 a night.

Open: May 1–October 31.

Directions: From the intersection of U.S. 1 and Duck Puddle Road in Nobleboro, drive 1.5 miles on Duck Puddle Road to the campground.

Contact: Sue and Jim Ferrier, Duck Puddle Campground, Duck Puddle Road, P.O. Box 176, Nobleboro, ME 04555, 207/563-5608, website: www.duckpuddlecampground.com.

33 LAKE PEMAQUID CAMPGROUND

🏊 🛶 🚤 ✖ 🐕 🏠 🚐 ⛰️

Rating: 6

On Lake Pemaquid in Damariscotta

This campground is located on a large (seven miles long) freshwater lake that boasts excellent bass, perch, pickerel, and brown trout fishing. The interconnected waterways actually provide access to more than 15 miles of lakes and streams for exploration. If you don't have your own boat, you can rent a motorboat, canoe, paddleboat, sailboat, or even an aqua bike from the campground. Some of the sites are situated directly along the shore, while others are tucked back in the woods of pine, white birch, and oak trees. For those who come to Maine for the seafood, lobsters and clams are sold in the campground store.

Campsites, facilities: There are 293 sites for tents and RVs, 120 with full hookups, 140 with water and electric hookups, and 10 with none. Flush toilets, metered hot showers, picnic tables, fireplaces, laundry facilities, a dump station, and a store are provided. Recreational facilities include a boat launch, swimming pool, canoe rentals, recreation room, volleyball, basketball, badminton, and horseshoes. Ice, firewood, and LP gas are available. Leashed pets are permitted.

Reservations, fees: Reservations are accepted. For stays of fewer than seven days, payment in full is required; for stays of over a week, send a 50 percent deposit. Sites are $24–40 a night.

Open: May 15–Columbus Day.

Directions: From the intersection of Business U.S. 1 and Biscay Road in Damariscotta, drive two miles on Biscay Road and then follow signs for .75 mile to the campground.

Contact: Lake Pemaquid Campground, Box 967, Damariscotta, ME 04543, 207/563-5202, website: www.lakepemaquid.com.

34 SALTWATER FARM CAMPGROUND

Rating: 8

On the St. George River in Thomaston

Saltwater Farm is an attractive campground set on a high, open meadow above the mouth of the St. George River, where it flows into the Atlantic Ocean. This is a lovely, scenic spot with wide-open views to the east and south. The campground has 500 feet of frontage on the St. George River, offering excellent saltwater fishing and sea kayaking access.

Campsites, facilities: There are 37 sites for tents and RVs, 25 with full hookups, six with water and electric hookups, and six with none. Flush toilets, hot showers, picnic tables, fireplaces, laundry facilities, a dump station, and a store are provided. Recreational facilities include a swimming pool, recreation room, volleyball, and horseshoes. Leashed pets are permitted.

Reservations, fees: Reservations are recommended. Sites are $20–32 a night.

Open: May 15–October 15.

Directions: From the intersection of U.S. 1 and Wadsworth Street in Thomaston, drive 1.5 miles southeast on Wadsworth Street to the campground.

Contact: Linda and Bruce Jennings, Saltwater Farm Campground, P.O. Box 165, Thomaston, ME 04861, 207/354-6735, website: www.mid coast.com.

35 MEGUNTICOOK CAMPGROUND BY THE SEA

Rating: 7

In Rockport

Unfortunately, this place is too close to busy U.S. 1. Megunticook Campground by the Sea is nonetheless an exceptionally attractive and well-run facility set among tall shade trees next to the shores of Penobscot Bay. But the real lure is the surrounding area, which offers almost too much to even contemplate doing. No matter what your preference, you will probably find it nearby: hiking in Camden Hills State Park; shopping, restaurants, and movies in Camden; strolling through the picturesque village of Rockport; enjoying a schooner cruise on Penobscot Bay; sea kayaking among the many offshore islands; deep-sea fishing and whale-watching—the list goes on.

Campsites, facilities: There are 82 sites for tents and RVs, 41 with full hookups, 22 with water and electric hookups, and 19 with none. Flush toilets, hot showers, tables, fireplaces, cable TV, laundry facilities, a dump station, and a store are provided. A heated swimming pool, kayak and bicycle rentals, a deck overlooking the ocean, recreation room, playing field, badminton, and horseshoes are also available. Leashed pets are permitted.

Reservations, fees: Reservations are recommended. A deposit of one night's fee is required. Sites are $32–42 a night.

Open: May 15–October 15.

Directions: From the junction of U.S. 1 and Highway 90 in Rockport, drive two miles south on U.S. 1 to the campground.

Contact: John Alexander, Megunticook Campground by the Sea, U.S. 1, Rockport, ME 04856, 207/594-2428 or 800/884-2428, fax 207/594-0549, email: mebythesea@midcoast.com, website: www.campgroundbythesea.com.

36 LOBSTER BUOY CAMPSITE

≈ 🎣 🚂 ✕ 🐕 🚐 ⛺

Rating: 10

On Penobscot Bay in South Thomaston

Here is the campground for those who want little more than direct and easy access to the ocean. Lobster Buoy is situated right where the Penobscot Bay waters empty into the wide Atlantic Ocean, separated from the open sea by Muscle Ridge, a line of rock-rimmed, spruce-covered granite islands jutting up from the cold depths. The campground has 400 feet of ocean frontage. Understandably, this is paradise for sea kayakers and sailors. But if seafaring isn't for you, don't forget to bring your fishing gear to try for various saltwater species. No campsite is more than 150 yards from the water, and all have expansive ocean views.

Campsites, facilities: There are 40 sites for tents and RVs, with full, partial, and no hookups. Flush toilets, hot showers, picnic tables, fireplaces, a dump station, and a store are provided. Leashed pets are permitted.

Reservations, fees: Reservations are recommended. A deposit of one night's fee is required. Sites are $17–27 a night.

Open: May 15–October 15.

Directions: From the junction of U.S. 1 and Highway 73 in Rockland, drive seven miles south on Highway 73 to the campground.

Contact: Mabel Batty and Eleanor Carpenter, Lobster Buoy Campsite, 280 Waterman Beach Road, South Thomaston, ME 04858, 207/594-7546.

37 OLD QUARRY OCEAN ADVENTURES INC.

✕ ≈ 🎣 🐕 ⛺

Rating: 10

On Webb Cove, Buckmaster Neck, in the Oceanville section of Stonington

Old Quarry is much more than a campground. It's arguably the finest sea kayaking destination in the United States. There are indeed campsites

here, but Old Quarry is really an adventure center where you can learn to sea kayak, rent sea kayaks, find specialty kayaking items in the store, or simply begin and end your own full-day or multi-day sea kayaking adventures among the dozens of granite islands of Merchant Row and the Deer Isle Thoroughfare just offshore. For tent campers with a sense of adventure hoping to explore the true off-the-beaten-path coast of Maine, there is simply no better choice.

Campsites, facilities: There are 10 campsites for tent camping. Seven of the sites are in the woods spread far apart so that you can have plenty of privacy on your Maine camping experience, while three of the sites are in an open area and are great for groups or those wanting lots of sun while camping. Facilities include flush toilets, hot showers, laundry facilities, Internet access, a swim pond, kayak launch sites, a camp store, tent platforms, picnic tables, deck chairs, and fire grills. Firewood and lobsters are available at the camp store.

Reservations, fees: Reservations are accepted. Sites are $16–32 a night.

Open: April 1–November 1.

Directions: From Bucksport, take U.S. 1 north for five miles to the intersection with Highway 15. At the intersection, drive south on Highway 15 for 38 miles to Oceanville Road. Drive east one mile on Oceanville Road to Settlement Quarry Road, then drive approximately 200 yards south on Settlement Quarry Road to the campground.

Contact: Captain Bill Baker, Old Quarry Ocean Adventures, RR 1, Box 700, Stonington, ME 04681, 207/367-8977, website: www.oldquarry.com.

38 BLACKBURN'S CAMPGROUND

🧗 ≈ 🎣 🚂 🐕 🚐 ⛺

Rating: 4

In Waterboro Center

This campground is situated on the shores of scenic Ossipee Lake, where you can play on a sandy beach or plunk in a canoe for a lazy day of paddling. The lake is home to landlocked salmon, togue, brook trout, bass, and pickerel, so come prepared to cast a line. Campsites on the upper level are wooded, and those on the lower level are set along the waterfront. Hiking trails that lead to the Ossipee Mountain summit begin at the campground.

Campsites, facilities: There are 85 sites for tents and RVs, 65 with full hookups and 20 with water and electric hookups. Many sites come with additional cable TV and telephone connections. Flush toilets, hot showers, picnic tables, fireplaces, and a dump station are provided. Recreational facilities include access to a private pond, canoe and paddleboat rentals, a dock, volleyball and badminton nets, and horseshoes. Leashed pets are permitted.

Reservations, fees: Reservations are accepted. Sites are $19 a night.

Open: May 1–October 1.

Directions: From U.S. 202 north of Waterboro, follow Highway 5 west to Waterboro Center. The campground is near the intersection of Highway 5 and Buxton Road.

Contact: Blackburn's Campground, Box 369, Ossipee Lake, Waterboro, ME 04030, 207/247-5875.

39 WALNUT GROVE CAMPGROUND

Rating: 4

In Alfred

Wooded and open sites are available at Walnut Grove. This campground is located in the lakes region of southern Maine, a mostly rural slice of the state that's dotted with 25 lakes, so anglers should bring their fishing gear. The beaches of southern Maine are a half-hour's drive away.

Campsites, facilities: There are 93 sites for tents and RVs, all with water and electric hookups. Facilities include flush toilets, hot showers, picnic tables, fireplaces, a dump station, laundry facilities, a snack bar, and a store. Recreational

facilities include a playground, recreation room, volleyball and basketball, horseshoe pits, and hiking trails. Leashed pets are permitted.

Reservations, fees: Reservations are recommended and require a deposit of $16.50. Sites are $25 a night.

Open: May 1–October 15.

Directions: From the intersection of U.S. 202 and Highways 4 and 111, drive one mile north on U.S. 202/4. Turn left on Gore Road and drive 2.75 miles northwest to the campground.

Contact: Arthur and Sandy Roberts, Walnut Grove Campground, Gore Road, Box 260, Alfred, ME 04002, 207/324-1207, website: www.gocampingamerica.com/walnut-groveme.

40 HIGHLAND LAKE PARK

Rating: 5

On Highland Lake in Windham

Located between Sebago Lake and Portland, this campground is situated within a short drive of woods, lakes, beaches, and the attractions of the city of Portland. Nearby you will find riding stables, golf courses, and the Windham Covered Bridge. Also within easy reach are the historic Portland Head Lighthouse, Old Orchard Beach, Two Lights State Park, and Crescent Beach State Park.

Campsites, facilities: There are 40 sites for tents and RVs, several of which offer full hookups. Facilities include flush toilets, hot showers, picnic tables, fireplaces, and a dump station. You will also find a lake and a playground. No pets are allowed.

Reservations, fees: Reservations are accepted. Sites are $18–26 a night.

Open: Year-round.

Directions: From the Maine Turnpike/I-95 near Portland, take Exit 8 and drive 4.5 miles north on U.S. 302 to the campground on the right.

Contact: Arthur and Pat McDermott, Highland Lake Park, 19 Roosevelt Trail, Windham, ME 04062, 207/892-8911.

41 WASSAMKI SPRINGS CAMPGROUND

🏊 🎣 🚣 🐴 ⛹ 🚐

Rating: 4

In Westbrook

Both lakefront and wooded sites are available at Wassamki Springs, a large campground with a private 30-acre lake. A mile of sandy beach borders these crystal-clear waters, which are stocked with trout for fishing. This is the closest campground to downtown Portland and puts campers within minutes of the Old Port area, fine shops and restaurants, historic sites, beaches, lighthouses, and the many attractions of the southern and midcoastal regions of Maine.

Campsites, facilities: There are 160 sites for tents and RVs with full, partial, and no hookups. Phone hookups are available. Flush toilets, hot showers, picnic tables, fireplaces, a dump station, laundry facilities, and a store are provided. Recreational facilities include a lake with a sand beach, a stocked trout pond, boat rentals, playgrounds, a recreation room, volleyball, basketball, and horseshoe pits. Leashed pets are permitted.

Reservations, fees: Reservations are required. You must leave a deposit of $10 for every night you plan to stay. Sites are $34–40 a night.

Open: May 1–October 15.

Directions: From the Maine Turnpike/I-95 west of Portland, take Exit 7, drive one mile south on Payne Road, and then head 2.5 miles north on Highway 114. Turn right on Saco Street and drive .5 mile north to the campground.

Contact: The Hillock Family, Wassamki Springs Campground, 855 Saco Street, Westbrook, ME 04092, 207/839-4276, website: www. wassamkisprings.com.

42 ORRS ISLAND CAMPGROUND

🚶 🏊 🎣 🚐 🎣 🐴 🚐 ⛺

Rating: 10

On Orrs Island

Catering to families, this campground is perched on a 42-acre bluff overlooking Harpswell Sound, one of the most scenic long reaches of saltwater on Maine's Midcoast. The 70 sites are both open and wooded, and many sit high above the water on a rocky bluff where visitors enjoy unbroken views over the sound. Saltwater swimming and fishing are within easy reach. And it's just a short drive to the town of Brunswick, home of Bowdoin College, and Bath, where guided missile cruisers are built at the venerable Bath Iron Works, one of the oldest shipbuilders in the country. Just off the southern tip of Bailey Island (which is connected to Orrs Island by a bridge) is Eagle Island, where Admiral Robert Peary, discoverer of the North Pole, used to live.

Campsites, facilities: There are 70 sites for tents and RVs, 35 with full hookups, 18 with water and electric hookups, and 17 with none. Flush toilets, hot showers, picnic tables, fireplaces, laundry facilities, a dump station, and a store are provided. Recreational facilities include canoe rentals, a floating dock, boat mooring, hiking trails, volleyball, badminton, and horseshoes. Leashed pets are permitted.

Reservations, fees: Reservations are accepted for stays of two or more days. A $30 deposit is required. Sites are $24–35 a night.

Open: Memorial Day–September 15.

Directions: From the junction of U.S. 1 and Highway 24 west of Bath, drive 11 miles south on Highway 24 to the campground.

Contact: Orrs Island Campground, RR 1, P.O. Box 650, Orrs Island, ME 04066, 207/833-5595, website: www.orrsisland.com.

43 HERMIT ISLAND CAMPGROUND

🚶 🏊 🎣 🚐 🎣 🐴 ⛺

Rating: 10

On Hermit Island in Casco Bay

This campground is on a 255-acre private island, where each site has been designed with maximum privacy in mind. Sites have been placed in the woods, in open fields, and directly on the shore of Casco Bay. This is the perfect setting for sailors, boaters, and especially sea kayakers, who can set up a base camp for long journeys among the plentiful islands strewn along this portion of the Maine coast. And don't forget to bring your fishing gear: the campground owns a 50-foot deep-sea fishing boat that sails daily from the on-site wharf in search of cod and giant bluefin tuna. For landlubbers, hiking trails extend through the green forest, along sandy beaches, and across rocky ocean bluffs.

Campsites, facilities: There are 275 tent sites, all without hookups. Trailers and RVs are not allowed, but pickup trucks and small campers are permitted. Flush toilets, hot showers, picnic tables, and fireplaces are provided. Recreational facilities include a boat launch, canoe and rowboat rentals, a recreation room, a pavilion, volleyball, basketball, badminton, and horseshoes. Leashed pets are permitted.

Reservations, fees: Reservations are accepted with full payment. Sites are $29–38 a night.

Open: May 15–Columbus Day.

Directions: From Bath, head south on Highway 209. When you reach the junction of Highways 209 and 216, continue south for four miles on Highway 216 to Hermit Island and the campground.

Contact: Hermit Island Campground, 42 Front Street, Bath, ME 04530, 207/443-2101, website: www.hermitisland.com.

44 OCEAN VIEW PARK CAMPGROUND

🚶 ⛵ 🛶 🚐 🍴 🐕 🚍 ⛺

Rating: 10

Near Popham Beach in Phippsburg

As they say in the real estate business, location is everything, and can you imagine a better location than this? Ocean View Park sits at the very end of the Phippsburg Peninsula, where the land gives way to the open Atlantic, and is situated right next to Popham Beach State Park, widely considered the most at-

tractive sandy beach in Maine. From your campsite, you can soon be swimming in the ocean or fishing for mackerel, bluefish, and striped bass. The campground is close to wildlife refuges, historic forts, and miles of scenic ocean drives. Need we say more?

Campsites, facilities: There are 48 sites for tents and RVs, 11 with full hookups, 31 with water and electric hookups, three with electric hookups only, and three with none. Flush toilets, hot showers, picnic tables, fireplaces, a dump station, and a store are provided. Leashed pets are permitted.

Reservations, fees: Reservations are recommended. Sites are $20–27 a night.

Open: May 10–September 23.

Directions: From the junction of U.S. 1 and Highway 209 in Bath, drive 13 miles south on Highway 209 to the campground.

Contact: Bernadette and Charlie Konzelman, Ocean View Park Campground, Highway 209, Phippsburg, ME 04562, 207/389-2564 or 207/443-1000.

45 GRAY HOMESTEAD OCEAN FRONT

🚶 ⛵ 🛶 🚐 🍴 🐕 🚍 ⛺

Rating: 10

On the island of Southport

Like several other campgrounds mentioned in this guide, a place like Gray Homestead could only be found in New England. Here, along the rockbound coast on your perch above the crashing swells, the salt tang of the sea blends with the scent of evergreens—and you know without a doubt that you are in Maine. Suzanne and Stephen Gray make you feel at home in New England, too, offering to order fresh Maine seafood for you to cook on your fire. And if you want to sample someone else's cooking, there are plenty of fine restaurants and other attractions in nearby Boothbay Harbor.

Campsites, facilities: There are 30 sites for tents and RVs, two with full hookups, 15 with water and electric hookups, and 13 with none. Flush toilets, hot showers, picnic tables, fireplaces, laundry facilities, a dump station, volleyball, basketball, and horseshoes are provided. Campers have access to the ocean and a sandy beach. Leashed pets are permitted.

Reservations, fees: Reservations are recommended June–August. Sites are $18–27 a night.

Open: May 1–October 10.

Directions: From U.S. 1 east of Wiscasset, drive south on Highway 27 to Southport. Take Highway 238 south for two more miles to the campground.

Contact: Suzanne and Stephen Gray, Gray Homestead Ocean Front, 21 Homestead Road, Southport, ME 04576, 207/633-4612, website: www.graysoceancamping.com.

46 SHERWOOD FOREST CAMPSITE

🚶 🚲 🏊 🎣 🚣 ✖ 🐕 🚐 ⛰

Rating: 10

On the ocean in New Harbor

Pemaquid Point is a long, rural peninsula pointing like an arrowhead into the Atlantic Ocean. Sherwood Forest Campsite, which lies on this peninsula, is an attractive campground with an enviable water location. From here, you have access to great saltwater fishing, sea kayaking, birding in the nearby Rachel Carson Salt Pond Preserve, puffin viewing trips out to Egg Rock, excursions to Monhegan Island—where the Wyeth family paints—bicycling on the lightly traveled roads that ring the peninsula, and much more.

Campsites, facilities: There are 80 sites for tents and RVs, 64 with water and electric hookups and 16 with none. Flush toilets, hot showers, picnic tables, fireplaces, laundry facilities, a dump station, and a store are provided. You will also find a swimming pool, canoe rentals, a recreation room, volleyball, basketball, badminton, and horseshoes. Ice and firewood are available. Leashed pets are permitted.

Reservations, fees: Reservations are accepted. Sites are $22–27 a night.

Open: May 15–October 1.

Directions: From Damariscotta, travel south on Highway 130. When you reach the intersection of Highways 130 and 32 in New Harbor, continue .25 mile south on Highway 130 and then head west on Pemaquid Beach Road for .75 mile. Go south from here on Pemaquid Trail for .25 mile to the campground.

Contact: Sherwood Forest Campsite, Pemaquid Trail, P.O. Box 189, New Harbor, ME 04554, 207/677-3642.

47 PEMAQUID POINT CAMPGROUND

🎣 🚐 ✖ 🏊 🚶 🐕 🚐 ⛰

Rating: 8

On Pemaquid Point in New Harbor

Located on beautiful and historic Pemaquid Point, this campground is ideally situated for those looking for all the attractions that the rugged Maine Coast has to offer. Situated near the historic Pemaquid Lighthouse, which was erected in 1827, this campground is also near Fort William Henry, a replica of the 1692 fort that played an important role in the centuries-long struggle between France and Great Britain for control of North America. Also nearby is the Rachel Carson Salt Marsh Preserve, where the famous naturalist and author of *Silent Spring* did much of her research among the granite outcrops, coves, salt ponds, and mixed coastal forests.

Campsites, facilities: There are 50 sites for tents and RVs, several of which offer full hookups. Facilities include flush toilets, hot showers, picnic tables, fireplaces, laundry facilities, a recreation hall, group area, and a modem connection.

Reservations, fees: Reservations are accepted. Sites are $23–33 a night.

Open: May 15–October 15.

Directions: From Damariscotta, travel south on Highway 130 for 14 miles to the campground.

Contact: Pemaquid Point Campground, 1850 Bristol Road, New Harbor, ME 04554, 207/677-2267, website: www.midcoast.com/~ed.

48 POTTER'S PLACE ADULT PARK

Rating: 7

In North Lebanon

Potter's Place provides an especially relaxed, pleasant, and peaceful camping experience in a classic rural New England locale. These spacious sites for adults—no children are permitted—are very well tended and are found in a mix of open and wooded settings. Maintained nature trails, a six-acre spring-fed pond, and floral gardens round out the surroundings. Come prepared to relax: this is one of the most restful campgrounds we visited.

Campsites, facilities: There are 100 RV sites, all with water and electric hookups. Flush toilets, hot showers, picnic tables, fireplaces, free firewood, and a dump station are provided. Recreational facilities include a playground, recreation room, pond, and nature trails. Leashed pets are permitted.

Reservations, fees: Reservations are not necessary. Sites are $21.40.

Open: May 1–October 15.

Directions: From the junction of Highway 109 and U.S. 202/11 in Sanford, drive west on U.S. 202 for six miles to Depot Road in East Lebanon. Turn right on Depot Road, drive two miles north, then turn right on Baker's Grant Road and continue one mile east to the campground.

Contact: Tom and Barbara Potter, Potter's Place Adult Park, RR 2, Box 490, North Lebanon, ME 04027, 207/457-1341, website: www.pottersplacecampground.com.

49 SCOTT'S COVE CAMPING AREA

Rating: 3

On Bunganut Lake in Alfred

A bustling campground, Scott's Cove Camping Area is situated in woods overlooking a freshwater lake. The place is popular with seasonal campers who enjoy fishing and paddling around in boats, and it has a very crowded, urban atmosphere.

Campsites, facilities: There are 50 sites for tents and RVs, two with full hookups and 48 with water and electric hookups. Flush toilets, hot showers, picnic tables, fireplaces, a dump station, and a store are provided. Recreational facilities include a playground, basketball and volleyball courts, horseshoe pits, a lake with a sandy beach, and rowboat, canoe, and paddleboat rentals. Firewood is available. No pets are allowed.

Reservations, fees: Reservations are accepted. Sites are $27–35 a night.

Open: May 1–Columbus Day.

Directions: From the junction of U.S. 202 and Highways 4 and 111 in Alfred, drive 2.5 miles north on U.S. 202/4. Turn right on Brock Road and drive .5 mile east to the campground.

Contact: Brenda and Stew Stoney, Scott's Cove Camping Area, Alfred, ME 04002, 207/324-6594, website: www.scottscovecamping.com.

50 BUNGANUT LAKE CAMPING AREA

Rating: 4

On Bunganut Lake in Alfred

The sites at Bunganut Lake Camping Area are perched on a steep, sloping wooded hillside above a freshwater lake. The grounds are well maintained, and the campground has a spacious, private feel. The lake is a great place to go for a swim or fish for your supper. Kids will enjoy visiting with the animals in the petting zoo, but we thought the cages looked awfully small.

Campsites, facilities: There are 110 sites for tents and RVs, all with water and electric hookups. Flush toilets, hot showers, picnic tables, fireplaces, a dump station, laundry facilities, and a store are provided. Recreational facilities include a playground, recreation room, volleyball, basketball, and horseshoe pits. The maximum RV length is 20 feet. Leashed pets are permitted.

Reservations, fees: Reservations are accepted. Sites are $25–27 a night.

Open: May 1–October 1.

Directions: From the junction of U.S. 202 and Highways 4 and 111 in Alfred, drive 2.5 miles north on U.S.4/202. Turn right on Brock Road and drive 1.5 miles east to Williams Road. Turn right on Williams Road and drive one mile south to the campground.

Contact: Bunganut Lake Camping Area, P.O. Box 141, Alfred, ME 04002, 207/247-3875.

51 KINGS AND QUEENS COURT VACATION RESORT

≈ 🎣 🐕 🚴 🚐 ⛺

Rating: 3

On the Salmon Falls River in South Lebanon

A Disneyland-type feeling pervades this very large RV park situated on the New Hampshire–Maine border, about an hour's drive from the ocean and an hour from the mountains. In fact, there's almost too much going on at Kings and Queens: among the numerous amenities, the park has two heated swimming pools, a giant water slide, four hot tubs, a pond with a sandy beach, and the Salmon Falls River, where you can cast out a fishing line. Wagon rides and arts and crafts are just some of the many scheduled activities to keep campers busy.

Campsites, facilities: There are 450 sites for tents and RVs, 200 with full hookups and 250 with water and electric hookups. Facilities include flush toilets, hot showers, picnic tables, fireplaces, a dump station, laundry facilities, a snack bar, and a store. Recreational facilities include two heated swimming pools, a playground, recreation room, volleyball, basketball, horseshoe pits, a water slide, whirlpool, miniature golf course, and a river and pond for swimming and fishing. Some sites come with cable TV hookups. LP gas and RV supplies are available on-site. Leashed pets are permitted.

Reservations, fees: Sites are $37 a night.

Open: May 17–September 29.

Directions: From the Spaulding Turnpike in Rochester, New Hampshire, take Exit 16 to Highway 16 heading north. Take the second right onto River Road and drive one mile east to the campground.

Contact: Ralph and Elinor Davis, Kings and Queens Court Vacation Resort, Flat Rock Ridge Road, R.F.D. 1, Box 763, East Lebanon, ME 04027, 207/339-9465, website: www.kingsandqueenscamping.com.

52 APACHE CAMPGROUND

≈ 🎣 🐕 🚴 🚐 ⛺

Rating: 4

On Estes Lake in Sanford

Large wooded sites on the shores of Estes Lake are offered at Apache Campground. Bring your fishing gear, because this part of the state is known as southern Maine's lakes region. Twenty-five lakes are sprinkled throughout the area. For a change of pace, or if you'd rather cast for bluefish instead of bass, ocean beaches are a mere 20 minutes away.

Campsites, facilities: There are 150 sites for tents and RVs, 113 with full hookups and 37 with water and electric hookups. Flush toilets, hot showers, picnic tables, fireplaces, a dump station, laundry facilities, and a store are provided. Recreational facilities include a lake with a sandy beach, a playground, recreation room, horseshoe pits, and volleyball, basketball, and bocce ball courts. Leashed pets are permitted.

Reservations, fees: Reservations are accepted and require a deposit of one night's fee. Sites are $24–28 a night.

Open: May 15–October 15.

Directions: From the junction of Highways 109 and 4 in Sanford, drive two miles north on Highway 4 and then 1.5 miles east on New Dam Road to Bernier Road. The campground is .6 mile ahead on the right.

Contact: Gerard and Rita Bernier, Apache Campground, Bernier Road, Sanford, ME 04073, 207/324-5652.

53 SACO/PORTLAND SOUTH KOA

Rating: 3

In Saco

No surprises here. KOA is a nationwide chain, just like McDonald's and Wal-Mart, and campers know what they are going to get. The large commercial facility is situated in 30 acres of woods two miles from the sand beaches, amusements, and souvenir shops of Old Orchard Beach.

Campsites, facilities: There are 120 sites for tents and RVs, 42 with full hookups, 46 with water and electric hookups, and 28 with none. Flush toilets, free hot showers, picnic tables, fireplaces, a dump station, laundry facilities, and a store are provided, as are a pool, playground, recreation room, volleyball, basketball, and horseshoe pits. LP gas is available. Leashed pets are permitted.

Reservations, fees: Reservations are recommended. Sites are $25–35 a night.
Open: May 9–October 17.
Directions: From the Maine Turnpike/I-95, take Exit 5 to I-195. After driving a short distance, take Exit 2B and continue north on U.S. 1 for 1.6 miles to the campground on the left.
Contact: Saco/Portland South KOA, 814A Portland Road, Saco, ME 04072, 207/282-0502 or 800/KOA-1886, website: /www.koa.com/where.

54 CASCADIA PARK CAMPGROUND

Rating: 3

In Saco

Although it has an unenviable location along a busy highway, Cascadia is still close to some very worthwhile places to visit. The Scarborough Marsh Nature Center in Scarborough and the Biddeford Pool tidal basin to the south, as well as several other nature preserves along the southern Maine coast, are all within easy reach. Old Orchard Beach, with its seven-mile-long sandy beachfront and associated shops and amusements, is just minutes away by car.

Campsites, facilities: There are 100 sites for tents and RVs, 47 with full hookups, 26 with water and electric hookups, and 27 with none. Flush toilets, hot showers, picnic tables, fireplaces, laundry facilities, and a dump station are provided. Volleyball and badminton nets are also available. Leashed pets are permitted.
Reservations, fees: Reservations are accepted. Sites are $19–23 a night.
Open: May 1–October 30.
Directions: From the Maine Turnpike/I-95, take Exit 5 to I-195. After driving a short distance, take Exit 2B and continue north on U.S. 1 for 2.5 miles to the campground.
Contact: Cascadia Park Campground, 911 Portland Road, U.S. 1, Saco, ME 04072, 207/282-1666.

55 BAYLEY'S CAMPING RESORT

Rating: 3

In Scarborough

Bayley's is a very large, private campground that's close to all the attractions of Old Orchard Beach and Maine's southern coast. Although virtually every camper spends much of the time at the seashore, the resort does offer enough activities to keep a family busy for weeks. The wide variety of water-related recreation options includes swimming pools, spas, trout ponds, and paddleboat ponds. An extensive activities program—from fishing derbies and wagon rides to soccer games and bike rodeos—is organized for children and adults alike. When you tire of the crowds, be sure to check out the nearby Scarborough Marsh Nature Center and Prouts Neck Bird Sanctuary.
Campsites, facilities: There are 470 sites for tents and RVs, 250 with full hookups, 100 with water and electric hookups, 40 with electric hookups only, and 80 with none. Flush toilets, free hot showers, wheelchair-accessible

restrooms, picnic tables, fireplaces, a dump station, laundry facilities, and a store are provided. Recreational facilities include a playground, recreation room, three pools, a stocked fishing pond, miniature golf, volleyball, basketball, and horseshoe pits. Ice, firewood, groceries, LP gas, and RV supplies are available. Leashed pets are permitted.

Reservations, fees: Reservations are accepted. A deposit of $150 is required, and reservations for four days and under must be paid in full. Sites are $20.50–48 a night.

Open: May 1–Columbus Day.

Directions: From the Maine Turnpike/I-95 in Scarborough, take Exit 6 and drive 1.5 miles south on U.S. 1 to Highway 9. Turn left on Highway 9 and drive three miles east to Pine Point. In Pine Point, follow the signs to the campground.

Contact: Bayley's Camping Resort, Box T-6, Ross Road, West Scarborough, ME 04074, 207/883-6043, website: www.bayleys-camping.com.

56 OLD ORCHARD BEACH CAMPGROUND

Rating: 3

In Old Orchard Beach

For those who want their fun prepackaged and in large doses, Old Orchard Beach is like heaven on earth. If you fit that description, this campground is bound to please. Take a shuttle bus from the campground and be sure to check out such tourist attractions as Funtown (an amusement park), Aquaboggan (a water slide), the Maine Mall, harness and stock-car racing tracks, and hundreds of T-shirt shops. For more information on the Old Orchard Beach area, see the Acorn Village listing in this chapter.

Campsites, facilities: There are 400 sites for tents and RVs, many with full hookups. Flush toilets, hot showers, picnic tables, fireplaces, a dump station, and laundry facilities are provided. Recreational facilities include a pool with a water slide, a playground, recreation

room, volleyball, basketball, and horseshoe pits. Leashed pets are permitted.

Reservations, fees: Reservations are recommended. Sites are $29–36 a night.

Open: May 1–Columbus Day.

Directions: From the Maine Turnpike/I-95 near Saco, take Exit 5 and drive east on I-195 for 2.5 miles. Turn left on Highway 5 and travel 100 feet east to the campground.

Contact: The Daigle Family, Old Orchard Beach Campground, Ocean Park Road, Old Orchard Beach, ME 04064, 207/934-4477, website: www.gocamping.com.

57 WAGON WHEEL CAMPGROUND AND CABINS

Rating: 3

In Old Orchard Beach

This large, popular trailer and RV park lies within two miles of the sandy beaches, rides, and amusements of Old Orchard Beach. For more information on the Old Orchard Beach area, see the Acorn Village listing in this chapter.

Campsites, facilities: There are 400 sites for tents and RVs, many with full hookups. Flush toilets, hot showers, picnic tables, fireplaces, a dump station, laundry facilities, and a store are provided. Two swimming pools, a playground, recreation room, volleyball, basketball, and horseshoe pits are among the recreational offerings. A shuttle bus service runs to the beach. Ice and firewood are available. Leashed pets are permitted.

Reservations, fees: Reservations are accepted. Sites range from $33–36 a night. Weekly and off-season rates also are available.

Open: May 1–Columbus Day.

Directions: From the Maine Turnpike/I-95 near Saco, take Exit 5 and drive about 2.5 miles east on I-195. Turn left on Highway 5, travel .25 mile east, then turn right and drive another .25 mile south on Saco Road to the campground entrance.

Contact: Wagon Wheel Campground and Cabins, 3 Old Orchard Road, Old Orchard Beach, ME 04064, 207/934-2160, website: www.go-camping.com.

58 VIRGINIA TENT AND TRAILER PARK

🏊 🎣 🚤 🏕️ 🚐 ⛺

Rating: 3

Near Old Orchard Beach

Yet another option in bustling downtown Old Orchard Beach, this campground offers a quiet, open setting with shaded sites. It's just half a mile from the area's sandy beaches. For more information on the area, see the Acorn Village listing in this chapter.

Campsites, facilities: There are 135 sites for tents and RVs, 48 with full hookups, 50 with water and electric hookups, and 37 with none. Flush toilets, hot showers, picnic tables, fireplaces, a dump station, laundry facilities, and a store are provided. Recreational facilities include a swimming pool, playground, and shuffleboard courts on the property. Leashed pets are permitted.

Reservations, fees: Reservations are accepted and require a $25 deposit. Sites are $30–37 a night.

Open: Memorial Day–September 24.

Directions: From the Maine Turnpike/I-95 near Saco, take Exit 5 and drive 2.5 miles east on I-195. Turn left on Highway 5, travel .5 mile east, then turn right on Temple Avenue and drive .5 mile south to the campground.

Contact: Virginia Tent and Trailer Park, P.O. Box 242, Temple Avenue, Old Orchard Beach, ME 04064, 207/934-479, website: www.virginiaparkcampground.com.

59 WILD ACRES FAMILY CAMPING RESORT

🏊 🎣 🚤 🐕 🏕️ 🚐 ⛺

Rating: 3

In Old Orchard Beach

Established in 1929, this is Old Orchard Beach's most venerable trailer park. The campground is located close to miles of sand beaches, amusement park rides, boating and deep-sea fishing excursions, restaurants, and shops. For more information on the Old Orchard Beach area, see the Acorn Village listing in this chapter.

Campsites, facilities: There are 485 sites for tents and RVs, 303 with full hookups, 152 with water and electric hookups, and 30 with none. Facilities include flush toilets, hot showers, picnic tables, fireplaces, a dump station, laundry facilities, and a store. Recreational facilities include two swimming pools, three whirlpools, a playground, adult recreation room, game room, tennis, volleyball, basketball, horseshoe pits, nature trail, and a stocked fishing pond. Leashed pets are permitted.

Reservations, fees: Reservations are accepted. Sites are $29–38 a night.

Open: May 15–Labor Day.

Directions: From the Maine Turnpike/I-95 near Saco, take Exit 5 and drive 2.5 miles east on I-195. Turn left on Highway 5 and travel .75 mile east to the campground.

Contact: Dick and Marion Ahearn, Wild Acres Family Camping Resort, 179 Saco Avenue, Old Orchard Beach, ME 04064, 207/934-2535, website: www.mainecamping.com.

60 NE'RE BEACH FAMILY CAMPGROUND

🏊 🐕 🚐 ⛺

Rating: 3

In Old Orchard Beach

Here's yet another option for those looking to camp near the sandy beaches and amusements of Old Orchard Beach. Sites are grassy and shaded by trees. For more information on the Old Orchard Beach area, see the Acorn Village listing in this chapter.

Campsites, facilities: There are 60 sites for tents and RVs, 13 with full hookups and 47 with water and electric hookups. Flush toilets, free hot showers, picnic tables, fireplaces, a dump station, laundry facilities, and a store are provided. There are sandy ocean beaches nearby and a pool on the property. Leashed pets are permitted.

Reservations, fees: Reservations are recommended July 1–Labor Day. A deposit of $20 is required. Sites are $23–27 a night.

Open: May 15–September 8.

Directions: From the Maine Turnpike/I-95 near Saco, take Exit 5, drive 2.5 miles east on I-195, then turn left on Highway 5 and go 1.75 miles east to the campground.

Contact: Phil and Michelle Boisjoly, Ne're Beach Family Campground, P.O. Box 537, 38 Saco Avenue/Highway 5, Old Orchard Beach, ME 04064, 207/934-7614.

61 PARADISE PARK RESORT CAMPGROUND

Rating: 3

In Old Orchard Beach

A large spring-fed pond is on the 40-acre grounds of this wooded campground for families (no campers traveling alone are allowed). Park your car and leave it until you are ready to depart: Paradise Park claims to be the area's closest campground to the beach and is only 800 feet from downtown with its boardwalk, pier, amusement park, and other attractions. For more information on the Old Orchard Beach area, see the next listing for Acorn Village.

Campsites, facilities: There are 200 sites for tents and RVs, 50 with full hookups, 100 with water and electric hookups, and 50 with none. Flush toilets, hot showers, picnic tables, fireplaces, a dump station, laundry facilities, and a store are provided. Recreational facilities include a swimming pool, playground, recreation room, volleyball, basketball, horseshoe pits, paddleboat rentals, and pond and saltwater fishing and swimming. Leashed pets are permitted.

Reservations, fees: Reservations are recommended. Sites range from $28–38 a night.

Open: Memorial Day–September 15.

Directions: From the Maine Turnpike/I-95 near Saco, take Exit 5 and drive 2.5 miles east on I-195. Take Highway 5 east for 4.2 miles, then turn left on Adelaide Road and continue .25 mile north to the campground entrance at the end of the road.

Contact: Paradise Park Resort Campground, P.O. Box 4, Adelaide Road, Old Orchard Beach, ME 04064, 207/934-4633, website: www.paradiseparkresort.com.

62 ACORN VILLAGE

Rating: 3

In Old Orchard Beach

While there are nearly 3,500 miles of shoreline in Maine, sandy beachfront covers fewer than 100 miles. Most of these beaches are found south of Portland and are open to the public. The silvery, sandy beaches of the South Coast stretch for miles and are very popular with locals and travelers, as well as French-Canadian visitors. (You are likely to hear French being spoken wherever you go in this area.) Old Orchard Beach is a resort town with a varied assortment of tacky tourist traps and an amusement park. The highlight of the area is the seven-mile-long white sand beach. Acorn Village, located within the town of Old Orchard Beach, is a cottage village and campground within walking distance of the beach, pier, and amusements.

Campsites, facilities: There are 75 sites for tents and RVs with full, partial, and no hookups. Twenty heated cottages are also available. Flush toilets, hot showers, picnic tables, fireplaces, a dump station, laundry facilities, and a pool are provided. No pets are allowed.

Reservations, fees: Reservations are accepted. Sites are $25–35 a night.

Open: Memorial Day–Labor Day.

Directions: From the Maine Turnpike/I-95 near Saco, take Exit 5 onto I-195 and then onto Highway 5. Follow Highway 5 east into the town of Old Orchard Beach. Make a quick left, then a quick right onto Walnut Street, and continue to the campground.

Contact: Lionel and Cynthia Bisson, Acorn

Village, 42 Walnut Street, Old Orchard Beach, ME 04064, 207/934-4154.

63 HID'N PINES CAMPGROUND

Rating: 3

In Old Orchard Beach

True to its name, Hid'n Pines is located on 25 acres of pine trees and apple orchards and is within easy walking distance of Old Orchard Beach's famous and very popular seven-mile-long sandy ocean beach. For more information on the Old Orchard Beach area, see the previous listing for Acorn Village.

Campsites, facilities: There are 260 sites for tents and RVs, many with full hookups. Flush toilets, free hot showers, picnic tables, fireplaces, a dump station, laundry facilities, and a store are provided. Recreational facilities include a heated pool, playground, recreation room, and a basketball hoop. Leashed pets are permitted.

Reservations, fees: Reservations are recommended and require a deposit of $30. There is a three-night minimum stay on holidays. Sites are $28–37 a night.

Open: May 15–September 15.

Directions: From the Maine Turnpike/I-95 near Saco, take Exit 5, drive 2.5 miles east on I-195, and then go two miles east on Highway 5. From the junction of Highways 5 and 98, drive 1.5 miles north on Highway 98 to the campground.

Contact: Larry and Lori Owen, Hid'n Pines Campground, 8 Cascade Road, P.O. Box 647, Old Orchard Beach, ME 04064, 207/934-2352, website: www.mainerec.com/hidnpines.

64 POWDER HORN FAMILY CAMPING

Rating: 3

In Old Orchard Beach

Set on 80 acres of pine groves and open fields, Powder Horn Family Camping is another of the large private campgrounds found near the sandy beaches, amusements, and souvenir shops of Old Orchard Beach. You can cool off in the pool, unwind in the hot tub, or putter around the 18-hole miniature golf course. For more information on the Old Orchard Beach area, see the Acorn Village listing in this chapter.

Campsites, facilities: There are 458 RV sites, 217 with full hookups, 104 with water and electric hookups, and 137 with none. Flush toilets, free hot showers, picnic tables, fireplaces, a dump station, laundry facilities, and a store are provided. Recreational facilities include nearby sand beaches, three pools, a hot tub, playground, recreation room, volleyball, basketball, badminton, shuffleboard, miniature golf, and horseshoe pits. Leashed pets are permitted.

Reservations, fees: Reservations are recommended on busy weekends. Sites are $29–45 a night.

Open: Memorial Day–Labor Day.

Directions: From the Maine Turnpike/I-95 near Saco, take Exit 5 to U.S. 1. Drive north on U.S. 1 to Highway 98. Turn right and drive 1.8 miles to the campground on the left.

Contact: David and Glenna Ahearn, Powder Horn Family Camping, P.O. Box 366, Highway 98, Old Orchard Beach, ME 04064, 207/934-4733, website: www.mainecampgrounds. com.

65 YANKEELAND CAMPGROUND

Rating: 2

Near Kennebunk

Many permanent summer retirement homes have been established in this large campground set on a flat, sandy plain in an unspectacular second-growth forest. Beaches and the other wonderful area attractions are approximately 20 minutes away by car.

Campsites, facilities: There are 200 sites for

tents and RVs with full, partial, and no hookups. Flush toilets, hot showers, picnic tables, fireplaces, a dump station, laundry facilities, and a store are provided. Recreational facilities include a playground, pool, recreation room, basketball, and horseshoe pits. Leashed pets are permitted.

Reservations, fees: Reservations are recommended and require a deposit of one day's fee. Sites are $20–30 a night.

Open: May 1–Columbus Day.

Directions: From the Maine Turnpike/I-95 near Kennebunk, take Exit 3 and drive 2.7 miles west on Alfred Road to the campground.

Contact: The Robinson Family, Yankeeland Campground, P.O. Box 829, Kennebunk, ME 04043, 207/985-7576 or 800/832-7059.

66 MOUSAM RIVER CAMPGROUND

🏊 🛶 🚙 🐕 🚐

Rating: 2

Near Kennebunk

A meandering river flows by the large wooded sites here. However, like several other nearby campgrounds, this place is not too attractive, as it's surrounded by a stunted, second-growth forest in a semirural area. Mousam River is also pretty far removed from all the great regional attractions and is some 20 minutes by car from Maine's attractive sand beaches.

Campsites, facilities: There are 115 sites for RVs with full hookups. Flush toilets, hot showers, picnic tables, fireplaces, laundry facilities, a dump station, and a store are provided. A swimming pool, recreation room, pavilion, badminton nets, and horseshoes are also on the grounds. Leashed pets are permitted.

Reservations, fees: Reservations are accepted. Sites are $28 a night.

Open: May 15–October 15.

Directions: From the intersection of U.S. 1 and Highway 35, drive two miles north on Highway 35 to an overpass on the Maine Turnpike/I-95. At the fork after the overpass, go straight onto Alfred Road and continue 1.5 miles north to the campground.

Contact: Mousam River Campground, West Kennebunk, ME 04094, 207/985-2507.

67 FRAN-MORT CAMPGROUND

🏊 🛶 🚙 🏕 🐕 🚹 🚐 ⛺

Rating: 5

In Kennebunkport

Fran-Mort is a large, open-field campground situated near beaches, picturesque coastal villages, and shops. The curious may opt for a drive along the shore past nearby Walkers Point, site of former president George Bush Sr.'s summer home, which you can glimpse from a scenic turnout on the road.

Campsites, facilities: There are 130 sites for tents and RVs, 90 with full hookups and 40 with water and electric hookups. Flush toilets, hot showers, picnic tables, fireplaces, a dump station, laundry facilities, and a playground are provided. Leashed pets are permitted.

Reservations, fees: Reservations are accepted. Sites are $25 a night.

Open: May 30–October 12.

Directions: From the junction of U.S. 1 and Highway 9A/35 in Kennebunk, drive north on U.S. 1 for about 1.25 miles. Turn right on Log Cabin Road, travel approximately one mile to the intersection with Sinnott Road, turn right, and continue to the campground.

Contact: Morrell Swain, Fran-Mort Campground, Sinnott Road, Kennebunkport, ME 04046, 207/967-4927.

68 SHAMROCK RV PARK

🏊 🛶 🚙 🏕 🐕 🚹 🚐 ⛺

Rating: 6

Near Biddeford

Offering quiet and secluded sites, Shamrock RV Park is a wooded campground situated in a rural area near some of the finest scenery along Maine's South Coast. Be sure to visit

Biddeford Pool, Fortunes Rocks Beach, and Goose Rocks Beach, and drive along the shore road to Cape Porpoise and Kennebunkport. In Kennebunkport Harbor, you can charter a deep-sea fishing boat or head out to open waters to look for whales.

Campsites, facilities: There are 60 sites for tents and RVs, 25 with full hookups, 19 with water and electric hookups, and 16 with none. Flush toilets, free hot showers, a dump station, picnic tables, and fireplaces are provided. Recreational facilities include a swimming pool, playground, recreation room, and fishing pond. Leashed pets are permitted.

Reservations, fees: Reservations are recommended. Sites are $25–35 a night.

Open: May 30–October 1.

Directions: From the intersection of Highway 111, U.S. 1, and West Street in downtown Biddeford, drive 4.5 miles east on West Street to the campground.

Contact: Irene Lamarche, Shamrock RV Park, 391 West Street, Biddeford, ME 04005, 207/284-4282, website: www.shamrockrvpark.com.

69 SALTY ACRES CAMPGROUND

Rating: 6

Near the ocean in Kennebunkport

One of southern Maine's prettiest, and possibly the most overlooked, stretches of coastline is home to Salty Acres, a very large full-service campground. Stay here and you are near Walkers Point, the summer home of former president George Bush Sr., and within minutes of both downtown Kennebunkport, with its shops and restaurants, and Kennebunkport Harbor, where you can join fishing charters or go on a boating excursion. There are fine opportunities for ocean swimming, fishing, and boating close by at Goose Rocks Beach and Fortunes Rocks Beach. Bicyclists find the lightly traveled roads in the area are good for riding.

Campsites, facilities: There are 400 sites for tents and RVs, 70 with full hookups, 90 with water and electric hookups, and 240 with none. Flush toilets, hot showers, picnic tables, fireplaces, laundry facilities, a dump station, and a store are provided on the grounds. Recreational facilities include a swimming pool, playground, sports field, volleyball and badminton nets, horseshoes, and access to the ocean and a river for fishing, boating, and swimming. Leashed pets are permitted.

Reservations, fees: Reservations are accepted. Sites are $22–32 a night.

Open: May 15–October 15.

Directions: From the junction of Highways 9A/35 and 9, drive five miles east on Highway 9 to the campground.

Contact: Priscilla Spang, Salty Acres Campground, Highway 9, 277 Mills Road, Kennebunkport, ME 04046, 207/967-2483.

70 BEAVER DAM CAMPGROUND

Rating: 4

On a small pond in Berwick

Beaver Dam is a pleasant little campground with sites spread out on 40 partially wooded acres. Kids will enjoy going for a hayride, just one of the camp's planned activities. There is a 20-acre pond for fishing and swimming, and, yes, beavers do live in the pond and streams here. Maine's beaches lie just half an hour's drive to the south, while the White Mountains of New Hampshire are only an hour away to the northwest.

Campsites, facilities: There are 60 sites for tents and RVs, 59 with water and electric hookups and one with none. Flush toilets, hot showers, picnic tables, fireplaces, a dump station, and a store are provided. Recreational facilities include a brook, fishing pond, sandy beach, playground, recreation room, paddleboat and canoe rentals, volleyball, basketball, horseshoe pits, and miniature golf. Leashed pets are permitted.

Reservations, fees: Reservations are accepted. Sites are $24–34 a night.

Open: May 15–September 30.

Directions: From the junction of Highways 236 and 9 in Berwick, drive five miles east on Highway 9 to the campground.

Contact: Larry and Letty Erwin, Beaver Dam Campground, 551 Highway 9, Berwick, ME 03901, 207/698-1985, website: www.beaverdamcampground.com.

71 KENNEBUNKPORT CAMPING

Rating: 6

Near the coast in Kennebunkport

There's plenty to do when you camp in Kennebunkport. Hit the beach, hop on a boat for a whale-watching or deep-sea fishing trip, poke around the picturesque villages of Kennebunkport and Cape Porpoise, and visit natural areas such as the Rachel Carson National Wildlife Refuge in nearby Wells. The campground is located close to former president George Bush Sr.'s summer home, which is visible from a turnout along the road.

Campsites, facilities: There are 82 sites for tents and RVs, 33 with full hookups, 26 with water and electric hookups, and 23 with none. Flush toilets, free hot showers, picnic tables, fireplaces, a dump station, and a store are provided. Recreational facilities include a play area, horseshoes, badminton, and volleyball. Ice and firewood are available. Leashed pets are permitted.

Reservations, fees: Reservations are accepted and require a deposit of one night's fee. Sites are $18–27 a night.

Open: May 15–October 15.

Directions: From the intersection of Highways 9A/35 and 9, drive two miles east on Highway 9, then turn left and drive .1 mile north on Old Cape Road to the campground.

Contact: The Roberge Family, Kennebunkport Camping, 117 Old Cape Road, Kennebunkport, ME 04046, 207/967-2732 or fax 207/967-3519.

72 BEACH ACRES

Rating: 3

On U.S. 1 in Wells

A large campground, Beach Acres is within walking distance of sandy ocean beaches that stretch for some nine miles. The resort town of Wells, where the campground is located, boasts plenty of antique stores and factory outlets. For those who want to escape the hectic pace of town and nearby U.S. 1, the Rachel Carson National Wildlife Refuge offers peace and quiet. This woodland retreat overlooks a salt marsh, tidal channels, and an estuary, and has a boardwalk that winds throughout the area. The Wells National Estuarine Research Reserve at Laudholm Farm is another great getaway. With seven miles of trails meandering through 1,600 acres of fields, woods, wetlands, and barrier beaches, the reserve is worth a visit.

Campsites, facilities: There are 400 sites for tents and RVs, most with full hookups and some with no hookups. Flush toilets, hot showers, picnic tables, fireplaces, a dump station, laundry facilities, and a store are provided. Recreational facilities include a swimming pool, playground, recreation room, shuffleboard, and a basketball hoop. Ice and firewood are available. No pets are allowed.

Reservations, fees: Reservations are recommended. Sites are $25–32 a night.

Open: Memorial Day–Labor Day.

Directions: From the Maine Turnpike/I-95 near Wells, take Exit 2 and drive 1.5 miles east on Highway 9/109. Turn right on U.S. 1 and travel two miles south to Eldridge Road. Turn left on Eldridge Road and drive one block east to the campground.

Contact: Marc and Sandy Batchelder, Beach Acres, 563 Post Road, Wells, ME 04090, 207/646-5612, website: www.beachacres.com.

73 OCEAN OVERLOOK

Rating: 3

On U.S. 1 in Wells

Ocean Overlook is one of several options for those who are looking for a place to set up camp near the popular sand beaches in Wells and Ogunquit. This facility has spacious, grassy sites set back from busy U.S. 1. While in Wells, check out the nearby Rachel Carson National Wildlife Refuge and the Webhannet River Marsh natural area. For more information on the Wells area, see the previous listing for Beach Acres.

Campsites, facilities: There are 50 sites for tents and RVs, most with full hookups. Flush toilets, hot showers, picnic tables, fireplaces, and a dump station are provided. Also on the grounds are two pools, a playground, recreation fields, and badminton and volleyball nets. Beaches are nearby. No pets are allowed.

Reservations, fees: Reservations are recommended. Weekly rentals require a deposit of $50. Sites are $28–30 a night.

Open: May 15–Columbus Day.

Directions: From the Maine Turnpike/I-95 near Wells, take Exit 2 and drive 1.5 miles east on Highway 9/109. Turn right on U.S. 1 and travel 1.5 miles south to the campground on the right.

Contact: The Martinez Family, Ocean Overlook, U.S. 1, P.O. Box 309, Wells, ME 04090, 207/646-3075.

74 WELLS BEACH RESORT

Rating: 3

On U.S. 1 in Wells

Wells Beach Resort is a popular commercial campground located on a major highway just one mile from the sandy beaches of Wells. Very clean and well maintained, the park is also close to deep-sea fishing and whale-watching excursion boats, summer playhouses, factory outlets, amusement parks, and wildlife refuges.

For more information on the Wells area, see the Beach Acres listing in this chapter.

Campsites, facilities: There are 215 sites for tents and RVs, 200 with full hookups and 15 with none. Cable TV hookups are available. Flush toilets, hot showers, tables, fireplaces, a dump station, laundry facilities, and a store are provided. Recreational facilities include a swimming pool, two playgrounds, a recreation room, fitness room, miniature golf, volleyball, basketball, and horseshoe pits. Leashed pets are permitted.

Reservations, fees: Reservations are accepted. A deposit of $50 is required for stays of three days or fewer, and a deposit of $100 is required for stays of four or more days. Sites are $28–52 a night.

Open: May 15–October 15.

Directions: From the Maine Turnpike/I-95 near Wells, take Exit 2 and drive 1.5 miles east on Highway 9/109. Turn right on U.S. 1 and travel 1.25 miles south to the campground on the right.

Contact: Ken and Shirley Griffen, Wells Beach Resort, 1000 Post Road, U.S. 1, Wells, ME 04090, 207/646-7570 or 800/640-CAMP (800/640-2267), website: www.wellsbeach.com.

75 OCEAN VIEW COTTAGES AND CAMPGROUND

Rating: 3

Near the beach in Wells

As the name suggests, this campground, which is situated above the Webhannet River Marsh natural area and two miles from sandy beaches, affords an ocean view. But not all the senses are pampered here, for the place is also just off busy, noisy U.S. 1. For more information on the Wells area, see the Beach Acres listing in this chapter.

Campsites, facilities: There are 108 sites for tents and RVs, 60 with full electric hookups, 35 with water and electric hookups, and 13 with none. Flush toilets, hot showers, picnic tables, fireplaces, a dump station, laundry facilities, and a store are provided. Recreational facilities include a pool, playground, recreation room, shuffleboard, and basketball and tennis courts. Leashed pets are permitted.

Reservations, fees: Reservations are recommended and must be for at least four nights in July and August. A deposit of $20 is required for stays of under a week; for a week or longer, it's $40. Sites are $28–30 a night.

Open: May 1–Columbus Day.

Directions: From the junction of U.S. 1 and Highway 9 in Wells, drive north on U.S. 1 for .1 mile. Turn right at the fire station and drive .25 mile east on Lower Landing Road to the campground.

Contact: Ocean View Cottages and Campground, P.O. Box 153, 84 Harbor Road, Wells, ME 04090, 207/646-3308, website: http://home.comcast.net/~oceanviewcampground.

76 SEA-VU CAMPGROUND

Rating: 3

Near the beach in Wells

Sea-Vu is another large, crowded campground situated to the side of a busy highway in a semi-wooded location close to sand beaches. The campground overlooks the salt marshes of Wells Harbor and is within five miles of Ogunquit and Kennebunkport. Nearby activities include deep-sea fishing and whale-watching excursions, hiking or canoeing in wildlife refuges, and strolling through picturesque villages. For more information on the Wells area, see the Beach Acres listing in this chapter.

Campsites, facilities: There are 225 sites for tents and RVs, 218 with full hookups, 36 with water and electric hookups, and seven with none. Flush toilets, hot showers, picnic tables, fireplaces, a dump station, laundry facilities, and a store are provided. Recreational facilities include a pool, playground, sports field, recreation room, library, aerobics classes, miniature golf, volleyball and basketball courts, and horseshoe pits. LP gas is available. Leashed pets are permitted.

Reservations, fees: Reservations are recommended. Sites are $33–50 a night.

Open: May 15–Columbus Day.

Directions: From the Maine Turnpike/I-95 near Wells, take Exit 2 and drive 1.5 miles east on Highway 9/109. Turn left and drive .5 mile north on U.S. 1 to the campground on the right.

Contact: Sea-Vu Campground, U.S. 1, P.O. Box 67, Wells, ME 04090, 207/646-7732, website: www.sea-vucampground.com.

77 GREGOIRE'S CAMPGROUND

Rating: 3

In Wells

Providing campsites in an open field setting, Gregoire's Campground is located within a short drive of sandy beaches. Also nearby is the Ogunquit Playhouse, one of the country's best summer-stock theaters. For more information on the Wells area, see the Beach Acres listing in this chapter.

Campsites, facilities: There are 130 RV sites, 31 with full hookups, 62 with water and electric hookups, and 37 with none. Flush toilets, hot showers, picnic tables, fireplaces, a dump station, laundry facilities, and a store are provided. A playground and a recreation room are also available. Leashed pets are permitted.

Reservations, fees: Reservations are accepted. Sites are $18–25 a night.

Open: May 15–September 15.

Directions: From the Maine Turnpike/I-95 in Wells, take Exit 2 and continue 100 yards north on Highway 109 to the campground.

Contact: Albert and Virginia Gregoire, Gregoire's Campground, Highway 109, Wells, ME 04090, 207/646-3711.

78 SEA BREEZE CAMPGROUND

Rating: 3

On U.S. 1 in Wells

Sea Breeze is a small campground located in a wooded area off busy U.S. 1 within minutes of sandy beaches, wildlife refuges, summerstock theaters, deep-sea fishing and whale-watching operators, and picturesque villages. For more information on the Wells area, see the Beach Acres listing in this chapter.

Campsites, facilities: There are 58 sites for tents and RVs, most with full hookups. Flush toilets, hot showers, picnic tables, fireplaces, a dump station, laundry facilities, and a store are provided. A heated swimming pool, playground, and recreation room are also on the property. Cable TV hookups are available. Leashed pets are permitted.

Reservations, fees: Reservations are recommended. A 50 percent deposit for weeklong stays and a full deposit for shorter stays is required. Sites range from $20–37 a night.

Open: May 15–Columbus Day.

Directions: From the Maine Turnpike/I-95 near Wells, take Exit 2 and drive 1.5 miles east on Highway 9/109. Turn left on U.S. 1 and drive 1.3 miles north to the campground.

Contact: Sea Breeze Campground, 2073 Post Road, Wells, ME 04090, 207/646-4301 or fax 207/646-4803.

79 STADIG CAMPGROUND

Rating: 3

Just off the U.S. 1 bypass in Wells

This campground is nestled in the woods off a busy highway and puts campers within a short drive of sandy beaches, deep-sea fishing and whale-watching excursions, summer theater playhouses, shops, and villages.

Campsites, facilities: There are 150 sites for tents and RVs, 37 with full hookups, five with water and electric hookups, 11 with electric hookups, and 97 with none. Flush toilets, hot showers, picnic tables, fireplaces, a dump station, laundry facilities, and a store are provided. You will also find a playground, recreation room, volleyball, basketball, shuffleboard, and horseshoe pits. No pets are allowed.

Reservations, fees: Reservations are accepted. Sites are $18–26 a night.

Open: May 30–October 1.

Directions: From the Maine Turnpike/I-95 near Wells, take Exit 2 to U.S. 1 and drive two miles north to the intersection with the U.S. 1 bypass. Drive .25 mile north on the U.S. 1 bypass to the campground.

Contact: Stadig Campground, R.F.D. 2, Box 850, Wells, ME 04090, 207/646-2298, website: www.stadig.com.

80 INDIAN RIVERS CAMPGROUND

Rating: 3

On the Piscataqua River in Eliot

This campground is set in the woods alongside a tidal stream within a short drive of the Maine and New Hampshire beaches. Bring your fishing gear and cast for bluefish or striped bass in the Piscataqua and Cocheco Rivers, or swim in the saltwater. There's no drop-off, so it's safe for children, and there is a sandy beach for sunbathing.

Campsites, facilities: There are 35 sites for tents and RVs, with full hookups available. Each site has a picnic table and fireplace. Flush toilets, hot showers, and a dump station are provided. Recreational facilities include a heated indoor swimming pool, playground, recreation room, horseshoe pits, sandy beach, canoe rentals, and a swimming float. The maximum length for trailers is 30 feet. Leashed pets are permitted.

Reservations, fees: Reservations are accepted. Sites are $20–27 a night, plus 50 cents for pets.

Open: May 1–November 1.

Directions: From I-95 in Kittery, take Exit 3

and travel seven miles north on Highway 236. Turn left on Highway 101 and drive .25 mile west to the campground.

Contact: Lloyd and Philice Burt, Indian Rivers Campground, Highway 101, Eliot, ME 03903, 207/748-0844.

81 PINEDEROSA CAMPING AREA

Rating: 4

Near Ogunquit

Family-owned Pinederosa is a wooded, riverside campground that enjoys a semirural setting. Private wooded sites are available in addition to those set in open fields. The campground is within a few minutes' drive of ocean beaches, summer theater, fine restaurants, and nature preserves. For more information on attractions in the Wells and Ogunquit area, see the Beach Acres listing in this chapter.

Campsites, facilities: There are 152 sites for tents and RVs, some with full hookups and others with water and electric. Flush toilets, hot showers, picnic tables, fireplaces, a dump station, laundry facilities, a swimming pool, and a store are provided. Sand beaches, natural areas, and deep-sea fishing boats are accessible nearby. Leashed pets are permitted.

Reservations, fees: Reservations are accepted. Sites are $21–27 a night.

Open: May 15–October 1.

Directions: From Ogunquit, drive one mile north on U.S. 1. Turn left on Captain Thomas Road and drive 1.5 miles west to the campground.

Contact: Barbara Stevens, Pinederosa Camping Area, RR 1, Box 1330, Wells, ME 04090, 207/646-2492, website: www.pinederosa.com.

82 DIXON'S CAMPGROUND

Rating: 4

Between Ogunquit and York

Another medium-sized campground in the York Beach area, this one caters to tenters and people with small campers and trailers. Stay here and you are close to beaches, restaurants, nature preserves, and summer theater. Bring your camera to photograph the Nubble Light, a lighthouse built in 1879 on a high rocky island.

Campsites, facilities: There are 100 sites for tents and RVs, 22 with water and electric hookups and 78 with no hookups. Flush toilets, metered hot showers, picnic tables, fireplaces, a dump station, store, and playground are provided. Ice is available. Campers have easy access to saltwater swimming, boating, and fishing. The maximum RV length is 30 feet. No pets are allowed.

Reservations, fees: Reservations are accepted for stays of three nights or more. If staying less than one week, the reservation must be paid in full. Sites are $26–30 a night.

Open: Memorial Day–September 15.

Directions: From the village of Ogunquit, drive two miles south on U.S. 1 to the campground.

Contact: Dixon's Campground, 1740 U.S. 1, Cape Neddick, ME 03902, 207/363-2131, website: www.dixonscampground.com.

83 CAPE NEDDICK OCEANSIDE CAMPGROUND

Rating: 4

On the oceanfront and along the Cape Neddick River

Tenters and those traveling with small self-contained campers or trailers will find that their needs are catered to at this campground. Many sites are located directly on the oceanfront and along the Cape Neddick River. Stay here and you are within easy walking distance of the various amusements and tourist-trap souvenir shops of York Beach, and within a short drive of fine restaurants, playhouses, and nature preserves in the town of York Harbor and in nearby Ogunquit to the north. Needless to add, dozens of miles of sand and surf are also close at hand for beach lovers who want to sunbathe, swim, or toss a Frisbee.

Campsites, facilities: There are 80 sites for tents and RVs, 50 with electric hookups and 30 with none. Flush toilets, hot showers, picnic tables, fireplaces, a dump station, and a store are provided. Campers have access to the ocean and saltwater swimming, boating, and fishing. The maximum RV length is 28 feet. No pets are allowed.

Reservations, fees: Reservations are required, and you must make a 20 percent deposit. The reservation must be for at least one week, starting on a Sunday. Sites are $25–27 a night.

Open: May 15–October 15.

Directions: From the intersection of U.S. 1A and Shore Road, drive 1.25 miles north on Shore Road to the campground.

Contact: Cape Neddick Oceanside Campground, P.O. Box 1, Cape Neddick, ME 03902, 207/363-4366, website: www.harbourview.com.

84 CAMP EATON

Rating: 4

Across from Long Sands Beach in York Harbor

Since 1923, this venerable campground has been a fixture above the sands of York Beach. Perched on a bluff overlooking the surf, the campground is ideally situated for those looking for a site within walking distance of the shops and restaurants in the picture-postcard village of York Harbor, as well as the rides, amusements, and tacky souvenir shops of York Beach. Long Sands Beach, just across U.S. 1A from the campground, extends for two miles. While you're here, be sure to take a short drive to the scenic Nubble Light on Cape Neddick.

Campsites, facilities: There are 307 sites for RVs, most with full hookups; cabins and tent sites are available. Flush toilets, hot showers, picnic tables, fireplaces, and a dump station are provided. You will also find a playground, recreation room, volleyball and basketball courts, horseshoe pits, and shuffleboard. Leashed pets are permitted.

Reservations, fees: Reservations are recommended. Sites are $38–48 a night.

Open: May 1–October 2.

Directions: From the Maine Turnpike/I-95 at York Village, take Exit 4 (the "Yorks"), drive .25 mile south on U.S. 1, then get on U.S. 1A and drive three miles northeast to the campground on the left.

Contact: Peter and Kathy Wagner, Camp Eaton, P.O. Box 626, Highway 1A, York Harbor, ME 03911, 207/363-3424, website: www.campeaton.com.

85 LIBBY'S OCEANSIDE CAMP

Rating: 4

Near Long Sands Beach in York Harbor

Like nearby neighbor Camp Eaton (see previous listing), this RV spot has overlooked the York Beach sands since 1923 from its blufftop perch above the surf. It is a good choice for those campers who are looking for an oceanside site within walking distance of both the shops and restaurants in the picturesque village of York Harbor and the tacky rides, amusements, and souvenir shops of touristy York Beach.

Campsites, facilities: There are 95 sites for tents and RVs with full hookups. Flush toilets, free hot showers, picnic tables, fireplaces, and a recreation room are provided. Campers enjoy easy access to long sandy beaches. Leashed pets are permitted.

Reservations, fees: Reservations are accepted for stays of one week or longer. A deposit of $50 per week is required. Sites are $35–60 a night.

Open: May 15–October 15.

Directions: From the Maine Turnpike/I-95 at York Village, take Exit 4 (the "Yorks"), drive .25 mile south on U.S. 1, then get on U.S. 1A and drive three miles northeast to the campground on the right.

Contact: Norm and Cindy Davidson, Libby's Oceanside Camp, P.O. Box 40, U.S. 1A, York Harbor, ME 03911, 207/363-4171, website: www.libbysoceancamping.com.

86 FLAGG'S TRAILER PARK

Rating: 3

In the town of York Beach

Yet another campground within walking distance of the sandy beaches, souvenir shops, and amusements of York Beach, Flagg's is a small trailer park with a family orientation. If you plan on singing around the campfire well into the wee hours, move on to the next spot, as Flagg's imposes quiet hours from 10 P.M. to 8 A.M. every night.

Campsites, facilities: There are 84 sites for RVs up to 35 feet in length, with full and partial hookups. Flush toilets, hot showers, picnic tables, fireplaces, and a playground are provided. Seasonal campers can obtain telephone and cable TV hookups. No pets are allowed.

Reservations, fees: Reservations are recommended. Sites are $28 a night.

Open: May 11–September 30.

Directions: From the Maine Turnpike/I-95 at York Village, take Exit 4 (the "Yorks"), drive .25 mile south on U.S. 1, then get on U.S. 1A

and drive 3.5 miles northeast to the campground on the left.

Contact: Flagg's Trailer Park, Webber Road, Box 232, York Beach, ME 03910, 207/363-5050.

87 YORK BEACH CAMPER PARK

Rating: 3

On U.S. 1A in York Beach

Found near the heart of York Beach's popular attractions, including restaurants, beaches, and York's Wild Kingdom and Amusement Park, the campground is central to all that this resort community has to offer. Also nearby are boat operators offering whale-watching and deep-sea fishing excursions.

Campsites, facilities: There are 46 sites for tents and RVs, 34 with full hookups, five with water and electric hookups, and seven with none. Flush toilets, hot showers, picnic tables, fireplaces, a dump station, laundry facilities, a store, and a playground are provided. Sandy beaches are within walking distance. Leashed pets are permitted.

Reservations, fees: Reservations are accepted. Sites are $26–34 a night.

Open: May 15–October 1.

Directions: From the Maine Turnpike/I-95 at York Village, take Exit 4 (the "Yorks") and drive north on U.S. 1 for 3.3 miles. Turn right on U.S. 1A and travel 1.1 miles east to the campground.

Contact: York Beach Camper Park, U.S. 1A, Box 127, York Beach, ME 03910, 207/363-1343.

Chapter 4

© MAINE OFFICE OF TOURISM/JEFF GREENBERG

Down East

Down East

This rugged, rocky coast is as far north and east as you can go in the United States. The roughly 1,000 miles of indented shoreline stretching from Penobscot Bay in the Midcoast region to Cobscook Bay and the New Brunswick border is a rich trove of dramatic sea cliffs and deep-cut coves, of dark shaggy spruce forests and gleaming granite islands. Though home to New England's only national park, Acadia, most of the region sees relatively few tourists, and lobster boats certainly outnumber pleasure craft by a wide margin.

Fewer than 10 percent of visitors to the Maine Coast proceed beyond Acadia and Bar Harbor, the last major coastal town. But those who do are amply rewarded with dramatic ocean scenery, spectacular wildlife viewing, and plenty of outdoor recreation opportunities.

Take a hike on Quoddy Head, the easternmost point in the United

States, up a high rocky bluff sticking far out into the cold North Atlantic. Watch the world's highest tides surge past as they flow in and out of the Bay of Fundy—which stretches from Down East Maine to Yarmouth, Nova Scotia—twice daily. Cast a line for Atlantic salmon in the many tidal rivers flowing to the sea. Take a ferry to nearby islands that are home to puffins, auks, and arctic terns. All the while keep an eye out for migrating whales as they breach and spout just offshore.

As elsewhere in Maine, the warmest days are in July and August. But don't come here expecting to find long, sandy beaches and fine swimming. The coast is beautiful, but it's also bold and rocky, more suitable for sailing and sea kayaking than beach walking. And the water is—well, let's just say the water is a bit on the chilly side.

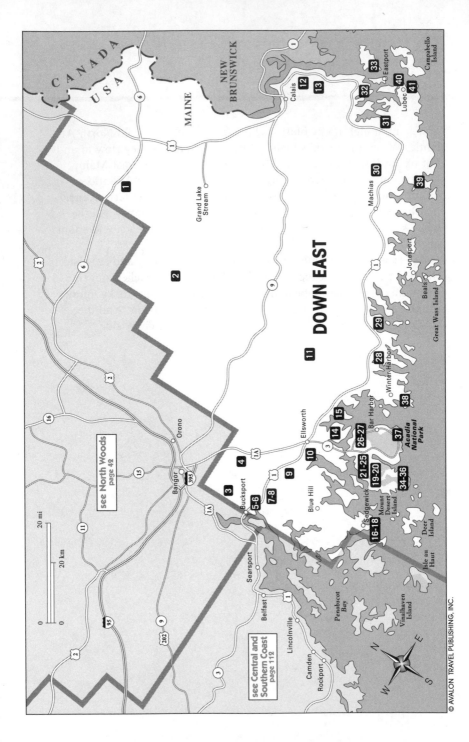

1 MAINE WILDERNESS CAMPS

Rating: 10
Between the towns of Topsfield and Springfield

Once you make it here, you appreciate the rough access road you were just cursing, because this camp bordering a wilderness lake is definitely way off the beaten path. For many people, this is as close as they ever come to a true wilderness experience. The rustic facility at the end of the road is the only sign of humanity on Pleasant Lake, and campers are surrounded by hundreds of square miles of unpopulated woodlands. It's a great spot for those who want to get away from it all, perhaps launching off on an extended canoe trip. A short portage out of Pleasant Lake leads to the Grand Lake Chain and more than 40 miles of wilderness waterways. If you want to begin a long canoe expedition here, Maine Wilderness Camps offers a full outfitting and shuttle service. Anglers and hunters will find full guide services at the campground, too. This is a sportsperson's paradise, where the fishing for landlocked salmon, brook and lake trout, bass, and white perch is excellent. In the fall, make this your base camp for deer, moose, bear, and game-bird hunting. And during winter, explore the dirt roads and lakes (if frozen) by snowmobile or cross-country skis. For those who want their own rustic lakeside retreat, several housekeeping cabins are rented out.

Campsites, facilities: There are 19 sites for tents and RVs, four with water and electric hookups and 15 with none. Flush toilets and hot showers are located at the main campground, while the wilderness sites, which are accessible by trail or boat, have pit toilets. Picnic tables and fireplaces are provided, and you will find a limited store and lodge at the main campground. Recreational facilities include horseshoes, a sandy beach, boat dock, and motorboat, canoe, and kayak rentals. Several housekeeping cabins are available for rent. Leashed pets are permitted.

Reservations, fees: Reservations are recommended. A deposit of one-third of the total cost is required. Sites are $15–20 a night.

Open: Year-round.

Directions: From I-95 near Lincoln, take Exit 55 to U.S. 2 and then Highway 6, and drive east for 34 miles until you enter Washington County. Continue 4.5 miles east of the county line on Highway 6, then turn right at the sign for Maine Wilderness Camps, and follow the very rough logging road for 3.5 miles. If you are unsure about your vehicle's ability to handle deep ruts, washboards, and rocks, call ahead.

Contact: Terry and Paula McGrath, Maine Wilderness Camps, HC 82 Box 1085, Topsfield, ME 04490, 207/738-5052 (this is a radio phone; let it ring), website: www.mainewildernesscamps.com.

2 DUCK LAKE MANAGEMENT UNIT

Rating: 10
East of Burlington

Duck Lake is a 25,000-acre preserve in the remote and sparsely populated eastern woodlands of Maine. In addition to the namesake pond, several other small lakes with sand beaches—including Gassabias Lake, the Unknown Lakes, and Fourth Machias Lake—are contained in the unit's boundaries. Duck Lake is more popular with campers than the others, and thus more crowded. Renowned for its excellent cold-water fishing for landlocked salmon and brook trout, Duck Lake lures many visitors who arrive armed with fishing rods. Equally good warm-water fishing is available on the other lakes. For a pleasant canoe trip in which you float through a variety of wildlife habitats, put your canoe and paddles into Gassabias Stream.

Campsites, facilities: There are six primitive tent sites on the shores of Duck Lake, Gassabias Lake, and Upper and Lower Unknown Lake. Pit toilets, picnic tables, and fire rings are provided. Pets are permitted.

Reservations, fees: Sites are first come, first served. There is no fee.

Open: Year-round.

Directions: From the village of Burlington northeast of Bangor, follow rough logging roads east for several miles to access the unit.

Contact: Maine Bureau of Parks and Lands, 22 State House Station, Augusta, ME 04333, 207/287-3821, website: www.state.me.us/doc/parks.

3 MASTHEAD CAMPGROUND

🏊 🛶 🚐 🐴 🏃 🚃 ⛰️

Rating: 7

On Hancock Pond in Bucksport

Masthead is one of those quiet, established, rather small campgrounds that makes visitors feel right at home as soon as they enter. The entire grounds are very well tended, sites are spacious and private, and the mix of open fields, tall trees, and sparkling waters creates a feeling of remoteness and seclusion. Two beaches on Hancock Pond are the star attractions, and a day at the waterfront is made even more pleasant by the prohibition of motorboats. The rule prevents buzzing engines from disturbing those who simply want to cast out a fishing line or read a book on the shore. Canoes and kayaks are always welcome. This splendid campground is near picturesque fishing villages and Acadia National Park.

Campsites, facilities: There are 38 sites for tents and RVs, all with partial hookups. Flush toilets, hot showers, picnic tables, fireplaces, a dump station, laundry facilities, and a store are provided. Recreational facilities include two beaches, canoe rentals, a pavilion, playground, volleyball and badminton nets, and horseshoe pits. Leashed pets are permitted.

Reservations, fees: Reservations are recommended. Sites are $18–22 a night.

Open: Memorial Day–September 15.

Directions: From the intersection of Highway 15 and U.S. 1 in Bucksport, drive two miles east on U.S. 1 and then 5.5 miles north on Highway 46. Turn right on Mast Hill Road and go .75 mile east to the campground.

Contact: Annette and Bob Valenotte, Mast-

head Campground, P.O. Box 418, Bucksport, ME 04416, 207/469-3482.

4 BRANCH LAKE CAMPING AREA

🏃 🚲 🏊 🛶 🚐 🐴 🏃 🚃 ⛰️

Rating: 5

On Branch Lake in Ellsworth

Branch Lake is a breezy, shaded campground set in rolling forested countryside on a large freshwater lake. The usual array of waterfront activities is available. Cool off in Branch Lake, launch a motorboat or canoe, or grab your fishing rod to catch that night's supper. The campground is located midway between the city of Bangor and Acadia National Park.

Campsites, facilities: There are 55 sites for tents and RVs with full and partial hookups. Flush toilets, hot showers, picnic tables, fireplaces, a dump station, and a store are provided. Recreational facilities include a large freshwater lake with a sandy beach, a boat launch, boat rentals, and a playground. Leashed pets are permitted.

Reservations, fees: Reservations are recommended. Sites are $16–25 a night.

Open: May 1–October 15.

Directions: From the junction of Highway 46 and U.S. 1A in Holden, drive south on U.S. 1A for approximately six miles. Turn right and head west on Winkumpaugh Road, then go south on Landing Road and follow signs to the campground.

Contact: Dick and Brenda Graves, Branch Lake Camping Area, R.F.D. 5, Box 473, Ellsworth, ME 04605, 207/667-5174.

5 FLYING DUTCHMAN

🏃 🚲 🏊 🛶 🚐 ❌ 🐴 🏃 🚃 ⛰️

Rating: 7

On the banks of the Penobscot River in Bucksport

Ⓕ Flying Dutchman is a small, well-kept campground located directly on the banks of the Penobscot River just downstream of

Fort Knox, an impressive stone fort built during the Civil War era. A sandy beach and boat launch are available across the street at Fort Knox State Park. The heated pool and hot tub at the campground offer welcome warmth after a day in Maine's chilly ocean waters. From Flying Dutchman, you can take day trips to the beautiful Penobscot Bay area and several nearby seaside communities and attractions, including historic Castine, Blue Hill, and Deer Isle. Acadia National Park is a short drive away.

Campsites, facilities: There are 35 sites for tents and RVs, 14 with full hookups, 20 with water and electric hookups, and one with none. Flush toilets, hot showers, a whirlpool, picnic tables, fireplaces, a dump station, laundry facilities, and a store are provided. Recreational facilities include a heated swimming pool, boat launch, saltwater fishing, a recreation room, playground, volleyball, basketball, badminton, and horseshoe pits. Leashed pets are permitted.

Reservations, fees: Reservations are recommended. For stays of up to three days, send one night's fee as a deposit; for four or more days, a $40 deposit is required. Sites are $18–26 a night.

Open: May 1–Columbus Day.

Directions: From the junction of U.S. 1 and Highway 15 in Bucksport, drive one mile south on U.S. 1 to the campground.

Contact: Hans and Glee Honders, Flying Dutchman, P.O. Box 549, Bucksport, ME 04416, 207/469-3256.

⑥ SHADY OAKS CAMPGROUND
🚶 🏊 🚐 🔺

Rating: 5

In Orland

Small, clean, and not at all noisy, the Shady Oaks Campground is within easy driving distance of many midcoast attractions, including Fort Knox, a Civil War-era fort guarding the Penobscot River, the Deer Isle and Blue Hill areas with their coastal scenery and pretty fishing villages, and Acadia National Park. The campground offers many amenities to families including a swimming pool, nature trail, and a schedule of planned activities.

Campsites, facilities: There are 50 sites for tents and RVs, 41 with full hookups and nine with water and electric hookups. Flush toilets, free hot showers, picnic tables, fireplaces, laundry facilities, a dump station, and a store are provided. Recreational facilities include a swimming pool, recreation room, volleyball, basketball, badminton, and horseshoes. No dogs are allowed.

Reservations, fees: Reservations are recommended. Sites are $18–26 a night.

Open: May 1–October 1.

Directions: From the junction of U.S. 1 and Highway 15 in Bucksport, drive two miles east on U.S. 1 to the campground.

Contact: Joyce and Don Nelson, Shady Oaks Campground, RR 1, P.O. Box 1874, Orland, ME 04472, 207/469-7739.

⑦ WHISPERING PINES CAMPGROUND
🏊 🚣 🏊 🐕 🚐 🔺

Rating: 8

On Toddy Pond in the township of East Orland

Whispering Pines is a quiet, well-maintained, spacious campground set among stately mature white pines and hemlocks. The campground is situated along the shores of Toddy Pond, a wild and undeveloped 10-mile-long lake. Two other lakes lie within walking distance, and all three waters offer superb trout, salmon, and bass fishing. Campers are granted free use of rowboats and canoes, allowing children plenty of time to learn how to row or paddle. The sandy beach, with its swimming floats and gradually sloping bottom, is a safe place for children to swim and play. This is an exceptional facility located within easy reach of midcoast Maine's finest attractions.

Campsites, facilities: There are 50 sites for tents

and RVs, 40 with full hookups, six with water and electric hookups, and four with none. Facilities include flush toilets, hot showers, picnic tables, fireplaces, and a dump station. Recreational facilities include a large lake with a sandy beach, a boat launch, free use of canoes and rowboats, a recreation room, volleyball, badminton, and horseshoes. Leashed pets are permitted.

Reservations, fees: Reservations are accepted. Sites are $22–27 a night.

Open: May 20–September 30.

Directions: From the junction of U.S. 1 and Highway 15 in Bucksport, drive 7.5 miles east on U.S. 1 to the campground.

Contact: Dwight and Sandy Gates, Whispering Pines Campground, East Orland, ME 04431, 207/469-3443, website: www.campmaine.com/whisperingpines.

8 BALSAM COVE CAMPGROUND

Rating: 5

On Toddy Pond in the township of East Orland

With plenty of space between sites, this rustic campground offers welcome peace and privacy for families. The large waterfront sites are very popular. The swimming area, complete with a float and slide, provides access to 10-mile-long Toddy Pond. Bring your canoe and launch it from the beach or reserve dock space for your motorboat. When you tire of freshwater swimming, drive the short distance to the ocean for a day of swimming, boating, and fishing in saltwater. Spectacular Acadia National Park is not too far from here. Note: Be sure to check out the expansive blueberry fields on the drive into the campground.

Campsites, facilities: There are 60 sites for tents and RVs, 30 with water and electric hookups, 20 with electric hookups only, and 10 with none. Flush toilets, hot showers, picnic tables, fireplaces, a dump station, laundry facilities, and a store are provided. Recreational facilities include

a large lake with a sandy beach, a playground, recreation room, volleyball, basketball, and horseshoe pits. Leashed pets are permitted.

Reservations, fees: Reservations are recommended. Sites are $18–25 a night.

Open: May 24–September 30.

Directions: From the intersection of U.S. 1 and Highway 15 in Bucksport, drive south on Highway 15 for one mile, then turn left on a dirt road and follow the signs to the campground.

Contact: Sharon and Charlie, Balsam Cove Campground, P.O. Box C, East Orland, ME 04431, 207/469-7771, website: www.balsamcove.com.

9 PATTEN POND CAMPING RESORT

Rating: 7

On Lower Patten Pond in Ellsworth

This campground is located on the shores of Lower Patten Pond, a freshwater lake within easy driving distance of the coast. This is a good base camp for day trips to Acadia National Park, but don't overlook other attractions in the immediate area. Here you're just north of the village of Blue Hill, with its attractive colonial town center and picturesque harbor, and Castine, home of the Maine Maritime Academy and scene of naval battles that were waged in the American Revolution and Civil War.

Campsites, facilities: There are 145 sites for tents and RVs, 105 with partial hookups and 40 with no hookups. Flush toilets, hot showers, picnic tables, fireplaces, laundry facilities, a dump station, and a store are provided. Recreational facilities include a boat launch, canoe rentals, a playground and sports field, hiking trails, a recreation room, volleyball, basketball, badminton, and horseshoes. Leashed pets are permitted.

Reservations, fees: Reservations are accepted. Sites are $16–23 a night.

Open: Mid-May–mid-October.

Directions: From the junction of U.S. 1 and U.S. 1A in Ellsworth, drive 7.5 miles west on U.S. 1 to the campground.

Contact: Patten Pond Camping Resort, Ellsworth, ME 04605, 207/667-5745, website: www.barharborcampgrounds.com.

10 THE GATHERINGS FAMILY CAMPGROUND

🚶 🚵 🏊 ⛵ 🛶 🛶 🐕 🛶 🚐 ⛺

Rating: 9

On Weymouth Point in the village of Surry

Aside from boasting a spectacular setting on Weymouth Point's tip at the northern end of Blue Hill Bay, this spacious campground offers fairly secluded waterfront sites with expansive views over the ocean. With more than a quarter mile of ocean frontage on Patten Bay accessible from this campground, it's difficult to think of a reason to leave. But after staring at Cadillac Mountain and the other peaks of Acadia National Park from your site here, you'll be tempted to head to the nearby park to explore its other natural wonders, including lakes, streams, cliffs, tidepools, and forests. Hiking trails and carriage roads for hiking and biking weave throughout the park. This is a peaceful place with remarkably easy access to the coastal gems of Maine.

Campsites, facilities: There are 110 sites for tents and RVs, five with full hookups and 105 with water and electric hookups. Flush toilets, hot showers, picnic tables, fireplaces, a dump station, laundry facilities, and a store are provided. Recreational facilities include a boat launch, beach, saltwater swimming and fishing, boat and canoe rentals, a playground, recreation room, volleyball, basketball, and horseshoe pits. Leashed pets are permitted.

Reservations, fees: Reservations are recommended. Full payment is required for stays of up to three days; for up to 13 days, send three days' fee as a deposit, and for two weeks or more, send 25 percent of the total fee. Sites are $22–28 a night.

Open: May 1–October 15.

Directions: From the junction of U.S. 1 and Highway 172 in Ellsworth, drive four miles south on Highway 172 to the campground.

Contact: Ralph and Ann Jacobsen, The Gatherings Family Campground, R.F.D. 3, Box 69, Ellsworth, ME 04605, 207/667-8826.

11 DONNELL POND MANAGEMENT UNIT

🚶 🚵 🛶 🚐 🎣 ❄️ 🐕 ⛺

Rating: 10

East of Ellsworth

Donnell Pond is an extremely scenic land parcel that displays a great diversity of natural attractions, all of it open to campers who are willing to hike or boat to one of the preserve's primitive campsites. Located just a few miles from the ocean, the unit includes miles of undeveloped shoreline on several wilderness lakes. A private boat ramp, which at this time the public can use, is located just outside the management unit at the Card Mill site in Franklin. While there is no prohibition on high-powered boats, this is a remote area that attracts wildlife and many species of birds, making a smaller boat or canoe the preferred method of travel. The preserve also encompasses Schoodic, Black, and Caribou Mountains. A hiking trail system accesses the Black Mountain area, while other trails climb Schoodic Mountain from Schoodic Beach. In addition to these routes, some old roads and former trails offer plenty of opportunities to explore the unit on foot, mountain bike, snowshoes, or cross-country skis.

Campsites, facilities: Several primitive campsites for tents are available. They are currently undeveloped and have no facilities. Pets are permitted.

Reservations, fees: Sites are available on a first-come, first-served basis. There is no fee.

Open: Year-round.

Directions: From Ellsworth, drive 12 miles east on Highway 182 or Highway 183 to access the management unit.

Contact: Maine Bureau of Parks and Lands, 22 State House Station, Augusta, ME 04333, 207/287-3821.

12 KEENE'S LAKE CAMPGROUND

⚊ ⚊ ⚊ ⚊ ⚊ ⚊ ⚊

Rating: 8

In Calais

This campground is located on a wilderness lake with sheltered inlets and coves surrounded by miles of woodlands. Fish in the lake or in nearby Passamaquoddy Bay, launch a canoe from the campground or a kayak from the town landing in Robbinston, or spend a day helping the U.S. Fish and Wildlife Service band woodcocks at nearby Moosehorn National Wildlife Refuge. Be sure to visit Quoddy Head State Park and check out Campobello Island, the summer home of President Franklin Delano Roosevelt. For more information on the area, see the Cobscook Bay State Park listing in this chapter.

Campsites, facilities: There are 151 sites for tents and RVs, 142 with water and electric hookups and nine with no hookups. Flush toilets, hot showers, picnic tables, fireplaces, laundry facilities, a dump station, and a store are provided. A boat launch, canoe rentals, a recreation room, volleyball, basketball, miniature golf, and horseshoes are among the recreational offerings. Leashed pets are permitted.

Reservations, fees: Reservations are recommended. Sites are $16 a night.

Open: May 15–October 1.

Directions: From Calais, drive eight miles south on U.S. 1. Turn right on Shattuck Road and drive one mile west.

Contact: Keene's Lake Campground, Shattuck Road, RR 1, Box 179, Calais, ME 04619, 207/454-8557, website: www.geocities.com/keeneslakecampground.

13 HILLTOP CAMPGROUND

⚊ ⚊ ⚊ ⚊ ⚊ ⚊ ⚊ ⚊

Rating: 7

Near the hamlet of Robbinston

This place is popular with seasonal campers from Canada who flock to the United States in the summer months and stay long enough to legally buy American merchandise duty-free. The campground sits high atop an open ridge overlooking the broad reaches of Passamaquoddy Bay and the New Brunswick shore off in the distance across the water. Don't forget to bring your fishing tackle so you can catch your dinner. Or bring a sea kayak to launch at the town dock in Robbinston. For more information on the area, see the Cobscook Bay State Park listing in this chapter.

Campsites, facilities: There are 117 sites for tents and RVs, 34 with full hookups, 69 with water and electric hookups, and 14 tent platforms. Flush toilets, wheelchair-accessible restrooms, hot showers, picnic tables, fire rings, a dump station, laundry facilities, a playground, recreation hall, swimming pool, horseshoe pits, basketball, volleyball, and a store are provided. Leashed pets are permitted.

Reservations, fees: Reservations are recommended. A deposit of 50 percent of the total fee is required. One-night reservations are not accepted for weekends in July or August unless approved by management. Sites are $18–22 a night.

Open: Mid-May–late September.

Directions: From the intersection of U.S. 1 and Ridge Road in Robbinston, drive one mile west on Ridge Road to the campground.

Contact: Harold and Pamela Brooks, Hilltop Campground, RR 1, Box 298, Robbinston, ME 04671, 207/454-3985.

14 LAMOINE STATE PARK

⚊ ⚊ ⚊ ⚊ ⚊ ⚊ ⚊ ⚊ ⚊ ⚊

Rating: 10

On Frenchman Bay in Ellsworth

Found on a beautiful peninsula that juts out into Frenchman Bay, Lamoine State Park is the perfect alternative to Acadia National Park for those who wish to enjoy the same stunning scenery and ocean access, but also want to get away from the summer crowds. Some sites are right next to the water and, as with other state parks in Maine, all sites afford a good measure of privacy. The day-use area, which stretches along the shoreline, has a large picnic area as well as many hibachi-style grills for barbecues. If you are looking for a splendid campground with easy access to the water, this is the place. Acadia National Park and Bar Harbor are less than an hour away by car.

Campsites, facilities: There are 61 sites for tents and RVs up to 20 feet long, all without hookups. Picnic tables, fire rings, restrooms, a dump station, boat ramp, group camping area, playground, and swimming area are provided. Leashed pets are permitted.

Reservations, fees: Reservations are accepted, and the total amount due must accompany your request. Contact the Maine Bureau of Parks and Lands at 207/287-3821. The State of Maine allocates some sites on a first-come, first-served basis. Sites are $15 a night for Maine residents and $20 for nonresidents.

Open: May 15–October 15.

Directions: From the junction of U.S. 1 and Highway 184 in Ellsworth, drive 10 miles south on Highway 184 to the park entrance.

Contact: Lamoine State Park Ranger, 207/667-4778; Maine Bureau of Parks and Lands, 22 State House Station, Augusta, ME 04333, 207/287-3821, website: www.state.me.us/doc/parks.

15 MOUNTAINVIEW CAMPGROUND

Rating: 10

On Frenchman Bay in East Sullivan

As the name would suggest, the views of the mountains in Acadia National Park across Frenchman Bay are exceptional from this campground. If you have traveled this far east along the Maine coast, by now you probably realize that you've left the crowds and the modern world behind. From here to the New Brunswick border, the roads are emptier, the little towns smaller, and the scenery more spectacular than what you encounter to the west. Mountainview Campground is just what you might ex-

pect in this part of Maine, a rather worn and somewhat weather-beaten, no-frills place right on the water.

Campsites, facilities: There are 50 sites for tents and RVs, four with full hookups and 46 with water and electric hookups. Flush toilets, hot showers, picnic tables, fireplaces, a dump station, and a store are provided. Recreational facilities include a beach, playground, horseshoe pits, and miniature golf. Leashed pets are permitted.

Reservations, fees: Reservations are not necessary. Sites are $19–29 a night.

Open: Memorial Day–October 1.

Directions: From the junction of U.S. 1 and Highway 185 in Sullivan, drive one mile east on U.S. 1 to the campground.

Contact: Mountainview Campground, U.S. 1, East Sullivan, ME 04607, 207/422-6215, website: www.acadia.net/flandersbay/campground.htm.

16 SUNSHINE CAMPGROUND

Rating: 9

On Deer Isle

Small and intimate Sunshine Campground sits at the end of a long, narrow peninsula jutting into Blue Hill Bay, one of the prettiest bodies of water anywhere on the Maine coast. The campground is set in a thick maritime forest on several bumpy knolls, and none offer water views or oceanfront locales. Instead, you must access the water across the road from the campground. This is a clean, well-kept facility, perfect for those looking to literally get away from it all by heading to land's end. As a point of departure for sea kayakers, Sunshine Campground is hard to beat: after pushing off from this spot, kayakers are soon surrounded by dozens of islands.

Campsites, facilities: There are 22 sites for tents and RVs, 15 with partial hookups and seven with none. Facilities include flush toilets, hot showers, picnic tables, fireplaces, laundry facilities, a dump station, and a limited store.

Recreational facilities include a recreation room, access to the water, and horseshoes. Leashed pets are permitted.

Reservations, fees: Reservations are accepted. Sites are $22–26 a night.

Open: Memorial Day–October 15.

Directions: From U.S. 1 in Bucksport, follow Highway 175 all the way south to Deer Isle. Take Highway 15 south, then turn left on Sunshine County Road, and drive 5.75 miles east to the campground.

Contact: Sunshine Campground, RR 1, Box 521D, Deer Isle, ME 04627, 207/248-6681, website: www.sunshinecampground.com.

17 GREENLAW'S MOBILE AND RV PARK

Rating: 8

In the small fishing village of Stonington on Deer Isle

Stonington is truly a place that has been untouched by time, a little fishing village at the very tip of Deer Isle overlooking Merchant Row, a cluster of dozens of islands floating in Penobscot Bay. Those islands, along with miles of secluded bays, coves, and inlets, are part of why this area is considered the finest sailing and sea kayaking territory on the East Coast—and possibly in all of North America. So, if you want to get down to the sea, check out this campground with wooded sites at land's end.

Campsites, facilities: There are 50 sites for tents and RVs, 15 with full hookups, 17 with water and electric hookups, and 18 with none. Flush toilets, hot showers, picnic tables, fireplaces, and a dump station are provided. You will also find hiking trails, badminton nets, and horseshoes. Leashed pets are permitted.

Reservations, fees: Reservations are accepted. Sites are $18–28 a night.

Open: April–November.

Directions: From U.S. 1 in Bucksport, follow Highway 175 all the way south to Deer Isle. Take Highway 15 south for 10.75 miles to Ston-

ington and then go 1.5 miles west on County Road to the campground.

Contact: Greenlaw's Mobile and RV Park, Airport Road, Box 72, Stonington, ME 04681, 207/367-5049.

18 ISLE AU HAUT CAMPGROUND

Rating: 10

On Isle au Haut in Acadia National Park

French Explorer Samuel de Champlain dubbed this place Isle au Haut, or the High Island, in 1603 because of the way its rocky summit looms more than 500 feet above the ocean swells. Footpaths and hiking trails crisscross the island, tracing the shore of its bays and inlets, traversing thick maritime forests, and climbing some of the higher points. This is a wild and serene place at the edge of the open ocean, and memories of a stay here will not soon be forgotten. For sea kayakers, it's a very popular destination.

Campsites, facilities: There are five lean-tos accommodating up to six people each. Pit toilets, picnic tables, and fireplaces are provided. Hiking trails leave from the campground. Leashed pets are permitted.

Reservations, fees: Reservations are required. Sites are $25 a night per lean-to.

Open: Mid-May–mid-October.

Directions: The campground is accessible by boat only. From U.S. 1 in Bucksport, follow Highway 175 all the way south to Deer Isle. Take Highway 15 south to Stonington and then catch the mail boat to Duck Harbor Landing on Isle au Haut. Or paddle your own canoe or sea kayak through the islands of Merchant Row to the campground.

Contact: Acadia National Park, P.O. Box 177, Bar Harbor, ME 04609, 207/288-3338, website: www.nps.gov/acad.

19 SPRUCE VALLEY CAMPGROUND

Rating: 7

In Bar Harbor

Spruce Valley is a clean, quiet family campground centrally located near Bar Harbor and Acadia National Park. Although there are no water views or oceanfront sites, this is an attractive park within easy reach of hiking, biking, sea kayaking, whale-watching, and other Mount Desert Island attractions. Children love the heated swimming pool with slide as well as the cedar playground.

Campsites, facilities: There are 100 sites for tents and RVs, 15 with full hookups, 33 with water and electric hookups, and 52 with none. Flush toilets, hot showers, picnic tables, fireplaces, laundry facilities, a dump station, and a camp store are provided. Recreational facilities include a heated swimming pool with slide, recreation room, volleyball, basketball, and horseshoes. Leashed pets are permitted.

Reservations, fees: Reservations are recommended in July and August. A deposit of two nights' fees is required. Sites are $22–32 a night.

Open: May 10–October 31.

Directions: From Ellsworth, drive south on Highway 3 onto Mount Desert Island. At the intersection of Highways 3 and 102/198, follow Highway 102/198 south for 1.5 miles to the campground on the left.

Contact: Harry and Paula Luhrs, Spruce Valley Campground, Highway 102, Box 2420, Bar Harbor, ME 04609, 207/288-5139, website: www.sprucevalley.com.

20 SMUGGLER'S DEN CAMPGROUND

Rating: 8

In Southwest Harbor on Mount Desert Island

Smuggler's Den is a spacious, attractive campground lying at the foothills of some of Mount Desert Island's mountains. Campsites, which are set in the woods bordering a large open field, afford a feeling of openness and privacy. The campground claims an ideal location about halfway down the western, or quiet, side of the island, very near freshwater lakes, hiking trails, ocean access points, and the pretty villages of Somesville and Southwest Harbor.

Campsites, facilities: There are 100 sites for tents and RVs, 22 with full hookups, 43 with water and electric hookups, and 35 with none. Flush toilets, hot showers, picnic tables, fireplaces, laundry facilities, a dump station, and a store are provided. Recreational facilities include a heated swimming pool, volleyball, badminton, and horseshoes. Leashed pets are permitted.

Reservations, fees: Reservations are recommended and require a $30 deposit. Sites are $26–34 a night.

Open: Memorial Day–Columbus Day.

Directions: From Ellsworth, drive south on Highway 3 onto Mount Desert Island. Follow Highway 102/198 south and then follow Highway 102 south for five more miles to the campground.

Contact: Jean Conroy, Smuggler's Den Campground, P.O. Box 787, Southwest Harbor, ME 04679, 207/244-3944, website: www.campmaine.com/smugglersden.

21 MOUNT DESERT CAMPGROUND

Rating: 10

At the tip of Somes Sound on Mount Desert Island

It is not possible to be more centrally located on Mount Desert Island than right here at Mount Desert Campground. Located at the very tip of Somes Sound—the only fjord on the East Coast—the campground is within minutes of the villages of Bar Harbor, Northeast Harbor, and Southwest Harbor, in addition to being close to the natural and scenic attractions of Acadia National Park, including hiking and biking trails, freshwater lakes, sand beaches, and ocean cliffs. The sites are well spaced and set beneath tall trees, offering a tremendous sense of privacy and seclusion.

Campsites, facilities: There are 150 sites for tents and RVs, some with water and electric hookups and some without. Flush toilets, hot showers, picnic tables, fireplaces, and a store are provided. Recreational facilities include a boat launch, canoe rentals, and saltwater swimming. The maximum RV length is 20 feet. Dogs are not permitted during July and August.

Reservations, fees: Reservations are accepted for stays of three or more days from Memorial Day–Labor Day. There is a $30 reservation fee. Waterfront sites must be reserved for a week or more and require a $50 reservation fee. Sites are $28–40 a night.

Open: May 15–October 1.

Directions: From Ellsworth, drive south on Highway 3 onto Mount Desert Island. Follow Highway 102/198 south and then drive .75 mile south on Highway 198 to the campground.

Contact: Owen and Barbara Craighead, Mount Desert Campground, Highway 198, Mount Desert, ME 04660, 207/244-3710, website: www.mountdesertcampground.com.

22 SOMES SOUND VIEW CAMPGROUND

Rating: 6

On Somes Sound in Mount Desert

The campground is perched on a rocky hill directly above Somes Sound, a deep arm of the Atlantic Ocean that reaches into the very center of Mount Desert Island and is the only fjord on the East Coast. The road down to the campground is steep, with several narrow turns, and is not suitable for large campers or RVs. Kayakers, canoeists, and sailors are in their element here, for the water access is unsurpassed in this area. If you left your canoe or sailboat at home, rent one at the campground and explore the nooks and crannies of Somes Sound.

Campsites, facilities: There are 60 sites for tents and RVs, 20 with partial hookups and 40 without hookups. Flush toilets, hot showers, picnic tables, fireplaces, and a dump station are provided. A boat launch is available, and sailboats and canoes can be rented. The maximum RV length is 16 feet. Leashed pets are permitted.

Reservations, fees: Reservations are accepted and require a $20 deposit. Sites are $22–26 a night.

Open: Memorial Day–Columbus Day.

Directions: From Ellsworth, drive south on Highway 3 onto Mount Desert Island. Follow Highway 102/198 south and then follow Highway 102 south for two more miles. Turn left on Hall Quarry Road and continue .75 mile east to the campground entrance.

Contact: Sharon Musetti, Somes Sound View Campground, Hall Quarry Road, Mount Desert, ME 04660, 207/244-3890, website: www.acadiainfo.com/ssview.htm.

23 NARROWS TOO CAMPING RESORT

Rating: 7

Near Bar Harbor in Trenton

Like its sister resort across the water, Mount Desert Narrows Camping Resort (see listing in this chapter), Narrows Too guards the ocean narrows separating Mount Desert Island from the mainland. And as at Mount Desert Narrows, there's something for everyone here, from well-developed RV sites to spacious sites along the water's edge. The park feels spacious, with lots of open space to roam. This is a good base camp for outings to Bar Harbor and Acadia National Park.

Campsites, facilities: There are 120 sites for tents and RVs, 50 with full hookups, 60 with water and electric hookups, and 10 with none. Flush toilets, hot showers, picnic tables, fireplaces, laundry facilities, a dump station, and a store selling groceries and RV supplies are provided. Recreational facilities include a boat launch, heated swimming pool, canoe rentals, a recreation room, miniature golf, volleyball, basketball, badminton, and horseshoes. Ice, firewood, and LP gas are available. Leashed pets are permitted.

Reservations, fees: Reservations are recommended for July and August. A $45 deposit is required for stays of up to three days; for four or more days, send a $90 deposit. Sites are $22–46 a night.

Open: Memorial Day–Columbus Day.

Directions: From the junction of Highway 3 and Highway 230 in Ellsworth, drive .25 mile south on Highway 3 to the campground.

Contact: Narrows Too Camping Resort, RR 1, Box 193, Trenton, ME 04605, 207/667-4300, website: www.barharborcampgrounds.com.

24 BARCADIA CAMPGROUND

Rating: 7
On Western Bay, north of Bar Harbor

Barcadia bills itself as the "gateway to Acadia National Park," and there is some truth to the claim, as this is the first campground you encounter after crossing the bridge to Mount Desert Island from the mainland. This is a large park with open and wooded sites, many set directly along the shore of Western Bay. A waterfront site on the private beach is worth the extra fee, given the panoramic views of the bay you gain. A shuttle bus provides regular service to Bar Harbor.

Campsites, facilities: There are 200 sites for tents and RVs, 25 with full hookups, 150 with water and electric hookups, and 25 with none. Flush toilets, hot showers, picnic tables, fireplaces, a dump station, laundry facilities, and a store are provided. Recreational facilities include a boat launch, private beach, a playground, recreation room, volleyball, basketball, and horseshoe pits. Ice, firewood, and LP gas are available. Leashed pets are permitted.

Reservations, fees: Reservations are recommended and require a deposit of two days' fees. Sites are $25–36 a night for four people. Pets are $2 a day.

Open: May 17–October 15.

Directions: From Ellsworth, drive south on Highway 3 onto Mount Desert Island. The campground is at the intersection of Highways 3 and 102/198 at the island's northern tip.

Contact: Pete and Lynn Desroches, Barcadia Campground, RR 1, Box 2165, Bar Harbor, ME 04609, 207/288-3520, website: www.acadiainfo.com/barcadiacamp.htm.

25 MOUNT DESERT NARROWS CAMPING RESORT

Rating: 7
In Bar Harbor near the bridge to Mount Desert Island

Situated directly on the ocean narrows separating Mount Desert Island from the mainland, this large campground has something for everyone. The park offers distinct RV and wilderness tenting areas, a full range of amenities and amusements, and oceanfront and oceanview sites on an expansive shoreline. It's a quick drive to the center of Bar Harbor and the entrance to Acadia National Park.

Campsites, facilities: There are 239 sites for tents and RVs, 50 with full hookups, 136 with water and electric hookups, and 53 with none. Flush toilets, hot showers, picnic tables, fireplaces, laundry facilities, a dump station, and a store selling groceries and RV supplies are provided. Recreational facilities include a heated swimming pool, saltwater swimming and fishing, miniature golf, canoe rentals, volleyball, basketball, badminton, and horseshoes. Ice, firewood, and LP gas are available. Leashed pets are permitted.

Reservations, fees: Reservations are recommended. A $45 deposit is required for stays of up to three days; for four or more days, it's a $90 deposit. Sites are $18–45 a night.

Open: May 1–October 25.

Directions: From Ellsworth, drive south on Highway 3 onto Mount Desert Island. After you reach the intersection of Highways 3 and

102/198, drive another 1.5 miles east on Highway 3 to the campground.

Contact: Mount Desert Narrows Camping Resort, Highway 3/Bar Harbor Road, RR 1, Box 2045, Bar Harbor, ME 04609, 207/288-4782, website: www.barharborcampgrounds.com.

26 HADLEY'S POINT CAMPGROUND

🚶 🚴 🏊 ⛴ 🛶 🎣 🏕 🐕 ♿ 🚐 ⛺

Rating: 6

In Bar Harbor

Just four miles from the entrance to Acadia National Park, Hadley's is well situated for those who want to take advantage of Mount Desert Island's scenic and recreational opportunities. The sites are set in open fields and woods near, but not on, the waterfront. A public saltwater beach is just a five-minute stroll from the campground. If chilly saltwater doesn't appeal to you, take a dip in the campground's pool. Shuttle service from Hadley's to Bar Harbor runs daily from late June to Labor Day. Christian campers will appreciate that church services are held every Sunday at the campground.

Campsites, facilities: There are 180 sites for tents and RVs, 15 with full hookups, 117 with water and electric hookups, and 48 with none. Flush toilets, hot showers, picnic tables, fireplaces, a dump station, laundry facilities, a store, and Sunday church services are provided. The property also has a playground, swimming pool, shuffleboard, basketball, and horseshoe pits. Leashed pets are permitted.

Reservations, fees: Reservations are recommended. Sites are $20–28 a night.

Open: May 15–October 15.

Directions: From Ellsworth, drive south on Highway 3 onto Mount Desert Island. After you reach the intersection of Highways 3 and 102/198, drive another three miles east on Highway 3 to the campground on the left.

Contact: The Baker Family, Hadley's Point Campground, Hadley's Point Road, Box 1790,

Bar Harbor, ME 04609, 207/288-4808, website: www.hadleyspoint.com.

27 BAR HARBOR CAMPGROUND

🚶 🚴 🏊 ⛴ 🛶 🎣 🏕 🐕 ♿ 🚐 ⛺

Rating: 6

Just outside the town of Bar Harbor

The designers of this very large campground have managed to create sites in a maritime spruce-fir forest that offer plenty of privacy yet have a spacious feel. Located just north of the village of Bar Harbor and close to the Nova Scotia ferry terminal, the campground is well placed for folks who seek quick access to all that the region has to offer, including the wondrous features of Acadia National Park—among them its forests, beaches, mountains, cliffs, wildlife, lakes, and offshore islands. By walking a short distance from here, campers can soon be exploring the town of Bar Harbor and sampling the food at the wonderful restaurants there. A lobster pound, just across the street from Bar Harbor Campground, is a great place to shop for a Down East dinner.

Campsites, facilities: There are 300 sites for tents and RVs, 60 with full hookups, 100 with water and electric hookups, and 140 with none. Flush toilets, hot showers, picnic tables, fireplaces, a dump station, laundry facilities, and a store are provided. Recreational facilities include a swimming pool, playground, recreation room, shuffleboard, basketball, and horseshoe pits. Leashed pets are permitted.

Reservations, fees: Reservations are not accepted. Sites are $20–28 a night.

Open: Memorial Day–Columbus Day.

Directions: From Ellsworth, drive south on Highway 3 onto Mount Desert Island. After you reach the intersection of Highways 3 and 102/198, drive another five miles east on Highway 3 to the campground on the left.

Contact: Craig Robbins, Bar Harbor Campground, R.F.D. 1, Box 1125, Bar Harbor, ME 04609, 207/288-5185, website: www.barharborcamping.com.

28 MAINAYR CAMPGROUND

Rating: 10

On Joy Cove near Steuben

Mainayr is situated on a tidal cove emptying into the open Atlantic Ocean. The feeling here is one of wildness, woods and waters, and fresh sea breezes. Wildlife abounds in the estuary, salt marshes, and forested uplands that surround campers. This is a real retreat, an off-the-beaten-path refuge that provides peace and quiet in an unspoiled Maine coast setting.

Campsites, facilities: There are 32 sites for tents and RVs, five with full hookups, five with water and electric hookups, seven with electric only, and 13 with none. Flush toilets, hot showers, picnic tables, fireplaces, a dump station, laundry facilities, and a store are provided. Recreational facilities include a beach, playground, recreation room, volleyball and badminton nets, and horseshoe pits. Leashed pets are permitted.

Reservations, fees: Reservations are recommended. Sites are $18.25 a night.

Open: Memorial Day–Columbus Day.

Directions: From the intersection of U.S. 1 and Steuben Road in Steuben, drive .5 mile east on Steuben Road to the campground.

Contact: David and Kathy Ayers, Mainayr Campground, RR 1, P.O. Box 69, Steuben, ME 04680, 207/546-2690, website: www.mainayr.com.

29 ROCKY LAKE PUBLIC RESERVED LAND

Rating: 9

North of East Machias

The Rocky Lake Management Unit is an 11,000-acre wildland typical of this portion of eastern Maine. A glacial landscape dotted with rocky, jagged-edged lakes and with watersheds divided by low ridges, the unit is laced by meandering streams bordered by abundant natural wetlands. The preserve incorporates Rocky Lake, a beautiful and remote body of water with numerous coves, inlets, and islands that offer excellent fishing. Also within the unit's boundaries are stretches of the East Branch of the Machias River, a stream renowned as a great canoeing and fishing destination.

Campsites, facilities: There are six primitive campsites. Four are reachable by water only, while two are accessible by vehicle. Pit toilets, picnic tables, and fire rings are provided. Pets are permitted.

Reservations, fees: Registration is not required; sites are available on a first-come, first-served basis. There is no fee.

Open: Year-round.

Directions: From East Machias, drive six miles north on Highway 191 to access the management unit.

Contact: Maine Bureau of Parks and Lands, Eastern Region Office, Airport Road, Box 415, Old Town, ME 04468, 207/827-5936, fax 207/827-8441, website: www.state.me.us/doc/parks.

30 BAYVIEW CAMPGROUND

Rating: 8

In the town of Milbridge on Narraguagus Bay

This campground has open sites overlooking the sparkling waters of Narraguagus Bay, a long reach of the Atlantic Ocean where the Narraguagus River flows into the sea. Enjoy a view over the dark blue swells, watch lobstermen ply their trade, or launch your sea kayak and explore this unspoiled slice of the Maine coast. And if you think Maine's coastal communities are all chock-full of tourist traps and lobster pounds, Milbridge is a pleasant surprise. This is truly a Down East Maine town, home to one of the region's last surviving sardine canneries as well as a Christmas wreath factory, two examples of the state's traditional industries. While in the area, be sure to visit the Petit Manan National Wildlife Refuge, where a five-mile hiking path clings to the shoreline. Bicyclists find lots of little-traveled roads and logging routes in the campground's vicinity.

Campsites, facilities: There are 24 sites for tents and RVs, 14 with water and electric hookups and 10 with none. Flush toilets, hot showers, picnic tables, fireplaces, recreation pavilion, and a dump station are provided. Leashed pets are permitted.

Reservations, fees: Reservations are accepted. Sites are $17–20 a night.

Open: May 15–October 15.

Directions: From the intersection of U.S. 1 and U.S. 1A in Milbridge, drive .25 mile north on U.S. 1A, then turn right on Bayview Street and go .5 mile east to the campground.

Contact: Bayview Campground, Box 243, Milbridge, ME 04658, 207/546-2946.

31 COBSCOOK BAY STATE PARK

🏕️ 🛶 🚐 ⛏️ 🐕 👫 🚙 ⛺

Rating: 10

South of Dennysville on Cobscook Bay

Twenty-four-foot tides—the highest in the state—and the famous Reversing Falls near Pembroke make this one of the most scenic and dramatic natural areas in the country. And this park, located in undeveloped Down East Maine, is a real gem. Camping spots are perched above the water as well as in the maritime boreal forest of thick spruce and fir. Launch your boat, canoe, or kayak on the bay, or hike one of the nature trails that leaves right from the campground. Additionally, be sure to take a day trip to Quoddy Head State Park, the easternmost point in the United States and the first place in the country to be struck by the sun's rays every morning. Also a short drive away are Roosevelt-Campobello International Park, where President Franklin Delano Roosevelt and his family spent their summers, and Moosehorn National Wildlife Refuge. To the southwest is Roque Bluffs State Park, which boasts sugary sand beaches and both saltwater and freshwater swimming. The campground is a delectable spot to stay while traveling to or from Canada's Maritime Provinces.

Campsites, facilities: There are 125 sites for tents and RVs, all without hookups. Each site has a picnic table and fire ring. Pit toilets, hot showers, a dump station, boat launch, nature trails, and a playground are also provided. Leashed pets are permitted.

Reservations, fees: Reservations are accepted. Contact the Maine Bureau of Parks and Lands at 207/287-3821. The State of Maine allocates some sites on a first-come, first-served basis. Sites are $14 a night for Maine residents and $19 for nonresidents.

Open: May 15–October 15.

Directions: From the junction of Highway 86 and U.S. 1 in Dennysville, drive south on U.S. 1 for six miles to the park.

Contact: Cobscook Bay State Park Ranger, 207/726-4412; Maine Bureau of Parks and Lands, 22 State House Station, Augusta, ME 04333, 207/287-3821, website: www.state.me.us/doc/parks.

32 KNOWLTON'S SEASHORE CAMPGROUND

🏊 🛶 🚐 ⛏️ 🐕 👫 🚙 ⛺

Rating: 10

Near the tiny hamlet of Perry

From its prime location on a narrow peninsula jutting out into the water, Knowlton's Seashore Campground offers splendid views up and down Cobscook Bay. Campsites are strung along the shore in a grassy, open field, giving you a sensation of being out at sea. Fish, canoe, kayak, and swim right from the campground if you wish, or explore the broad expanses and hidden coves, islands, and inlets of Cobscook and Passamaquoddy Bays. For more information on the area, see the Cobscook Bay State Park listing in this chapter.

Campsites, facilities: There are 80 sites for tents and RVs, 50 with full hookups, 10 with water and electric hookups, and 20 with none. Flush toilets, hot showers, picnic tables, fire rings, a dump station, and a playground are provided. Leashed pets are permitted.

Reservations, fees: Reservations are recommended. A $5 deposit is required. Sites are $14–$18 a night.

Open: May 21–mid-October.

Directions: From Calais, drive south on U.S. 1 to Perry. After you reach the junction with Highway 190 in town, continue three miles south on U.S. 1 to the campground.

Contact: Mr. and Mrs. Lloyd Knowlton, Knowlton's Seashore Campground, U.S. 1, Perry, ME 04667, 207/726-4756.

33 THE SEAVIEW

Rating: 7

In Eastport

Located on a slight hill overlooking the broad blue reaches of Passamaquoddy Bay, The Seaview has sites in an open field sloping toward the water. The campground does afford great views, but because the park is tucked away on a long, narrow strip of waterfront property, there is a lack of open space and the trailers, rental houses, and cabins are packed quite close together. With its good boating access, the waterfront is the recreational focal point for campers. If you like shellfish, try digging for clams in the flats of Passamaquoddy Bay at low tide. For more information on the area, see the Cobscook Bay State Park listing in this chapter.

Campsites, facilities: There are 80 sites for RVs with full hookups, plus some tent sites and cabins. Flush toilets, hot showers, picnic tables, fire rings, a dump station, laundry facilities, cable TV hookups, a playground, recreation room, boat ramp, horseshoe pits, and a store are provided. Leashed pets are permitted.

Reservations, fees: Reservations are recommended. Sites range from $18–25 a night.

Open: May 15–October 15.

Directions: From Calais, drive south on U.S. 1 to Perry. At the junction of U.S. 1 and Highway 190, bear left and drive five miles south on Highway 190, then turn left on Norwood Road and go .25 mile east to the campground.

Contact: The Seaview, 16 Norwood Road, Eastport, ME 04631, 207/853-4471.

34 QUIETSIDE CAMPGROUND

Rating: 7

On the western side of Mount Desert Island in West Tremont

The name refers to the fact that this small, peaceful campground is located on the far edge of the western side of Mount Desert Island, known as the quiet side. Most of the sites are tucked into the woods, affording a good deal of privacy. Fresh Maine food is available nearby: check out the wild blueberry fields to see if the delicious fruit is in season (you can buy berries from roadside stands or pick wild ones yourself) and travel to one of the working harbor towns for fresh fish or lobster. Still within a short drive of the action in touristy Bar Harbor village and the natural and scenic splendors of Acadia National Park, the campground is a haven of relaxation after a day pursuing the myriad activities available to visitors on Mount Desert Island.

Campsites, facilities: There are 37 sites, six for RVs with water and electric hookups and 31 tent sites with none. Flush toilets, hot showers, picnic tables, fireplaces, laundry facilities, a playground, and a dump station are provided. The maximum RV length is 22 feet. Leashed pets are permitted.

Reservations, fees: Reservations are recommended, and you must send a 50 percent deposit. Sites are $19–24 a night. Pets are $5 a night.

Open: June 15–Columbus Day.

Directions: From Ellsworth, drive south on Highway 3 onto Mount Desert Island. Follow Highway 102/198 south and then go south on Highway 102. From the intersection with Highway 102A in Southwest Harbor, drive 3.25 miles south on Highway 102 to the campground.

Contact: Hugh and Susan McIsaac, Quietside Campground, Highway 102, P.O. Box 8, West Tremont, ME 04690, 207/244-5992, website: www.quietsidecampground.com.

35 BASS HARBOR CAMPGROUND

🚶 🚴 🛶 🎣 🚐 ✕ 🏕 🚗 ⛺

Rating: 8

In Bass Harbor, on the western side of Mount Desert Island

The western, or quiet, side of Mount Desert Island is home to this attractive campground located near many of Acadia National Park's finest natural jewels, including mountains, beaches, and the pounding surf of the Atlantic Ocean. Also nearby are the picturesque Bass Harbor Head Lighthouse, scenic fishing village of Bernard, and hiking trails that trace the oceanside at Ship Harbor. While you are close to the hustle and bustle of the national park, you're not in the center of the action, a plus for those who want to get away from the crowds. The park's Seawall section is a short drive away. A long, sandy beach nearby makes the perfect spot for an evening picnic when you return to the campground after a day of exploring.

Campsites, facilities: There are 130 sites for tents and RVs, 58 with water and electric hookups and 74 without hookups. Flush toilets, free hot showers, picnic tables, fireplaces, a dump station, laundry facilities, and a store are provided. Cable TV is available. You will find a heated swimming pool, playground, recreation room, miniature golf, shuffleboard, basketball, and horseshoe pits on the grounds. No pets are allowed.

Reservations, fees: Reservations are recommended. Sites are $24–32 a night.

Open: Memorial Day–September 30.

Directions: From Ellsworth, drive south on Highway 3 onto Mount Desert Island. Follow Highway 102/198 south and then continue south on Highway 102. From the intersection with Highway 102A in Southwest Harbor, drive five miles south on Highway 102A.

Contact: The McAfee Family, Bass Harbor Campground, P.O. Box 122, Highway 102A, Bass Harbor, ME 04653, 207/244-5857, website: www.bassharbor.com.

36 SEAWALL CAMPGROUND

🚶 🚴 🛶 🎣 🚐 ✕ 🐕 ♿ 🚗 ⛺

Rating: 10

In Acadia National Park near Southwest Harbor

While most of Acadia National Park is on the eastern peninsula of Mount Desert Island, a few of its gems dot the western peninsula. Here on the "quiet" side of the island, separated from the hustle and bustle of Bar Harbor and the park's main attractions, Seawall is the kind of place where you can relax and enjoy all that the coast of Maine has to offer. As you look out across the street, you soon realize how the campground got its name: a natural seawall, formed by the piling up of rocks and boulders set loose by winter storms, stretches along the coastline in the vicinity. The beach across the road is perfect for picnics, photography, beachcombing, kayaking, windsurfing, and—for hardy souls—swimming. The campsites are spacious, well maintained, and afford a good deal of privacy. And an extensive array of programs that interests both adults and children takes place on summer evenings at the campground's amphitheater. In a short drive, you can be back on the eastern side of the park, hiking Cadillac Mountain, biking or horseback riding on the carriage trails, canoeing in Somes Sound, or simply driving the loop road. Be sure to stop at the charming town of Southwest Harbor.

Campsites, facilities: There are 212 sites for tents and RVs, all without hookups. A group camping area is also available. Facilities include wheelchair-accessible flush toilets, picnic tables, and fireplaces. A self-guided nature trail leaves from the campground, and a picnic area is located across the street at the beach. Leashed pets are permitted.

Reservations, fees: Sites are available on a first-come, first-served basis. The fee is $20 a night.
Open: Late May–late September.
Directions: From Ellsworth, drive south on Highway 3 onto Mount Desert Island. Follow Highway 102/198 to Southwest Harbor and continue south on Highway 102. At the fork, bear left onto Highway 102A/Manset Road and continue approximately five miles to the campground, on your right.
Contact: Acadia National Park, P.O. Box 177, Bar Harbor, ME 04609, 207/288-3338, website: www.nps.gov/acad.

37 BLACKWOODS CAMPGROUND

🥾 🚲 🏊 🛶 🛥 🗙 ♿ 🐕 🚐 ⛰

Rating: 9

In Acadia National Park

Blackwoods Campground bears an appropriate name, as it is situated in a thick maritime forest of dark spruce and fir trees. This place definitely has a northern feel, and even on the hottest summer days the air is cool and fresh. As with virtually every public campground in Maine, whether run by state or federal authorities, the sites at Blackwoods are very well spaced and afford a remarkable amount of privacy. Staying here puts you on Mount Desert Island's east side, and from the campground you can hop on the long, gentle trail that leads to the Cadillac Mountain summit, which rises 1,530 feet above the sea.
Campsites, facilities: There are 306 sites for tents and RVs, all without hookups. Facilities include wheelchair-accessible flush toilets, picnic tables, fireplaces, and a dump station. Hiking trails and bike paths leave from the campground. Leashed pets are permitted.
Reservations, fees: Reservations are strongly recommended. Contact Ticketron or Acadia National Park at the numbers below. Sites are $20 a night.
Open: Year-round.
Directions: From Ellsworth, drive south on

Highway 3 to the town of Bar Harbor on Mount Desert Island. After you reach the intersection of Highways 3 and 233, continue another five miles south on Highway 3 to the campground.
Contact: Ticketron, 800/365-2267; Acadia National Park, P.O. Box 177, Bar Harbor, ME 04609, 207/288-3338, website: www.nps.gov/acad.

38 OCEAN WOOD CAMPGROUND

🥾 🚲 🏊 🛶 🛥 🗙 🚐 🐕 ⛰

Rating: 10

On the Schoodic Peninsula in Birch Harbor

One section of Acadia National Park that most people never see is the Schoodic Peninsula, which lies across Frenchman Bay from Bar Harbor and Mount Desert Island. This lovely, windswept point juts out into the frothy Atlantic, a rocky, pine-covered headland far from the summer crowds you see elsewhere. Just one mile from the park boundary in Birch Harbor, Ocean Wood Campground caters to those who can't wait to get off the beaten path. The spacious sites cover more than a quarter acre on average, and many are located right on the waterfront. This is definitely a place for someone looking to get away from it all.
Campsites, facilities: There are 70 sites for tents and RVs, 20 with partial hookups and 50 with none. Flush toilets, hot showers, picnic tables, and fireplaces are provided. Leashed pets are permitted.
Reservations, fees: Reservations are accepted. Sites are $18–32 a night.
Open: May 1–October 31.
Directions: From Ellsworth, drive east on U.S. 1 and then turn right on Highway 186 heading south toward Schoodic Point. At the intersection of Highway 186 and Birch Harbor Road in Birch Harbor, turn south on Birch Harbor Road and drive .5 mile to the campground.
Contact: Ocean Wood Campground, P.O. Box 111, Birch Harbor, ME 04613, 207/963-7194, website: www.jabinc.org/oceanwood/ow_campground.htm.

39 CUTLER COAST MANAGEMENT UNIT

Rating: 10
Near the village of Cutler and the ocean

Located on Down East Maine's Bold Coast—the easternmost region in the United States—this unit encompasses almost five miles of undeveloped ocean shoreline. A trail network traces along the shore, providing access to remote hike-in campsites that allow intrepid souls to have a wild maritime camping experience. After you break camp, return via the trail as it crosses overland through the thick forests and open meadows of the interior to gain a full perspective on all that the area has to offer.

Campsites, facilities: There are three primitive tent sites accessible by foot only. Each site has a pit toilet, picnic table, and fire ring. Pets are permitted.

Reservations, fees: Registration is not required; sites are available on a first-come, first-served basis. There is no fee.

Open: Year-round.

Directions: From Cutler, drive approximately three miles north on Highway 191 to access the management unit.

Contact: Maine Bureau of Parks and Lands, 22 State House Station, Augusta, ME 04333, 207/287-3821, website: www.state.me.us/doc/parks.

40 SUNSET POINT TRAILER PARK

Rating: 8
On a peninsula jutting into Cobscook Bay in Lubec

Ⓕ Sunset Point is a small campground sitting on a peninsula in Cobscook Bay. Open and airy with gorgeous views over the pine-and-spruce-rimmed bay, this quiet place enjoys a setting of stunning natural beauty. Campers get good water access and can easily swim, fish, canoe, or kayak in the ocean from here. Anglers also find a small freshwa-

ter pond for fishing. The tiny town of Lubec is the gateway to Campobello Island, site of Roosevelt-Campobello International Park. And just down the road from the campground is Quoddy Head State Park. For more information on the area, see the previous listing for Cobscook Bay State Park.

Campsites, facilities: There are 40 sites for tents and RVs, 30 with water and electric hookups and 10 with none. Facilities include flush toilets, hot showers, picnic tables, fire rings, a dump station, laundry facilities, cable TV hookups, horseshoe pits, and badminton nets. Leashed pets are permitted.

Reservations, fees: Reservations are accepted. Sites are $18–27 a night.

Open: Memorial Day–Columbus Day.

Directions: From East Machias, follow U.S. 1 northeast to Whiting. Bear right onto Highway 189 and travel nine miles east to the campground.

Contact: Jane Hallett, Sunset Point Trailer Park, Highway 189, Lubec, ME 04652, 207/733-2150.

41 SOUTH BAY CAMPGROUND

Rating: 8
On South Bay, a part of Cobscook Bay, in Lubec

Large private sites with views of Cobscook Bay make this campground a kayaker's dream. Just offshore there is seemingly endless coastline and protected water to paddle with virtually no visible sign of humanity. Bring your binoculars and watch the seals and the eagles. For more information on the area, see the the Cobscook Bay State Park listing in this chapter.

Campsites, facilities: There are 82 sites for tents and RVs, 15 with full hookups, 20 with water and electric hookups, and 47 with no hookups. Facilities include flush toilets, hot showers, picnic tables, fire rings, a dump station, laundry facilities, a recreation hall, modem connection, horseshoes, hiking trails, and a swimming pool. Pets are permitted.

Reservations, fees: Reservations are accepted. Sites are $20–25 a night.
Open: May 15–October 15.
Directions: From East Machias, follow U.S. 1 northeast to Whiting. Bear right onto Highway 189 and travel 7.5 miles to the campground.
Contact: J. T. Wilson, South Bay Campground, 591 County Road, Lubec, ME 04652, 207/733-1037.

New Hampshire

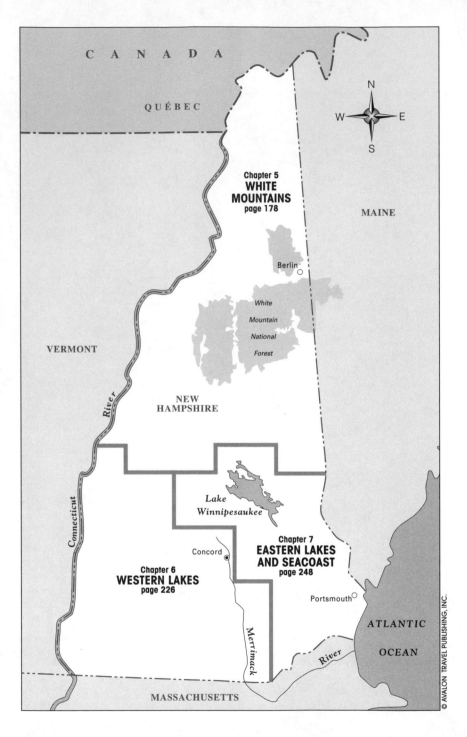

Within the image:

C A N A D A

QUÉBEC

N
W   E
S

Chapter 5
**WHITE
MOUNTAINS**
page 178

MAINE

Berlin

White

Mountain

National

Forest

VERMONT

River

NEW
HAMPSHIRE

Connecticut

Lake
Winnipesaukee

Chapter 7
**EASTERN LAKES
AND SEACOAST**
page 248

Concord

Chapter 6
WESTERN LAKES
page 226

Portsmouth

ATLANTIC

OCEAN

Merrimack

River

MASSACHUSETTS

© AVALON TRAVEL PUBLISHING, INC.

JEFFEREY E. BLACKMAN/© NEW HAMPSHIRE OFFICE OF TRAVEL AND TOURISM DEVELOPEMENT

White Mountains

White Mountains

N ew Hampshire's majestic White Mountains are truly the roof of
New England. Austere, remote, and visible from more than 30
miles out to sea, the White Mountains are a jumble of jagged
peaks and sharp, bare summits. Located in the northern-central part
of the state, they sprawl north to the Canadian border and reach well
into Maine.

Unlike the gentler Green Mountains in Vermont—which are essentially a smooth ridgeline running north-south, forming the spine of
that state—the White Mountains are a collection of wild and rugged
individual peaks and distinct ranges. Formed by cataclysmic volcanic
activity, these mountains are solid granite and are the source of New
Hampshire's nickname "The Granite State." The peaks and ranges
are separated by forested valleys and sheer mountain passes—the
rough-hewn products carved from the living rock by the last great Ice
Age that departed the region some 10,000 years ago.

As a four-season playground, the White Mountains are hard to beat.
Winter, the longest season, lasts nearly half the year and buries the region in snow, which is perfect for downhill and cross-country skiing,
snowshoeing, snowmobiling, and dogsledding. In spring the skiing continues on the high summits and in the glacial ravines on Mount Washington and the Presidential Range, while down below in the valleys, the
raging rivers attract white-water boaters and fly fishers. Summer means

biking, mountain climbing, hiking on the Appalachian Trail and myriad other footpaths, and swimming in the region's many lakes. For many, autumn is the finest season, when the fiery colors attract leaf-peepers by the thousands.

The State of New Hampshire operates 18 campgrounds. The campgrounds are generally open from mid-May through Columbus Day, except where specially noted in the text. The phone numbers given for each campground are in service during this period, but cannot be used to make reservations. All reservations for state park campgrounds are made through the New Hampshire State Parks Camping Reservation Center, P.O. Box 1856, Concord, NH 03302-1856, 603/271-3628 or website: www.nhparks.state.nh.us. Reservations are accepted by phone Monday through Friday, excluding holidays according to the following dates and hours: January, 9 A.M.–10 P.M.; February–mid-May, 9 A.M.–4 P.M.; mid-May–Labor Day, 9 A.M.–10 P.M. and Saturday, 9 A.M.–7 P.M.; Labor Day–October 1, 9 A.M.–4 P.M. Reservations must be made at least seven days prior to the beginning of your stay, and reservation phone calls are limited to two reservations per call. Be ready to pay the site fee when you make your reservation. To make reservations by mail, call and request an official prereservation form. Reservations are also accepted via email from the state park website at www.nhparks.state.nh.us.

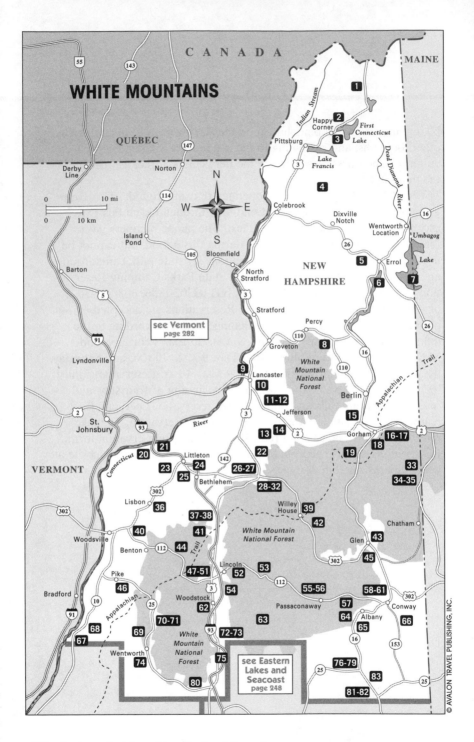

1 DEER MOUNTAIN CAMPGROUND

Rating: 10

North of the Second Connecticut Lake

These primitive wooded sites are found along the Connecticut River between the First and Second Connecticut Lakes. Hiking trails leave from the campground and explore Moose Falls, a small and lovely waterfall. Fishing in the river and the lakes is allowed; be sure to check on regulations before you cast a line, though, as some areas are restricted to fly-fishing and catch-and-release, and you can keep only one salmon and one lake trout from the lakes. Moose viewing is a popular pastime in this area just south of the Canadian border. The rangy beasts usually come out for a bite to eat around dusk. In late August, the North Country holds a Moose Festival with parades, mock moose stew, and dancing in the street. For many years, this portion of the northern forest was heavily logged. Today the abandoned logging roads make good mountain biking trails.

Campsites, facilities: There are 26 sites for tents and RVs, all without hookups. Piped water and primitive toilets are provided. Water is not available after mid-October. Leashed pets are permitted.

Reservations, fees: For reservations, contact the New Hampshire State Parks Camping Reservation Center, P.O. Box 1856, Concord, NH 03302-1856, 603/271-3628, website: www.nhparks.state.nh.us. Sites are $13 a night.

Open: Early May-early December.

Directions: From Pittsburg, travel north on U.S. 3 for 20 miles to the campground entrance.

Contact: Deer Mountain Campground, Connecticut Lakes State Forest, U.S. Highway 3, Pittsburg, NH 03592, 603/538-6965; New Hampshire Division of Parks and Recreation, 603/271-3628.

2 MOUNTAIN VIEW CABINS AND CAMPGROUND

Rating: 10

North of Pittsburg

A variety of spacious sites, from wooded to open and grassy, are available just off U.S. 3. This makes a great jumping-off point to explore the wilderness area known as the Great North Woods stretching across northern Vermont, New York, and New Hampshire, and over the Canadian border. Boaters and anglers are especially drawn to the string of Connecticut Lakes and numerous streams nearby. This was once a heavily logged area, and miles of old logging roads make for excellent mountain biking.

Campsites, facilities: There are 60 sites for tents and RVs, some with water and electric hookups, and 16 year-round housekeeping cabins. A dump station, restrooms, and hot showers are provided, and canoes are available for rent. Ice and firewood are sold on the property. Leashed pets are permitted.

Reservations, fees: Reservations are accepted. Sites start at $16 a night for two people; cabins are $60-125 for two people.

Open: The campground is open May-October; the cabins are open year-round.

Directions: From Pittsburg, travel three miles north on U.S. 3. The campground entrance is on the left (west) side of the road.

Contact: Mountain View Cabins and Campground, RR 1, Box 30, Pittsburg, NH 03592, 603/538-6305, website: www.mountainviewcabinsandcampground.com.

3 LAKE FRANCIS STATE PARK

Rating: 10

On the northwest tip of Lake Francis

Water, water everywhere. Lake Francis is a pristine, undeveloped tall drink of water. These sites are scattered along an odd arm that juts north from the eastern end of the lake's main body.

Five of the 43 sites are "hike-ins," set about a two-minute walk from the parking lot; these sites are near the Connecticut River and have tent platforms. A boat launch is located at the day-use area south of the campground. The shoreline is heavily wooded, and boaters should be watchful of high winds when out on the water. Trout and salmon are the primary game fish. This 2,051-acre body of water is the last in the chain of lakes that forms the Connecticut River headwaters. Fittingly, the lake was named for Saint Francis, the patron saint of wildlife. Some of the many creatures who call the area home include beavers, hawks, eagles, osprey, herons, otters, fisher cats, and moose.

Campsites, facilities: There are 41 sites for tents and RVs, all without hookups. A dump station, restrooms, and tables are provided. Services and supplies are available in Pittsburg. Water is not available after mid-October. Leashed pets are permitted.

Reservations, fees: For reservations, contact the New Hampshire State Parks Camping Reservation Center, P.O. Box 1856, Concord, NH 03302-1856, 603/271-3628, website: www.nh-parks.state.nh.us. Sites are $13–20 a night.

Open: Mid-May–mid-December.

Directions: From Pittsburg, travel north on U.S. 3 for seven miles to the campground sign. Turn right on River Road and continue south to the campground entrance.

Contact: Lake Francis State Park, Connecticut Lakes State Forest, 37B River Road, Pittsburg, NH 03592, 603/538-6965; New Hampshire Division of Parks and Recreation, 603/271-3628.

4 COLEMAN STATE PARK

Rating: 10

Northeast of Colebrook

Anglers are the primary customers at these backcountry campsites. Self-contained RVs up to 35 feet in length can make it into the wooded area near Little Diamond Pond. That loch is noted for its excellent trout fishing, home to both rainbows and browns. Diamond Pond and Little Diamond Pond are named for Isaac Diamond, who shot a bull moose in the area in 1778. Man and beast had a good scrap in which Isaac lost all his clothing before the moose went down. These campsites make a good jumping-off point for hunting trips into the surrounding heavily timbered wilderness. The state snowmobile corridor crosses the park and continues through spruce-fir country to the Canadian border. "Roads" are mostly old skidder routes cut through the hills and dales.

Campsites, facilities: There are 30 sites for tents and self-contained RVs, all without hookups. Pit toilets, piped water, a dump station, and a playground are provided. Water is not available after mid-October. The maximum RV length is 35 feet. Leashed pets are permitted.

Reservations, fees: For reservations, contact the New Hampshire State Parks Camping Reservation Center, P.O. Box 1856, Concord, NH 03302-1856, 603/271-3628, website: www.nh-parks.state.nh.us. The fee is $15 a night per family.

Open: Early May–early December.

Directions: From Colebrook, travel east on Highway 26 for seven miles. Turn left on Diamond Pond Road and head north for five miles to the campground.

Contact: Coleman State Park, c/o Connecticut Lakes State Forest, 37B River Road, Pittsburg, NH 03592, 603/538-6965.

5 LOG HAVEN CAMPGROUND

Rating: 8

West of Errol

Smack in the middle of the north country, Log Haven offers sites set beside Clear Stream. You can fish for trout at the campground, but anglers may want to try Akers Pond to the east for some serious pickerel wrangling. The pond has a beach and boat launch and is just west of the town of Errol. In winter, this is a popular spot for snowmobilers, since the campground has direct access to the state-groomed snowmobile trail system. Log Haven lies at the foot of Dixville Notch State Park, where the Heritage Trail leads hikers past such highlights as cascades, outlooks, and the craggy profiles of Martha Washington and Daniel Webster. Though lesser known than their cousin in Franconia, the Old Man of the Mountain, these countenances are nonetheless spectacular. The campground is studded with tall pine trees that provide shade for these mostly grassy sites. A restaurant and lounge with live entertainment are also operated on the property. At last visit in 2004, this property was for sale, so be sure to call for up-to-date information.

Campsites, facilities: There are 90 sites for tents and RVs, 40 with full hookups. Each site has a picnic table and fire ring. A dump station, restrooms, hot showers, laundry facilities, a lounge, pool, and playground are provided. A camp store on the grounds carries ice and firewood. Leashed pets are permitted.

Reservations, fees: Reservations are accepted. Tent sites are $15 a night and RV sites with full hookups are $25 a night per family.

Open: Year-round.

Directions: From Errol, travel west on Highway 26 for 5.5 miles to the campground on the right (north) side of the road.

Contact: Log Haven Campground, P.O. Box 239, Errol, NH 03579, 603/482-3294, website: www.loghaven.com.

6 MOLLIDGEWOCK STATE PARK

🏊 🚣 ✖️ 🐕 🚐 ⛺

Rating: 10

South of Errol

Located in the Thirteen Mile Woods Scenic Area south of Errol, these primitive wooded sites are on the bank of the mighty Androscoggin River. Five remote sites are accessible by either canoe or car. Once used to float logs from out of the north woods to paper mills in Berlin, the Androscoggin is now a whitewater playground. From Errol to Berlin, the river offers 30 miles of excellent paddling or kayaking, with dependable Class III white water, three stretches of rapids, and views of the Presidential Range to the south. The Thirteen Mile Woods is also known for the many moose that venture out to the road to watch the passing cars. A small natural beach is available at the campground, and anglers will find many spots where they can cast for trout and salmon.

Campsites, facilities: There are 47 sites for tents and RVs up to 30 feet in length, all without hookups. Piped water and pit toilets are provided. Ice and wood are sold at a grocery store. Supplies and services can be found in Errol. Leashed pets are permitted.

Reservations, fees: For reservations, contact the New Hampshire State Parks Camping Reservation Center, P.O. Box 1856, Concord, NH 03302-1856, 603/271-3628, website: www.nhparks.state.nh.us. Sites are $13 a night per family.

Open: Mid-May–mid-October.

Directions: From Errol, travel three miles south on Highway 16 to the campground.

Contact: Mollidgewock State Park, P.O. Box 29, Errol, NH 03579, 603/482-3373; New Hampshire Division of Parks and Recreation, 603/271-3628.

7 UMBAGOG LAKE STATE PARK

🏊 🚣 🚐 ✖️ 🐕 🚐 ⛺

Rating: 10

On the south shore of Umbagog Lake

Umbagog Lake straddles the Maine-New Hampshire border east of the town of Errol, and these campsites put you at its southern end. Nearly 8,000 acres of water are available for wildlife viewing, canoeing, boating, fishing, and swimming. There are RV-equipped sites on the lakeshore at base camp and remote sites on secluded shores and islands accessible only by boat. If you don't bring your own canoe or rowboat, you can rent one at the campground, or use the camp's shuttle service.

Most of the New Hampshire shoreline is

protected by the Umbagog Lake National Wildlife Refuge and conservation easements stipulating that the land remains as it is. (Most of the Maine shoreline is privately owned but remains virtually undeveloped.) The landscape consists of rolling hills with a distant mountain backdrop, all blanketed in thick pine forest. There's fair to good fishing on the lake for landlocked salmon, trout, perch, and pickerel. The Androscoggin River, which flows out of the lake on the northwest shore, is open to fly-fishing; it's one of two area waterways that support salmon. The lake is known for its pair of nesting bald eagles and the more than 15 pairs of loons. Osprey, ducks, herons, moose, and deer are other common wildlife. Be aware that winds can come up instantly on this large lake and create treacherous boating conditions. There are numerous inlets and islands to explore by canoe, including the Androscoggin River.

Campsites, facilities: There are 35 sites for tents and RVs at the base campground, most with water and electric hookups, and 32 wilderness sites, some on islands accessible only by boat. The park offers transportation to remote sites for a fee. Each base site has a picnic table and fire ring. A dump station, restrooms, hot showers, and laundry facilities are provided. A small grocery store sells ice. Rental boats are available at the campground. Leashed pets are allowed.

Reservations, fees: Reservations are recommended. For reservations, contact the New Hampshire State Parks Camping Reservation Center, P.O. Box 1856, Concord, NH 03302-1856, 603/271-3628, website: www.nhparks.state.nh.us. Per family, fees range from $20–22 a night.

Open: Late May–mid-September.

Directions: From Errol, travel eight miles southeast on Highway 26 to the campground.

Contact: Umbagog Lake Campground, P.O. Box 181, Errol, NH 03579, 603/482-7795.

8 NAY POND CAMPGROUND

Rating: 8

North of Berlin

Set in a mix of hard- and softwood trees on 62-acre Nay Pond, these sites are secluded and quiet. A beach, boat ramp, and picnic grove are available to campers. Nay Pond owns a private island equipped with a cabin (no electricity) and a stone fireplace available for rent by the week ($1,000) or weekend ($250). The warm-water pond is open to motorized boating and supports rock bass, smallmouth bass, black crappie, pickerel, and horned pout. From the park, the northern reaches of the White Mountain National Forest are visible including the Mahoosuc and Kilkenney Ranges. For a short scenic hike, head northwest of the campground to the South Pond Recreation Area off Highway 110. From there, the Devil's Hopyard Trail is a moderate 2.6-mile hike that passes by a mossy, boulder-strewn gorge and cascade.

Campsites, facilities: There are 50 sites for tents and RVs up to 30 feet long, some with full hookups. Air conditioner and heater use is allowed. A dump station, restrooms, hot showers, laundry facilities, and a playground are provided. Ice and firewood are available. Leashed pets are permitted.

Reservations, fees: Reservations are accepted. For two people, tent or walk-in sites are $15 a night, and sites with full hookups are $20 a night.

Open: June 1–October 1.

Directions: From the junction of Highways 16 and 110 in Berlin, travel nine miles northwest on Highway 110 to the campground.

Contact: Nay Pond Campground, 7 Nay Pond Road, West Milan, NH 03588, 603/449-2122, website: www.naypond.com.

9 BEAVER TRAILS CAMPGROUND

Rating: 8
On the Connecticut River in Lancaster

The Connecticut River flows by these sites in a grassy meadow, so campers can cool off in natural water in addition to the campground pool. Bring your own boat, or rent a canoe and paddle the Connecticut through pastoral farmland with panoramic mountain views. Don't forget to drop in a line while you're at it—trout, bass, and many other species live in the river. A few miles north of the campground on U.S. 3 you'll find the Lancaster Fairgrounds, which hosts an agricultural fair usually on Labor Day weekend. To the east of the campground lies the northern reaches of the White Mountain National Forest, including the Pliny and Pilot mountain ranges, with extensive and little-used hiking trails for day or overnight trips into the backcountry.

Campsites, facilities: There are 46 sites for tents and RVs, 40 with full hookups. Each site has a picnic table and fire ring. Air conditioner and heater use is allowed. A dump station, restrooms, hot showers, laundry facilities, a pool, and a playground are provided. Volleyball and horseshoes are available. A general store sells LP gas, gasoline, ice, and firewood. Leashed pets are permitted.

Reservations, fees: Reservations are recommended. Sites start at $25 a night. Seasonal rates are available on request.

Open: May 1–October 15.

Directions: From the junction of U.S. 3 and U.S. 2 in Lancaster, travel west on U.S. 2 for .75 mile to the campground entrance.

Contact: Beaver Trails Campground, Route 2, Bridge St., Box 315, Lancaster, NH 03584, 603/788-3815 or 888/788-3815, website: www.beavertrailsnh.com.

10 ROGER'S CAMPGROUND AND MOTEL

Rating: 8
Southeast of Lancaster

Rumpled mountain ridges surround this 300-acre campground and motel resort. Most sites are pull-throughs that can accommodate any size RV. Sites are grassy, open, and don't afford much privacy, especially for tenters. On the grounds are a water slide, miniature golf course, and a large arcade area. Group RV caravans are welcome to stay in a field equipped with hookups and portable grills. Two on-site function halls can accommodate groups of up to 200 and 1,000 people, respectively. To the immediate southwest is Weeks State Park, the former estate of John Wingate Weeks. This mountaintop park commemorates the onetime secretary of war and U.S. congressman who introduced legislation that established the White Mountain National Forest. From atop the park's Prospect Mountain's fire tower, you can gaze for miles in every direction. About four miles south of the campground on U.S. 2 is Santa's Village, a Christmas theme park with rides, live reindeer, shows, and the jolly red-suited man himself.

Campsites, facilities: There are over 500 sites for tents and RVs, over half with full hookups. Each site has a table, fire ring, and grill. Air conditioner and heater use is allowed, and phone hookups are available. A dump station, restrooms, hot showers, laundry facilities, a recreation hall, pools, and a playground are provided. Off-season RV storage and a group rally site for tents and RVs are located on the property. Courts for basketball, tennis, badminton, shuffleboard, volleyball, and horseshoes are available. A store carries LP gas, ice, and firewood. Entry is controlled by a traffic gate. Leashed pets are permitted.

Reservations, fees: Reservations are recommended July 1–Labor Day and require a prepaid deposit. Sites start at $24–30 a night.

Open: Late April–late October.

Directions: From Lancaster, travel southeast on U.S. 2 for about two miles to the campground entrance.

Contact: Roger's Campground and Motel, 10 Roger's Campground Road, Lancaster, NH 03584, 603/788-4885, website: www.rogerscampground.com.

11 MOUNTAIN LAKE CAMPGROUND

Rating: 7

On Blood Pond south of Lancaster

Mountains surround Blood Pond and provide the dominant scenery for these wooded and open sites on and near the shore. Canoe, rowboat, and paddleboat rentals are available at the campground, and a dock is provided for campers with boats. The pond supports a variety of warm-water fish species. You can swim at the campground beach, but on colder days you'll probably opt for the heated pool. To sample some of the local produce, check out the farmer's market in Lancaster, held on most weekends during the summer. About three miles south off U.S. 3, the Mountain View Golf Course has nine scenic holes open to the public.

Campsites, facilities: There are 97 sites for tents and RVs, most with hookups. Each site has a picnic table and fire ring. Air conditioner and heater use is allowed, and cable TV is available. A dump station, restrooms, hot showers, laundry facilities, a recreation hall, heated pool, and a playground are provided. Courts for basketball, badminton, volleyball, and horseshoes are available. Rental kayaks, pedal boats, and canoes are available for rent. A grocery store carries LP gas, RV supplies, tackle, ice cream, ice, and firewood. Log cabins and tepees are also for rent. Leashed pets are permitted.

Reservations, fees: Reservations are recommended and require a nonrefundable deposit. Sites start at $26 a night, with surcharges for hookups, air conditioners, heaters, and guests.

Lakefront and prime sites cost extra. Seasonal rates are available.

Open: May 1–October 31.

Directions: From Lancaster, travel four miles south on U.S. 3 to the campground.

Contact: Mountain Lake Campground, P.O. Box 475, Lancaster, NH 03584, 603/788-4509, website: www.greatnorthwoods.org/mountainlake.

12 LANTERN MOTOR INN AND CAMPGROUND

Rating: 8

Northwest of Jefferson

You're in big-view country now: Lantern Motor Inn and Campground is set on a grassy plain with a view of the surrounding White Mountains. The facility is located between the public Waumbek Golf Course and Santa's Village. The latter is a Christmas theme park operated under the guise of Mr. Claus's summer residence. There are trained tropical birds, a roller coaster, shows, and the Skyway Sleigh Monorail. For more natural recreation, head into the northern reaches of the White Mountain National Forest east of the campground.

Campsites, facilities: There are 64 sites for tents and RVs, 23 with full hookups, 30 with water and electric hookups, and 11 with none. Each site has a picnic table, fire ring, and grill. A dump station, restrooms, hot showers, laundry facilities, a recreation hall, video arcade, pool, and playground are provided. Courts for badminton, volleyball, and horseshoes are available. A camp store carries ice and firewood. Leashed pets are permitted.

Reservations, fees: Reservations are accepted with prepaid deposits. Sites are $22–35 a night.

Open: May 15–October 15.

Directions: From the junction of U.S. 2 and Highway 115 south of Jefferson, travel 4.5 miles northwest on U.S. 2 to the campground entrance.

Contact: Lantern Motor Inn and Campground, P.O. Box 97, Jefferson, NH 03583, 603/586-7151, website: www.thelanternresort.com.

13 ISRAEL RIVER CAMPGROUND

Rating: 9

In the Jefferson Meadows

In these graceful meadowlands, the peaks of the Presidential Range rise into full view. Campers swim in the pool, while trout swim in the Israel River, which flows through the grounds. You can hike on rugged forest trails or take easy swings on 18 public holes at the Waumbek Golf Course in Jefferson. Six Gun City and Santa's Village, two theme amusement parks, are within a few miles.

Campsites, facilities: There are 120 sites for tents and RVs, some with full hookups and most with water and electric hookups. Each site has a picnic table and fire ring. A dump station, restrooms, hot showers, laundry facilities, a recreation hall, pool, horseshoe pits, and a playground are provided. Courts for volleyball, basketball, horseshoes, and croquet are also on the property. A camp store carries ice and firewood. Leashed pets are permitted.

Reservations, fees: Reservations are recommended. Sites start at $20 a night. Weekly rates are available.

Open: May 1–October 15.

Directions: From the junction of Highway 115A and U.S. 2 in Jefferson, travel southwest on Highways 115A and 115B for 2.5 miles to the campground.

Contact: Israel River Campground, P.O. Box 179A, Jefferson, NH 03583, 603/586-7977.

14 JEFFERSON CAMPGROUND

Rating: 9

In Jefferson

Frustrated cowboys will think they've died and gone to heaven when they arrive at these campsites next to Six Gun City. The campground boasts mountain views and is just off U.S. 2, but the main attraction is the Wild West theme park next door. Six Gun City features a fort, Indian camp, ranch animals, cowboy skits, frontier show, and burro rides. If that's not enough excitement, a few miles to the northwest is Santa's summer home; Santa's Village is a Christmas theme park with sleigh rides, live tropical birds, elves, and reindeer. In addition to the campground, the owners operate an RV sales office and service garage. One drawback is that the sites are small—only about 20 feet wide—and lack privacy. In addition to renting out campsites, Jefferson is a Fleetwood RV dealer.

Campsites, facilities: There are 100 sites for tents and RVs, 32 with full hookups, 25 with water and electric hookups, and 43 with none. Each site has a picnic table, fire ring, and grill. Air conditioner and heater use is allowed. A dump station, restrooms, hot showers, laundry facilities, a pool, and a playground are provided. Courts for basketball, badminton, volleyball, and horseshoes are available. A small grocery store carries RV supplies, LP gas, ice, and firewood. Leashed pets are permitted.

Reservations, fees: Reservations are accepted. Sites are $18–23 a night.

Open: Memorial Day–Labor Day.

Directions: From the junction of U.S. 2 and Highway 115 south of Jefferson, travel .5 mile northwest on U.S. 2 to the campground entrance.

Contact: Jefferson Campground, P.O. Box 112A, Jefferson, NH 03583, 603/586-4510, website: www.jeffersoncampground.com.

15 MOOSE BROOK STATE PARK

Rating: 9

South of Berlin

Moose Brook and Perkins Brook flow through this wooded campground, and anglers can pull trout from either one. The sites are a good base camp for those who want to make treks into the White Mountain National Forest, but there are also miles of multiuse trails in the park itself. Mountain bikers will find plenty of challenging terrain. A pool on Moose Brook serves as a swimming area.

Campsites, facilities: There are 59 sites for tents and RVs up to 35 feet long, all without hookups. Each site has a picnic table and fire ring. Restrooms, metered hot showers, and horseshoe pits are provided, as are badminton, volleyball, and basketball courts. A camp store carries ice and firewood. Leashed pets are permitted.

Reservations, fees: For reservations, contact the New Hampshire State Parks Camping Reservation Center, P.O. Box 1856, Concord, NH 03302-1856, 603/271-3628, website: www.nhparks.state.nh.us. Sites are $15 a night per family.

Open: Mid-May–mid-October.

Directions: From the junction of Highway 16 and U.S. 2 in Gorham, head west for two miles on U.S. 2 to the park on the right (north) side of the road.

Contact: Moose Brook State Park, R.F.D. 1, 30 Jimtown Road, Gorham, NH 03581, 603/466-3860.

16 WHITE BIRCHES CAMPING PARK
🏃 🚴 🏊 🎣 🐕 🛶 🚐 ⛺

Rating: 9

East of Gorham in the White Mountain National Forest

The campground is divided into three sections: The "village" area has full hookups and grassy pull-through sites for RVs. The "rendezvous" sites are wooded, set in the high meadow of a birch and hemlock forest. And the "topknot" area has wilderness sites in the foothills of Mount Moriah—the most private spots in the whole park. There is a short hiking and biking trail on the property, but just a short drive from here, miles of trails await on the lands of the White Mountain National Forest. Not only is this the only campground offering RV hookups in winter, it's also right on a state-maintained snowmobile trail. The Wildcat Ski Area is 10 miles south of here, and Maine's

Sunday River Ski Resort is 30 miles to the east.

Campsites, facilities: There are 110 sites, about half with hookups. Each site has a picnic table and fire ring. Air conditioner and heater use is allowed. A dump station, restrooms, hot showers, laundry facilities, a recreation hall, pool, and playground are provided. Group sites are available for tents and RVs. Courts for basketball, badminton, volleyball, and horseshoes are on the property. A camp store carries RV supplies, LP gas, ice, and firewood. Leashed pets are permitted.

Reservations, fees: Reservations are recommended. Sites start at $22–27 a night.

Open: Year-round.

Directions: From the junction of U.S. 2 and Highway 16 in Gorham, travel east for 2.5 miles on U.S. 2 to the campground.

Contact: White Birches Camping Park, 218 State Street, Shelburne, NH 03581, 603/466-2022, website: www.gocampingamerica.com/whitebirches.

17 TIMBERLAND CAMPING AREA
🏃 🏊 🎣 🐕 🛶 🚐 ⛺

Rating: 9

West of Shelburne

You'll find large wooded sites with mountain views at Timberland. Equally suited to tents and RVs, these spots look out over the Androscoggin River before it heads into Maine. The Androscoggin Valley Country Club west of the campground is open to the public with 18 holes on a grassy riverside meadow. The Appalachian Trail crosses U.S. 2 near the campground and offers good day hikes or longer treks into the White Mountain National Forest.

Campsites, facilities: There are 133 sites for tents and RVs, 41 with full hookups, 37 with water and electric hookups, and 55 with none. Each site has a picnic table, fire ring, and grill. Air conditioner and heater use is allowed, and full-hookup sites also have satellite TV. A dump station, restrooms, hot showers, laundry facilities, a recreation hall, pool, and playground are provided. Courts for basketball, badminton, croquet, volleyball, and horseshoes are available. A general store carries ice and firewood. Supplies are available in Gorham, four miles west. Leashed pets are permitted.

Reservations, fees: Reservations are recommended and require a prepaid deposit. Sites start at $18–25 a night. Weekly and monthly rates are available.

Open: May 1 late October.

Directions: From the junction of U.S. 2 and Highway 16 in Gorham, travel five miles east on U.S. 2 to the campground entrance.

Contact: Timberland Camping Area, Route 2, P.O. Box 303, Gorham, NH 03581, 603/466-3872, website: www.ucampnh.com/timberland.

18 APPALACHIAN TRAIL

Rating: 10

From the New Hampshire–Vermont border, the trail crosses central New Hampshire on a northeast tack, meeting the Maine border at Success in the Mahoosuc Range

From Springer Mountain in Georgia to Mount Katahdin in Maine, the Appalachian Trail traverses the Appalachian Mountain chain on a continuous 2,158-mile marked footpath. The trail and its adjacent lands—about 270,000 acres—link more than 75 parks and forests in 14 states, including eight units of the national forest system and six units of the national park system. Countless wild, scenic, historic, and pastoral settings are enjoyed along the footpath by through-hikers—those who typically start in Georgia and make a six-month trek to Maine—day hikers, and overnight backpackers. On average, fewer than 200 through-hikers complete the 2,000-mile journey each year.

From the Vermont–New Hampshire line at the Connecticut River, the trail is surrounded by farms, roads, and houses, traverses cleared fields, and passes through some wilderness before entering the White Mountain National Forest in Warren. The first major peak encountered from this direction is Mount Moosilauke, after which the trail crosses Highway 112 and heads into Kinsman Notch. From here, the trail continues northeast through Franconia Notch, the Pemigewasset Wilderness, and Crawford Notch before running over the tallest peak on the entire trail, Mount Washington at 6,288 feet. For the next 10 or so miles, the trail doesn't descend below 5,000 feet and thus is one of the most treacherous portions. After crossing Mount Madison at the north end of the Presidential Range, the trail veers south to Pinkham Notch. Shortly after crossing Highway 16, it heads northeast again through the Carter and Mahoosuc Ranges to the Maine border.

The New Hampshire section of the trail offers an exercise in polar extremes; some of the wildest sections of the entire route are in this state, including the Mount Washington alpine garden, a rare Arctic ecosystem. But summiting Washington can be a bit of a disappointment, for once on top you'll find a snack bar, a visitors center, and hordes of tourists who drive up the auto road each year or take the Cog Railway. Because it has become so developed, some locals call the summit the "slummit" and refer to the railway as the "smog Railway." However, once you turn your back to the commercialization, the views in all directions are breathtaking.

Campsites, facilities: Numerous lean-tos, tent platforms, cabins, and huts are located along the New Hampshire section of the Appalachian Trail. Most of this portion lies within the White Mountain National Forest, and backcountry camping is permitted below tree line away from trails and streams. Primitive toilets and an untreated water source are provided at most formal sites; topographic maps and published guides indicate sites where water may not be available. Leashed pets are permitted.

Reservations, fees: Most tent and lean-to sites are available free of charge on a first-come, first-served basis. Huts and shelters operated by the

Appalachian Mountain Club (AMC), and some of the national forest cabins, have caretakers and charge an overnight fee; some also require reservations (see listing for AMC Huts and Lodges in this chapter). For reservations, contact the Appalachian Mountain Club Pinkham Notch Visitor Center, P.O. Box 298, Gorham, NH 03581, 603/466-2721, email: information@amcinfo.org, website: www.outdoors.org; White Mountain National Forest Supervisor, 719 North Main Street, Laconia, NH 03246, 603/528-8721, TDD for hearing impaired 603/528-8722.
Open: Year-round.
Directions: The Appalachian Trail comes into New Hampshire from Norwich, Vermont, at Hanover on a small bridge over the Connecticut River near the Dartmouth College boathouses. The trail crosses into Maine from New Hampshire on the ridge of the wild, rugged Mahoosuc Range at a shallow notch between Mounts Carlo and Success, in Maine and New Hampshire respectively. The 31-mile section of the Appalachian Trail in the Mahoosucs is unbroken by roads. This portion is accessible at its crossing of U.S. 2 and the Androscoggin River near Shelburne.
Contact: Appalachian Trail Conference, P.O. Box 807, Harpers Ferry, WV 25425, 304/535-6331, website: www.appalachiantrail.org. This nonprofit group publishes 10 sectional guides, which are accompanied by topographic maps. The Appalachian Mountain Club, 5 Joy Street, Boston, MA 02108.

19 DOLLY COPP CAMPGROUND

Rating: 9
In Pinkham Notch in the White Mountain National Forest

Large wooded sites are separated into several areas at this campground along the Peabody River, a stream that is stocked with rainbow, brook, and brown trout. This is one of the largest campgrounds in the entire national forest system, and as many as 1,000 people may be camped here at any time on busy summer weekends. The campground is named for a member of the colorful Copp family who lived here during the 1800s. Remnants of the Copp homestead still exist. Dolly and Hayes Copp were married for five decades, toiling as innkeepers and farming the land. On their 50th anniversary, Dolly decided enough was enough, and the two parted possessions and ways. The Forest Service provides ample information about the region's history. Other nearby attractions include the Mount Washington Auto Road, Tuckerman's Ravine, Crystal Cascade, and hiking trails in the Presidential and Carter Ranges. Interpretive programs are offered at the campground in summer. The Barnes Field group camping area is nearby, and sites there can be reserved through the Androscoggin Ranger District office.
Campsites, facilities: There are 176 RV and tent sites surrounding the historic Dolly Copp homestead. Picnic tables, fire rings, vault toilets, and piped water are provided. Coin-operated hot showers, topographic maps, and camping supplies are available at the AMC Pinkham Notch Visitor Center to the south. Leashed pets are permitted.
Reservations, fees: Reservations are necessary from June–September for some sites. Call Reserve USA, 877/444-6777, or visit www.reserveusa.com. For each reservation, an $8.65 fee is charged. Sites are $18 a night.
Open: Mid-May–mid-October.
Directions: From Gorham, travel six miles south on Highway 16 to the campground.
Contact: White Mountain National Forest, Androscoggin Ranger District, 80 Glen Road, Gorham, NH 03581, 603/466-2713, website: www.fs.fed.us/r9/white/.

20 CONNECTICUT RIVER CANOE SITES

Rating: 10
Connecticut River, at the border of New Hampshire and Vermont

The valley where the Connecticut River forms

the border between New Hampshire and Vermont is a place of beauty and history. Once a through-way for log drives headed to sawmills in Massachusetts, this section of the 410-mile-long liquid highway is New England's largest renewable energy system. Except for a few well-marked breached dams and a set of rapids below White River Junction, the river is an easy to moderate journey in canoe, kayak, or small motorboat.

Though the river begins in the Fourth Connecticut Lake on the New Hampshire–Quebec border in Pittsburg, most canoe trips start below the dam in Canaan, Vermont. From here to the Massachusetts border, river campsites are maintained on a 278-mile river stretch by different groups including the Upper Valley Land Trust, Pacific Gas and Electric, and the Student Conservation Association.

From north to south, they are:

• **Dodge Falls** (Ryegate Dam, Monroe, New Hampshire): Two shelters and a chemical toilet are provided at this campsite.

• **Howard Island** (Haverhill, New Hampshire): A cleared tent site, a box privy, and fire ring are provided.

• **Harkdale Farm** (Newbury, Vermont): Amenities include a cleared tent site, box privy, fire ring, and picnic table.

• **Vaughan Meadow** (South Newbury, Vermont): The site is located about a mile south of the Bedell Bridge abutment. Look for a broad wooded riverbank above a curving beach.

• **Bugbee Landing** (Bradford, Vermont): Behind the Bugbee campsite, the commercial district of Bradford is visible across a golf course. This camping facility is large enough to accommodate groups and is also accessible by car.

• **Underhill Campsite** (Piermont, New Hampshire): Look for the site immediately above Eastman Brook; the town of Piermont is high above on a hill.

• **Birch Meadow** (Fairlee, Vermont): This site is set above marshland at the outlet of Lake Morey.

• **Esther Salmi Campsite** (Thetford, Vermont):

This site lies on a straight stretch of wooded shoreline several hundred meters beyond a white frame house on the New Hampshire side. Watch out for poison ivy here. No open fires are allowed.

• **Loveland Point Campsite** (in Vermont just north of Hanover, New Hampshire): You'll find this campsite on a piney point on the west shore just south of the Ompompanoosuc River mouth in Norwich, Vermont.

• **Gilman Island Campsites** (on Gilman Island): This site is on the south end of the island about a mile below Ledyard Bridge. The northern river section gets a lot of use by crew teams and powerboaters in addition to being the Dartmouth College's Ledyard Canoe Club site. The Ledyard Bridge is also where the Appalachian Trail crosses from Vermont into New Hampshire.

• **Burnap's Island Campsite** (south of White River Junction in Plainfield, New Hampshire): Just below the campsite—located at the mouth of the Ottauquechee River—there are huge boulders in the river known as "Chicken and Hens." The Sumner Falls/Hartland rapids are just ahead.

• **Burnham Meadow** (Windsor, Vermont): You'll get a good view of Mount Ascutney to the west from this site. Three miles south of here there's a covered bridge and the village of Windsor.

• **Wilgus State Park** (Weathersfield, Vermont): The state park campground is located on the west bank, about a mile below the Ascutney bridge. A fee is charged.

• **Student Conservation Association Canoe Camp** (Charleston, New Hampshire): Two small, separate campsites are located approximately two miles below Hubbard Island.

• **Lower Meadow Campsite** (South Charleston, New Hampshire): This site is in a thicket of small trees near the lower end of a series of hayfields. It is isolated from the mainland by a backwater marsh.

• **Windyhurst Farm** (Putney, Vermont): The red barns of Windyhurst Farm are set on a hill above this campsite, which is located in low woods downstream from a large tilled field.

• **Wantastiquet Campsite** (Hinsdale, New Hampshire): A large lumberyard stands opposite this site about a mile below the girder railroad bridge, which angles across the river just below downtown Brattleboro.

• **Stebbin Island Campsite** (in Hinsdale, New Hampshire, just north of the Ashuelot River outlet): Two sites are on this large island a mile below the Vernon dam. A one-mile paddle up the Ashuelot River brings you to the town of Hinsdale.

Experienced paddlers can cover up to 30 miles a day. Plan on significantly less mileage if you want to stop frequently or make side trips to some of the interesting and accessible towns and natural or historic sites along the river valley. The water is clean but must be treated for consumption. Swim wherever you please, using good judgment. The only time you might not want to swim is following heavy rains when some of the agricultural agents used at riverside farms get washed into the river. Many fish species live in this waterway, including bass, trout, walleye, and northern pike. Check New Hampshire and Vermont state laws regarding fishing on the river; you will need a license.

Location: Along the Connecticut River; see White Mountains map.

Campsites, facilities: There are 17 primitive tent sites on the river from East Ryegate, Vermont, south to the Massachusetts border. Most sites have pit or chemical toilets and fire rings. At several sites, supplies can be obtained by walking a short distance into nearby towns. Sites are designated by a blue-on-yellow sign with a tent and river symbol. Pets are allowed.

Reservations, fees: Sites are available on a first-come, first-served basis. A fee is charged at Wilgus State Park.

Open: Year-round as weather and river conditions permit.

Directions: Sites are located on either bank of the Connecticut River, which forms the boundary between Vermont and New Hampshire.

Contact: Upper Valley Land Trust, 19 Buck Road, Hanover, NH 03755, 603/643-6626, website: www.uvlt.org; Pacific Gas and Electric's toll-free river line: 888/FLO-FONE (888/356-3663).

21 CRAZY HORSE CAMPGROUND

Rating: 8

On Moore Reservoir west of Littleton

Moore Reservoir is a 12-mile lake on the Connecticut River open to powerboating, fishing, and swimming. These rural sites are set back from the lake in a heavily forested area. Most are shaded, but a few are grassy and more open. The campground, which is crisscrossed by paved roads, has a pool and patio, canoe rentals, and, a quarter mile away, a boat launch. When you get out on the lake, bass, trout, and other warm-water species are fair game. Nature trails on the property are open to snowmobiling and skiing in season, and the state corridor of snowmobile trails is accessible nearby in Littleton. Franconia Notch State Park is a short ride south of here, and paddlers may want to consider embarking on longer trips down the Connecticut River from this home base. Littleton is a large city where campers can obtain all goods and services.

Campsites, facilities: There are 150 sites for tents and RVs, two-thirds with hookups. Each site has a picnic table, fire ring, and grill. Air conditioner and heater use is allowed, and phone hookups are available. A dump station, restrooms, hot showers, laundry facilities, a recreation hall, sports field, pool, pavilion, and playground are provided. Courts for badminton, volleyball, and horseshoes are available. A camp store carries LP gas, RV supplies, ice, and firewood. Tepees and RVs may also be rented. Leashed pets are permitted.

Reservations, fees: Reservations are accepted. Sites start at $22–29 a night. Weekly, monthly, and seasonal rates are available on request.

Open: Year-round.

Directions: From I-93 west of Littleton, take Exit 43. Head east and then southwest on Highway 135 for 1.5 miles. Take a right onto Hilltop Road and continue 1.25 miles to the campground.

Contact: Crazy Horse Campground, 788 Hilltop Road, Littleton, NH 03561, 800/639-4107, website: www.ucampnh.com/crazyhorse.

22 TWIN MOUNTAIN KOA KAMPGROUND

Rating: 8

North of Twin Mountain

Cherry Mountain rises to an elevation of 3,050 feet behind these level campsites in the woods. Part of the national KOA chain, this campground caters to families with a well-stocked store, sturdy playground equipment, and a game room. The pool and patio offer a view of the surrounding peaks. On weekends, campers gather in the amphitheater for singalongs and bonfires, or at the recreation hall for pancake breakfasts. Head into the mountains for day hikes, drive along scenic byways dotted with many picnic spots and pull-offs, or visit nearby commercial attractions such as the Mount Washington Cog Railway off U.S. 302 or Six Gun City, a western amusement park with roller coasters, water slides, and a miniature horse show just north of here in Jefferson.

Campsites, facilities: There are 65 sites for tents and RVs, eight with full hookups, 35 with water and electric hookups, and 22 with none. Each site has a picnic table and fire ring. A dump station, restrooms, hot showers, a recreation hall, amphitheater, pool, laundry facilities, and a playground are provided. Courts for badminton, volleyball, and horseshoes are available. A camp store carries ice and firewood. Leashed pets are permitted.

Reservations, fees: A deposit of one night's fee is required for reservations. Sites start at $27–39 a night.

Open: Mid-May–mid-October.

Directions: From the intersection of U.S. 3 and U.S. 302 in Twin Mountain, travel north for two miles on U.S. 3. Turn right on Highway 115 and head northeast for .75 mile to the campground entrance.

Contact: Twin Mountain KOA Kampground, P.O. Box 148, Twin Mountain, NH 03595, 603/846-5559, reservations: 800/KOA-9117, website: www.twinmountainkoa.com/.

23 LITTLETON KOA KAMPGROUND

Rating: 8

On the Ammonoosuc River southwest of Littleton

RVers and families especially will appreciate these meadowland campsites scattered along the Ammonoosuc River. At the campground you can enjoy a heated swimming pool, hot tub, and full amenities, including meal service if you want dinner catered at your site. From here, scenic drives explore Franconia Notch State Park or the various attractions of Vermont across the Connecticut River.

Campsites, facilities: There are 60 sites for tents and RVs, 12 with full hookups, 29 with water and electric hookups, and 19 without hookups. Each site comes with a picnic table, fire ring, and grill. A dump station, restrooms, hot showers, laundry facilities, a recreation room, heated swimming pool, and a playground are provided. Cable TV is available. Courts for badminton, volleyball, and horseshoes are provided on the property. A grocery store carries LP gas, ice, and firewood. Leashed pets are permitted.

Reservations, fees: Reservations are accepted with prepaid deposits. For two people, sites start at $27 a night without hookups and $30 a night for full hookups.

Open: Early May–mid-October.

Directions: From I-93 at Littleton, take Exit

42. Travel southwest for five miles on U.S. 302 to the campground.

Contact: Littleton KOA Kampground, 2154 U.S. 302, Littleton, NH 03561, 603/838-5525 or 800/562-5836 (for reservations).

24 APPLE HILL CAMPGROUND

🏃 🏊 ❄️ 🐕 🐎 🚐 ⛺

Rating: 8

North of Bethlehem

This rural, wooded campground in the town of Bethlehem offers level sites and provides separate areas for tents and RVs. From here, several North Country attractions are within a short drive, including the western theme amusement park Six Gun City in Jefferson. A small pond on the property can be used for swimming (or skating in winter), and nature trails weave through the woods. For a lakeside picnic in birch groves, head north to Forest Lake State Park in Dalton where you'll also find a swimming beach and good warm-water fishing.

In Bethlehem, two golf courses are open to the public. The downtown area has several junk and antique shops, funky restaurants, and an art deco movie theater. A number of historic oddities exist in town, such as a 160-year-old patched pine tree (reinforced with steel retaining rods) at the Bretzfelder Memorial Park off Main Street, and The Rocks, an estate that now serves as a working Christmas tree farm. Self-guided nature trails at The Rocks double as ski trails in the winter. Both The Rocks and Bretzfelder are owned by the Society for the Protection of New Hampshire Forests. Apple Hill Campground is open year-round, and snowmobilers and skiers will find trails at the campground in addition to many more in the surrounding mountains and valley. Perhaps inspired by its name, Bethlehem puts on an old-time Christmas celebration each year with tours of decorated homes, sleigh rides at The Rocks, and ice-skating parties.

Campsites, facilities: There are 65 sites for tents and RVs, 20 with full hookups. Each site has a picnic table and fire ring. A dump station, restrooms, hot showers, laundry facilities, a recreation room, and a playground are provided. Badminton, volleyball, and horseshoe pits are available. A small grocery store carries ice and firewood. Leashed pets are permitted.

Reservations, fees: A nonrefundable deposit is required with all reservations. Sites start at $18–23 a night.

Open: Year-round.

Directions: From I-93 in Bethlehem, take Exit 40 and travel east on U.S. 302 for three miles. Turn left when you see the campground sign and head north for one mile to the campground entrance.

Contact: Apple Hill Campground, Route 142N, P.O. Box 388, Bethlehem, NH 03574, 603/869-2238 or 800/284-2238, website: www.musar.com/applehill.

25 SNOWY MOUNTAIN CAMPGROUND AND MOTEL

🏃 🏊 🐕 🐎 🚐 ⛺

Rating: 8

West of Bethlehem

Operated in conjunction with a small motel, these landscaped and wooded sites just off the interstate can accommodate any size RV. Southwest of the motel and campground is a protected property known as The Rocks. This former estate is owned by the Society for the Protection of New Hampshire Forests. In summer, the public may use picnic areas and three miles of self-guided educational nature trails. The Rocks is also a working Christmas tree farm with more than 50,000 trees in the ground. Special programs include the Wildflower Festival, held in early June, and the Shakespeare Festival, which hits the boards in July. Bethlehem is a good jumping-off point for excursions into the White Mountain National Forest. Stop in at the Ammonoosuc Ranger Station off U.S. 3 for free maps and information.

Campsites, facilities: There are 37 sites for tents

and RVs, 16 with water and electric hookups. Each site has a picnic table, fire ring, and grill. A dump station, restrooms, hot showers, a recreation hall, pool, and playground are provided. Courts for badminton, volleyball, and horseshoes are available. A small grocery store carries ice and firewood; additional supplies and services are available in Bethlehem or Littleton. Leashed pets are permitted.

Reservations, fees: Reservations are recommended. Sites start at $16 a night.

Open: May 1–October 31.

Directions: From I-93 at Exit 40 in Bethlehem, travel one mile east on U.S. 302 to the campground entrance.

Contact: Snowy Mountain Campground and Motel, P.O. Box 300, 1225 Main Street, Bethlehem, NH 03574, 603/444-7789, website: www.snowymountainvacation.com.

26 BEECH HILL CAMPGROUND AND CABINS

Rating: 8

West of Twin Mountain

Surrounded by deep piney woods and mountain vistas, these campsites are available year-round. The Ammonoosuc River is 100 yards from the campground entrance. Twin Mountain is on the state's maintained snowmobile corridor—from here you can drive your sled to the Canadian border and almost as far south as Massachusetts, as long as there's enough snow. Wilderness and day hiking is available in the White Mountain National Forest to the southeast of the campground, while country comforts are served up a short drive to the west in the funky little town of Bethlehem, known as the poetry capital of New Hampshire, probably because it gives an annual stipend to its "poet laureate." Several good restaurants, antique and junk shops, and a summer movie theater line the main street.

Campsites, facilities: There are 125 sites, two-thirds with hookups. Each site has a picnic table and fire ring. A dump station, restrooms, hot showers, a recreation hall, laundry facilities, an indoor pool, and a playground are provided. Courts for badminton, volleyball, and horseshoes are available. A camp store carries ice and firewood. Several cabins are also available for rent. Leashed pets are permitted.

Reservations, fees: Reservations are recommended. Sites start at $25 a night.

Open: Year-round.

Directions: From the intersection of U.S. 3 and U.S. 302 in Twin Mountain, travel west on U.S. 302 for two miles to the campground entrance on the right (north) side of the road.

Contact: Beech Hill Campground and Cabins, P.O. Box 129, Twin Mountain, NH 03595, 603/846-5521, website: www.beechhill.com.

27 TWIN MOUNTAIN MOTOR COURT AND RV PARK

Rating: 8

Near the junction of U.S. 302 and U.S. 3 in Twin Mountain

This motor court for RVers only is on the way to many North Country attractions. Sites are paved and level and set beside a motel. The Ammonoosuc River flows by the property and is open for trout fishing to anglers with licenses. Hotel clients and RVers share a pool. Twin Mountain has a small municipal airport that offers scenic rides—a real color feast during the fall foliage display in early October. This is moose and bear country, so keep a watchful eye on the roads at dusk and make sure your food and garbage are tightly sealed.

Campsites, facilities: There are 18 sites for RVs, and only full-hookup units are welcome. Each site has a picnic table and fire ring. Restrooms, hot showers, a recreation hall, pool, and laundry facilities are provided. You will also find courts for basketball, badminton, shuffleboard, volleyball, and horseshoes. A camp store carries ice and firewood. Leashed pets are permitted.

Reservations, fees: Reservations are strongly

recommended. Sites start at $27 a night for two people.

Open: May 15–October 15.

Directions: From the intersection of U.S. 3 and U.S. 302 in Twin Mountain, travel south on U.S. 3 for one mile to the campground entrance.

Contact: Twin Mountain Motor Court and RV Park, Route 3 Box 104, Twin Mountain, NH 03595, 603/846-5574 or 800/332-TWIN/8946, website: www.twinmountainmotorcourtrvpark.com.

28 AMMONOOSUC CAMPGROUND

🚶 ≈ ❄ 🐕 👫 🚐 ⛺

In Twin Mountain

Rating: 8

Ammonoosuc Campground is located at the crossroads of U.S. 3 and U.S. 302 in Twin Mountain, which boasts an elevation of 1,400 feet. The bulk of the White Mountain National Forest lies south and east of these campsites; from here you can see the foothills of Mount Hale, the Twin Mountains, and the Sugarloafs. Some sites are in the woods, while others are more open and grassy, providing several camping habitats for RVers and tenters. Go for a dip in the swimming pool or take a short walk north to the Ammonoosuc River for a more natural way to cool off. Any number of day and overnight hikes are accessible within a short drive. The campground is also open in winter and is situated directly on a state-maintained snowmobile corridor—in fact, Twin Mountain is known as the snowmobile capital of New Hampshire. If you need a warm meal after zooming around all day, a pizza restaurant is operated on the property.

Campsites, facilities: There are 112 sites for tents and RVs, 75 with full hookups, 13 with water and electric hookups, and 24 with none. Each site has a picnic table, fire ring, and grill. Air conditioner and heater use is allowed. A dump station, restrooms, hot showers, a recreation hall, laundry facilities, a pool, and a play-

ground are provided. Courts for badminton, volleyball, and horseshoes are also available. A general store is located a quarter mile north of the campground. Leashed pets are permitted.

Reservations, fees: Reservations are encouraged and may be made by phone or by mail. They must be accompanied by a nonrefundable $10 deposit, and fees are payable in full upon arrival. Tent sites are $20 a night, and RV sites with full hookups are $24 a night per family.

Open: Year-round.

Directions: From the intersection of U.S. 3 and U.S. 302 in Twin Mountain, head south on U.S. 3 for just .25 mile to the campground on the left (east) side of the road.

Contact: Ammonoosuc Campground, P.O. Box 178N, Twin Mountain, NH 03595, 603/846-5527, website: www.ucampnh.com/ammonoosuc.

29 TARRY-HO CAMPGROUND AND COTTAGES

🚶 🚴 ≈ 🎣 ❄ 🐕 👫 🚐 ⛺

West of Twin Mountain

Rating: 8

Cottages and campsites share the mountain views from this grassy meadow flanking the Ammonoosuc River, where you can fish for trout from your own site. With hundreds of miles of backcountry trails, the nearby White Mountain National Forest is an ideal destination for outdoors people, from mountain bikers to backpackers. And a few miles west on U.S. 302 is Bretton Woods, a four-season recreation center. In summer, visitors can hike in the Rosebrook and Presidential mountain ranges or, for something more gentrified, stop in at the grand old Mount Washington Hotel, which resembles a fairy-tale castle in the rosy light of evening alpenglow. In winter, Bretton Woods Resort is a Nordic and alpine ski center with a large number of wide, intermediate trails.

Campsites, facilities: There are 55 sites, most with hookups. Each site has a picnic table, fire ring, and grill. A dump station, restrooms, hot showers, a recreation hall, pool, and nicely outfitted playground are provided. Courts for badminton, volleyball, and horseshoes are also available. A camp store carries ice and firewood. Leashed pets are permitted.

Reservations, fees: Reservations are recommended. Sites start at $24–33 a night.

Open: Year-round, except for the month of April and from October 15–November 15.

Directions: From the intersection of U.S. 3 and U.S. 302 in Twin Mountain, travel west on U.S. 302 for .75 mile to the campground entrance on the left (south) side of the road.

Contact: Tarry-Ho Campground and Cottages, P.O. Box 369, Route 302, Twin Mountain, NH 03595, 603/846-5577, website: www.tarryho.com.

30 LIVING WATER CAMPGROUND

Rating: 8

On the Ammonoosuc River in Twin Mountain

Mountain views and grassy, riverside sites greet campers at Living Water, a quiet alcohol-free family campground with clean, safe facilities. The operative word here is quiet: minibikes, scooters, ATVs, chainsaws, firearms, fireworks, and anything that goes "Bang" are expressly prohibited. Don't even think about listening to your music unless you have headphones. The Ammonoosuc River, a healthy trout stream, runs along the property. Alas, this isn't a good place to swim as there are no pools and it's shallow, but wading in the mountain waters is a great way to cool off. A motel is operated in conjunction with the campground. Numerous White Mountain attractions, both natural and man-made, are within a short drive. To the east, the Mount Washington Cog Railway chugs up to the summit of the tallest peak in the northeast (elevation 6,288 feet). A scenic drive heads southeast through Crawford Notch with great views throughout the gap. Much of the land on either side of the byway is part of Crawford Notch State Park, and several pull-offs offer hikes to gushing falls or other points of interest.

Campsites, facilities: There are 86 sites for tents and RVs, 13 with full hookups, 29 with water and electric hookups, and 44 with none. Each site has a picnic table and fire ring. A dump station, restrooms, hot showers, laundry facilities, a recreation hall, pool, and playground are provided. Courts for basketball, badminton, volleyball, and horseshoes are also available. A grocery store carries camping supplies, ice, and firewood. No pets are allowed.

Reservations, fees: An advance deposit of $26 is required with all reservations. Sites start at $27 a night. Visitors are not permitted during holiday weekends.

Open: Open year-round with limited camping in winter.

Directions: From the intersection of U.S. 3 and U.S. 302 in Twin Mountain, travel east on U.S. 302 for 1,000 feet to the campground entrance on the right (south) side of the road.

Contact: Living Water Campground, P.O. Box 158, Twin Mountain, NH 03595, 603/846-5513, website: www.livingwatercampground.com.

31 ZEALAND CAMPGROUND

Rating: 9

East of Twin Mountain in the White Mountain National Forest

Shaded, grassy sites are located directly on scenic byway U.S. 302, making this a good place to catch moose in action. The large beasts are frequently observed feeding near lakes and streams at dusk. Zealand is open through December and serves as a good base camp for early winter trips into the Pemigewasset Wilderness. With reservations you can also get overnight accommodations at the Zealand Falls Appalachian Mountain Club hut. The sites are close to the cog railway and Mount Washington, New Hampshire's highest peak at 6,288 feet. Also nearby, the Mount Washington Hotel and Resort offers golf, tennis, gourmet dining, and nightlife in the summer.

Campsites, facilities: There are 11 RV sites along the Ammonoosuc River with picnic tables, fire rings, vault toilets, and piped water. No pets are allowed.

Reservations, fees: Sites are available on a first-come, first-served basis. The fee is $16 a night.

Open: May–mid-December.

Directions: From the intersection of U.S. 302 and U.S. 3 in Twin Mountain, travel east for two miles on U.S. 302. The campground is on the right (south) side of the road.

Contact: White Mountain National Forest, Ammonoosuc Ranger District, Box 230, Bethlehem, NH 03574, 603/869-2626, website: www.fs.fed.us/r9/white/recreation/camping.

32 SUGARLOAF CAMPGROUNDS I AND II

Rating: 9

East of Twin Mountain in the White Mountain National Forest

These wooded sites make good base camps for treks into the Pemigewasset Wilderness; with reservations you can also get overnight accommodations at the Zealand Notch Appalachian Mountain Club hut. The sites are close to the cog railway and Mount Washington (New Hampshire's highest peak), as well as the Mount Washington Hotel and Resort, where golf, tennis, gourmet meals, and nightlife are available in summer. The Sugarloaf Peak trails are short, moderate hikes, and both rocky summits afford views of the wilderness area and the Franconia Ridge to the southwest.

Campsites, facilities: There are 29 sites at Sugarloaf I and 32 sites at Sugarloaf II for tents and RVs. Each site has a picnic table and fire ring. Wheelchair-accessible vault toilets are provided at Sugarloaf II, and flush toilets are provided at Sugarloaf I. Piped water is available at both campgrounds. No pets are allowed.

Reservations, fees: Reservations are necessary from June–September for some sites. Call Reserve USA, 877/444-6777, or visit www.re-serveusa.com. For each reservation, an $8.65 fee is charged. Sites are $16–18 a night.

Open: Sugarloaf I is open from mid-May–mid-October, and Sugarloaf II stays open through mid-December.

Directions: From the intersection of U.S. 302 and U.S. 3 in Twin Mountain, travel east for two miles on U.S. 302. Turn right on Zealand Road and continue .5 mile to the campgrounds.

Contact: White Mountain National Forest, Ammonoosuc Ranger District, Box 230, Bethlehem, NH 03574, 603/869-2626, website: www.fs.fed.us/r9/white/recreation/camping.

33 WILD RIVER

Rating: 8

On the Wild River in Beans Purchase in the White Mountain National Forest

You will find plenty of peace, quiet, and privacy at these wilderness sites tucked away in the woods along the Wild River. Brook and rainbow trout dwell in the river, so you can try to catch something for an evening fish fry on your campfire. From here, several trails lead deep into the Wild River Valley and remote wilderness areas of Beans Purchase.

Campsites, facilities: There are 12 sites, two suitable for RVs, but no hookups. One site has a lean-to. Picnic tables, fire rings, vault toilets, and piped water are provided. Leashed pets are permitted.

Reservations, fees: Sites are available on a first-come, first-served basis. The fee is $16 a night.

Open: Mid-May–mid-October.

Directions: From the junction of U.S. 2 and Highway 113 in Gilead, Maine, follow Highway 113 southwest for three miles. Turn right onto a dirt Forest Service road and continue five miles west to the campground.

Contact: White Mountain National Forest, Evans Notch Ranger District, 18 Mayville Road, Bethel, ME 04217, 207/824-2134, website: www.fs.fed.us/r9/white/recreation/camping.

34 BASIN CAMPGROUND

Rating: 7

North of Fryeburg, Maine, in the White Mountain National Forest

Sites here are nestled in the woods on Basin Pond, which has a boat ramp and a wheelchair-accessible fishing dock. Nonmotorized boating is allowed on this 23-acre impoundment. Anglers will find brook trout in Basin Pond, the Cold River, and other small streams. Just east of the campground is Brickett Place, a 175-year-old brick building constructed by one of the first settlers in this area.

Campsites, facilities: There are 21 sites for tents and RVs, all without hookups. Picnic tables, fire rings, flush toilets, and piped water are provided. Leashed pets are permitted.

Reservations, fees: Reservations are necessary from June–September for some sites. Call Reserve USA, 877/444-6777, or visit www. reserveusa.com. For each reservation, an $8.65 fee is charged. Sites are $18 a night.

Open: Mid-May–mid-October.

Directions: From Fryeburg, Maine, travel 15 miles north on Highway 113. Following the signs, turn left, and continue to the campground entrance.

Contact: White Mountain National Forest, Evans Notch Ranger District, 18 Mayville Road, Bethel, ME 04217, 207/824-2134, website: www.fs.fed.us/r9/white/recreation/camping.

35 COLD RIVER

Rating: 7

In White Mountain National Forest near the Maine border in North Chatham

Located at the foot of Evans Notch in North Chatham, these open and wooded campsites are close to excellent hiking terrain in the Caribou–Speckled Mountain Wilderness, offering campers plenty of day-hiking options. Trails lead

to the summits of Mount Meader and Ragged Jacket from Basin Pond. Trout fishing is good in both the Cold River and Basin Pond; the latter has a boat ramp and is open to nonmotorized boating. Cold River is one of the first Forest Service campgrounds to become snow-free each year, making it a favorite destination of early season fishing enthusiasts. A small picnic shelter is provided at the campground.

Campsites, facilities: There are 14 sites, 12 suitable for RVs, but none with hookups. Picnic tables, fire rings, flush toilets, and piped water are provided. You will also find an open grassy area for sports and a picnic shelter for small groups. Leashed pets are permitted.

Reservations, fees: Reservations are necessary from June–September for some sites. Call Reserve USA, 877/444-6777, or visit www. reserveusa.com. For each reservation, a service fee is charged. Sites are $16 a night.

Open: Mid-May–mid-October.

Directions: From Fryeburg, Maine, travel 15 miles north on Highway 113 to the campground on the left.

Contact: White Mountain National Forest, Evans Notch Ranger District, 18 Mayville Road, Bethel, ME 04217, 207/824-2134, website: www.fs.fed.us/r9/white/recreation/camping.

36 MINK BROOK FAMILY CAMPGROUND

Rating: 8

North of Lisbon

With the White Mountains at their back, these open and shaded campsites for tenters and RVers claim a rural location yet are close to many North Country attractions. The small campground has a swimming pool on the grounds, but the Ammonoosuc River is just across the road if you want to try for trout or take a dip in natural water. To the south in Bath, a 376-foot-long bridge built back in 1832 spans the river. For a breathtaking drive through this peaceful countryside, head north to Sugar Hill and take Highway 117 east to Franconia. You'll pass old inns, mountain vistas, and the Sugar Hill Historical Museum before descending into the valley and Franconia.

Campsites, facilities: There are 54 sites for tents and RVs, 26 with water and electric hookups, and 28 without hookups. Each site has a picnic table, fire ring, and grill. A dump station, restrooms, hot showers, a recreation hall, swimming pool, playground, horseshoe pits, and a court for volleyball and badminton are provided. A camp store sells groceries, ice, and firewood. Leashed pets are permitted.

Reservations, fees: Reservations are recommended. Sites start at $20 a night for two people.

Open: Early May–mid-October.

Directions: From the junction of Highway 117 and U.S. 302 in Lisbon, travel 1.25 miles southwest on U.S. 302 to the campground on the left.

Contact: Mink Brook Family Campground, U.S. Highway 302, Lisbon, NH 03585, 603/838-6658.

37 FRANSTED FAMILY CAMPGROUND

🚲 🏊 🛶 🎣 ❄ 🐕 🚶 🚐 ⛺

Rating: 9

On Meadow Brook in Franconia

From their setting in a riverside meadow, these grassy sites offer a front-row view of the Franconia Range from the north. Meadow Brook babbles through the campground, allowing campers access to prime trout habitat. The stream feeds into the spirited Gale River just north of the campground. A moderate 8.5-mile paddle with Class II rapids on the Gale starts below the bridge in Franconia and passes through undeveloped land as it flows toward Twin Mountain, affording Kinsman Ridge views along the way. By far, the most spectacular scenery is in Franconia Notch to the south. Land on either side of this gap is protected by the state. A good way to take it all in is on an eight-mile-long bike path extending from the Cannon Mountain tram to The Flume, a scenic gorge north of Lincoln. Bike rentals are available in Franconia. Winter

sites are open to seasonal campers, there are numerous cross-country skiing trails in the immediate area, and the Cannon Mountain alpine ski center a few miles south has the biggest vertical drop—2,146 feet—of any lift-served area in the state. In summer, the state maintains a swimming beach nearby on Echo Lake.

Campsites, facilities: There are 96 sites for tents and RVs, 26 with full hookups. Air conditioner and heater use is allowed. A dump station, restrooms, hot showers, laundry facilities, and a playground are provided. A miniature golf course, horseshoe pits, and a badminton and volleyball court are located on the property. A small grocery store sells bait, ice, and firewood. Leashed pets are permitted.

Reservations, fees: Reservations are accepted with prepaid deposits. Sites are $20–31 a night for two people. Groups are welcome, but in July and August they may consist of no more than 12 people.

Open: Tent sites are available May 1–Columbus Day, but seasonal RV campers are welcome year-round.

Directions: From I-93 at Franconia, take Exit 38. Travel 50 feet west and then head south on Highway 18 for one mile to the campground.

Contact: Fransted Family Campground, P.O. Box 873, Highway 18, Franconia, NH 03580, 603/ 823-5675, website: www.franstedcampground. com.

38 CANNON MOUNTAIN

🚶 🚲 🏊 🛶 🚐 ❄ 🚐

Rating: 10

North of Echo Lake in Franconia Notch State Park

From fly-fishing on Profile Pond to hiking high in the mountains, campers can experience Franconia Notch State Park to the utmost when they stay in one of these sites. The sites themselves aren't anything special since they're at the edge of a big dirt parking lot, but mountains stand in full view in every direction, and there's a pristine swimming lake, boat ramp, and fly-fishing pond a short walk from your RV door. Echo Lake is next to these sites and has a swimming beach, snack bar, boat rentals, and good trout fishing. There's also a boat ramp on its southern end.

A short walk south, Profile Pond is set beneath the remains of one the White Mountains' most recognizable attractions, the Old Man of the Mountain. The rocky countenance succumbed to gravity in May 2003. For an easy high, take the five-minute ride on the Cannon Mountain aerial tram, which you'll find at state park headquarters. It ascends more than 2,000 vertical feet. On the mountaintop, you can take a short walk to an observation tower. To explore the eight-mile-long notch, try the paved bike path running north to south with many points of interest along the way. In winter, these RV sites are staked out by skiers, as Cannon Mountain is one of two state-owned alpine ski centers. The bike path doubles as a cross-country skiing trail in winter.

Campsites, facilities: There are seven sites for RVs, and only full-hookup units are accepted. Tables and a public phone are provided. No pets are allowed.

Reservations, fees: For reservations, contact the New Hampshire State Parks Camping Reservation Center, P.O. Box 1856, Concord, NH 03302-1856, 603/271-3628, website: www. nhparks.state.nh.us. Sites are $24 a night.

Open: Year-round.

Directions: From the Franconia Notch Parkway/I-93 south of Franconia, take Exit 3 heading toward Echo Lake. Travel west for about .25 mile to the campground entrance.

Contact: Cannon Mountain, c/o Lafayette Campground, U.S. 3, Franconia, NH 03580, 603/823-9513; New Hampshire Division of Parks and Recreation, 603/271-3628 website: franconianotchstatepark.com.

39 DRY RIVER CAMPGROUND

Rating: 10

In Crawford Notch State Park

Primitive wooded sites are strung along the Dry

River, a tempting trout stream. Crawford Notch State Park serves as a centrally located base camp for excursions into the Presidential Range and surrounding national forestlands. From here, the Mount Washington summit is 16 miles northeast. Close by, Arethusa Falls—at more than 200 feet high the tallest falls in the state—are accessible on a moderate three-mile loop trail that starts a half mile south of the campground near the Willey House site. This site was once the home of an early settler, Samuel Willey Jr., who moved his family here in 1825. The family died in a great storm and slide in 1828. They had left the house to find safety and, ironically, the house was the only untouched object in the valley.

Campsites, facilities: There are 36 sites for tents and RVs, all without hookups. Pit toilets, piped water, and picnic tables are provided. Leashed pets are permitted.

Reservations, fees: For reservations, contact the New Hampshire State Parks Camping Reservation Center, P.O. Box 1856, Concord, NH 03302-1856, 603/271-3628, website: www.nh-parks.state.nh.us. The fee is $15 a night.

Open: Mid-May–mid-December.

Directions: From the junction of U.S. 302 and Highway 16 in Glen, travel northwest on U.S. 302 for 16 miles. The campground is on the right (east) side of the highway.

Contact: Dry River Campground, Crawford Notch State Park, P.O. Box 177, Twin Mountain, NH 03595, 603/374-2272.

40 TWIN RIVER CAMPGROUND & COTTAGES

Rating: 8

South of Bath

Located at the junction of U.S. 302 and Highway 112 on the banks of the Ammonoosuc and Wild Ammonoosuc Rivers, this campground caters to families. Sites are spacious and mostly flat and grassy, and kids will love panning for gold in the Ammonoosuc River right from the campground. Bath is the unofficial covered-bridge capital of New Hampshire. It claims the 1832 Bath Village Bridge, at 400 feet the longest covered bridge in the state, as well as the 1827 Bath-Haverhill Bridge, the oldest standing covered bridge in use in America.

Campsites, facilities: There are over 70 RV sites (and more under construction on the riverfront) with water and electric hookups, and some with sewer also. On-site you'll find a playground, pool, store, laundry facilities, hot showers, horseshoes, shuffleboard, volleyball, mini-golf, and modem access. Leashed pets are allowed.

Reservations, fees: Reservations are recommended. Sites range from $20–27 a night for a family of four.

Open: Mid-May–mid-October.

Directions: From I-93, take Exit 32 near Lincoln and follow Highway 112 west for 21 miles.

Contact: Twin River Campground & Cottages, P.O. Box 212, U.S. 302 and Highway 112, Bath, NH 03740, 603/747-3640 or 800/811-1040, website: www.ucampnh.com/twinriver.

41 LAFAYETTE CAMPGROUND

Rating: 10

In Franconia Notch State Park

Stunning mountain views await you at this location at the bottom of the notch on the Pemigewasset River. Sites are sandy and tucked into the woods at the base of the Cannon Balls, two massive rolling summits. The notch walls rise more than 4,000 feet on either side of I-93, with Mount Lafayette the tallest peak on the gap's east side at 5,260 feet. The eight-mile-long Franconia Notch State Park receives a lot of traffic due to its many pull-offs and interest points. At the park's south end there's The Flume, a dramatic, skinny gorge with footpaths and boardwalks. The Basin, just south of the campground, is a deep glacial pothole nearly 30 feet across.

Several good day hikes leave from the campground, including a short hike to Lonesome Lake, where you'll find an Appalachian Moun-

tain Club hut, and the longer Falling Waters/Bridle Path loop on the east side of the notch, which crosses the summits of Little Haystack, Lincoln, and Lafayette on the narrow, rocky Franconia Ridge. Campers may swim and boat in Echo Lake at the notch's north end by showing their campground pass. The lake has a lifeguard, boat ramp, sandy beach, and snack bar.

Campsites, facilities: There are 97 sites for tents and RVs, all without hookups. Each site has a picnic table, fire ring, and grill. Restrooms, hot showers, and a playground are provided. A small grocery store carries ice and firewood. No pets are allowed.

Reservations, fees: For reservations, call the New Hampshire Division of Parks and Recreation at 603/271-3628. Sites are $16 a night.

Open: Mid-May–mid-December.

Directions: Take the Tramway exit/Exit 2 off the Franconia Notch Parkway/I-93. Reverse your direction and head south on the parkway for 2.5 miles to the Lafayette Place/Campground exit.

Contact: Lafayette Campground, U.S.3, Franconia, NH 03580, 603/823-9513; New Hampshire Division of Parks and Recreation, 603/271-3628, website: www.franconianotchstatepark.com.

42 CRAWFORD NOTCH GENERAL STORE AND CAMPGROUND

Rating: 10

In Crawford Notch State Park

Here at the only privately owned campground in Crawford Notch State Park, secluded and roomy sites are set either beside or near the Saco River. Fish and swim in the river at the campground, or take one of the many nearby hiking trails into the mountains. Numerous other trails and forest roads in the area are open to mountain biking.

Campsites, facilities: There are 80 sites for tents and RVs up to 35 feet long, 30 with electric hookups. Each site has a table, fire ring, and grill. Chemical toilets, piped water, dish-washing stations, hot showers, and a public phone are provided. A general store carries groceries, ice, and firewood. Leashed pets are permitted ($3).

Reservations, fees: Reservations are recommended. Sites start at $18–24 a night.

Open: May 1–mid-October.

Directions: From the junction of Highway 16 and U.S. 302 in Glen, travel northwest on U.S. 302 for 14.5 miles to the campground.

Contact: Crawford Notch General Store and Campground, U.S. 302, Harts Location, NH 03812, 603/374-2779, website: www. crawfordnotchcamping.com

43 GREEN MEADOW CAMPING AREA

Rating: 9

North of Glen

The craggy contours of New Hampshire's White Mountains are in full view of these meadow sites. Of the two campgrounds in the immediate Glen area, this one is probably better suited to adults, though there are some sports courts and a swimming pool to keep campers with children happy. It's also the only year-round option for RVs. While hiking, biking, and canoeing are popular summer pursuits, in winter the valley comes to life in a different way. To the north in Jackson, there are miles of maintained cross-country ski trails in and out of town, challenging backcountry skiing in Pinkham Notch, and alpine ski areas in Conway and Pinkham Notch. This campground is next door to Story Land, a theme park with rides and costumed characters based on favorite tales including Humpty Dumpty and the Old Woman in the Shoe.

Campsites, facilities: There are 93 sites for tents and RVs, 31 with full hookups, 32 with water and electric hookups, and 30 with none. Each site has a picnic table, fire ring, and grill. Cable TV is available. A dump station, restrooms, hot showers, a basketball hoop, volleyball and

badminton court, horseshoe pits, and a pool are provided. A camp store carries RV supplies, ice, and firewood. Leashed pets are permitted.

Reservations, fees: Reservations are recommended during the summer months. Sites are $21–27 a night per family.

Open: Year-round.

Directions: From the junction of Highway 16 and U.S. 302 in Glen, travel .25 mile north on Highway 16, then turn right and go another .25 mile east to the campground entrance.

Contact: Green Meadow Camping Area, P.O. Box 246, Route 16, Glen, NH 03838, 603/383-6801, website: www.ucampnh.com/greenmeadow.

44 WILDWOOD CAMPGROUND

Rating: 8

West of North Woodstock in the White Mountain National Forest

Set in Kinsman Notch across the road from the Ammonoosuc River, these sites are wooded and offer good mountain views. Try to catch a trout for dinner in the river, and when you're ready for a hike, head three miles south to where the Appalachian Trail crosses Highway 112. From there, the challenging Beaver Brook Trail ascends Mount Moosilauke. An easier trek to the north ascends Mount Wolf via the Kinsman Ridge Trail.

Campsites, facilities: There are 26 sites for tents and RVs, all without hookups. Picnic tables, fire rings, vault toilets, and piped water are provided. Leashed pets are permitted.

Reservations, fees: Sites are available on a first-come, first-served basis. The fee is $16 a night.

Open: Mid-May–mid-December.

Directions: From Lincoln, travel west on Highway 112 for seven miles to the campground entrance.

Contact: White Mountain National Forest, Ammonoosuc Ranger District, Box 230,

Bethlehem, NH 03574, 603/869-2626, website:
www.fs.fed.us/r9/white/recreation/camping.

45 GLEN-ELLIS FAMILY CAMPGROUND

🏊 🛶 🎣 🏕 🚴 🚐 ⛺

Rating: 9

South of Glen

This campground is at an important crossroads in the White Mountains. To the north lies the resort town of Jackson and, beyond that, Pinkham Notch. To the northwest lie Crawford Notch and the Presidential Range. And to the south lies the town of North Conway, known for its outlet shopping, restaurants, and hotels. Glen-Ellis is on a mountain meadow nestled between the Ellis and Saco Rivers and offers many waterfront sites. A wilderness tent area (sites 101–110) is right on the Saco, which is open to fishing and canoeing. Large play areas, a gazebo, pool, and a patio make this campground both attractive and practical for families. Just north are two commercial attractions: the Heritage New Hampshire Museum retraces the state's history from the colonial voyage from England to America in 1634, and Story Land is a theme park with rides that bring such tales as Cinderella and Humpty Dumpty to life.

Campsites, facilities: There are 200 sites for tents and RVs, 99 with water and electric hookups. Each site has a picnic table, fire ring, and grill. Air conditioner and heater use is allowed. A dump station, restrooms, hot showers, a recreation hall, pool, pavilion, sports field, and playground are provided. Courts for basketball, badminton, shuffleboard, tennis, volleyball, and horseshoes are available, as are group tent sites. A grocery store carries RV supplies, ice, and firewood. There's a traffic control gate at the entrance. Leashed pets are permitted.

Reservations, fees: Reservations are accepted. Per family, sites start at $24 a night. Add $2 for waterfront sites. Seasonal rates are available on request.

Open: Late May–mid-October.

Directions: From the junction of Highway 16 and U.S. 302 in Glen, travel .25 mile west on U.S. 302 to the campground.

Contact: Glen-Ellis Family Campground, P.O. Box 397, Glen, NH 03838, 603/383-4567, website: www.glenelliscampground.com.

46 OLIVERIAN VALLEY CAMPGROUND

🥾 🏊 🛶 🎣 🚐 ⛺

Rating: 9

West of Glencliff

These wooded sites set in a 2,000-acre preserve are strictly for the privacy-conscious. The preserve surrounds a working farm, maple sugaring operation, and organic garden. A self-guided nature trail on the property was developed with the Department of Fish and Game to create wildlife habitat demonstration areas. Guided tours and trail lunches are available on request. More than 10 miles of trails traverse marsh, stream, field, and forest and present views of the Connecticut River Valley, Mount Moosilauke, and other scenic spots along the way. On weekends, the sugar shack serves breakfast, and a cabin a mile into the woods serves refreshments in the evening while campers swap stories and stoke a communal fire.

Campsites, facilities: There are 24 sites for tents and self-contained RVs, all without hookups. Each site has a picnic table, privy, and fire ring or grill. Restrooms, hot showers, a volleyball court, horseshoe pits, and a recreation hall are provided. Leashed pets are permitted.

Reservations, fees: Reservations are accepted with a 25 percent deposit. Sites start at $22 a night per family.

Open: May 15–October 15.

Directions: From the junction of Highways 10 and 25 in Haverhill, travel east on Highway 25 for approximately eight miles to the campground entrance.

Contact: Oliverian Valley Campground, P.O. Box 97, East Haverhill, NH 03765, 603/989-3351.

47 AMC HUTS AND LODGES

🏃 🏊 🛶 📷 ❄️

Rating: 10

Between Crawford and Pinkham Notch

More than a century ago, the Appalachian Mountain Club (AMC) opened its first hut in the White Mountains with the aim of providing comfortable accommodations for hikers much like the alpine huts of Europe. Back then, a night's stay at the Madison Springs cabin cost 50 cents and you had to bring your own food. Today, hikers can carry little more than a light backpack and lunches for an extended hiking tour of the White Mountains, and accommodations can cost more than $70 a night. Trail and ecology information is available at all huts, as the AMC has a dual mission of education and responsible recreation. Accommodations include shared bunk rooms, common rooms, and hot meals. Suppers include homemade bread, salad, vegetables, and dessert in addition to a main dish of chicken, fish, beef, turkey, or lasagna. A hiker shuttle operates June–October between Crawford and Pinkham Notch, stopping at numerous points in between.

From west to east, AMC accommodations include:

• **Lonesome Lake hut** (on Lonesome Lake in Franconia Notch State Park): This is the most popular destination for families since the hike in is short and easy.

• **Greenleaf hut** (below the summit of Mount Lafayette): Greenleaf is located at tree line and offers spectacular sunsets.

• **Galehead hut** (on the north edge of the Pemigewasset Wilderness): The most remote hut in the system, Greenleaf offers views of the Pemigewasset Wilderness.

• **Zealand Falls hut** (near the Pemigewasset Wilderness): The easy hike to the hut in summer makes it a favorite with families. It's open year-round and is a popular destination for backcountry skiers.

• **Crawford Hostel** (off U.S. 302 north of Crawford Notch): The facility is open year-round and offers bunk rooms, showers, and a self-service kitchen.

• **Mizpah Spring hut** (on Mount Clinton): Moderate hiking leads to this scenic outlook over Crawford Notch—a great fall foliage destination.

• **Lakes of the Clouds hut** (on the southern shoulder of Mount Washington): This is the AMC's highest, largest, and most popular hut. It sleeps 90.

• **Madison Springs hut** (above the sheer walls of Madison Gulf): After a strenuous trek in to this hut, hikers are rewarded with sunsets over the Presidentials.

• **Pinkham Notch Visitors Center Lodge** (off Highway 16 in the Mount Washington Valley): Bunk rooms, hot showers, hot meals, a trading post (selling books and outdoor gear), and an information desk are available at this year-round facility.

• **Carter Notch hut** (below the summit of Wildcat Mountain): Open year-round, this is a good base for exploring nearby mountains and ponds.

Location: In the White Mountain National Forest and Franconia Notch State Park; see White Mountains map.

Campsites, facilities: There are eight huts, one hostel, and one lodge. Bunk beds, wool blankets, pillows, and cold running water are provided. Self-service huts have fully equipped kitchens, partially heated common rooms, and unheated bunk rooms. Some huts have pit or flush toilets. Full-service stays include hot meals at dinner and breakfast. Lights and appliances are solar powered or run on propane gas. Other facilities differ from hut to hut. Pets are not allowed in any AMC facility.

Reservations, fees: Reservations are strongly recommended. Prepayment is encouraged and is required for package plans. Prepaid deposits must be received within seven days of reserving by phone. For adults, full-service rates range from $75 a night for members to $82 for nonmembers. Self-service rates (no meals) are offered at some huts. Discounted rates apply for package stays and children. Stays during August weekends are slightly more expensive.

Open: Most huts are open May–October; the Zealand and Carter huts are open year-round, as are the Crawford Hostel and Pinkham Notch Lodge.

Directions: The AMC huts and lodges are strung along 56 miles of the Appalachian Trail. Trailheads are accessible on I-93, Highways 112 and 16, U.S. 302, and U.S. 2 in the state's White Mountains region.

Contact: The Appalachian Mountain Club, 5 Joy Street, Boston, MA 02108; for reservations, contact P.O. Box 298, Gorham, NH 03581, 603/466-2727, website: www.outdoors.org. White Mountain National Forest Supervisor, 719 North Main Street, Laconia, NH 03246, 603/528-8721, TDD for hearing impaired 603/528-8722.

48 COUNTRY BUMPKINS CAMPGROUND AND COTTAGES

Rating: 7

In North Woodstock on U.S. 3

The busy interstate and the Pemigewasset River border these wooded sites. Some sites are located along Bog Brook. There's a small artificially constructed duck pond in the campground center. From here, wild and contrived attractions abound, from the Whale's Tale water park—complete with games, rides, and shows—to The Flume, an 800-foot-long gorge with walls up to 90 feet high and in places only 12 feet wide; both are north of the campground on U.S. 3. The Flume is about three miles north and lies at the south end of Franconia Notch State Park, a spectacular eight-mile-long mountain pass.

Campsites, facilities: There are 45 sites for tents and RVs, some with full hookups. Each site has a picnic table and fireplace. A dump station, restrooms, hot showers, laundry facilities, a game room, horseshoe pits, and a playground are provided. A camp store carries ice and firewood. Leashed pets are permitted.

Reservations, fees: Reservations are accepted.

Sites are $19–25 a night per family of four. Weekly, monthly, and seasonal rates are available.

Open: April 1–November 1.

Directions: From I-93, take Exit 33 for Lincoln. Travel south on U.S. 3 for .5 mile to the entrance.

Contact: Country Bumpkins Campground and Cottages, U.S. 3, Lincoln, NH 03251, 603/745-8837, website: www.countrybumpkins.com.

49 COLD SPRING CAMPGROUND

Rating: 7

On the Pemigewasset River in Lincoln

If it's the middle of July and all the other campgrounds around here are full, try Cold Spring. This small family campground has seasonal campsites and a few primitive spots for overnighters. The Pemigewasset River flows by the property, should you be in the mood to fish. The towns of North Woodstock and Lincoln are within a short car or bike ride.

Campsites, facilities: There are 37 sites for tents and RVs, five with full hookups, 12 with water and electric hookups, and 20 with none. Restrooms, hot showers, picnic tables, fire rings, and grills are provided. Leashed pets are permitted.

Reservations, fees: Reservations are accepted. Sites start at $20 a night.

Open: April 15–October 15.

Directions: From I-93, take Exit 33 for Lincoln. Travel south on U.S. 3 for .5 mile to the entrance.

Contact: Cold Spring Campground, R.F.D. 3, Box 84, Lincoln, NH, 03251, 603/745-8351.

50 MAPLE HAVEN RESORT

Rating: 8

West of North Woodstock

The Maki family became the new owners of this facility in 2002 and have been renovating and improving the property ever since. Moosilauke Brook, also known as the Lost River, passes by this campground, as does Highway 112. Operated in conjunction with cabins and a lodge, these sites are set in wooded areas and several of them offer mountain views. While Highway 112 can get busy in the summer, campers here remain off the beaten paths of Lincoln and North Woodstock. Another plus is that you can fish for trout from your campsite. Five minutes away are natural interest points including Loon Mountain and Lost River Reservation, a series of caves on Moosilauke Brook. All supplies and services are available in North Woodstock, about half a mile away.

Campsites, facilities: There are 44 sites for tents and RVs, many with water and electric hookups. Each site has a picnic table and fire ring. A dump station, restrooms, indoor and outdoor hot showers, a recreation area, and courts for badminton, volleyball, and horseshoes are provided. A recreation hall and camp store carry ice and firewood. Leashed, well-behaved, and picked-up-after pets are welcome.

Reservations, fees: Reservations are recommended. For two people, tent sites start at $18 a night; RV sites start at $25 a night, with surcharges for wooded and waterfront sites and electric and sewer services.

Open: April 15–October 31.

Directions: From I-93 at North Woodstock, take Exit 32. Turn right and head west on Highway 112 for one mile to the campground entrance. You pass through a stoplight in North Woodstock on the way.

Contact: Maple Haven Resort, 109 Lost River Road (Route 112), North Woodstock, NH 03262, 800/221-3350, website: www.maplehavenresort.com.

51 LOST RIVER VALLEY CAMPGROUND

Rating: 8

West of Woodstock at the confluence of the Lost River and Walker Brook

Not one, but two mountain streams are at your disposal when you bed down at Lost River Valley Campground. Walker Brook flows to one side, and the namesake Lost River is on the other; there's also a swimming pond and a sandy beach for additional aquatic recreation. Private wooded sites line this peninsula, once the site of a turn-of-the-century lumber mill. The water wheel still operates. Sites 107–117 and the mid-50s are the most remote. With the woods and mountain views to yourself, it's hard to believe you're only a half mile from one of the White Mountains' most popular family attractions: west of the campground, Lost River Reservation features a chaotic jumble of glacially sculpted boulders on Moosilauke Brook. For a nominal fee, you can follow the river through a series of boardwalks and caves, including the so-called Lemon Squeezer. West of Lost River, the Appalachian Trail crosses Highway 112; a challenging day hike leads up some steep and rocky steps on the Beaver Brook Trail to the summit of Mount Moosilauke.

Campsites, facilities: There are 130 sites for tents and RVs, eight with full hookups, 51 with water and electric hookups, and 71 with none. Each site has a picnic table and fire ring. Air conditioner and heater use is allowed. A dump station, restrooms, hot showers, laundry facilities, a recreation hall, sports field, and playground are provided. Courts for tennis, basketball, badminton, shuffleboard, volleyball, and horseshoes are located on the property. A grocery store carries ice and firewood. An entry gate controls traffic. Leashed pets are permitted.

Reservations, fees: Reservations are accepted for stays of three or more days with prepaid deposits. Overnight sites are available on a first-come, first-served basis. Sites start at $23 a night for two people. Weekly stays are subject to a 10 percent discount.

Open: Mid-May–Columbus Day weekend.

Directions: From I-93 at North Woodstock, take Exit 32. Turn right and head west on Highway 112 for four miles to the campground entrance. You pass through a stoplight in North Woodstock on the way.

Contact: Lost River Valley Campground, 951

Lost River Road, North Woodstock, NH 03262, 603/745-8321 in the summer, or 407/286-1825 in the winter, website: www.lostriver.com.

52 HANCOCK CAMPGROUND

🏕 🏊 🛶 ❄ 🏠 ♿ 🚐

Rating: 9

East of Lincoln on the Kancamagus Highway in the White Mountain National Forest

A hardwood tree grove shades these sites situated near the Pemigewasset River, which is open to fishing. A five-minute walk from the campground leads to Upper Lady's Bath, a secluded swimming hole. This calm pool of water has a rocky ledge bottom. Just a few miles east of I-93, Hancock Campground is close to many White Mountain attractions including the natural rock formations of Indian Head and the Old Man of the Mountain. In winter, nearby Loon Mountain offers all levels of downhill skiing while the Lincoln Woods Visitor Center, across Highway 112 from the campground, maintains eight miles of cross-country ski trails. From the center, multiuse trails lead to several interest points, among them Black Pond, with its panoramic views of the mountains, Franconia Falls, and beaver ponds.

Campsites, facilities: There are 56 RV sites, all without hookups; 35 offer easy access for trailers. Fire grills, picnic tables, vault toilets, and piped water are provided. Leashed pets are permitted.

Reservations, fees: Sites are available on a first-come, first-served basis. The fee is $18 a night.

Open: Year-round. The roads are plowed in winter.

Directions: From I-93 at Lincoln, take Exit 32 and travel east on the Kancamagus Highway/Highway 112 for four miles to the campground.

Contact: White Mountain National Forest, Pemigewasset Ranger District, R.F.D. 3, Box 15, Plymouth, NH 03264, 603/536-1310, website: www.fs.fed.us/r9/white/recreation/camping.

53 BIG ROCK CAMPGROUND

🛶 🏕 ❄ 🏠 🚐 ⛺

Rating: 9

East of Lincoln on the Kancamagus Highway/Highway 112 in the White Mountain National Forest

Glacial erratics, or large boulders, were sprinkled here during the last ice age and inspired the name of this campground. Tiers of campsites are set in a hardwood forest and can serve as convenient base camps for winter and summer forays into the Whites. Big Rock is two miles east of the Lincoln Woods Visitor Center, a haven of homey hospitality, especially during the cold winter months. Eight miles of maintained cross-country ski trails start at the center, where a woodstove cranks out warmth and heats up water for hot chocolate. From the center, multiuse trails lead to several natural interest points including Black Pond, which affords a panoramic mountain view, Franconia Falls, and beaver ponds housing busy or hibernating inhabitants, depending on the season.

Campsites, facilities: There are 28 sites for tents and RVs, all without hookups. Fire grills, picnic tables, vault toilets, and piped water are provided. Leashed pets are permitted.

Reservations, fees: Sites are available on a first-come, first-served basis. Fees are $16 a night in spring, summer, and fall, and $6 a night in winter.

Open: Year-round, but the roads are not plowed in the winter.

Directions: From I-93 at Lincoln, take Exit 32 and travel east on the Kancamagus Highway/Highway 112 for six miles to the campground.

Contact: White Mountain National Forest, Pemigewasset Ranger District, R.F.D. 3, Box 15, Plymouth, NH 03264, 603/536-1310, website: www.fs.fed.us/r9/white/recreation/camping.

54 RUSSELL POND

Rating: 9

In Woodstock in the White Mountain National Forest

Russell Pond is a spring-fed pool stocked with brook and brown trout. There's a beach area for swimmers, and paddlers will have enough room to drop in a canoe. Some short trails explore the immediate area surrounding the wooded campsites, but for great hiking you should continue east on Tripoli Road to check out a bowl formed by Mounts Tripyramid, Tecumseh, and Osceola. The Mount Osceola Trail is a challenging 6.4-mile trek that climbs 2,000 vertical feet to the peak's summit at 4,340 feet.

Campsites, facilities: There are 86 sites for tents and RVs, all without hookups. Piped water, flush toilets, metered hot showers, picnic tables, and fire rings are provided. Leashed pets are permitted.

Reservations, fees: Reservations are accepted for some sites from May–October; call the National Forest Reservation Center at 800/280-2267. Sites are $18 a night plus service charge.

Open: Mid-May–mid-October.

Directions: From I-93 north of Woodstock, take Exit 31. Head east on Tripoli Road for 1.5 miles. Turn left at Russell Pond Road and continue about two miles to the campground.

Contact: White Mountain National Forest, Pemigewasset Ranger District, R.F.D. 3, Box 15, Plymouth, NH 03264, 603/536-1310, website: www.fs.fed.us/r9/white/recreation/camping.

55 PASSACONAWAY CAMPGROUND

Rating: 7

On the Kancamagus Highway/Highway 112 in the White Mountain National Forest

Directly across the Kancamagus Highway from the Potash Mountain Trail, Passaconaway Campground offers access to some of the best hiking terrain in the White Mountain National Forest southern reaches. A covered picnic pavilion at the site is surrounded by balsam and white pine trees.

Campsites, facilities: There are 33 sites for tents or trailers with no hookups. Fire grills, tables, vault toilets, and piped water are provided. Leashed pets are permitted.

Reservations, fees: Sites are available on a first-come, first-served basis. The fee is $16 a night.

Open: May–October.

Directions: From the junction of Highways 16 and 112 in Conway, travel 16 miles west on the Kancamagus Highway/Highway 112.

Contact: White Mountain National Forest, Saco Ranger Station, 33 Kancamagus Highway, Conway, NH 03818, 603/447-5448, website: www.fs.fed.us/r9/white/recreation/camping.

56 JIGGER JOHNSON CAMPGROUND

Rating: 8

On the Kancamagus Highway/Highway 112 in the White Mountain National Forest

Named for an old logging boss, Jigger Johnson is set in a dense white pine forest near the historic Russell-Colbath House, a restored homestead from 1830. Interpretive talks are offered during the summer months.

Campsites, facilities: There are 75 sites for tents or trailers with no hookups. Fire grills, tables, flush toilets, and piped water are provided. Leashed pets are permitted.

Reservations, fees: Sites are available on a first-come, first-served basis. The fee is $18 a night.

Open: May–October.

Directions: From the junction of Highways 16 and 112 in Conway, travel 12.5 miles west on the Kancamagus Highway/Highway 112.

Contact: White Mountain National Forest, Saco Ranger Station, 33 Kancamagus Highway, Conway, NH 03818;603/447-5448, website: www.fs.fed.us/r9/white/recreation/camping.

57 BLACKBERRY CROSSING

Rating: 9

On the Kancamagus Highway/Highway 112 west of Conway in the White Mountain National Forest

These wooded sites are large and private. Located at the southwest edge of the White Mountain National Forest, Blackberry Crossing is close to wilderness hiking and biking as well as scenic byways to the north and south. Members of Franklin Roosevelt's Civilian Conservation Corps "Tree Army" originally settled this site. In 1941, 200 men lived here in military camp fashion while they worked on various projects in the White Mountains. Two immense stone chimneys remain from the headquarters and recreation hall buildings; now they serve campers as grand outdoor fireplaces.

Campsites, facilities: There are 26 sites for tents or trailers with no hookups. Fire grills, tables, and vault toilets are provided. Piped water is available in spring, summer, and fall. Leashed pets are permitted.

Reservations, fees: Sites are available on a first-come, first-served basis. The fee is $16 a night from May–October; there is no fee in winter when there are no services.

Open: Year-round, with limited service after mid-October.

Directions: From the junction of Highways 16 and 112 in Conway, travel six miles west on the Kancamagus Highway/Highway 112 to the campground entrance on the left (south) side of the road.

Contact: White Mountain National Forest, Saco Ranger Station, 33 Kancamagus Highway, Conway, NH 03818, 603/447-5448, website: www.fs.fed.us/r9/white/recreation/camping.

58 COVERED BRIDGE CAMPGROUND

Rating: 9

West of Conway in the White Mountain National Forest

To reach the campground, you must drive over the 1858 Albany Covered Bridge, hence the name. Sites are set in a white pine forest nestled between the base of a granite cliff and the aptly named Swift River, a good trout stream. You will find a fishing pier within a short walk of here. The campground is located off a Forest Service road, which makes a challenging mountain biking route up to and over Bear Notch and into Bartlett.

Campsites, facilities: There are 49 sites for tents or small trailers with no hookups. Fire grills, picnic tables, vault toilets, and piped water are provided. Leashed pets are permitted.

Reservations, fees: Reservations are necessary for 20 sites located directly on the Swift River; call the National Forest Reservation Center at 800/280-2267. Sites are $16 a night plus a reservation service charge.

Open: May–October.

Directions: From the junction of Highways 16 and 112 in Conway, travel six miles west on the Kancamagus Highway/Highway 112. Signs will lead you over a bridge across the Swift River and into the campground.

Contact: White Mountain National Forest, Saco Ranger Station, 33 Kancamagus Highway, Conway, NH 03818, 603/447-5448, website: www.fs.fed.us/r9/white/recreation/camping.

59 THE BEACH CAMPING AREA

Rating: 9

On the Saco River north of Conway

Aptly named, this campground on the eastern edge of the White Mountain National Forest has a gigantic sandy beach on the Saco River. About a third of the sites are right beside the water, and many have mountain views. The Saco is clean and refreshing, a great place to swim or fish for trout. Trees, a mix of hardwoods and softwoods, provide shade. The best way to explore the Saco is by canoe. You may bring your own or rent one nearby. It's a quiet-water paddle from here to Maine, and you'll pass under two covered bridges just south of the campground in Conway Village. On weekends, organized activities at the campground range from square dances to bonfires. Numerous day hikes are accessible a short drive west in the national forest.

Campsites, facilities: There are 120 sites for tents and RVs, 87 with full hookups, 21 with water and electric hookups, and 12 with none. Each site has a picnic table, fire ring, and grill. Air conditioner and heater use is allowed. A dump station, restrooms, hot showers, laundry facilities, a recreation hall, pavilion, and a playground are provided. Courts for basketball, badminton, shuffleboard, volleyball, and horseshoes are available. A camp store carries RV supplies, ice, and firewood. Leashed pets are permitted.

Reservations, fees: Reservations are recommended. Sites range from $22-32 a night.

Open: Mid-May–mid-October.

Directions: From Conway, travel north on Highway 16 for 1.5 miles to the campground entrance on the left (west) side of the road.

Contact: The Beach Camping Area, 98 Eastern Slope Terrace, North Conway, NH 03818, 603/447-2723, website: www.ucampnh.com/thebeach.

60 SACO RIVER CAMPING AREA

Rating: 8

On the Saco River north of Conway

Set in the thick of the North Conway factory outlet shopping district, these campsites allow consumers to enjoy mountain views while they spend. Highway 16 is commercially developed here with many hotels, restaurants, and strip malls. Dense stands of trees buffer the campsites from the busy road. Sites 29-57 are right on the Saco River, a good trout stream, though sites 29-31 abut the sandy beach that's open to all campers. Most spots are roomy and shaded and can handle any size RV. From here, you can walk to eateries, grocery stores, a movie theater, and shops. On weekends and holidays, a staff recreation director organizes bonfires, games, and theme events. Two miles north, the North Conway Country Club has a public golf course; there's also a racquet club nearby.

Canoes may be rented at the campground, and from here the Saco River offers 12 miles of quiet water to paddle to the Maine border. In North Conway, the Conway Scenic Railroad conducts one-hour rides through Crawford Notch and the Conway-Bartlett Valley. For lake swimming in breathtaking surroundings, head north to Echo Lake State Park in North Conway. With White Horse Ledge in the background, you can swim in the clear lake and use the beach for a nominal fee. Hiking trails lead to the top of the cliff; White Horse and neighboring Cathedral Ledge are heavily used rock climbing routes.

Campsites, facilities: There are 146 sites for tents and RVs, most with full hookups. Each site has a picnic table, fire ring, and grill. Air conditioner use is allowed, and cable TV hookup is available. A dump station, restrooms, hot showers, laundry facilities, a recreation hall, sports field, and a playground are provided. Courts for basketball, badminton, shuffleboard, volleyball, and horseshoes are available. Group sites are available for tents and RVs. A camp store carries LP gas, RV supplies, ice, and firewood. A guarded gate controls traffic at the campground entrance. Leashed pets are permitted.

Reservations, fees: Reservations are recommended May–October. A prepaid nonrefundable deposit equal to one night's stay is required for a reservation. Sites are $21-29 a night per family, depending on services and proximity to the river.

Open: May 1–October 15.

Directions: From the southern junction of Highway 16 and U.S. 302 north of Conway, travel .25 mile south on Highway 16/302 to the campground entrance on the right (west) side of the road.

Contact: Saco River Camping Area, P.O. Box 546, Highway 16, North Conway, NH 03860, 603/356-3360, website:www.sacorivercampingarea.com.

61 EASTERN SLOPE CAMPING AREA

Rating: 8

On the Saco River in Conway

The Saco River loops around this campground full of wooded sites—many set right beside the river—with mountain views. Each site has a sheltered picnic table. Two large beaches are available for swimming and sunbathing, and canoeists can take long and short paddles on the Saco River; it's quiet water from this point into Maine. Two covered bridges are just south of the campground: the Saco River bridge, which was built in 1890, and the Swift River bridge, which dates back just as far and was completely restored in 1991. From Conway, drive west on the Kancamagus Highway/Highway 112, New England's only national forest scenic byway. The paved road rises to 3,000 feet and overlooks falls, notches, and valleys. Numerous day hikes and picnic areas are marked along the roadway. At the junction of Highway 112 (the Kanc) and Highway 16, the Saco Ranger Station has all the information you need to take advantage of the national forest, and most of it is free.

Campsites, facilities: There are 210 sites for tents and RVs. Each site has a sheltered picnic table and fire ring. A dump station, restrooms, hot showers, a recreation hall, and a playground are provided. Courts for badminton, volleyball, and horseshoes are available. A grocery store

carries ice and firewood. Pets are allowed after Labor Day.

Reservations, fees: Reservations are recommended and require a nonrefundable deposit. Sites start at $26 a night per family. Seasonal rates are available on request. Special discount lodging packages which include admission to local attractions are offered; reservations are required.

Open: Late Memorial Day–Columbus Day.

Directions: From Conway, travel a mile north on Highway 16 to the campground entrance on the left (west) side of the road.

Contact: Eastern Slope Camping Area, P.O. Box 1127, Conway, NH 03818, 603/447-5092, website: www.easternslopecamping.com.

62 BROKEN BRANCH KOA KAMPGROUND

Rating: 7

South of Woodstock

Pull up a lawn chair and look out over the Pemigewasset River from these plateau sites with mountain views. The rocky river is accessible from the campground for fishing and inner tubing. Clean modern facilities, a safe pool, and a miniature golf course cater to families with young kids. A variety of scheduled events occurs on weekends, including occasional Saturday night bonfires. The campground is right off the highway, and both I-93 and U.S. 3 lead north to North Woodstock and Lincoln, where manmade attractions are as plentiful as the White Mountain National Forest surrounding wilderness. In North Woodstock, Clark's Trading Post features the only trained bears in New England. In Lincoln, the Whale's Tale water park has rides, games, shows, and a petting zoo.

Campsites, facilities: There are 144 sites for tents and RVs, over half with hookups. Each has a table and fire ring. A dump station, restrooms, hot showers, laundry facilities, a recreation hall, pool, pavilion, and playground are provided. Courts for badminton, volleyball, and horseshoes are available. A store sells LP gas, ice, and wood. Leashed pets are permitted.

Reservations, fees: Reservations are accepted. Sites start at $28 a night for two people. There are surcharges for hookups, air conditioners, heaters, extra campers, and guests. Seasonal rates are available.

Open: May 1–mid-October.

Directions: From I-93 at Exit 31 at Woodstock, travel south on Highway 175 for two miles to the campground.

Contact: Broken Branch KOA Kampground, P.O. Box 6, Woodstock, NH 03293, 603/745-8008, reservation only: 800/KOA-9736, website: www.brokenbranchcampground.com.

63 WATERVILLE CAMPGROUND
🏃 🚴 🎣 ⛽ ❄ 🐕 🚐 ⛰

Rating: 8

South of Waterville Valley in the
White Mountain National Forest

A scenic bowl formed by Mounts Tecumseh, Osceola, Kancamagus, Tripyramid, and Sandwich Dome cradles these wooded campsites near the town and ski resort of Waterville Valley. The Mad River flows by the campground and is open to fishing and boating. Multiuse trails for biking, hiking, cross-country skiing, and horseback riding cut through the valley. In spring, summer, and fall, the biggest attraction is hiking. There are miles of hiking trails that traverse the Sandwich Range Wilderness, all accessible within a quarter mile of here. One 1.2-mile hike starts across the road from the campground entrance and leads to Fletcher's Cascades, a beautiful waterfall. Nearby are golf courses, shopping, and the Waterville Valley Alpine Ski Center. These sites are open in the winter, but campers must hike in when the roads are not cleared of snow.

Campsites, facilities: There are 27 sites for tents and RVs up to 22 feet long, all without hookups. Fire grills, picnic tables, piped water, and vault toilets are provided. The campground is across

the street from a convenience store and a gas station. Leashed pets are permitted.

Reservations, fees: Most sites are available on a first-come, first-served basis, but reservations are accepted for a few sites; call the National Forest Reservation Center at 800/280-2267. Campsites are $16 a night per family.

Open: Year-round, but roads are not plowed in winter.

Directions: From I-93 at Campton, take Exit 28 and travel northeast on Highway 49 for nine miles. Turn left on Forest Service Road 30 and continue .25 mile to the campground.

Contact: White Mountain National Forest, Pemigewasset Ranger District, R.F.D. 3, Box 15, Plymouth, NH 03264, 603/536-1310, website: www.fs.fed.us/r9/white/recreation/camping.

64 WHITE LEDGE
🏃 🐕 ♿ 🚐 ⛰

Rating: 7

South of Conway in the
White Mountain National Forest

Though these campsites are wooded, there isn't much of a buffer between busy Highway 16 and the campground. Still, this is a popular base camp for hikers who come to make overnight treks into the White Mountains, as several trails lead from here into the Mount Chocorua Scenic Area.

Campsites, facilities: There are 28 sites for tents or trailers with no hookups. Fire grills, tables, vault toilets, and piped water are provided. Leashed pets are permitted.

Reservations, fees: Certain sites may be reserved from May–October; call the National Forest Reservation Center at 800/ 280-2267. For each reservation, an $8 fee is charged. Sites are $16 a night.

Open: Mid-May–mid-October.

Directions: From Conway, travel five miles south on Highway 16. The campground entrance is on the right (west) side of the road.

Contact: White Mountain National Forest, Saco Ranger Station, 33 Kancamagus Highway, Conway, NH 03818, 603/447-5448, website: www.fs.fed.us/r9/white/recreation/camping.

65 PINE KNOLL CAMPGROUND AND RV RESORT

Rating: 7

On the north shore of Iona Lake in Albany

Iona Lake is surrounded by oak and pine trees and is a haven for smallmouth bass, pickerel, horned pout, and trout. Some of these large wooded sites are right on the lake, while others are set back a bit from the water on grassy, more open plots. Swimmers have a huge sandy beach at their disposal, and nonmotorized boats can be launched at the campground. Canoes and rowboats are available for rent. To the southeast at Madison Boulder Natural Area, you'll find the largest known glacial erratic in North America, standing 23 feet high and 83 feet long. The granite enormity has an estimated weight of 7,650 tons. To the north, the Kancamagus Highway/Highway 112 links Conway and Lincoln on a 34.5-mile route featuring dramatic vistas from 3,000 feet. Make the return trip on a loop via U.S. 302 to the north through more gaps and valleys, but watch for moose if you're driving at night.

Campsites, facilities: There are 175 sites for tents and RVs, all with hookups. Each site has a picnic table and fire ring. Air conditioner and heater use is allowed, and phone hookups are available. A dump station, restrooms, hot showers, laundry facilities, a recreation hall, sports field, and playground are provided. Courts for basketball, badminton, volleyball, and horseshoes are available. A camp store carries ice and firewood. A guarded gate controls traffic at the entrance. Leashed pets are permitted.

Reservations, fees: Reservations are accepted. Base rates are $21–27 per site each night.

Open: Year-round.

Directions: From Conway, travel four miles south on Highway 16 to the campground entrance on the left.

Contact: Pine Knoll Campground and RV Resort, Highway 16, Conway, NH 03818, 603/447-3131, website: http://pineknollcampground.com.

66 COVE CAMPING AREA

Rating: 8

On the west shore of Conway Lake

Laughing loons may rouse you in the morning at these heavily wooded lakeside sites. Set on 1,300-acre Conway Lake, this campground is well away from the hustle and bustle of commercial North Conway. Mountain views, abundant wildlife, and great fishing are the spoils at this location. Canoeing is the best way to explore the lake's islands, marshy inlets, and wooded shoreline. Winds can get ornery on this large body of water, so be aware of quickly changing weather. Piscine residents include rainbow trout, salmon, pickerel, horned pout, and smallmouth bass. There are two boat ramps and a dock in case you bring your own vessel; if not, canoes and rowboats are for rent at the campground.

Campsites, facilities: There are 95 sites for tents and RVs up to 30 feet long, half with hookups. Each site has a picnic table and fire ring. A dump station, restrooms, hot showers, laundry facilities, a recreation hall, pavilion, horseshoe pits, two boat ramps, and a playground are provided. A camp store carries ice and firewood. Rental tents are available. Dogs are allowed after Labor Day.

Reservations, fees: Reservations require a prepaid deposit. Sites are $22–48 a night for two adults with surcharges for children, guests, air conditioners, heaters, and dock space.

Open: Memorial Day–Columbus Day.

Directions: From the junction of Highways 16 and 113 in Conway, travel one mile east on Highway 113. Turn right on Stark Road and head south for 1.75 miles. Make a left onto Cove Road and continue a mile to the campground.

Contact: Cove Camping Area, P.O. Box 778, Conway, NH 03818, 603/447-6734, website: www.covecamping.com.

67 THE PASTURES CAMPGROUND

Rating: 8

On the Connecticut River in South Orford

Throughout the summer, campers here gather to enjoy community meals. Then they bed down for the night at campsites that line the grassy banks of the Connecticut River, which forms the boundary between Vermont and New Hampshire. Docks are provided, so campers will have a place to tie up their own boats or sit for a few hours of fishing. The river is home to numerous species of warm-water and cold-water fish; just be sure to obtain a fishing license before dropping in a line. You can't swim right at the campground, but once you get out on the water, you're free to jump in. From here, the river is navigable by canoe for 20 miles in either direction. Goods and services are available nearby in Orford.

Campsites, facilities: There are 58 sites for tents and RVs, all with water and electric hookups. Each site has a picnic table and fire ring. A dump station, restrooms, and hot showers are provided. You will also find courts for basketball and horseshoes. Firewood is sold on the property. Leashed pets are permitted.

Reservations, fees: Reservations are recommended. Tent sites are $18 a night per family, $22 for RV sites. Weekly, monthly, and seasonal rates are available.

Open: Mid-May–mid-October.

Directions: From I-91 north of White River Junction in Vermont, take Exit 15 for Fairlee-Orford. Turn left onto U.S. 5 and head north for .75 mile to Highway 25A. Turn right onto the green bridge, cross the Connecticut River, and then turn right and head south on Highway 10 for a mile to the campground entrance.

Contact: The Pastures Campground, 499 Highway 10, Orford, NH 03777, 603/353-4579, website: www.thepastures.com.

68 JACOBS BROOK CAMPGROUND

Rating: 8

On the Vermont–New Hampshire border along Jacobs Brook

Shady campsites are set along Jacobs Brook, which feeds into the Connecticut River about a mile to the west, making this a good jumping-off point for those who want to embark on longer canoeing and fishing river outings. The brook itself features several waterfalls and natural pools that make ideal swimming spots. Orford is largely an agricultural community, and the town's many farms indirectly support a sizable wild turkey population. If you come during May, don't be surprised by the hordes of turkey hunters you're likely to encounter around town. A few miles to the east, the Appalachian Trail intersects Highway 25. From this trailhead, Mount Cube to the south is a good destination for a day hike.

Campsites, facilities: There are 75 sites for tents and RVs, 15 with full hookups, 35 with water and electric hookups, and 25 with none. Each site has a picnic table and fireplace. Air conditioner and heater use is allowed. On-site facilities include a dump station, a laundry room, restrooms, hot showers, a pool, and a playground. A camp store sells ice and firewood. Courts for basketball, badminton, and horseshoes are located on the property, as are a sports field and hiking trails. The maximum RV length is 36 feet. Leashed pets are permitted.

Reservations, fees: Reservations are recommended. Tent sites are $20 a night, and RV sites start at $28 a night. Weekly, monthly, and seasonal rates are available.

Open: May 15–October 15.

Directions: From I-91 north of White River Junction in Vermont, take Exit 15 for Fairlee-Orford. Turn left onto U.S. 5 and head north for .75 mile to Highway 25A. Turn right onto the green bridge, cross the Connecticut River, turn left onto Highway 10, and travel north for a mile. Turn right on Archertown Road and head east for a mile to the campground entrance.

Contact: Jacobs Brook Campground, P.O. Box 167, High Bridge Road, Orford, NH 03777, 603/353-9210.

69 SWAIN BROOK CAMPGROUND

Rating: 8

On Swain Brook north of Wentworth

Swain Brook runs through this 417-acre privately owned nature preserve. Sites are natural and wooded and set near a small fishing hole, Downing Pond. In all, there are five mountain brooks on the property, and over a mile of hiking trails leading to cascades, potholes, and trout habitat. Wild apple trees, berry patches, blue herons, and deer are common sights. More extensive day hikes are a few miles west of the campground on the Appalachian Trail.

Campsites, facilities: There are 75 sites for tents and RVs, some with full hookups. Each site has a picnic table and fire ring. A dump station, restrooms, hot showers, a recreation hall, pool, horseshoe pits, tetherball, a TV room, and a playground are provided. A camp store carries groceries, sporting goods, ice, and firewood. Group sites are available for tents and RVs. Leashed pets are permitted.

Reservations, fees: Reservations are recommended and require prepaid deposits. Sites start at $24 a night per family. Weekly, monthly, and seasonal rates available.

Open: Late April–early November.

Directions: From the junction of Highways 25 and 25A in Wentworth, travel north on Highway 25 for .5 mile to Beech Hill Road. Take a left and continue north for .75 mile to the campground entrance.

Contact: Swain Brook Campground, P.O. Box 157, Beech Hill Road, Wentworth, NH 03282, 603/764-5537, website: www.swainbrook.com.

70 SCENIC VIEW CAMPGROUND

Rating: 8

In Warren on the Baker River and Patch Brook

Choose from grassy, sunny sites with hookups along the brook, or wilderness tent sites in the woods along the Baker River, a renowned trout stream. Scenic View is in Warren, a sleepy town on the west side of the White Mountain National Forest. A mix of seasonal and vacation campers gathers here for nature programs, fishing derbies, campfires, and tournaments in the shadow of the mountains. Down the road is the Warren Fish Hatchery, which has interpretive programs and a self-guided science center. The hatchery land is also open to hunting, and the local wildlife includes deer, fox, and coyote. Mount Moosilauke rises to the north of town, a bald, broad 4,810-footer offering sweeping views of the Whites.

Campsites, facilities: There are 98 sites for tents and RVs. Each site has a picnic table and fire ring. Air conditioner and heater use is allowed, and cable TV is available. A dump station, restrooms, hot showers, laundry facilities, a recreation hall, pool, sports field, and playground are provided. Courts for basketball, badminton, volleyball, and horseshoes are available. A camp store carries LP gas, ice, and firewood and rents mountain bikes. Leashed pets are permitted.

Reservations, fees: Reservations are accepted with a prepaid deposit. Holiday weekend stays require full prepayment. Sites are $24–36 a night per family. Weekly, monthly, and seasonal rates available.

Open: May 1–October 15.

Directions: From I-93 at Plymouth, take Exit 26. Travel northwest on Highway 25 for 18 miles to the campground, just south of the Warren town center.

Contact: Scenic View Campground, 193AA South Main Street, Warren, NH 03279, 603/764-9380, website: www.scenicviewnh.com.

71 MOOSE HILLOCK CAMPGROUND

Rating: 8

North of Warren

Mount Moosilauke, the state's 10th highest peak at elevation 4,810 feet, is visible through a break in the trees on the campground duck pond, which is shaped like the United States. Sites at Moose Hillock are exceptionally private and wooded, each with its own driveway and yard area. Some spots are on the water, and the most remote sites are reserved for tenters. Batchelder Brook tumbles over rocks and forms pools on its way through the property. There's fishing and swimming in the brook, but the campground also has three swimming pools, including one with a natural rock slide, cave, and waterfall. A 200-year-old post-and-beam barn serves as the recreation hall. Planned events abound for parents and kids, including visits from the costumed character Bruce the Moose and dancing to cover bands in the barn. Trailheads for Moosilauke are within a short drive. Miles of logging and dirt roads offer challenging mountain biking. And, yes, this is moose country, so keep your eyes peeled for the large gangly beasts.

Campsites, facilities: There are 227 sites for tents and RVs. Each site has a picnic table and fire ring. Air conditioner and heater use is allowed. A dump station, restrooms, hot showers, laundry facilities, a recreation hall, sports field, swimming pools, and a playground are provided. Courts for basketball, badminton, volleyball, and horseshoes are available. A camp store carries RV supplies, LP gas, ice, and firewood. Leashed pets are permitted.

Reservations, fees: Reservations are recommended. Sites are $28–37 a night per family.

Open: Mid-May–September 9.

Directions: From I-93 at Plymouth, take Exit 26. Travel northwest on Highway 25 for 20 miles through the towns of Rumney, Wentworth, and Warren. Take a right onto Highway 118 and continue north for a mile to the campground entrance.

Contact: Moose Hillock Campground, 98 Batcheldor Brook Road, Highway 118, Warren, NH 03279, 603/764-5294, website: www.moosehillock.com.

72 PEMI RIVER CAMPGROUND

Rating: 7

On the Pemigewasset River in Thornton

Tenters will find wooded sites on the Pemigewasset River, while RVers are accommodated in grassy, shaded pull-throughs. The Pemi is the main attraction here, and the campground rents kayaks, canoes, and inner tubes to suit any camper's preferred style of exploration. The White Mountain National Forest lies to the north, east, and west of the campground with endless options for short, long, and overnight hikes.

Campsites, facilities: There are 73 sites for tents and RVs. Each site has a table and fireplace. A dump station, restrooms, hot showers, a game room, and a playground are provided. Sports facilities include a soccer field, a court for badminton and volleyball, horseshoe pits, and inner tube and kayak rentals. A small store carries ice and firewood. Leashed pets are permitted.

Reservations, fees: Reservations are accepted. Sites start at $28 a night per family. Weekly, monthly, and seasonal rates are available.

Open: May 15–Labor Day.

Directions: From I-93 at Exit 29 for Campton-Thornton, head north on U.S. 3 for several yards to the campground entrance on the right side of the road.

Contact: Pemi River Campground, 2458 Highway 3, Thornton, NH 03223, 603/726-7015 in the summer, or 603/625-2879 in the winter, website: www.pemirivercampground.com.

73 CAMPTON CAMPGROUND

🧍🏊🚣🚗🐕✖🚐⛺

Rating: 8

In the White Mountain National Forest north of Campton Pond

Towering white pines dominate this heavily wooded campground at the westerly edge of the White Mountain National Forest. Interpretive programs are offered on Saturday evenings in the summer, and a playing field provides room for a variety of team sports. Stores and restaurants are close by in Waterville Valley and Campton. The Mad River flows through Campton Campground and is open to fishing, swimming, and boating. Many hiking trails can be accessed in the vicinity, including the wilderness areas of the Sandwich Range to the east. A short loop is just northeast of the campground off Mad River Road. Dickey and Welch Mountains are accessible on this moderate 4.4-mile round-trip hike; there's a parking area on Orris Road.

Campsites, facilities: There are 58 sites for tents and RVs up to 30 feet long, all without hookups. Piped water, metered hot showers, fire rings, tables, and a playing field are provided. A small store sells ice and firewood. Across Highway 49 there are three group sites. Leashed pets are permitted.

Reservations, fees: Reservations are recommended; call the National Forest Reservation Center at 800/280-2267. Sites are $18 a night per family. Group rates range from $15–80 for up to 100 people.

Open: Mid-May–mid-October, but the group sites are open year-round.

Directions: From I-93 at Campton, take Exit 28 and travel two miles east on Highway 49 to the campground entrance.

Contact: White Mountain National Forest, Pemigewasset Ranger District, R.F.D. 3, Box 15, Plymouth, NH 03264, 603/536-1310, website: www.fs.fed.us/r9/white/recreation/camping.

74 PINE HAVEN CAMPGROUND

🚲🏊🚣✖🏠🐕🏃🚐⛺

Rating: 8

On the Baker River west of Rumney

A pine forest envelops these sites on the Baker River. Some sites are occupied by seasonal campers who gather for group events including tournaments and dinners. Canoes may be rented at the campground for an easy to moderate paddle on the Saco River from West Rumney to Plymouth. One of the region's prettiest lakes lies northeast of the campground. Stinson Lake is ringed by perky mountains and has a public boat launch at its southern end. The Stinson Mountain Trail is an old logging road that leaves from south of the lake to a 2,900-foot summit affording views of the region.

Campsites, facilities: There are 100 sites for tents and RVs. Each site has a picnic table, fire ring, and grill. Air conditioners are allowed, but heaters are prohibited. A dump station, restrooms, hot showers, laundry facilities, a recreation hall, pool, and playground are provided. Courts for basketball, badminton, shuffleboard, volleyball, and horseshoes are available. A grocery store carries LP gas, RV supplies, ice, and firewood. Leashed pets are permitted.

Reservations, fees: Reservations are accepted. Sites start at $28 a night per family. Weekly, monthly, and seasonal rates are available on request.

Open: May 15–October 15.

Directions: From I-93 at Plymouth, take Exit 26 and travel west on Highway 25 toward Wentworth for 12 miles. The campground is on the left side of the road, about .75 mile north of the junction of Highways 25 and 118.

Contact: Pine Haven Campground, P.O. Box 43, Wentworth, NH 03282, 603/786-2900, reservations only: 800/370-PINE (800/370-7463), website: www.pinehavencampground.com.

75 BRANCH BROOK CAMPGROUND

🏊 🛶 🎿 ❄️ 🐕 🚴 🚐 ⛺

Rating: 7
On the Pemigewasset River in West Campton

On a typical hot day, the Pemigewasset River is full of campers floating on inner tubes to keep cool. Branch Brook intersects the campground, and a small five-acre pond on the brook is open to fishing. Full-hookup RV sites are set in a pine-forested area accessible by a road or a pretty footpath that crosses the brook on a covered bridge. A second area offers grassy meadow sites on the brook, while yet another section is in the woods near the shores of the Pemi.

There's a swimming beach on the river, and canoes may be rented at the campground for those who want to explore the waterway. The White Mountain National Forest lies to the north, east, and west of the campground, offering myriad options for short, long, and overnight hikes.

Campsites, facilities: There are 168 sites for tents and RVs, most with hookups. Each site has a picnic table and fire ring. A dump station, restrooms, hot showers, a large pool, laundry facilities, a recreation hall, and a playground are provided. Courts for basketball, badminton, volleyball, and horseshoes are available. A small grocery store carries LP gas, RV supplies, ice, and firewood. RV storage and RV rentals are available. Leashed pets are permitted.

Reservations, fees: Reservations are recommended Memorial Day–Labor Day and require a prepaid deposit. Holiday weekend reservations must be prepaid in full. Sites are $27–32 a night per family. Weekly, monthly, and seasonal rates are available.

Open: May 1–late October, but seasonal sites are open year-round.

Directions: From I-93 in Campton at Exit 28, travel west on Highway 49 for .5 mile to the campground.

Contact: Branch Brook Campground, P.O. Box 390, Campton, NH 03223, 603/726-7001, website: www.campnh.com.

76 CHOCORUA CAMPING VILLAGE

🚶 🏊 🛶 🚐 ❄️ 🐕 🚴 🚐 ⛺

Rating: 7
On Moores Pond in Tamworth

Two hundred wooded acres on the north shore of Moores Pond provide a scenic backdrop to Chocorua Camping Village. Sites are spacious, private, and set either beside or near the pond. Boats and canoes are available for rent at the campground, and there's a designated swimming area with a sandy beach. The campground caters to families, with three directed activities for kids daily, from arts and crafts to organized games and recreation. Walkers will find shaded nature trails in the surrounding woodlands. For good cold-water fishing, try the Chocorua River north of the campground, or White Lake State Park across Highway 16 to the south. Not only does White Lake have a boat launch, it's also the site of a National Natural Landmark: a stand of mature pitch pines covers 72 acres, some trees with diameters measuring up to two feet. Such an uncut area is a rare occurrence in the Northeast.

Campsites, facilities: There are 150 sites for tents and RVs, most with water and electric hookups. Each site has a picnic table and fire ring. A dump station, laundry facilities, restrooms, hot showers, a recreation hall, and a playground are provided. A camp store sells LP gas, ice, and firewood. Leashed pets are permitted.

Reservations, fees: Reservations are recommended. Sites start at $28 a night. Rental trailers are available.

Open: May 1–October 15.

Directions: From the northern junction of Highways 16 and 25 in West Ossipee, travel three miles north on Highway 16 to the campground entrance on the right (east) side of the road.

Contact: Chocorua Camping Village, P.O. Box

484, Chocorua, NH 03817, 603/323-8563, website: www.chocoruacamping.com.

77 FOOTHILLS CAMPGROUND

🏔 🏊 🚣 🐕 🚴 🚐 ⛺

Rating: 7

North of White Lake State Park

Here's another camping option right off busy Highway 16. Tall pines tower over these sites located north of White Lake State Park. A small pond on the property is open to fishing, but more adventuresome anglers will want to check out White Lake to the south. There's a pool on-site for those who want to cool off on hot summer days, as well as many lakes and rivers for natural swimming. Several trails explore the surrounding pine forest; for longer treks head north to Hemenway State Forest and hike through groves of white pines. A 125-acre forest section that holds 150-year-old conifers is protected as the Big Pines Natural Area. In nearby Tamworth, you will find the state's oldest summer theater, the Barnstormers. It stages a different comedy, musical, or mystery every week in July and August.

Campsites, facilities: There are 84 sites with a special primitive area set aside for tenters. All RV sites have hookups. Each site has a picnic table and fire ring. A dump station, restrooms, hot showers, a pavilion, pool, horseshoe pits, a basketball court, and a playground are provided. A small grocery store sells ice, LP gas, and firewood. The maximum RV length is 33 feet. Leashed pets are permitted.

Reservations, fees: Reservations are accepted. Sites range from $22–35 a night per family.

Open: Mid-May–mid-October.

Directions: From the northern junction of Highways 16 and 25 in West Ossipee, travel 1.5 miles north on Highway 16 to the campground on the left (west) side of the road.

Contact: Foothills Campground, 506 Maple Road, Tamworth, NH 03886, 603/323-8322, website: www.thefoothills.com.

78 TAMWORTH CAMPING AREA

🏊 🚣 ❄ 🐕 🚴 🚐 ⛺

Rating: 7

On the Swift River in Tamworth

Private campsites are set in a woodsy meadow on or near the Swift River. A sandy beach is available for swimming, but many riverside sites come with their own individual small beaches. Popular pursuits include trout fishing and tubing on the river. Kids can feed and visit with sheep, lambs, and goats at the campground's petting zoo. There are open areas for group camping. Numerous sites are rented by seasonal campers who join together on weekends for parades, dances, pig roasts, and tournaments. In the winter, snowmobilers and cross-country skiers can head to nearby White Lake State Park; the state snowmobile corridor (running parallel to Highway 16) is also not too far to the east.

Campsites, facilities: There are 100 sites for tents and RVs, many with hookups. Each site has a picnic table, fire ring, and a grill. Air conditioner and heater use is allowed. A dump station, laundry facilities, restrooms, hot showers, a recreation hall, and a playground are provided. A small grocery store sells LP gas, RV supplies, ice, and firewood. Off-season RV storage is available. Courts for basketball, shuffleboard, badminton, volleyball, and horseshoes are located on the property. Traffic is controlled by an entry gate. Leashed pets are permitted.

Reservations, fees: Reservations are recommended, especially during holiday weekends and in July and August. A 50 percent deposit is required for all reservations, and full prepayment is required on three-day holiday weekends. Sites range from $25–36 a night.

Open: Mid-May–November.

Directions: From the northern junction of Highways 16 and 25 in West Ossipee, go north on Highway 16 for .75 mile. Turn left on Depot Road and head west for three miles to the campground entrance.

Contact: Tamworth Camping Area, P.O. Box

99, Depot Road, Tamworth, NH 03886, 603/323-8031, website: www.tamworthcamping.com.

79 WHITE LAKE STATE PARK

Rating: 7

On White Lake in West Ossipee

The wooded sites here in the foothills of the White Mountains are linked by dirt and paved roads. Many campsites are right on the shore of pristine White Lake. Trolling motors are allowed on the water, and canoes may be rented at the park. Swimming, however, is the main attraction—the park maintains a clean, sandy beach. There's also good trout fishing in these waters. Hiking trails explore the surrounding forest and the White Lake Pitch Pine Area, a National Natural Landmark; this stand of native pines covers 72 acres and includes several trees with trunk diameters of nearly two feet. White Lake is one of the most popular state park campgrounds; to snag a waterfront site you must reserve very early in the year.

Campsites, facilities: There are 200 sites for tents and RVs, all without hookups. Each site has a picnic table, and some are also equipped with fire rings. Restrooms and a playground are provided. A camp store sells ice and firewood. The maximum RV length is 30 feet. No pets are allowed.

Reservations, fees: For reservations, contact the New Hampshire State Parks Camping Reservation Center, P.O. Box 1856, Concord, NH 03302-1856, 603/271-3628, website: www.nhparks.state.nh.us. Sites are $16–22 a night per family.

Open: Mid-May–mid-October.

Directions: From the northern junction of Highways 16 and 25 in West Ossipee, travel north on Highway 16 for one mile to the campground entrance on the left (west) side of the road.

Contact: White Lake State Park, P.O. Box 41, West Ossipee, NH 03890, 603/323-7350; New Hampshire Division of Parks and Recreation, 603/271-3628, website: www.nhparks.state.nh.us.

80 PLYMOUTH SANDS CAMPGROUND

Rating: 7

On the Baker River in Plymouth

A sandy beach on the Baker River is the center of action at this campground. You just need an inner tube to take advantage of the cooling currents. This clear mountain stream also provides healthy habitat for trout. All but beginner canoeists can enjoy Class II paddling on the Baker River between West Rumney and Plymouth. The waterway offers mountain views and passes beneath a covered bridge just before you reach Plymouth. To get the lay of the land, head up Plymouth Mountain. From the trailhead located to the south off Highway 25 in Hebron, the Plymouth Mountain Trail ascends the 2,187-foot summit on a moderate six-mile walk through protected wilderness.

Campsites, facilities: There are 84 sites for tents and RVs, some with full hookups. Each site has a picnic table and fire ring. A dump station, restrooms, hot showers, and a playground are provided, and a camp store sells ice, firewood, and snacks. The maximum RV length is 26 feet. Leashed pets are permitted.

Reservations, fees: Reservations are accepted. Sites are $16–21 a night per family. Weekly and seasonal rates are available on request.

Open: May 15–September 15.

Directions: From I-93 at Plymouth, take Exit 26, head west on Highway 25 for a short distance, and then follow U.S. 3 north for .1 mile to Fairground Road. Turn left and head west on Fairground for three miles to the campground entrance on the left (south) side of the road, just past the junction with Smith Bridge Road.

Contact: Plymouth Sands Campground, RR 1, Box 3172, Plymouth, NH 03264, 603/536-2605.

81 BEARCAMP RIVER CAMPGROUND

🏃 🏊 ⛵ 🚣 🎿 ❄ 🐕 🚶 🚐 ⛺

Rating: 7

On the Bearcamp River

Nearly half of these large sites are located on the Bearcamp River, a clear mountain stream. Towering hemlocks, pines, and spruce trees shade the campground. An easy two-hour paddle down-river brings canoeists to Ossipee Lake to the south; boats may be rented at the campground. Trout inhabit the Bearcamp River, and many ponds and lakes in the area offer remote spots for warm-water and cold-water fishing. All are easily explored in a cartop boat. The Mount Whittier Waterslide—where you can hop into a bumper boat if that's your preference—is located near the campground. For hiking, the Mount Whittier summit lies just to the west of here and can be reached in an easy to moderate hike. Many seasonal campers roost at Bearcamp, thus reservations are strongly suggested.

Campsites, facilities: There are 68 sites for tents and RVs, most with water and electric hookups. Each site has a picnic table and fire ring. A dump station, restrooms, hot showers, a recreation hall, and a playground are provided. Courts for basketball, badminton, volleyball, and horseshoes are also on the property. Supplies can be purchased in West Ossipee and Center Ossipee. Leashed pets are permitted.

Reservations, fees: Reservations are accepted. Sites range from $22–26 a night. Seasonal rates are available.

Open: Year-round, but winter sites are available for seasonal campers only.

Directions: From the southern junction of Highways 16 and 25 at Center Ossipee, travel northwest on Highway 16 for 3.5 miles to Newman Drew Road. Turn left (west) and enter the campground on the right. It's next to Gitchee Gumee Campground.

Contact: Bearcamp River Campground, P.O. Box 104, West Ossipee, NH 03890, 603/539-4898, website: www.bearcamp.com.

82 WHIT'S END CAMPGROUND

🏊 ⛵ 🚣 🎿 ❄ 🐕 🚶 🚐 ⛺

Rating: 7

On the Bearcamp River in West Ossipee

The Bearcamp River flows by these wooded, spacious sites shaded by hemlock, pine, and spruce trees. An easy two-hour paddle on this clear mountain stream brings canoeists to Ossipee Lake to the south. Whit's End offers rental boats and maintains a large sandy beach on the Bearcamp River. If you like fishing, bring your gear, as this is a good trout stream. Winter sites are available to seasonal campers who want to take advantage of the vast network of snowmobile trails accessible from the campground. The area's many ponds and lakes offer unlimited ice-fishing opportunities.

Campsites, facilities: There are 156 sites for tents and RVs, most with water and electric hookups. Each site has a table and fire ring. A dump station, laundry facilities, restrooms, hot showers, a recreation hall, playground, snack bar, and a game room are provided. Firewood, LP gas, and ice are sold on-site. Leashed pets are permitted.

Reservations, fees: Reservations are accepted. Sites are $24–28 a night. Seasonal rates are available.

Open: Mid-May–mid-September, and Columbus Day weekend.

Directions: From the southern junction of Highways 16 and 25 at Center Ossipee, travel northwest on Highway 16 for 3.5 miles to Newman Drew Road. Turn left (west) and continue to the campground entrance on the right. It's next to Bearcamp River Campground.

Contact: Whit's End Campground, Newman Drew Road, West Ossipee, NH 03890, 603/539-6060, website: www.whitsendcampground.com.

83 WESTWARD SHORES CAMPGROUND

Rating: 8

On the northwest shore of Ossipee Lake

Birch trees provide welcome shade for these sites near the shore of Ossipee Lake. A small marina, an expansive sandy beach, and boat rentals give campers several different ways to enjoy the open water. Fishing enthusiasts will find bass, horned pout, perch, pickerel, salmon, and trout in the lake, while fly fishers will want to head south to the Lovell River for some of the state's best trout fishing; the Lovell feeds into the lake just near a road bearing the same name. Also to the south, the Indian Mound Golf Club is open to the public; it was built on an old Ossipee Indian burial ground. The southeast lakeshore, called Heath Pond Bog, is a protected area. This National Natural Landmark is fragile and undeveloped; a floating mat of peat is covered with moss and provides habitat for a unique plant community including orchids and insectivorous plants. A nature trail explores the bog and the surrounding spruce and tamarack forest. Seasonal renters may use sites in the winter months, maybe as a base camp for excursions on the area's extensive snowmobiling and cross-country skiing trails, or to enjoy ice fishing and skating on the lake.

Campsites, facilities: There are 260 sites for tents and RVs. Each site has a picnic table and fire ring. Air conditioners and heaters are allowed, and cable TV hookups are available. A dump station, laundry facilities, restrooms, hot showers, a recreation hall, pavilion, and a playground are provided, and a camp store sells ice and firewood. Courts for basketball, badminton, volleyball, and horseshoes are located on the property. Off-season RV storage is available. Traffic is controlled by an entry gate. Leashed pets are permitted.

Reservations, fees: All reservations must be accompanied by a 33 percent deposit. A minimum three-day stay is required during holiday weekends. Sites are $35 a night per family. Boat slips are $10 a day. Seasonal rates are available.

Open: Year-round.

Directions: From the northern junction of Highways 16 and 25 in West Ossipee, travel 3.5 miles south on Highway 16. Turn left on Nichols Road and head east for a short distance to the campground entrance.

Contact: Westward Shores Campground, P.O. Box 308, West Ossipee, NH 03890, 603/539-6445.

Chapter 6

DAVID BROWNELL/© STATE OF NEW HAMPSHIRE

Western Lakes

Western Lakes

Visitors are often surprised by the rural character of southwestern New Hampshire. But if you look at a map, you'll see why: No major interstate cuts through the area; thus, travelers don't flock here as they do New Hampshire's White Mountains or Vermont's Green Mountains. That's good news for campers who like freshwater lakes, rolling hills, and a minimum of traffic. Come here to pass a summer's vacation on the water, spend afternoons shopping for antiques or picking berries, or go for hikes in the hills.

Of course, the lack of an interstate doesn't mean this part of the state is a backwater. To the north, the region is anchored by Hanover, home to Dartmouth College and a renowned medical community. To the south, the city of Keene is home to a state college, with a gorgeous view of Mount Monadnock. People who live here feel like they have the best of both worlds: enough culture in the small cities, but boundless opportunities to explorc outdoors. Because most campgrounds are set on water in this region, you'll find many cater to seasonal campers, families who return year after year to the same spot. As they say: If it ain't broke, don't fix it.

For detailed information on New Hampshire State Parks, see the introductiom to the White Mountains chapter.

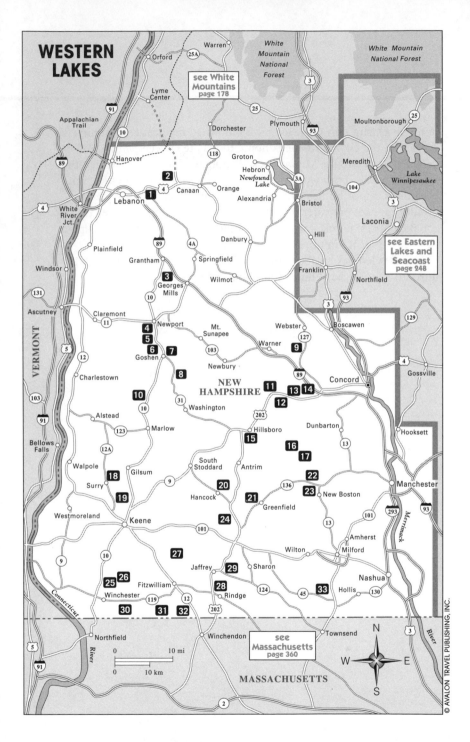

WESTERN LAKES

see White Mountains page 178

White Mountain National Forest

White Mountain National Forest

Warren
Orford
25A

Lyme Center

Appalachian Trail
91
10
Hanover

Dorchester

Plymouth
93
25
3

Moultonborough
25

118
Groton
Hebron
Newfound Lake
Meredith
Lake Winnipesaukee
104
3

2
4
Canaan
Orange
Alexandria
3A
Bristol

1
Lebanon

Laconia

Plainfield
89
4A
Danbury
Hill

see Eastern Lakes and Seacoast page 248

White River Jct.
4

Windsor

Grantham
Springfield
Wilmot
Franklin
Northfield

131

3
Georges Mills
10

VERMONT
5
12
Ascutney
Claremont
11
4
Newport
Mt. Sunapee
103
Webster
127
9
Boscawen
129

Charlestown

6
7
Goshen
Newbury
Warner
89
Concord
4
Gossville

8

103
91
10
10
Alstead
31
Washington
NEW HAMPSHIRE
11
13
14
12
202

Bellows Falls
123
Marlow
Hillsboro
15
Dunbarton
13
Hooksett

Walpole
12A
Gilsum
9
16
17

18
Surry
South Stoddard
Antrim
22
Manchester
293
93

19
Keene
20
Hancock
21
23
New Boston
136
Greenfield
101
Amherst

Westmoreland
24
13
Milford

9
10
101
Wilton
Sharon

27
Jaffrey
29
Merrimack

25
26
Fitzwilliam
28
Rindge
124
45
33
Hollis
130
Nashua

Winchester
119
12
202

30
31
32

Northfield
Winchendon
see Massachusetts page 360
Townsend
3

N
W E
S

5

91

MASSACHUSETTS

0   10 mi
0   10 km

© AVALON TRAVEL PUBLISHING, INC.

226   Foghorn Outdoors New England Camping

◉ MASCOMA LAKE CAMPGROUND

🥾 🏊 🛶 🚐 🐕 ♿ 🚗 ⛺

Rating: 8

In Enfield on the western shore of Mascoma Lake

The campsites here are set in tiers on the mountainside, allowing each one to have a view of Mascoma Lake. Water sports, including swimming, boating, and paddling around in a canoe, are the focus of summertime activities, and boat owners may dock their craft at the campground for a fee. Mascoma Lake is home to smallmouth and largemouth bass, rock bass, and trout. Nature hikes on the mountain leave from the campground. For those who like to stay close to home, group activities such as crafts and community dinners are organized for adults and children from May–September. Just south of the campground on Route 4A you will find the Enfield Shaker Museum, a cluster of historic buildings, including the largest Shaker stone dwelling house ever built.

Campsites, facilities: There are 96 sites for tents and RVs, 46 with full hookups, 26 with water and electric hookups, and 24 with none. Each site has a picnic table and fireplace. Air conditioner and heater use is allowed. A recreation hall, dump station, laundry facilities, restrooms, hot showers, and a playground are provided. A camp store sells ice and firewood. Courts for basketball, volleyball, and horseshoes are located on the property. Leashed pets are permitted.

Reservations, fees: Reservations are recommended and must be accompanied by one night's fee. Holiday stays must be prepaid in full. Sites range from $22–29 a night. Cabin and cottage rentals are $55–75 a night.

Open: May–mid-October.

Directions: From I-89 at Lebanon, take Exit 17 and travel east on U.S. 4 for approximately two miles to Highway 4A. Turn right onto Highway 4A and head south for .7 mile to the campground entrance.

Contact: Mascoma Lake Campground, 92 U.S. Route 4A, Lebanon, NH 03766, 603/448-5076 or 800/769-7861, website: www.mascomalake.com.

◉ CRESCENT CAMPSITES

🏊 🛶 🚐 🐕 ♿ 🚗 ⛺

Rating: 8

On Canaan Street Lake in Canaan

Grassy, wooded campsites beside Canaan Street Lake offer easy access for boaters. The waterway is open to powerboating, waterskiing, and canoeing, and a sandy swimming beach is also provided. Anglers can try to catch their dinners here, as bass, pickerel, and perch inhabit the lake. Summer weekends are filled with organized meals and dances for campers. Excellent hiking routes are found a short drive to the east in Mount Cardigan State Park. Moderate and easy trails for hikers of all ages and abilities include a 3,121-foot summit hike on the West Ridge Trail. Panoramic Lakes Region views can be had from the fire tower atop the mountain. Another popular family attraction is Ruggles Mine, located south of Canaan off U.S. 4. Nearly 200 years old, this open pit mine contains more than 150 minerals including mica, amethyst, and garnet. Giant rooms and tunnels in the mine are open for exploration, and visitors are welcome to collect minerals.

Campsites, facilities: There are 82 sites, all with hookups. Each site has a table and fireplace. A dump station, laundry facilities, restrooms, free hot showers, a sports field, boat ramp, and a playground are provided. There's also a recreation room with video games, a jukebox, and a pool table. A small grocery store sells ice and firewood. Courts for basketball and horseshoes and a pool are located on-site. Leashed pets are permitted.

Reservations, fees: Reservations are recommended. Tenters may stay for up to two weeks, and one tent per site is allowed. Sites start at $22–26 a night.

Open: Mid-May–mid-October.

Directions: From I-89 at Lebanon, take Exit 17 and travel 12 miles east on U.S. 4 to Canaan. At the blinking yellow light in the center of town, turn left on Canaan Street, just west of the junction of U.S. 4 and Highway 118. Head north for one-eighth mile on Fernwood Street, bear right at the fork in the road, and continue about a mile to the campground.

Contact: Crescent Campsites, P.O. Box 238, Canaan, NH 03741, 603/523-9910 or 800/494-5118, website: www.ucampnh.com/crescent/.

3 OTTER LAKE CAMPGROUND
🏞 🚣 🎣 🛶 🏕 🐕 🚶 🚐 ⛺

Rating: 7
On the west side of Otter Lake near Georges Mills

Both open and wooded sites are offered at this campground set near Otter Lake. There's a sandy beach for sunning and swimming, and campers may rent rowboats, canoes, and paddleboats here. Nature trails explore Phillips Memorial Preserve, which lies adjacent to the campground. Just south of the campground is Sunapee Lake, with its three working lighthouses and numerous hidden coves. Several outfitters rent powerboats, canoes, sailboats, and sailboards for day use on the water. Head to Mount Sunapee State Park at that lake's south end to take advantage of hiking trails and a scenic chairlift ride. At the same end of the lake, an easy hike leads into the John Hay National Wildlife Refuge, a preserve for upland birds. Besides great bird-watching, the preserve—once a summer retreat for former Secretary of State John Hay—features gardens and a marvelous view of Mount Sunapee.

Campsites, facilities: There are 28 sites for tents and RVs, 12 with water and electric hookups. Each site has a picnic table and fireplace. A dump station, recreation hall, restrooms, hot showers, horseshoe pits, rental boats, and a playground are provided. Ice and firewood are sold on site. The maximum RV length is 30 feet. Leashed pets are permitted.

Reservations, fees: Reservations are accepted. Campsites start at $17 a night per family.
Open: Mid-May–mid-October.
Directions: From I-89 south of Lebanon, take Exit 12 for New London. Head west for a mile on Highway 11. Turn right on Otterville Road and proceed a short distance to the campground.
Contact: Otter Lake Campground, 55 Otterville Road, New London, NH 03257, 603/763-5600.

4 LOON LAKE CAMPGROUND
🏞 🚴 🚣 🎣 🏕 🐕 🚶 🚐 ⛺

Rating: 8
On an artificial pond north of Newport

One-hundred-acre artificially constructed Loon Lake is the hub of activity for campers here, offering fishing enthusiasts a place to try for smallmouth and largemouth bass, horned pout, brook trout, and rainbow trout. Swimmers and sunbathers have access to a sandy beach. And for those who want to get out on the water, there are four small islands and many inlets to explore by nonmotorized boats. All campsites have lake views, and a separate primitive area is reserved for tents. In season, campers gather for potluck dinners and dances. Miles of trails lacing the surrounding woodlands provide forested terrain for hikers and mountain bikers to explore. Mount Sunapee State Park, seven miles to the southeast, is the northern terminus of the Monadnock-Sunapee Greenway, a 51-mile trail connecting two of southern New Hampshire's most notable peaks. Campers can take a scenic chairlift ride to the top of the mountain, hike, or hop aboard a boat for a cruise on 4,085-acre Sunapee Lake at the foot of the mountain.

Campsites, facilities: There are 102 sites for tents and RVs, 88 with full hookups and the rest with either water and electric hookups or no hookups. Each site has a picnic table and fireplace. Air conditioner use is allowed. Facilities include a dump station, restrooms, hot showers, and a playground. A camp store sells fishing licenses, ice, and firewood. Courts for basketball, volleyball, and horseshoes are located on the property. A recreation hall, library, and large screened pavilion are also on the grounds. Leashed pets are permitted.

Reservations, fees: Reservations are recommended. Rates range from $17 a night per family for sites without hookups to $22 and $29 for limited- and full-hookup sites, respectively. Weekly, monthly, and seasonal rates are available. Deposits are required for a security gate pass and pets.

Open: Mid-May–mid-October.

Directions: From I-89 at Newport, take exit 12. Follow Route 11 west for nine miles. Turn right onto Reed's Mill Road. The campground entrance is 2.4 miles ahead on the left.

Contact: Loon Lake Campground, P.O. Box 345, Newport, NH 03773, 603/863-8176, website: www.camploonlake.com.

5 CROW'S NEST CAMPGROUND

Rating: 8

On the Sugar River in Newport

Riverside and grassy, these wooded sites have access to an extensive multiuse trail system available year-round for such activities as snowmobiling and cross-country skiing. You won't suffer frostbite at Crow's Nest Campground, because winter campers can get a break from the cold by sitting around the fireplace in the warm-up lodge. In the summer, free concerts are performed every Sunday evening on the town common. There's good fishing for brown, lake, and rainbow trout on the Sugar River, and 18 holes and greens are located nearby at the John H. Cain Golf Club in Newport.

Campsites, facilities: There are 95 sites for tents and RVs, most with hookups. Each site has a picnic table and fireplace. Air conditioners are allowed, but heaters are prohibited. A dump station, laundry facilities, restrooms, hot showers, a pool, wading pool, and a playground are on the grounds. There's also a recreation hall with coin games and a small camp store selling ice and firewood. Volleyball courts, horseshoe pits, a sports field, and a miniature golf course are located on the property. Leashed pets are permitted.

Reservations, fees: Reservations are recommended from Memorial Day–Labor Day. Sites start at $20–27 a night. Weekly, monthly, and seasonal rates are available.

Open: Year-round.

Directions: From the intersection of Highways 10 and 11/103 in Newport, travel two miles south on Highway 10. The campground is on the right (west) side of the road.

Contact: Crow's Nest Campground, 529 South Main Street, Newport, NH 03773, 603/863-6170 or 800/424-0900, website: www.crowsnestcampground.com.

6 NORTHSTAR CAMPGROUND

Rating: 8

In South Newport on Coon Brook and the Sugar River

Roomy, private campsites are set either in a grassy meadow or in the woods alongside Coon Brook or the Sugar River. There's excellent trout fishing in the river and a spring-fed swimming pond that was formed when part of the brook was cordoned off. Live entertainment is featured at such events as the annual pig roast, held each September. Other organized activities include theme weekends, cookouts, and a fishing derby in October. Foot trails lead into the woods surrounding the campground; you will discover more challenging hikes if you drive 15 minutes southeast at Mount Sunapee State Park. In early August, the park hosts one of the largest crafts fairs in New England.

Campsites, facilities: There are 56 sites for tents and RVs, 31 with water and electric hookups. Each site has a picnic table and fireplace. A dump station, restrooms, hot showers, a pavilion, and a playground are provided. Courts for badminton, volleyball, tetherball, and horseshoes are located on the property, as are a softball field and a croquet lawn. Ice and firewood are available. Leashed pets are permitted.

Reservations, fees: Reservations are accepted. Sites start at $22 a night. Seasonal and club rates are available.

Open: Mid-May–mid-October.

Directions: From the intersection of Highways 10 and 11/103 in Newport, travel 3.5 miles south on Highway 10. Turn right on Coon Brook Road and head west for .25 mile to the campground entrance on the right side of the road.

Contact: Northstar Campground, 43 Coon Brook Road, Newport, NH 03773, 603/863-4001, website: www.northstarcampground.com.

7 RAND POND CAMPGROUND

🚶 🏊 🚣 ❄ 🐕 🥾 🚐 ⛺

Rating: 7

On the south shore of Rand Pond in Goshen

Campers can choose from open, wooded, and shoreline sites beside Rand Pond. A boat ramp, dock, and sandy swimming beach are maintained at the water's edge. There's good trout fishing in these waters, and rental boats are available at the campground. Winter sites attract snowmobilers, for the state snowmobile corridor (a network of groomed trails) is accessible right from the campground. Once the pond is frozen over in the winter, it is cleared for skating. Four miles north of here, Mount Sunapee State Park has hiking trails and a scenic chairlift that runs in the summer. In winter, the mountain's alpine ski center is known for its abundant intermediate trails, but there are also a few challenging chutes for the expert skier.

Campsites, facilities: There are 100 sites for tents and RVs, 21 with full hookups and 79 with water and electric hookups. Each site has a table, fire ring, and grill. A dump station, laundry facilities, restrooms, hot showers, a recreation hall, sports field, and a playground are provided. A store sells ice and wood. Courts for badminton, shuffleboard, volleyball, and horseshoes are located on-site. Leashed pets are permitted.

Reservations, fees: Reservations are recom-

mended for stays on weekends and holidays and require a deposit equal to one night's fee. Sites are $17–20 a night for two people. Seasonal rates are available on request.

Open: Year-round; fully operational April 30–October 15.

Directions: From the intersection of Highways 10 and 11/103 in Newport, follow Highway 10 south for five miles to Goshen. Turn left on Brook Road and head east for 2.5 miles to the campground.

Contact: Rand Pond Campground, P.O. Box 10, Brook Road, Goshen, NH 03752, 603/863-3350.

8 PILLSBURY STATE PARK

🚶 🏊 🎣 🚣 🐕 🚐 ⛺

Rating: 8

Northwest of Hillsborough

Wooded, primitive sites are located beside May Pond, and three of them are accessible only by canoe, providing a quiet retreat for campers who want to get away from it all. This 2,400-acre parcel of land was deeded to the state by a former sawmill owner and a founder of the Society for the Protection of New Hampshire Forests, and much of it remains undeveloped. In the 1930s, the Civilian Conservation Corps cleared and restored ponds that were once clogged with sawdust. Several ponds are open to nonmotorized boating and support largemouth bass, horned pout, perch, and pickerel populations. The 51-mile Monadnock-Sunapee Greenway hiking trail passes through the park's boundaries.

Campsites, facilities: There are 38 sites for tents and RVs, all without hookups. Pit toilets, piped water, tables, and fire rings are provided. Firewood is available. The maximum RV length is 30 feet. Leashed pets are permitted.

Reservations, fees: For reservations, contact the New Hampshire State Parks Camping Reservation Center, P.O. Box 1856, Concord, NH 03302-1856, 603/271-3628, website: www.nhparks.state.nh.us. The fee is $13 a night.

Open: Early May–mid-October.

Directions: From Hillsborough, travel northwest on Highway 31 to Washington and then continue another 17 miles on the same road to the park entrance on the right (east) side.
Contact: Pillsbury State Park, P.O. Box 83, Hillsborough, NH 03244, 603/863-2860.

9 COLD BROOK CAMPGROUND

Rating: 7

South of Webster

Roomy sites with plenty of shade line the Blackwater River banks. From here, canoeists can venture north to Lake Winnepocket on quiet water. Rent a boat at the campground or bring your own; no motors are allowed. Swimmers have a private beach on the Blackwater, which is also open to fishing.
Campsites, facilities: There are 60 sites for tents and RVs, 28 with full hookups and 32 with water and electric hookups. Each site has a picnic table and fire ring. Air conditioner use is allowed. A dump station, laundry facilities, restrooms, hot showers, and a playground are provided. You will also find basketball and shuffleboard courts and horseshoe pits. Firewood is sold on-site. Leashed pets are permitted.
Reservations, fees: Reservations are recommended. Sites are $15–$20 a night. Weekly and seasonal rates are available.
Open: May 1–November 1.
Directions: From I-89 at Davisville, take Exit 7, travel .75 mile east on Highway 103, and then go three miles north on Highway 127. The campground entrance is on the left (west) side of the road.
Contact: Denny and Kathy Stevens, Cold Brook Campground, 541 Battle Street (Highway 127), Webster, NH 03303, 603/529-2528.

10 TAMARACK TRAILS CAMPING PARK

Rating: 7

On Dodge Brook in East Lempster

An 83-acre tree farm on Dodge Brook surrounds 15 RV sites and five tent sites. Except for three RV sites in an open grassy field, all of the spaces are shaded by tall pine trees. Trails explore the tree farm and nearby Dodge Brook State Forest, where black bear, moose, coyotes, bobcats, and beavers have been sighted. There's good trout fishing in Dodge Brook, and nearby Dodge Pond and Long Pond are open to fishing, swimming, and boating.
Campsites, facilities: There are 20 sites for tents and RVs, 15 with water and electric hookups. Each site has a picnic table and fire ring. A dump station, laundry facilities, restrooms, hot showers, a recreation area, and a playground are provided. Firewood is sold at the office. Leashed pets are permitted.
Reservations, fees: Reservations are recommended. Sites start at $12 a night per family. Water and electric hookups are $3 extra. Weekly, monthly, and seasonal rates are available.
Open: Mid-May–mid-October.
Directions: From the junction of Highways 123 and 10 in Marlow, travel 5.5 miles north on Highway 10 and turn left on Dodge Brook Road. The campground is .4 mile ahead.
Contact: Tamarack Trails Camping Park, P.O. Box 24, East Lempster, NH 03605, 603/863-6443.

11 LAKE MASSASECUM CASINO PARK CAMPGROUND

Rating: 7

On the southwest shore of Lake Massasecum

Partially wooded sites allow for easy access to the Lake Massasecum shore, known for it's fabulous mountain views across the water. Campers and locals alike are welcome to use the sandy swimming beach, so it can get pretty crowded here, especially on weekends when the weather is good. Massasecum's 402 acres of warm-water habitat support horned pout and largemouth and smallmouth bass. Plunk a canoe into the water and you might catch something for an evening fish fry at your campsite grill. To the northwest, a short hiking trail at Harriman Chandler State Forest leads to the summit of Stewarts Peak.

Campsites, facilities: There are 50 sites for tents and RVs, 35 with water and electric hookups. Each site has a picnic table, fire ring, and grill. There are also six cabins for rent. Facilities include a dump station, restrooms, hot showers, and a recreation room. A small camp store sells ice and firewood. Horseshoe pits and a play area are located on the property. Leashed pets are permitted.

Reservations, fees: Reservations are recommended. Sites start at $20 a night. Seasonal rates are available.

Open: Mid-May through mid-September.

Directions: From the intersection of U.S. 202 and Highway 114 in Henniker, travel six miles north on Highway 114 to Bradford. Turn right on Massasecum Road and travel east for half a mile. The campground entrance is on the left.

Contact: Bob and Jane Laurendeau, Lake Massasecum Casino Park and Campground, Lake Massasecum Road, RR 1, Box 499, Bradford, NH 03221, 603/938-2571.

12 MILE-AWAY CAMPGROUND
🚶 ⛵ 🏊 🚐 ❄️ 🏠 🚴 ♿ 🚌 ⛺

Rating: 7

North of U.S. 202 in Henniker

Mile-Away Campground has an old-fashioned air. The lounge in the main lodge comes complete with a large stone fireplace, player piano, and Yamaha organ, and weekend activities include wine and cheese parties and square dancing. There's a swimming beach on French Pond, which is also stocked with trout. Boats

may be rented here or you can bring your own; motors up to six horsepower are allowed. In winter, skaters take to the ice while snowmobilers and cross-country skiers journey through the surrounding country woods on miles of trails. All sites are heavily wooded, and some are set on the pond shore.

Campsites, facilities: There are 190 sites for tents and RVs, 53 with full hookups, 131 with water and electric hookups, and six with none. Each site has a picnic table and fire ring. Air conditioner and heater use is allowed, and phone hookups are available. Tent and RV groups can be accommodated. A dump station, laundry facilities, restrooms, hot showers, a recreation hall, pavilion, and playground are provided. A small grocery store carries LP gas, sandwiches, ice, and firewood. Courts for volleyball, basketball, badminton, shuffleboard, and horseshoes are located on the property, as is a miniature golf course. Leashed pets are permitted.

Reservations, fees: Reservations are recommended. Sites are $26–33 a night.

Open: Year-round.

Directions: From I-89 west of Concord, take Exit 5 and travel west on Highway 9/U.S. 202 for about five miles. At the intersection with Highway 114, turn right on Old West Hopkinton Road and travel northeast for a mile to the campground entrance.

Contact: Mile-Away Campground, 41 Old West Hopkinton Road, Henniker, NH 03242, 603/428-7617 or 800/787-4679, website: www.mileaway.com.

13 SANDY BEACH FAMILY CAMPGROUND
⛵ 🏊 🚐 🍴 🐕 🚴 🚌 ⛺

Rating: 6

On Rolf Pond in Hopkinton

Crystal-clear Rolf Pond sees most of the action at Sandy Beach Family Campground, where wooded sites set beneath tall pines are close to the water's edge. Contoocook is a small country village where you can find supplies and services. The river bearing the same name runs just south of the campground; it passes by the Hopkinton–Everett Lake Project, a national landholding surrounding Hopkinton Lake. The waterways are open to all types of boating, swimming, and fishing. Duston Country Club, also a few miles south of here, offers nine holes of laid-back greens.

Campsites, facilities: There are 180 sites for tents and RVs with water and electric hookups. Each site has a picnic table and fire ring. A dump station, recreation hall, restrooms, hot showers, arcade, and a playground are provided. A camp store carries RV supplies, LP gas, ice, and firewood. RV parts and service are also available. Leashed pets are permitted.

Reservations, fees: Reservations are accepted with prepaid deposits. Sites start at $20 a night per family. Seasonal rates are available on request.

Open: May 1–Columbus Day.

Directions: From the junction of U.S. 202/Highway 9 and Highway 127 in Contoocook, travel north on Highway 127 for about four miles into the village. Go past the fire station and turn left on Pine Street. Travel west for two miles to Clement Hill Road. Take another left and travel south about .5 mile to the campground entrance.

Contact: Sandy Beach Family Campground, 677 Clement Hill Road, Contoocook, NH 03229, 603/746-3591.

14 KEYSER POND CAMPGROUND

🧍 🏊 🛶 🚤 🐕 🚣 🚐 ⛺

Rating: 6

South of U.S. 202 in Henniker

A wooded hillside above Keyser Pond is terraced with roomy sites for all types of campers. Recreation is centered around the freshwater pond; electric motors are allowed, and canoes, rowboats, and paddleboats are available for rent at the campground. You can also play a round or two of miniature golf on the grounds. Many sites are rented by seasonal campers.

Small pockets of land are protected in the immediate area: Ames, Contoocook, and Craney Hill State Forests offer some short hikes.

Campsites, facilities: There are 116 sites for tents and RVs, 107 with water and electric hookups and nine with none. Each site has a picnic table and fire ring. Air conditioner and heater use is allowed, and phone hookups are available. A dump station, laundry facilities, restrooms, hot showers, a recreation hall, pool, miniature golf course, and a playground are provided. A small grocery store carries LP gas, ice, and firewood. Courts for volleyball, basketball, badminton, shuffleboard, and horseshoes are located on the property. Leashed pets are permitted.

Reservations, fees: Nonrefundable deposits are required for all reservations. Sites start at $20–30 a night per family. Seasonal rates are available.

Open: May 15–October 15.

Directions: From Concord, take I-89 north to Exit 5. Travel west on U.S. 202/Highway 9 to the intersection with Highway 127. Take a left (there's a blinking yellow light); the campground is just ahead.

Contact: Keyser Pond Campground, 47 Old Concord Road, Henniker, NH 03242, 603/ 428-7741 or 800/272-5221, website: www.ucampnh.com/keyserpond.

15 OXBOW CAMPGROUND

🧍 🏊 🛶 🏠 🐕 🚐 ⛺

Rating: 7

Near Hillsborough

A mix of lawns and thick woodlands surrounds the roomy sites at Oxbow, where campers can choose from open or shaded settings. A spring-fed swimming pond on the property is flanked by a sandy beach, and more than 100 forestland acres are traversed by trails for hiking and cross-country skiing; one favorite destination is a giant red oak tree. For longer hikes and excellent birding, head north to Fox State Forest in Hillsborough. More than 20 miles of foot trails explore the moderate hills of this 1,432-acre sanctuary studded with hardwoods and orchards. The north-flowing Contoocook River runs through downtown Hillsborough just to the north of Oxbow Campground and offers challenging and technical white-water canoeing above the bridge; it's also a good place to fish for trout. South of town on U.S. 202, the Angus Lea nine-hole golf course is open to the public. Hillsborough is a quiet country town for the most part, but in late September when the neighboring Deerfield community hosts the annual Deerfield Fair, both towns swell with visitors who attend agricultural events including tractor pulls, mutant and prize vegetable exhibits, harness racing, and horse, sheep, and cow shows.

Campsites, facilities: There are 74 sites for tents and RVs, 60 with full hookups and 14 with none. Each site has a picnic table, fire ring, and grill. Air conditioners are allowed, but heaters are prohibited. Cable TV and telephone hookups are available. Facilities include a dump station, a laundry room, restrooms, hot showers, a recreation hall, pavilion, and playground. A store sells ice, firewood, and snacks. Courts for basketball, volleyball, badminton, shuffleboard, and horseshoes are provided. Leashed pets are permitted.

Reservations, fees: Reservations are accepted. Sites are $25–28 a night. Weekly, monthly, and seasonal rates are available.

Open: Fully operational May 15–October 15 and open for winter camping November 15–April 15; closed two months of the year.

Directions: From the junction of U.S. 202 and Highway 149 in Hillsborough, travel .75 mile south on Highway 149 to the campground entrance.

Contact: Oxbow Campground, 8 Oxbow Road, Deering, NH 03244, 603/464-5952, website: www.ucampnh.com/oxbow.

16 COLD SPRINGS CAMP RESORT

Rating: 6

West of Goffstown

Operated in conjunction with a full-blown RV sales office, Cold Springs draws hordes of peo-

ple in motor homes. The campground is well forested, and the sites are scattered beside the pond shore. Pull-through sites and paved roads are designed to handle vehicles of any size. Once you park, you will find a wide array of recreational offerings from tennis courts (you can rent equipment) and two heated pools, to a sundeck and a whirlpool. Regularly organized events include live entertainment, bingo tournaments, scavenger hunts, and special meals. There is also a family restaurant on the property.

Campsites, facilities: There are 400 sites for tents and RVs, all with full hookups. Each site has a table and fire ring. A dump station, laundry facilities, restrooms, hot showers, a recreation hall, pavilion, two heated pools, and a playground are provided. A camp store carries LP gas, ice, and wood. Courts for volleyball and horseshoes are located on the property. Leashed pets are permitted.

Reservations, fees: Nonrefundable deposits are required for all reservations. Sites are $38–42 a night. Seasonal rates are available on request.

Open: Mid-April–Columbus Day.

Directions: From the junction of Highways 101 and 114 in Bedford, travel north on Highway 114 through Goffstown. Five miles north of Goffstown Center, take the first right after the Cold Springs RV Sales Center onto Barnard Hill Road. Signs will lead to the campground entrance.

Contact: Cold Springs Campground, 22 Wildlife Drive, Weare, NH 03281, 603/529-2528, website: www.coldspringscampresort.com.

17 AUTUMN HILLS CAMPGROUND

Rating: 6

South of Weare Center

Rolling woodlands of tall oak and pine trees shade the sites at this full-service RV park near Horace Lake and Clough State Park. Huse Brook forms a small pond on the property and is open to fishing. A few miles to the north, Clough State Park is situated on a river pool that is stocked with trout. Sandy beaches for swimming are available at the state park and also at larger Horace Lake to the west. A public boat launch and wide, clear waters at Horace Lake attract powerboaters and water-skiers, especially on weekends. The community of seasonal campers at Autumn Hills takes part in dancing, dinners, and theme weekends. They also crown an annual winner in a male beauty contest.

Campsites, facilities: There are 97 sites for tents and RVs, 76 with full hookups and 21 with water and electric hookups. Each site has a picnic table, grill, and fire ring. A dump station, restrooms, metered hot showers, a recreation hall, pavilion, pool, and playground are provided. A camp store carries LP gas, ice, and firewood. Courts for volleyball, basketball, badminton, and horseshoes are located on the property. Leashed pets are permitted.

Reservations, fees: Prepaid deposits must accompany reservations. Sites start at $24 a night per family. Weekly, monthly, and seasonal rates are available.

Open: Early May–mid-October.

Directions: From the junction of Highways 114 and 149 in South Weare, travel 2.5 miles east on Highway 149 to the campground entrance on the left (north) side of the road.

Contact: Autumn Hills Campground, 285 South Stark Highway, South Weare, NH 03281, 603/529-2425, website: www.autumnhillscampground.com.

18 SURRY MOUNTAIN CAMPING AREA

🚶 🏊 🛶 🎣 🐕 🚐 ⛺

Rating: 8

On Surry Mountain Lake

Spacious and wooded sites offer maximum privacy and access to almost 2,000 acres of protected land in the neighboring Surry Mountain Lake Project, a U.S. Army Corps of Engineers holding. Good warm-water fishing for largemouth bass, pickerel, horned pout, and yellow perch is offered on the 265-acre lake. If trout is your preferred game, head south of the dam and wade into the spirited Ashuelot River. Motors up to 10 horsepower are welcome on Surry Mountain Lake, and you'll find a maintained beach and picnic area on project land. Several hiking trails traverse the protected area. For golfers, fewer than two miles south of here on Highway 12A, the 27-hole Bretwood Golf Course is open to the public.

Campsites, facilities: There are 43 sites for tents and RVs, 38 with water and electric hookups. Each site has a picnic table, fire ring, and grill. A portable dump service, flush toilets, and hot showers are provided. Ice and firewood are sold on-site. Horseshoe pits and a volleyball court are located on the property. Leashed pets are permitted.

Reservations, fees: Reservations are recommended. Sites start at $20 a night.

Open: May 15–October 15.

Directions: From the junction of Highways 12 and 12A north of Keene, head north on Highway 12A for four miles. Take a right turn onto the entrance road and head southeast for .25 mile to the campground.

Contact: Surry Mountain Camping Area, East Shore Road, Keene, NH 03431, 603/352-9770.

19 HILLTOP CAMPGROUND AND ADVENTURE GAMES

🚶 🏊 🛶 🎣 🐕 🚐 ⛺

Rating: 7

South of Sullivan

Mountain views and a choice of open and shaded sites are just some of the features of this campground located in a rural, rolling countryside setting. Ferry Brook runs through the property and is open to fishing, but better fishing can be found by driving a short distance northeast to Otter Brook, a healthy trout stream near East Sullivan. Just south of the campground is the Otter Brook Lake Project and dam; the lake is open to nonmotorized boating and has a swimming beach and a ball field near the shore. Hilltop Campground also operates a paintball adventure game company on the grounds. Campers can rent "guns" in the pro shop and play a souped-up version of capture the flag. Staff members are well trained and use radio communication to ensure that games run safely and smoothly.

Campsites, facilities: There are 39 sites for tents and RVs, 32 with water and electric hookups and seven with none. Each site has a picnic table and fire ring. Facilities include a dump station, restrooms, hot showers, a pavilion, pool, and a playground. A store sells ice and firewood. Courts for volleyball, badminton, and horseshoes are provided. Services and supplies are available in Sullivan, a few miles north of the campground. Leashed pets are permitted.

Reservations, fees: Reservations are recommended. Sites without hookups start at $15 a night per family, and sites with hookups start at $18 a night.

Open: May 1–October 1.

Directions: From the northern junction of Highways 9 and 10 north of Keene, travel a mile east on Highway 9, turn left on Sullivan Road, and drive another two miles northeast. The campground is on the east side of the road.

Contact: Hilltop Campground and Adventure Games, H.C.R. 33, Box 186, Keene, NH 03431, 603/847-3351.

20 SEVEN MAPLES CAMPING AREA

🏃 🏊 ⛵ 🎣 🐕 🚐 ⛺

Rating: 6

North of Hancock on Norway Pond

Seasonal campers are the main customers at these tightly clustered sites tucked into the woods near Norway Pond. If you're looking to join an established camping community in a rural setting, this is a good choice. A swimming pool, tennis courts, and hiking trails are right on the property. Moose Brook flows through the campground before emptying into Norway Pond. Brook trout live in the stream, while the pond

is home to warm-water species including bass and perch; both waters are open to fishing. A short drive to the west gets you to a prime powerboating destination: Nubanusit Lake, which you can access by using a public boat launch. Prize rainbow trout have been pulled from that lake, so bring your fishing gear.

Campsites, facilities: There are 100 sites for tents and RVs, 80 with water and electric hookups. Each site has a picnic table, fire ring, and grill. A dump station, recreation hall, restrooms, hot showers, a pool, and a playground are provided. A store sells LP gas, ice, and firewood. The grounds also have courts for volleyball, badminton, shuffleboard, and horseshoes. Leashed pets are permitted.

Reservations, fees: Reservations are accepted and require a nonrefundable deposit. Sites start at $22–30 a night. Weekly, monthly, and seasonal rates are available.

Open: Early May through mid-October.

Directions: From the intersection of Highways 137 and 123 in Hancock, travel north for .5 mile on Highway 137 to Longview Road. Turn left and head northwest for a short distance to the campground entrance.

Contact: Seven Maples Camping Area, 24 Longview Road, Hancock, NH 03449, 603/525-3321, website: www.sevenmaples.com.

21 GREENFIELD STATE PARK

🏃 🏊 ⛵ 🚣 🐕 🐾 🚐 ⛺

Rating: 7

On Otter Lake in Greenfield

Natural campsites are set in the woods near Otter Lake. Canoes and rowboats are rented out at the campground, and you may launch your own boat at Greenfield State Park's public ramp. Many youth groups organize overnight outings here, so be forewarned that the park is often overrun with young campers during the summer months. Hiking trails explore the surrounding woods and marshlands. Otter Brook supports several warm-water fish species and attracts anglers who come to cast out a line.

To get a bird's-eye view of the area, drive to the Crotched Mountain Rehabilitation Center via the road across from the park entrance. Leave your car at the hillcrest and follow a trail to the summit of Crotched Mountain. You will see old ski trails on the hillside, and, on clear days, Franconia Notch in the White Mountains will be visible to the north.

Campsites, facilities: There are 252 sites for tents and RVs, all without hookups. Each site has a picnic table and fire ring. Facilities include a dump station, restrooms, hot showers, and a playground. A store sells ice, firewood, and limited supplies. Youth group camping and day-use areas are available by reservation. Leashed pets are permitted in designated areas.

Reservations, fees: For reservations, contact the New Hampshire State Parks Camping Reservation Center, P.O. Box 1856, Concord, NH 03302-1856, 603/271-3628; website: www.nhparks.state.nh.us. Sites are $16 a night for up to four people.

Open: Mid-May–Columbus Day.

Directions: From the center of Greenfield, travel a mile west on Highway 31 to the state park entrance.

Contact: Greenfield State Park, P.O. Box 203, Greenfield, NH 03047, 603/547-3497; New Hampshire Division of Parks and Recreation, 603/271-3628.

22 WILDWOOD CAMPGROUND

Rating: 5

Southwest of New Boston

Camping in the southern New Hampshire sticks is what you find at Wildwood. Tall pine trees shade densely settled campsites in the backwoods of New Boston. Kids can fish in a small pond on the property, but grown-ups will have to head to other nearby brooks and rivers to cast a line. There's a swimming pool on the grounds. The resident country band Pony Express plays regularly for campers, and bonfires,

hayrides, and bingo games round out the planned activities schedule. Sites are open for overnight and seasonal camping in winter.

Campsites, facilities: There are 100 sites for tents and RVs, 35 with full hookups, 62 with water and electric hookups, and three with none. Each site has a picnic table, fire ring, and grill. Air conditioner and heater use is allowed. A dump station, laundry facilities, restrooms, metered hot showers, a recreation room, pool, and playground are provided. A grocery store carries LP gas, ice, and firewood. Courts for volleyball, badminton, and horseshoes are located on the property. Leashed pets are permitted.

Reservations, fees: Advance reservations are accepted with a 50 percent prepaid deposit. Tent sites are $18 a night, and full-hookup sites are $22 a night for a family of four. In winter, all sites start at $22 a night. Weekly, monthly, seasonal, and group rates are available.

Open: Year-round; fully operational May 1–October 15.

Directions: From the junction of Highways 77, 136, and 13 (known as the Southwest Corner in New Boston), travel 3.5 miles southwest on Old Coach Road to the campground entrance on the left.

Contact: Wildwood Campground, 540 Old Coach Road, New Boston, NH 03070, 603/487-3300.

23 FRIENDLY BEAVER CAMPGROUND

Rating: 5

Northwest of New Boston

Closely settled campsites at Friendly Beaver are tucked in under the trees, providing adequate privacy. Numerous sites are occupied by seasonal campers who use the facility year-round. An aquatic compound featuring an open-air deck with umbrellas and tables is the action center in both winter and summer, offering three outdoor pools for sports, wading, and swimming, and an indoor heated pool and hot tub. Miles of multiuse trails leave from the campground; in winter they are popular with snowmobilers who rejuvenate in the whirlpool after a day out in the elements. The playground is surrounded by a chain-link fence and features natural wood play structures such as Noah's Ark, airplanes, castles, and trucks. Families can choose from a long organized activities list including sing-alongs, carnivals, dances, parades, and competitions. Ceramics classes are conducted at an on-site studio.

Campsites, facilities: There are 172 sites for tents and RVs, 131 with full hookups and 41 with water and electric hookups. Each site has a picnic table and fire ring. Group sites are available. Air conditioner use is allowed. A dump station, laundry facilities, restrooms, hot showers, a recreation hall, patio area, four pools, and a playground are provided. A small camp store carries groceries, LP gas, ice, and firewood. Courts for basketball, badminton, and horseshoes are located on the property. There's also a sports field and recreation director. Leashed pets are permitted.

Reservations, fees: Prepaid deposits are required for all reservations, and holiday weekend reservations must be prepaid in full. Sites are $31–36 a night per family. Weekly, monthly, and year-round seasonal rates are available.

Open: Year-round.

Directions: From the junction of Highways 77, 136, and 13 (known as the Southwest Corner in New Boston), travel two miles west on Old Coach Road, following signs to the campground entrance on the right.

Contact: Friendly Beaver Campground, Old Coach Road, New Boston, NH 03070, 603/487-5570, website: www.friendlybeaver.com.

24 FIELD 'N' FOREST RECREATION AREA

🚶 🏊 🛶 🐕 🚐 ⛺

Rating: 6

South of Hancock near Beaver Pond

Tranquillity and privacy reign at this small rural campground. Campers can select from open, wooded, or grassy sites. Whichever you choose, you are near Beaver Pond, which is open to swimming and fishing. Nature trails meander into a mixed forest abutting the pond and head south into protected lands around the Edward MacDowell Lake Project. Operated by the U.S. Army Corps of Engineers, MacDowell Dam is the site of nature and interpretive programs held in the summer months, including story programs for kids.

Campsites, facilities: There are 40 sites for tents and RVs, eight with water and electric hookups and the rest with none. Each site has a picnic table, fire ring, and grill. A dump station, sports field, restrooms, and hot showers are provided. Ice and firewood are sold on-site. You will also find volleyball and badminton courts and horseshoe pits. Leashed pets are permitted.

Reservations, fees: Reservations are accepted and require a nonrefundable deposit. Sites start at $18 a night per family. Weekly, monthly, and seasonal rates are available.

Open: Memorial Day–Labor Day.

Directions: From the intersection of Highways 137 and 123 in Hancock, travel south for three miles on Highway 137 to the campground entrance on the left (east) side of the road.

Contact: Field 'N' Forest Recreation Area, Highway 137, Hancock, NH 03449, 603/525-3568.

25 FOREST LAKE CAMPGROUND

🚶 🚲 🛶 🎣 🚭 🐕 🏌 🚐 ⛺

Rating: 8

On the north shore of Forest Lake in Winchester

Boat rentals, a boat launch, and a big beach on Forest Lake center the action here at water's edge. Roomy wooded sites are set back from the shoreline, and some even boast mountain views. This warm-water lake near the Massachusetts border is home to pickerel, smallmouth bass, and horned pout. Just west of the campground on the other side of Highway 10 lies Pisgah State

Park, formerly called the Pisgah Wilderness. Twenty square miles of low ridges, dividing valleys, and ponds, streams, and marshes are accessed by more than 30 miles of old logging roads perfect for moderate mountain bike rides.

Campsites, facilities: There are 150 sites for tents and RVs, 85 with full hookups, 55 with water and electric hookups, and 10 with none. Each site has a picnic table, fire ring, and grill. Air conditioners are allowed, and phone hookups are available. A dump station, restrooms, hot showers, a pool, ball field, recreation hall, and playground are provided. There are also courts for basketball, shuffleboard, and horseshoes. A store sells ice, LP gas, and firewood. Supplies and services can be obtained 1.5 miles south in Winchester. The maximum RV length is 35 feet. Leashed pets are permitted.

Reservations, fees: Reservations are recommended in July and August and are accepted with a nonrefundable two-days' deposit. Sites start at $20 a night. Monthly and seasonal rates are available.

Open: May 1–October 1.

Directions: From the junction of Highways 10 and 9 in Keene, travel south for 10 miles on Highway 10 to the campground entrance on the left (east) side of the road.

Contact: Forest Lake Campground, 331 Keene Road, Winchester, NH 03470, 603/239-4267.

26 SWANZEY LAKE CAMPING AREA

🚶 🚴 🏊 🎣 🛶 🐕 🚐 ⛰️

Rating: 7

On Swanzey Lake

Gentle green hills surround spring-fed Swanzey Lake, which is home to trout and bass. Wooded sites are set near and on the shoreline. Sink your toes into cool sand, dive into the crystal-clear water, or ply the surface for a few hours in a rented boat. A number of dirt roads to the north of the lake are good routes for mountain bike excursions; three nearby covered

bridges can be reached on a 10-mile loop. For more extensive rides, head west to Pisgah State Park, once known as the Pisgah Wilderness. With more than 30 miles of old logging roads, summits, valleys, marshes, and ponds, it makes a great day-trip destination.

Campsites, facilities: There are 75 sites for tents and RVs, 30 with full hookups, 10 with water and electric hookups, and 35 with none. A dump station, pit toilets, a recreation hall, metered hot showers, tables, and fire rings are provided. Also on the grounds are a ball field and a volleyball court. Ice and firewood are sold on-site. The maximum RV length is 35 feet. Pets are allowed before Memorial Day and after Labor Day.

Reservations, fees: Reservations are recommended. Sites start at $20 a night for two people.

Open: Mid-May–mid-October.

Directions: From the intersection of Highways 10 and 12 in Keene, travel south on Highway 12 for a mile. Bear right on Highway 32 and continue south for five more miles. Take a right onto Lake Road and head southwest for two miles. Take another right onto East Shore Road and head north to the campground on the left side of the road at number 88.

Contact: Swanzey Lake Camping Area, East Shore Road, Keene, NH 03431, 603/352-9880, website: www.swanzeylake.com.

27 MONADNOCK STATE PARK

🚶 ❄️ ⛰️

Rating: 8

At the base of Mount Monadnock in Jaffrey

Ⓕ Mount Monadnock has the dubious distinction of being one of the most-hiked mountains in the world. Summit trails here are challenging, though relatively short. Since the mountain is a solitary peak (or a monadnock), unobstructed long-distance views are attainable from the summit. In fact, on a clear day, you can see points in all six New England states. Fire and deforestation have left behind a bare, rocky top. Heavily used trails leave from the campground, but for less-traveled routes you need only drive a short distance west to either Dublin or Marlborough. Monadnock State Park's campsites are set in the woods near the state park headquarters. In winter, 14 miles of challenging trails are open to cross-country skiing in the lower elevations.

Campsites, facilities: There are 21 individual sites for tents and several group camping areas. RVs are not allowed, and there are no hookups. Each site has a picnic table and fire ring. Pit toilets, flush toilets, and piped water are provided in summer, and pit toilets only are maintained in winter. A small camp store sells ice, firewood, and limited supplies. No pets are allowed.

Reservations, fees: For reservations, contact the New Hampshire State Parks Camping Reservation Center, P.O. Box 1856, Concord, NH 03302-1856, 603/271-3628, website: www.nhparks.state.nh.us. Sites are $12 a night for up to four people. Youth group sites must be reserved in advance through the campground office.

Open: Year-round.

Directions: From the intersection of U.S. 202 and Highway 124 in Jaffrey, travel four miles west on Highway 124 to Slade Road. Turn right and head north, following signs to the state park and the campground.

Contact: Monadnock State Park, P.O. Box 181, Jaffrey, NH 03452, 603/532-8862.

28 WOODMORE CAMPGROUND

Rating: 6

On the southwest shore of Contoocook Lake in Rindge

Sun-dappled sites are set near and along the Contoocook Lake shore in rural Rindge. Boats may be rented at the campground, and a dock is provided in case you bring your own boat (motors up to 35 mph are allowed on the lake). The cove in front of the campground is prime habitat for bass and horned pout; the best time to

fish for the latter species is late at night. On weekends, potluck dinners and tournaments bring Woodmore's campers together. Mount Monadnock to the northwest is the most striking feature in this area; you can see it from the northeast end of Contoocook Lake. Monadnock is also one of the most-hiked mountains in the world. The state park entrance and hiking trails are located off Highway 124 in Jaffrey.

Campsites, facilities: There are 130 sites for tents and RVs, 90 with full hookups, 20 with water and electric hookups, and 20 with none. Each site has a table, fire ring, and grill. Air conditioners are allowed, but heaters are prohibited. A dump station, laundry facilities, restrooms, hot showers, a pool, and a playground are provided. A grocery store sells RV supplies, LP gas, ice, and firewood. RV storage is available as are group tent and RV sites. Courts for basketball, volleyball, badminton, shuffleboard, and horseshoes are provided. Leashed pets are permitted.

Reservations, fees: Reservations are recommended Memorial Day–Labor Day. Sites start at $24–30 a night. Weekly, monthly, and seasonal rates are available.

Open: May 15–September 20, and then weekends only through Columbus Day.

Directions: From the intersection of U.S. 202 and Highway 119 in Rindge, travel north for a mile on U.S. 202 and then turn right on Davis Crossing Road. After .25 mile, turn left on Woodbound Road and continue .5 mile to the campground entrance.

Contact: Woodmore Campground, P.O. Box 830, Rindge, NH 03461, 603/899-3362, website: www.woodmorecampground.com.

29 EMERALD ACRES CAMPGROUND

Rating: 6

On Cheshire Pond in Jaffrey

These pondside sites set in the shade of pine trees are favored by seasonal campers, so be sure to call ahead and find out if there are any openings. Campers can take a dip in the pond or set out in a canoe. Paddleboats and canoes are rented at the campground. Better swimming and fishing can be found at any of the nearby lakes. Downtown Jaffrey is nearby and offers all the necessary services and supplies. The town is also home to Mount Monadnock, one of the most-hiked peaks in the world. Named for a Native American word meaning "stands alone," this isolated peak affords views of all six New England states on a clear day. In summer, Jaffrey hosts several cultural events including a bandstand concert series, a lecture forum, and the largest fireworks show on the northeast coast.

Campsites, facilities: There are 52 sites for tents and RVs, 44 with full hookups and eight with none. Each site has a picnic table and fire ring. A dump station, laundry facilities, restrooms, hot showers, a recreation hall, and a playground are provided. Supplies can be obtained less than a mile away in Jaffrey. Leashed pets are permitted.

Reservations, fees: Reservations are recommended. Sites start at $10 a night for two people, with surcharges for all services. Seasonal rates are available.

Open: May 1–October 14.

Directions: From the intersection of U.S. 202 and Highway 124 in Jaffrey, travel north on U.S. 202 for .75 mile to Ridgecrest Road. Turn left and continue to the campground at the end of the street.

Contact: Emerald Acres Campground, 39 Ridgecrest Road, Jaffrey, NH 03452, 603/532-8838.

30 SHIR-ROY CAMPING AREA

Rating: 7

On Cass Pond in Richmond

You will find lakeside campsites under pine trees at Shir-Roy, where fishing, boating, and swimming on Cass Pond are the main activities. Anglers can try for largemouth bass, pickerel, horned pout, and perch; fishing licenses are for sale at the campground. A sandy beach welcomes swimmers and sunbathers at the water's edge. Canoes, rowboats, and paddleboats may be rented by the hour or the half day, and for a small fee you may dock your own vessel on-site. To the northeast of Shir-Roy lies Rhododendron State Park and Little Monadnock Mountain. Nature trails weave through more than 16 acres of wild rhododendrons, and a mile hike leads to the Little Monadnock Mountain summit; this peak offers a view of Mount Monadnock and the smaller peaks in the area from the south.

Campsites, facilities: There are 110 sites for tents and RVs, 107 with water and electric hookups and three with none. Each site has a picnic table, fire ring, and grill. Air conditioners are allowed, but heaters are prohibited. A dump station, laundry facilities, restrooms, hot showers, and a playground are provided. You'll also find courts for volleyball, badminton, and horseshoes and a camp store selling groceries, RV supplies, ice, and firewood. Tent cottages and tent trailers are also for rent. Off-season RV storage is available. Leashed pets are permitted.

Reservations, fees: Reservations are recommended Memorial Day–Labor Day and require a 50 percent deposit. There is a three-day minimum stay during holiday weekends. Sites with hookups start at $20 a night per family.

Open: Late May–early October.

Directions: From the center of Richmond at the intersection of Highways 32 and 119, travel a mile south on Highway 32 to the campground entrance on the left (east) side of the road.

Contact: Shir-Roy Camping Area, 100 Athol Road, Richmond, NH 03470, 603/239-4768.

31 LAUREL LAKE CAMPGROUND

Rating: 7

South of Fitzwilliam near the Massachusetts border

Cottages, homes, and a girls' camp dot the wooded shoreline of crystalline Laurel Lake. This spring-fed beauty is small enough to be private, yet large enough for waterskiing. You compete with lots of local fishermen for the resident brown and rainbow trout, smallmouth bass, pickerel, and horned pout. Campsites are tucked into the woods behind a grassy area on the lake. A dock is provided, and there's also a group area for tents. Fitzwilliam is a classic New England town with a hospitable inn and several churches on its picturesque common. It's also home to Rhododendron State Park, a National Natural Landmark; a walking path there explores more than 16 acres of wild rhododendrons that are usually in full bloom by mid-July.

Campsites, facilities: There are 65 sites for tents and RVs, 54 with water and electric hookups and the rest with none. Each site has a table and fire ring. Air conditioner and heater use is allowed. A dump station, laundry facilities, restrooms, hot showers, and a playground are provided. There are also courts for basketball, volleyball, and horseshoes. A snack bar and a store are nearby. The maximum RV length is 32 feet. Leashed pets are permitted.

Reservations, fees: Reservations are recommended July 1–Labor Day. Sites start at $19 a night per family.

Open: May 15–October 15.

Directions: From the intersection of Highways 12 and 119 in Fitzwilliam (at the blinking light), travel 1.5 miles west on Highway 119, then turn left on East Lake Road and go 1.5 miles south to the campground.

Contact: Laurel Lake Campground, P.O. Box 114, Fitzwilliam, NH 03447, 603/585-3304.

32 HUNTER'S STATE LINE CAMPGROUND

🏊 🚤 🚣 🎣 ❄️ 🐕 🚴 🚐 ⛺

Rating: 6
On Sip Pond near the Massachusetts border

Year-round camping in the sticks beside Sip Pond is what's offered at Hunter's State Line. In the summer months, campers enjoy the swimming beach, dock, and rental paddleboats on this undeveloped lake. Many warm-water fish species lurk in the shallow waters. In fall and spring, hunters can comb miles of woods and marshland in search of deer and hare. Then in winter, ice fishers try for pickerel and perch. An easy family day hike is located west of the campground at Rhododendron State Park. The park itself is in full bloom in mid- to late July. A trail on the park's north side leads into Little Monadnock State Park, where a mile hike through a hardwood forest over moderate terrain brings you to the 1,833-foot summit of Little Monadnock Mountain for an outstanding view of Mount Monadnock from the south.

Campsites, facilities: There are 100 sites for tents and RVs, some with full hookups. Each site has a picnic table and fire ring. A dump station, laundry facilities, restrooms, hot showers, a snack bar, and a playground are provided. A store sells ice, firewood, and bait. Leashed pets are permitted.

Reservations, fees: Reservations are recommended. Sites start at $18 a night per family. Weekly, monthly, and seasonal rates are available.

Open: Year-round.

Directions: From Fitzwilliam, travel four miles south on Highway 12 to the campground.

Contact: Hunter's State Line Campground, Highway 12, Box 132, Fitzwilliam, NH 03447, 603/585-7726.

33 FIELD AND STREAM TRAVEL TRAILER PARK

🏊 🚤 🎣 ❄️ 🐕 🚴 🚐 ⛺

Rating: 7
Near Pontanipo Pond in Brookline

Any size RV can be accommodated at Field and Stream. The campground is aptly named, as most of the sites are on grassy plots in a lightly wooded area along Gould Mill Brook, which is stocked with trout. Canoeists can put in at the campground and paddle a short distance southwest to Pontanipo Pond, a warm-water habitat supporting bass and horned pout.

A few miles from the Massachusetts border, this campground is located in a small town but is close to Nashua, New Hampshire's second largest city. Winter sites are open to seasonal campers only.

Campsites, facilities: There are 54 sites for tents and RVs, 19 with full hookups and 35 with water and electric hookups. Each site has a picnic table and fire ring. Air conditioner and heater use is allowed. A dump station, laundry facilities, restrooms, metered hot showers, a recreation hall, pavilion, pool, and playground are provided. A camp store sells LP gas, ice, and firewood. Courts for volleyball, basketball, badminton, and horseshoes are located on the property. A gate controls traffic at the entrance. Leashed pets are permitted.

Reservations, fees: Reservations are required from November–April and accepted at other times. Sites start $25 a night per family.

Open: Year-round; fully operational May 1–October 31.

Directions: From the intersection of Highways 13 and 130 in Brookline, travel a mile west on Highway 130 (Mason Road) to Dupaw Gould Road. Turn right and travel .25 mile north to the campground entrance.

Contact: Field and Stream Travel Trailer Park, 5 Dupaw Gould Road, Brookline, NH 03033, 603/673-4677, website: fieldnstream.hypermart.net.

Chapter 7

BROOKS DODGE/© NEW HAMPSHIRE OFFICE OF TRAVEL & TOURISM DEVELOPMENT

Eastern Lakes
and Seacoast

Eastern Lakes and Seacoast

South of the White Mountains, the glaciers of the last ice age carved huge basins that are now filled with sparkling blue waters dotted by islands and ringed by forested hillsides. These are the more than 270 lakes that give the Lakes Region its name.

Lake Winnipesaukee, near the center of New Hampshire, is the largest of these gorgeous bodies of water. Sprawling for some 72 square miles and boasting at least 240 islands (as yet there is no official tally), Winnipesaukee is a boater's paradise. Though much of the lake is undeveloped, those who prefer prepackaged amusements and summer fun will find the town of Weirs Beach an irresistible attraction. It's a boisterous playground where kids can get their fill of cotton candy and hot dogs, water slides and go-carts, arcades, and miniature golf.

Farther south, the land flattens out as it begins its slow descent to the Atlantic Ocean. And though New Hampshire claims a mere 18-mile piece of seacoast between Massachusetts and Maine, those 18 north-south miles actually stretch into a whopping 131 miles of meandering coastal shoreline. Though the season is relatively short here (roughly

July and August), and the water is bracingly cold, the New Hampshire seacoast is a beautiful region popular with both suntanners and sailors, sea kayakers and striped-bass fishers.

There are several state parks and fine sandy beaches along the New Hampshire seacoast, from honky-tonk Hampton Beach to the wide open stretches of sand in Rye. Access to the beaches and waterfront sites is along highly scenic Highway U.S. 1A.

And don't drive through the seacoast without stopping in stately Portsmouth. While in town, take a scenic boat tour of this historic port and harbor. You'll hear about Portsmouth's impressive naval history and its roles during all of the major wars of the last three centuries. If you have a full day, take the boat out to the Isles of Shoals, the islands a dozen miles out to sea, where Blackbeard left a wife and where poets and writers took the salt airs in the 19th century. And there's plenty of great dining in this port town.

For detailed information on New Hampshire State Parks, see the introduction to the White Mountains chapter.

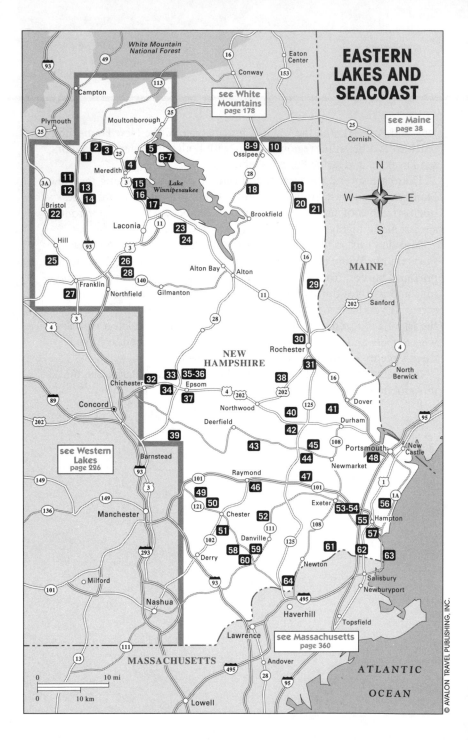

EASTERN
LAKES AND
SEACOAST

see White
Mountains
page 178

see Maine
page 38

see Western
Lakes
page 226

see Massachusetts
page 360

ATLANTIC

OCEAN

© AVALON TRAVEL PUBLISHING, INC.

❶ AMES BROOK CAMPGROUND

🏊 🚣 🏕 ⛺ 🚐 ⛰

Rating: 7

Southeast of Ashland on Ames Brook

Ames Brook tumbles by wooded campsites, some of which are set right beside the water. A separate tent area has larger, more private campsites underneath the trees. On weekends, campers awake to the smell of bacon and eggs, for a small restaurant on the property serves breakfast. Weekend organized activities include hay-wagon rides, water aerobics in the pool, sundae festivals, and candy bar bingo. Ames Brook is open to fishing, but for more lively waters try Little Squam Lake to the north; there's a public boat launch in Holderness, and the lake supports both warm-water and cold-water species. Ashland is a sweet old mill town; there's still a five-and-dime on Main Street that sells penny candy. Just a few miles off I-93, this campground makes a good jumping-off point for day trips to the White Mountains and to the Lakes Region's various attractions.

Campsites, facilities: There are 52 sites for tents and RVs, most with hookups. Each site has a picnic table and fire ring. Cable TV hookups are available. A dump station, restrooms, laundry facilities, hot showers, a recreation hall, pool, and playground are provided. A camp store sells LP gas, ice, and firewood. Courts for badminton, volleyball, and horseshoes are located on the property. Leashed pets are permitted.

Reservations, fees: Reservations are accepted. Sites are $30–32 a night. Off-season, weekly, monthly, and seasonal rates are available.

Open: May 1–October 31.

Directions: From I-93 at Ashland, take Exit 24 and travel .75 mile south on U.S. 3. Continue south for another .25 mile on Highway 132, turn left on Winona Road, and head east. The campground is .5 mile ahead on the road's south side.

Contact: Ames Brook Campground, 104 Winona Road, R.F.D. 1, Box 102, Ashland, NH 03217, 603/968-7998 or 800/234-7998, website: www.amesbrook.com.

❷ SQUAM LAKES CAMP RESORT

🥾 🏊 🚣 🚐 🛶 ❄ 🏕 ⛺ 🚐 ⛰

Rating: 8

On Little Squam Lake

Squam Lakes Camp Resort is located at Lakeside Farm on Little Squam Lake. In addition to shaded campsites on a hill above the shore, the facility includes a restaurant, ice-cream shop, and full-service marina. Bring your own boat or use one of the rental canoes, motorboats, or pontoon boats to explore public islands, secluded coves, and sandy beaches. This is a four-season resort, and amenities include a heated pool, outdoor hot tub with a sprawling sundeck, and a lodge with an exercise room, indoor hot tub, billiard room, and a big-screen TV. To the northeast lies Squam Lake, the state's second largest body of water; it's famous as the setting for the Hollywood film *On Golden Pond.* Loons are the unofficial Squam Lakes mascot, and visitors are asked to take special care not to disturb nests or young families. For a spectacular view of the entire Lakes Region, head north from Holderness on Highway 113 for about four miles to the Old Bridle Path Trailhead. From here, an easy 1.8-mile hike ascends 1,260-foot West Rattlesnake Mountain.

Campsites, facilities: There are 119 sites for tents and RVs, 66 with full hookups, 41 with water and electric hookups, and 12 with none. Each site has a picnic table, fire ring, and grill. A dump station, laundry facilities, restrooms, hot showers, a recreation hall, pool, and playground are provided. Leashed pets are permitted.

Reservations, fees: Reservations are recommended and require a deposit. Sites are $35 a night for two people.

Open: Year-round.

Directions: From the junction of Highway 113 and U.S. 3/Highway 25 in Holderness, travel .5 mile southeast on U.S. 3/Highway 25 to the campground entrance.

Contact: Squam Lakes Camp Resort, R.F.D. 1, Box 42, Ashland, NH 03217, 603/968-7227, website: www.squamlakesresort.com.

3 BETHEL WOODS CAMPGROUND

🏊 🏕 ⛹ 🚐 ⛰

Rating: 8

Near Little Squam Lake

Though many seasonal campers have claimed these natural wooded sites close to the recreational offerings of the Lakes Region, Bethel Woods does have room for overnight campers; just be sure to call ahead. Squam Lake and Little Squam Lake provide access to powerboating, fishing, and canoeing within a mile or two radius, but it's also possible to have water-based fun right at the campground. A pool, sauna, and whirlpool complex is complemented by a spacious sundeck. Your vehicle can get in on the wet action with Bethel Woods' RV steam wash, part of a full-service RV repair shop next to the campground.

Putters will find a campground green where they can practice their shots before teeing off at the White Mountain Country Club, an 18-hole public golf course to the north in Ashland. Church services are another on-site amenity. For an educational family day trip, try the Science Center of New Hampshire in Holderness. Using hands-on exhibits, games, and puzzles, staff members teach visitors about native New Hampshire plants and animals. It includes a 200-acre wildlife sanctuary and a short walking trail that leads past black bear, white-tailed deer, owls, foxes, otters, and bald eagles living in natural enclosures. The facility hosts field trips, courses, and lectures, as well as a regularly scheduled natural history cruise on Squam Lake.

Campsites, facilities: There are 58 sites for tents and RVs, 50 with water and electric hookups. Each site has a picnic table and fire ring. Air conditioner and heater use is allowed. A dump station, laundry facilities, restrooms, hot show-

ers, a recreation hall, pool, and a playground are provided. A small grocery store sells RV supplies, LP gas, ice, and firewood. Courts for basketball, badminton, volleyball, and horseshoes are located on the property. A gate controls traffic at the campground entrance. The maximum RV length is 35 feet. Leashed pets are permitted.

Reservations, fees: Reservations are recommended at all times. Sites are $28–30 a night.

Open: May 15–October 15.

Directions: From I-93 at Ashland, take Exit 24. Travel east on U.S. 3/Highway 25 for four miles to the campground entrance on the left (north) side of the road.

Contact: Bethel Woods Campground, P.O. Box 201, Holderness, NH 03245, 603/279-6266, website: www.bethelwoods.com.

4 HARBOR HILL CAMPING AREA

🏊 ⛹ 🚐 ⛰

Rating: 7

North of Meredith

Dirt roads wind through a mixed hardwood forest of beech, birch, and oak trees, accessing these small but private campsites. Most are fully equipped for RVs up to 35 feet long, but tenters are offered spots in a wilderness hilltop area. A public boat launch is available just north of the campground at Leavitt Park on Lake Winnipesaukee, and you are free to explore the more than 44,500 acres of freshwater and islands by powerboat (with a license), kayak, or canoe. Numerous marinas rent every waterborne mode of transport, from sailboards and sailboats to Jet Skis and powerboats with cuddy cabins. Harbor Hill is within easy driving distance of several Lakes Region attractions, including bustling Weirs Beach and the Castle in the Clouds (a stone mansion built in the early 1900s and now open for tours, with panoramic Lake Winnipesaukee views), yet it is far enough away that you aren't bothered by the crowds.

Campsites, facilities: There are 140 sites for

tents and RVs, 81 with full hookups, 26 with water and electric hookups, and 33 with none. Each site has a picnic table and fire ring. Air conditioners are allowed, but heaters are prohibited. Phone hookups are available. A dump station, laundry facilities, restrooms, hot showers, a recreation hall, pool, and playground are provided. A grocery store sells LP gas, ice, and firewood. Courts for basketball, shuffleboard, badminton, volleyball, and horseshoes are located on the property, and the entrance has a traffic control gate. The maximum RV length is 35 feet. Leashed pets with rabies vaccination certification are permitted.

Reservations, fees: A 50 percent deposit is required for all reservations. Tent sites are $25–32 a night per family. Cabins are available for $45 a night. There are fees for guests and air conditioner use.

Open: Mid-May–mid-October.

Directions: From the junction of Highway 25 and U.S. 3 in Meredith, travel two miles east on Highway 25 to the campground.

Contact: Harbor Hill Camping Area, 189 Highway 25, Meredith, NH 03253, 603/279-6910, website: www.hhcamp.com.

5 CAMP IROQUOIS CAMPGROUND

🛶 🏊 🚻 🎣 🐕 🎮 🚐 ⛺

Rating: 8

On Moultonborough Neck on Lake Winnipesaukee

Pine trees shade these campsites scattered along the giant Lake Winnipesaukee northern shore on Moultonborough Neck's Ash Cove. A boat ramp and swimming beach are provided for campers. Casting from shore is prohibited, but once you're out on the state's largest body of water, you find excellent fishing for many species including salmon, bass, and trout. The lake's 44,586 acres are open to every kind of boating as well as Jet Skiing in certain areas. A marina close to the campground sells boat licenses and provides rule booklets. Just south

of the campground is the Kona Wildlife Management Area, which is open to hunting in season. Supplies and services are available in the village of Center Harbor.

Campsites, facilities: There are 90 sites for tents and RVs, all with water and electric hookups. Each site has a picnic table and fire ring. A dump station, restrooms, warm showers, and a pavilion are provided. Some provisions, including firewood, are sold on-site. Courts for basketball, tennis, and horseshoes are located on the property. The maximum RV length is 35 feet. Leashed pets are permitted.

Reservations, fees: Reservations are accepted for stays of a week or longer and must include a $40 deposit. For stays shorter than a week, or for weekends, sites are available on a first-come, first-served basis. Sites start at $22 a night per family.

Open: Mid-May–October 1.

Directions: From Center Harbor, travel 1.5 miles northeast on Highway 25. Turn right on Moultonborough Neck Road and continue 1.5 miles southeast to the campground entrance on the right side of the road.

Contact: Camp Iroquois Campground, P.O. Box 150, Center Harbor, NH 03226, 603/253-4287.

6 PINE WOODS CAMPGROUND

🛶 🏊 🚻 🎣 🐕 🎮 🚐 ⛺

Rating: 8

On Moultonborough Neck on Lake Winnipesaukee

Tucked into the woods, these small, quiet sites are a short distance from the shore of giant Lake Winnipesaukee, at 44,586 acres the state's largest body of water. Campers have access to an on-site pool and recreation area, or they can opt to swim in the lake at several nearby public access points. The campground's lands are adjacent to the Kona Wildlife Management Area, where hunting is permitted for big and small game, fur-bearing animals, and game birds.

Campsites, facilities: There are 97 sites for tents and RVs, 80 with water and electric hookups and 12 with none. Each site has a picnic table and fire ring. A dump station, laundry facilities, restrooms, hot showers, a recreation hall, pool, and a playground are provided. A camp store sells ice and firewood. Courts for shuffleboard, badminton, volleyball, and horseshoes are located on the property. Leashed pets are permitted.

Reservations, fees: Reservations are recommended. Sites are $25–27 a night for two people.

Open: May 1–October 31.

Directions: From Center Harbor, travel 1.5 miles northeast on Highway 25. Turn right on Moultonborough Neck Road and continue four miles southeast to the campground entrance.

Contact: Pine Woods Campground, P.O. Box 776, Moultonborough, NH 03254, 603/253-6251, website: www.pinewoods.com.

7 LONG ISLAND BRIDGE CAMPGROUND

🌊 🛶 🎣 🏕 🦌 🏠 ♿ 🚐 ⛺

Rating: 8
On Long Island on Lake Winnipesaukee

Pine trees protect the open and shaded sites on Long Island, one of the largest islands on Lake Winnipesaukee. On either side of Long Island are numerous smaller islands, making this a favorite area among kayakers. At the campground, a boat ramp, dock, and swimming beach are provided for campers. Out on the lake, there's excellent fishing for many species including salmon, bass, and trout. Lake Winnipesaukee is the state's largest, and its 44,586 acres are open to every kind of boating including personal watercraft in certain areas. Be sure to check the rules and regulations before you head out; booklets are available at any marina on the lake. The Kona Wildlife Management Area just south of the campground is open to hunting in season. Sup-

plies and services are available in the village of Center Harbor.

Campsites, facilities: There are 112 sites for tents and RVs, 76 with full hookups, 23 with water and electric hookups, and 12 with none. Each site has a picnic table and fire ring. Air conditioner and heater use is allowed. A dump station, laundry facilities, restrooms, hot showers, and a playground are provided. A camp store sells ice and firewood. Courts for basketball, volleyball, and horseshoes are located on the property. The maximum RV length is 32 feet. Leashed pets are permitted.

Reservations, fees: Reservations are accepted. Sites are $25–35 a night per family.

Open: May 15–October 15.

Directions: From Center Harbor, travel 1.5 miles northeast on Highway 25. Turn right on Moultonborough Neck Road and travel southeast for 6.5 miles to the campground.

Contact: Long Island Bridge Campground, H.C.R. 62, Box 455, Center Harbor, NH 03226, 603/253-6053, website: www.ucampnh/longislandbridge.com.

8 TERRACE PINES CAMPGROUND

🧗 🌊 🛶 🎣 🦌 ♿ 🚐 ⛺

Rating: 8
Between Big and Little Dan Holes in Center Ossipee

Lake lovers can have the best of both worlds at Terrace Pines. The campground offers sites in hilly wooded areas beside and near both Big and Little Dan Hole ponds. The bigger lake is open to powerboating and waterskiing, while only nonmotorized boating is allowed on Little Dan Hole. There are three beach areas for swimming as well as a boat launch and dock. Anglers can try for lake trout and salmon in Big Dan Hole. North of the campground, a short footpath leads to the summit of Sentinel Mountain.

Campsites, facilities: There are 184 sites for tents and RVs, 178 with full hookups and five with water and electric hookups. Cabins and A-frame shelters are also for rent. Each site has a picnic table and fire ring. Phone hookups are available. Air conditioner and heater use is allowed. A dump station, laundry facilities, restrooms, hot showers, a recreation hall, and a playground are provided, and a camp grocery store sells LP gas, ice, and firewood. Courts for basketball, badminton, volleyball, and horseshoes are located on the property. The maximum RV length is 29 feet. Leashed pets are permitted.

Reservations, fees: A 50 percent prepaid deposit is required with all reservations except for those on holiday weekends, which must be prepaid in full. Sites are $32–38 a night per family. Seasonal rates are available on request.

Open: Mid-May–September 9.

Directions: From Center Ossipee near the southern junction of Highways 16 and 25, travel 1.5 miles southwest on Moultonville Road. Stay left at the fork and continue southeast for 1.75 miles on Valley Road. Bear left on Bents Road and continue .5 mile to the campground entrance.

Contact: Terrace Pines Campground, P.O. Box 98, Center Ossipee, NH 03814, 603/529-6210, website: www.terracepines.com.

9 DEER CAP CAMPGROUND

South of Center Ossipee

Rating: 7

Deer Cap Campground doubles as a cross-country ski center and camping facility. Note that winter sites are available for seasonal campers only, however. Sites are roomy and shaded by tall pine trees beside the Beech River, a small trout-filled stream. In winter, campers can ski on miles of groomed trails that leave from the campground and afterward soak in Deer Cap's heated outdoor pool. For summer recreation, Ossipee Lake to the north is open to powerboating, fishing, and swimming and has a public boat launch on Deer Cove. The

Indian Mound Golf Club offers 18 holes beside the lake and is open to the public.

Campsites, facilities: There are 75 sites for tents and RVs, some with full hookups. Each site comes with a picnic table and fire ring. A dump station, restrooms, hot showers, a recreation hall, heated swimming pool, and a playground are provided, as are courts for volleyball and horseshoes. Ice and firewood are sold on the grounds. Leashed pets are permitted.

Reservations, fees: Reservations are accepted. Sites start at $18 a night for two people.

Open: Year-round, but winter sites are available for seasonal campers only.

Directions: From the junction of Highways 16 and 28 in Ossipee, travel north for approximately 3.5 miles on Highway 16 to the campground entrance on the left (west) side of the road.

Contact: Deer Cap Campground, P.O. Box 332, Center Ossipee, NH 03814, 603/539-6030, website: www.members.ttlc.net/~deercap.

10 BEAVER HOLLOW CAMPGROUND

Northeast of Ossipee

Rating: 6

Busy Highway 16, a major thoroughfare for travelers headed to the White Mountains, borders this campground. Campsites are set far enough back in the woods so road noise isn't a nuisance, but you should be prepared to deal with traffic, especially on weekends, once you leave the campground. Frenchman's Brook runs through the grounds, with sites 70–77 set right on the shore. You can fish in the stream, but you'll find two really good cold-water ponds just north and east of here: White Pond and Duncan Lake are stocked with brook and rainbow trout. Pine River State Forest is northeast of the campground and has some multiuse trails. State-maintained snowmobile trails are also accessible from the campground. On weekends, organized activities include live entertainment and group dinners.

Campsites, facilities: There are 132 sites for tents and RVs, all with water and electric hookups. Each site has a picnic table, fire ring, and grill. Air conditioner and heater use is allowed. A dump station, laundry facilities, restrooms, hot showers, a recreation hall, pool, picnic pavilion, and a playground are provided. A small grocery store sells RV supplies, ice, and firewood. Courts for basketball, shuffleboard, badminton, volleyball, bocce ball, and horseshoes are located on the property. Leashed pets are permitted.

Reservations, fees: Reservations are recommended Memorial Day–Labor Day and require a nonrefundable deposit. Sites are $26 a night per family. Weekly, monthly, and seasonal rates are available.

Open: Year-round; fully operational May 15–Columbus Day.

Directions: From the junction of Highways 16 and 28 in Ossipee, travel south for a mile on Highway 16 to the campground entrance on the left (east) side of the road.

Contact: Beaver Hollow Campground, P.O. Box 437, Ossipee, NH 03864, 603/539-4800 or 800/226-2557.

11 YOGI BEAR'S JELLYSTONE PARK CAMP RESORT

Rating: 7
On the Pemigewasset River south of Ashland

Yogi Bear's is a family camping theme park. The resort is located on the Pemigewasset River, which is open to canoeing, swimming, and fishing; you can rent boats at the campground. Sites are small and mostly open, though some offer shade trees. A full slate of organized activities includes visits from Yogi Bear every day, movies and cartoons, dances, outdoor concerts, bingo marathons, and ceramics. In addition to the services listed above, baby-sitting is available. There's a restaurant on-site as well as a 19-hole miniature golf course. Many sites are rented by seasonal campers. The camp-

ground caters to families who want to stay busy from dawn to dusk. A new water playground includes fountains, slides, and more—a real hit with kids.

Campsites, facilities: There are 275 sites for tents and RVs, 19 with full hookups, 204 with water and electric hookups, and the rest with none. RVs and cabins are also available for rent. Each site has a picnic table and fire ring. Air conditioner and heater use is allowed. A dump station, laundry facilities, restrooms, hot showers, a recreation hall, pool, game room, and playground are provided. A store sells groceries, ice, LP gas, RV supplies, and firewood. You will also find courts for basketball, shuffleboard, badminton, volleyball, and horseshoes. Roads are paved within the park, and a guard controls the front entrance. Leashed pets are permitted.

Reservations, fees: Reservations are recommended Memorial Day–Labor Day. Sites are $53–58 a night per family, with discounts in spring and fall.

Open: Early May–early October.

Directions: From I-93 south of Ashland, take Exit 23 for the Lakes Region. Travel east on Highway 104 for 500 yards, and then head north for four miles on Highway 132. The campground entrance will be on the left (west) side of the road.

Contact: Yogi Bear's Jellystone Park Camp Resort, RR 1, Box 396, Ashland, NH 03217, 603/968-9000, website: www.jellystonenh.com.

12 DAVIDSON'S COUNTRYSIDE CAMPGROUND

Rating: 7
On the Pemigewasset River

All full-hookup sites at Davidson's are occupied by seasonal campers, but about 30 sites with water and electricity are reserved for overnighters and vacation travelers. Overnight sites 54, 54A, and 55 are on the Pemigewasset River shoreline. Campers will find a variety of settings here, from open and grassy to wooded and riverfront. Swift-flowing and clear, the Pemi winds south to Franklin, where it meets the Merrimack River. Fish for trout from the shoreline or float for hours in an inner tube. From the campground, you can paddle on Class II and III rapids to Franklin just before the falls; canoes and one rowboat are available for rent at the campground. Northwest of the campground lies Newfound Lake, a 4,000-acre waterway renowned for its trout fishing. Wellington State Park is on the west shore and offers a swimming beach and a birding trail. One other perk: Davidson's owners make and sell maple syrup at the campground.

Campsites, facilities: There are 130 sites for tents and RVs, five with full hookups, 110 with water and electric hookups, and 15 with none. Each site has a picnic table and fire ring. A dump station, restrooms, hot showers, a recreation hall, pool, and playground are provided. A small grocery store sells snacks, ice, RV supplies, and firewood. Courts for basketball, badminton, volleyball, and horseshoes are located on the property. Leashed pets are permitted.

Reservations, fees: Reservations are accepted. Sites are $26–35 per night. Monthly and seasonal rates are available on request. Off-season RV storage is $2 per day.

Open: May 24–October 14.

Directions: From I-93 south of Ashland, take Exit 23 heading toward Bristol and travel west on Highway 104 for two miles. Take a right onto River Road and travel north to the campground entrance .5 mile ahead.

Contact: Davidson's Countryside Campground, 100 Schofield Road, Bristol, NH 03222, 603/744-2403, website: www.worldpath.net/~davcamp.

13 MEREDITH WOODS FOUR SEASON CAMPING AREA

Rating: 8

Near the north shore of Pemigewasset Lake

Four seasons of recreation await visitors to this campground in the Lakes Region. Most sites are rented seasonally, so call ahead to see if they have space. The facility is co-owned with Clearwater Campground across the street (see next listing), thus Meredith Woods' campers have full use of the large sandy beach on Pemigewasset Lake. Boats may be docked across the street at Clearwater Campground for $4 a night. Sandy, wooded sites are tightly settled, averaging about 25 feet wide. The owners take measures to control dust and mosquitoes in the park. Though tent spaces are available, the campground is dominated by RVers. For winter users, Meredith Woods offers an indoor heated pool and spa. Snowmobilers can get on the state's trail corridor from the campground, and cross-country skiers will find bountiful tracks through the surrounding pine forest. Pemigewasset Lake is an ice-fishing mecca from January–March.

Campsites, facilities: There are 64 sites for tents and RVs, all with full hookups. Each site has a picnic table and fire ring. Air conditioner and heater use is allowed, and cable TV and telephone hookups are available. A dump station, laundry facilities, restrooms, hot showers, a pavilion, recreation hall, pool, and playground are provided. A camp store sells ice and firewood. Courts for basketball, shuffleboard, badminton, volleyball, and horseshoes are located on the property. There's a traffic control gate at the campground entrance. Leashed pets are permitted.

Reservations, fees: Reservations for stays of a week or longer require a $75 deposit per week. For stays shorter than a week, or for weekends, full prepayment is required. Per family, sites are $40 a night. Weekly and seasonal rates are available.

Open: Year-round.

Directions: From I-93 at New Hampton, take Exit 23 and travel east on Highway 104 for three miles to the campground entrance on the left.

Contact: Meredith Woods Four Season Camping Area, 26 Campground Road, Meredith, NH 03253, 603/279-5449, website: www.meredithwoods.com.

14 CLEARWATER CAMPGROUND

Rating: 8

On the north shore of Pemigewasset Lake

Rolling mountains are in full view of the campground's large sandy beach on Pemigewasset Lake. The beach is well suited for waterskiing and is also the site of group campfires and activities. Sites are tightly settled (about 25 feet wide) in the woods by the lake, and campers have access to a boat launch and a 36-slip dock. This location is ideal for families who want to take day trips north to the White Mountains, or to the boardwalk beach scene at Lake Winnipesaukee's Weirs Beach. Conveniences and courtesies at the campground include dust control on the facility's dirt roads, mosquito control, and a night manager at the gated entrance.

Campsites, facilities: There are 153 sites for tents and RVs, 144 with water and electric hookups, and some with full hookups, including cable TV. Each site has a picnic table and fire ring. Air conditioner and heater use is allowed. A dump station, laundry facilities, restrooms, hot showers, a sports field, pavilion, recreation hall, and playground are provided. A grocery store sells ice, firewood, and RV supplies. Courts for basketball, shuffleboard, badminton, volleyball, and horseshoes are located on the property. Leashed pets are permitted.

Reservations, fees: Reservations for stays of a week or longer require a $75 deposit per week. For stays of three nights or fewer, and on holidays, full prepayment is required. Sites are $38–42 a night per family. A limited number of sites offer sewer and cable TV connections for $3 extra. Weekly and seasonal rates are available. In the spring and fall, off-season rates start at $20 a night. The boat docking fee is $4 a night.

Open: Mid-May–mid-October.

Directions: From I-93 at New Hampton, take Exit 23 and travel east on Highway 104 for three miles to the campground entrance on the right (south) side of the road.

Contact: Clearwater Campground, 26 Campground Road, Meredith, NH 03253, 603/279-7761, website: www.clearwatercampground.com.

15 HACK-MA-TACK FAMILY CAMPGROUND

Rating: 7

North of Weirs Beach

These roomy wooded sites are right in the thick of the Lakes Region's booming commercial district. Arcades, entertainment centers, a beach boardwalk, shops, restaurants, and boat cruises are available fewer than two miles south in bustling Weirs Beach, a resort area on the shore of giant Lake Winnipesaukee. Campers in search of quieter surroundings may want to try campgrounds located in less boisterous resort towns on the lake such as Moultonborough or Center Harbor.

Campsites, facilities: There are 80 sites for tents and RVs. Each site has a picnic table and fire ring. A dump station, restrooms, hot showers, a recreation hall, pool, and a playground are provided. A small grocery store sells RV supplies, ice, charcoal, and firewood. Courts for shuffleboard, basketball, and horseshoes are located on the property. Leashed pets are permitted.

Reservations, fees: Reservations require a $25 deposit for stays of fewer than seven days and $50 per full week. Full prepayment is required on holiday weekends. Sites start at $26 a night for two people, with discounted rates after three days. There are surcharges for guests and sewer connections. Refunds are given within one hour of registration if you are unhappy with your site.

Open: Mid-May–mid-October.

Directions: From the junction of U.S. 3 and Highway 104 in Meredith, travel 2.5 miles south on U.S. 3 to the campground entrance on the left (east) side of the road.

Contact: Hack-Ma-Tack Family Campground, U.S. 3, Box 90, Laconia, NH 03246, 603/366-5977.

16 WEIRS BEACH TENT AND TRAILER PARK

Rating: 7

Just north of Weirs Beach

Small sites are organized in rows separated by birch, oak, maple, pine, and beech trees amid the melee of the Weirs Beach commercial resort district. Arcades, entertainment centers, a beach boardwalk, shops, restaurants, and boat cruises are a short walk south of here on the shore of Lake Winnipesaukee. These campsites offer few amenities since all goods and services can be obtained nearby in Weirs Beach. Swimming areas and marinas are close by.

Campsites, facilities: There are 184 sites for tents and RVs. Each site has a picnic table and fire ring. A dump station, restrooms, hot showers, and horseshoe pits are provided. The maximum RV length is 31 feet. Leashed pets are permitted.

Reservations, fees: Reservations require one night's fee as a nonrefundable deposit. For two people, primitive sites are $24 a night, sites with water and electric hookups are $24 a night, and those with full hookups are $28 a night. The boat docking fee is $5 a night. Seasonal rates are available.

Open: May 15–September 15; self-contained units can stay from September 15–Columbus Day.

Directions: From the junction of U.S. 3 and Highway 104 in Meredith, travel four miles south on U.S. 3 to the campground.

Contact: Weirs Beach Tent and Trailer Park, R.F.D. 3, Box 98, Laconia, NH 03246, 603/366-4747, website: www.ucampnh/weirsbeach.com.

17 PAUGUS BAY CAMPGROUND

Rating: 8

On Paugus Bay in Lake Winnipesaukee

Sites here are staggered on a hillside beside Paugus Bay and most with full hookups are occupied by seasonal campers, so be sure to call ahead. All the attractions at Weirs Beach—water slides, arcades, a beach boardwalk, and go-carts—are a short walk away. Boaters can dock their craft at the campground, and others may explore the bay and Lake Winnipesaukee in rental canoes. This is the state's largest lake with more than 44,500 freshwater acres open to fishing, boating, and swimming. Check rules and regulations on boating and fishing before setting out; booklets are available at all marinas.

Campsites, facilities: There are 130 sites for tents and RVs, 102 with full hookups and 25 with water and electric hookups. Each site has a picnic table and fire ring. A dump station, laundry facilities, restrooms, hot showers, a recreation hall, pavilion, horseshoe pits, and a playground are provided. A small grocery store sells ice and firewood. Leashed pets are permitted.

Reservations, fees: A $50 deposit is required with all reservations. In July and August, sites must be reserved for a minimum of seven days. Sites are $28–32 a night per family. Weekly, monthly, and seasonal rates are available. After Labor Day, sites start at $20 a night.

Open: May 15–October 15.

Directions: From the junction of U.S. 3 and Highway 104 in Meredith, head southeast on U.S. 3 toward Weirs Beach for four miles. Turn right on Hilliard Road and continue .2 mile to the campground.

Contact: Paugus Bay Campground, Hilliard Road, Laconia, NH 03246, 603/366-4757, website: www.geocities.com/weirs_pbc.

18 WOLFEBORO CAMPGROUND

Rating: 7

North of Lake Wentworth

Secluded and rural, these sites are enveloped in tall pine tree stands. This is the ideal spot for RVers who want to tour the Lakes Region, but desire a quiet, private place to return to at the end of the day. To the south, Wentworth State Park is a small, state-owned parcel of land on Lake Wentworth. A picnic area and swimming beach there are open to the public. World War II buffs should pay a visit to the Wright Museum of American Enterprise in Wolfeboro, where scenes of American life are re-created using authentic uniforms, vehicles, periodicals, and memorabilia.

Campsites, facilities: There are 50 sites for tents and RVs, 40 with water and electric hookups and 10 with none. Each site has a table, fire ring, and grill. A dump station, restrooms, hot showers, a recreation hall, and a playground are provided. A store sells LP gas, ice, and firewood. Courts for badminton, volleyball, and horseshoes are located on the property. The maximum RV length is 40 feet. Leashed pets are permitted.

Reservations, fees: Reservations are recommended. Sites are $20–25 a night per family, plus charges for whatever electricity is used. Weekly, monthly, and seasonal rates are available.

Open: May 15–October 15.

Directions: From Wolfeboro, travel north for 4.5 miles on Highway 28 to Haines Hill Road. Bear right heading uphill, and the campground is 1,000 feet ahead.

Contact: Wolfeboro Campground, 61 Haines Hill Road, Wolfeboro, NH 03894, 603/569-9881, website: www.wolfborocampground.com.

19 BEACHWOOD SHORES CAMPGROUND

🏍 🏊 🛶 🚤 🎣 🐴 🚴 🚐 ⛺

Rating: 7

On the southwest shore of Province Lake

Choose from lakefront, lakeview, wooded, and riverfront sites at Beachwood Shores Campground. All sites are large and sandy, shaded by tall pine trees beside Province Lake. The lake is open to warm-water fishing, powerboating, and swimming. Boats are available for rent at the campground, and there's a ramp near the beach. Hiking trails lead into Pine

River State Forest to the west. The Pine River flows through that parcel of land and is canoeable over a 20-mile stretch during high water; it's also favored by local trout fishermen. To the east of the campground on the Maine border is the Province Lake Country Club, with its public golf course and tennis courts.

Campsites, facilities: There are 87 sites for tents and RVs, all with full hookups. Each site has a picnic table, fire ring, and grill. A dump station, laundry facilities, restrooms, hot showers, a recreation hall, and a playground are provided. A camp store sells RV supplies, limited groceries, LP gas, ice, and firewood. Courts for basketball, badminton, volleyball, and horseshoes are located on the property. Leashed pets are permitted.

Reservations, fees: Reservations are accepted. Sites start at $28 a night per family. Seasonal rates are available on request.

Open: Mid-May–mid-October.

Directions: From north of Union at the junction of Highway 16 and Highway 153 (which turns into Mountain Laurel Road), travel north for 12 miles on Highway 153. Turn left on Bonnyman Road and head west for two miles to the campground entrance.

Contact: Beachwood Shores Campground, HC Box 228, East Wakefield, NH 03830, 603/539-4272 or 800/371-4282, website: www.ucampnh.com/beachwoodshores.

20 LAKE IVANHOE CAMPGROUND

🚲 🏊 🛶 🚤 🐴 🚴 🚐 ⛺

Rating: 7

On the north shore of Lake Ivanhoe near the Maine border

Pine trees tower above these large sites near the Lake Ivanhoe north shore. Campers can get out on the 100-acre spring-fed lake by rental rowboats, canoes, or paddleboats. A large sandy swimming beach is a short walk from the campsites. Group activities at Lake Ivanhoe Campground include hay-wagon rides, sports tournaments, and adult bingo. Wakefield has several bicycle routes for visitors to explore the town's 11 lakes, passing by rivers, rolling pastures, and forests; maps are available at the campground office. One rainy day option is a visit to the Museum of Childhood in Wakefield. The collection includes 3,000 dolls, dollhouses, teddy bears, puppets, and music boxes.

Campsites, facilities: There are 74 sites for tents and RVs, 49 with full hookups, 18 with water and electric hookups, and eight with none. Each site has a picnic table and fire ring. Air conditioner and heater use is allowed. A dump station, laundry facilities, restrooms, hot showers, a recreation hall, and a playground are provided. Also on the property are an 18-hole miniature golf course and courts for basketball, shuffleboard, badminton, volleyball, and horseshoes. A camp store carries LP gas, RV supplies, ice, and firewood. Leashed pets are permitted.

Reservations, fees: Reservations are recommended in July and August and require a 50 percent deposit. Sites are $28–38 a night for two people. Weekly, monthly, and seasonal rates are available.

Open: Mid-May–mid-October.

Directions: From north of Union at the junction of Highway 16 and Mountain Laurel Road, travel .5 mile east on Mountain Laurel Road. Turn left and travel north for 2.5 miles on Highway 153. Turn right on Acton Ridge Road and travel 1.2 miles east to the campground entrance.

Contact: Lake Ivanhoe Campground, 631 Acton Ridge Road, East Wakefield, NH 03830, 603/522-8824, website: www.lakeivanhoe.com.

21 LAKE FOREST RESORT

Rating: 7

On Great East Lake near the Maine border

Lake Forest's sites are nestled in the woods on Great East Lake, a seven-mile-long body of clear water with a sandy bottom straddling the New Hampshire–Maine border. Adult seasonal campers are the predominant clientele; no tents

or pop-up trailers are allowed, and only family members are welcome as guests. A short golf course on-site is a good place to warm up for action on any of the six 18-hole courses in the greater Wakefield area. There's also a post-and-beam clubhouse (much like an old-style barn) that's used for pancake breakfasts, bingo tournaments, suppers, and dances. At the shore, a long wooden dock and deck make comfy places to look out upon the lake and, in the distance, the rolling hills. The lake is open to swimming, fishing, and all types of boating.

Campsites, facilities: There are 160 sites for RVs only, 130 with full hookups and a group area containing 30 sites with water and electric hookups. Each site has a picnic table and fire ring. A dump station, laundry facilities, restrooms, hot showers, and a recreation hall are provided. Leashed pets are permitted.

Reservations, fees: Reservations are recommended. Sites are $26–30 a night for two people. Seasonal rates are available.

Open: May 10–October 14.

Directions: From north of Union at the junction of Highway 16 and Mountain Laurel Road, travel .5 mile east on Mountain Laurel Road. Turn left and travel north for 2.5 miles on Highway 153. Turn right on Acton Ridge Road and travel east for 1.6 miles to Dearborn Road. Turn right and follow signs to the campground entrance.

Contact: Lake Forest Resort, HC 66, Box 115A, East Wakefield, NH 03830, 603/522-3306 in the summer, or 603/569-6186 in the winter, website: www.ucampnh.com/lakeforestresort.

22 TWIN TAMARACK FAMILY CAMPING AND RV RESORT

Rating: 7

On Pemigewasset Lake

Pine-shaded sites in the woods, across Highway 104 from Pemigewasset Lake, are private and roomy. Twin Tamarack maintains a boat launch, beach, and dock area for lakeshore campers. Sites are fully equipped to handle RVs of any size, yet the dirt roads and natural landscaping maintain a rustic appearance. Paddleboats, canoes, and rowboats may be rented at the campground. RV rallies are welcome to pull in at a spacious group area and can contact the campground owners on CB channel 14. The pool and recreation hall complex includes a hot tub and game room. Seasonal campers occupy most of the full-hookup sites during the summer.

Campsites, facilities: There are 256 sites for tents and RVs. Each site has a picnic table and fire ring. Air conditioners are allowed, but heaters are prohibited. A dump station, laundry facilities, restrooms, hot showers, a pool, sports field, recreation hall, and playground are provided. A small grocery store sells RV supplies, ice, and firewood. You will also find courts for basketball, badminton, volleyball, and horseshoes on the property. Off-season RV storage is available. Leashed pets are permitted.

Reservations, fees: Prepaid deposits of $75 a week are required for all reservations except for stays of three days or fewer, which require full prepayment. Sites are $32–36 a night per family.

Open: Late May–early October.

Directions: From I-93 at New Hampton, take Exit 23 and travel east for 2.5 miles on Highway 104 to the campground.

Contact: Gene and Bev Sands, Twin Tamarack Family Camping and RV Resort, Highway 104, Box 121, New Hampton, NH 03256, 603/279-4387, website: www.ucampnh.com/twintamarack.

23 ELLACOYA STATE RV PARK

Rating: 8

On the southwest shore of Lake Winnipesaukee

These RV sites look out on the Ossipee and Sandwich Mountains across Lake Winnipesaukee. Only vehicles with full hookups are allowed. There is a swimming beach, a boat launch for cartop vessels, and a picnic area at the campground. To launch larger boats, head north to Sanders Bay, which has a public boat ramp. Once out on the state's largest lake, you find that these 44,000-plus acres offer anglers both warm-water and cold-water habitat, supporting numerous fish species. On good weather weekends, the lake is crowded with powerboats, personal watercrafts, and sailors. Before you head out find out about rules and regulations at any of the many local marinas.

Campsites, facilities: There are 38 sites for RVs only, all with full hookups. Each site has a picnic table. Laundry facilities, restrooms, hot showers, and a community fire pit are provided. A camp store sells ice and firewood. Pets, tents, and tent trailers are not allowed.

Reservations, fees: For reservations, contact the New Hampshire State Parks Camping Reservation Center, P.O. Box 1856, Concord, NH 03302-1856, 603/271-3628, website: www.nhparks.state.nh.us. Sites are $37 a night per family.

Open: Mid-May–mid-October.

Directions: From the junction of Highway 11 and U.S. 3 at Weirs Beach, travel five miles south on Highway 11.

Contact: Ellacoya State RV Park, P.O. Box 7277 Gilford, NH 03246, 603/293-7821; New Hampshire Division of Parks and Recreation, 603/271-3628, website: www.nhparks.state.nh.us.

24 GUNSTOCK CAMPGROUND

Rating: 9

At the base of Gunstock Mountain in Gilford

Gunstock Mountain rises from the Lake Winnipesaukee south shore, the state's largest body of water, providing a dramatic backdrop to these campsites. They are located in the woods at the mountain's base, which is also home to a four-season recreational facility. In winter, the mountain offers alpine and Nordic skiing at two different centers. In spring and summer, mountain bikers take to the ski trails, earning verdant views of Lake Winnipesaukee after a rugged ride to the top. Motorcyclists participate in a Hill Climb in June during Motorcycle Week, when the entire Lakes Region is overrun with two-wheeled enthusiasts. At the campground, a pool and a small pond can be used for swimming, fishing, boating, and canoeing. Boats are for rent on-site. In the fall, visitors climb Gunstock Mountain to get colorful views of the region dressed in its bright foliage hues. This campground can feel crowded because all the facilities are also open for day use. To escape the throngs, hike up the Red Trail to Belknap Mountain south of Gunstock Mountain. It's a moderate 1.5-mile trek to a summit fire tower.

Campsites, facilities: There are 300 sites for tents and RVs, 113 with water and electric hookups. Each site has a picnic table, fire ring, and grill. Air conditioners are allowed, but heaters are prohibited. A dump station, restrooms, hot showers, a recreation hall, pavilion, pool, sports field, and a playground are provided. A grocery store sells RV supplies, LP gas, ice, and firewood. Group sites for tents and RVs are available. You will also find courts for basketball, badminton, volleyball, and horseshoes. A traffic control gate and security guard are posted at the entrance. Leashed pets with rabies vaccination certification are permitted.

Reservations, fees: A nonrefundable deposit must accompany all reservations. For two adults or a family, sites start at $22 a night without hookups and $27 a night with water and electricity.

Open: Mid-May–mid-October, then mid-December–ski season.

Directions: From the north edge of town in Gilford, travel east on Highway 11A for 3.5 miles to the campground.

Contact: Gunstock Campground, P.O. Box 1307, Gilford, NH 03247, 800/GUN-STOCK (800/486-7862), extension 191, website: www.gunstock.com.

25 PINE GROVE CAMPGROUND

Rating: 6

West of the Pemigewasset River and north of Franklin

Quiet, peaceful camping in an open grassy area is offered at Pine Grove. Swim in the campground's pool, or head east to the Pemigewasset River for a day of tubing, canoeing, fishing, or swimming. Part of the Franklin Falls Dam Project, the river is enveloped in protected lands and provides habitat for horned pout, bass, pickerel, and perch.

Campsites, facilities: There are 29 sites for tents and RVs, seven with full hookups and 11 with water and electric hookups. Each site has a table and fire ring. A dump station, laundry facilities, restrooms, hot showers, a pavilion, and a playground are provided. A camp store sells ice and wood. Courts for badminton, volleyball, and horseshoes are located on-site. Leashed pets are permitted.

Reservations, fees: Reservations are accepted, and weekly, monthly, and seasonal rates are available for sites with hookups. Sites start at $18 a night for two people.

Open: May 15–October 15.

Directions: From Franklin, travel five miles north on Highway 3A to the campground entrance on the left.

Contact: Pine Grove Campground, 14 Timberlane Drive, Franklin, NH 03235, 603/934-4582.

26 WINNISQUAM BEACH RESORT

Rating: 7

On the southwest shore of Winnisquam Lake

Here's another lakeside campground with shady sites near the water. A boat launch, beach, and dock space are available for campers. Winnisquam Lake has both cold-water and warm-water piscine habitats supporting bass, salmon, trout, and several other species.

Campsites, facilities: There are 146 sites for tents and RVs, some with full hookups. Each site has a picnic table and fire ring. A dump station, laundry facilities, restrooms, hot showers, and a playground are provided. No pets are allowed.

Reservations, fees: Reservations are accepted. Sites are $25 a night per family. Seasonal rates are provided on request.

Open: Year-round, but winter sites are available to seasonal campers only.

Directions: From I-93 near Tilton, take Exit 20 and head north on U.S. 3 for two miles to Grey Rock Road. Turn right and look for the campground just ahead.

Contact: Winnisquam Beach Resort, P.O. Box 67, Lochmere, NH 03252, 603/524-0021.

27 THOUSAND ACRES FAMILY CAMPGROUND

🏊 🚣 🚐 🏕 🚴 🚌 ⛺

Rating: 6

South of Franklin on Shaw Brook

Family fun and games are the main attraction at Thousand Acres. Campsites are set amid the trees and have sandy driveways. Weekend events at the campground include free hayrides, ice-cream socials, ceramics, movies, bingo for all ages, a golf league, and sporting competitions. A small pond on Shaw Brook is privately owned, so you can fish there without a license. There's a sandy swimming beach on the pond and canoes for rent.

Campsites, facilities: There are 150 sites for tents and RVs, 47 with full hookups, 74 with water and electric hookups, and 29 with none. Each site has a table and stone fireplace. Air conditioner and heater use is allowed. A dump station, restrooms, hot showers, a recreation hall, and playground are provided. A grocery store sells ice and wood. Group camping areas for tents and RVs are available. Courts for basketball, badminton, volleyball, and horseshoes

are located on the property. Leashed pets are permitted.

Reservations, fees: Reservations are recommended July 1–Labor Day. Per family, sites range from $32 a night with no hookups to $34 with full hookups. Weekly and seasonal rates are available.

Open: May 15–October 1.

Directions: From I-93 at Penacook, take Exit 17. Travel north on U.S. 3 toward Franklin for 10 miles to the campground entrance on the left.

Contact: Thousand Acres Family Campground, Highway 3, Franklin, NH 03235, 603/934-4440, website: www.thousandacrescamp.com.

28 SILVER LAKE PARK CAMPGROUND

🏊 🚣 🚐 🏕 🚌 ⛺

Rating: 7

On the east shore of Silver Lake south of Laconia

Shrubs, lawns, and flower gardens punctuate many of the seasonal sites on a hillside overlooking the campground's sandy beach on Silver Lake. The warm-water loch supports smallmouth and largemouth bass and is big enough for good waterskiing. A quiet-water canoe excursion leads south out of the lake on the Winnipesaukee River. To the north, the Lakeview Golf Club is open to the public and offers nine holes overlooking Winnisquam Lake. If you're feeling lucky, take a short drive south to the Lakes Region Greyhound Park and place a bet on your favorite canine.

Campsites, facilities: There are 77 sites for tents and RVs, 70 with full hookups, five with water and electric hookups, and two with none. Each site has a table and fire ring. Air conditioner and heater use is allowed, and cable TV hookups are available. A dump station, laundry facilities, restrooms, hot showers, a recreation hall, and a playground are provided. A store sells ice and wood. Courts for badminton, volleyball, and horseshoes are located on site. Dogs are not allowed.

Reservations, fees: Reservations are recommended July 1–Labor Day weekend and must be accompanied by a nonrefundable deposit. Sites start at $25–35 a night. There are surcharges for air conditioners, cable TV, and boat ramps. Seasonal rates are available.

Open: Early May–mid-October.

Directions: From I-93 near Tilton, take Exit 20 and travel north on U.S. 3 for two miles. Turn right on Silver Lake Road and travel a mile south to the campground entrance.

Contact: Silver Lake Park Campground, P.O. Box 7, 64 Jamestown Road, Lochmere, NH 03252, 603/524-6289, website: www.onlinevacation. com/silverlake.

29 MI-TE-JO CAMPGROUND

Rating: 7

On Milton Pond in Milton

Mi-Te-Jo is an out-of-the-way lakeside campground with wooded sites. Milton Pond is open to fishing, swimming, and boating; a ramp and dock are provided at the campground. There are also a few canoes and rowboats for rent. Hiking trails explore the streams and forests in the area, including land across the border in Maine. Milton is famous as the New Hampshire Farm Museum site, located off the Spaulding Turnpike at Exit 18. This National Historic Site offers guided tours of connected farm buildings, blacksmith and cobbler shops, a country store, animals, and a nature trail. On weekends, visitors can learn old-time farm skills and crafts at demonstrations and workshops.

Campsites, facilities: There are 179 sites for tents and RVs, 46 with full hookups and 133 with water and electric hookups. Each site has a picnic table and fire ring. Air conditioner and heater use is allowed. A dump station, restrooms, hot showers, a recreation hall, sports field, and playground are provided. A camp store sells LP gas, RV supplies, ice, and firewood. Courts for basketball, shuffleboard, badminton, volleyball, and horseshoes are lo-

cated on the property. Leashed pets are permitted.

Reservations, fees: Reservations are recommended June–September. Sites are $30–38 a night per family.

Open: May 10–October 15.

Directions: From the Spaulding Turnpike/Highway 16 in Milton, take Exit 17 and travel east on Highway 75 for .75 mile. Take a left onto Highway 125 and head north for 3.25 miles to Townhouse Road. Turn right and head east for one mile to the campground entrance on the left.

Contact: Mi-Te-Jo Campground, P.O. Box 830, Milton, NH 03851, 603/652-9022, website: www. mi-te-jo.com.

30 GRAND VIEW CAMPING AREA

Rating: 7

On Baxter Lake west of Rochester

Wooded sites are set on the Baxter Lake shore, looking out across the water and to the mountains in the distance. Baxter is a warm-water habitat that supports several bass species as well as pickerel and perch. Boats are available for rent at the campground. The prominent feature on the western horizon is Blue Job Mountain. An easy hike starts at First Crown Point Road and ascends the 1,356-foot peak, where a fire tower on top affords ocean views on a clear day.

Campsites, facilities: There are 150 sites for tents and RVs, most with water and electric hookups. Each site has a picnic table and fire ring. A dump station, restrooms, hot showers, a recreation hall, and a playground are provided. A camp store sells ice and firewood. Leashed pets are permitted.

Reservations, fees: Reservations are accepted. Sites are $25–$28 a night per family. Seasonal and yearly rates are available.

Open: Mid-May–October 1.

Directions: From the Spaulding Turnpike/Highway 16 in Rochester, take Exit 14 to Ten Rod

Road and travel south for 1.5 miles. Take a right on Four Rod Road; the campground entrance is .5 mile ahead on the west side of the road. **Contact:** Grand View Camping Area, 51 Four Rod Road, Rochester, NH 03867, 603/332-1263, website: www.grandviewcamping.com.

31 CROWN POINT CAMPGROUND

🏊 🚣 🚐 🐕 🚵 🚙 ⛺

Rating: 6

West of the Rochester Reservoir

A clear 6.5-acre pond on Berrys Brook is the activity center for campers at Crown Point. The privately owned pond is flanked by woods and grass, and anglers may pull fish from its waters without a license. While away a few hours on the pond by paddling or pedaling in a rental boat, or join in a beach volleyball game. At night, campers gather for dances, bonfires, and barbecues. There's a snack bar on the premises, and breakfast is available on weekends. If you're looking for a low-key family camping experience in undeveloped countryside, this is a good choice.

Campsites, facilities: There are 135 sites for tents and RVs, 100 with full hookups and 35 with water and electric hookups. Each site has a picnic table and fire ring. A dump station, restrooms, hot showers, a recreation hall, and a playground are provided. A camp store sells LP gas, limited groceries, ice, and firewood. Courts for badminton, volleyball, and horseshoes are located on the property. Leashed pets are permitted.

Reservations, fees: Reservations are recommended and require a nonrefundable deposit. Sites are $28-32 a night. Seasonal rates are available.

Open: Mid-May–mid-October.

Directions: From the junction of the Spaulding Turnpike/Highway 16 and Ten Rod Road in Rochester at Exit 14, travel .2 mile south on Highway 11, .2 mile west on Twombley Street, and then four miles southwest on Highway 202A. Take a right onto First Crown Point Road and the campground entrance will be just ahead on the left.

Contact: Crown Point Campground, 44 First Crown Point Road, Rochester, NH 03867, 603/332-0405, website: www.crownpointcampground.com.

32 CASCADE PARK CAMPING AREA

🏊 🚣 🚐 🐕 🚙 ⛺

Rating: 5

Just west of Chichester

These shaded sites are located near the Soucook River shore, where anglers can try for rainbow, brook, and brown trout. A swimming hole at the campground has a small sandy beach. Many campers at Cascade Park are race fans; a few miles north of here in Loudon, the New Hampshire International Speedway revs up crowds all summer long with an international lineup of auto and motorcycle races.

Campsites, facilities: There are 191 sites for tents and RVs, all with full hookups. Each site has a picnic table and fire ring. A dump station, restrooms, hot showers, a recreation hall, dance pavilion, and playground are provided. A camp store carries LP gas, ice, and firewood. Courts for shuffleboard and horseshoes are located on the property. Leashed pets are permitted.

Reservations, fees: Reservations are accepted. Sites start at $25 a night per family. Seasonal rates are available.

Open: Mid-May–October 1.

Directions: From I-93 at Concord, take Exit 14 and travel east on Highway 393/U.S. 4 to Highway 106. Turn left and continue north for two miles. The campground is just ahead on the right side of the road.

Contact: Cascade Park Camping Area, 379 Highway 106, South Loudon, NH 03301, 603/224-3212, website: www.cascadecampground.com.

33 HILLCREST CAMPGROUND

🏊 🎣 �"⃗ 🏘 🐕 🚐 ⛺

Rating: 5

West of Epsom Four Corners

Hillcrest Campground is located right off U.S. 4, a busy thruway from central New Hampshire to the seacoast. Trees buffer the campsites from much of the noise, but campers have to contend with traffic, especially on weekends, once they leave the campground. The swimming pool, some rental cabins, and group areas are close to the highway, but sites 58–68 and those in the 20s and low 30s are set far back from the road near Marsh Brook and Great Meadow Pond. Canoes, rowboats, and paddleboats are available for rent at the campground for people who want to explore the quiet pond waters. Every weekend the campground organizes activities with a family theme such as Christmas in July or Lobster Boil Weekend. Concord, the state capital, is a short drive west of here and has several educational family attractions including the Christa McAuliffe Planetarium and the Canterbury Shaker Village. The latter is a living history museum just north of Concord and features 24 historic buildings built by Shakers. Programs, events, and meals help visitors interpret Shaker culture. Candlelight dinners and tours are also offered.

Campsites, facilities: There are 120 sites for tents and RVs, 70 with full hookups. Each site has a picnic table and fire ring. Air conditioner and heater use is allowed. Cable TV and phone hookups are available. A dump station, laundry facilities, restrooms, hot showers, a recreation hall, pavilion, pool, and a playground are provided. A small grocery store carries RV supplies, LP gas, ice, and firewood. There's a traffic control gate at the entrance. Courts for volleyball, basketball, badminton, shuffleboard, and horseshoes are located on the property. Leashed pets are permitted.

Reservations, fees: Prepaid deposits are required for all reservations. Sites are $30–35 a night. There are surcharges for guests, air conditioners, and heaters. Weekly, monthly, and seasonal rates are available.

Open: May 1–October 15.

Directions: From I-93 at Concord, take Exit 14 and travel east on Highway 393/U.S. 4 for six miles to the campground entrance on the left (north) side of the road.

Contact: Hillcrest Campground, 78 Dover Road, Chichester, NH 03234, 603/798-5124; for information and reservations from outside of New Hampshire, call 800/338-9488, website: www.ucampnh.com/hillcrest.

34 CIRCLE 9 RANCH CAMPGROUND

🏇 🏊 🎣 ❄ 🏘 🐕 🚲 🚐 ⛺

Rating: 4

At Epsom Four Corners

If you're a country music fan, Circle 9 Ranch Campground just might be your kind of place. Choose from a mix of open, grassy, and shaded campsites, all located behind a full-scale dance hall. The dance hall is open to the public for country two-stepping every weekend, and guests should bring their own beverages. Located off a main thruway to the White Mountains, the campground is near a commercial district, but a pine tree grove does provide something of a buffer zone to shield visitors from the traffic noise. Year-round organized activities will appeal to campers of every age group; there are live bands, dancing, dinners, and ice skating in winter. Young anglers are welcome to try their luck on two small campground ponds where they can drop in a fishing line.

Campsites, facilities: There are 145 sites for tents and RVs, 60 with full hookups and 85 with water and electric hookups. Each site comes with a picnic table and fire ring. Air conditioner and heater use is allowed. A dump station, laundry facilities, restrooms, metered hot showers, a recreation hall, dance hall, swimming pool, and a playground are provided. A camp store carries

LP gas, ice, and firewood. Courts for volleyball, basketball, and horseshoes are located on the property. Leashed pets are permitted.
Reservations, fees: Reservations are recommended. Sites are $32–54 a night. Weekly, monthly, and seasonal rates are available.
Open: Year-round.
Directions: From I-93 at Concord, take Exit 14 and travel east on Highway 393/U.S. 4. At the Epsom traffic circle, head south on Highway 28 for .25 mile. The campground will be on the right (west) side of the road on Windymere Drive.
Contact: Circle 9 Ranch Campground, Windymere Drive, P.O. Box 282, Epsom, NH 03234, 603/736-9656, website: www.circle9ranch.com.

35 LAZY RIVER CAMPGROUND

🏊 🎣 🛶 🐕 🚴 🚐 ⛺

Rating: 6

North of Highway 9 in Epsom

Piney woods surround both shaded and open sites, which are scattered along the banks of the Suncook River. Canoeists can explore the river and its many tributaries in search of brook, brown, and rainbow trout. Many seasonal and overnight campers are drawn to Lazy River Campground for its proximity to the New Hampshire International Speedway about 12 miles north in Loudon. For hiking and biking trails, head south to Bear Brook State Park (see listing in this chapter); although the park's day-use areas can get quite crowded in summer, the paths that weave through hilly forests, bogs, and marshlands are little used.
Campsites, facilities: There are 112 sites for tents and RVs, 45 with full hookups and 67 with water and electric hookups. Each site has a picnic table, fireplace, and grill. Air conditioners are allowed, but electric heaters are prohibited. A dump station, restrooms, hot showers, a recreation hall, pool tables, two playgrounds, and a swimming pool are provided. Courts for volleyball, badminton, and horseshoes are located on the property. The campground sells ice and firewood. Leashed pets are permitted.

Reservations, fees: Reservations are accepted. Per family, sites are $25–30 a night. Weekly, monthly, and seasonal rates are available.
Open: May 1–October 1.
Directions: From I-93 at Concord, take Exit 14 and travel east on Highway 393/U.S. 4. At the Epsom traffic circle, head north on Highway 28 for two miles to Depot Road. Take a right and head east for .5 mile to the campground entrance.
Contact: The Blomstrom Family, Lazy River Campground, RR 2, Box 173, Epsom, NH 03234, 603/798-5900 or 800/972-4873.

36 EPSOM VALLEY CAMPGROUND

🏊 🎣 🛶 🐕 🚴 🚐 ⛺

Rating: 6

North of Highway 9 in Epsom

Lofty pine trees shade these grassy sites lining the bank of the Suncook River. Canoeists can explore the river and its numerous tributaries in this valley south of the Lakes Region. Brook, brown, and rainbow trout are fair game for anglers in these waters. Boat rentals and a beach are available at the campground. Among the many seasonal campers at Epsom Valley are loyal race fans: the New Hampshire International Speedway is about 12 miles north of here in Loudon. Bear Brook State Park to the south offers a trail network for mountain biking, horseback riding, and hiking across hilly forests, bogs, and marshland.
Campsites, facilities: There are 65 sites for tents and RVs, 60 with water and electric hookups. Each site has a picnic table, fire ring, and grill. Air conditioner and heater use is allowed. A dump station, restrooms, metered hot showers, a miniature golf course, and a playground are provided. Courts for basketball, volleyball, badminton, and horseshoes are located on the property. Ice and firewood are sold on-site. A gate controls traffic at the entrance. Leashed pets are permitted.
Reservations, fees: Reservations are recom-

mended in the summer. Sites are $25–27 a night per family. Weekly, monthly, and seasonal rates are available.

Open: Memorial Day–Columbus Day.

Directions: From I-93 at Concord, take Exit 14 and travel east on Highway 393/U.S. 4. At the Epsom traffic circle, head north on Highway 28 for 1,500 feet to the campground entrance on the right side of the road.

Contact: John and Dwyna Arvanitis, Epsom Valley Campground, R.F.D. 2, Box 132, Epsom, NH 03234, 603/736-9758 in the summer, or 508/658-4396 in the winter, website: www.ucampnh/epsomvalley.

37 BLAKE'S BROOK FAMILY CAMPGROUND

Rating: 5

East of Concord

Thickly settled brookside sites are scattered among the trees at this campground. Campers can cool off in the swimming pool or head a short distance south to Bear Brook State Park to take a refreshing dip in natural water. Swimming and picnicking draw crowds to the park in the summer, and families can enjoy a host of nature programs. Boat rentals are also available. The park has an extensive trail system for mountain biking, horseback riding, and moderate hikes through bogs and marshes. Most visitors stick to the day-use areas, so even in summer you are likely to have these trails to yourself.

Campsites, facilities: There are 50 sites for tents and RVs, 33 with full hookups, 12 with water and electric hookups, and five with none. Each site has a picnic table and fire ring. Air conditioner use is allowed. A dump station, restrooms, metered hot showers, a recreation hall, swimming pool, and a playground are provided. Ice and firewood are available. Courts for volleyball, basketball, and horseshoes as well as a small game room are located on the property. Leashed pets are permitted.

Reservations, fees: A 50 percent deposit is required for all reservations. Sites are $28 a night per family. There are surcharges for guests and air conditioners. Weekly, monthly, and seasonal rates are available.

Open: May 1–mid-October.

Directions: From I-93 at Concord, take Exit 14 and drive east on Highway 393/U.S. 4 to the Epsom traffic circle. Travel halfway around the circle, staying on U.S. 4/202 east. Turn right at the campground sign two miles east of the circle. Continue south for 1.5 miles and then head west for another .25 mile, following signs to the campground entrance.

Contact: Blake's Brook Family Campground, 76 Mountain Road, Epsom, NH 03234, 603/736-4793, website: www.blakesbrook.com.

38 AYERS LAKE FARM CAMPGROUND

Rating: 5

Southwest of Rochester on Ayers Lake

Fifteen acres of forest, field, and shoreline envelop these sites set in a pine tree grove near and next to Ayers Lake. Anglers can pull perch, horned pout, and pickerel from the pond if they have a New Hampshire license. To get out on the lake, rent a canoe at the campground or launch your own; a public boat ramp is available just to the south of the campground. Many sites are right beside the water, and four "island" sites are found on a private wooded peninsula. A rambling New England farmhouse holds the campground headquarters. The Nippo Lake Golf Course, located a bit farther down U.S. 202, has nine holes for casual chippers.

Campsites, facilities: There are 50 sites for tents and RVs up to 32 feet long, 44 with water and electric hookups. Each site has a picnic table and fire ring. A dump station, restrooms, hot showers, and a playground are provided. Ice and firewood are available. Leashed pets are permitted.

Reservations, fees: Reservations are accepted.

Sites are $32–37 a night per family. Seasonal rates are available.

Open: Late May–late September.

Directions: From the junction of U.S. 202 and the Spaulding Turnpike/Highway 16 in Rochester, travel five miles southwest on U.S. 202 to the campground entrance.

Contact: Ayers Lake Farm Campground, U.S. 202, Barrington, NH 03825, 603/332-5940, website: www.ucampnh.com/ayerslake.

39 BEAR BROOK STATE PARK

Rating: 7

Southeast of Concord

Wooded campsites at Bear Brook State Park are located on Beaver Pond. The park encompasses 10,000 acres and is traversed by an extensive multiuse trail system open to hikers, mountain bikers, and horseback riders. These paths access summits, bogs, marshlands, and ponds. Visitors can rent canoes at Beaver and Catamount Ponds, and rowboats are also available at the campground. The New Hampshire Department of Fish and Game maintains two public archery ranges at Bear Brook, the only two in the state. A museum complex at the park includes a 4-H Nature Center with exhibits on the park's natural history, the New Hampshire Antique Snowmobile Museum, a Museum of Family Camping, and a Civilian Conservation Corps Museum; all are housed in historic CCC buildings.

Campsites, facilities: There are 93 sites for tents and RVs, all without hookups. Each site has a picnic table and fire ring. A dump station, laundry facilities, restrooms, and hot showers are provided. Some facilities are wheelchair accessible. Within the park you will find picnic areas, ball fields, and play areas. A small grocery store carries ice and firewood. Leashed pets are permitted.

Reservations, fees: For reservations, contact the New Hampshire State Parks Camping Reservation Center, P.O. Box 1856, Concord, NH 03302-1856, 603/271-3628, website: www.nh-

parks.state.nh.us. Sites are $15 a night per family. Extra adults pay $7 each.

Open: Mid-May–mid-October.

Directions: From the northern junction of Highway 28 and U.S. 3 in Suncook, travel eight miles northeast on Highway 28 to the campground entrance.

Contact: Bear Brook State Park, R.F.D. 1, Box 507, Allenstown, NH 03275, 603/845-9869; New Hampshire Division of Parks and Recreation, 603/271-3628.

40 BARRINGTON SHORES CAMPING AREA

Rating: 6

On Swains Lake in Barrington

Gentle hills covered with a white pine, oak, and maple tree mixed forest above Swains Lake are terraced with roomy tent and RV campsites at Barrington Shores Camping Area. Clubs and organizations can stay in a group area with hookups. Three-mile Swains Lake is a haven for powerboaters; slips, boat rentals, and a boat launch are provided at the campground. There are two beaches for swimming and sunbathing, and great bass fishing can be found in the lake's many shadowy nooks and crannies. Ocean beaches and coastal attractions are about a half-hour drive to the east.

Campsites, facilities: There are 145 sites for tents and RVs. Each site has a picnic table and fire ring. Air conditioner and heater use is allowed. A dump station, laundry facilities, restrooms, hot showers, a recreation hall, boat rentals, and a playground are provided. A camp store sells LP gas, ice, and firewood. Courts for volleyball, basketball, badminton, and horseshoes are located on the property. Leashed pets are permitted.

Reservations, fees: For reservations during holiday weekends and for stays of fewer than three days, full prepayment is required. Longer stays require a 50 percent deposit. Sites are $34–40 a night per family.

Open: Mid-May–late September.

Directions: From the intersection of U.S. 4 and Highway 125 in Lee, travel three miles north on Highway 125, turn left on Beauty Hill Road, and go a mile west. Take another left onto Hall Road and travel a mile south to the campground.

Contact: Barrington Shores Camping Area, 70 Hall Road, Barrington, NH 03825, 603/664-9333, website: www.barringtonshores.com.

41 OLD STAGE CAMPGROUND

West of Dover

Rating: 5

The tent and RV campsites in this rural and quiet area on the Dover outskirts are wooded and offer welcome privacy. In addition to a pool, the grounds hold a small pond for fishing and swimming. A recreation director plans group activities in the summer months. The city of Dover to the east has several historical buildings along the Cocheco River and offers all manner of goods and services. Portsmouth, the hub of cultural activity on the seacoast, lies just a short drive to the east; earthy shops and eateries line that city's small streets, some of which are cobblestoned. At night those streets are filled with pub crawlers and theatergoers, and young crowds from a host of coffeehouses encroach on the sidewalks.

Campsites, facilities: There are 157 sites for tents and RVs, 81 with full hookups and 46 with water and electric hookups. Each site has a picnic table and fire ring. Air conditioner and heater use is allowed. A dump station, laundry facilities, restrooms, metered hot showers, a recreation hall, pool, sports field, and a playground are provided. A small grocery store carries RV supplies, ice, and firewood. Courts for volleyball, basketball, badminton, shuffleboard, and horseshoes are located on the property. Group sites for tents and RVs are available. Traffic is controlled by a gate at the entrance. Leashed pets are permitted.

Reservations, fees: Reservations are recom-

mended in July and August and must be accompanied by a prepaid deposit. Sites start at $28 a night per family.

Open: Memorial Day–Columbus Day.

Directions: From the Spaulding Turnpike/ Highway 16 in Dover, take Exit 8W and travel northwest on Highway 9 for approximately 1.5 miles. Turn left on Old Stage Road and continue to the campground entrance .5 mile ahead.

Contact: Old Stage Campground, 46 Old Stage Road, Dover, NH 03820, 603/742-4050.

42 FOREST GLEN CAMPGROUND

On Wheelright Pond in Lee

Rating: 5

Wheelright Pond is a fishing refuge carved into a pine forest. Warm waters support bass, white perch, pickerel, and horned pout. Campers can launch and dock their boats at the campground if they pay a surcharge and are staying for more than a few days. The town of Durham to the east is home to the University of New Hampshire, where summer cultural offerings include nationally booked musical acts.

Campsites, facilities: There are 130 sites for tents and RVs with water and electric hookups. Each site has a table and fire ring. A dump station, laundry facilities, restrooms, metered hot showers, a recreation hall, and a playground are provided. LP gas, ice, and wood are sold on-site. You'll also find courts for volleyball, basketball, badminton, and horseshoes. Leashed pets are permitted.

Reservations, fees: Reservations are recommended in the summer. Sites are $26–30 a night per family. Weekly and seasonal rates are available on request.

Open: May 1–October 1.

Directions: From the center of Lee on Highway 155, travel a mile north to the campground entrance on the left.

Contact: Forest Glen Campground, P.O. Box 676, Durham, NH 03824, 603/659-3416.

43 PAWTUCKAWAY STATE PARK

🏃 🚲 🏊 🛶 ⛵ ⛺

Rating: 7

On Pawtuckaway Lake in Raymond

Most of the woodsy, private sites at this state park are set along the shores of Pawtuckaway Lake. Campers may not swim at their sites, but there is a beach area for those who want to jump in. Canoes and paddleboats are available for rent at the campground, and a boat launch is provided; motors are permitted. Pawtuckaway Lake has many small islands and houses smallmouth and largemouth bass, so fishing enthusiasts should bring their gear. Mountain bikers and hikers can explore the 6,500-acre state park on several loop trails. The Pawtuckaway Mountains, especially the south peak which has a fire tower, offer sweeping views over this otherwise flat part of the state.

Campsites, facilities: There are 193 tent sites at three locations. Each site has a picnic table and fire ring. Restrooms, metered hot showers, and boat rentals are provided. Within the park you will find picnic areas, ball fields, and play areas. A small grocery store carries ice and firewood. No pets are allowed.

Reservations, fees: For reservations, contact the New Hampshire State Parks Camping Reservation Center, P.O. Box 1856, Concord, NH 03302-1856, 603/271-3628, website: www.nhparks.state.nh.us. Sites are $16–22 per night. Campers 65 and older are offered a $2 discount per site from Sunday–Thursday.

Open: Mid-May–mid-October.

Directions: From the junction of Highways 101 and 156 in Raymond, travel 3.5 miles north on Highway 156 to Mountain Road. Turn left and follow the road into the park.

Contact: Pawtuckaway State Park, 128 Mountain Road, Nottingham, NH 03290, 603/895-3031; New Hampshire Division of Parks and Recreation, 603/271-3628, website: www.nhparks.state.nh.us.

44 WADLEIGH FALLS CAMPGROUND

🏊 🔥 🏠 🐾 🚐 ⛺

Rating: 5

West of the town of Newmarket

Wadleigh Falls features a primitive tenting area and tent sites set beside the river in addition to many fully equipped RV sites. This is a fisherman's dream campground with 2,200 feet of shoreline along the Lamprey River where you can fish for trout, bass, and pickerel. The river follows a roundabout course but eventually veers southeast and enters Great Bay. For paddlers, there is an easy canoe route that starts at Newmarket and ends on the bay, passing through urban and undeveloped areas on the shallow estuary.

Campsites, facilities: There are 117 sites for tents and RVs. Each site has a picnic table and fire ring. A dump station, laundry facilities, restrooms, metered hot showers, a recreation hall, sports field, pool, and playground are provided. A camp store carries LP gas, ice, and firewood. Courts for volleyball and badminton and horseshoe pits are located on the property. Leashed pets are permitted.

Reservations, fees: Reservations are recommended. Sites are $25–30 a night per family. Weekly, monthly, and seasonal rates are provided on request.

Open: May 15–October 15.

Directions: From the junction of Highways 125 and 152 in South Lee, travel just under two miles east on Highway 152. At the campground road, take a right and head south to the campground entrance less than .25 mile ahead.

Contact: Wadleigh Falls Campground, 16 Campground Road, Lee, NH 03824, 603/659-1751, website: www.wadleighfalls.com.

45 FERNDALE ACRES CAMPGROUND

Rating: 5

Near the center of Lee

A pine tree canopy provides cooling shade at these campsites found here in the boondocks of Lee. The Little River flows right by the retreat, offering trout fishing and easy flows for paddling lazily in a canoe. Swimmers can cool off in the campground pool or in the river itself. Just to the east in Durham, the Wiswall Dam and Packers Falls flank a pretty swimming hole complete with sunbathing rocks. For four-wheeled entertainment, take the entire family to the New England Speedway to the south in Epping. Special events there include the Funny Car Nationals and Corvette Day. Campers can also find fun closer to home on the weekends when the campground hosts organized activities.

Campsites, facilities: There are 150 sites for tents and RVs. Each site has a picnic table and fire ring. A dump station, laundry facilities, restrooms, hot showers, a recreation hall, pool, and a playground are provided. A small grocery store carries LP gas, ice, and firewood. Courts for volleyball, basketball, badminton, and horseshoes are located on the property. Leashed pets are permitted.

Reservations, fees: Reservations require a non-refundable deposit. Sites start at $25 a night for two people. Weekly, monthly, and seasonal rates are available on request.

Open: May 15–September 15.

Directions: From the intersection of U.S. 4 and Highway 155 north of Lee, travel 2.5 miles south on Highway 155, turn left on Wednesday Hill Road, and go 1.5 miles east of the center of town. Turn right on the campground road at the sign and continue south for .75 mile to the campground.

Contact: Ferndale Acres Campground, 132 Wednesday Hill Road, Lee, NH 03824, 603/659-5082, website: www.ferndaleacres.com.

46 PINE ACRES FAMILY CAMPGROUND

Rating: 6

On Dead Pond in Raymond

Tall pine trees cloak this large campground in cool shade beside Dead Pond, which is anything but what its name suggests. Action-oriented campers can choose from a long list of organized activities, from mountain bike rides and arm-wrestling tournaments, to candlelight parades and hog-calling competitions. Most folks take to the water for bass fishing, swimming, or boating (motorized cruising up to 7 mph is allowed). There are separate docks for fishing and boating, as well as canoes, rowboats, and paddleboats for rent. A 19-hole miniature golf course is located on the property, and several miles of old railroad beds near the campground double as mountain bike trails; yes, Pine Acres also rents bikes. A giant water slide was recently added to the recreational lineup. About half the sites are occupied by seasonal campers, and a separate area near a small pond is reserved for tents. Adult-oriented events include live bands and DJ dancing.

Campsites, facilities: There are 382 sites for tents and RVs, 330 with water and electric hookups and 20 with none. Each site has a picnic table and fire ring. A dump station, laundry facilities, restrooms, metered hot showers, a recreation hall, pavilion, pool, sports field, and playground are provided. A grocery store carries LP gas, ice, and firewood. Courts for volleyball, badminton, and horseshoes are located on the property. There is a guard at the front gate. Leashed pets are permitted.

Reservations, fees: Reservations are recommended July 1–Labor Day. Holiday reservations must be paid in full within a week of making a reservation. Deposits are required for all other reservations, and there is a $10 service charge for cancellations with 30 days' notice. Sites are $34–46 a night. Seasonal rates are available.

Open: April 15–November 15.

Directions: From Highway 101 in Raymond, take Exit 5. Head south on Highway 107 for .75 mile to the campground entrance on the left.

Contact: Pine Acres Family Campground, 74 Freetown Road, Raymond, NH 03077, 603/895-2519, website: www.pineacresrecreation.com.

47 THREE PONDS CAMPGROUND

🧍🏊⛵🎣🚤🐕🚣🚐⛺

Rating: 7

South of Epping

Acres of green lawns surround the three small, clear ponds here. Gravel roads lead to roomy sites, some of which have shade trees. The largest pond offers a swimming beach and is stocked with largemouth bass. One of the smaller ponds is also open to fishing. Boats are available for rent at the campground. Campers can take part in bonfires, tugs-of-war, and bocce ball tournaments, relax in the golf-course-like landscape, or explore the surrounding countryside on nature trails.

Campsites, facilities: There are 135 sites for tents and RVs with full hookups. Each site has a picnic table and fire ring. A dump station, laundry facilities, restrooms, hot showers, a pavilion, recreation hall, gazebo, ball field, and playground are provided. A camp store carries ice cream, ice, and firewood. Courts for volleyball, bocce ball, basketball, badminton, and horseshoes are located on the property. Leashed pets are permitted.

Reservations, fees: Reservations are accepted. Sites start at $27 a night for a family of four. Seasonal rates are provided on request.

Open: May 15–October 15.

Directions: From Exeter, travel five miles west on Highway 101. At the Rockingham County Complex sign, turn left onto North Road. The campground entrance will be just ahead on the right.

Contact: Three Ponds Campground, 146 North Road, Brentwood, NH 03833, 603/679-5350, website: www.3pondscampground.com.

48 GREAT BAY CAMPING

🏊🎣⛵🎣🐕🚣🚐⛺

Rating: 5

Near Great Bay in Newfields

Tall oaks and pines shade these sites located either right beside or near the Squamscott River. A special area has been set aside for seasonal campers, and natural tent sites are nearer to the water. Bluefish and striped bass are among the tasty saltwater game fish that thrive in the Squamscott, and the tidal flats at the campground are prime for oyster digging. Campers have use of a boat launch and dock on the property. One of the best methods of exploring the river and Great Bay is by kayak. You encounter protected lands, large marinas, and, finally, the open ocean. The Newfields town center is postcard perfect with its white clapboard church and stone bridge, but you have to go into Exeter to obtain most goods and services.

Campsites, facilities: There are 105 sites for tents and RVs, 69 with full hookups, 18 with water and electric hookups, and 28 with none. Each site has a picnic table and fire ring. Air conditioner and heater use is allowed. A dump station, laundry facilities, restrooms, metered hot showers, a recreation hall, pool, pavilion, and playground are provided. A convenience store carries LP gas, gasoline, groceries, ice, and firewood. Also on the property are courts for volleyball, basketball, badminton, and horseshoes. One leashed pet per site is allowed.

Reservations, fees: Reservations are accepted. Per family, rates start at $25 a night for tent sites and $30 a night for sites with full hookups.

Open: May 15–October 15.

Directions: From I-95 at Exit 2 in Hampton, travel 7.5 miles west on Highway 101. At the intersection with Highway 108, exit and travel north on Highway 108 for four miles. The campground driveway is directly behind the Citgo gas station.

Contact: Great Bay Camping, P.O. Box 331, Newfields, NH 03856, 603/778-0226, website: www.greatbaycamping.com.

49 CALEF LAKE CAMPING AREA

🚶 🚲 🏊 🛶 � 🏕 🚐 ⛺

Rating: 7

East of Massabesic Lake in Auburn

Primarily occupied by seasonal campers, the sites at Calef Lake are set in thick woods near and on a privately owned lake. Because the lake belongs to the campground, you are welcome to fish without a license. Canoes, paddleboats, and rowboats may be rented on-site; only electric motors are allowed on the water. Wildlife flourishes in these quiet environs, so you see everything from small mammals to songbirds. Beavers have built lodges on another small pond on the property. Several miles of old logging roads are a good pick for short hikes and mountain bike rides.

Campsites, facilities: There are 130 sites for tents and RVs up to 29 feet long, 121 with water and electric hookups. Each site has a picnic table, fire ring, and grill. A dump station, laundry facilities, restrooms, metered hot showers, and a pavilion are provided. A small camp store carries LP gas, ice, and firewood. Courts for basketball, badminton, volleyball, and horseshoes are located on the property. Leashed pets are permitted.

Reservations, fees: Reservations are recommended. Sites are $24–28 a night per family. Weekly and seasonal rates are available.

Open: May–October.

Directions: From the junction of Bypass Highway 28 and Highway 121 near Auburn, travel 5.5 miles south on Highway 121. The campground is on the left (east) side of the road.

Contact: Calef Lake Camping Area, 593 Chester Road (Route 121), Auburn, NH 03032, 603/483-8282.

50 SILVER SANDS CAMPGROUND

🏊 🛶 🚐 🏕 � 🚐 ⛺

Rating: 6

On North Pond east of Derry

North Pond is a privately owned bass pond on the grounds at Silver Sands, so campers can hook their dinner without having to obtain a license. Most of the clientele are seasonal family campers from the region who retreat to the pond's sandy beach on hot weekends. Sites are both open and wooded, and all are close to the water. Whether paddling the calm surface waters or gathering for a Silver Sands barbecue, campers here kick back in the company of tall trees—and little else—for miles around.

Campsites, facilities: There are 100 sites for tents and RVs, 50 with full hookups, 20 with water and electric hookups, and 30 with none. Each site has a picnic table and fire ring. A dump station, laundry facilities, restrooms, metered hot showers, a recreation hall, pavilion, pool, and playground are provided. A camp store carries LP gas, ice, and firewood. Courts for volleyball, basketball, badminton, and horseshoes, as well as a ball field are located on the property. Leashed pets are permitted.

Reservations, fees: Reservations are recommended. Sites start at $22 a night.

Open: May 1–October 1.

Directions: From I-93 in Derry, take Exit 4 and travel 10 miles east on Highway 102 to North Pond Road. The campground entrance is just ahead.

Contact: Silver Sands Campground, 603 Raymond Road, Chester, NH 03036, 603/887-3638.

51 HIDDEN VALLEY RV AND GOLF PARK

🚶 🏊 🛶 🚐 🏕 � 🚐 ⛺

Rating: 7

Northeast of Derry

Golfers will appreciate these RV sites set beside a pond and bordering a nine-hole par-three golf course. Rolling woods on a country lane provide the scenery. A beach is provided for campers, and the pond is open to fishing and boating—but only electric motors are allowed. Church services are offered on the premises every Sunday. Robert Frost fans should pay a visit to the poet's farm just east of the campground in Derry Village. This simple, white clapboard two-story house was Frost's home from 1900–1909. Guides conduct tours in season, but you can also head out on your own on the nature-poetry interpretive trail through fields and woodlands and get a sense of Frost's rural muse.

Campsites, facilities: There are 280 sites for tents and RVs, 250 with full hookups, 10 with water and electric hookups, and 20 with none. Each site has a picnic table and fire ring. Air conditioner and heater use is allowed. A dump station, laundry facilities, restrooms, metered hot showers, a recreation hall, game room, and playground are provided. A camp store carries LP gas, RV supplies, ice, and firewood. Courts for volleyball, basketball, badminton, shuffleboard, and horseshoes are located on the property. The entrance has a traffic control gate. Leashed pets are permitted.

Reservations, fees: Reservations are accepted. Sites are $34 a night.

Open: May 1–October 15.

Directions: From I-93 in Derry, take Exit 4 and travel two miles east on Highway 102. Continue east for 4.5 miles on East Derry Road. Turn left on Damren Road and head north for a mile.

Contact: Hidden Valley RV and Golf Park, 81 Damren Road, Derry, NH 03038, 603/887-3736 in the summer, or 904/423-3170 in the winter, website: www.ucampnh.com/hiddenvalley.

52 EXETER RIVER CAMPING AREA

🏊 ⛵ ✖ 🦌 🎣 🚐 ⛺

Rating: 6

Near Fremont Station

Near the origin of the Exeter River, campers can vie for brown, brook, and rainbow trout from these wooded sites set along the riverbank. The New Hampshire seacoast is about a 30-minute drive to the east.

Campsites, facilities: There are 50 sites for tents and RVs, some with hookups. Each site has a table and fire ring. A dump station, restrooms, hot showers, a recreation hall, and playground are provided. Ice and firewood are sold onsite. Leashed pets are permitted.

Reservations, fees: Reservations are recommended. Sites start at $20–22 a night per family. Weekly, monthly, and seasonal rates are available on request.

Open: May 15–October 1.

Directions: From the northern junction of Highways 111A and 107 in Fremont, travel south on Highway 111A for a mile to the campground entrance on the right (west) side of the road at the sign for Clough Road.

Contact: Exeter River Camping Area, 13 South Road, Fremont, NH 03044, 603/895-3448.

53 THE GREEN GATE CAMPING AREA

🏊 ⛵ ✖ 🦌 🚐 ⛺

Rating: 6

On the Exeter River

Here's another family campground on one of the region's major rivers, the Exeter. Sites, many of which are occupied by seasonal campers, are well shaded. Swimmers can choose from taking a dip in the river or in the swimming pool. You can cast a line for trout right from the campground. For cross-country running trails or short mountain bike rides, head north on Highway 108 for about a mile to Phillips Exeter Academy. Take Gilman Street to the school's stadium; behind the facility are miles of dirt roads and trails along the river.

Campsites, facilities: There are 118 sites for tents and RVs, 96 with full hookups and 22 with water and electric hookups. Each site has a picnic table and fire ring. A dump station, laundry facilities, restrooms, hot showers, a recreation hall, pool, canoe rentals, and a playground are provided. A camp store carries ice and firewood. Courts for volleyball, badminton, shuffleboard, and horseshoes are located on the property. No pets are allowed.

Reservations, fees: Nonrefundable deposits are required for all reservations. Sites start at $27.50 a night per family. Seasonal rates are provided on request.

Open: May 1–October 1.

Directions: From the junction of Highways 111 and 108 in Exeter, travel 1.5 miles south on Highway 108 to the campground entrance on the right (west) side of the road.

Contact: The Green Gate Camping Area, P.O. Box 185, Exeter, NH 03833, 603/772-2100, website: www.ucampnh/greengate.

54 EXETER ELMS CAMPGROUND

Rating: 6

On the Exeter River

Family fun and big wooded sites along the Exeter River put the Elms in high demand by both seasonal and vacation campers. If you are at one of the many waterfront sites, you can pull up your canoe or rowboat right on shore. A recreation director coordinates dances, live entertainment, tournaments, canoe races, and puppet shows as part of a full activities schedule. Other amenities include a wide-screen TV in the clubhouse, an insect control system, and a Ping-Pong table. No motors are allowed on the river here, but paddling is the best way to explore the Exeter anyway. For a classic excursion, put in your canoe below the bridge in town, where public parking is available. Paddle to the Squamscott River and head out toward Great Bay, a largely undeveloped, shallow estuary. Be sure to check the tide charts lest you risk getting beached on a mudflat.

Campsites, facilities: There are 200 sites for tents and RVs, 81 with full hookups, 52 with water and electric hookups, and 67 with none. Each site has a picnic table and fire ring. Air conditioner and

heater use is allowed. A dump station, laundry facilities, restrooms, hot showers, a recreation hall, pavilion, pool, boat rentals, and a playground are provided. A camp store carries RV supplies, ice, and firewood. Courts for volleyball, basketball, badminton, shuffleboard, and horseshoes are located on the property. There's also a security guard on duty. Leashed pets are permitted.

Reservations, fees: Reservations are recommended, and a prepaid 50 percent deposit must accompany them. Three-day minimum stays during holiday weekends must be prepaid in full. Per family, sites range from $23 a night for tents to $36 a night for full hookups, with surcharges for dogs, preferred and waterfront sites, and visitors. Seasonal rates are available.

Open: May 15–September 15.

Directions: From the junction of Highways 111 and 108 in Exeter, travel 1.5 miles south on Highway 108 to the campground entrance on the left (east) side of the road.

Contact: Exeter Elms Campground, 188 Court Street, Exeter, NH 03833, 603/778-7631, website: www.exeterelms.com.

55 WAKEDA CAMPGROUND

Rating: 7

East of Exeter

Wakeda Campground displays a unique rustic charm—all of the buildings and picnic tables here were fashioned by the owners' hands from cathedral pines grown and milled on-site. As you enter the campground, you are greeted by a colorful totem pole and a flowerbed of annuals. A seasonal camper carved the pole, also made from a Wakeda pine. Don't worry though, plenty of trees have been left untouched to tower over the roomy campsites. The majority of sites are suitable for trailers up to 40 feet long, plus there are a few primitive sites near a beaver pond and a special tent area.

The campground was named with the Native American word *wakeda,* which means "one who hunts." If you are *wakeda,* hunting grounds are located just to the east in the Saltmarsh Wildlife Management Area. Check on state laws before you set out; possible game includes deer, otter, hare, and ducks. Ocean beaches are eight miles to the east. You can find a boat launch and 350-foot fishing pier at the state-owned Hampton Marina, next to Hampton Beach State Park on Highway 1A. Day-use fees are $4 per car, $5 for cars with boats. From the commercial pier, many boats offer deep-sea fishing excursions. Hampton Beach State Park has swimming, picnicking, and fishing facilities, as well as several miles of sandy beach. Day-use fees are $5 midweek and $8 on the weekend. In the town of Hampton Beach, a lively boardwalk features restaurants, shops, arcades, and Wednesday night fireworks in the summertime.

Location: East of Exeter; see Eastern Lakes and Seacoast map.

Campsites, facilities: There are 400 sites for tents and RVs. Each site has a picnic table, fire ring, and grill. Air conditioner and heater use is allowed. A dump station, laundry facilities, restrooms, hot showers, a recreation hall, pavilion, miniature golf course, and playground are provided. In the off-season, RVs may be stored on-site. Rental RVs are available. A small grocery store carries ice and firewood. Courts for volleyball, basketball, badminton, shuffleboard, and horseshoes are located on the property. The entrance has a guarded gatehouse. Leashed pets are permitted.

Reservations, fees: Reservations are recommended in July and August and require a nonrefundable prepaid deposit. Tent sites start at $20 a night per family, and sites with full hookups start at $28 a night per family. Seasonal rates are available.

Open: May 15–October 1.

Directions: From the junction of Highways 88 and 101 in Exeter, travel 2.6 miles south on Highway 88 to the campground.

Contact: Wakeda Campground, 294 Exeter Road, Hampton Falls, NH 03844, 603/772-5274, website: www.wakedacampground.com.

56 SHEL-AL FAMILY CAMPGROUND

Rating: 6

Near Hampton Beach

Grassy, level sites are located right off busy U.S. 1 about three miles from the seacoast. They are densely settled in a grove of young trees. Head out Highway 111 to North Hampton State Beach to enjoy a day of sun and surf. For a floral detour, take a walk through Fuller Gardens in North Hampton. One of the few remaining early 20th-century estate gardens in the country, it features award-winning annuals and 1,500 rose bushes that are usually in their grandeur in mid- to late June.

Campsites, facilities: There are 213 sites for tents and RVs up to 31 feet long, 68 with full hookups, 66 with water and electric hookups, and 66 with none. Each site has a picnic table, all but the full-hookup sites have fireplaces, and some have grills. Restrooms, metered hot showers, and a playground are provided. A small grocery store carries ice and firewood. Courts for basketball, shuffleboard, and horseshoes are located on the property. Leashed pets are permitted.

Reservations, fees: A nonrefundable deposit is required with all reservations. No one-night reservations are accepted. Sites are $28–37 a night for two people.

Open: May 15–September 15.

Directions: From the junction of Highway 111 and U.S. 1 in Hampton, travel north for .5 mile on U.S. 1 to the campground.

Contact: Shel-Al Family Campground, U.S. 1, Hampton, NH 03842, 603/964-5730, website: www.shel-al.com.

57 TIDEWATER CAMPGROUND

Rating: 6

Near Hampton Beach

Yet another RV park near the beach, Tidewater Campground puts you close to all that the seaside has to offer. Just two miles to the east is Hampton Beach State Park, a sunbather's mecca all summer long. Spread out blankets in the sand dunes or on the beach; if you prefer to fish, head south to the Hampton State Pier just before the Seabrook Bridge. Day-use fees are $4 per car, $5 for cars with boats. You can park and launch your vessel or drop a line from the 350-foot fishing pier. Many deep-sea fishing charters leave from this dock. In summer, public concerts are staged at the Hampton Seashell, a state-owned amphitheater and information center. This is also the site of fireworks displays on Wednesday nights and holidays.

Campsites, facilities: There are 200 sites for tents and RVs. Each site has a picnic table and fire ring. Air conditioner and heater use is not allowed. A dump station, restrooms, metered hot showers, a recreation hall, pool, and playground are provided. A small grocery store carries RV supplies, ice, and firewood. Basketball courts and horseshoe pits are located on the property. Traffic is controlled by a gate at the entrance. No pets are allowed.

Reservations, fees: Reservations are accepted for stays of three or more nights and must be accompanied by a nonrefundable deposit. Sites are $34 a night per family. Seasonal rates are provided on request.

Open: May 15–October 15.

Directions: From the junction of Highway 101 and U.S. 1 in Hampton, head south on U.S. 1 for .25 mile to the campground entrance on the right (west) side of the road.

Contact: Tidewater Campground, 160 Lafayette Road, Hampton, NH 03842, 603/926-5474.

58 SANBORN SHORE ACRES CAMPGROUND

Rating: 6

On Island Pond in Hampstead

Shady sites on Island Pond are primarily occupied by seasonal campers. A few spots, however, are available for overnight stays, but be

sure to call ahead to see if there's room. All campers may fish, swim, and boat in the lake, and seasonals may rent dock space for the summer. Organized activities include pizza parties, horseshoe tournaments, and dancing to tunes spun by a DJ. A snack bar and ice-cream stand operated at the campground serves three meals a day. Canobie Lake Park, the state's only major amusement park, is located just 15 minutes away by car. In winter, the frozen lake teems with ice skaters, snowmobilers, cross-country skiers, and ice fishers in search of pickerel.

Campsites, facilities: There are 140 sites for RVs, most with full hookups and a limited number of transient sites available with water and electric hookups. Tents are allowed. Each site has a picnic table and fire ring. A dump station, restrooms, hot showers, a recreation hall, game room, and playground are provided. Ice and firewood are sold on-site. Courts for volleyball, basketball, badminton, shuffleboard, and horseshoes are located on the property. Leashed pets are permitted.

Reservations, fees: Reservations are accepted. Sites start at $25 a night per family. Weekly, monthly, and seasonal rates are available.

Open: April 15–October 15, and November 15–March 15.

Directions: From I-93 near the town of Salem, take Exit 3, travel east for eight miles on Highway 111, then turn left and head two miles north on Highway 121 to the campground entrance on the left (west) side of the road.

Contact: Sanborn Shore Acres Campground, P.O. Box 626, Main Street, Hampstead, NH 03841, 603/329-5247, website: www.ucampnh/ sanbornshore.com.

59 ANGLE POND GROVE CAMPING AREA

Rating: 5

On Angle Pond in Sandown

Small wooded sites are either near or right beside Angle Pond, a developed lake set in southern New Hampshire. This warm-water habitat supports horned pout and pickerel, fair game for anglers. Private homes line the shore of the 150-acre pond, which is open to all kinds of boating. The campground has a roped-off swimming area and a sloping sandy beach, but no boat launch. If you're not a fan of tents or pets, this is the place for you, as neither are welcome at Angle Pond Grove.

Campsites, facilities: There are 140 sites for RVs, all with full hookups. Each site has a picnic table and fire ring. Air conditioner use is allowed. Laundry facilities, restrooms, metered hot showers, a recreation hall, ball field, and playground are provided. A small grocery store carries LP gas, ice, and firewood. Courts for volleyball, bocce ball, basketball, badminton, shuffleboard, and horseshoes are located on the property. A gate controls traffic at the campground entrance. No tents or pets are allowed.

Reservations, fees: A 50 percent deposit must accompany all reservations. Sites start at $24 a night for two people and top out at $38 per night for a waterfront site with a dock for your own boat. Weekly and seasonal rates are available.

Open: May 15–October 15.

Directions: From I-495 near Plaistow, take Exit 51, head north on Highway 125 for 1.5 miles, and then continue north on Highway 121A to East Hampstead. Stay on this road for another .6 mile, passing through the intersection with Highway 111. Turn left on Pillsbury Road and look for the campground just ahead.

Contact: Angle Pond Grove Camping Area, P.O. Box 173, East Hampstead, NH 03826, 603/887-4434, website: www.anglepondgrove.com.

60 SUNSET PARK CAMPGROUND

🏊 🚣 🛶 🐕 🧺 🚐 ⛺

Rating: 6

On Wash Pond in Hampstead

The roomy, shaded sites next to Wash Pond are occupied mostly by seasonal campers. For a fee, you can bring your own canoe, rowboat, or powerboat to use on the pond, and large powerboats are admitted with permission from the owners. A 400-foot swimming beach is provided. To the southwest in North Salem is an interesting natural attraction, America's Stonehenge. Considered by many the oldest stone-constructed site in North America, it can still be used to determine solar and lunar events. Ongoing research is being conducted to determine whether the structure was built by Native Americans or a migrant European population.

Campsites, facilities: There are 140 sites with water and electric hookups occupied largely by seasonal campers; five sites for tents or RVs are available for overnight stays. Each has a table and fire ring. A dump station, laundry facilities, restrooms, hot showers, a recreation hall, and a playground are provided, as are volleyball and basketball courts, a softball field, and horseshoe pits. Leashed pets are permitted.

Reservations, fees: Reservations are recommended. Sites are $26 for two people.

Open: Memorial Day–Columbus Day.

Directions: From I-93 near Salem, take Exit 3, travel east for eight miles on Highway 111, and then go a mile north on Highway 121. Turn right on Emerson Road and head .25 mile east.

Contact: Sunset Park Campground, P.O. Box 16N, 104 Emerson Road, Hampstead, NH 03841, 603/329-6941.

61 TUXBURY POND CAMPING AREA

🏊 🚣 🛶 🐕 🧺 ♿ 🚐 ⛺

Rating: 6

On Tuxbury Pond east of Kingston

Lanky pine trees shelter waterside sites at Tuxbury Pond Camping Area, which draws a mix of seasonal and vacation campers. They're all after the same thing: swimming, fishing, and quiet boating on a spring-fed pond. Some open, grassy sites are set right beside the water, and there's even a separate "adult community" park section that's child-free. Canoes and rowboats may be rented near the beach.

Campsites, facilities: There are 208 sites for tents and RVs, 149 with full hookups and 59 with water and electric hookups. Each site has a picnic table and fire ring. Air conditioner use is allowed. A dump station, laundry facilities, restrooms, metered hot showers, a recreation hall, pavilion, and playground are provided. A small grocery store carries LP gas, ice, and firewood. Courts for volleyball, basketball, badminton, shuffleboard, and horseshoes are located on the property. A traffic control gate is at the entrance, and personnel conduct night patrols. Leashed pets are permitted.

Reservations, fees: Reservations are recommended Memorial Day–Labor Day and require a nonrefundable deposit. Sites start at $25 a night for four people.

Open: Mid-May–mid-October.

Directions: From the junction of I-495 and Highway 150 in Amesbury, Massachusetts, take Exit 54 and head north on Highway 150. In .75 mile, turn left at the blinking yellow light onto Highland Street and travel northwest for .25 mile to Lions Mouth Road. Turn left again and head west a little over a mile to Newton Road. Turn right, travel north for a mile, then follow signs into the campground.

Contact: Tuxbury Pond Camping Area, 88 Whitehall Road, South Hampton, NH 03827, 603/394-7660, website: www.tuxburypondcampground.com.

62 NEW HAMPSHIRE SEACOAST CAMPGROUND

Rating: 4

A mile inland from Seabrook Beach

A mile-long bike, drive, or shuttle-bus ride on a busy road takes campers from these level, wooded sites to Seabrook Beach on the ocean. The sandy beach is open to the public, and a boat launch is located just north of the Hampton River on Highway 1A. Fish for stripers and bluefish right from the shore, or head out on the open water. Seabrook is commercially developed along the beach road, where you find some eateries and shops, but it's not as oppressive as Hampton with its honky-tonk strip, nightclubs, surf shops, and arcades. Seabrook is famous for two things: the Seabrook Nuclear Power Plant, which has sparked several decades of debate, and the Seabrook Greyhound Park on Highway 107, which features live dog races and simulcast horse races. To learn more about nuclear power and New Hampshire's seacoast, pay a visit to the Science and Nature Center at Seabrook Station. Exhibits, aquariums, self-guided trails, and a guided tour through a control room simulator are some of the educational highlights.

Campsites, facilities: There are 100 sites for tents and RVs up to 35 feet long, 80 with full hookups and 20 with none. Each site has a picnic table and fire ring. A dump station, restrooms, hot showers, a recreation hall, horseshoe pits, and a playground are provided. A camp store carries ice and firewood. There's also shuttle service between the campground and ocean beaches. Leashed pets are permitted.

Reservations, fees: Reservations are recommended and must be accompanied by a nonrefundable deposit. Sites start at $28 a night per family.

Open: May 15–September 15.

Directions: From I-95 at Exit 60 near the Massachusetts border, head east on Highway 286. At the second stoplight turn left into the campground entrance.

Contact: New Hampshire Seacoast Campground, P.O. Box 235, Seabrook, NH 03874, 603/474-9813 or 800/313-6306.

63 HAMPTON BEACH STATE RV PARK

Rating: 8

On the Atlantic Ocean near the Massachusetts border

Miles of sandy beach for saltwater fishing and swimming are directly accessible from these open sites on the Atlantic Ocean. It's a short walk, bike, or skate up to the hub of beachdom along the Hampton Beach boardwalk. Sunbathers parade the commercial strip in colorful and skimpy attire, hawkers sell fried dough and cotton candy, lights flash from pinball arcades, machines twist and pull saltwater taffy in storefront windows, and limousines deliver big-name musical acts to the Casino Ballroom, a 1,800-seat nightclub. In the summer, public concerts are staged at the seashell on various evenings, and fireworks displays light up the sky every Wednesday night and on holidays.

Campsites, facilities: There are 20 sites for RVs; only units with full hookups are allowed. A park store carries some supplies including ice. Groceries and services can be obtained in Hampton Beach. Campfires, tents, trailers, and pets are not allowed.

Reservations, fees: For reservations, contact the New Hampshire State Parks Camping Reservation Center, P.O. Box 1856, Concord, NH 03302-1856, 603/271-3628, website: www.nhparks.state.nh.us. The minimum stay is two nights, and on holiday weekends it is three nights; the maximum allowable stay is 14 days. A nonrefundable deposit is required with all reservations. Sites are $35 a night.

Open: Mid-May–mid-October.

Directions: From I-95 at Hampton, take Exit 2 and head south on Highway 101 for three miles. Take a right onto Highway 1A and then travel a mile south to the park.

Contact: Hampton Beach State RV Park, P.O. Box 606, Rye Beach, NH 03871, 603/926-8990, website: www.nhparks.state.nh.us.

64 COUNTRY SHORE CAMPING AREA

Rating: 6

On Country Pond in Kingston

This seasonal RV camping destination in the woods beside Country Pond is designed especially for boaters. You can keep your vessel at the campground dock and head out on the water to fish, water-ski, or simply explore. There's also a separate fishing dock at the water's edge. Bake Park, a wildlife and natural area on the north shore of the lake, is home to numerous species of birds and small and large mammals. For hiking or mountain biking, an old railroad grade crosses the wildlife area and then continues into some surrounding undeveloped land.

Campsites, facilities: There are 100 sites for RVs, all with full hookups. Each site has a picnic table and fire ring. A dump station, restrooms, metered hot showers, a recreation hall, and a playground are provided. Courts for volleyball, basketball, softball, badminton, shuffleboard, and horseshoes are located on the property. One leashed pet per site is allowed.

Reservations, fees: A $200 deposit must be paid by May 1 to reserve seasonal sites. Other reservations require a 50 percent deposit. Sites are $30 a night per family, plus $3 a day for guests. Per season, dock space is $100 for boats without motors and from $110–120 for powerboats. Weekly and seasonal rates are available.

Open: Memorial Day–October 1.

Directions: From the junction of Highways 125 and 111 in Kingston, travel southwest on Highway 125 for about four miles to the campground entrance on the left.

Contact: Country Shore Camping Area, P.O. Box 559, Plaistow, NH 03865, 603/642-5072, website: www.ucampnh.com/countryshore.

Vermont

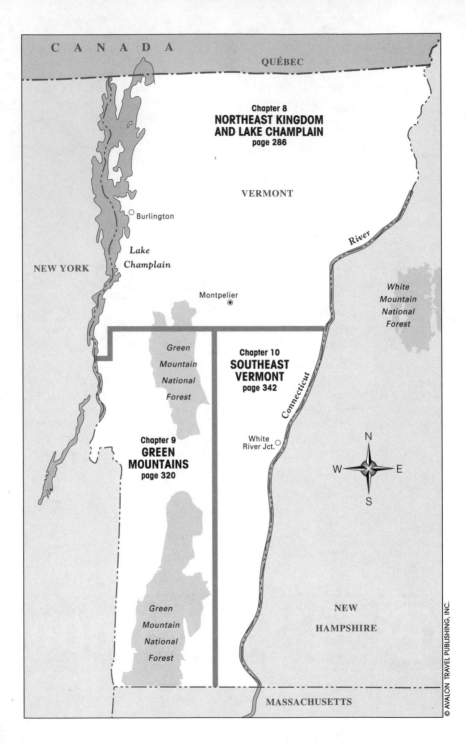

Chapter 8
**NORTHEAST KINGDOM
AND LAKE CHAMPLAIN**
page 286

CANADA

QUÉBEC

VERMONT

○ Burlington

Lake
Champlain

NEW YORK

River

White
Mountain
National
Forest

Montpelier
◉

Green
Mountain
National
Forest

Chapter 10
**SOUTHEAST
VERMONT**
page 342

Connecticut

White
River Jct. ○

Chapter 9
**GREEN
MOUNTAINS**
page 320

Green
Mountain
National
Forest

N
W   E
S

NEW
HAMPSHIRE

MASSACHUSETTS

© AVALON TRAVEL PUBLISHING, INC.

Chapter 8

© STATE OF VERMONT AGENCY OF NATURAL RESOURCES

Northeast Kingdom and Lake Champlain

Northeast Kingdom and Lake Champlain

A
pproximately half of all the campgrounds in Vermont are located
in the northern region. The plethora of clear lakes and streams
and achingly beautiful mountains make it a camper's mecca.
You'll find both wilderness campgrounds and fully equipped RV parks
to accommodate every kind of experience. The eastern half of northern Vermont is known as the Northeast Kingdom. This is the most
wild and rural part of the state, with large tracts of undeveloped land.
The woods have been heavily logged over the years, and the miles
of old dirt logging roads make this area a favorite with hunters and
fishermen.

Travelers so love exploring the rural northern reaches of the Green
Mountain range and the many small villages that dot the landscape
that it's easy to forget that northern Vermont is also home to the
state's largest city. Burlington offers urban delights, like live music
and fine dining, yet it's located on the shore of Lake Champlain, one
of the state's most prized natural treasures. You'll find a number of
public and private campgrounds along Champlain's shoreline, perfect
destinations for anglers, swimmers, and boaters of every stripe. The
other highlight of this region is its proximity to the Canadian border.
Take a day trip a few miles north and you end up in another country,
complete with a foreign language (French).

The state of Vermont operates nearly 40 campgrounds for public
use. Most are open from mid-May through early September or October, though a few offer year-round sites where noted. Reservations
are encouraged, especially in summer and during the fall foliage season in early October. You may reserve by mail or phone through the

appropriate regional office; telephone reservations are only accepted on Tuesday and Thursday from 9 A.M.–4 P.M. from the first Tuesday in January through May 14. After that, contact the park directly. Requests made through the mail must be postmarked no earlier than January 1. All parks will accept reservation requests for specific sites for stays of four or more consecutive nights. Most parks (except Branbury, Burton Island, Lake St. Catherine, and Silver Lake) will accept requests for fewer than four nights beginning May 15, but may not guarantee a specific site.

Mailed reservations are accepted in order of receipt of a completed application with full payment at the appropriate regional office or at a particular park after May 15. A nonrefundable processing fee must accompany each request. Refunds are issued in the form of credit vouchers for unused days, but a charge is assessed on all refunds.

The following regional office addresses and phone numbers should be used when reserving between the first Tuesday in January through May 14 (after that, contact the park directly). Northwest: Ranger Supervisor, 111 West Street, Essex Junction, VT 05452, 802/879-5674. Northeast: Ranger Supervisor, 324 North Main Street, Barre, VT 05641, 802/479-4280. Southwest: Ranger Supervisor, RR 2, Box 2161, Pittsford, VT 05763, 802/483-2001. Southeast: Ranger Supervisor, RR 1, Box 33, North Springfield, VT 05150, 802/ 886-2434.

For additional information or reservation applications, contact the Vermont Department of Forests, Parks, and Recreation, 103 South Main Street, Waterbury, VT 05671-0601, 802/241-3665, website: www.vtstateparks.com.

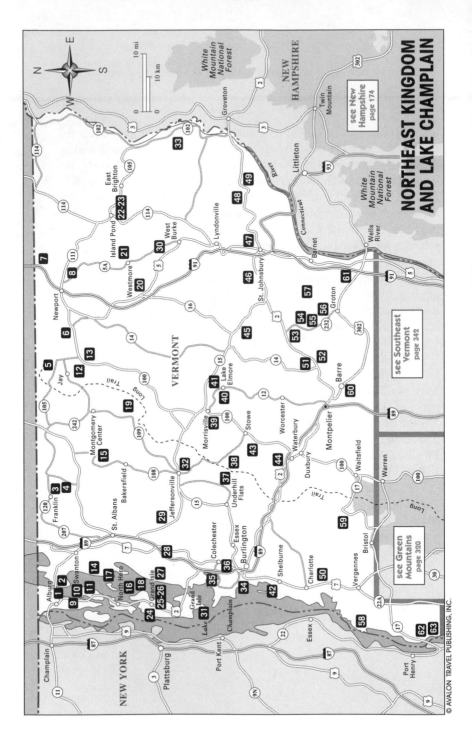

see New
Hampshire
page 174

see Southeast
Vermont
page 342

see Green
Mountains
page 320

NEW
HAMPSHIRE

NEW YORK

VERMONT

White
Mountain
National
Forest

White
Mountain
National
Forest

© AVALON TRAVEL PUBLISHING, INC.

1 ALBURG RV RESORT

Rating: 7

On Lake Champlain near the Canadian border

Shoreline is plentiful at Alburg, a well-manicured camping resort set on the northern shore of Lake Champlain. The grassy, tidy sites are tucked in the trees along the shore, and many are occupied by seasonal campers, some with large permanent trailers. A nearby boat ramp provides lake access to larger craft, but windsurfers, kayakers, and canoeists can launch right from the campground's 1,500-foot sandy beach. Alburg's protected location on Lake Champlain makes it a popular spot for all types of sailing. On a clear day, you enjoy Green Mountain views from the beach. Tent sites are available, but the soft-roof set might want to camp at less RV-centric sites in North Hero State Park (see listing in this chapter) on Grand Isle to the south. Camping in the Champlain Islands can prove to be a cultural experience, as many Canadians vacation here too.

Campsites, facilities: There are 175 sites for tents and RVs, 150 with full hookups. Each site has a picnic table and fire ring. Air conditioners are allowed, but heaters are not. RV storage, dump stations, hot showers, laundry facilities, a grocery store, playground, pool, recreation hall, sports courts, an athletic field, and horseshoe pits are provided. RV supplies, an RV sales office, LP gas, ice, and firewood are available. Leashed pets are permitted.

Reservations, fees: Reservations are recommended July 1–Labor Day. Sites start at $24 a night for two people, with surcharges for additional campers and services. Weekly, monthly, and seasonal rates are available.

Open: May 1–October 1.

Directions: From the junction of U.S. 2 and Highway 78 in Alburg Center, travel east for two miles on Highway 78. Turn right and drive .5 mile south on Blue Rock Road.

Contact: Alburg RV Resort, P.O. Box 50,.Alburg, VT 05440, 802/796-3733.

2 LAKEWOOD CAMPGROUND

Rating: 6

On Lake Champlain in Swanton

Yet another RV park in the heart of Lake Champlain country, this one is landscaped with perennials and hardwood trees—with at least one tree per site to provide campers with cooling shade. Paved roads lead through a grid of pull-through sites near the lakeshore; only Tabor Road comes between the campground and the lake. For water lovers, there's a swimming pool with a water slide and a lakeside boat dock and swimming beach.

Just to the northeast of here is the Missisquoi National Wildlife Refuge, which protects the Missisquoi River delta with the goal of enhancing feeding and nesting areas for migratory waterfowl. The refuge consists primarily of marshy, wooded swampland traversed by numerous creeks that are ideal for bird-watching by canoe in spring and fall (the bird population is slim at the height of summer). A nature trail loops beside two of the creeks.

Campsites, facilities: There are 281 sites for tents and RVs, 179 with full hookups. A dump station, recreation hall, pool, restrooms, hot showers, a baseball field, and laundry facilities are provided. A small grocery store carries LP gas, ice, and firewood. On the grounds are a playground and tennis courts. Leashed pets are permitted. Management is fluent in both French and English.

Reservations, fees: Reservations are recommended. Campsites range from $15–22 a night.

Open: May 1–October 1.

Directions: From Swanton, travel eight miles west on Highway 78. Turn left on Tabor Road and head south to the campground entrance.

Contact: Colette R. Levesque, Lakewood Campground, 122 Champlain Street, Swanton, VT 05488, 802/868-7270; off-season 802/868-5125.

3 MILL POND CAMPGROUND

🏊 🚣 ⛵ 🐕 🚶 🚐

Rating: 8

North of Lake Carmi

This peaceful campground is a good option for families who wish to access Lake Carmi but would like a few more amenities than those offered at the state park. Choose from open and wooded sites and then head for the lake to boat, fish, and swim to your heart's content.

Campsites, facilities: There are 58 RV sites, some with full hookups. A playground, pool, sports courts, hot showers, flush toilets, a dump station, and an arcade are provided. Leashed pets are permitted.

Reservations, fees: Reservations are recommended. Sites range from $16–21 a night.

Open: May 1–October 1.

Directions: From St. Albans, head east on Highway 105 to the junction of Highway 120. Head north on Highway 120 for four miles to the campground entrance.

Contact: Mill Pond Campground, 75 Mill Pond Road, Route 120, Franklin, VT 05457-9726, 802/285-2240.

4 LAKE CARMI STATE PARK

🚴 🏊 🚣 ⛵ 🍴 🐕 🚶 ♿ 🚐 ⛰

Rating: 8

Northwest of Enosburg Falls on Lake Carmi

Families with a penchant for water sports flock to Lake Carmi in the summertime. Big, wooded sites set back from the lake and easy water access draw campers to this spot just shy of the Canadian border. The state park includes two miles of shoreline on Vermont's fourth largest natural lake. If you are interested in exploring the Missisquoi River (to the south) by canoe, the state park is a good jumping-off point, as there's a popular put-in at Enosburg Falls. Be sure to bring your mountain bike—the main roads around here are sparsely traveled, and many "secondary" roads are scenic dirt byways.

Campsites, facilities: There are 178 sites for tents and RVs, including 35 lean-tos and two cabins, all without hookups. Each site has a table and fire ring. Facilities include a dump station, playground, beach, boat ramp, boat rentals, a snack bar, metered hot showers, and flush toilets. Leashed pets with rabies vaccination certification are permitted, but not in day-use areas.

Reservations, fees: Reservations are accepted for two-night minimum stays. Tent sites are $16 a night and lean-tos are $23 a night for four people. The maximum allowable number of people at a site is eight, and there must be one person at least 18 years of age with each camping party. Two cabins are rented for $35 per cabin per night. See the introduction to this chapter for more information on state regulations.

Open: Mid-May–Labor Day.

Directions: From Enosburg Falls, travel three miles west on Highway 105. Turn right on Highway 236 and head north for three more miles to the campground.

Contact: Lake Carmi State Park, 460 Marsh Farm Road, Enosburg Falls, VT 05450, 802/933-8383 or 888/409-7579.

5 LONG TRAIL

🚶 🏊 🚣 🍴 ❄ 🐕 ⛰

Rating: 10

Along the ridge of the Green Mountains

Known as the "Footpath in the Wilderness," Vermont's Long Trail is the oldest long-distance hiking trail in America. The 270-mile track follows the main ridge of the Green Mountains north from the Massachusetts-Vermont state line to the Canadian border. This backwoods path crosses rugged summits, follows clear streams, traverses alpine bogs, and cuts through deep rolling woodlands. An end-to-end hike on the Long Trail usually takes a month or less to complete. Many people hike the trail in its entirety, but certain sections are heavily used by day hikers and overnight backpackers, as the highway crosses most of the state's highest peaks and penetrates its most remote wilderness reaches. The Green Mountain Club blazed the trail from 1910–1930, inspiring the construction of the Appalachian Trail in the process. The two trails converge at the Massachusetts border and work their way north on a single footpath for 100 miles. At Sherburne Pass near Pico Peak they diverge at Maine Junction, with the Appalachian Trail veering east and the Long Trail continuing north.

Campsites, facilities: There are 70 campsites along the 270-mile footpath. Some have lodges with woodstoves, many have Adirondack-style lean-tos, and others are wooded tent sites. Primitive toilets are provided at most of them. Group camping is allowed by permit; many campgrounds can accommodate small groups. All sites offer some kind of water source, but not all are reliable or pure. Off-trail camping is allowed in the Green Mountain National Forest and on state-owned lands under an elevation of 2,500 feet. Leashed pets are permitted.

Reservations, fees: All sites are available on a first-come, first-served basis. Use of any overnight facility operated by the Green Mountain Club (GMC) is limited to three consecutive nights. In the summer months, some of the more heavily used sites are staffed by caretakers and charge fees of $4 a night for Green Mountain Club members and $5 for nonmembers. Some of the sites on Green Mountain National Forest property charge a nightly fee and offer no discounts for GMC members.

Open: The Long Trail is open in summer, fall, and winter. Travel is discouraged during mud season, usually from late March–early May.

Directions: The southern starting point of the trail can be reached via the Appalachian Trail (AT) or the Pine Cobble Trail. To reach the AT trailhead: From the junction of U.S. 7 and Highway 2 at the traffic circle in Williamstown, Massachusetts, travel three miles east to a traffic light at Phelps Avenue. There is no parking at the trailhead; parking is available with permission at the Greylock Community Club, .1 mile east of the trail, or at the Holy Family Catholic Church adjacent to the AT. To reach the Pine Cobble Trailhead: From the junction of U.S. 7 and Highway 2 at the traffic circle in Williamstown, Massachusetts, follow Highway 2 east for .6 mile to Cole Avenue. Turn left and travel north for .8 mile to where Cole Avenue ends at North Hoosac Road. Turn right, proceed .3 mile, turn on Pine Cobble Road, and continue .2 mile to the trailhead; parking is available.

Contact: The Green Mountain Club, 4711 Waterbury-Stowe Road, Waterbury Center, VT 05677, 802/244-7037, website: www.greenmountainclub.org.

6 PROUTY BEACH CAMPGROUND

Rating: 8

On Lake Memphremagog in Newport

Thirty-two-mile Lake Memphremagog was a travel route and fishing ground for Native Americans long before settlers arrived. Today, the lake's trout and landlocked salmon populations still attract anglers, while boaters of every sort traverse the northern waters. The city owns and operates sandy Prouty Beach and the campground, in addition to maintaining tennis courts and picnic areas for all to enjoy. In July the beach is the site of the annual Summer Fest, a seasonal celebration with family events. Several hundred yards west of the beach is a city-run dock and launching area, complete with boat supplies and slips. The Gateway Center at the dock has a snack bar and open-air deck beside the lake. The lake's main body and South Bay offer excellent conditions for windsurfing, and a group of islands off Eagle Point to the north is a kayaker's playground. A paved scenic bike path is accessible from the campground. Canada and Vermont share the lake with the local legend of Memphre, a large serpentlike creature occasionally spotted out on the water.

Campsites, facilities: There are 52 sites, four for tents and the rest for RVs; 18 have full hookups and 28 have water and electric hookups. Each site has a fire ring, grill, and picnic table. Facilities include a dump station, a laundry room, boat rentals, a playground, tennis courts, a sports field, horseshoe pits, volleyball courts, and shuffleboard. Ice and firewood are available. Leashed pets are permitted.

Reservations, fees: Reservations are recommended. Sites start at $20 a night for two people. Seasonal rates are available.

Open: Early May–mid-October.

Directions: From I-91 at Derby Center east of Lake Memphremagog, take Exit 27 and travel three miles northwest on Highway 191 into Newport. Turn left, head west on Freeman Street, take another left on Veterans Avenue, and drive south to the park.

Contact: Prouty Beach Campground, Newport City Recreation Department, Newport, VT 05855, 802/334-7951, website: www.newportvermont. org/recreation/proutybeach.htm.

◼ FIRESIDE CAMPGROUND
🏊 ➡ 🐕 🚐 ⛺

Rating: 5

East of Lake Memphremagog in Derby

Ten sites at Fireside are set aside for tents, and the rest are level pull-throughs for RVs. The campground accommodates trailers up to 40 feet in length. Though not a booming metropolis, downtown Derby does have restaurants, stores, bowling lanes, and tennis courts, all within walking distance of the campground. Lake Derby nearby is open for swimming and boating. To the north in the town of Derby Line, the world's only international opera house and library straddles the Canadian border: the Haskell Free Library and Opera House has seats on U.S. soil and a stage in Rock Island, Quebec.

Campsites, facilities: There are 34 sites for tents and RVs, 10 with full hookups and 14 with water and electric hookups. Flush toilets, a dump station, and hot showers are provided. Firewood is available. Leashed pets are permitted.

Reservations, fees: Reservations are recommended. Sites start at $16 a night.

Open: Mid-May–October 1.

Directions: From I-91 near Derby, take Exit

28 and drive north on U.S. 5 for a mile to the campground.

Contact: Fireside Campground, 3300 U.S. Route 5, Derby, VT 05829, 802/766-5109.

◼ CHAR-BO CAMPGROUND
🏊 🚤 ➡ 🐕 🎣 🚐 ⛺

Rating: 7

East of Derby overlooking Lake Salem

From this hilltop perch, campers have panoramic views of Lake Salem and Mounts Pisgah and Hor towering above Lake Willoughby. Grassy sites are divvied up according to camper type: RV sites are open while tent sites have shade trees and more privacy. The campground rents boats for lake use, and a path leads down the hill to a swimming beach. In Derby, the Cow Town Elk Ranch is the only elk farm in the state. These animals roamed freely in Vermont in the early 1800s until settlement pushed them north; a good time to visit the ranch is during the 4 P.M. feeding.

Campsites, facilities: There are 44 sites for tents and RVs, 18 with full hookups and 15 with water and electric hookups. Each site has a table, fire ring, and grill. Air conditioner use is permitted. Facilities include a laundry room, dump station, restrooms, hot showers, a game room, horseshoe pits, a basketball hoop, playground, and pool. RV rentals, RV storage, RV supplies, limited groceries, ice, and firewood are available. Leashed pets are permitted.

Reservations, fees: Reservations are recommended. Sites start at $18–23 a night per family of four. Weekly, monthly, and seasonal rates are available.

Open: Mid-May–October 15, weather permitting.

Directions: From I-91 at Derby, take Exit 28, travel four miles east on Highway 105, turn left on Haywood Road, and head north to the campground.

Contact: Char-Bo Campground, P.O. Box 438, Derby, VT 05829, 802/766-8807, or in winter, 352/347-0930, website: www.char-bo.com.

9 GOOSE POINT CAMPGROUND

Rating: 7

In South Alburg

Goose Point is a 117-acre outcrop of land facing north toward Missisquoi Bay. Sites are varied, from sunny and parklike to lakefront; tent spaces are in a separate, well-shaded area. Sailing is especially popular on Lake Champlain's northern reaches, and Missisquoi Bay to the north is a destination for anglers in search of northern pike, walleye, and lake trout. Take a dip in the campground pool or the invigorating waters of Lake Champlain. There are walking trails at the campground as well as a boat launch. If you're tenting and get rained out, you can escape to the bed-and-breakfast on the premises.
Campsites, facilities: There are 143 sites for tents and RVs, 50 with full hookups, 46 with water and electric hookups. Each site has a table and fire ring. Air conditioners are not allowed. A dump station, recreation hall, flush toilets, hot showers, a camp store, laundry facilities, and a playground are on the grounds. A small store carries bait, tackle, ice, and firewood. Recreational facilities include a pool, shuffleboard, horseshoe pits, and badminton and volleyball courts. The owners speak French as well as English. Leashed pets are permitted.
Reservations, fees: Reservations are recommended and require a 50 percent deposit. Sites start at $18 a night for four people; beach sites start at $20.
Open: May–mid-October.
Directions: From the junction of U.S. 2 and Highway 78 in Alburg Center, travel three miles southeast on U.S. 2.
Contact: Gordon and Pauline Beyor, Goose Point Campground, 526 U.S. Route 2, South Alburg, VT 05440, 802/796-3711.

10 NORTH HERO STATE PARK

Rating: 7

On the Lake Champlain Islands

Though it does fill up in the summer, this 400-acre state park is less of a mob scene than Grand Isle. Sites are set in a lowland forest near a beach on Lake Champlain. If you have a boat or wish to rent one, consider spending a day island-hopping to the other state-owned properties of Knight, Woods, and Burton Islands.
Campsites, facilities: There are 117 sites for tents and RVs, including 18 lean-tos, all without hookups. Each site has a table and fire ring. A dump station is provided. Facilities include a playground, beach, boat ramp, metered hot showers, and flush toilets. Ice, firewood, and boat rentals are available. Leashed pets with rabies vaccination certification are permitted, but not in day-use areas.
Reservations, fees: Reservations are recommended. Tent sites are $14 a night and lean-tos are $21 a night for four people. The maximum allowable number of people at a site is eight, and there must be one person at least 18 years of age with each camping party. See the introduction to this chapter for more information on state park regulations.
Open: Late May–Labor Day.
Directions: From North Hero, travel four miles north on U.S. 2. Bear left on Town Road and continue northeast for four more miles to the park.
Contact: North Hero State Park, 3803 Lakeview Drive, North Hero, VT 05474, 802/372-8727 in summer, 888/409-7579 October–May.

11 KING'S BAY CAMPGROUND

Rating: 8

In North Hero on the east shore of Lake Champlain

Lakeside and shaded, these sites are occupied mostly by seasonal campers, so absolutely call ahead if you want to stay here. King's Bay offers 1,300 feet of shoreline, and a few docks for boats, on Lake Champlain. To the east are views of the Cold Hollow Mountains; this chain extends into Canada and is called by many the Northern Green Mountains. Canadians and Americans aren't the only ones who take time off in the islands: the Royal Lipizzan Stallions of Austria have a summer home on North Hero. These horses perform a hoofed ballet on summer weekends.

Campsites, facilities: There are 40 sites for tents and RVs with full hookups. Hot showers, a dump station, and flush toilets are provided. Leashed pets are permitted.

Reservations, fees: Seasonal reservations require a $100 deposit. Sites start at $16 a night for two people. Weekly and seasonal rates are available.

Open: May 15–September 15.

Directions: From North Hero, travel north on U.S. 2 for 3.3 miles to Lakeview Drive. Continue north one mile more on Lakeview Drive to the campground entrance.

Contact: King's Bay Campground, 1088 Lakeview Drive, North Hero, VT 05474, 802/372-3735.

12 MILL BROOK CAMPGROUND

🏃 🚴 🏊 🛶 ✕ 🏕 🚐 ⛰

Rating: 7

In the village of Westfield

Grassy, spacious sites for RVs are set along Mill Brook, which is open to trout fishing. Tenters are offered more secluded, wooded sites. A short wade or stroll upstream leads to a waterfall and gorge. Road biking is at its best in this part of the state, where highways are both scenic and lightly traveled. Easy bike routes explore nearby Newport on Lake Memphremagog, Jay Peak, and the verdant farmland of the Northeast Kingdom (the northern reaches of Vermont that lie east of the Green Mountains). For long hikes, hop on the Long Trail and scamper up Jay Peak, the last

big rise before the trail's end at the Canadian border.

Campsites, facilities: There are 30 sites for tents and RVs, 16 with full hookups, 12 with water and electric hookups. Each site has a fireplace and picnic table. Free hot showers, a play area, dump station, restrooms, and sports courts are provided. Ice and firewood are available. There's also a general store next to the campground. Leashed pets are permitted.

Reservations, fees: Reservations are recommended. Tent sites start at $12 a night for two people, and sites with full hookups start at $16 a night. Seasonal rates are available.

Open: Mid-May–mid-September.

Directions: From I-91 at Orleans, take Exit 26 to U.S. 5. North of Coventry, turn left on Highway 14 and head north to Highway 100. Follow Highway 100 as it leads south to Westfield. The campground is in the middle of the village.

Contact: Mill Brook Campground, Highway 100, P.O. Box 133, Westfield, VT 05874, 802/744-6673.

13 BARREWOOD CAMPGROUND

🏃 🏊 🛶 🐕 🏕 ♿ 🚐 ⛰

Rating: 7

South of Jay Peak

Bilingual hospitality is offered at this campground only 10 miles from the Canadian border. Sites are open and grassy. A fishing stream runs through the property, and there's also a swimming pool for cooling off after hiking in the hills to the west. Nature trails leave from here and pass a triple-decker waterfall. The Long Trail's northernmost reaches are just to the west of the campground. This section crosses over the summit of Jay Peak and continues on to the trail's end at the Canadian border, making for a challenging day hike. You can also drive to Jay Peak, park at the bottom, make your ascent, and take the tram back to the parking lot or hike down the ski trails.

Campsites, facilities: There are 45 sites for tents

and RVs, six with full hookups and 39 with water and electric hookups. Each site has a picnic table and fire ring. Laundry facilities, hot showers, a recreation hall, pavilion, playground, group camping areas, and a dump station are provided. There are also horseshoe pits, a volleyball court, and a badminton net. LP gas, ice, and firewood are for sale. The owners speak French as well as English. Leashed pets are permitted.

Reservations, fees: Reservations are recommended. Sites start at $20 a night per family. Seasonal rates are available.

Open: May 1–mid-October.

Directions: From the intersection of Highways 58 and 100 in Lowell, travel four miles north on Highway 100 to the campground entrance on the left (west) side of the road.

Contact: Barrewood Campground, 3102 Route 100, Westfield, VT 05874, 802/744-6340 or 802/744-2068.

14 CHAMPLAIN VALLEY CAMPGROUND

Rating: 7

On Lake Champlain south of Swanton

Ideal RV sites are strung along the Lake Champlain shore, all with hookups. Views of Grand Isle and some of the smaller islands to the south are at your front door, and campers have use of a boat launch. This RV park is dominated by seasonal campers; tenters will want to try for a spot at one of the state parks to the south.

Campsites, facilities: There are 79 sites for RVs up to 32 feet in length, 40 with full hookups and 39 with water and electric hookups. A dump station, recreation hall, restrooms, free hot showers, and a playground are provided. LP gas and firewood are available. Leashed pets are permitted.

Reservations, fees: Reservations are recommended. Sites start at $22 a night.

Open: Mid-May–mid-October.

Directions: From Swanton, travel four miles south on Highway 36 to the campground entrance.

Contact: Champlain Valley Campground, 600 Mcquam Shore Road, Swanton, VT 05488, 802/524-5146.

15 BROOKSIDE CAMPGROUND

Rating: 6

On Bogue Brook south of Enosburg Center

Grassy, level plots are carved out beside Bogue Brook, where campers select either open, sunny sites or ones that are shaded and more private. You can cast a fishing line in the brook, or explore the surrounding hardwood forest on a nature trail. This is close to the Canadian border town of Richford, a popular put-in location for canoe trips on the lower Missisquoi River to Lake Champlain.

Campsites, facilities: There are 35 sites for tents and RVs, 21 with full hookups and 14 with water and electric hookups. Each site has a table and fire ring. A dump station, horseshoe pits, laundry facilities, a group area, and a playground are provided, and ice and firewood are available. Leashed pets are permitted.

Reservations, fees: Reservations are recommended. Sites are $12–16 a night. Seasonal rates are available.

Open: May 1–October 1. Hunters, however, may reserve sites into late fall.

Directions: From Enosburg Falls, travel three miles east on Highway 105 to Boston Post Road. Turn right and head south for six miles to the campground entrance.

Contact: Brookside Campground, 680 Sand Hill Road, Enosburg Falls, VT 05450, 802/933-4376.

16 KNIGHT ISLAND STATE PARK

Rating: 10

East of North Hero

Knight Island is a mile long and nearly half a mile wide. It was farmed long ago, then remained uninhabited for many years. Before being purchased by the state in 1990, the island was operated privately as a nudist campground, and unofficially remains clothing optional. Ten acres on the southern tip of the island are still privately owned. Campsites dot the isolated shoreline, and each has a private access path. Plan on anchoring your boat offshore or pulling up on the campsite shore. Dead and down wood is available for campfires. Human waste must be buried in cat holes dug in the top six inches of soil at least 100 feet from shore. Day users are welcome at a picnic area on the island but must leave before sundown. There are some marked trails on the island for short hikes that lead to scenic views of the Green and Adirondack Mountains.

Campsites, facilities: There are seven primitive tent sites, six with lean-tos, all with fire rings but no other facilities. Firewood is available on the island. Leashed pets with rabies vaccination certification are permitted, but not in day-use areas.

Reservations, fees: Camping is by permit only on designated sites, and setting up camp prior to permit acquisition is not allowed. Obtain permits at the caretaker's residence. Reservations are handled through Burton Island State Park. The minimum stay is three nights and the maximum stay is 14 nights. Sites are $14–21 a night for four people and can accommodate up to eight people. See the introduction to this chapter for more information on state park regulations.

Open: Mid-May–Labor Day.

Directions: From St. Albans Bay, travel west on Highway 36 and take a left onto Point Road to Kill Kare State Park. Parking spaces and a boat ramp are provided. Take your own boat over to Knight Island or catch the passenger ferry (no vehicles) that runs to the island once a day, twice on weekends and holidays.

Contact: Knight Island State Park, c/o Burton Island State Park, P.O. Box 123, St. Albans Bay, VT 05481, 802/524-6353.

17 WOODS ISLAND STATE PARK

Rating: 10

East of North Hero

Five open, primitive campsites offer ultimate privacy on the formerly farmed mile-long preserve. The campsites are connected by scenic trails. The sites are cleared areas big enough for a tent or two. Endangered plant species are protected on Woods Island, so no fires are allowed. A trail traces the perimeter of the island and crosses over its center where a former owner attempted to build a landing strip. Vestiges of the runway are still visible. Human waste must be buried in cat holes dug in the top six inches of soil at least 100 feet from shore. Day users are welcome at a picnic area on the island but must leave before sundown. This is a great spot for nature study.

Campsites, facilities: There are five primitive tent sites and no facilities. Fires are prohibited. Leashed pets with rabies vaccination certification are permitted, but not in day-use areas.

Reservations, fees: Camping is by permit only on designated sites, and setting up camp prior to permit acquisition is not allowed. Obtain permits at Burton Island State Park. Sites are $14 a night for up to eight people. See the introduction to this chapter for more information on state park regulations.

Open: Late May–Labor Day.

Directions: From St. Albans Bay, travel west on Highway 36 and then Point Road to Kill Kare State Park. Parking spaces and a boat ramp are provided. There is no ferry service to the island; you must take your own boat.

Contact: Woods Island State Park, c/o Burton Island State Park, P.O. Box 123, St. Albans Bay, VT 05481, 802/524-6353.

18 BURTON ISLAND STATE PARK

Rating: 9

Near St. Albans Bay on Lake Champlain

Cows, pigs, and chickens roamed 253-acre Burton Island in the early 1900s when it served as pastureland. Now the state-owned island is a unique camping spot offering both a full-service marina and natural tent and lean-to sites along the mostly open northern shore. The island is home to an abundant bird population as well as deer and small mammals. In addition to boat rentals, a swimming beach, and other water-oriented offerings, the island has a resident naturalist who hosts interpretive programs, and a nature trail network that allows visitors to explore the island. Remnants of Burton Island's agricultural past are evident in the woods, from rusted farm implements to an old barn foundation. Because of the marina, the island is a popular stopover for big-boat enthusiasts. Don't worry, the tent and lean-to sites are set apart from the busy recreation area.

Campsites, facilities: There are 17 tent sites, 26 lean-to sites, 15 boat moorings, and a 100-slip marina with dockside electricity, fuel service, and a dump station for boats with septic tanks. All tent and lean-to sites have fireplaces and picnic tables. Restrooms, metered hot showers, a snack bar, playground, and rowboat and canoe rentals are provided on the island. A park store sells firewood, marine maps of the lake, and staples. Leashed pets with rabies vaccination certification are permitted, but not in day-use areas.

Reservations, fees: Reservations are recommended. Sites and slips range from $16–23 a night. The maximum allowable number of people at a site is eight, and there must be one person at least 18 years of age with each camping party. See the introduction to this chapter for more information on state park regulations.

Open: Late May–Labor Day.

Directions: From St. Albans Bay, travel west on Highway 36 and take a left onto Point Road to Kill Kare State Park. Parking spaces and a boat ramp are provided. Take your own boat over to Burton Island, or catch the passenger ferry (no vehicles) that runs from 8:30 A.M.–6:30 P.M. at two-hour intervals.

Contact: Burton Island State Park, P.O. Box 123, St. Albans Bay, VT 05481, 802/524-6353.

19 LAKEVIEW CAMPING AREA

Rating: 5

On Lake Eden

Highway 100 intersects this campground on Lake Eden. Grassy, open field–type sites are set either beside the lake or across the street in a slightly more wooded area. Most have a view of Lake Eden, but the parking lot setup precludes privacy. On the lake, there are sandy beaches, a large play area, and a small gift shop and grocery store. The campground gives mountain bikers a price break: if you're touring on two wheels, you can set up camp for $4 a person. For a challenging day hike and a great view, the Long Trail is just five miles to the west. Take the Asbestos Mine Road out of Eden Mills to the Frank Post Trailhead. In two miles, this highway meets the Long Trail. Head south to Belvedere Mountain and then take the Forester's Trail back to your car. It's seven miles round-trip.

Campsites, facilities: There are 68 sites for tents and RVs up to 30 feet in length, all with water and electric hookups. Each site has a garbage can, fire ring, grill, and picnic table. Facilities include a dump station, restrooms, hot showers, a limited grocery store, shuffleboard, badminton courts, and horseshoe pits. Ice, firewood, and bait are available. Leashed pets are permitted, but not in the beach area.

Reservations, fees: Reservations require a deposit. Sites start at $23 a night. Weekly and monthly rates are available.

Open: May 15–September 15.

Directions: From I-89 at Colbyville, take Exit 10 and travel north on Highway 100. When you reach the junction with Highway 118, continue two miles north on Highway 100 to the campground entrance.

Contact: Lakeview Camping Area, 4902 Route 100, Eden Mills, VT 05653, 802/635-2255.

20 BELVIEW CAMPGROUND

Rating: 8

On the north end of Crystal Lake

Overlooking Crystal Lake, these sites are set back from the water in the woods. The lake is flanked by rolling hills to the east and flatter farmland to the west. Just west of Belview, Crystal Lake State Park has two sandy beaches, picnic areas, and a boat launch. The lake is open to powerboating as well as fishing; for more of a wilderness experience, explore May Pond and May Pond Mountain just to the east of the campground. Some of Vermont's elusive moose have been spotted here. If you're camping at Belview in August, be sure to check out the Barton Fair, an old-fashioned country event held at the village's extensive fairgrounds.

Campsites, facilities: There are 50 sites for tents and RVs, some with full hookups, as well as on-site rental units. Some sites have cable TV hookups. Metered hot showers, a dump station, restrooms, and a playground are provided. Firewood and ice are available. Leashed pets are permitted.

Reservations, fees: Reservations are recommended and require a 50 percent deposit. Sites are $17–23 a night.

Open: Mid-May–mid-October.

Directions: From I-91, take Exit 25 toward Barton. Travel north for a mile on Highway 16 to the village of Barton. Turn right onto U.S. 5, head south for .5 mile, then turn right on Highway 16 and follow it east over the railroad tracks to the campground entrance .5 mile ahead.

Contact: Belview Campground, P.O. Box 222, Barton, VT 05822, 802/525-3242, website: www.belviewcampground.com.

21 WILL-O-WOOD CAMPGROUND

Rating: 8

North of Lake Willoughby

Roomy sites are perched on a grassy hill overlooking Lake Willoughby a half mile to the south. Mounts Pisgah and Hor rise steeply from opposite ends of the lake, creating a fjord-like vista. Open fields and woodlands at Will-O-Wood provide ample room to relax. Willoughby Beach on the lake's north shore is a short walk or drive away. Five miles long and 300 feet deep in some spots, the lake attracts windsurfers, powerboaters, anglers, and swimmers. A group called the Westmore Association maintains many miles of hiking trails in the woods and on the five peaks in the immediate area; trail maps are available at the campground. Bald Mountain, the highest summit at 3,315 feet, is accessible by the Long Pond and Mad Brook Trails. A fire tower atop the peak provides 360-degree views of the Green and White Mountains and Lake Memphremagog to the north.

Campsites, facilities: There are 117 sites for tents and RVs, 60 with full hookups and 24 with water and electric hookups. Each site has a picnic table, fire ring, and grill. Air conditioner and heater use is allowed. The camp provides a recreation hall, dump stations, laundry facilities, a pool, playground, sports courts, and horseshoe pits. A camp store sells groceries, LP gas, ice, and firewood. RV rentals are available. Leashed pets are permitted.

Reservations, fees: Nonrefundable deposits are required for reservations. Tent sites are $18 a night per family, and sites with full hookups start at $24. Weekly, monthly, and seasonal rates are available.

Open: May 1–October 15.

Directions: From I-91 at Orleans, take Exit 26 and travel 6.25 miles east on Highway 58. Turn left on Highway 5A and drive north for .5 mile to the campground.

Contact: Will-O-Wood Campground, 227 Will-O-Wood Lane, Orleans, VT 05860, 802/525-3575, website: www.will-o-woodcampground.com.

22 LAKESIDE CAMPING

Rating: 7

On the north side of Island Pond

Offering both wooded and open sites on Island Pond, Lakeside Camping focuses on water-based recreation. The campground rents boats and maintains a long, sandy beach for swimming. Cruises are regularly scheduled. The lake is somewhat developed near the town of Island Pond, but miles of wilderness lie just east of the lake, where seemingly endless old logging roads provide entertainment for mountain bikers, and, in season, are fruitful hunting grounds. Check in at the general store in Island Pond for bait, ammo, licenses, and maps.

Campsites, facilities: There are 200 sites for tents and RVs, many with full hookups. A dump station, playground, hot showers, a recreation hall, game room, laundry facilities, and boat rentals are provided. A grocery store sells LP gas, ice, and firewood. Leashed pets are permitted.

Reservations, fees: Reservations are recommended. Sites start at $16–22 a night. Seasonal rates are available.

Open: Mid-May–mid-September.

Directions: From the town of Island Pond, travel two miles east on Highway 105 to the campground entrance on the left.

Contact: Lakeside Camping, 1348 Route 105, East Brighton Road, Island Pond, VT 05846, 802/723-6649, website: www.lakesidecamping.com.

23 BRIGHTON STATE PARK

Rating: 8

Between Island and Spectacle Ponds in Brighton

Wilderness surrounds the campground at Brighton State Park. Land to the east is virtually devoid of streets and towns, and logging roads access wooded mountains and deep, quiet valleys. In winter, snowmobilers flock to the area. Campsites hug the woods at the edge of Spectacle Pond, an excellent fishing hole. Campers may use a small beach and plunk a canoe into the water, but no motors are allowed. Nature trails, a natural history museum, and a garage theater are located at park headquarters. A resident naturalist helps interpret the local flora and fauna, including loons that live on the lake. A half mile south of the campground, the park operates a day-use area on Island Pond, which is open to all boating and has a snack bar and boat rentals. The town of Island Pond used to be a major crossroads of rail commerce; it was the site of the first international railroad junction in the United States. A historic district there features a grand two-story railway station.

Campsites, facilities: There are 63 tent and RV sites and 21 lean-tos, all without hookups. Each site has a picnic table and fireplace. Facilities include a dump station, flush toilets, hot showers, a playground, and horseshoe pits. Firewood is available. There's a snack bar half a mile away at the day-use area, and supplies can be purchased in the town of Island Pond, two miles to the west. Leashed pets with rabies vaccination certification are permitted, but not in day-use areas.

Reservations, fees: Reservations are recommended. Sites are $16–23 a night for four people. The maximum allowable number of people at a site is eight, and there must be one person at least 18 years of age with each camping party. See the introduction to this chapter for more information on state park regulations.

Open: Mid-May–Columbus Day.

Directions: From the center of Island Pond, travel two miles east on Highway 105 and then .75 mile south on a local road. There's no name to this road; par for the course in Vermont. It's the only road near the 2.0 mile mark out of town, and you can't miss it. However, if you do miss it, folks in Island Pond will redirect you.

Contact: Brighton State Park, Island Pond, VT 05846, 802/723-4360.

24 CHAMPLAIN ADULT CAMPGROUND

Rating: 8

North of Keeler Bay in Grand Isle

Flanked by the ferry to the south and a public golf course to the north, these campsites are set on and back from the shore of 120-mile-long Lake Champlain. A grove of cedars and an old orchard provide shade and privacy. The campground caters to retired people and adult couples without children; you must be 18 or older to stay here. A beach and dock provide front-row seats for watching salmon-colored skies as the sun disappears behind the Adirondack Mountains. Keep your eyes peeled for Champ, the elusive lake monster and probable cousin of Scotland's Nessie. The campground owners are sensitive to environmental issues; all sites sport fresh grass, and the roads winding through the campground are gravel. For several years, a prime lakefront site has been occupied by a pileated woodpecker and thus has not been rented out.

Campsites, facilities: There are 79 sites for tents and RVs, some with full hookups. Each site has a table and fireplace. A dump station, restrooms, hot showers, and a recreation hall are provided. Firewood is available. The owners speak French as well as English. Leashed pets are permitted.

Reservations, fees: Reservations are recommended. Sites start at $20 a night. Veterans of World War I and II camp for free.

Open: Mid-May–early October.

Directions: From I-89 north of Burlington, take Exit 17 and follow U.S. 2 to the Lake Champlain Islands and the intersection with Highway 314. Bear left and follow Highway 314 north for 2.5 miles to the campground entrance.

Contact: Champlain Adult Campground, Champlain Landing, Grand Isle, VT 05458, 802/372-5938, website: www.champlainresort.com.

25 GRAND ISLE STATE PARK

Rating: 6

On the Lake Champlain Islands

Grand Isle is one of the most developed state parks in Vermont. Campsites line the east shore and are close to the main attraction, a lake beach where swimming, fishing, and boating are the favored activities. This is Vermont's only state park with a recreation hall used for group events. Exercise nuts can work out on the fitness trail that winds through the 226-acre park. One of the isle's more interesting tourist attractions is found north of the park on the east shore: Hyde Log Cabin is believed to be the oldest log cabin in the United States.

Campsites, facilities: There are 156 sites for tents and RVs, including 34 lean-tos, all without hookups. Each site has a table and fire ring. A dump station is provided. A playground, beach, boat ramp, boat rentals, recreation hall, metered hot showers, and flush toilets are provided. Ice and firewood are available. Leashed pets with rabies vaccination certification are permitted, but not in day-use areas.

Reservations, fees: Reservations are recommended. Tent sites are $16 a night and lean-to sites are $23 a night for four people. The maximum allowable number of people at a site is eight, and there must be one person at least 18 years of age with each camping party. One cabin is available for $35 a night. See the introduction to this chapter for more information on state park regulations.

Open: Mid-May–mid-October.

Directions: From the town of Grand Isle, travel a mile south on U.S. 2 to the park entrance on the left.

Contact: Grand Isle State Park, 36 East Shore South, Grand Isle, VT 05458, 802/372-4300.

26 APPLE ISLAND CAMPGROUND

Rating: 7

On the southern end of Grand Isle

Mountain views and magnificent Lake Champlain greet campers at Apple Island. This full-service RV park caters to boaters with an on-site marina, dock, ramp, and boat supply store, as well as a place to gas up. A nine-hole golf course and a clubhouse are also located on the 188-acre Apple Island Resort, of which the campground is part. Take a dip in the brisk lake or opt for the resort's heated pool. The lake's northern end is shared by powerboaters, kayakers, and canoeists. Fishing guides are available for hire at the marina for campers who want to penetrate the deep waters of the 120-mile-long lake and perhaps take home a cooler full of lake trout, landlocked salmon, walleye, smelt, northern pike, or any of several other species. Throughout the summer, bingo, dancing, special dinners, and other group activities are organized.

Campsites, facilities: There are 200 sites, most with hookups. Each site has a picnic table, fire ring, and grill. Air conditioners are allowed. Facilities include RV storage, dump stations, hot showers, laundry facilities, a grocery store, playground, heated pool, recreation hall, sports courts, athletic field, and horseshoe pits. Group sites for tents and RVs, RV supplies, LP gas, gasoline, ice, and firewood are available. An on-site marina has a dock, ramp, gas, and boat rentals. Leashed pets are permitted.

Reservations, fees: Reservations are recommended Memorial Day–Labor Day. Sites start at $27 a night. Weekly, monthly, and seasonal rates are available.

Open: May 1–October 20.

Directions: From I-89 north of Burlington, take exit 17 toward South Hero and travel six miles west on U.S. 2 to the resort on the right (north) side of the road.

Contact: Apple Island Campground, P.O. Box 183, 71 Route 2, South Hero, VT 05486-0183, 802/372-5398, website: www.appleislandresort.com.

27 COVENTRY RESORT

Rating: 7

North of Burlington

This family-oriented nudist resort offers tent and RV sites plus rental cabins near the shore of Long Pond.

Campsites, facilities: There are 22 RV sites with hookups, 30 tent sites, and 12 rental cabins. Each site has a picnic table; fires are limited to a shared fire pit. Facilities include dump stations, restrooms, hot showers, a laundry room, recreation room, hot tub, and sports courts. Leashed pets are allowed.

Reservations, fees: Reservations are required for cabins and RV sites. For nonmembers, tent sites start at $35 a night, RV sites at $45 a night, and cabins at $75 a night. Discounts apply for members and multiple night stays.

Open: May 1–October 1.

Directions: From Milton Center .5 mile past the bridge, take a left onto Lake Road. After three miles, take a left onto Everest Road and follow for two miles. Take a right on Beebe Hill Road. The resort is one mile ahead on the right.

Contact: Coventry Resort, 468 Beebe Hill Road, Milton, VT 05468, 802/893-7773, website: www.coventryresort.com.

28 HOMESTEAD CAMPGROUND

Rating: 5

At the north end of Arrowhead Mountain Lake in Milton

Family-oriented camping is found right off the highway at Homestead. Level grassy sites are close together under a canopy of trees. Myriad activities are available on weekends: planned events include flea markets, wagon rides, bingo, and more. Sports courts, pools, athletic fields, and an on-site arcade keep campers of all ages entertained. Across the street is a driving range and a miniature golf plaza with a snack bar and go-carts. Though tenters are welcome, RVs and seasonal mobile homes dominate the park. The campground is conveniently located near many of northwest Vermont's bigger attractions, such as Lake Champlain, Burlington, and the Green Mountains.

Campsites, facilities: There are 160 sites for tents and RVs, all with water and electric hookups. Each site has a picnic table and fire ring. Air conditioners are allowed, but heaters are not. Cable TV hookups are available. Facilities include a dump station, laundry room, hot showers, restrooms, a recreation hall, arcade, two pools, sports courts, horseshoe pits, and a playground. Also available are group sites for tents and RVs, RV rentals, and RV storage. A small grocery store sells RV supplies, LP gas, ice, and firewood. Leashed pets are permitted.

Reservations, fees: Reservations are recommended. Sites start at $26 a night per family.

Open: May 1–mid-October.

Directions: From I-89 north of Burlington, take Exit 18 and travel .25 mile south on U.S. 7 to the campground entrance.

Contact: Homestead Campground, 864 Ethan Allen Highway, Milton, VT 05468, 802/524-2356, website: www.homesteadcampground.net.

29 MAPLE GROVE CAMPGROUND

🛶 🏕 🐕 ⛺ 🚐 ⛰

North of Fairfax

Rating: 7

With just 25 sites, Maple Grove is fully equipped for RV camping. RV sites are shaded and level, and there are a few grassy spaces for tents under maple trees. Just to the south, the Lamoille River flows through Fairfax on its way to Malletts Bay. Canoeists can put in at Fairfax Falls for day trips or full-scale excursions to Lake Champlain. The Lamoille is also open to trout fishing.

Campsites, facilities: There are 25 sites for tents and RVs, 12 with full hookups and 13 with water and electric hookups. Each site has a fire ring and table. Air conditioners, but not heaters, are allowed. Facilities include a dump station, laundry room, basketball hoop, playground, badminton and volleyball courts, and horseshoe pits. Limited groceries, RV supplies, ice, and wood are available. Leashed pets are permitted.

Reservations, fees: Reservations are recommended. Sites range from $19–23 a night per family.

Open: May 1–mid-October.

Directions: From I-89 north of Burlington, take Exit 18 and drive five miles east on Highway 104A. Turn left on Highway 104 and head north for less than a mile to the campground entrance on the right (east) side of the road.

Contact: Maple Grove Campground, 1627 Main Street, Fairfax, VT 05454, 802/849-6439, website: www.vtcampgrounds.com/maplegrove/index.htm.

30 WHITE CAPS CAMPGROUND

🏃 🚴 🏊 🎣 🚐 🐕 🧗 🚙 ⛺

Rating: 9

On the southern tip of Lake Willoughby

Lake Willoughby is sandwiched dramatically between glacially sculpted mountains. White Caps Campground lies at the southern end of the five-mile-long lake, and most sites have superb views. Some of the trailer sites are small, only 20 feet wide, while others can accommodate RVs up to 40 feet in length. White birch trees shade much of the grounds. Across U.S. 5 there's a sandy beach and a boat launch owned by the campground. The Lake Willoughby area is an outdoorsperson's playground: there are craggy cliffs for rock climbing, 300-foot lake depths for scuba diving, five miles of open water for waterskiing and sailing, and miles of quiet country roads for biking. In 1996, a 29-pound lake trout was hooked at Willoughby, setting the world record for ice fishing.

Campsites, facilities: There are 52 sites for tents and RVs, 35 with full hookups. Each site has a picnic table and fire ring. Hot showers, flush toilets, a dump station, laundry facilities, and a playground are provided. A camp store carries ice and firewood. Leashed pets are permitted.
Reservations, fees: Reservations are accepted. Sites range from $18–26 a night.
Open: May 15–September 15.
Directions: From I-91 north of St. Johnsbury, take Exit 23 and head north on U.S. 5 about 10 miles to West Burke. From the junction of U.S. 5 and Route 5A, travel north for six more miles on Route 5A to the campground entrance on the right (east) side of the road.
Contact: White Caps Campground, 5659 Route 5A, Westmore, VT 05860, 802/467-3345, website: www.whitecapscampground.com.

31 CAMP SKYLAND ON LAKE CHAMPLAIN

Rating: 9

On the southern tip of land in Grand Isle County on Lake Champlain

Enjoy unspoiled views at Camp Skyland on Grand Isle's southernmost peninsula. The vistas of Malletts Bay, Lake Champlain, and the mountains beyond are seemingly infinite. A boat launch for small vessels and canoes is provided at the campground for those who wish to explore the peaceful horizon. On the lakeshore, there's a swimming area, dock, and boat rentals. This is one of the most pastoral places in all of Vermont. Revolutionary War hero Ethan Allen's cousin, Ebenezer, homesteaded the island of South Hero in 1783, and farms, orchards, and hamlets still abound.
Campsites, facilities: There are 33 sites for tents and RVs, 13 with full hookups and nine with water and electric hookups. Each site has a picnic table and fireplace. A recreation hall, flush toilets, hot showers, laundry facilities, boat rentals, and a playground are provided, but there is no dump station. There are also

12 rustic cabins available for rent that can accommodate two–six people each. Leashed pets are permitted.
Reservations, fees: Reservations are recommended. Sites start at $20 a night per family of four.
Open: Late May–mid-September.
Directions: From I-89 north of Burlington, take Exit 17, head west on U.S. 2, and cross the Sandbar Bridge. In South Hero, turn left on South Street and drive 3.5 miles to the campground.
Contact: Camp Skyland on Lake Champlain, 398 South Street, South Hero, VT 05486, 802/372-4200.

32 BREWSTER RIVER CAMPGROUND

Rating: 8

Northwest of Stowe

Twenty quiet sites are set along the Brewster River. A few sites can accommodate RVs, but tenters will be happiest here. Notably, this campground practices "green" camping and strongly encourages energy conservation, recycling, and composting of organic waste.
Campsites, facilities: There are 20 sites, three with water and electric hookups; a few can accommodate trailers up to 18 feet in length. Several lean-tos can sleep six people. A modern bathhouse with flush toilets and free hot showers is available. Each site has a picnic table and fireplace. Pets are not permitted.
Reservations, fees: Reservations are encouraged for weekends; there is a two-night minimum stay. Sites are $20–30 a night.
Open: Mid-May–early October, with winter camping by arrangement.
Directions: From the village of Jeffersonville, head three miles south on Route 108 to the campground entrance opposite Burnor Road.
Contact: Brewster River Campground, 110 Campground Drive, Jeffersonville, VT 05464-9422, 802/644-2126.

33 MAIDSTONE STATE PARK

🏃 🚴 🏊 🛶 🚣 🐕 🦽 🚐 ⛺

Rating: 6

On Maidstone Lake northeast of St. Johnsbury

Covering almost 800 acres, Maidstone Lake offers the full gamut of water sports from fishing (there are 25-pound lake trout, landlocked salmon, rainbow, and brook trout in these waters) to sailing and powerboating. Campsites are near the shore; besides the park, much of the shoreline is occupied by seasonal camps, but Maidstone has the distinction of being Vermont's most remote park. Boat rentals and a public ramp are provided. If you tire of the busy lake, head into the surrounding wilderness. There are no roads in the woods to the west, save for old logging roads that are suitable for mountain bikes and hiking boots. Beaver flowages and ponds, wetlands, and 2,000-foot hills are inhabited by deer, black bear, moose, fisher cat, and other mammals and birds. Be prepared to enjoy the call of the loons in the early morning and early evening.

Campsites, facilities: There are 82 sites for tents and RVs, including 37 lean-tos, all without hookups. Each site has a picnic table and fireplace. A dump station, boat rentals, a group camping area, and a playground are provided. Firewood can be purchased at the park. Leashed pets with rabies vaccination certification are permitted, but not in day-use areas.

Reservations, fees: Reservations are recommended. For reservations, phone 800/658-6934. Tent sites are $16 a night and lean-to sites are $21 a night for four people. The maximum allowable number of people at a site is eight, and there must be one person at least 18 years of age with each camping party. See the introduction to this chapter for more information on state park regulations.

Open: Mid-May–Labor Day.

Directions: From Guildhall, travel north on Highway 102 for 11 miles. Turn left and head southwest on State Forest Highway for five miles to the park entrance.

Contact: Maidstone State Park, 4858 Maidstone Lake Road, Guildhall, VT 05905, 802/676-3930.

34 BURLINGTON'S NORTH BEACH CAMPGROUND

🏃 🚴 🏊 🛶 🚣 🐕 🦽 🚐 ⛺

Rating: 8

North of Burlington

Owned and operated by the Burlington Parks and Recreation Department, this campground offers sites right beside Lake Champlain and access to a long sandy beach on the lake. Sites are wooded even though this is an urban location.

Campsites, facilities: There are 137 sites, with half outfitted for RVs. Each site has a picnic table, and fire grills are available. On-site are flush toilets, hot showers, a seasonal snack bar, a playground, and a pump-out service. Ice and firewood are available at the campground. Leashed pets are permitted.

Reservations, fees: Reservations are recommended. Sites start at $20–30 a night.

Open: May 1–mid-October.

Directions: From I-89, take Exit 14 at Burlington. Head west on Route 2 until you come to the end of the road at Lake Champlain. Head north on Lake Street, which turns into North Avenue. Follow signs to North Beach Park.

Contact: Burlington's North Beach Campground, 60 Institute Road, Burlington, VT 05401, 802/862-0942 or 800/571-1198.

35 MALLETTS BAY CAMPGROUND

🏊 🚣 🚐 🐕 🦽 ♿ 🚐 ⛺

Rating: 6

On Malletts Bay

Both open and wooded spots are offered at this full-service RV park laid out in a tight grid of sites and streets across a street from Lake Champlain. Water-view sites look out across the bay and boat moorings to the Champlain

Islands and New York state. Tent campers can stay on grassy lawns around the RV lots. The campground is bordered to the north by Bayside Park, which has a public beach and boat launch. The surrounding area is developed, offering access to nearby golf courses, shopping centers, ferries, and churches. Malletts Bay Campground is especially popular with seasonal campers.

Campsites, facilities: There are 119 sites for tents and RVs, 77 with full hookups and 32 with water and electric hookups. Each site has a table and fire ring. Cable TV hookups are available. Facilities include a dump station, restrooms, hot showers, laundry facilities, a recreation hall, playground, horseshoe pits, and basketball courts. A camp store sells LP gas, ice, and firewood. Leashed pets are permitted.

Reservations, fees: Reservations are recommended. Sites are $25–32 a night per family. Weekly, monthly, and seasonal rates are available.

Open: May 1–mid-October.

Directions: From I-89 north of Burlington, take Exit 16 to U.S. 7. Travel two miles north, turn left on Highway 127, and continue north for three miles to the campground entrance.

Contact: Malletts Bay Campground, 88 Malletts Bay Campground Road, Colchester, VT 05446, 802/863-6980.

36 LONE PINE CAMPSITES

Rating: 5

Near Malletts Bay

Paved roads and campsites are laid out in grid fashion with one shade tree per lot. Campsites are level and grassy, and a thick row of trees buffers the facility from I-89. A short drive to the southwest takes you to the Lake Champlain shore, where boating and fishing are allowed with the proper state licenses. Organized activities for the whole family are scheduled daily from May–September. Typical planned functions include fire engine rides on Friday and Saturday, line-dancing instruction,

and cribbage tournaments with cash prizes. A counselor-directed day camp for kids ages 6–15 is open on summer weekdays and features workshops in drama, arts and crafts, and nature exploration. The city of Burlington to the south is home to University Mall, Vermont's largest enclosed shopping center. In summer, the University of Vermont hosts the Champlain Shakespeare Festival at the Royall Tyler Theatre; Tyler, a native Vermonter, was America's first professional playwright.

Campsites, facilities: There are 265 sites for tents and RVs, 200 with full hookups and 65 with water and electric hookups. Each site has a picnic table, grill, and fire ring. Air conditioners are allowed, and phone hookups are available. Facilities include dump stations, restrooms, hot showers, laundry facilities, a recreation room, pavilion, two pools, miniature golf, sports courts, athletic fields, and horseshoe pits. LP gas, RV rentals, RV storage, RV supplies, ice, and firewood are available. Two pets per site are allowed.

Reservations, fees: Reservations are recommended July 1–Labor Day and are accepted through the mail or over the phone. Sites start at $28 a night for a family of four.

Open: May 1–October 15.

Directions: From I-89 north of Burlington, take Exit 16 and travel north on U.S. 2/7 for 3.5 miles. Turn left on Bay Road and continue one mile north to the campground entrance.

Contact: Lone Pine Campsites, 52 Sunset View Road, Colchester, VT 05446, 802/878-5447, website: www.lonepinecampsites.com.

37 UNDERHILL STATE PARK

Rating: 8

To the southeast of Mount Mansfield

The steep entry road into the campground makes this a poor choice for those with trailers or RVs. Campsites are in a wooded glen on Mount Mansfield's lower slopes. Nine large lean-to sites set above the other spaces are reserved for use by organized groups. The state park, located at the headwaters of the trout-jammed Brown River, is part of 34,000-acre Mount Mansfield State Forest. Four popular trails lead from the campground to the summit ridge of Mount Mansfield, Vermont's tallest peak at 4,393 feet; they branch off above the group camping area. The Sunset Ridge Trail is the most popular and scenic, offering views for much of the way. Vermont's Long Trail crosses the summit, and a trail network on the other side makes many hiking loops possible. The harsh summit-ridge climate has fostered rare Arctic vegetation; once you summit, you see the Stowe Ski Area on the west side of the mountain. The campground includes a day-use area and a large log picnic shelter built by the Civilian Conservation Corps in the late 1930s.

Campsites, facilities: There are 25 sites for tents including 15 lean-tos and a group camping area. Flush toilets, piped water, fireplaces, and picnic tables are provided. Down and dead wood in the state forest can be used for campfires. Supplies are sold in Underhill Center, and more extensive goods and services can be obtained in Jeffersonville. Leashed pets with rabies vaccination certification are permitted, but not in day-use areas.

Reservations, fees: Reservations are recommended. Tent sites are $14 a night and lean-to sites are $21 a night for four people. The maximum allowable number of people at a site is eight, and there must be one person at least 18 years of age with each camping party. See the introduction to this chapter for more information on state park regulations.

Open: Late May–mid-October.

Directions: From Highway 15 in Underhill Center, travel four miles east on Town Road. When the pavement turns to gravel, continue east for another four miles on the same road to the state park.

Contact: Underhill State Park, P.O. Box 249, Underhill Center, VT 05490, 802/899-3022.

38 SMUGGLERS NOTCH STATE PARK

🚶 🐴 ♿ 🚐 ⛺

Rating: 8

Northwest of Stowe

The rocky walls of Mount Mansfield and Spruce Peak are separated by a skinny path that makes for a dramatic entrance to the park. These wooded sites lie at the north end of the notch and are the perfect jumping-off point for any number of day and overnight treks in the Green Mountains, as the Long Trail and its many side trails are accessible from the park. According to local lore, bootleggers cached contraband goods during the War of 1812 in a set of rocks known as the Smugglers Caves behind the information booth at Smugglers Notch. Now the notch is one of the state's designated natural areas. Arctic tundra, rare and endangered plants, and interesting rock formations are highlights, and this is also a nesting spot for peregrine falcon. Note: High winds often whip through the notch and campground.

Campsites, facilities: There are 35 sites for tents and RVs, including 14 lean-tos and 15 hike-in sites, all without hookups. A dump station, hot showers, flush toilets, a playground, fireplaces, and picnic tables are provided. Ice and firewood are available. Leashed pets with rabies vaccination certification are permitted, but not in day-use areas.

Reservations, fees: Reservations are recommended. Sites are $14–21 a night for four people. The maximum allowable number of people at a site is eight, and there must be one person at least 18 years of age with each camping party. See the introduction to this chapter for more information on state park regulations.

Open: Mid-May–mid-October.

Directions: From the village of Stowe, head northwest on Highway 108 for eight miles to the park entrance on the right.

Contact: Smugglers Notch State Park, 7248 Mountain Road, Stowe, VT 05672, 802/253-4014.

39 COMMON GROUND CAMPING RESORT

Rating: 4

In Hyde Park

Kids will love Common Ground, for it's more of an amusement park than a campground. Twenty RV sites flank a recreation complex with bumper boats, go-carts, miniature golf, and a swimming pool. For more natural amusements, the Long Trail is located just to the west, offering day hikes up Mount Mansfield and the surrounding peaks, while Elmore State Park to the southwest has a boat ramp and swimming beach. The glitziest town in Vermont's north country lies just to the south: Stowe's streets are lined with expensive shops and gourmet restaurants.

Campsites, facilities: There are 20 RV sites with hookups. A dump station, recreation hall, miniature golf, volleyball, horseshoes, shuffleboard, and a swimming pool are provided. Ice is available, and firewood is sold nearby. Leashed pets are permitted.

Reservations, fees: Reservations are recommended. Tent sites start at $15 a night, and sites with water and electric start at $23 a night.

Open: Mid-April–October 15.

Directions: From the junction of Highways 15 and 100 north of Morrisville, travel 1.7 miles north on Highway 100 to the park entrance on the left.

Contact: Common Ground Camping Resort, 1781 Route 100, Hyde Park, VT 05655, 802/888-5210.

40 ELMORE STATE PARK

Rating: 7

On the north shore of Lake Elmore

Surrounded by forested hills and mountains, Lake Elmore is open to all types of water-based sports. Sites are set in the woods just above the north shore, and the park offers a public boat ramp as well as rowboat and canoe rentals. Most of the lake's shoreline is privately owned and developed. A hiking trail leaves from the campground and ascends 2,608-foot Mount Elmore to the southeast. When you reach the summit, climb 55 feet higher on one of Vermont's last remaining fire towers. The cabin offers a near 360-degree view of the surrounding mountains. Given the campground's location in the central section of northern Vermont, it provides a scenic base camp for day-trip explorations of the Green Mountains and the northeastern reaches of the state.

Campsites, facilities: There are 60 sites for tents and RVs, including 15 lean-tos, all without hookups. Each site has a table and fire ring. A dump station is provided. Facilities include a playground, beach, boat ramp, boat rentals, snack bar, metered hot showers, and flush toilets. Ice is available at the park. Leashed pets with rabies vaccination certification are permitted, but not in day-use areas.

Reservations, fees: Reservations are recommended. Tent sites are $16 a night, and lean-to sites are $23 a night for four people. The maximum allowable number of people at a site is eight, and there must be one person at least 18 years of age with each camping party. See the introduction to this chapter for more information on state park regulations.

Open: Mid-May–mid-October.

Directions: From I-89 north of Montpelier, take Exit 10 and travel north on Highway 100 to Morrisville. Follow Highway 12 south for five miles.

Contact: Elmore State Park, P.O. Box 93, Lake Elmore, VT 05657, 802/888-2982.

41 MOUNTAIN VIEW CAMPGROUND

Rating: 8

In Morrisville on the Lamoille River

Bordered by the Lamoille River and Bugbee Brook, these campsites offer mountain views and full amenities in the country. Tent sites line the river, where rainbow trout and smallmouth bass are often hooked, and RV sites with shade trees lie between the river and Highway 15. The facilities are spotless and upscale, including a hot tub, heated pool, and a nine-hole miniature golf course. Canoeing on the Lamoille is easy enough for paddlers of any skill level; the river flows through miles of pastoral farmland west of Morrisville. Just to the south, Stowe offers more commercial attractions such as the Mount Mansfield alpine slide and a new outdoor amphitheater for summer concerts on the mountain. A good way to explore the country around Morrisville is by bicycle on little-traveled secondary roads. Though family oriented, Mountain View has rules that are less restrictive than those at many private campgrounds: motorcycles are allowed to travel into and out of the park, and campfires can burn until 1 A.M.

Campsites, facilities: There are 63 sites for tents and RVs, 19 with full hookups, 24 with water and electric hookups, and 20 with none. There are also cabins available for rent. Each site has a fire ring and table. Air conditioners are allowed, but heaters are not. Phone hookups are available. Facilities include a dump station, laundry facilities, heated restrooms, hot showers, two pools (one heated), a whirlpool, miniature golf, a playground, badminton and volleyball courts, a recreation hall, camp store, and horseshoe pits. There are also seven cabins for rent. Leashed pets are permitted.

Reservations, fees: Reservations are recommended. Sites start at $25 per night; cabins $75–90 for two people.

Open: Early May–October 15.

Directions: From I-89 north of Montpelier, take Exit 10 and travel north on Highway 100 through Stowe and Morrisville. At the junction with Highway 15, take a right and travel east for three miles to the campground entrance.

Contact: Mountain View Campground, 3154 Route 15E, Morrisville, VT 05661, 802/888-2178, website: www.MountainViewCamping.com.

42 SHELBURNE CAMPING AREA

Rating: 6

North of Shelburne Village

It's hard to miss the entrance—just look out for the Dutch-style windmill. The campground is owned and operated by the proprietors of the Dutch Mill Motel and family restaurant, and large, grassy sites with shade trees line up behind the facility in RV-park fashion. Seasonal campers tend to favor this place for its proximity to Lake Champlain, Burlington, and lake beaches. One mile south of the campground is the Shelburne Museum. Founder Electra Havermayer Webb was an eccentric heiress who traveled all over the country in the early part of this century, snapping up canoes, toys, furniture, paintings, quilts, decoys, scrimshaw, weather vanes, and many other folk art items. More than 80,000 pieces are contained in three galleries and seven furnished historic houses on 45 country acres.

Campsites, facilities: There are 76 sites for tents and RVs, 30 with full hookups, 40 with water and electric hookups, and six with none. Each site has a picnic table and fire ring. Air conditioner and heater use is allowed. Laundry facilities, a dump station, recreation room, two pools, a basketball hoop, badminton and volleyball courts, and horseshoe pits are provided. Cable TV, phone, and modem hookups are available. A small grocery store sells LP gas, ice, and firewood. Leashed pets are permitted.

Reservations, fees: Reservations are recommended July 1–Labor Day. Sites start at $20 a night for two people.

Open: March 1–November 1.

Directions: From Shelburne Village, travel a mile north on U.S. 7.

Contact: Shelburne Camping Area, 4385 Shelburne Road, Shelburne, VT 05482, 802/985-2540, website: www.shelburnecamping.com.

43 GOLD BROOK CAMPGROUND

🚶 🏊 🚣 📷 ❄ 🐕 🚴 🚐 ⛺

Rating: 8

South of Stowe

Gold Brook and the Little River, two waterways that are teeming with trout, skirt the campground property. Most sites have frontage on either stream as well as shade trees around the edge of a large grassy lawn that begs for a game of ultimate Frisbee. There's a small pool at the campground, but swimming is also permitted in Gold Brook and the Little River. Operated in conjunction with Nichols Lodge, the facility offers a breakfast plan during the winter by reservation and runs an ice-cream stand during the summer. In snowy months, the winter sports office at the lodge rents out snowmobiles for use on the miles of trails that are accessible from the campground. Several alpine and Nordic ski centers operate in the area and, to the immediate west, the Long Trail ascends the state's tallest peak, Mount Mansfield. Stowe, just two miles north of here, is one of the state's oldest and most posh resort towns, known for its expensive hotels, shops, and fine restaurants.

Campsites, facilities: There are 79 sites for tents and RVs, 30 with full hookups and 20 with water and electric hookups. Each site has a table, fireplace, and grill. Facilities include a dump station, free hot showers, laundry facilities, a recreation room, pool, playground, shuffle board, badminton and volleyball courts, and horseshoe pits. Cable TV and telephone connections are available. LP gas, ice, and firewood are for sale on-site. Leashed pets are permitted.

Reservations, fees: Reservations are recommended and must be accompanied by a one-day deposit. Tent sites start at $20 a night. Weekly, seasonal, and ski-season rates are available.

Open: Year-round.

Directions: From I-89 at Waterbury, take Exit 10 and head north on Highway 100 for 7.5 miles to the campground entrance on the left (west) side of the road.

Contact: Gold Brook Campground, P.O. Box 1028, Route 100, Stowe, VT 05672, 802/253-7683 or 800/483-7683.

44 LITTLE RIVER STATE PARK

🚶 🏊 🚣 🚻 🐕 🚴 ♿ 🚐 ⛺

Rating: 8

Northwest of Montpelier on the Waterbury Reservoir

The Waterbury Reservoir was created when a dam was placed on the Little River. This campground is located across the cove from the day-use area and has its own beach and boat launch. Some of the northern sites are on remote stretches of shoreline, while the majority are well shaded and roomy, set in the hilly forest on steep banks above the water. At night, join the captain of the park pontoon boat for a two-hour sunset tour of the reservoir. On dry land, a history hike leads to stone walls and foundations from a 6,000-acre farming community that dates back to the 1700s. The park is part of Mount Mansfield State Forest and is a good jumping-off point for day hikes or overnight backpacking trips on the Long Trail. A maintained nature trail explores Stevenson Brook, which flows from the west into the reservoir. If you are screaming for ice cream, the Ben and Jerry's Ice Cream Factory churns out its world-famous treats to the south in Waterbury. Tours of the facility include free samples.

Campsites, facilities: There are 101 sites for tents and RVs, including 20 lean-tos, all without hookups. Each site has a picnic table and fireplace. A dump station, metered hot showers, restrooms, boat rentals, a boat ramp, playground, and beach are provided. The contact station sells ice and firewood. Leashed pets with rabies vaccination certification are permitted at sites, but not in day-use areas.

Reservations, fees: Reservations are recommended. Tent sites are $16 a night and lean-to sites are $21 a night for four people. The maximum allowable number of people at a site is eight, and there must be one person at least

18 years of age with each camping party. See the introduction to this chapter for more information on state park regulations.

Open: Mid-May–Columbus Day.

Directions: From Waterbury, travel west on U.S. 2 for .5 mile, then turn right on Little River Road. Drive 3.5 miles north to the campground entrance.

Contact: Little River State Park, 3444 Little River Road, Waterbury, VT 05676, 802/244-7103.

45 IDLE HOURS CAMPGROUND
🐟 🛥 🏕 🐕 🚶 🚐 🏕

Rating: 6

Near Mackville Pond in Hardwick

Secluded, wooded sites at Idle Hours are popular with seasonal campers, so call ahead to find out if space is available. There's a pool on the grounds for swimming, but if you seek true peace and quiet, spend an afternoon canoeing on Mackville Pond. Should you desire a little culture, Hardwick hosts a group of local chamber musicians at the town hall every Thursday night in July and August. Anglers can cast flies on the Lamoille River, which flows through downtown, for smallmouth bass, brown trout, and rainbow trout. This waterway eventually empties into Lake Champlain.

Campsites, facilities: There are 22 sites for tents and RVs, nine with full hookups and 13 with water and electric hookups. A dump station, laundry facilities, playground, pool, hot showers, and flush toilets are provided. Ice and firewood are available. Leashed pets are permitted.

Reservations, fees: Reservations are recommended. Sites start at $20 a night.

Open: Late May–mid-September.

Directions: From the junction of Highways 14 and 15 in Hardwick, travel south on Highway 15 for about .5 mile to Mackville Pond Road. Turn left and go east for one mile. From the camping sign, continue another .75 mile to the pond and then turn left.

Contact: Idle Hours Campground, 965

Mackville Road, Hardwick, VT 05843, 802/472-6732 in season or 802/388-0907 off-season.

46 SUGAR RIDGE RV VILLAGE AND CAMPGROUND, INC.
🚶 🚴 🛥 🏕 🐕 🚐 🏕

Rating: 7

West of St. Johnsbury

This brand new family campground offers sites set beneath tall pines and maple trees.

Campsites, facilities: There are 111 sites with hookups and phone and cable TV access. Most sites accommodate air-conditioning. Each site has a picnic table and campfire pit. On-site are restrooms, free hot showers, a snack bar, Laundromat, recreation building, and a grocery store (with firewood, ice, and LP gas). Leashed pets are permitted.

Reservations, fees: Reservations are recommended. Sites start at $27–34 a night.

Open: May 1–October 31.

Directions: From I-91, take Exit 21 and travel 4.5 miles west on Route 2 to the campground entrance.

Contact: Sugar Ridge RV Village and Campground, Inc., 24 Old Stagecoach Road, Danville, VT 05828, 802/684-2550, website: www.sugarridgervpark.com.

47 MOOSE RIVER CAMPGROUND
🚶 🛥 🏕 🚐 🐕 ♿ 🚐 🏕

Rating: 5

East of St. Johnsbury on the Moose River

These sites are set on a grassy bend in the Moose River on the outskirts of working-class St. Johnsbury. The campground caters to adult seasonal campers who enjoy the location between the White Mountains of New Hampshire and the Green Mountains, and the proximity to the Connecticut River. (Busy U.S. 2 does detract from the scenery, however.) You can fish on the Moose River. Moore Reservoir, a few miles southeast in New Hampshire, has a public launch and offers excellent powerboating and swimming; it is often a wild, rowdy scene on weekends. The Fairbanks Museum and Planetarium on Main Street in St. Johnsbury is a bit of a paradox: You step back in time upon entry into the historic building, but the state-of-the-art exhibits include collections from around the world, a weather center, and Vermont's only public planetarium. It's open daily all summer long.

Campsites, facilities: There are 50 sites for tents and RVs, 28 with full hookups and 14 with water and electric hookups. Each site has a table and fire ring. Phone hookups are available. A dump station, metered hot showers, badminton court, and horseshoe pits are provided. Ice and firewood are available. Supplies and services are found in St. Johnsbury. Campers need permission before displaying items for sale at their sites. Leashed pets are permitted.

Reservations, fees: Reservations are recommended. Sites range from $18–28 a night.

Open: May 1–October 15.

Directions: From I-91, take Exit 19 and head south on I-93 for two miles. At Exit 1, take Highway 18 north for about a third of a mile to U.S. 2. Turn left and continue to the campground entrance 200 feet ahead on the left.

Contact: Moose River Campground, 2870 Portland Street, St. Johnsbury, VT 05819, 802/748-4334 in summer or 802/472-3139 in winter, website: www.mooserivercampground.com.

48 RUSTIC HAVEN CAMPGROUND

Rating: 6

North of Concord

Grassy sites are shaded by tall pine trees in this small but pretty campground. If you are here during foliage season, head to nearby Kirby Mountain and surrounding farms for some lovely views.

Campsites, facilities: There are 38 RV sites with water and electric hookups. Each site has a picnic table and stone fireplace. A play-

ground, pool, hot showers, flush toilets, and a dump station are provided. Leashed pets are permitted.

Reservations, fees: Reservations are recommended. Sites range from $20–26 a night.

Open: Mid-May–mid-October.

Directions: From I-91, take Exit 20/St. Johnsbury to Route 2 east for seven miles to the campground.

Contact: Rustic Haven Campground, 1111 Main Street, Concord, VT 05824, 802/695-9933, website: www.members.tripod.com/rustichaven.

49 BREEZY MEADOWS CAMPGROUND

Rating: 7

North of Concord

Large grassy sites buffered by wooded ridges are perfect for family camping. You can rent canoes and paddleboats at the campground for use on the Moose River. This is a newly built campground (with modern, handicapped-accessible facilities), and when construction is finished, there will be over 100 campsites.

Campsites, facilities: There are currently 51 sites for tents and RVs, some with hookups. Tent and pop-up sites are along the river. Each site has a picnic table and fireplace. A playground, heated pool (through Labor Day), hot showers, laundry facilities, a pavilion, sports courts, hiking trails, flush toilets, and a dump station are provided. Wood, ice, and LP gas available on-site. Leashed pets are permitted.

Reservations, fees: Reservations are recommended. Sites start at $20–28 a night.

Open: May–October.

Directions: From I-91, take exit 20 to Route 2. Follow for eight miles east to the campground entrance.

Contact: Breezy Meadows Campground, 23 Wendel Road, Concord, VT 05824, 802/695-9949, website: www.gocampingamerica.com/breezymeadows.

50 MOUNT PHILO STATE PARK

Rating: 7

Near Lake Champlain in North Ferrisburgh

These campsites are set near the top of Mount Philo. And though the summit elevation is only 980 feet, the mountain's proximity to the Lake Champlain shores makes it an ideal lookout for panoramic views to the west of the Adirondack Mountains in New York state. Note that a steep roadway leads into the park, prohibiting access to camping vehicles more than 30 feet in length.

Campsites, facilities: There are 10 sites for tents and RVs, including three lean-tos, all without hookups. Each site has a table and fireplace. No dump station is available. Metered hot showers, flush toilets, recycling bins, a picnic shelter, and a playground are provided. Firewood is available. Leashed pets with rabies vaccination certification are permitted, but not in day-use areas.

Reservations, fees: Reservations are recommended. Sites are $14–21 a night for four people. The maximum allowable number of people at a site is eight, and there must be one person at least 18 years of age with each camping party. See the introduction to this chapter for more information on state park regulations.

Open: Early May–mid-October.

Directions: From North Ferrisburgh, travel a mile north on U.S. 7. Turn right on the town road and drive a mile east to the park entrance, following the signs.

Contact: Mount Philo State Park, 5425 Mount Philo Road, Charlotte, VT 05445, 802/425-2390.

51 GREEN VALLEY CAMPGROUND

Rating: 5

Northeast of Montpelier

For people traveling on I-89, this is the perfect place to stop for the night. A green hill rises behind the campground, and sites are grassy, wide open, and snug—only about 30 feet wide. Some sites have a shade tree. To the south is the state capital of Montpelier, which has the smallest population of any capital city in the country. To the immediate south in Barre, the Rock of Ages company conducts tours of their granite quarry, the largest in the world.

Campsites, facilities: There are 35 sites for tents and RVs, most with hookups. Cable TV access is available. Air conditioner and heater use is allowed. A dump station, laundry facilities, a playground, pool, hot showers, horseshoe pits, a grocery store with limited supplies, and tables are provided. There's also a community fireplace and recreation hall. Ice and LP gas are available. Leashed pets are permitted.

Reservations, fees: Reservations are recommended. Sites start at $25 a night. There are surcharges for electric heaters, air conditioners, cable TV, and additional campers.

Open: May 1–November 1.

Directions: From the junction of I-89 and U.S. 2 in Montpelier (Exit 8), travel northeast on U.S. 2 for six miles to the campground entrance on the right.

Contact: Green Valley Campground, P.O. Box 21, U.S. 2, East Montpelier, VT 05651, 802/223-6217, website: www.greenvalleyrvpark.com.

52 ONION RIVER CAMPGROUND

Rating: 6

East of Montpelier

Smallmouth bass and trout are the sought-after prey in the Winooski River, which you can cast into from your campsite at Onion River. Here, small and grassy sites are set at the water's edge. Groton State Forest is adjacent to the campground, and multiuse trails for hiking and mountain biking lead through the surrounding hills. In addition to having some glorious swimming holes, the Winooski is also open to paddlers; most people put in at Montpelier and head west to Lake Champlain.

Campsites, facilities: There are 48 RV sites, some with full hookups. A dump station, hot showers, laundry facilities, a small store, tables, fire rings, and grills are provided. Recreational facilities include horseshoe pits, hiking trails, and badminton and volleyball courts. LP gas, ice, and firewood are available. Leashed pets are permitted.

Reservations, fees: Reservations are recommended. Sites start at $18 a night.

Open: April 1–November 30.

Directions: From the junction of U.S. 2 and Highway 14 east of Montpelier, travel 5.25 miles east on U.S. 2 to the campground entrance on the right (south) side of the road.

Contact: Onion River Campground, 61 Onion River Road, Plainfield, VT 05667, 802/426-3232.

53 GROTON FOREST ROAD CAMPGROUND

Rating: 6

North of Groton State Forest

Set on nine acres just outside Groton State Forest, half of these sites are open and grassy while the rest are tucked in the woods. The small and clean campground is a good choice for RVers who need hookups (the state forest campgrounds only have dump stations) and want to enjoy the many lakes, ponds, streams, and trails in the 25,000-acre forest. Various wildlife species inhabit the state's second largest contiguous landholding, including moose, black bear, deer, loons, mink, and grouse. The ponds are open to fishing and swimming. A good rainy day side trip for cheese lovers is just to the north in Cabot, where the Cabot Creamery churns out a line of dairy products; you can tour the factory and watch cheese being made, then sample your way through the gift shop. (For information, call 800/242-2740.)

Campsites, facilities: There are 35 sites for tents

and RVs with water and electric hookups. A dump station, metered hot showers, flush toilets, picnic tables, fire rings, free firewood, a playground, pool, horseshoe pits, and courts for volleyball, badminton, and croquet are provided. Leashed pets are permitted.

Reservations, fees: Reservations are recommended. Sites start at $18 a night.

Open: May–mid-October, weather permitting. Sites are available during the fall deer-hunting season by reservation.

Directions: From the junction of U.S. 2 and Highway 232 in Marshfield, travel three miles south on Highway 232 to the campground entrance on the right.

Contact: Groton Forest Road Campground, 2654 Route 232, Marshfield, VT 05658, 802/426-4122 in the summer.

54 NEW DISCOVERY STATE PARK

Rating: 7

In Groton State Forest

Of the three campgrounds within the state forest, this is the only one not on a swimming lake and thus is the last to fill up. All three make good jumping-off points for those who want to explore this 25,000-acre tract of land dominated by rolling and steep hills. Open year-round, a network of multiuse trails traverses summits, bogs, and streams. From the campground, the Osmore Pond Trail travels downhill through a stand of spruce and fir and an old logging area to the pond; remote hike-in camping is allowed here with a permit ($25/night for four people). From here, you can ascend Little or Big Deer Mountains. Warm-water fish can be caught in the park's ponds, while the streams are stocked with trout. The camping fee includes a day-use charge that allows you to visit any of the other state parks here during your stay, such as Stillwater State Park (see next listing) and Ricker Pond State Park (see listing in this chapter).

Campsites, facilities: There are 61 sites for tents and RVs, including 14 lean-tos, all without hookups. Each site has a picnic table and fireplace. Metered hot showers, flush toilets, recycling bins, a dump station, picnic shelter, and playground are provided. Firewood is available. Leashed pets with rabies vaccination certification are permitted, but not in day-use areas.

Reservations, fees: Reservations are recommended. Sites are $14–$21 a night for four people. The maximum allowable number of people at a site is eight, and there must be one person at least 18 years of age with each camping party. See the introduction to this chapter for more information on state park regulations.

Open: Mid-May–Labor Day.

Directions: From Marshfield, travel a mile east on Highway 232, bear right, and continue south on the same road for 5.5 miles to the campground entrance on the left (east) side of the road.

Contact: New Discovery State Park, Groton State Forest, 4239 Route 232, Marshfield, VT 05658, 802/426-3042.

55 STILLWATER STATE PARK

🚶 🚲 🛶 🎣 🛶 ✕ 🎣 🐕 ⛺ ♿
🚐 ⛺

Rating: 8

In Groton State Forest

These wooded sites are extremely popular in summertime with campers who want to swim and boat on Lake Groton, the largest body of water in the 25,000-acre state forest. Flanked by hills and acres of forestland, this clear gem offers the chance to canoe in a spectacular setting. Sites are set in the woods on or near the lake, and there is a sandy beach at the campground. More than 40 miles of multiuse trails traverse the park. From the nature center at the northern tip of Lake Groton, the Peacham Bog Trail leads to one of Vermont's largest natural bogs.

Campsites, facilities: There are 79 sites for tents and RVs, including 17 lean-tos, all without hookups. Each site has a picnic table and fireplace. Metered hot showers, flush toilets, recycling bins, a dump station, picnic shelter, boat rentals, a boat ramp, snack bar, and playground are provided. Firewood is available. You will find general stores in Marshfield and Groton; more extensive services are offered in Montpelier and Barre. Leashed pets with rabies vaccination certification are permitted, but not in day-use areas.

Reservations, fees: Reservations are recommended. Sites are $16–23 a night for four people. The maximum allowable number of people at a site is eight, and there must be one person at least 18 years of age with each camping party. See the introduction to this chapter for more information on state park regulations.

Open: Mid-May–mid-October.

Directions: From Groton, travel two miles west on U.S. 302. Take a right onto Highway 232 and head north for six miles. Turn right on Boulder Beach Road and head east for .5 mile to the campground.

Contact: Stillwater State Park, Groton State Forest, 126 Boulder Beach Road, Groton, VT 05046, 802/584-3822.

56 RICKER POND STATE PARK

🚶 🚲 🛶 🎣 🛶 🎣 🐕 ⛺ ♿ 🚐

Rating: 8

In Groton State Forest

The sites at this campground, one of three in the state forest, are located on the south side of Ricker Pond, where boat rentals and a ramp are available. Campers also have access to several hiking and multiuse trails. The trailhead for the nearby Silver Ledge Trail is across the road from the camp. Starting out level, it then climbs steeply to a lookout over Lake Groton and Beaver Meadows. The campground bounds the Montpelier/Wells River Railroad, now a multiuse trail popular with mountain bikers.

Campsites, facilities: There are 55 sites for tents and RVs, including 23 lean-tos, all without hookups. Each site has a picnic table and fireplace. Metered hot showers, flush toilets, recycling bins, a dump station, picnic shelter, boat rentals, a boat ramp, and playground are provided. Firewood is available. Leashed pets with rabies vaccination certification are permitted, but not in day-use areas.

Reservations, fees: Reservations are recommended. Sites are $16–23 a night for four people. The maximum allowable number of people at a site is eight, and there must be one person at least 18 years of age with each camping party. See the introduction to this chapter for more information on state park regulations.

Open: Mid-May–mid-October.

Directions: From Groton, travel two miles west on U.S. 302. Take a right onto Highway 232 and drive north for 2.5 miles to the park entrance on the right (east) side of the road.

Contact: Ricker Pond State Park, Groton State Forest, 526 State Forest Road, Groton, VT 05046, 802/584-3821.

57 HARVEYS LAKE CABINS AND CAMPGROUND

Rating: 8

On the north end of Harveys Lake in Barnet

Harveys Lake is Vermont's oldest private campground. In addition to sites for tents and RVs, 11 furnished cabins are also available for rent. Most of the cabins are set in the woods above the beach area on Harveys Lake, and campsites 8–13 also have water frontage. Several others are next to a river channel. These small sites (about 20 feet wide) are buffered by large pine trees. The big draw is Harveys Lake, a quiet 350-acre pool that's more than 100 feet deep in places and is perfect for fishing and swimming. Guarded by hills and forest, the lake has no public access and is not overdeveloped, so it's peaceful even in the summer.

Recently, someone pulled a 17-pound lake trout out of these waters. The atmosphere at Harveys is low-key.

Campsites, facilities: There are 53 sites for tents and RVs up to 30 feet in length, 15 with full hookups, 26 with water and electric hookups, and 12 with none. Each site has a fire pit, table, and grill. A dump station, hot showers, flush toilets, video games, a recreation hall, pool and Ping-Pong tables, a basketball court, and horse shoe pit are provided. Eleven cabins are for rent. Leashed pets are permitted.

Reservations, fees: Reservations are recommended and require a 50 percent deposit. Sites start at $19 a night per family; cabins $55–125 for two people. Seasonal rates are available.

Open: May 15–October 15.

Directions: From I-91 at Barnet, take Exit 18 and travel five miles west. In West Barnet, turn left at the white church, cross a small bridge, and then turn right on the first dirt road at the orange "narrow road" sign.

Contact: Harveys Lake Cabins and Campground, 109 Camper's Lane, West Barnet, VT 05821, 802/633-2213, website: www.harveyslakecabins.com.

58 BUTTON BAY STATE PARK

Rating: 10

On Lake Champlain west of Vergennes

Located on the Lake Champlain south shore, these campsites offer stunning views of the Adirondack Mountains across the water in New York. Water-skiers and powerboaters sometimes clog the park's boat ramp and dock on summer weekends. Most visitors are drawn to Button Bay for the views and the water sports, while the resident naturalist, nature center, and interesting geography and history only add to the campground's popularity. A footpath at the Button Bay Natural Area leads through a small, but impressive, oak-hickory woodland with lake vistas. The bedrock here is limestone, formed about 450 million years ago. Some of the oldest fossilized coral in the world, as well as the remains of other marine organisms, are found here. "Buttons" were clay deposits, left by retreating glaciers some 10,000 years ago, that cemented into circular shapes with holes in the middle. A collection of these now rare formations is on display at the nature center. Button Bay is where General Benedict Arnold sank America's first naval fleet; British soldiers named the sheltered, strategic location for the button like clay formations.

Campsites, facilities: There are 72 sites for tents and RVs, including 13 lean-tos, all without hookups. Each site has a picnic table and fireplace. Metered hot showers, flush toilets, recycling bins, a dump station, picnic shelter, snack bar, pool, and playground are provided. Leashed pets with rabies vaccination certification are permitted, but not in day-use areas.

Reservations, fees: Reservations are recommended. Sites are $16–21 a night for four people. The maximum allowable number of people at a site is eight, and there must be one person at least 18 years of age with each camping party. See the introduction to this chapter for more information on state park regulations.

Open: Mid-May–Columbus Day.

Directions: From Vergennes, travel .5 mile south on Highway 22A. Turn right and head west for six miles to the campground, following the signs.

Contact: Button Bay State Park, 5 Button Bay State Park Road, Vergennes, VT 05491, 802/475-2377 or 800/658-1622.

59 MAPLE HILL CAMPSITES

East of Bristol

Rating: 7

Private and small, this campground is best suited to tents and pop-up campers. There are woodland paths through the 150-acre campground, and the Long Trail is accessible from the nearby Jerusalem Trail. Take a five-minute walk to a great swimming hole or a trout fishing spot. Come sunset, the view of the Adirondacks is spectacular. In mid- to late May and again in September, Native Americans gather for a four-day event at Maple Hill, and all are welcome to join in the healing circles and sweat lodges. For information, contact Elder Dominique Dedam at 802/453-6337.

Campsites, facilities: There are 15 sites for tents and RVs, a few with electric hookups. Each site has a picnic table and fireplace; flush toilets, hot showers and a playground are provided. Leashed pets are allowed.

Reservations, fees: Reservations are recommended. Sites range from $18–20 a night.

Open: Mid-May–October.

Directions: From Bristol, take Highway 17 east for approximately five miles. Follow signs off Highway 17 to the campground entrance.

Contact: Maple Hill Campsites, 3825 Quaker Street, Bristol, VT 05443, 802/453-3687, website: www.sover.net/~maplehil/.

60 LAZY LIONS CAMPGROUND

South of Barre

Rating: 5

Wooded, grassy sites are divided into two separate areas for tents and RVs. Children are welcome, but the campground bills itself as "adult-oriented." Between the campsites and Highway 63, the owners operate the Lazy Lions Cafe, so if you are feeling a little lackadaisical, let them cook breakfast for you. Just south of the campground is the world's largest granite quarry, Rock of Ages. Take a free self-guided tour of the quarry or, for a small fee, a narrated shuttle tour. An observation deck over the Craftsman Center lets visitors watch master stonecutters at work.

Campsites, facilities: There are 34 RV and tent sites, 21 with full hookups. Each site has a table and fire ring. The campground offers a dump station, metered hot showers, restrooms, laundry facilities, a café, and a playground. Ice and firewood are available. Leashed pets are permitted.

Reservations, fees: Reservations are recommended in the summer. Site base rates range from $15–25 a night.

Open: May 15–November 1.

Directions: From I-89 south of Montpelier, take Exit 6 and travel east on Highway 63. Approximately four miles later, you arrive at a stop signal at the junction with Highway 14. Continue east for exactly a mile to the campground entrance on the left.

Contact: Lazy Lions Campground, 281 Middle Road, Graniteville, VT 05654, 802/479-2823, website: www.gocampingamerica.com/lazylions.

61 PLEASANT VALLEY CAMPGROUND

Rating: 7

On the north end of Ticklenaked Pond

Open to boating, swimming, and fishing, Ticklenaked Pond is as fun as its name sounds. Sites are set on 100 wooded acres next to the lake, and many are occupied by seasonal campers. You can rent paddleboats at the campground. For a livelier boating experience, trek a short distance east to the Connecticut River. Here in the northern reaches, the river is less developed and flows through lush farm country.

Campsites, facilities: There are 50 sites for tents and RVs, 30 with water and electric hookups. Each has a table and fireplace. A dump station, laundry facilities, a playground, recreation hall, hot showers, restrooms, paddleboat rentals, a volleyball court, and horseshoe pits are provided. A store sells ice and firewood. Leashed pets are permitted.

Reservations, fees: Reservations are recommended. Sites are $15–20 a night; seasonal rates are available.

Open: Mid-May–mid-October.

Directions: From I-91 north of Wells River, take Exit 17 and travel one mile west on U.S. 302. Turn right on Ryegate Center Road and continue north for 1.5 miles to the campground entrance.

Contact: Pleasant Valley Campground, 964 Wallace Hill Road, Wells River, VT 05081, 802/584-3884, in winter 802/866-5991.

62 D.A.R. STATE PARK

Rating: 8

On Lake Champlain north of the Chimney Point Bridge

D.A.R. State Park is on the Lake Champlain shore. Campers can launch boats near the campground onto the 120-mile-long lake, as well as go swimming and fishing. Sites are partly shaded and roomy and are in high demand in midsummer, so be sure to reserve.

Campsites, facilities: There are 70 sites for tents and RVs, including 24 lean-tos, all without hookups. Dump stations, tables, fire rings, and a playground are provided, and ice can be purchased nearby. Firewood is available on-site. Leashed pets with rabies vaccination certification are permitted, but not in day-use areas.

Reservations, fees: Reservations are recommended. For reservations, phone 800/658-1622. Sites are $16–21 a night for four people. The maximum allowable number of people at a site is eight, and there must be one person at least 18 years of age with each camping party. See the introduction to this chapter for more information on state park regulations.

Open: Mid-May–Labor Day.

Directions: From the junction of Highways 22A and 17 in Addison, travel seven miles southwest on Highway 17 to Lake Champlain. The campground borders the water.

Contact: D.A.R. State Park, 6750 Route 17W, Addison, VT 05491, 802/759-2354.

63 GRIFFIN'S TEN ACRE CAMPGROUND

Rating: 7

Near the Chimney Point Bridge

Set in a wooded niche surrounded by rolling, cleared farmland, this campground is just across the road from 120-mile-long Lake Champlain. Both open and shaded spots are available, and all sites are grassy. A small, stocked fishing pond on the grounds will please the kids, while grown-ups will want to get out on the big lake. Docks are located across the road from the campground, and all types of boats are welcome. Sailing and powerboating are the most popular activities.

Campsites, facilities: There are 78 RV sites with full hookups and 12 tent sites, including two lean-tos. Each site has a picnic table and fire ring. Hot showers, laundry facilities, a heated pool, pavilion, game room, horseshoe pits, shuffleboard, and miniature golf are provided. LP gas, ice, and firewood are available. Leashed pets are permitted.

Reservations, fees: Reservations are recommended. Sites are $16–$22 a night for two people.

Open: May 1–mid-October.

Directions: From the Chimney Point Bridge, which crosses Lake Champlain, travel a mile south on Highway 125 to the campground entrance across the street from the lake.

Contact: Griffin's Ten Acre Campground, 9 Ten Acres Drive, Addison, VT 05491, 802/759-2662.

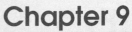

Chapter 9

© STATE OF VERMONT AGENCY OF NATURAL RESOURCES

Green Mountains

Green Mountains

Like a string of emeralds, Vermont's Green Mountains shimmer in the sunlight, dominating the western half of the state. Geographically they represent a physical hurdle, but they serve to bind together the people and towns of the region.

Camp here if you love to hike; seemingly endless miles of trails explore the green spine of Vermont. But you'll also find extensive lake recreation . . . all that water running down the hillsides has to end up somewhere! Most campgrounds take advantage of the mountain views or access to rivers and lakes. The landscape is a mix of working farmland, cozy villages, mountain passes, and historic sites. There are also several well-known colleges here (Middlebury, Bennington College) that add to the region's air of culture.

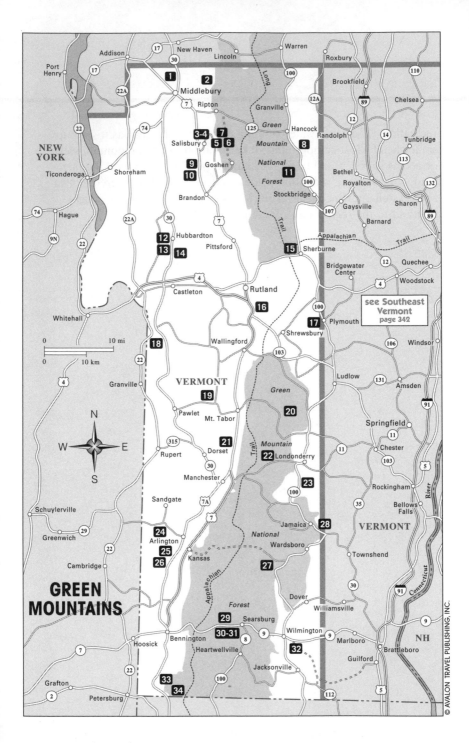

NEW
YORK

VERMONT

**GREEN
MOUNTAINS**

see Southeast
Vermont
page 342

VERMONT

NH

Port
Henry

Addison

New Haven

Lincoln

Warren

Roxbury

Brookfield

Chelsea

Middlebury

Ripton

Granville

Hancock

Randolph

Tunbridge

Ticonderoga

Shoreham

Salisbury

Goshen

Green

Bethel

Royalton

Sharon

Brandon

Mountain

Stockbridge

Gaysville

Barnard

Hague

Hubbardton

Pittsford

National

Sherburne

Bridgewater
Center

Quechee

Woodstock

Whitehall

Castleton

Rutland

Forest

Plymouth

Shrewsbury

Windsor

Granville

Wallingford

Ludlow

Amsden

Pawlet

Mt. Tabor

Green

Springfield

Rupert

Dorset

Chester

Manchester

Mountain

Londonderry

Rockingham

Sandgate

Jamaica

Bellows
Falls

Townshend

Schuylerville

Arlington

National

Wardsboro

Greenwich

Kansas

Cambridge

Forest

Dover

Williamsville

Searsburg

Bennington

Heartwellville

Wilmington

Marlboro

Brattleboro

Jacksonville

Guilford

Hoosick

Grafton

Petersburg

0   10 mi

0   10 km

N
W   E
S

© AVALON TRAVEL PUBLISHING, INC.

1 RIVERS BEND CAMPGROUND

🚶 🏊 🛶 🗡 🏕 🚴 🚐 ⛺

Rating: 7

At the confluence of Otter Creek and the New Haven River

About half the sites at this campground, located in a bend in Otter Creek, are right on the water and are grassy and partially shaded. The campground owns about 4,000 feet of river frontage on waters that are ripe for swimming, fishing, tubing, and canoeing. Otter Creek, which flows north to Lake Champlain, is especially known for its pace: easy enough for paddlers of all levels to handle. Rivers Bend also maintains a sandy beach. Two nature trails explore the hills around the river valley. The Morgan Horse Farm, operated by the University of Vermont, is nearby. Established in the 1870s, the farm is devoted to breeding Morgan horses, the first American breed. Guided tours are given through the stately and historic main barn.

Campsites, facilities: There are 67 sites for tents and RVs with water and electric hookups. Each site has a fire ring and table. Air conditioners are allowed. Facilities include a dump station, restrooms with hot showers, laundry facilities, a pavilion, playground, horseshoe pits, and volleyball. Ice and firewood are available. Leashed pets are permitted.

Reservations, fees: Reservations are recommended. Sites start at $22 a night.

Open: May 1–mid-October.

Directions: From the junction of Highway 125 and U.S. 7 at Middlebury, travel four miles north on U.S. 7. Turn left on Dog Team Road and drive a mile to the entrance.

Contact: Rivers Bend Campground, P.O. Box 110, 1000 Dog Team Road, New Haven, VT 05472, 802/388-9092, website: www.riversbendcampground.com.

2 GREEN MOUNTAIN CAMPING AREA

🚶 🏊 🏕 🚴 🚐 ⛺

Rating: 6

South of Bristol in the Green Mountain National Forest

Peaceful family camping in the heart of the Green Mountain National Forest is what you'll find here. The sites are well shaded and have ample natural buffer for privacy. A small brook runs through the property, but most campers swim in either of the two brand-new pools. Hiking trails are accessible from the campground. In fact, one of the most striking Long Trail stretches lies just to the east of Elephant Mountain: the ridge from Lincoln Gap to Appalachian Gap is as precipitous as it is beautiful, a skinny catwalk that offers sweeping views in every direction.

Campsites, facilities: There are 50 sites, most for RVs and a few for tents; all have electric hookups, and some have full hookups. Each site has a fireplace and picnic table. A pavilion, playground, pool, trails, sports courts, athletic fields, and horseshoe pits are provided. Ice and firewood are available. Leashed pets are permitted.

Reservations, fees: Reservations are recommended and require a $10 deposit. Sites are $18–23 a night.

Open: May 1–mid-October.

Directions: From Bristol, drive about three miles south on Highway 116. The campground entrance is on the left (east) side of the highway.

Contact: Green Mountain Family Campground, 4817 Route 116 South, Bristol, VT 05443, 802/453-3123, website: www.familycampground.com.

3 LAKE DUNMORE KAMPERSVILLE

🚶 🏊 🛶 🚐 🎿 🏕 🚴 🚐 ⛺

Rating: 6

North of Lake Dunmore

Lake Dunmore and the surrounding green hills provide the setting for this full-service, family-oriented campground. Sparkling clean facilities and sites, most of them wooded, are located across the street from the lake. In summer, colorful beds of annuals punctuate the grounds. Campers have access to beaches and docks where a host of organized activities takes place, from guided pontoon boat rides to fishing and waterskiing. The lake is fed by a spring and supports landlocked salmon and trout. Most mornings in the summer, the owner of the campground gives guided tours of Kampersville, while recreation personnel lead frequent nature walks to nearby scenic destinations such as secluded Silver Lake and Cascade Falls, both of which are open to swimming. There are tournaments both for kids and adults, from shuffleboard and horseshoes to whist and Ping-Pong, as well as craft classes and yo-yo lessons. Theme weekends are organized throughout the summer. As you've probably guessed, this is a high-energy, high-activity campground.

Campsites, facilities: There are 210 sites for tents and RVs, 39 with full hookups, 65 with water and electric hookups. Newly renovated Tarky's Lodge log cabin sleeps 28. Air conditioner and heater use is allowed. Cable TV and telephone connections are available. Facilities include a laundry room, picnic tables, fire rings, grills, a recreation hall, snack bar, restrooms, free hot showers, a pavilion, and a playground. For recreation, there are pools, boat rentals, planned group activities, movies, sports courts, athletic fields, and miniature golf. RV storage, RV supplies, ice, firewood, LP gas, and groceries are available. Recycling is mandatory. Leashed pets with rabies vaccination certification are permitted.

Reservations, fees: Reservations are recommended July–Labor Day. Sites are $19–33 a night.
Open: Year-round; the pools (one heated) are open Memorial Day through Labor Day.
Directions: From the junction of U.S. 7 and Highways 125 and 30 in Middlebury, travel six miles south on U.S. 7. Turn left on Highway 53 and head south for 1.5 miles to the campground entrance on the left.
Contact: Lake Dunmore Kampersville, P.O.

Box 56, Route 53, Salisbury, VT 05769, 802/352-4501 or 877/250-2568, website: www.kampersville.com.

4 WATERHOUSES CAMPGROUND AND MARINA

≋ 🎣 🛶 🏹 🐴 🚶 🚐 ⛺

Rating: 8

North of Lake Dunmore

Waterhouses has been located on the shore of Lake Dunmore since 1876 when Loyal N. Waterhouse established his marina and boat building operation across the lake from Mount Moosalamoo. Now, campsites dot Sunset Hill; you'll find deeply wooded sites as well as some strung along the riverfront at the north end of the lake. This is a great place for boaters since a marina is connected to the campground. Walk or bike to the top of Sunset Hill for a "two lake view" of Dunmore and the southern end of Lake Champlain.

Campsites, facilities: There are 60 sites for tents and RVs, most with hookups. Facilities include a laundry room, picnic tables, fire rings, grills, a recreation hall, snack bar/deli, restrooms, hot showers, and a playground. For recreation, there are pools, boat rentals, and miniature golf. Ice, firewood, LP gas, and groceries are available. Leashed pets with rabies vaccination certification are permitted.

Reservations, fees: Reservations are recommended in summer. Sites start at $28 a night.
Open: Mid-May–mid-October.
Directions: From Middlebury, take Route 7 south to Route 53 (you'll see signs for Lake Dunmore). Travel east on Route 53 and stay to the right when the road forks in .25 mile. The marina will be on the left, the campground on your right.
Contact: Waterhouses Campground and Marina, 937 West Shore Road, Salisbury, VT 05769, 802/352-4433, website: www.waterhouses.com.

⑤ BRANBURY STATE PARK
🚶 🏊 🛶 🚤 🐴 🎣 ♿ 🚙 ⛺

Rating: 7

On the south end of Lake Dunmore

About half the campsites, including the lean-tos, are tucked into the woods west of Highway 53 and are accessible to hiking trails. Another 17 sites are set in an open grassy area near Lake Dunmore. This spring-fed lake holds landlocked salmon and trout, and offers a sandy beach and large, protected swimming area well away from the boating action. You can launch or beach your boat at the campground, or rent one of the canoes, rowboats, or paddleboats. For easy hiking, try a self-guided half-mile nature trail or the route to the Falls of Lana. For more of a challenge, head up to the Mount Moosalamoo summit (2,640 feet) past Rattlesnake Point; the trail is studded with waterfalls and caves. Another hike leads to secluded Silver Lake in the mountains.

Campsites, facilities: There are 39 sites for tents and RVs, including six lean-tos, all without hookups. Each site has a picnic table and fireplace. Metered hot showers, flush toilets, recycling bins, a dump station, picnic shelter, snack bar, small store, and playground are provided. Leashed pets with rabies vaccination certification are permitted, but not in day-use areas.

Reservations, fees: Reservations are recommended. Sites are $16–23 a night for four people. See the introduction to the Northeast Kingdom and Lake Champlain chapter for more information on state park regulations.

Open: Mid-May–Columbus Day.

Directions: From the junction of U.S. 7 and Highway 73 in Brandon, travel north for four miles on U.S. 7 to the park entrance on the right (east) side of the road.

Contact: Branbury State Park, 3570 Lake Dunmore Road, Route 53, Salisbury, VT 05743, 802/247-5925.

⑥ SILVER LAKE CAMPGROUND
🚶 🚴 🏊 🎣 ⛺

Rating: 8

East of Lake Dunmore

These hike-in sites are set just south of a day-use picnic area where campers can fish and swim. Wooded and private, they are near the starting point of several hiking trails. From the campground, the Leicester Hollow Trail heads south and is open to mountain bikers as well as hikers.

Campsites, facilities: There are 15 primitive tent sites. An outhouse and piped water are provided. No pets are allowed.

Reservations, fees: Sites are offered on a first-come, first-served basis. There is no fee, but donations are accepted.

Open: Mid-May–October.

Directions: From U.S. 7 south of Middlebury, travel six miles east on Highway 125, passing through Ripton. Turn left on Road 32, drive past the Moosalamoo parking area, and continue south past the Blueberry Hill Ski Touring Center to Highway 27. Take a right and travel northwest to the campground parking area.

Contact: Green Mountain National Forest, Middlebury Ranger District, RR 4, Box 1260, Middlebury, VT 05753, 802/388-4362, website: www.fs.fed.us/r9/gmfl.

⑦ MOUNT MOOSALAMOO CAMPGROUND
🚶 🏊 ⛺

Rating: 8

East of Lake Dunmore in the Green Mountain National Forest

These primitive backcountry sites are a hiker's playground. Many trail miles can be accessed from the campground, including routes to secluded Silver Lake and up Mount Moosalamoo (elevation 2,640 feet). Sugar maple, beech, and birch trees grow in the surrounding woods, while the limestone-rich earth supports many wildflower varieties as well as wild ginger and low-bush blueberries. Watch for the animals that feed on this flora; you might spot black bears, moose, deer, rabbits, hawks, and the endangered peregrine falcon. This camp makes a great jumping-off point for overnight treks on the Long Trail in the surrounding Green Mountains. By the way, the area is named for an Abenaki word that means "the moose departs."

Campsites, facilities: There are an undetermined number of primitive tent sites. An outhouse and piped water are provided. No pets are allowed.

Reservations, fees: Sites are offered on a first-come, first-served basis and are $5 a night.

Open: Memorial Day–Labor Day.

Directions: From U.S. 7 south of Middlebury, travel six miles east on Highway 125, passing through Ripton. Turn left on Road 32 and follow the signs to the campground.

Contact: Green Mountain National Forest, Middlebury Ranger District, RR 4, Box 1260, Middlebury, VT 05753, 802/388-4362, website: www.fs.fed.us/r9/gmfl.

8 MOUNTAIN TRAILS

🏃 🏊 🎣 🐕 🚐 ⛰

Rating: 7

West of Randolph

When the sun goes down, campers at Mountain Trails can stargaze and enjoy the natural glow of their campfires—just remember to bring a flashlight because there are no lights here. This unsophisticated campground is small and clean. There is no water access on-site, but the White River boasts trout fishing and excellent swimming holes nearby. Fifteen sites are for tents and are set in a stand of spruce and maple trees. RV sites are more open, but they do have shade trees. A hiking trail leads from the campground to the rocky summit of Mount Cushman (elevation 2,750 feet).

Campsites, facilities: There are 25 sites for tents and RVs, five with full hookups and 10 with water and electric hookups. A dump station, hot showers, flush toilets, picnic tables, fireplaces, a sandbox and swings, horseshoe pits,

and a badminton court are provided. Firewood is available. Leashed pets are permitted.

Reservations, fees: All fees must be paid in advance. Tent sites start at $12 a night, and RV sites start at $15 a night. Prices are per family (two parents, three kids), with surcharges for extra campers.

Open: May 1–November 30; facilities are limited after archery season, a special deer-hunting season in early fall.

Directions: From I-91 near White River Junction, Vermont, head northwest on I-89. At Exit 3, drive west on Highway 107 through Bethel and up to Rochester (at the junction of Highways 12 and 107 north of Bethel, be sure to take a left to stay on Highway 107). Head north from Rochester on Highway 100 for 2.75 miles. Turn right on Quarry Road and continue east for 1.5 miles to the campground.

Contact: Mountain Trails, 1375 Quarry Hill Road, Rochester, VT 05767, 802/767-3352, website: www.mountaintrailscamping.com.

9 COUNTRY VILLAGE CAMPGROUND

🏊 🐕 🚣 ♿ 🚐 ⛰

Rating: 6

North of Brandon

As its name implies, Country Village has a rural flavor. With open meadows and wooded sites, the campground caters to RVers who want to stay awhile. Many seasonal campers return to these cozy sites because of their proximity to several natural attractions. Lake Dunmore, about four miles away, is open to boating, fishing, and canoeing. About the same distance to the west is slow-moving Otter Creek, which can be paddled by canoeists of all skill levels. A popular auto tour is the drive on Highway 73 between Rochester and Brandon; the road passes over Brandon Gap and overlooks Mount Horrid and Lake Champlain.

Campsites, facilities: There are 41 sites for tents and RVs, most with water and electric hookups. A dump station, fire rings, grills, and tables are provided. Air conditioner and heater use is allowed. Facilities include a solar-heated pool, miniature golf, sports courts, horseshoe pits, a playground, and metered hot showers. Limited groceries, ice, and firewood are available. Leashed pets are permitted.

Reservations, fees: Reservations are recommended in the summer. Sites range from $14–20 a night. Weekly, monthly, and seasonal rates are available.

Open: Mid-May–mid-October.

Directions: From the junction of U.S. 7 and Highway 73 in Brandon, travel three miles north on U.S. 7 to the campground entrance on the left (west) side of the road.

Contact: Country Village Campground, 40 U.S. 7, Leicester, VT 05733, 802/247-3333.

10 SMOKE RISE FARM RESTAURANT AND CAMPGROUND

Rating: 6

North of Brandon

Cleared, grassy farmland is open to campers in this rural locale. Developed sites are for RVs, while unlimited tent camping, ideal for large groups, is available in a separate, rolling field. If you're not in the mood to light a campfire, the Smoke Rise Restaurant across the street serves a mean breakfast. Nearby Lake Dunmore to the north is open to boating, fishing, and canoeing, while slow-moving Otter Creek to the west can be paddled by even novice canoeists.

Campsites, facilities: There are 50 sites for tents and RVs, 21 with full hookups and 29 with water and electric hookups. A dump station, pavilion, laundry facilities, fire rings, tables, a pool, athletic field, and sports courts are provided. LP gas, ice, and firewood are available. Leashed pets are permitted.

Reservations, fees: Reservations are recommended. Sites are $12–25 a night.

Open: May 15–October 15.

Directions: From the town of Brandon, travel

two miles north on U.S. 7. The campground entrance is on the right.

Contact: Smoke Rise Farm Restaurant and Campground, 2111 Grove Street, Brandon, VT 05733, 802/247-6472.

11 CHITTENDON BROOK RECREATION AREA

Rating: 8

North of Rutland on the Long Trail in Green Mountain National Forest

Secluded, wooded sites are set along cascading Chittendon Brook, named for Vermont's first governor, Thomas Chittendon. A wetland area across the brook from the campground offers a chance to view beavers, tree swallows, and the occasional moose. Several hikes leave from the campground; the Chittendon Brook Trail cuts through a spruce and fir forest to the Long Trail about three miles away.

Campsites, facilities: There are 17 tent sites. Tent pads, tables, fire grates, garbage and recycling bins, outhouses, and water pumps are provided. No pets are allowed.

Reservations, fees: Sites are available on a first-come, first-served basis. The fee is $5 a night.

Open: Mid-May–mid-November.

Directions: From Brandon, travel east on Highway 73 for 12 miles. Turn right on Chittendon Brook Road and drive two miles to the recreation area and campground.

Contact: Green Mountain National Forest, Rochester Ranger District, Route 100, Rochester, VT 05767, 802/767-4261.

12 HALF MOON POND STATE PARK

Rating: 8

On Half Moon Pond northwest of Lake Bomoseen

Though this tucked-away campground does attract crowds on summer weekends, you'll find it's a peaceful place during the week. Campsites are set near the shore of three-acre Half Moon Pond, which is open to canoeing, swimming, and fishing. Don't be surprised if you hear a gobble in these woods, because this is prime wild turkey country. Anglers will find trout, bass, and pike in the pond. If you want to head deeper into the hills, take a short hike from the park to High Pond.

Campsites, facilities: There are 70 sites for tents and RVs, including 10 lean-tos, all without hookups. Each site has a picnic table and fireplace. Metered hot showers, flush toilets, recycling bins, a dump station, picnic shelter, and playground are provided. You can rent boats at the campground. Leashed pets with rabies vaccination certification are permitted at sites, but not in day-use areas.

Reservations, fees: Reservations are recommended. Sites are $16–23 a night for four people. The maximum allowable number of people at a site is eight, and there must be one person at least 18 years of age with each camping party. See the introduction to the Northeast Kingdom and Lake Champlain chapter for more information on state park regulations.

Open: Mid-May–mid-October.

Directions: From Rutland, take U.S. 4 west to Highway 30. At the intersection, turn south on Highway 30 to Highway 4A and then go west on Highway 4A for a mile. Turn right on Town Road and travel north for seven miles, past Bomoseen State Park, to the Half Moon State Park entrance.

Contact: Half Moon Pond State Park, 1621 Black Pond Road, Hubbarton, VT 05743, 802/273-2848.

13 BOMOSEEN STATE PARK

Rating: 7

On the west side of Lake Bomoseen

Many privately owned cabins dot the shoreline of large, developed Lake Bomoseen. Camp-

sites are secluded, set well back from the shore. Because of its size, Bomoseen is popular with powerboaters and sees a lot of action on summer weekends. There's a ramp at the state park where you can launch your own boat. Fishing is a big attraction; the lake is home to rainbow, brown, brook, and lake trout, black bass, northern pike, perch, pickerel, bluegill, and bullhead. Roughly 10 miles of trails can be hiked at the state park; the Slate History Trail visits former slate quarries that were active in the 1800s.

Campsites, facilities: There are 66 sites for tents and RVs, including 10 lean-tos, all without hookups. Each site has a picnic table and fireplace. Metered hot showers, flush toilets, recycling bins, a dump station, picnic shelter, snack bar, and playground are provided. Boats can be rented at the campground. Leashed pets with rabies vaccination certification are permitted, but not in day-use areas.

Reservations, fees: Reservations are recommended. Sites are $16–23 a night for four people. The maximum allowable number of people at a site is eight, and there must be one person at least 18 years of age with each camping party. See the introduction to the Northeast Kingdom and Lake Champlain chapter for more information on state park regulations.

Open: Mid-May–Labor Day.

Directions: From Rutland, take U.S. 4 west to the intersection with Highway 30. Turn south on Highway 30 to Highway 4A and then go west on Highway 4A for a mile. Turn right and travel north to the park entrance.

Contact: Bomoseen State Park, 22 Cedar Mountain Road, Fair Haven, VT 05743, 802/265-4242.

14 LAKE BOMOSEEN CAMPGROUND

Rating: 6

On the north end of Lake Bomoseen

Bomoseen is the state's largest lake, and this campground is set back from the water in the woods at its northern end. A separate tenting area and roomy RV sites are spread out on 33 acres. Boaters and RVers will feel right at home because a marina and RV sales office are operated in conjunction with the campground. Dock space and a boat launch are available. Campers are also welcome to rent boats—pontoon boats, bass boats, fishing boats, rowboats, paddleboats, and canoes are available by the day or half day.

There is no beach for swimming here, as weeds grow profusely at this corner of the lake, but once you're out on the water you'll want to jump right in, or take a dip in the campground's 100,000-gallon swimming pool. A swimming complex boasts a slide pool, barrel slides, kiddie wading pool, and spa. Fishing is also a popular draw; the lake is home to trophy-size rainbow, brown, brook, and lake trout, black bass, northern pike, perch, pickerel, bluegill, and bullhead.

Campsites, facilities: There are 143 sites for tents and RVs, many with hookups. Each site has a picnic table and fire ring. Air conditioner and heater use is allowed. Cable and satellite TV hookups are available. Facilities include a dump station, laundry room, restrooms, hot showers, a traffic control gate, recreation hall, game room, miniature golf, swimming pool, sports courts, an athletic field, and horseshoe pits. LP gas, ice, firewood, RV storage and supplies, and boat supplies are available onsite. There's also a grocery store nearby. Leashed pets are permitted.

Reservations, fees: Reservations are recommended and can be made through the mail or by telephone; a deposit is required. Sites range from $24–36 a night per family. Pets are $1 extra per day; boat launch/dock permits cost $7 and are good for your entire stay.

Open: Mid-May–mid-October.

Directions: From the junction of U.S. 4 and Highway 30 near Castleton, travel five miles north on Highway 30 to the campground entrance on the left.

Contact: Lake Bomoseen Campground, Ma-

rine and RV Sales, Service, and Rentals, 18 Campground Drive, Highway 30, Lake Bomoseen, VT 05732, 802/273-2061, website: www.lakebomoseen.com/campground.

15 GIFFORD WOODS STATE PARK

Rating: 7

Northeast of Rutland

No-frills Gifford Woods is a centrally located, wooded campground with private sites near Kent Pond, which is open to bass and trout fishing. The park also includes a seven-acre natural area with stands of virgin hardwood. Short trails lead throughout the woods, but hikers are also conveniently close to trailheads for the Long and Appalachian Trails; the two footpaths diverge nearby at Sherburne Pass. In summer, this camp is popular with mountain bikers who ride at the Killington Ski and Summer Resort and in the surrounding Green Mountains.

Campsites, facilities: There are 48 sites for tents and RVs, including 21 lean-tos, all without hookups. Each site has a picnic table and fireplace. Metered hot showers, flush toilets, recycling bins, a dump station, picnic shelter, and playground are provided. Firewood is available. Leashed pets with rabies vaccination certification are permitted, but not in day-use areas.

Reservations, fees: Reservations are recommended. Sites are $14–21 a night for four people. The maximum allowable number of people at a site is eight, and there must be one person at least 18 years of age with each camping party. See the introduction to the Northeast Kingdom and Lake Champlain chapter for more information on state park regulations.

Open: Mid-May–Columbus Day.

Directions: From the junction of U.S. 4 and Highway 100 west of Sherburne Center, travel .5 mile north on Highway 100 to the state park entrance on the right (east) side of the road.

Contact: Gifford Woods State Park, 34 Gifford Woods, Killington, VT 05751, 802/775-5354.

16 IROQUOIS LAND FAMILY CAMPING

Rating: 6

Southeast of Rutland

A variety of sites is offered at Iroquois, some set amid pine trees, but the most popular are the large, mowed grassy sites for RVs with full hookups. Though there's a good view of the surrounding Green Mountains, some may find the campground too densely settled. A swimming pool is provided on the grounds, and there's also a large field for flying kites and playing. Downtown Rutland is only minutes from here. On U.S. 4 in town, the Norman Rockwell Museum has a comprehensive display of the artist's magazine covers, advertisements, and other published works—more than 2,000 pieces in all.

Campsites, facilities: There are 50 sites for tents and RVs, 12 with full hookups and 38 with water and electric hookups. Restrooms, hot showers, a dump station, pool, recreation room, sports courts, a playing field, and horseshoe pits are provided. Also available are a camp store, ice, firewood, and RV parts and supplies. Leashed pets with rabies vaccination certification are permitted.

Reservations, fees: Reservations are recommended. Send $20 by check or money order and be sure to note your arrival date, camper type, needed hookups, and stay length; reservations are confirmed by return mail. Sites start at $28 a night. Weekly and monthly rates are available.

Open: May 1–October 15.

Directions: From the southern junction of U.S. 4 and U.S. 7 near Rutland, travel .5 mile south on U.S. 7. At the stoplight, turn left on North Shrewsbury Road and head east for one mile. Turn right on East Road and continue to the campground entrance .75 mile ahead on the left.

Contact: Iroquois Land Family Camping, 2334 East Clarendon Road, North Clarendon, VT 05759, 802/773-2832.

17 SUGARHOUSE CAMPGROUND

Rating: 6

North of Plymouth

Folks who like catching trout like these sites near the Black River. The campground is shaded by sugar maples and is just up the road from historic Plymouth. A laid-back atmosphere and informal organized events make Sugarhouse popular with seasonal campers. Potluck suppers, the Strawberry Social, and theme dinners are just a few of the offerings. This is one of only a handful of central Vermont RV campgrounds open year-round with winterized services. At Sugarhouse you are just minutes from the Killington Ski and Summer Resort—a grand six-mountain ski center—and are also close to Okemo and Pico, two mid-sized alpine ski areas. Multiuse trails are found to the north at Coolidge State Park (see listing in the Southeast Vermont chapter).

Campsites, facilities: There are 45 sites for tents and RVs with full hookups. Hot showers, fire rings, picnic tables, and a playground are provided. Leashed pets are permitted.

Reservations, fees: Reservations are required in the winter. Sites are $12–15 a night in the summer, $20 a night in the winter. Weekly, monthly, and seasonal rates are available.

Open: May 1–Columbus Day.

Directions: From the junction of Highways 100 and 100A in Plymouth, travel .5 mile north on Highway 100 to the campground entrance on the left (west) side of the road.

Contact: Sugarhouse Campground, Highway 100, Plymouth, VT 05056, 802/672-5043.

18 LAKE ST. CATHERINE STATE PARK

Rating: 8

South of Poultney

At seven miles long, Lake St. Catherine is a boater's paradise. You will find a boat ramp at

this campground, where sites are set right on the shore, and a sandy beach welcomes swimmers. Anglers can try for a variety of species including smallmouth and largemouth bass, perch, pike, and walleye. The aptly named Big Trees Nature Trail traverses the campground as it meanders through stately pines, maples, and a few red oaks.
Campsites, facilities: There are 50 sites for tents and RVs, including eight lean-tos, all without hookups. Each site has a picnic table and fireplace. Facilities include a dump station, flush toilets, metered hot showers, a boat ramp, sports field, and playground. Firewood, boat rentals, and a snack bar are available. Ice and LP gas can be obtained nearby. Leashed pets with rabies vaccination certification are permitted, but not in day-use areas.
Reservations, fees: Reservations are recommended. Sites are $16–23 a night for four people. The maximum allowable number of people at a site is eight, and there must be one person at least 18 years of age with each camping party. See the introduction to the Northeast Kingdom and Lake Champlain chapter for more information on state park regulations.
Open: Mid-May–mid-October.
Directions: From Poultney, travel three miles south on Highway 30 to the state park entrance.
Contact: Lake St. Catherine State Park, 3034 Route 30 South, Poultney, VT 05764, 802/287-9158.

19 OTTER CREEK CAMPGROUND
🚤 🏊 ⛏ 🎆 🦌 🚐 ⛺

Rating: 5
North of Danby

Though these sites are located directly on Otter Creek, they lose some of their scenic value due to the "wheel-to-wheel" feel—sites are only about 20 feet wide. The river flows north to Lake Champlain and is ripe for quick-water canoeing in springtime when it's swollen from snowmelt and runoff. There are some small swimming holes at the campground, as well as

warm-water fishing for smallmouth bass and northern pike.
Campsites, facilities: There are 50 sites for tents and RVs, 35 with water and electric hookups and 15 with none. Each site has a fire ring, grill, and table. Facilities include a dump station and laundry room. Also provided are a recreation hall, swimming pool, boat rentals, badminton and volleyball courts, a sports field, and horseshoe pits. Limited groceries, LP gas, ice, and firewood are available. Leashed pets are permitted.
Reservations, fees: Reservations are recommended, especially in summer and fall. There are no refunds. Sites start at $14 a night per family in summer, higher in winter.
Open: Year-round; fully operational May 1–October 1.
Directions: From the northern town limits of Danby, travel north on U.S. 7 for .75 mile to the campground entrance.
Contact: Otter Creek Campground, U.S. 7, Danby, VT 05739, 802/293-5041.

20 GREENDALE CAMPGROUND
🚤 🐕 🏃 ♿ 🚐 ⛺

Rating: 9
West of Ludlow in the Green Mountain National Forest

Spacious, wooded campsites are strung out along Greendale Brook. The waterway is inhabited by native trout and is also the target of an effort to reintroduce the endangered Atlantic salmon. Along the brook you notice logs or rocks deliberately placed to create and cover deep pools for the protected fish; the salmon are off-limits, but you can cast for trout with a valid Vermont fishing license. The campground is at the edge of the White Rocks National Recreation Area, which is traversed by an extensive trail system and is home to the Big Branch and Peru Peak Wilderness Areas.
Campsites, facilities: There are 11 sites for tents and trailers. Pit toilets, piped water, grills, and tables are provided. A picnic area also serves

as a group tenting area. Leashed pets are permitted.

Reservations, fees: Sites are available on a first-come, first-served basis. The maximum stay is 14 days. Self-service payment is $5 a night.

Open: Spring, summer, and fall. The access road is not maintained for winter travel.

Directions: From Weston, head north on Highway 100 for three miles. Turn left on Forest Service Road 18 and drive northwest for two miles to the campground.

Contact: Green Mountain National Forest, Manchester Ranger District, 2538 Depot Street, Manchester Center, VT 05255, 802/362-2307.

21 EMERALD LAKE STATE PARK

Rating: 7

On Emerald Lake in Dorset

This park is located in the narrowest stretch of the Vermont Valley, the groove that separates the Taconic Range (which continues into New York) from the Green Mountains. Campsites are set atop a heavily wooded ridge above Emerald Lake, the Otter Creek headwaters. There are two no-pet zones near the park's day-use area, so campers with animals in tow will need to stay in Area B. Area A is closest to the lake beach, but the other two sections have hiking trails that lead to the water through a forest of ash and hickory. The lake is open to nonmotorized boating and is a haven for quiet-water canoeing. A wheelchair-accessible beach house and play area are provided by the water.

Campsites, facilities: There are 105 sites for tents and RVs, including 36 lean-tos, all without hookups. Facilities include a dump station, metered hot showers, picnic tables, fireplaces, boat rentals, a snack bar, and playground. Firewood is available. Small grocery stores are located in Danby and East Dorset. Leashed pets with rabies vaccination certification are permitted, but not in day-use areas.

Reservations, fees: Reservations are recommended. Tent sites start at $16 a night and lean-tos start at $23 a night for four people. The maximum allowable number of people at a site is eight, and there must be one person at least 18 years of age with each camping party. See the introduction to the Northeast Kingdom and Lake Champlain chapter for more information on state park regulations.

Open: Mid-May–mid-October.

Directions: From the junction of U.S. 7 and Highway 7A in Dorset, travel four miles north on U.S. 7 to the state park entrance on the left.

Contact: Emerald Lake State Park, 65 Emerald Lake Lane, East Dorset, VT 05253, 802/362-1655.

22 HAPGOOD POND RECREATION AREA

Rating: 9

West of Londonderry in the Green Mountain National Forest

Hapgood Pond offers a family wilderness camping experience. Wooded, private sites are set back from the pond in the woods. Down at the water there's a beach and a boat launch for your canoe or rowboat (inflatable floats are not allowed). A lifeguard is on duty from 10 A.M.–5 P.M. from Memorial Day–Labor Day. This is trout-stocked water, and with a Vermont fishing license, you can hook up to five fish a day. A short nature trail winds around the pond's north edge and crosses Flood Brook.

Campsites, facilities: There are 28 sites for tents and trailers. Pit toilets, piped water, tent pads, grills, and tables are provided. Also on the property are an amphitheater, pavilion, and restrooms. Leashed pets are permitted.

Reservations, fees: Sites are available on a first-come, first-served basis. The maximum stay is 14 days. Sites are $5 a night for up to six people.

Open: Memorial Day–Columbus Day.

Directions: From Manchester, travel east on Highway 11 for six miles, bearing left into Peru. Continue two miles north of town on Hapgood Pond Road to the campground.

Contact: Green Mountain National Forest, Manchester Ranger District, RR 1, Box 1940, Manchester Center, VT 05255, 802/362-2307, website: www.fs.fed.us/r9/gmfl.

23 WINHALL BROOK CAMPING AREA

Rating: 8

On Ball Mountain Lake in South Londonderry

The handiwork of the U.S. Army Corps of Engineers gives these grassy streamside campsites their no-nonsense appeal. Located north of the Ball Mountain Dam, which controls the West River, the shaded sites are surrounded by reservoir lands open to hunting in season. The West River provides fishing for brown trout downstream of the dam and is stocked with Atlantic salmon as part of a restoration program. Smallmouth bass inhabit the 75-acre reservoir. The surrounding forest is traversed by multiuse trails that are open year-round. Each week during summer months, Army Corps personnel present programs on the dam project in the campground amphitheater.

Campsites, facilities: There are 109 sites for tents and RVs, all without hookups. Each site has a table and fire grill. Facilities include a dump station, showers, piped water, horseshoe pits, picnic areas, and restrooms. Firewood is sold at the campground office. Leashed pets with rabies vaccination certification are permitted.

Reservations, fees: Reservations are not accepted. Sites start at $16 a night for four people.

Open: Mid-May–early September.

Directions: From South Londonderry, travel 2.5 miles south on Highway 100 to the campground entrance on the left.

Contact: Upper Connecticut River Basin Office, RR 1, Box 164B, Perkinsville, VT 05151, 802/874-4881, reservations: 877/444-6777.

24 CAMPING ON THE BATTENKILL

Rating: 6

In Arlington on the Batten Kill River

Seasonal campers make up about a third of the summer population at Batten Kill. Many of the wooded sites are located on the river and are favored by people who like to cast a fishing line from their campsite. The only drawback is the tight quarters along the riverfront, where sites are rarely more than 25 feet wide. The Battenkill River (derived from an English word meaning "to grow prosperous" and the Dutch word for river) is a good choice for intermediate canoeists in search of quick water, but you might want to tease the brook trout as well, so bring a fishing pole along with your paddles. From Manchester to the campground and on to the New York border, this stretch of water is narrow and challenging, especially where it meets Roaring Brook in the town of Arlington. The town is known for its association with artist Norman Rockwell, who lived there from 1939–1953. Arlington's town meeting is depicted in Rockwell's famous *Four Freedoms* series as representing Freedom of Speech, and visitors can view his work at the Norman Rockwell Exhibition on Main Street.

Campsites, facilities: There are 100 sites for tents and RVs, most with hookups. Each site has a picnic table, garbage can, gravel pad, and fire ring. Air conditioners are allowed, but heaters are not. Facilities include a dump station, hot showers, and restrooms. LP gas, ice, fishing licenses, and firewood are available. Groups can rent sites in May, June, and September. Leashed pets are permitted.

Reservations, fees: Reservations are recommended for holiday weekends and during July and August; a deposit of one-day's fee is required. No single-day or weekend reservations are taken for July or August. Sites range from $20–26. Two camping units (a unit is a tent, van, or trailer) may occupy one site, but each will be charged as if it had its own site.

Open: Mid-April–mid-October.

Directions: From U.S. 7 north of Bennington, take Exit 3 to Highway 7A, heading west and then north into the town of Arlington, then turn left on Highway 313. The campground entrance is on the right, .75 mile from the junction of Highways 313 and 7A.

Contact: Camping on the Battenkill, Inc., 48 Camping on the Battenkill, Arlington, VT 05250, 802/375-6663 or 800/830-6663, website: www.campvermont.com/battenkill.

25 HOWELL'S CAMPING AREA

Rating: 6

Southwest of Arlington

Campsites are set beside a small pond that is open to fishing, swimming, and boating with electric motors only. Campers have use of a sandy beach as well as a boat ramp where they can launch their own vessels. Several canoes and paddleboats are also available for rent. Canoeing on the pond is a quiet affair, but the Batten Kill River is a short drive to the north and offers quick-water adventures. There's a put-in at downtown Arlington, a classic Vermont village full of historic charm.

Campsites, facilities: There are 73 sites for tents and RVs, 40 with full hookups and 33 with water and electric hookups. Dump stations, laundry facilities, LP gas, and firewood are available. The property also has a recreation room, boat rentals, horseshoe pits, picnic tables, and fire rings. Leashed pets are permitted.

Reservations, fees: Reservations are recommended. Sites start at $20 a night for four people.

Open: Mid-April–mid-October.

Directions: From U.S. 7 north of Bennington, take Exit 3, travel two miles west and then one mile north on Highway 7A. Turn left on Highway 313 and make a quick left (after 200 feet) onto School Street, heading south. Continue to the road's end and the campground entrance.

Contact: Howell's Camping Area, P.O. Box

133, School Street, Arlington, VT 05250, 802/375-6990.

26 LAKE SHAFTSBURY STATE PARK

Rating: 6

South of Arlington

This campground is now available to groups only. The cool waters of Lake Shaftsbury border this handful of campsites. A snack bar, boat rentals, and a boat ramp make the area popular for day use. A short nature trail circumnavigates the lake and crosses through several terrain types, including swamp and hardwood forest, as well as passing over a glacial "esker," or curious rogue ridge.

Campsites, facilities: There are 15 groups-only sites for tents and trailers, all with lean-tos. There are no hookups or dump stations. Pit toilets, fireplaces, tables, a playground, and a boat ramp are provided. Boat and canoe rentals are available, as is a snack bar. No pets are allowed.

Reservations, fees: Reservations are recommended. Sites start at $16 a night for four people. The maximum allowable number of people at a site is eight, and there must be one person at least 18 years of age with each camping party. See the introduction to the Northeast Kingdom and Lake Champlain chapter for more information on state park regulations.

Open: Mid-May–Labor Day.

Directions: From Arlington, travel two miles south on Highway 7A to the state park entrance.

Contact: Lake Shaftsbury State Park, 262 Shaftsbury State Park Road, Shaftsbury, VT 05262, 802/375-9978.

27 GROUT POND

Rating: 8

West of Stratton in the Green Mountain National Forest

Like pearls, these tent sites are strung along

the shoreline of small, pristine Grout Pond. Aside from fire rings and a few lean-tos, there are no amenities. But you will find an abundance of peace and quiet disturbed only by the sounds of frogs, birds, and other wildlife. Beavers have established a lodge at the pond's south end, while other nooks and crannies house sunfish, yellow perch, and a few wise bass. Easy hiking trails circle the pond and lead south to Somerset Reservoir. If you are looking for a backwoods respite without having to backpack in, this is a good choice.

Campsites, facilities: There are 11 primitive walk-in sites, 7 accessible by canoe, one suitable for wheelchair users, and two have shelters that sleep up to six people. A cabin with a fireplace is available year-round. Water can be obtained from a hand pump but should be treated before drinking. Outhouses are provided. Leashed pets with rabies vaccination certification are permitted.

Reservations, fees: Sites are available on a first-come, first-served basis. There is no fee.

Open: Year-round.

Directions: From West Wardsboro east of Arlington, travel seven miles west through the town of Stratton on Highway 100. Turn left on Grout Pond Road and proceed to the campsites.

Contact: Green Mountain National Forest, Manchester Ranger District, 2538 Depot Street, Manchester Center, VT 05255, 802/362-2307, website: www.fs.fed.us/r9/gmfl.

28 JAMAICA STATE PARK

Rating: 7

On the West River in Jamaica

Underneath a thick canopy of tall pine trees and next to the West River, these sites are dotted with flower boxes. Upriver from the campground is Ball Mountain Dam; in the last weeks of April and September, water releases turn the river into a gnarly white-water rip on which canoeing and kayaking competitions are often held. A fine swimming hole at the campground

bears some historical significance: during the French and Indian Wars, three Frenchmen and several Native Americans ambushed British soldiers at Salmon Hole. The most spectacular feature at the park is Hamilton Falls, the state's longest waterfall—a 125-foot cascade tumbling down a series of granite ledges. From the campground, the Overlook Trail leads to the Little Bald Mountain summit. The trail then links up with an old railroad bed that leads along the river all the way to the dam. The trail is a good vantage point for watching paddlers during the spring and fall.

Campsites, facilities: There are 61 sites for tents and RVs, including 18 lean-tos, all without hookups. Facilities include a dump station, metered hot showers, flush toilets, a picnic shelter, playground, horseshoe pits, and recycling bins. Ice and firewood are available. Leashed pets with rabies vaccination certification are permitted, but not in day-use areas.

Reservations, fees: Reservations are recommended. Sites are $16–23 a night for four people. The maximum allowable number of people at a site is eight, and there must be one person at least 18 years of age with each camping party. See the introduction to the Northeast Kingdom and Lake Champlain chapter for more information on state park regulations.

Open: Late April–mid-October.

Directions: From Highway 30 in Jamaica, head .5 mile north on the town road to the park entrance.

Contact: Jamaica State Park, P.O. Box 45, 285 Salmon Hole Lane, Jamaica, VT 05343, 802/874-4600.

29 RED MILL BROOK CAMPGROUND

Rating: 8

East of Bennington in the Green Mountain National Forest

Wooded campsites are set along Red Mill Brook in an area known for its many beaver ponds that are home to native brook trout. At-risk youth from Bennington help maintain the area in summertime to earn high school credits through the ACE (Alternative Community Experience) program. Just to the west of the campground is the Long Trail, which makes this a good base camp for backpacking excursions into the Green Mountains.

Campsites, facilities: There are 31 tent sites, some of which will accommodate small trailers. Pit toilets, piped water, tent pads, grills, and tables are provided. Sites are wheelchair accessible with assistance.

Reservations, fees: Sites are available on a first-come, first-served basis. Sites are $5 a night.

Open: May 15–late fall.

Directions: From Bennington, travel 10 miles east on Highway 9 to the campground entrance.

Contact: Green Mountain National Forest, Manchester Ranger District, RR 1, Box 1940, Manchester Center, VT 05255, 802/362-2307, website: www.fs.fed.us/r9/gmfl.

30 GREENWOOD LODGE AND CAMPSITES
🏕 🚴 🏊 🛶 🚐 🍴 🚌 ⛰

Rating: 7

East of Bennington

Two ponds on the property are open to swimming, boating, fishing, and canoeing. The campground is operated in conjunction with a lodge that offers rooms and meal plans in a rustic, home-style atmosphere. Campsites are secluded, set in a wooded, mountaintop glen; some are right on the ponds, and a small number of sites near the lodge have water and electric hookups. The facility is adjacent to the Green Mountain National Forest and is three miles from the Appalachian Trail, both of which offer excellent hiking and backpacking. If you're a history buff, head north to Bennington; the town's museum houses what is thought to be the oldest surviving Stars and Stripes, flown at the Battle of Bennington in 1777.

Campsites, facilities: There are 40 sites for tents and RVs, a few of which have water and electric hookups. Each site has a fire ring, picnic table, and trash container. Flush toilets, hot showers, and a dishwashing sink are provided. Also on the property are horseshoe pits, a playing field, and a volleyball court. Supplies can be purchased across the street at True's General Store. Quiet, leashed pets are allowed, but their owners must pick up after them.

Reservations, fees: Reservations are recommended. A 100 percent deposit is required for the first three nights and 50 percent for each consecutive night. Sites start at $18 a night for two people with surcharges for extra campers, firewood, and hookups.

Open: May through the fall foliage season.

Directions: From Bennington, travel eight miles east on Highway 9 to the Prospect Mountain Ski Area sign on the south side of the road. The entrance to the campground is off the ski area entrance; follow the signs.

Contact: Greenwood Lodge and Campsites, P.O. Box 246, Bennington, VT 05201, 802/442-2547, website: www.campvermont.com/greenwood.

31 WOODFORD STATE PARK
🏕 🏊 🛶 🚐 🍴 🚣 ♿ 🚌 ⛰

Rating: 8

East of Bennington

Adams Reservoir, which is open to nonmotorized boating and swimming, is the focal point of Woodford State Park. Campsites are set in two heavily wooded areas east of the reservoir. The park is perched on a plateau at an elevation of 2,400 feet and supports stands of high-elevation spruce, fir, and birch trees. A 2.7-mile trail loops around the reservoir, while more trails are available in the surrounding Green Mountain National Forest.

Campsites, facilities: There are 103 sites for tents and RVs, including 20 lean-tos, all without hookups. Facilities include a dump station, flush toilets, metered hot showers, piped water, picnic tables, fireplaces, a playground, and boat ramp. Firewood is available, and there's a store

nearby. Leashed pets with rabies vaccination certification are permitted, but not in day-use areas. **Reservations, fees:** Reservations are recommended. Sites are $16–23 a night for four people. The maximum allowable number of people at a site is eight, and there must be one person at least 18 years of age with each camping party. See the introduction to the Northeast Kingdom and Lake Champlain chapter for more information on state park regulations.
Open: Mid-May–mid-October.
Directions: From Bennington, travel 10 miles east on Highway 9 to the park entrance.
Contact: Woodford State Park, 142 State Park Road, Woodford, VT 05201, 802/447-7169.

32 MOLLY STARK STATE PARK

🚶 🚣 🐕 🚴 ♿ 🚐 ⛺

East of Wilmington   **Rating: 7**

Open lawns, the surrounding woods, and Mount Olga to the east are part of the striking landscape at Molly Stark State Park. From the campground, a short hiking trail ascends Mount Olga (2,145 feet), where a fire tower on the summit is a popular destination during peak foliage season. The park's first structures (fireplaces and a toilet building) were built by the Civilian Conservation Corps in the 1930s. Highway 9 and the park were named for Molly, the famous wife of General John Stark, a Revolutionary War hero who led troops to the Battle of Bennington in Vermont; it's said that she followed him to nurse the sick and wounded. On the 158-acre preserve, Beaver Brook offers the best cold-water fishing.
Campsites, facilities: There are 34 sites for tents and RVs, including 11 lean-tos, all without hookups. Each site has a fireplace and picnic table. On the grounds are a dump station, playground, volleyball court, horseshoe pits, and a large group picnic pavilion. Ice, firewood, flush toilets, and metered hot showers are available. A general store and laundry facilities are located in Wilmington. Leashed pets with rabies vac-

cination certification are permitted; they are not allowed in day-use areas and may be restricted to certain areas within the campground. **Reservations, fees:** Reservations are recommended. Sites are $14 a night and lean-tos are $21 a night for four people. The maximum allowable number of people at a site is eight, and there must be one person at least 18 years of age with each camping party. See the introduction to the Northeast Kingdom and Lake Champlain chapter for more information on state park regulations.
Open: Mid-May–mid-October.
Directions: From Wilmington, travel east on Highway 9 for three miles. Turn right into the state park entrance.
Contact: Molly Stark State Park, 705 Highway 9 East, Wilmington, VT 05363, 802/464-5460.

33 PINE HOLLOW CAMPGROUND

🏊 🚣 🚐 🐕 🚴 🚐 ⛺

South of Bennington   **Rating: 7**

Grassy meadows and mixed hardwoods meet at this campground on a spring-fed pond. Sites are compact and close together but have ample shade. Trout may be caught and released from the pond, which is also open to swimming and nonmotorized boating. Nearby is the southern starting point of the Long Trail, the country's first long-distance hiking route. Extending from the Massachusetts border into Canada, the Long Trail accesses 265 miles of rugged, scenic terrain. This southernmost section is shared with the 2,158-mile Appalachian Trail (see next listing) before it forks northeast in Sherburne Center.
Campsites, facilities: There are 60 sites for tents and RVs, 20 with full hookups and 38 with water and electric hookups. Big rigs are welcome. Each site has a picnic table and fire ring. A dump station, playground, cable TV hookups, restrooms, metered hot showers, boat rentals, and group areas are available. On the property, you will

find shuffleboard and badminton courts, a sports field, volleyball, and horseshoe pits. Quiet, leashed pets are permitted.

Reservations, fees: Reservations are recommended and require a nonrefundable deposit. Sites start at $20 a night.

Open: Mid-May–mid-October.

Directions: From the junction of Highway 9 and U.S. 7 in Bennington, travel six miles south on U.S. 7 and then 1.5 miles east on Barbers Pond Road. Turn right on Old Military Road and follow it .75 mile south to the campground entrance on the right.

Contact: Pine Hollow Campground, 342 Pine Hollow Road, Pownal, VT 05261, 802/823-5569, website: www.pinehollowcampground.net.

34 APPALACHIAN TRAIL

Rating: 10

The trail runs north-south along the Green Mountains' southern ridge to Sherburne Pass near Pico Peak and then veers west toward Hanover, New Hampshire, where it crosses the Connecticut River

From Springer Mountain in Georgia to Mount Katahdin in Maine, the Appalachian Trail traverses the Appalachian Mountain chain on a 2,158-mile continuous, marked footpath. The trail and its adjacent lands—about 270,000 acres—link more than 75 parks and forests in 14 states, including eight units of the national forest system and six units of the national park system. Countless wild, scenic, historic, and pastoral settings are enjoyed along the footpath by through-hikers—those who typically start in Georgia and make a six-month trek to Maine—day hikers, and overnight backpackers. On average, fewer than 200 through-hikers complete the 2,000-mile journey each year.

For the first 100 miles north of the Vermont-Massachusetts border, the Appalachian Trail and Vermont's Long Trail (see listing in the Northeast Kingdom and Lake Champlain chapter) share a common path. The Long Trail is the oldest long-distance hiking highway in America and served as the inspiration for the Appalachian Trail; the 270-mile track follows the Green Mountains' main ridge from the state line north to the Canadian border. At Sherburne Pass near Pico Peak, the trails diverge and the Appalachian Trail leads east while the Long Trail continues north. Most of the 100-mile stretch shared by the two trails is located in the Green Mountain National Forest. On a south-to-north route, the first major summit encountered is Glastonbury Mountain. From here, the trail ascends several peaks dominated by spruce groves and descends into a number of hardwood valleys. After topping out at Pico Peak, the trail travels across the low hills of the Green Mountains, passing through former farms and reverting woodlands. The trail crosses into New Hampshire from Norwich, Vermont, on a small bridge over the Connecticut River near the Dartmouth College boathouses.

Campsites, facilities: There are several dozen campsites along the 100-mile section of the Appalachian Trail (AT) that joins with the Long Trail at the Massachusetts border, none more than a moderate day hike apart. Some of these have lodges with woodstoves, many have Adirondack-style lean-tos, and others are wooded tent sites. Primitive toilets are provided at most sites. On the 40-mile stretch from Sherburne Pass to Hanover, New Hampshire, Adirondack-style shelters are located no more than a moderate day hike apart. Most of the sites offer some kind of water source, as indicated in guides and on topographic maps, but not all are reliable or pure. Off-trail camping is allowed in the Green Mountain National Forest and on state-owned lands under an elevation of 2,500 feet. Leashed pets are permitted.

Reservations, fees: All sites are available on a first-come, first-served basis. Use of any overnight facility operated by the Green Mountain Club is limited to three consecutive nights. In the summer months, some of the more heavily used sites on the Long Trail portion of the AT are staffed by caretakers and charge fees of $4 a night for Green Mountain Club members and $5 for nonmembers. Some of the Green Mountain National Forest sites charge a nightly fee.

Open: The Long Trail portion of the Appalachian Trail is open in summer, fall, and winter. Travel is discouraged during mud season, usually between late March and early May. The rest of the AT is open year-round. Hikers should note that trail use during mud season abets erosion.

Directions: To reach the Appalachian Trail's southern starting point, from the junction of U.S. 7 and Highway 2 at the traffic circle in Williamstown, Massachusetts, travel three miles east to a traffic light at Phelps Avenue. There is no parking at the trailhead; parking is available with permission at the Greylock Community Club, .1 mile east of the trail, or at the Holy Family Catholic Church adjacent to the AT.

Contact: Green Mountain Club, 4711 Waterbury-Stowe Road, Waterbury Center, VT 05677, 802/244-7037, website: www.greenmountainclub.org. Appalachian Trail Conference, P.O. Box 807, Harpers Ferry, WV 25425, 304/535-6331, website: www.appalachiantrail.org. The nonprofit Appalachian Trail Conference publishes 10 sectional guides, which are accompanied by topographic maps.

Southeast Vermont

Southeast Vermont

Your sleep in the arms of history when you camp in southeastern Vermont. If you listen closely, you might hear the cries of the Green Mountain Boys as they set off for New York to fight courageously in Revolutionary War battles. Look around you: Many things have historical names, from the Molly Stark Trail (Route 9) and Coolidge State Park (named after Vermont's presidential son, Calvin) to Fort Dummer State Park, named after the first white settlement in Vermont.

The region is dominated by the watery border between Vermont and New Hampshire: the Connecticut River. Outdoors enthusiasts come here to fish and canoe. Other smaller rivers, like the White River, offer springtime white water for kayakers. Campgrounds are clustered along the shorelines to offer access to this great resource. There are more private RV-oriented campgrounds in the southeastern part of the region than elsewhere in the state, due to the proximity of I-91. But all the campgrounds take advantage of the essence of Vermont: forested rolling hills, clear lakes and streams, and villages where the locals treat you like one of their own.

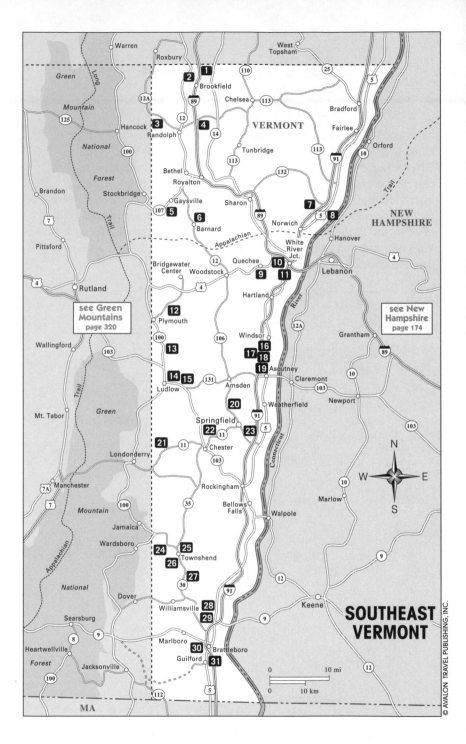

◻1 LIMEHURST LAKE CAMPGROUND

🚶 🏊 🚣 🚐 🐕 🚍 ⛺

Rating: 7

South of Williamstown

Campers at Limehurst Lake can use the 250-foot water slide next to the campground's sandy beach. Swimming and fishing are popular pursuits here, and no licenses are required to fish the privately owned pond. The sites, most of which are shaded by trees, are level, grassy, and set back from the shoreline of the 13-acre lake. You can rent rowboats, canoes, and paddleboats at the beach, or play around on the swimming raft and diving board. From the campground, several trails lead into the surrounding Green Mountains.

Campsites, facilities: There are 73 sites for tents and RVs, all with hookups. Each site has a fire ring and table. Cable TV and telephone connections are available. Air conditioner and heater use is allowed. On-site, you will find a camp store, snack bar, laundry facilities, restrooms, hot showers, LP gas, picnic and safari areas, a recreation room, pavilion, sports courts, and horseshoe pits. Trailers can be rented. Leashed pets are permitted.

Reservations, fees: Reservations are recommended July–mid-October. Sites are $20–29 a night per family.

Open: Mid-April–October.

Directions: From I-89 south of Barre, take Exit 6 and drive east on Highway 63 for four miles to Highway 14. Turn right (south) on Highway 14 and continue six miles to Limehurst Lake and the campground entrance.

Contact: Limehurst Lake Campground, 4104 Route 14, Williamstown, VT 05679, 802/433-6662, website: www.limehurstlake.com.

◻2 ALLIS STATE PARK

🚶 🐕 🚣 ♿ 🚍 ⛺

Rating: 8

In Brookfield on Bear Mountain

Families who want to introduce the little ones to hiking will find these mountaintop sites the ideal place to camp. Originally a farm, Bear Mountain (elevation 2,020 feet) is now adorned with a fire tower that affords views of Mount Mansfield and Camel's Hump to the north, Killington and Ascutney Mountains to the south, and New Hampshire's White Mountains to the east. The campground is small and quiet, set in the woods just off the summit near the fire tower. Two moderate loop trails, Bear Hill and Little Spruce, explore hardwood and softwood forests. Bear Hill passes a limestone outcrop and a shallow cave that once served as a bear den and now makes an interesting resting spot for hikers walking with kids. At the base of Bear Mountain are several lakes open to fishing, boating, and swimming.

Campsites, facilities: There are 18 sites for tents and RVs, including eight lean-tos, all without hookups. Each site has a picnic table and a stone or brick fireplace. Metered hot showers, flush toilets, recycling bins, a dump station, picnic shelter, and a playground are provided. Supplies are available in Randolph and Brookfield. Leashed pets with rabies vaccination certification are permitted, but not in day-use areas.

Reservations, fees: Reservations are recommended. Sites are $14 a night and lean-tos are $21 a night for four people. The maximum allowable number of people at a site is eight, and there must be one person at least 18 years of age or older with each camping party. See the introduction to the Northeast Kingdom and Lake Champlain chapter for more information on state park regulations.

Open: Mid-May–Labor Day.

Directions: From I-89 south of Brookfield, take Exit 4 and travel two miles west on Highway 66. Turn and drive north on Highway 12 for

12 miles to Highway 65. Turn right and head east on Highway 65 for 1.5 miles to the park entrance on the right (south) side of the road. A park road leads to the mountaintop.
Contact: Allis State Park, R.D. 2, Box 192, Randolph, VT 05060, 802/276-3175.

3 ABEL MOUNTAIN CAMPGROUND

Rating: 4
On the Third Branch of the White River in Randolph

Tents are welcome at Abel Mountain. But unless they don't mind camping in the thick of mobile homes and RVs, tenters will want to head north to Allis State Park (see previous listing) for wilder, more natural environs. Many of these sites are rented seasonally, and organized activities—including specialty potlucks, ice-cream socials, and theme weekends—keep campers busy. This dual mobile home park and RV campground is located on the Third Branch of the White River, offering direct access to boating, fishing, and freshwater swimming.
Campsites, facilities: There are 93 sites for tents and RVs, most with hookups. Each site has a picnic table and fire ring. Dump stations, laundry facilities, a pool, two playgrounds, restrooms, hot showers, a pavilion, sports field, and horseshoe pits are located on the grounds. LP gas, ice, firewood, and free RV storage are available. Leashed pets are permitted.
Reservations, fees: Reservations are recommended. Sites with full hookups start at $21 a night. Seasonal and monthly rates are available.
Open: May 15–mid-October.
Directions: From I-89, take Exit 4 onto Highway 66 and drive 2.5 miles west. When you reach Highway 12A, continue west for another 2.5 miles to the campground entrance on the left (south) side of the road.
Contact: Abel Mountain Campground, 354 Mobile Acres Road, Braintree, VT 05060, 802/728-5548.

4 LAKE CHAMPAGNE CAMPGROUND

Rating: 7
East of Randolph

Terraced sites adorn a hillside above secluded Lake Champagne, where campers can use a small sandy beach for swimming and sunning. Most of the slopes around the lake are open and grassy, but tall hardwood trees provide shade for the majority of the campsites. Rustic fencing helps the campground maintain a natural appearance. The upper sites afford good views of the Green Mountains. The Second Branch of the White River, which flows through East Randolph, is a popular fly-fishing waterway. Also worth a visit is the Floating Bridge at Sunset Lake in nearby Brookfield. First built in 1820, it's been replaced six times and is the most heavily used bridge of its type in the country; it's also where the locals go to swim.
Campsites, facilities: There 123 sites for tents and RVs, 66 with full hookups and 43 with water and electric hookups. Each site has a picnic table and fire ring. Hot showers, flush toilets, a dump station, playground, laundry facilities, a recreation hall, pavilion, shuffleboard, volleyball courts, and horseshoe pits are provided. LP gas, firewood, and ice are available. Leashed pets are permitted.
Reservations, fees: Reservations are recommended. A deposit of one days' fee will hold a site for a weekend; two days' fee holds one for a week. Sites start at $20 a night per family. There are surcharges for additional adults. Weekly and monthly rates are available.
Open: Late May–mid-October.
Directions: From I-89 south of Montpelier, take Exit 4 and drive a mile east on Highway 66 to the campground entrance.
Contact: Lake Champagne Campground, P.O. Box 250, Furnace Road, Randolph Center, VT 05061, 802/728-5293, website: www. lakechampagne.com.

5 WHITE RIVER VALLEY CAMPGROUND

🚶 🏊 🎣 🏕 🐕 👫 🚐

Rating: 7

On the White River in Gaysville

The frequently held special events at White River Valley Camping are pretty creative, including free pig roasts, bonfires, special meals, and ice-cream socials. But then there's the so-called Peanuts from Heaven, in which pilot Dan, one of the owners, flies overhead and drops peanut shells that contain prizes. The White River flows through the campground, and tubing here is a major family attraction. These waters are renowned for their trout fishing, but anglers might also like to visit the Bethel National Fish Hatchery in Gaysville, which releases a million salmon smelts into the Connecticut River annually.

Campsites, facilities: There are 102 RV sites, 19 with full hookups, 39 with water and electric hookups, and 44 with none. Air conditioner and heater use is allowed. Laundry facilities, a dump station, hot showers, a snack bar, restrooms, a whirlpool spa, recreation hall, playground, gaming equipment and courts, and horseshoe pits are provided. Leashed pets are permitted.

Reservations, fees: Reservations are recommended in the summer. Sites start at $22 a night for two people. Weekly, monthly, and seasonal rates are available.

Open: May 1–October 15.

Directions: From I-89, take Exit 3 and follow Highway 107 west for 8.3 miles. Turn right and proceed to the campground entrance on the right.

Contact: White River Valley Campground, P.O. Box 106, Highway 107, Gaysville, VT 05746, 802/234-9115, website: www.sover.net/~river.

6 SILVER LAKE STATE PARK

🏊 🎣 🏕 🐕 👫 ♿ 🚐 ⛰

Rating: 7

North of Woodstock on the east side of Silver Lake

Silver Lake is for swimmers. Flanked by Vermont's quintessential rolling green hills, this sparkling loch is open to nonmotorized boating only. A beach, diving board, boat rentals, and day-use picnic area are provided, and kids can catch sunfish and perch all day long right from shore. Campsites are in the woods near the lake. To learn about the people who settled these rural hills, visit the Billings Farm and Museum and the Sugarbush Cheese and Maple Syrup Farm to the south in Woodstock. The former has a restored farmhouse and holds many family events highlighting Vermont's agricultural history. Sugarbush demonstrates the modern family farm in action; visitors can watch cheese being hand cut and learn the maple sugaring process.

Campsites, facilities: There are 47 sites for tents and RVs, including seven lean-tos, all without hookups. A dump station, metered hot showers, flush toilets, fireplaces, a playground, snack bar, picnic shelter, and boat rentals are provided. Firewood is sold on-site. Leashed pets with rabies vaccination certification are permitted, but not in day-use areas.

Reservations, fees: Reservations are recommended. Sites are $16–23 a night for four people. The maximum allowable number of people at a site is eight, and there must be one person at least 18 years of age with each camping party. See the introduction to the Northeast Kingdom and Lake Champlain chapter for more information on state park regulations.

Open: Mid-May–Labor Day.

Directions: From I-89 northwest of White River Junction, Vermont, take Exit 3 for South Royalton. Travel 3.5 miles west on Highway 107 to the junction with Highway 12 and then head south through the town of Barnard. From the town center, drive north on Town Road for .25 mile to the campground and state park entrance.

Contact: Silver Lake State Park, P.O. Box 67, Barnard, VT 05031, 802/234-9451.

7 THETFORD HILL STATE PARK

Rating: 7

North of White River Junction, Vermont

Open, grassy sites flanked by woods are located near the Thetford Hill District, a historic section of town where most of the buildings predate the Civil War. A historic log picnic shelter is located at the top of the park, which also provides a beautiful vista. The award-winning cross-country trail developed in conjunction with Thetford Academy is ideal for hiking. Anglers like this location for fishing the West River. Just down the road to the south, the Union Village Dam Recreation Area is open to swimming and fishing in a six-mile stretch of water that is stocked with brown and rainbow trout and supports a resident natural brook trout population.

Campsites, facilities: There are 16 sites for tents and RVs, including two lean-tos, all without hookups. Each site has a picnic table and fireplace. Metered hot showers, flush toilets, recycling bins, a dump station, picnic shelter, and playground are provided. Firewood is available. Leashed pets with rabies vaccination certification are permitted, but not in day-use areas.

Reservations, fees: Reservations are recommended. Sites are $14–21 a night for four people. The maximum allowable number of people at a site is eight, and there must be one person at least 18 years of age with each camping party. See the introduction to the Northeast Kingdom and Lake Champlain chapter for more information on state park regulations.

Open: Mid-May–Labor Day.

Directions: From I-91, take Exit 14 and drive west on Highway 113 to Thetford Hill. In the center of town, turn south on Academy Road and travel a mile to the park entrance.

Contact: Thetford Hill State Park, P.O. Box 132, Thetford, VT 05074, 802/785-2266.

8 REST 'N' NEST CAMPGROUND

Rating: 6

Near the Connecticut River in Thetford

Tall pines keep campers cool during the summer months at Rest 'N' Nest. The spacious sites are separated into different sections for seasonal campers, RVers, and, in more heavily wooded areas, tenters. A small spring-fed, artificially constructed pond on the grounds is open for swimming. Great fishing can be had by traveling a mile in either direction: the Ompompanoosuc River and West Brook are about a mile to the west, and the Connecticut River lies to the east. On the Ompompanoosuc, Union Village Dam is operated by the U.S. Army Corps of Engineers and more than six miles of water are stocked with brown and rainbow trout.

Campsites, facilities: There are 90 RV and tent sites, 46 with full hookups and 29 with water and electric hookups. Each site has a picnic table and fire grill. Air conditioner and heater use is allowed. Facilities include a laundry room, metered hot showers, restrooms, a recreation hall, playground, badminton and basketball courts, and horseshoe pits. RV storage, group sites for tents and RVs, limited groceries, ice, and firewood are available. Leashed pets are permitted.

Reservations, fees: Reservations are recommended the second week in August and require a nonrefundable deposit. Sites range from $20–29 a night.

Open: Late April–late October.

Directions: From I-91 north of White River Junction, Vermont, take Exit 14 and head east on Highway 113 for approximately 200 feet. Turn left (north) on Latham Road; the campground entrance is less than .25 mile ahead.

Contact: Ramona Jacobs, Rest 'N' Nest Campground, P.O. Box 258, Latham Road, East Thetford Center, VT 05043, 802/785-2997, website: www.restnnest.com.

9 QUECHEE GORGE STATE PARK

🏃 🛶 🎣 🚴 ♿ 🚐 ⛺

Rating: 8

Near Quechee Gorge in White River Junction

Located next to the geological phenomenon of 200-foot-deep Quechee Gorge on the Ottauquechee River, the sites at this campground are set in a northern hardwood forest interspersed with conifers. A mile loop trail provides views of the gorge from the river and the rim. You can cast a line in the river for brook, rainbow, and brown trout, or head to the gorge's north end to try out a swimming hole. North Hartland Lake Recreation Area is a stone's throw to the southeast; maintained by the U.S. Army Corps of Engineers, the lake there has a developed swimming and recreation area that includes ball fields and a boat ramp.

Campsites, facilities: There are 54 sites for tents and RVs, including seven lean-tos, all without hookups. Each site has a picnic table and fireplace. Metered hot showers, flush toilets, recycling bins, a dump station, picnic shelter, and playground are provided. Firewood is available. Leashed pets with rabies vaccination certification are permitted, but not in day-use areas.

Reservations, fees: Reservations are recommended. Sites are $14–21 a night for four people. The maximum allowable number of people at a site is eight, and there must be one person at least 18 years of age with each camping party. See the introduction to the Northeast Kingdom and Lake Champlain chapter for more information on state park regulations.

Open: Mid-May–mid-October.

Directions: From I-89 in White River Junction, Vermont, take Exit 1 and head west on U.S. 4 for three miles to the park entrance on the left (south) side of the road.

Contact: Quechee Gorge State Park, 764 Dewey Mills Road, White River Junction, VT 05001, 802/295-2990.

10 PINE VALLEY RV RESORT

🏃 🛶 🎣 🛶 🐕 🚴 ♿ 🚐

Rating: 5

In White River Junction

Pine trees buffer these sites from the noise of nearby I-89 and U.S. 4. A small pond here is open to fishing, swimming, and boating and the campground rents out paddleboats and canoes. The pond is stocked with trout—you can keep any fish you catch for 50 cents an inch—and is circumnavigable by a short nature walk. Though tents are welcome, these sites are more suited to RVs—any size can be accommodated—and the campground owners say they cater to overnight travelers. A few miles to the west is Quechee Gorge, a mile-long chasm on the Ottauquechee River. You can hike and walk along the trails, or picnic overlooking waterfalls. The Vermont Raptor Center in nearby Woodstock is home to nonreleasable owls, hawks, eagles, and falcons; visitors are welcome.

Campsites, facilities: There are 90 RV sites, most with full hookups. Each site has a fire ring and picnic table. Air conditioner and heater use is allowed. Recycling bins, dump stations, restrooms, hot showers, laundry facilities, a recreation hall, pool, and playground are provided. Cable TV hookups, limited groceries, rental boats, LP gas, ice, and firewood are available. Leashed pets are permitted.

Reservations, fees: Sites start at $28–33 a night.

Open: May–late October.

Directions: From I-89 in White River Junction, Vermont, take Exit 1 and drive .25 mile west on U.S. 4 to the campground entrance on the left (south) side of the road.

Contact: Pine Valley RV Resort, 3700 Woodstock Road, White River Junction, VT 05001, 802/296-6711.

11 MAPLE LEAF MOTEL AND CAMPGROUND

🐕 🚣 🚐 ⛺

Rating: 3

In White River Junction

Partially shaded and grassy, these sites are located next to a motel on a busy road. While a few sites are suitable for tents, RVers will feel the most comfortable in this exposed campground. If you're looking for a place to pull off the interstate for the night, Maple Leaf Motel and Campground is a convenient option. Attention train buffs: White River Junction is home to the Vermont Railroad Museum, a repository of train-related historical artifacts and memorabilia.

Campsites, facilities: There are 20 sites for tents and RVs, four with full hookups and 10 with water and electric hookups. Some RV sites have cable TV hookups. Hot showers, a dump station, tables, and fire rings are provided. There's also a playground, badminton court, and horseshoe pits. Ice and firewood are available. Leashed pets are permitted.

Reservations, fees: Reservations are recommended. Sites are $16–24 a night.

Open: May–late October.

Directions: From the interchange of I-91 and I-89 in White River Junction, travel 2.5 miles south on U.S. 5 to the motel and campground driveway.

Contact: Maple Leaf Motel and Campground, 2374 North Hartland Road, White River Junction, VT 05001-3815, 802/295-2817.

12 COOLIDGE STATE PARK

🚶 🐕 🚣 ♿ 🚐 ⛺

Rating: 7

In Plymouth

🚴 Ⓕ As part of Calvin Coolidge State Forest, the campground offers secluded campsites and log lean-tos in a forest of spruce, hemlock, fir, birch, beech, and sugar maples. From the campground, hikes lead to Slack Hill, where some primitive "wilderness" campsites are lo-

cated. A trail network explores the preserve's more than 16,000 acres, including a route to Shrewsbury Peak northwest of Plymouth, one of the highest points in the forest. A trail leads to the summit, and connector trails meet up with the Long and Appalachian Trails. Nearby Plymouth is the birthplace of Calvin Coolidge, the 30th president of the United States and the man for whom the park was named. Learn about him at the Calvin Coolidge Homestead historical museum. This campground is the site of the third Civilian Conservation Corps camp built in Vermont; CCC workers established the camp in June 1933.

Campsites, facilities: There are 60 sites for tents and RVs, including 35 lean-tos, all without hookups. Each site has a picnic table and fireplace. Metered hot showers, flush toilets, recycling bins, a dump station, picnic shelter, snack bar, and playground are provided. Leashed pets with rabies vaccination certification are permitted, but not in day-use areas.

Reservations, fees: Reservations are recommended. Sites are $14–21 a night for four people. The maximum allowable number of people at a site is eight, and there must be one person at least 18 years of age with each camping party. See the introduction to the Northeast Kingdom and Lake Champlain chapter for more information on state park regulations.

Open: Mid-May–Columbus Day.

Directions: From Highway 100 in Plymouth, travel north for two miles on Highway 100A to the park entrance on the right.

Contact: Coolidge State Park, 855 Coolidge State Park Road, Plymouth, VT 05056, 802/672-3612.

13 CAMP PLYMOUTH STATE PARK

🚶 🏊 🎣 🚤 🚣

Rating: 7

South of Plymouth on the east side of Echo Lake

Not everyone would call this camping. The

state rents out four cottages in Tyson at the edge of Echo Lake, which is open to boating, fishing, canoeing, and swimming. Hiking trails follow the shore and traverse about 300 woodland acres. One trail leads to the abandoned town of Five Corners where visitors can pan for gold.

Campsites, facilities: There are four fully equipped cottages with flush toilets and hot showers. A playground and boat rentals are provided. Ice is available. No pets are allowed.

Reservations, fees: Reservations are necessary. Cottages are $560 a week, $80 a day. See the introduction to the Northeast Kingdom and Lake Champlain chapter for more information on state park regulations.

Open: Mid-May–mid-October.

Directions: From Highway 100 approximately 5.5 miles north of Ludlow, take a right onto Kingdom Road. Head east on Kingdom for one mile, then take a left and head north on Billings Scout Camp Road to the park entrance.

Contact: Camp Plymouth State Park, 2008 Scout Camp Road, Ludlow, VT 05149, 802/228-2025.

14 HIDEAWAY "SQUIRREL HILL" CAMPGROUND

🏃 🏠 🌲 🚐 ⛰️

East of Ludlow   Rating: 7

Small, quiet, and unadorned, this wooded campground is host to many seasonal campers. Be sure to call ahead if you want a spot. Located near the Green Mountain National Forest and the town of Ludlow, Hideaway is convenient for both wilderness and nightlife. Okemo State Forest is home to Okemo Ski Mountain, and the town of Ludlow at its base bustles with shops and restaurants. While the skiers wait for the white stuff to appear, hikers can venture to the 3,343-foot Okemo summit, also known as Ludlow Mountain, in spring, summer, and fall.

Campsites, facilities: There are 30 sites for tents

and RVs, most with hookups. Hot showers, a dump station, and a playground are provided. Firewood is available. Leashed pets are permitted.

Reservations, fees: Reservations are recommended. Sites start at $18 a night.

Open: Late May–mid-October.

Directions: From Ludlow, travel 1.5 miles southeast on Highway 103 to Bixby Road. Turn left and go to the campground entrance about 500 feet ahead on the left.

Contact: Hideaway "Squirrel Hill" Campground, P.O. Box 176, Bixby Road, Ludlow, VT 05149, 802/228-8800.

15 CATON PLACE CAMPGROUND

🚲 🏊 🏠 🌲 🚐 ⛰️

East of Ludlow   Rating: 8

Choose from either mountain-view sites or shaded sites in a grove of white pines at this family-oriented campground in the foothills of the eastern slope of the Green Mountains.

Campsites, facilities: There are 81 sites, most with hookups. On-site are a pool, sports courts, a playground, hot showers, and laundry facilities. Firewood and ice are available at the campground. Leashed pets are permitted.

Reservations, fees: Reservations are recommended. Sites start at $12 a night.

Open: Late May–November 1.

Directions: From Ludlow, take Route 101 East. Bear left on Route 131 just before Proctorsville. Follow Route 131 for 2.25 miles to Tarbell Hill Road. Follow it for 1.5 miles to East Road. Make a left on East Road and follow signs to campground entrance on the north (right) side of the road.

Contact: Caton Place Campground, 2419 East Road, Cavendish, VT 05142-9718, 802/226-7767.

16 RUNNING BEAR CAMPING AREA

Rating: 5

In Ascutney

Set in hilly woodlands, this campground is less than a mile from the Connecticut River. The area is densely formatted—sites are only about 25 feet wide—but it is fully equipped for RVers who want a spot close to the interstate. Some sites are rented seasonally in summer and in winter. A short drive inland on Highway 44A leads to Mount Ascutney State Park. In summer, the summit hike is a good way to spot hawks; in winter the privately owned ski area is a fun family destination with plenty of easy and moderate terrain. Since the freestanding mountain is not part of any range, it affords sweeping views in all directions.

Campsites, facilities: There are 107 RV sites, 45 with full hookups and 42 with water and electric hookups. Each site has a table, fire ring, and grill. Facilities include a dump station, hot showers, restrooms, and a recreation hall. Also on the property are a heated pool, sports field, and horseshoe pits. LP gas, groceries, ice, and firewood are available. Leashed pets are permitted.

Reservations, fees: Reservations are recommended and in winter are necessary. Sites are $20–28 a night for two people.

Open: Year-round.

Directions: From I-91 at Ascutney, take Exit 8 and travel .5 mile east on Highway 131 to U.S. 5. Drive a mile north to the campground entrance on the right (east) side of U.S. 5.

Contact: Running Bear Camping Area, P.O. Box 378, Ascutney, VT 05030, 802/674-6417, website: www.runningbearvermont.com.

17 MOUNT ASCUTNEY STATE PARK

Rating: 7

Northwest of Ascutney

Because of the excellent hiking opportunities at the park and the panoramic views from the Mount Ascutney summit, these campsites are in high demand. In addition to the wooded, spacious sites at the campground, trailside camping is permitted. The trails here are well established—some historians claim this was the first American mountain with a developed footpath—and moderate in difficulty for the most part, with some steep sections. Several routes lead to the 3,144-foot summit. There is also an auto road (fee) that ends about half a mile from the summit and a trail that leads from the main parking lot to the top. You see some notable sights as you hike, including the Steam Donkey—a machine used for logging in the early 1900s—on the Futures Trail and Crystal Cascade Falls, an 84-foot waterfall on the Weathersfield Trail. The mountain is a monadnock, not part of any ridge or chain, and thus provides an ideal launch for hang gliders (there are two established launch sites). You can hike to the gliders' takeoff points and observe their flights, or bring your own set of wings. An observation tower and other communication towers are atop Ascutney's summit.

Campsites, facilities: There are 39 sites for tents and trailers with no hookups, and 10 additional sites with lean-tos. Facilities include a dump station, restrooms, metered hot showers, piped water, a playground, fireplaces, and tables. Firewood is available on-site, and ice and LP gas can be obtained nearby in Ascutney. No generators or firearms are allowed, and only two vehicles are permitted at each campsite. Leashed pets with rabies vaccination certification are permitted, but not in day-use areas.

Reservations, fees: Reservations are recommended. Sites are $14–21. The maximum allowable num-

ber of people at a site is eight, and there must be one person at least 18 years of age with each camping party. See the introduction to the Northeast Kingdom and Lake Champlain chapter for more information on state park regulations.
Open: Mid-May–early October.
Directions: From I-91 at Ascutney, take Exit 8 and drive two miles north on U.S. 5. Head northwest on Highway 44A for a mile to Mount Ascutney Road. The park entrance is about a mile ahead on the left.
Contact: Ascutney State Park, 1826 Back Mountain Road, Windsor, VT 05089, 802/674-2060 or 800/299-3071.

18 WILGUS STATE PARK

Rating: 7
South of Ascutney on the Connecticut River

At Wilgus State Park, pitch your tent along the Connecticut River. Both open, grassy sites and private, wooded sites overlook the river, making this a popular destination for sportspeople and canoeists. Trout, walleye, pike, bass, and shad make their home in the river and are fair game for anglers. If you plan on canoeing the Connecticut, you'll want a good guide (AMC publishes a river guide for the New Hampshire and Vermont section) because certain areas, such as one spot near Bellows Falls, cannot be run. The abundant wildlife here includes river otters, beavers, and various birds. Within the park are two foot trails, each less than a mile long, leading to the 600-foot pinnacle. This peak offers a view of the Connecticut River and across to New Hampshire. To the north, the town of Windsor lays claim to the longest covered bridge in the United States; it crosses the Connecticut River and connects New Hampshire and Vermont.
Campsites, facilities: There are 26 sites for tents and RVs, including nine lean-tos, all without hookups. Facilities include a dump station, flush toilets, metered hot showers, a group area, playground, tables, and fireplaces. Fire-

wood is available, and ice and supplies can be obtained in Ascutney. Leashed pets with rabies vaccination certification are permitted at sites, but not in day-use areas.
Reservations, fees: Reservations are recommended. Sites are $14–21 a night for four people. The maximum allowable number of people at a site is eight, and there must be one person at least 18 years of age with each camping party. See the introduction to the Northeast Kingdom and Lake Champlain chapter for more information on state park regulations.
Open: Mid-May–mid-October.
Directions: From I-91 in Ascutney, take Exit 8 and travel .5 mile east on Highway 131 to U.S. 5. Drive two miles south to the park entrance on the left (east) side of U.S. 5.
Contact: Wilgus State Park, Box 196, Ascutney, VT 05030, 802/674-5422.

19 GETAWAY MOUNTAIN AND CAMPGROUND

Rating: 6
South of Ascutney on U.S. 5

Getaway Mountain and Campground offers full RV amenities and clean, partially shaded sites. Bring your berry pail—there are lots of native berries at the campground. Facilities include a pool, canoe rentals, and miniature golf. Some sites look out over the Connecticut River. Boaters and anglers who want to get out on the water should head a short distance north to Wilgus State Park (see previous listing). In addition to hiking and nature trails, the state-owned parcel includes frontage on the Connecticut River and boat access.
Campsites, facilities: There are 52 sites for tents and RVs, all with hookups. Flush toilets, metered hot showers, a dump station, playground, and recreation room are provided. Ice and firewood are available. Leashed pets are permitted.
Reservations, fees: Reservations are recommended. Sites start at $21 a night.

Open: Early May–late October.

Directions: From I-91 in Ascutney, take Exit 8 and travel .5 mile east on Highway 131 to U.S. 5. Drive south on this road to the campground two miles ahead on the left (east).

Contact: Getaway Mountain and Campground, P.O. Box 372, Route 5 South, Ascutney, VT 05030, 802/674-2812.

20 CROWN POINT CAMPING AREA

Rating: 7

South of Ascutney near the Connecticut River

The smell of pine trees will lull you to sleep at these level shaded sites overlooking Stoughton Pond. The pond, a half mile away, is a great place for cooling off on a hot summer day and is also open to fishing and boating.

Campsites, facilities: There are 143 sites for tents and RVs, 77 with full hookups and 43 with water and electric hookups. Three bathhouses with hot showers and laundry facilities are provided. A playground is provided at the campground, as are boat and bike rentals. Leashed pets are permitted.

Reservations, fees: Reservations are recommended. Sites range from $19–24 a night.

Open: Early May–late October.

Directions: From Perkinsville, travel a mile east on Highway 106.

Contact: Crown Point Camping Area, 131 Bishop Camp Road, Perkinsville, VT 05151, 802/263-5555, website: www.crownpointcamping.com.

21 HORSESHOE ACRES

Rating: 6

Between Weston and Andover

Horseshoe Acres is set deep in the woods and has a pond and swimming pool to cool off in during the summer. Utilizing a pavilion and a large lawn, the campground specializes in hosting camping safaris, reunions, receptions, and other group functions. In winter, the lodge becomes the center of activity for campers who wish to cross-country ski and snowmobile on trails that leave from the campground. Inside you will find a fireplace, heated restrooms, showers, and hot tubs. A limited number of sites are available in the winter, so reservations are suggested. This is an ideal spot for RVers who want to hit the slopes at nearby Nordic and alpine centers.

Campsites, facilities: There are 175 sites for tents and RVs, 25 with full hookups and 150 with water and electric hookups. Each site has a table, fire ring, and grill. Facilities include a dump station, laundry room, recreation hall, pavilion, pool, playground, sports field, adult lounge, game room and arcade, and horseshoe pits. Limited groceries, ice, firewood, RV supplies, RV storage, cable TV, and LP gas are available. Leashed pets are permitted.

Reservations, fees: Reservations are recommended in summer and winter. Sites range from $25–28 a night.

Open: Mid-April–November.

Directions: From I-91, take Exit 6 and travel north on Highway 103 to Chester. Head west on Highway 11 for four miles, and then turn right and go north on the Andover-Weston Road for 3.5 miles to the entrance.

Contact: Horseshoe Acres, 1978 Weston Andover Road, Andover, VT 05143, 802/875-2960.

22 HIDDEN VALLEY CAMPGROUNDS

🏊 🎣 🐕 🚴 🚐 ⛺

West of Springfield

Rating: 6

Seasonal campers dominate these shaded sites on or near a freshwater pond where they can swim and fish. The North Springfield Lake and Stoughton Pond Recreation Areas just to the north are open to powerboating.

Campsites, facilities: There are 36 sites for tents and RVs, 20 with water and electric hookups and 16 with none. A dump station, metered hot showers, a playground, and volleyball court are provided. Firewood is available on-site, and ice is for sale nearby. Leashed pets are permitted.

Reservations, fees: Reservations are recommended. Sites start at $17 a night.

Open: May 1–October 15.

Directions: From I-91 near Bellows Falls, take Exit 6 and follow Highway 103 north to Chester. Continue north through town on the same road for 4.5 miles to Gassetts. Turn right on Highway 10, heading east for a mile, then turn right on Mattson Road and bear left at the fork. The campground is two miles ahead.

Contact: Hidden Valley Campgrounds, Mattson Road, Chester, VT 05143, 802/886-2497.

23 TREE FARM CAMPGROUND

🚶 🚵 ⛷ 🐕 🚴 🚐 ⛺

East of Springfield

Rating: 8

Tree Farm Campground is nestled at the foot of one of Vermont's famous green hillsides. Sites are shaded by a tall pine tree canopy and are surrounded by more than 100 pine-forest acres crisscrossed by a multiuse trail system. In the summer, mountain bikers and hikers fill the paths. In the winter, skiers and snowmobilers enjoy the white woods; the campground also serves as a registration station for snowmobiles. A fireplace in the heated log cabin lodge and recreation room welcomes campers in the winter. Nearby is the Baltimore Covered Bridge, which links Springfield to Baltimore and was built over Great Brook in 1870.

Campsites, facilities: There are 118 sites for tents and RVs, 85 with full hookups and 33 with water and electric hookups. Each site has a table and fire ring. There's also an open camping area for clubs and groups. Sixty-six sites are open for winter camping. Facilities include a pavilion, heated recreation room, restrooms, and free hot showers. Also on the property are a playground, horseshoe pits, a sports area, and a dump station. Firewood, ice, cable TV, limited groceries, RV storage, and LP gas are available. Leashed pets are permitted.

Reservations, fees: Reservations are recommended. Sites with full hookups including cable TV are $18 a night per family. Ask about special rates for groups and clubs.

Open: Year-round. The winter season is November 1–May 1.

Directions: From I-91 at Springfield, take Exit 7 and travel three miles west on Highway 11. Turn right at Bridge Street and drive about .5 mile, crossing the Black River, then turn right again on Highway 143 and drive another .5 mile northeast to the campground entrance on the right.

Contact: Tree Farm Campground, 53 Skitchewaug Trail, Springfield, VT 05156, 802/885-2889.

24 TOWNSHEND STATE PARK

🚶 🏊 🎣 🪓 🐕 🚐 ⛺

On the West River north of Townshend

Rating: 7

Set along the West River, the campsites in Townshend State Park are favored by canoeists and anglers alike. Rainbow and brown trout live in this waterway. The U.S. Army Corps of Engineers maintains a dam and recreation area north of the state forest, and during water releases in spring and fall, the river offers exciting white-water canoeing for intermediate and expert paddlers. A loop trail leads from the campground to the Bald Mountain summit

(1,680 feet) through a forest of hemlock, white pine, and mixed hardwoods. Along the trail are waterfalls, chutes, and pools. Views to the north, south, and east await on the summit. The Scott Covered Bridge spans the West River on the approach to the campground and is open to foot traffic only. There's a beach for swimming and a boat ramp for larger vessels at the recreation area north of the forest.

Campsites, facilities: There are 34 sites for tents and RVs, four with lean-tos. There are no hookups or dump stations. Flush toilets, metered hot showers, picnic tables, and fire rings are provided. Ice and firewood are available. Leashed pets with rabies vaccination certification are permitted, but not in day-use areas.

Reservations, fees: Reservations are recommended. Sites are $14–21 a night for four people. The maximum allowable number of people at a site is eight, and there must be one person at least 18 years of age with each camping party. See the introduction to the Northeast Kingdom and Lake Champlain chapter for more information on state park regulations.

Open: Mid-May–mid-October.

Directions: From Brattleboro, take Exit 2 to Highway 30 and travel north for 15 miles. Turn left on State Forest Road, bearing right after .4 mile. The state park road is ahead on the left.

Contact: Townshend State Park, 2755 State Forest Road, Townshend, VT 05353, 802/365-7500.

25 BALD MOUNTAIN CAMPGROUND

🚶 🚲 ⛱ 🎣 🍴 🐕 🛶 🚐 ⛰

Rating: 8

On the West River in Townshend

Meadows and forest make up the landscape at Bald Mountain Campground. Formerly used for farming, this parcel offers sites on the West River or beside a beaver pond, sites in wooded areas, and open spaces with mountain views. Swimming, tubing, and fishing are popular

river activities here. Miles of dirt roads ideal for mountain biking surround the campground and neighboring Townshend State Park, and two hiking trails leave the park and ascend Bald Mountain. The hike climbs 1,100 vertical feet and features waterfalls, chutes, and pools along the way. The Scott Covered Bridge, built in 1870, spans the West River just north of the campground and state park.

Campsites, facilities: There are 200 sites for tents and RVs, 16 with full hookups and 184 with water and electric hookups. Each site has a picnic table and fire ring. There are group sites for tents and RVs, and a separate tenting area. Air conditioners are allowed, but heaters are not. Facilities include a dump station, laundry machines, hot showers, restrooms, a recreation hall, playground, horseshoe pits, swimming pool, volleyball and badminton, and a basketball hoop. RV storage, LP gas, limited groceries, ice, and firewood are available. Leashed pets are permitted.

Reservations, fees: Reservations are accepted. Sites start at $17 a night.

Open: Late April–Columbus Day.

Directions: From Brattleboro, take Exit 2 to Highway 30 and travel north for 15 miles. Turn left on State Forest Road, bearing right after .4 mile. The campground is 1.3 miles ahead.

Contact: Bald Mountain Campground, State Park Road, Townshend, VT 05353, 802/365-7510.

26 CAMPERAMA FAMILY CAMPGROUND

⛱ 🎣 🍴 🐕 🛶 🚐 ⛰

Rating: 7

On the West River in Townshend

With cows for company, you camp alongside a river and have access to full RV amenities at Camperama. Bordered by a barnyard on one side and the West River on another, the campsites are well shaded, and many enjoy mountain views. Sites 148–175 are right on the river, and all campers are encouraged to fish and swim in the refreshing current. A short drive to the north is Townshend State Park, complete with hiking trails. From the dam above the park to I-91 in Brattleboro, the river offers white-water canoeing for intermediate or better paddlers during water releases in the spring and fall.

Campsites, facilities: There are 219 sites for tents and RVs, 59 with full hookups and 160 with water and electric hookups. Each site has a table and fire ring. Air conditioners are allowed, but heaters are not. Facilities include a dump station, laundry room, grocery store, free hot showers, restrooms, a recreation hall, playground, horseshoe pits, two shuffleboard courts, a pool, volleyball and badminton, and a basketball hoop. Cable TV, RV supplies, LP gas, ice, and wood are available. Leashed pets are permitted.

Reservations, fees: Reservations are recommended; call 800/63-CAMPS (800/632-2677). Sites range from $21–$25 a night per family.

Open: Mid-April–mid-October.

Directions: From the junction of Highways 30 and 35 in Townshend, travel .75 mile south on Highway 30, turn right on Depot Road, and drive .25 mile west. The campground is just ahead after you cross the river.

Contact: Camperama Family Campground, P.O. Box 282, Depot Road, Townshend, VT 05353, 802/365-4315.

27 KENOLIE VILLAGE

🏊 ⛵ 🎣 🐕 🚴 🚐 ⛺

Rating: 7

In Newfane on the West River

Designed with RVers in mind, these sites are located in the West River Valley, and many look out onto the surrounding Green Mountains. Campers can fish and swim in the refreshing West River or take a short drive north to Townshend State Park, where multiuse trails attract bikers and hikers. The U.S. Army Corps of Engineers maintains a dam and recreation area north of the state forest, and when they release water in the spring and fall the river is an exciting place for intermediate and expert paddlers to canoe. Every weekend mid-May–Labor Day there are family-oriented activities at the campground.

Campsites, facilities: There are 150 sites for tents and RVs, 80 with water and electric hookups, and some sites just for tents. Flush toilets, hot showers, a dump station, playground, pavilion, recreation hall, and laundry facilities are provided. LP gas, limited groceries, ice, and firewood are available. Leashed pets are permitted.

Reservations, fees: Reservations are recommended. Sites start at $15 a night for two people.

Open: April 1–December 1.

Directions: From Townshend, travel southeast on Highway 30 for 3.5 miles to the campground entrance on the left.

Contact: Kenolie Village, 16 Kenolie Campground Road, Newfane, VT 05345, 802/365-7671.

28 BRATTLEBORO NORTH KOA

🏊 🏠 🚴 🚐 ⛺

Rating: 5

South of Putney on U.S. 5

Against a backdrop of Vermont's lush green hills, each of the campsites has a manicured grass plot and a shade tree. The roomy sites are separated by gravel roads, but have no natural buffers, so privacy is at a minimum. Superclean facilities add to the civilized feel; this is a good choice for travelers who want to regroup before heading to wilder destinations. Nearby tourist attractions include Basketville, a specialty store featuring all manner of woven works, and Santa's Land, a theme park with rides, elves, Santa's workshop, and real reindeer to feed; both are just north of Putney.

Campsites, facilities: There are 42 sites for tents and RVs, 12 with full hookups, 29 with water and electric hookups, and one with none. Each site has a shade tree, picnic table, and charcoal grill. Air conditioner and heater use is allowed. Facilities include a dump station, laundry room, pool, limited groceries, free hot showers, restrooms, a recreation hall, playground, horseshoe pits, volleyball court, and basketball hoop. Ice and wood are available. Leashed pets are permitted.

Reservations, fees: Reservations are strongly recommended. Sites start at $27 a night for two people.

Open: Mid-April–late October.

Directions: From I-91 north of Brattleboro, take Exit 3 and travel 3.5 miles north on U.S. 5 to the campground entrance on the right.

Contact: Brattleboro North KOA, 1238 U.S. Route 5, East Dummerston, VT 05346, 802/254-5908 or reservations 800/562-5909, website: www.koakampgrounds.com.

29 HIDDEN ACRES CAMPGROUND

🧑‍🤝‍🧑 🏊 🐕 ♿ 🚐 ⛰️

Rating: 5

North of Brattleboro

This full-service RV park has mostly open and many pull-through sites near the interstate. It's a good choice for travelers heading north who need to stop for the night. Families can keep busy with all the on-site recreation and nearby tourist attractions, especially the Santa's Land theme park a short drive north. The Connecticut River is conveniently close for people who enjoy fishing and boating. For those who like river cruising in a more leisurely style, there's the *Belle of Brattleboro,* a small-scale, open-air, motor-driven cruise boat that offers a variety of tours on the river separating Vermont and New Hampshire. Knowledgeable captains share history about the town of Brattleboro and the river itself.

Campsites, facilities: There are 40 sites for tents and RVs, all with hookups. Each site has a picnic table and fire ring. Group sites are available for tents and RVs. Air conditioner and heater use is allowed. Facilities include a dump

station, hot showers, and restrooms. Also on the property are a pool, miniature golf, nature trails, shuffleboard, basketball and volleyball courts, and horseshoe pits. RV storage, limited groceries, ice, and firewood are available. Leashed pets are permitted.

Reservations, fees: Reservations are recommended and require a nonrefundable deposit. Sites start at $20 a night.

Open: May 1–October.

Directions: From I-91 north of Brattleboro, take Exit 3 and travel 2.5 miles north on U.S. 5 to the campground entrance on the left.

Contact: Hidden Acres Campground, 792 U.S. 5, Brattleboro, VT 05301, 802/254-2098, website: www.hiddenacresvt.com.

30 MOSS HOLLOW CAMPGROUND

🧑‍🤝‍🧑 🚴 🏊 🎣 🐕 🚐 ⛰️

Rating: 7

West of Brattleboro

Swimming holes and fishing holes are some of the perks at these rustic and private sites near a stream. On some weekends, the owners offer hayrides through the countryside. Mountain bikers and hikers will find an abundance of dirt roads and trails that leave from the campground. In the summer, Mount Snow north of Wilmington swaps boards for bikes and becomes a fat-tire mecca. With more than 140 miles of trails, guided tours, lessons, and chairlift rides to the top (3,600 feet), the Mount Snow Mountain Bike Center appeals to riders of all skill levels; for information, call 802/464-3333.

Campsites, facilities: There are 50 sites for tents and RVs with water and electric hookups. Each site has a fire ring and table. Flush toilets, hot showers, horseshoe pits, a dump station, and small store are provided. Ice and firewood are available. Leashed pets are permitted.

Reservations, fees: Reservations are recommended. Sites are $15–20 a night.

Open: May 15–October 15.

Directions: From I-91 near Brattleboro, travel west on Highway 9 for 1.4 miles. Turn left on Greenleaf Street and follow the paved road to its end. Cross the bridge to continue on the dirt road. After crossing three more concrete bridges, take the first right and drive to the campground entrance 300 feet ahead on the right.

Contact: Moss Hollow Campground, 449 Thurber Road, Brattleboro, VT 05301, 802/368-2830.

31 FORT DUMMER STATE PARK

🏞 🛖 ♿ 🚐 ⛺

Rating: 6

Near the Connecticut River in Brattleboro

Fort Dummer is a small park, only 217 acres, that offers a forested oasis just outside of Brattleboro. These sites are private, yet provide easy access to nearby historic sites as well as fishing and boating on the Connecticut River. The park was named after Fort Dummer, the first white settlement in Vermont, and overlooks the fort site. There are hiking trails around the park.

Campsites, facilities: There are 61 sites for tents and RVs, including 10 lean-tos, all without hookups. Each site has a table and fireplace. A dump station, flush toilets, metered hot showers, and a playground are provided. Firewood is available. Leashed pets with rabies vaccina-tion certification are permitted, but not in day-use areas.

Reservations, fees: Reservations are recommended. Sites are $14–21 a night. The maximum allowable number of people at a site is eight, and there must be one person at least 18 years of age. See the introduction to the Northeast Kingdom and Lake Champlain chapter for more information on state park regulations.

Open: Mid-May–early September.

Directions: From I-91 in Brattleboro, take Exit 1 and travel .1 mile north on U.S. 5. Turn right on Fairground Road and drive .5 mile east. Take another right on Main Street and continue south for one mile on Old Guilford Road. The park entrance is just ahead.

Contact: Fort Dummer State Park, 517 Old Guilford Road, Brattleboro, VT 05301, 802/254-2610.

32 CONNECTICUT RIVER CANOE SITES

🚣 🎣 🏊 ✂ 🛖 ⛺

Rating: 10

For more information on a series of canoe campsites along the Connecticut River, which forms the border between Vermont and New Hampshire, see Connecticut River Canoe Sites in the White Mountains chapter of New Hampshire.

Massachusetts

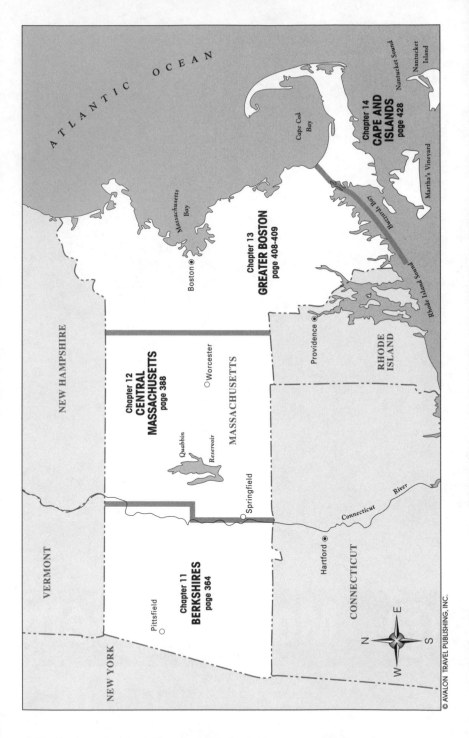

Chapter 11

© ROBIN TRAVERS

Berkshires

Berkshires

They're called the "Berkshire Hills" even though they're really mountains. The range runs the vertical length of the region, beckoning hikers and lovers of high places. The Appalachian Trail runs along this spine. Yet though the Berkshires claim some of the wildest land in the state, it is the region's dynamic art community that draws most visitors here, and has for well over a century.

Lenox and Stockbridge are well-known cultural meccas, home to the likes of the Norman Rockwell Museum, Tanglewood (summer home of the Boston Symphony Orchestra), Jacob's Pillow Dance Festival, and Shakespeare and Company theater troupe. North Adams near the Vermont border is home to Mass MoCA, the Massachusetts Museum of Contemporary Art (1040 Mass MoCA Way, 413/662-2111, website: www.massmoca.org). Housed in acres of old mill buildings, the site is perfect for large outdoor and indoor installations, as well as concerts, dance parties, and other special events. Campers come here to access both the natural and cultural gifts of the region.

For the most part, campsites reflect the topography of the region.

Most are set either in the rolling hills or along the flat river and streambed valleys. A few are set on ponds and lakes. Though the area has been heartily logged over the years, the landscape is one of forest: both hard- and softwoods. Much of it has been protected in dozens and dozens of state parks and thousands of acres of state forestland.

Massachusetts offers camping in 28 state forest and state park campgrounds. Reservations for campsites in any Massachusetts state park are accepted through the campground reservation system, Camp Massachusetts. Reservations can be made up to six months in advance of the date of your stay and as late as two days before your arrival. Reservations are limited to 14 cumulative days in any one park between Memorial Day and Labor Day. For a free copy of the "Massachusetts State Forests and Parks Guide to Recreation" and other publications, contact 617/626-1250, website: www.state.ma.dus/dem. For campsite reservations, contact 877/422-6762, website: www. reserveamerica.com.

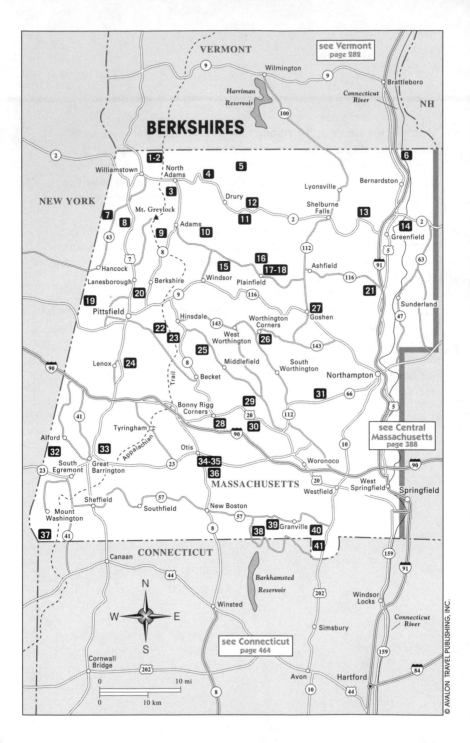

BERKSHIRES

1 APPALACHIAN TRAIL

🚶 ≈ ⛵ 🍴 ❄ 🐕

Rating: 10

From the Connecticut border in the south, the Appalachian Trail leads north through the Berkshires, over Mount Greylock, and on to the Vermont border where it intersects with the Long Trail

Some say the Berkshires are a state unto themselves. Geographically this is true, as the region is separated from the rest of Massachusetts by the low hills for which the area is named. This 87-mile-long portion of the Appalachian Trail hits the highlights of the Berkshires. Geologists claim that this region and the Green Mountains to the north are remnants of an ancient Cambrian sea, making them one of the oldest lands on earth, emerging some half a billion years ago. You may sense this timelessness when walking through second-growth forests, passing by chipper brooks and impromptu gorges, and summitting on Mount Greylock, which affords a sweeping view of western Massachusetts—all of which you experience on the Appalachian Trail.

Campsites, facilities: Lean-tos are located all along the Massachusetts portion of the trail, never more than a moderate day hike apart. Primitive toilets are provided. Current topographic maps show reliable and seasonal water sources. You will find formal campsites at October Mountain and Beartown State Forests, Clarksburg State Park, and Mount Greylock State Reservation. Pets are permitted.

Reservations, fees: Lean-to sites are available on a first-come, first-served basis. Sometimes a nominal nightly fee is charged in summer. Check with the Appalachian Trail Conference for up-to-date fees and conditions.

Open: Year-round.

Directions: In the western part of the state, the trail extends northward from Mount Everett State Reservation near the Connecticut border to Clarksburg State Park on the Vermont border. Easily accessible trailheads are on U.S. 7 in Sheffield, Highway 8 south of Washington,

Highway 9 east of Dalton, Highway 8 north of Cheshire, and Highway 2 at Blackinton.

Contact: Appalachian Trail Conference, P.O. Box 807, Harpers Ferry, WV 25425-0807, 304/535-6331, website: www.appalachiantrail.org. This nonprofit group publishes 10 sectional guides, which are accompanied by topographic maps.

2 CLARKSBURG STATE PARK

🚶 ≈ ⛵ 🚐 🐕 🚌 ⛰

Rating: 8

On the Vermont border in Clarksburg

You fall asleep among a smorgasbord of hardwoods and red and white pines at this heavily forested campground. Clarksburg State Park within the state forest consists mainly of mountain uplands overlooking the Hoosic River, which runs parallel to Highway 8. The Appalachian Trail crosses the westernmost portion of the forest, and a trail network carries hikers to altitudes between 1,000 and 2,000 feet for views of the Berkshire Hills and Vermont's Green Mountains. The hardwood mix makes Clarksburg a colorful place to be during foliage season. Campers can fish, swim, and boat in nonmotorized craft (canoes and kayaks) on Mauserts Pond next to the campground. Trout fishing is excellent in the many streams that wind through the unspoiled forestlands, once home to the Mohawk Indians.

Campsites, facilities: There are 44 sites for tents and RVs, all without hookups. Each site has a picnic table and fire grill. Piped water, flush toilets, and hot showers are provided. Leashed pets are permitted.

Reservations, fees: Reservations aren't usually necessary except in late fall during leaf-peeping season. For campsite reservations, contact 877/422-6762, website: www.reserveamerica. com. Sites are $12 a night.

Open: Mid-May–mid-October.

Directions: From Highway 8 north of North Adams, turn left on Middle Road. Signs will lead you to the campground entrance on the right.

Contact: Clarksburg State Park, Middle Road, Clarksburg, MA 02155, 413/664-8345.

3 HISTORIC VALLEY CAMPGROUND

🏃 🏊 🚣 ✕ 🐕 🚐 ⛺

Rating: 7

Southeast of North Adams on Windsor Lake

Windsor Lake is open to nonmotorized boating only, making it a peaceful spot to fish, canoe, and swim. Hiking trails surround the campground. Some of the RV sites are a little crowded, but the wilderness areas offer relief for tenters. The campground is near many attractions in western Massachusetts, including the Mohawk Trail and Mount Greylock State Reservation. One bizarre wonder can be found at Natural Bridge State Park a half mile north of North Adams: a natural marble bridge spans Hudson Brook—beautiful evidence of 550 million years of erosion.

Campsites, facilities: There are 103 large, wooded, and shaded sites for tents and RVs with water and electric hookups, plus a special wilderness section set aside for tents. Air conditioner and heater use is allowed. Facilities include restrooms, laundry machines, a dump station, boat and canoe rentals, a lake beach with lifeguards, pavilion, arcade, and scheduled activities. Firewood and ice are available. Motorcycles are prohibited. Dogs and cats are allowed but must be leashed at all times.

Reservations, fees: Reservations are recommended. Sites are $12–30 a night. Visitors, pets, air conditioners, and heaters are $2 extra per day. Weekly, monthly, and seasonal rates are available.

Open: May 15–October 15.

Directions: From the east on Highway 2 approaching downtown North Adams, turn onto East Main Street at Ed's Variety. After .25 mile, take a quick left on Kemp Avenue. The campground is 1.5 miles ahead.

Contact: Historic Valley Campground, 10 Main Street, North Adams, MA 01247, 413/662-3198.

4 MOHAWK PARK

🏊 🚣 🚐 ⛺

Rating: 5

West of Charlemont on Highway 2

Find just the basic amenities at this tidy, wooded campground located a few miles east of Mohawk Trail State Forest. Ask for a site right on the Deerfield River. On the property there is a full restaurant and nightclub with weekend entertainment. Mohawk Park is perfect for RVers who want to access the state forest but need hookups that aren't available at the state forest campground. For recreation, the state forest has over 18 miles of rivers and streams for excellent trout fishing, a swimming area, and a day-use picnic area. Many of the original Indian trails, including the Mohawk Trail, are open for hiking.

Campsites, facilities: There are 80 sites for tents and RVs, including some riverside sites. Ten sites have full hookups, 25 have water and electric hookups, and hot showers are available in the restrooms. There is no on-site dump station. Seasonal sites are available. Pets are not allowed.

Reservations, fees: Reservations are recommended July–Labor Day. Sites are $20 and up.

Open: Year-round.

Directions: From I-91, take Exit 26 and travel 21 miles west on Highway 2/Mohawk Trail to the campground entrance on the north side of the road.

Contact: Mohawk Park, P.O. Box 668, Charlemont, MA 01337, 413/339-4470.

5 MONROE STATE FOREST

🏃 🏊 🎣 🚶 🐕

Rating: 10

East of North Adams

Your backcountry camping experience in Monroe State Forest will most likely result in wildlife sightings. Campers here share the mountainous hardwood forest with deer, snowshoe hares, raccoons, woodcocks, and other small game and birds, as well as the occasional black bear. Nine miles of designated trails cross more than 4,000 acres at elevations up to 2,730 feet. Raycroft Lookout is a good vantage point from which to see the Deerfield River gorge, and Spruce Hill offers one of the most magnificent views in the state. Dunbar Brook, which traverses the forest, is known for its many small falls and rapids. In the winter months, these trails are frequented by cross-country skiers and snowmobilers. Hunting and fishing are allowed in season, and the streams are stocked with trout.

Campsites, facilities: There are three hike-in sites with shelters, but no facilities. Pets are allowed in the park.

Reservations, fees: Reservations are recommended; contact 877/422-6762, website: www.reserveamerica.com. Sites are $6 a night.

Open: Year-round.

Directions: From North Adams, travel about four miles east on Highway 2 to Tilda Hill Road. Continue east to the forest entrance two miles ahead.

Contact: Monroe State Forest Headquarters, c/o Mohawk Trail State Forest, P.O. Box 7, Charlemont, MA 01339, 413/339-5504.

6 TRAVELER'S WOODS OF NEW ENGLAND
🛶 🐕 ⛹ 🚐 ⛰

Rating: 6

Directly north of Greenfield

These open, grassy sites beside the Falls River are in close proximity to the interstate and numerous attractions such as the Yankee Candle flagship store and Historic Deerfield. This campground caters to families with low-key events like crafts for kids and potluck dinners. Anglers can cast a fishing line into the stream from the campground, though canoeists will have to look elsewhere for a put-in. The campground is only for short-term stays, so you won't be mingling with a seasonal camping crowd.

Campsites, facilities: There are 84 sites for tents and RVs, most with hookups. Facilities include a playground, laundry machines, a recreation hall, and game room. Firewood, ice, and RV supplies are available on the premises. Leashed pets are permitted.

Reservations, fees: Reservations are recommended. Tent sites start at $16 a night and RV sites start at $21 a night.

Open: May 1 through the third week in October.

Directions: From I-91 north of Greenfield, take Exit 28 south and make a right turn onto Highway 10. A quick left on River Road (after the Bernardston Auto Exchange) takes you to the campground entrance .7 mile ahead.

Contact: Traveler's Woods of New England, P.O. Box 88, Bernardston, MA 01337, 413/648-9105, website: www.travelerswoods.com.

7 BERKSHIRE VISTA NUDE RESORT AND CAMPGROUND
🚶 🏊 ⛹ 🚐 ⛰

Rating: 8

On the New York border north of Hancock

Berkshire Vista welcomes members of the American Association for Nude Recreation (AANR), The Naturist Society (TNS), and newcomers to enjoy recreational nudism. Campsites are in a field edged with trees adjacent to a year-round historic inn, all located on a high meadow in the lovely Berkshire Hills. Grounds include a sunning lawn, pool deck, solar heated pool, hot tubs, a sauna, fitness center, hiking trails, snack bar, volleyball, and tennis. Nearby cultural attractions include Tanglewood (summer home to the Boston Pops Symphony Orchestra), the Williamstown Theatre Festival, and the Norman Rockwell Museum.

Campsites, facilities: There are 180 sites for tents and RVs, most with full hookups and the rest with water and electric hookups. There is a dump station on-site as well as restrooms with hot showers, laundry facilities, a swimming pool, recreation hall, and a playground. Sites have picnic tables and fire rings. Pets are not permitted.

Reservations, fees: Campsites are $57–140 a night. Advance reservations are required.

Open: May 1–October 15.

Directions: From Hancock, take Highway 43 north to Kittle Road. Turn left on Kittle Road and follow it 1.5 miles to the end at the Berkshire Vista security gate.

Contact: Berkshire Vista Nude Resort and Campground, P.O. Box 1177, Hancock, MA 01237, 413/738-5154, website: www.berkshirevista.com.

8 BRODIE MOUNTAIN RESORT

🏃 ≋ 🎣 ➡ 🐕 ⛺ 🚐 ⛺

Rating: 8

On Highway 7 in New Ashford

In winter months, this is a ski and snowboard resort; in summer, it offers mountainside camping for RVers only. Sites are just minutes from trout fishing, golf courses, hiking and mountain biking, and cultural attractions. Brodie Mountain offers 150 rustic campsites with water and electric hookups and two restroom facilities.

Campsites, facilities: There are 150 sites with water and electric hookups. Each site has a picnic table and fire grill. Facilities include a heated pool, hot showers, a playground, horseshoes, and volleyball.

Reservations, fees: Sites are $22 a night.

Open: Mid-May–mid-October.

Directions: Take I-90 (the Mass Pike) west to Exit 2 (Berkshire Spur). Travel north on U.S. Route 7 to New Ashford and follow signs to the resort.

Contact: Brodie Mountain Resort, Route 7, New Ashford, MA 01237, 413/443-4752, website: www.skibrodie.com.

9 MOUNT GREYLOCK STATE RESERVATION

🏃 🚲 🎣 🐕 ♿ 🚐 ⛺

Rating: 9

West of Adams

Mount Greylock State Reservation was Massachusetts' first state park. For years, this rustic setting has inspired artists and writers, among them Henry David Thoreau and Herman Melville. Campsites are set at the foot of Stony Ledge, next to the Hopper, a protected region of old-growth forest with trees as old as 150 years. The Money Brook Trail crosses the Hopper from north to south and leaves from the campground. Mountain biking is allowed on designated trails only; one route departs from West Mountain Road and connects to a paved road just before the summit of Mount Greylock, the state's tallest peak. There are 45 trail miles in all. Atop the mountain, you will find the 92-foot War Veterans Memorial Tower and Bascom Lodge, a 1937 Civilian Conservation Corps (CCC) project. On a clear day, the summit offers views of the Green Mountains of Vermont to the north and the Adirondacks to the far west in New York. Since you can drive to the top, the summit gets crowded in the summer. The Appalachian Trail bisects the reservation, and there are several shelters for backpackers. Make sure you have a blueberry pail with you if you're here in late July.

Campsites, facilities: There are 35 sites for tents and RVs with no hookups or sewage disposal. Primitive toilets, piped water, picnic tables, and fireplaces are provided. Five group sites open to nonprofit organizations only can accommodate 25 people each. Backcountry lean-tos are open to backpackers for wilderness camping with no facilities. Leashed pets are permitted.

Reservations, fees: Reservations are recommended; lean-tos are first come, first served. Reserve by contacting 877/422-6762, website: www.reserveamerica.com. Sites are $12 a night. Group sites ($25 a night) must be reserved.

Open: Memorial Day weekend–mid-October.

Directions: From the Massachusetts Turnpike/I-90, take Exit 2 to U.S. 20/7 west/north. Take this road north to Lanesborough and follow signs to the park.

Contact: Mount Greylock State Reservation, P.O. Box 138, Highway 7, Lanesborough, MA

01237, 413/499-4262. For campsite reservations, contact 877/422-6762, website: www.reserveamerica.com.

10 SAVOY MOUNTAIN STATE FOREST

Rating: 9

North of Savoy

Encompassing more than 11,000 forestland acres, Savoy Mountain is one of the state's largest undeveloped parcels. Its extensive trail system designated for various uses attracts many kinds of outdoor enthusiasts. The terrain is rugged—most of the park is at an elevation of 2,000 feet or higher—and trails lead to several peaks and interest points such as Crooked Forest, a stand of misshapen trees most likely contorted by a severe ice storm. Colonists settled this tract of land, as evidenced by the cellar holes, stone walls, and family graveyards found throughout the forest. Campsites are set in an old apple orchard, so campers wake to the heady scent of apple blossoms in springtime. Spectacular natural features include Bog Pond with its floating bog islands, and Tannery Falls, which cascades through a deep chasm, finally plunging over a precipice to a clear pool below. You are camped out next to South Pond (one of two swimming ponds in the forest), which has a boat ramp. Streams and ponds in the area are stocked with trout for fishing.

Campsites, facilities: There are 45 sites for tents and RVs, all without hookups. Flush toilets, showers, piped water, picnic tables, and fireplaces are provided. A group site open to nonprofit organizations only can accommodate up to 50 people. Four cabins with fireplaces are also available. Leashed pets are permitted.

Reservations, fees: Reservations are recommended for cabins. The group site ($25 a night) must be reserved. Cabins are $25–35 a night and can sleep four people; campsites are $12

a night. Reserve by contacting 877/422-6762, website: www.reserveamerica.com.

Open: Memorial Day–mid-October. Cabins may be rented year-round.

Directions: From Highway 2 east of North Adams, travel south on Central Shaft Road and follow signs to the park entrance and the campground.

Contact: Savoy Mountain State Forest, R.F.D. 2, North Adams, MA 02147, 413/664-9567 in summer, 413/663-8469 year-round.

11 MOHAWK TRAIL STATE FOREST

Rating: 8

East of North Adams

Wooded sites by the Cold River offer campers plenty of wilderness and privacy. There's a swimming beach near the campground and good trout fishing in the Cold and Deerfield Rivers. Hiking trails leave from the far end of the campground and ascend both Clark and Todd Mountains. These trails are used by myriad woodspeople: horseback riders, bicyclists, hikers, anglers, and hunters. Some of the trails are original Mohawk Indian footpaths. In addition to the thick forest of beech, birch, maple, oak, and assorted softwoods, the park is colored by seasonal wildflowers such as violets, orchids, and lilies of the valley. Mountain laurel, blueberries, and wild roses embellish the landscape in season. Bears inhabit these woods, as do foxes and raccoons, so be sure to securely pack up your foodstuff at night.

Campsites, facilities: There are 56 sites for tents and RVs, all without hookups. Sixteen sites are open for self-contained RVs year-round. One group site open to nonprofit organizations only can accommodate up to 50 people. Six log cabins are also available. Flush toilets, showers, picnic tables, piped water, and fireplaces are available. Leashed pets are permitted.

Reservations, fees: Reservations are recommended for cabins. Cabins are $25–35 a night, campsites are $12 a night, and the winter fee for self-contained RVs is $5 a night. Reserve by contacting 877/422-6762, website: www.reserveamerica.com.

Open: Year-round for cabins and self-contained RVs, May 1–Columbus Day for all other sites.

Directions: From Charlemont, travel four miles west on Highway 2 and follow signs to the campground.

Contact: Mohawk Trail State Forest, P.O. Box 7, Highway 2, Charlemont, MA 01339, 413/339-5504.

12 COUNTRY AIRE

Rating: 5

West of Shelburne Falls on Highway 2

Most of the RV sites are strung out along the edge of pine woods while tent-only sites are more wooded and private. There are nature trails on the grounds, and the nearby Deerfield River offers swift water for canoeing, rafting, and tubing, as well as spots for fishing. Throughout the summer months, campers can partake in special theme meals, such as a strawberry shortcake social.

Campsites, facilities: There are 95 sites for tents and RVs, both open and shaded, all with water and electric hookups and 70 with additional sewer connections. Each site has a table and fire ring. Laundry facilities, hot showers, restrooms, LP gas, and a dump station are provided. You will find a pavilion, concrete swimming pool, horseshoe pits, a playground, and a camp store on-site. Leashed pets are permitted.

Reservations, fees: Reservations are recommended. Sites start at $22 a night.

Open: Year-round; fully operational May 15–October 15.

Directions: From I-91 near Greenfield, take Exit 26 and travel 13 miles west on Highway 2/Mohawk Trail to Charlemont. The campground is directly behind the Oxbow Motel and Restaurant.

Contact: Country Aire, P.O. Box 286, Charlemont, MA 01339, 413/625-2996, website: www.countryairecampground.com.

13 SPRINGBROOK FAMILY CAMPING AREA

Rating: 9

North of Shelburne Falls

Farmland stretches forth in the panorama before you at Springbrook. Set atop a cleared hill, the campground looks out upon the Holyoke Range to the south and Mount Monadnock to the north. Picturesque farms and meadows dot the landscape of the fertile Connecticut River Valley below. Springbrook is popular with seasonal campers, though there are some developed short-term RV sites and a secluded tent area for overnighters. Most sites have some shade but are grassy, spacious, and open. Hikers and mountain bikers will find trails and dirt roads that leave from the campground. One two-mile route leads to High Ledges, the Audubon Society Sanctuary, where the Lady Slipper Trail is especially memorable in the spring. The village of Shelburne Falls is a popular tourist destination in itself. The "Bridge of Flowers" spans the Deerfield River there, and streets are lined with artisans' studios, shops, and restaurants. Also worthy of note is a series of glacial potholes in the riverbed below the falls for which the town is named.

Campsites, facilities: There are 85 sites for tents and RVs, all with water and electric hookups. Each site has a table and fire ring. A dump station and pump service are available, as are LP gas, ice, and firewood. On-site you will find a traffic control gate, swimming pool, recreation and game rooms, a playground, sports courts and athletic fields, and RV storage. Leashed pets are permitted.

Reservations, fees: Reservations are recommended in summer. Sites start at $22 a night for two people.

Open: May 15–October 15.

Directions: From I-91 at Greenfield, take Exit 26 and head west on Highway 2 for 5.5 miles. Turn right on Little Mohawk Road. Travel 1.5 miles to the Patten Road sign and turn left; take the next left onto Tower Road and go to the campground entrance on the left.

Contact: Springbrook Family Camping Area, R.F.D. 1, 32 Tower Road, Shelburne, MA 01370, 413/625-6618.

14 BARTON COVE
🏃 🚲 🏊 🚤 🎣 🐕 ⛰️

Rating: 8

North of Greenfield on the Connecticut River

Lovely, natural campsites are set along a wooded peninsula on the Connecticut River, part of a land parcel that's maintained by the Northfield Mountain Recreation and Environmental Center owned by Northeast Utilities System. Campers have access to a nature trail featuring dinosaur footprints and nesting bald eagles. Another 25 miles of trails at the center are open for mountain biking and hiking. Staff members teach outdoor courses in orienteering, guide riverboat cruises, lead power-station tours, and operate a museum. Northeast Utilities also maintains Munns Ferry, a small campground with five sites on the Connecticut River in Northfield for canoeists and boaters only.

Campsites, facilities: There are 27 family tent sites, two pop-up sites, and two group sites for tents only. There are no hookups. Each site has a picnic table, hibachi, and fireplace. Showers, a recreation area, ice, firewood, and canoe and rowboat rentals are available on the property. Leashed pets are permitted.

Reservations, fees: Reservations are recommended for Barton Cove, and required at Munns Ferry. Sites start at $15 a night.

Open: The third weekend in May–Labor Day.

Directions: From I-91 at Greenfield, take Exit 27 and travel four miles east on Highway 2. Watch for the campground sign on your right.

Contact: Barton Cove, c/o Northfield Mountain, 99 Millers Falls Road, Northfield, MA 01360, 413/863-9300 or 800/859-2960, website: www.nu.com/northfield/camping.asp.

15 WINDSOR STATE FOREST
🏃 🚲 🏊 🚤 🎣 🎿 🐕 🚗 ⛰️

Rating: 8

Southeast of Savoy

The forest is known for the Windsor Jambs, a gorge formed by the brook that is the outlet of Windsor Pond. The falls cascade through a granite-walled gorge just 25 feet wide. Of the three large state forests in the immediate area—the other two are Dubuque Memorial and Savoy Mountain—Windsor is the smallest and affords the most privacy. You can easily drive or bike to the others to take advantage of extensive trail systems, but for the most peace and quiet, you will want to return here at the end of the day. It's also a popular spot to fish and canoe, and swimmers love the 100-foot-wide sandy beach on the Westfield River. Most RVers shy away from the campground with its unimproved facilities, so your neighbors will most likely be tenters.

Campsites, facilities: There are 24 sites for tents and RVs with no hookups or dump stations. Primitive toilets, piped water, picnic tables, and fireplaces are provided. A group site open to nonprofit organizations only can accommodate up to 25 people. Leashed pets are permitted.

Reservations, fees: Reservations are recommended. Reserve by contacting 877/422-6762, website: www.reserveamerica.com. Sites are $6 a night. The group site ($25 a night) must be reserved.

Open: Memorial Day weekend–Columbus Day.

Directions: From I-91 at Northampton, take Highway 9 west to West Cummington. Follow signs to River Road, which leads north into the forest.

Contact: Windsor State Forest, River Road, Windsor, MA 01270, 413/684-0948 in summer, 413/442-8928 mid-October–mid-April.

16 DUBUQUE MEMORIAL STATE FOREST

🚶 🚴 ⛴ ✂ 📷 ❄ 🐕 ⛰

Rating: 8

South of West Hawley

Backcountry enthusiasts will love these sites set on rugged, heavily wooded land crossed by several brooks. Nearly 8,000 forest acres are protected here, and the camping pavilions are several miles into the thick of it, accessed by little-used roads. There are eight miles of designated hiking trails and another 35 miles of woods, roads, and bridle paths used by snowmobilers, mountain bikers, and skiers. Several ponds and streams can be fished for trout, perch, and pickerel. The forest is home to plentiful wildlife, including the occasional bear and coyote, so hunters flock here in season; know when to wear your blaze orange. There is an abundance of historic and archaeological points of interest in this forest. These include many cellar holes which make up the now abandoned village of South Hawley, a rare "beehive" charcoal kiln, Moody Spring (a natural mineral spring said to have healing qualities), and mill and factory structure remains at Hallockville Pond.

Campsites, facilities: There are three hike-in sites at designated backcountry pavilions with no facilities. Leashed pets are permitted.

Reservations, fees: Sites are $6 a night. Reserve by contacting 877/422-6762, website: www.reserveamerica.com.

Open: Year-round.

Directions: From Highway 2 near Charlemont take Highway 8A south to the park entrance on the left.

Contact: Dubuque Memorial State Forest, P.O. Box 7, Charlemont, MA 01339, 413/339-5504.

17 SHADY PINES CAMPGROUND

🚶 ≈ ❄ 🐕 ♿ 🚐 ⛰

Rating: 6

Northeast of Savoy

Most of the campsites are in open fields at Shady Pines so there's not a lot of privacy. A few sites have natural pine tree buffers. Nature trails from the campground access thousands of acres of surrounding state-run forestlands and are used year-round by hikers, cross-country skiers, and snowmobilers. Dubuque Memorial State Forest lies to the north, Savoy Mountain State Forest to the northwest, and Windsor State Forest to the south. On the weekends, the adults-only lounge on the premises features live bands and dancing. In the winter, this is a popular spot for snowmobilers who can hop on the state-groomed trails right from the campground.

Campsites, facilities: There are 150 sites for tents and RVs in a mix of grassy, open, and partially open settings, 38 with full hookups and the rest with water and electric hookups. Each site has a picnic table and fire ring. You will find RV storage, group sites, restrooms, dump stations, laundry facilities, a limited grocery store, recreation hall, pavilion, pool, and sports courts on the property. Ice and firewood are available. Group activities are planned on weekends. Seasonal sites are available. Leashed pets are permitted.

Reservations, fees: Reservations are recommended June 1–Labor Day. Sites start at $25 a night for two people.

Open: Year-round; fully operational May 1–November 1.

Directions: From the west junction of Highways 8A and 116, travel three miles east on Highway 116 to the campground entrance on the left.

Contact: Bill and Edna Daniels, Shady Pines Campground, 547 Loop Road, Savoy, MA 02156, 413/743-2694, website: www.shady pinescampground.com.

18 PEPPERMINT PARK

Rating: 6

Northeast of Plainfield Center

Peppermint Park takes its name from the community that inhabited this hillside in the early 1800s and was a major producer of peppermint oil. The park spans 80 acres, 60 wooded and 20 grassy. Campsites are roomy and mostly wooded. Families choose this campground for its tranquil setting.

Campsites, facilities: There are 200 RV sites, most with full hookups. Each site has a picnic table, fireplace, and concrete patio. Seasonal sites are available, as are group sites for tents and RVs. Facilities include RV storage, a dump station, recreation hall, sports fields and courts, a pool, hot tub, and horseshoe pits. Some limited groceries, LP gas, gasoline, ice, and firewood are available. Leashed pets are permitted.

Reservations, fees: Reservations are recommended May–October. Sites are $22–30 a night per family.

Open: Year-round.

Directions: From the east junction of Highway 116 and Highway 8A, travel four miles southeast on Highway 116 through Plainfield. Turn left on Bow Street and drive one mile to the campground entrance.

Contact: The Bulissa Family, Peppermint Park, Grant Street, Plainfield, MA 01019, 413/634-5385, website: www.peppermintpark.net.

19 PITTSFIELD STATE FOREST

Rating: 8

South of Hancock on the New York border

Hikers especially will enjoy camping at Pittsfield State Forest, where sites are woodsy and rustic. In all, about 30 miles of trails lead through woods punctuated by streams, waterfalls, and flowering shrubs. In June, 65 acres of azaleas are a riot of pink blossoms. Mount Lebanon stands at the park's south end; the Taconic Skyline Trail runs the entire length of the ridge, providing lots of ledges from which to enjoy the scenic, rolling Berkshire Hills. Caves and rocky outcrops are one reason why bears seem to like it here. At 2,150 feet, Berry Pond is one of the highest natural bodies of water in the state. It's stocked with trout, and a dam holds the water of Lulu Brook in a basin for swimming near the campground. At the campground there's a three-quarter-mile paved trail that's popular with wheelchair users. In the northeast corner of the forest is Balance Rock, a 165-ton limestone rock balanced on a point of bedrock only three feet wide.

Campsites, facilities: There are 31 sites for tents and RVs with no hookups or dump stations. Flush and primitive toilets, piped water, picnic tables, and fireplaces are provided. Two group sites open to nonprofit organizations only can accommodate up to 20 and 50 people, respectively. Leashed pets are permitted.

Reservations, fees: Reservations are required for group sites, which are $25 a night. For regular sites, reservations are recommended in summer; the fee is $6 a night. Reserve by contacting 877/422-6762, website: www.reserve america.com.

Open: Mid-May–mid-October, but 10 sites for self-contained RVs are available year-round.

Directions: From Pittsfield Center, take U.S. 20 west toward the New York border and follow signs to the park entrance on the right side of the road.

Contact: Pittsfield State Forest, 1041 Cascade Street, Pittsfield, MA 01201, 413/442-8992; Department of Environmental Management, Region Five Headquarters, South Mountain, 412/442-8928.

20 BONNIE BRAE CABINS AND CAMPSITES

Rating: 5

North of Pittsfield near Pontoosuc Lake

If "nothing fancy" describes what you're looking for, give Bonnie Brae a try. This is a clean, low-key campground particularly suited to RVers who aren't looking for a full schedule of organized activities. It's within striking distance of the area's many major attractions, including Tanglewood (summer home to the Boston Pops Symphony Orchestra) in Lenox and the Hancock Shaker Village in Pittsfield. Also in Pittsfield is Arrowhead, Herman Melville's home from 1850–1863. This National Historic Landmark has an outstanding view of Mount Greylock to the north. Melville wrote that the mountain's shape reminded him of a whale and inspired him to write his epic tale *Moby Dick*.

Campsites, facilities: There are 42 sites for tents and RVs in a mix of open and shaded settings, all with hookups. Each site has a table and fireplace. A dump station, laundry facilities, a pool, and restrooms are provided. Leashed pets are permitted.

Reservations, fees: Reservations are recommended. Sites start at $27 a night for two people. Trailers and cabins are also available for rent.

Open: May 1–October 31, but self-contained RVs are allowed year-round.

Directions: From Pittsfield, head north on U.S. 7 for three miles. Pontoosuc Lake will be on your left. Turn right on Broadway Street and drive to the campground.

Contact: Bonnie Brae Cabins and Campsites, 108 Broadway Street, Pittsfield, MA 01201, 413/442-3754; http://bonniebraecampground.tripod.com/.

21 WHITE BIRCH CAMPGROUND

🚶 🏊 🎣 🏕 🐕 👫 🚐 ⛺

Rating: 6

North of Whately

Mountainsides of mixed hardwood forest surround this valley of open fields. Campsites cater to a variety of users, from tenters to seasonal RV folks. All are set on mostly grassy plots at the edge of the woods. There is a stream for fishing on the property and hiking trails in the surrounding woods. Though you're only 10 minutes from the interstate, the setting feels miles away from anywhere.

Campsites, facilities: There are 40 sites for tents and RVs, all with water and electric hookups. Dump stations and services are provided. LP gas, laundry facilities, a store, recreation hall, game room, playground, and a snack bar are available. Leashed pets are permitted.

Reservations, fees: Reservations are available and should be accompanied by a $25 deposit. Sites start at $20 a night for two people.

Open: May 1–November 1.

Directions: From Greenfield, head south on I-91. Take Exit 25. Bear right on Highway 116 and take the first left onto Whately Road. The campground is two miles ahead.

Contact: White Birch Campground, 122 North Street, Whately, MA 01093, 413/665-4941.

22 FERNWOOD FOREST

🚶 🏊 🎣 🏕 🐕 👫 🚐 ⛺

Rating: 8

West of Hinsdale

Fernwood is clean, quiet, and private and open only to seasonal campers. From the campground, you can walk to a trout-stocked fishing hole or to Plunkett Reservoir for swimming and fishing.

Campsites, facilities: There are 30 secluded woodland sites with hookups. Each site has a fireplace and table. Restrooms, hot showers, a dump station, playground, horseshoe pits, sports fields, and game courts are available on the property. Ice and firewood are sold on the premises. Leashed pets are permitted.

Reservations, fees: Sites are offered seasonally, $1,000 per year.

Open: May 1–October 15.

Directions: From Hinsdale proper, drive west on Michael's Road. Turn left on Plunkett Reservoir Road and continue to the campground.

Contact: Fernwood Forest, Box 896, Hinsdale, MA 01235, 413/655-2292, website: www.fernwoodforest.com.

23 BISSELLVILLE

South of Hinsdale

Rating: 8

Here's another tidy, quiet, private campground in the heart of the Berkshire Hills. Sites are set on rural, wooded flatlands. These folks cater to visitors seeking the combination of arts, culture, history, and scenic beauty that the area offers, from the Shakespeare festivals held at The Mount (novelist Edith Wharton's home) in Lenox, to the One Cell Town Jail in Chester. Bissellville remembers Israel Bissell, who is buried in a cemetery on Highway 143 in Hinsdale. This unsung patriot outdid Paul Revere, galloping for five days to carry the news of Lexington to Connecticut, New York, and Philadelphia.

Campsites, facilities: There are 35 sites for tents and RVs, all with water and electric hookups and 13 with additional sewer connections. Air conditioner and heater use is allowed. A pool, ballpark, laundry facilities, free hot showers, and a dump station are located on the property. Campfires are allowed. Leashed pets are permitted.

Reservations, fees: Reservations are recommended. Sites start at $18 a night for two people with surcharges for air conditioners and heaters.

Open: Mid-May–mid-October.

Directions: From the junction of Highways 8 and 143 in Hinsdale, head south for three miles on Highway 8 to the campground.

Contact: Eugene and Lorraine Brunet, Bissellville, 1109 Washington Road, Hinsdale, MA 01235, 413/655-8396.

24 OCTOBER MOUNTAIN STATE FOREST

East of Lenox

Rating: 8

October Mountain State Forest is Massachusetts' largest protected tract. On more than 16,000 acres, you will find trails for every experience level, including a challenging Appalachian Trail section which crosses the forest. Campsites dot a sunny hillside and are broken out into three levels. The second and third levels are reserved for tents; hiking trails leave directly from the two upper areas. One of the most scenic forest hikes leads to Schermerhorn Gorge. Nonmotorized boating and fishing are best at Finerty Pond and Lake Felton. Once a privately owned game preserve, the forest remains a popular hunting destination, so wear blaze orange in season.

Campsites, facilities: There are 46 sites for tents and RVs, all without hookups. Each site has a table and fireplace. Flush toilets, showers, piped water, and a dump station are provided. Leashed pets are permitted.

Reservations, fees: Reservations are recommended. Reserve by contacting 877/422-6762, website: www.reserveamerica.com. Sites are $12 a night.

Open: Mid-May–mid-October.

Directions: From the Massachusetts Turnpike/I-90 near Lee, take Exit 2 and travel west on U.S. 20. Turn right on Center Street, which leads into the forest, following the signs.

Contact: October Mountain State Forest, RR 2, Box 193, Lee, MA 01238-9563, 413/243-1778.

25 SUMMIT HILL CAMPGROUND

East of Becket

Rating: 7

Summit Hill caters to seasonal campers, so you are rubbing elbows (literally, since sites are typically just over 20 feet wide) with people who stay here every year. Backpackers have their own area, which is more private and natural. Sites are shaded and grassy, set in mountain woodlands, and there are nature trails on and around the property.

Campsites, facilities: There are 106 sites for tents and RVs, most with hookups. Heaters and air conditioners are prohibited. On-site you will find a heated pool, recreation hall, free hot showers, restrooms, an adult lounge, sports courts, a dump station, and horseshoe pits. LP gas, ice, and firewood can be purchased on the premises. RV supplies and storage are available. Leashed pets are permitted.

Reservations, fees: Sites start at $24 a night for two people.

Open: May 1–September 30.

Directions: From Highway 8 at Washington, get on Stonehouse Road by the town hall and continue until it turns into Summit Hill Road. From here, the campground is 1.7 miles away.

Contact: Summit Hill Campground, Summit Hill Road, Washington, MA 01235, 413/623-5761, website: www.summithillcampground.com.

26 BERKSHIRE PARK CAMPING AREA

🚶 🏊 🛶 🏠 🐕 👫 🚐 ⛺

Rating: 8

Southeast of Worthington Corners

Cool and woodsy, the campsites at Berkshire Park are well distanced from the kind of noise and traffic congestion that can clog the area in summer. Campers sleep beside a small pond where they can swim and fish. Nature trails leave from the campground. Right down the road at Chesterfield Gorge, spectacular glacial action is evidenced by a 30-foot-deep canyon through which the Westfield River waters tumble past granite cliffs.

Campsites, facilities: There are 100 sites for tents and RVs, 25 with water and electric hookups and the rest with none. Each site has a table and fireplace. There is no dump station. Facilities include sports courts, a playground, horseshoe pits, laundry facilities, restrooms, and free hot showers. Firewood is available on the premises. Leashed pets are permitted.

Reservations, fees: Reservations are recommended. Sites start at $18 a night for two people. Seasonal rentals are encouraged; prices are available on request.

Open: May 1–mid-October.

Directions: From the junction of Highways 112 and 143 at Worthington Corners, travel 1.2 miles southeast on Old Post Road to the campground.

Contact: Bob and Dawn Brimmer, Berkshire Park Camping Area, P.O. Box 531, Harvey Road, Worthington, MA 01098, 413/238-5918 or 800/727-0067, website: http://users.erols.com/bpca/.

27 D.A.R. STATE FOREST

🚶 🏊 🛶 🚐 🐕 ♿ 🚐 ⛺

Rating: 9

Northwest of Northampton in Goshen

Second-growth forest with an understory of mountain laurel, ferns, witch hazel, and blueberry makes up the attractive surroundings at the D.A.R. Campground, one of the state's most popular. Campsites are located next to Upper Highland Lake, complete with a large swimming beach and boat launch. Both Upper and Lower Highland Lakes are open for non-motorized boating. Bass, perch, and trout live in these waters, while deer, mink, and weasel make their home in the surrounding forest, which is traversed by hiking trails, dirt roads, and bridle paths. A trail leads from the far end of the campground to a fire tower from which you can see into New Hampshire and Vermont. The campground is also near a nature center that conducts evening walks in the woods and around the pond. This is also the starting point for a three-mile self-guided nature trail.

Campsites, facilities: There are 50 sites for tents and RVs with no hookups or dump stations. Flush toilets, showers, piped water, picnic tables, and fireplaces are provided. A group site open to nonprofit organizations only can accommodate up to 75 people. Leashed pets are permitted. Wheelchair-accessible sites are available by reservation.

Reservations, fees: Forty of the 50 sites can be reserved. Reserve by contacting 877/422-6762, website: www.reserveamerica.com. Sites are $12 a night. The group site is $25 and must be reserved. For self-contained RVs, the fee is $5 a night from mid-October–May 1.

Open: May 1–Columbus Day; sites are open to self-contained RVs and groups year-round.

Directions: From Northampton, take Highway 9 west to Goshen. Just past town, turn right and head north on Highway 112, following signs to the park entrance on the right side of the road.

Contact: D.A.R. State Forest, 555 East Street, Williamsburg, MA 01096, 413/268-7098.

28 BONNIE RIGG CAMPGROUND

🚶 🏊 🛖 🐾 🚐 ⛺

In Becket

Rating: 5

Located at the intersection of two well-traveled roads, Bonnie Rigg is a member-owned campground that's open to nonmembers also. Most of the sites are in the woods, with 45 labeled as "safari sites"—open and grassy. Organized activities such as hayrides, horseshoe tournaments, a men's beauty contest in the summer, and a winter carnival in January make this a tight-knit community that encourages campers to meet one another.

Campsites, facilities: There are 200 wooded and open sites for tents and RVs with water and electric hookups. About half are occupied by seasonal campers. A dump station and sewage dumping service are provided. Facilities include four restrooms with free hot showers, a pool, TV lounge, recreation hall, general store, playground, game room, and horseshoe pits. LP gas, ice, and firewood are sold on the premises. Leashed pets are permitted.

Reservations, fees: Reservations are recommended. Tent sites are $25 a night, and RV sites with electric and water hookups are $30.

Open: May 15–October 15.

Directions: From the Massachusetts Turnpike/I-90 west of Springfield, take Exit 3. Follow Highway 10/U.S. 202 south for two miles and then turn right onto U.S. 20 heading west.

Continue to the junction with Highway 8. The campground is at the crossroads.

Contact: Bonnie Rigg Camping Club, P.O. Box 14, Chester, MA 01011-0014, 413/623-5366, website: www.bonnyriggcampground.com.

29 WALKER ISLAND CAMPING

🚶 🏊 🛖 🐾 🚐 ⛺

Just south of downtown Chester

Rating: 8

Mountain streams border the campsites at Walker Island. Choose from secluded tent sites or equipped RV sites shaded by maple trees and other hardwoods, and, if you have a sweet tooth, sample the syrup (made from trees on the property) in the sugar shack by the office. Swimmers can take a dip in the streams or in the heated pool on the premises. Trails leave the campground and ascend rocky ledges and mountain lookouts. Organized activities are offered all season long, many especially for kids, from parades to theme meals.

Campsites, facilities: There are 90 sites for tents and RVs, most with hookups. Each site has a table and fireplace. Facilities include a dump station, laundry room, free hot showers, a heated pool, miniature golf, horseshoe pits, a store, recreation hall, game room, snack bar, and RV storage. LP gas and firewood are available onsite. Cable TV is also offered. Leashed pets are permitted.

Reservations, fees: Reservations are recommended in July and August. Sites start at $25 a night for two people.

Open: May 1–October 31.

Directions: From the junction of Highway 8 and U.S. 20 west of Chester, travel east on U.S. 20 for 2.25 miles to the campground.

Contact: Walker Island Camping, P.O. Box 131, Chester, MA 01011, 413/354-2295, website: www.walkerisland.com.

30 CHESTER-BLANDFORD STATE FOREST

🏃 🛶 🎣 🐕 🚐 ⛺

Rating: 7

In Chester

You will hear traffic as you fall asleep under the mixed hardwood canopy, since the campground is located directly off U.S. 20. Once you penetrate the 2,000-plus acres of Chester-Blandford, however, those sounds will soon be forgotten. Trails and forest roads offer challenging and sometimes steep hiking. A paved road leads to Sanderson Brook, which is graced with a 100-foot cascade about a quarter mile from the parking area. This small campground is popular in spring and early summer with anglers who come to try their luck in the trout-stocked streams. You need to arrive early then to secure a spot.

Campsites, facilities: There are 15 RV and tent sites in mountainous woodlands. Primitive toilets, piped water, picnic tables, and fireplaces are provided. Leashed pets are permitted.

Reservations, fees: Reservations are recommended; contact 877/422-6762, website: www.reserveamerica.com. Sites are $6 a night.

Open: Mid-May–Columbus Day.

Directions: From the Massachusetts Turnpike/I-90 west of Springfield, take Exit 3. Follow Highway 10/U.S. 202 south for two miles and then turn right on U.S. 20 heading west. Pass through Huntington and follow signs to the state forest entrance.

Contact: Chester-Blandford State Forest, P.O. Box 371, Huntington, MA 01050, 413/354-6347.

31 WINDY ACRES CAMPGROUND

Rating: 6

West of Northampton

Roomy sites are set on a hillside in the small, rural town of Westhampton. A spring-fed swimming pond here has a small beach that's usually overrun with families in summer. You find hometown hospitality at organized events ranging from hayrides to horseshoe tournaments. Seasonal sites are landscaped, and some have permanent structures on them. There's also a safari field for group camping. If you want to get a historic sense of these hills, stop in at the restored Westhampton Blacksmith Shop Museum. Largely donated by area families, the museum's collection includes furniture, toys, books, photos, clothing, tools, and other town memorabilia handed down through the ages.

Campsites, facilities: There are 137 sites for tents and RVs, all with water and electric hookups and many with full hookups. Dump stations and pumping services are available. Air conditioners are allowed, but heaters are not. Facilities include laundry machines, recreation and game rooms, a heated pool, hot showers, a traffic control gate, sports courts, a pavilion, athletic fields, a playground, and a camp store. Firewood, ice, LP gas, and on-site RV storage are available. Leashed pets are permitted.

Reservations, fees: Reservations are recommended in the summer. Sites start at $22–25 a night per family.

Open: May 1–October 1.

Directions: From the junction of Highways 66 and 9 in Northampton, travel west on Highway 66 for nine miles. Turn right on South Road and drive one block north to the campground.

Contact: Windy Acres Campground, 139 South Street, Westhampton, MA 01027, 413/527-9862, website: www.windyacres.com/home.htm.

32 PROSPECT LAKE PARK

🏊 🛶 🚐 🐕 🚴 🚐 ⛺

Rating: 7

In North Egremont

Some of the either open or shaded sites are right on Prospect Lake, making this a good choice for campers who enjoy swimming, boating, or fishing. A lovely picnic area is shaded by tall cathedral pines, and there are two sandy beaches. Scheduled activities include bingo, dances, potluck suppers, and live music.

Campsites, facilities: There are 140 sites for tents and RVs, most with hookups. The tenting area is set off from the RV sites. Each site has a fire ring and picnic table. Facilities include dump stations, a laundry room, recreation hall, playground, sports courts, boat rentals, and a snack bar. Metered LP gas; a camp store selling firewood, ice, and bait; RV storage; and seasonal sites are available. You will find hot showers and restrooms at four locations. Leashed pets are permitted.

Reservations, fees: Reservations are recommended. Sites start at $25 a night. Monthly and seasonal rates are available.

Open: Early May–Columbus Day.

Directions: From the junction of Highways 71 and 23 in southwestern Massachusetts, travel three miles west on Highway 71 to Prospect Lake Road. Turn left here and drive less than a mile to the park entrance on the right.

Contact: Prospect Lake Park, Prospect Lake Road, North Egremont, MA 02152, 413/528-4158, website: www.prospectlakepark.com.

33 BEARTOWN STATE FOREST

Rating: 8
Southeast of Stockbridge

Spacious and wooded, these campsites in the Hoosac Range foothills are in high demand in spring and early summer; get here early if you want to spend the night. RVs tend to have trouble ascending the winding road to the campground, so you find mostly backpackers here. At the forest center, Mount Wilcox (2,150 feet) stands surrounded by trout-filled streams that lure anglers to their banks. You can swim in Benedict Pond below the campsites; the 1.5-mile loop trail around the shore is picturesque in any season. All-terrain vehicles and snowmobiles are permitted on the forest's multiuse trails, so skiers and hikers should use caution. The Appalachian Trail crosses the forest on a north-south track for five miles.

Campsites, facilities: There are 12 sites for tents and RVs with no hookups. Primitive toilets, piped water, and picnic tables are provided. One group site open to nonprofit organizations only can accommodate up to 100 people; groups are required to bring a commercial, portable toilet. Leashed pets are permitted.

Reservations, fees: Reservations are recommended; contact 877/422-6762, website: www.reserveamerica.com. Sites are $6 a night.

Open: Mid-May–Columbus Day; self-contained RVs are welcome year-round.

Directions: From the Massachusetts Turnpike/I-90 near Lee, take Exit 2 and head east on U.S. 20. Get on Highway 102, drive west to Stockbridge, and then take U.S. 7 south to Highway 23 heading east. Turn left on Blue Hill Road and follow signs to the forest.

Contact: Beartown State Forest, P.O. Box 97, Blue Hill Road, Monterey, MA 01245, 413/528-0904.

34 CAMP OVERFLOW

Rating: 6
West of the Otis Reservoir in East Otis

Overflow has some open safari-type sites as well as more wooded spots, though they tend to be close together. A large contingent of seasonal campers makes up this campground's clientele each year. That's because the Otis Reservoir is right across the street, offering excellent fishing and waters that are open to motorboating, and the streams and hills of Tolland State Forest are right down the road. The campground has a private beach and boat launch on the reservoir for boats up to 20 feet in length. Rowboats and canoes are available for rent at the campground.

Campsites, facilities: There are 150 sites for tents and RVs, 50 with water and electric hookups. Each site has a picnic table and fireplace. Facilities include dump stations, hot showers, a camp store, firewood, a recreation hall, playground, snack bar, sports courts, and boat rentals. Seasonal rentals are available, but there is no on-site RV storage. Leashed pets are permitted.

Reservations, fees: Reservations are recommended. Sites start at $22 a night.
Open: May 15–October 1.
Directions: From the Massachusetts Turnpike/I-90 in Westfield, take Exit 3 and drive south on Highway 10/U.S. 202. After a short distance, turn right and head west on Highway 23. Continue to Reservoir Road and follow signs to the campground down Tolland Road. The entrance will be on your right.
Contact: Camp Overflow, P.O. Box 645, Otis, MA 01253, 413/269-4036, website: www.campoverflow.com.

35 TOLLAND STATE FOREST

Rating: 8
Near the Otis Reservoir

This wooded campground set in the state forest's north end enjoys a locale on a lake peninsula. Thirty-five of the sites are right on the shore, and all campers have access to a beach and boat ramp. Anglers can try for trout, bass, bluegill, perch, and pickerel, while boaters with motorized craft can zip around the reservoir unhindered by speed limits. Ten miles of multiuse trails border the forest. A wide variety of birds lives in the area, including owls, blue herons, purple finches, and ruby-throated hummingbirds.
Campsites, facilities: There are 90 sites for tents and RVs with no hookups. Facilities include a dump station, flush toilets, showers, piped water, picnic tables, and fireplaces. Five group sites are open to nonprofit organizations. There's a boat ramp on the reservoir. Leashed pets are permitted.
Reservations, fees: Reservations are recommended; contact 877/422-6762, website: www.reserveamerica.com. Sites are $12 a night.
Open: Mid-May–mid-October.
Directions: From the Massachusetts Turnpike/I-90 in Westfield, take Exit 3 and drive south on Highway 10/U.S. 202. After a short distance, turn right and head west on Highway 23. Follow signs to Reservoir Road and the campground.

Contact: Tolland State Forest, P.O. Box 342, East Otis, MA 01029, 413/269-6002.

36 LAUREL RIDGE CAMPING AREA

Rating: 7
West of the Otis Reservoir in East Otis

Large, flat, wooded campsites near the Otis Reservoir and on the Tolland State Forest border are perfect for family camping. Some open, grassy safari sites are also available. Campers can take motorboats out on the reservoir, using a boat ramp located a mile from Laurel Ridge. See the previous listing for Tolland State Forest for information on fishing and hiking in the area.
Campsites, facilities: There are 180 sites for tents and RVs, all with water and electric hookups. Each site has a picnic table and fireplace. Facilities include a dump station, hot showers, restrooms, a store, pool, recreation hall, game room, playground, and snack bar. There's also a basketball court and horseshoe pits. LP gas, firewood, and RV storage are available. Campers can borrow sports equipment. Leashed pets are permitted.
Reservations, fees: Reservations are recommended in July and August. Sites start at $24 a night for a family of four.
Open: Mid-May–Columbus Day.
Directions: From East Otis Center on Highway 23, take Old Blandford Road south for .75 mile.
Contact: Laurel Ridge Camping Area, P.O. Box 519, East Otis, MA 01029, 413/269-4804 or 800/538-2267.

37 MOUNT WASHINGTON STATE FOREST

Rating: 10
West of Highway 41 in the southwesternmost corner of the state

The rocky ledges and steep slopes of this forest attract campers in summertime, when the sites tend to fill up. Bash Bish Falls, a water cascade that tumbles through a series of gorges and drops 60 feet over the falls and into a sparkling pool, is a tourist magnet in these parts. Just east of the forest boundary is Bartholomew's Cobble, a limestone cobble foundation that supports boulder ledges, craggy outcrops, and stone sculptures. Here, foot trails wind along hemlock-covered slopes. For a million-dollar view of western Massachusetts at a bargain-basement price, make an ascent of 2,624-foot Mount Everett in an auto: from the village of Mount Washington follow signs to the Mount Everett Reservation past Guilder Pond, one of the highest lakes in the state.

Campsites, facilities: There are 15 wilderness campsites for tents with no facilities. The park does have restrooms. Leashed pets are permitted.

Reservations, fees: Reservations are recommended; contact 877/422-6762, website: www.reserveamerica.com. Sites are $6 a night.

Open: Year-round.

Directions: From the Massachusetts Turnpike/I-90 near Lee, take Exit 2 and head east on U.S. 20. Get on Highway 102 and drive west. Head south on U.S. 7 and then take Highway 23 west to Highway 41. Drive south on Highway 41 for about 300 feet to the park entrance.

Contact: Mount Washington State Forest, East Street, Mount Washington, MA 01258, 413/528-0330.

38 GRANVILLE STATE FOREST

Rating: 8

South of West Granville on the Connecticut border

If you're in the mood for more of a wilderness experience, definitely opt for the state forest's Hubbard River Camping Area, where sites are right on the shore with a backdrop of towering hemlocks growing on steep slopes flanking the brook. Swimming is allowed. The 2,000-plus-acre forest has been sculpted by

streams that created ravines and drainages as they flowed to the Hubbard River. Hunters track deer, snowshoe hare, grouse, and woodcock, and the waterways are stocked with trout. The relatively easy Hubbard River Trail parallels the riverbed.

Campsites, facilities: There are 36 tent sites at two locations within the state forest. Halfway Brook offers hot showers, flush toilets, fireplaces, piped water, and picnic tables. Hubbard River has primitive toilets, piped water, fireplaces, and tables. Leashed pets are permitted.

Reservations, fees: Reservations are recommended; contact 877/422-6762, website: www.reserveamerica.com. Sites are $6 a night.

Open: May 1–Columbus Day.

Directions: From the Massachusetts Turnpike/I-90 at Westfield, take Exit 3 and head south on Highway 10/U.S. 202. At the junction with Highway 57 exit and drive west, following signs to the park entrance on West Harland Road.

Contact: Granville State Forest, West Harland Road, Highway 57, Granville, MA 01034, 413/357-6611.

39 PROSPECT MOUNTAIN CAMPGROUND

Rating: 7

West of Springfield in Granville

Mountaintop campsites offer great views. Two fishing ponds are located on the premises, with sites 39–50 and 60–65 on the shore of Peters Pond. For hikers, several miles of walking trails lead through the surrounding hilly woods. Special dinners, bingo, dances, and theme weekends are part of the long planned activities list coordinated seven days a week by a full-time recreation professional in season. The abundance of amenities and activities tends to attract RVers, so tenters might want to consider heading farther down Highway 57 to Granville State Forest (see previous listing). The 2,000-plus-acre forest has been sculpted by streams that created ravines and drainages en route to the Hubbard River; a relatively easy hike parallels the riverbed.

Campsites, facilities: There are 225 sites for tents and RVs, most with water and electric hookups and 24 with additional sewer connections. Each site has a table and fire ring. Dump stations and pumping services are available. Facilities include a laundry room, recreation and game rooms, hot showers, a traffic control gate, snack bar, sports courts, a pavilion, playground, heated pool, athletic fields, and a camp store. Firewood, ice, LP gas, and on-site RV storage are available. Leashed pets are permitted.

Reservations, fees: Reservations are recommended. There is a three-day minimum stay on holiday weekends. Sites start at $25 a night for two people.

Open: May 1–October 15.

Directions: From I-91 south of Springfield, take Exit 5 and follow U.S. 5 through North Agawam. This road turns into Highway 57. Follow Highway 57 west through Southwick to Granville Center, then continue another four miles to the campground entrance, which will be on your left.

Contact: Prospect Mountain Campground, Highway 57, West Granville, MA 01034, 413/357-6494, website: www.prospectmtncampground. com.

40 SODOM MOUNTAIN CAMPGROUND

🏃 ≈ 🐕 🚣 🚐 ⛺

Rating: 7

West of Springfield in Southwick

Families flock to this campground because of its proximity to the Six Flags New England amusement park and the Eastern States Expo (site of fairs, trade shows, horse shows, big-name entertainers, and circuses) in West Springfield, so reservations are necessary in the summertime. Discount tickets to the amusement park are available through the campground. Camp-

sites are situated on a plateau on the side of Sodom Mountain and are spacious and mostly wooded, though some open areas do exist. Hiking trails lead from the campground to the mountaintop; the summit hike is moderate, with some steep sections, and takes about an hour. Planned activities, including pig roasts and live entertainment, fill the weekends.

Campsites, facilities: There are 150 sites for tents and RVs, most with water and electric hookups and 15 with additional sewer connections. Each site has a fire ring and picnic table. Dump stations and pumping services are available. Facilities include a laundry room, recreation and game rooms, hot showers, sports courts, a pool, athletic fields, a playground, and a camp store. Firewood, ice, LP gas, and on-site RV storage are available. Leashed pets are permitted.

Reservations, fees: Reservations are recommended. Sites start at $26 a night per family.

Open: May 1–Columbus Day.

Directions: From I-91 south of Springfield, take Exit 5 and follow U.S. 5 through North Agawam. This road turns into Highway 57. Follow Highway 57 west to Southwick Center and then continue another 3.5 miles to South Loomis Street. Turn left and go .25 mile to the campground entrance.

Contact: Janice LaFrance, Sodom Mountain Campground, 227 South Loomis Street, P.O. Box 702, Southwick, MA 01077, 413/569-3930, website: www.sodommountain.com.

41 SOUTHWICK ACRES

≈ 🐕 🚐 ⛺

Rating: 7

South of Southwick

Facilities are tailored to senior citizens at Southwick. Older campers appreciate the oversized sites (up to 60 feet) and the large L-shaped pool with stairs and a generous shallow end. Price discounts are also given to seniors. Though right off a major thoroughfare, Highway 10/U.S. 202, these wooded campsites are set back far enough to escape most of the traffic noise. The Congamond Lakes are nearby and offer fishing and boating.

Campsites, facilities: There are 65 sites for tents and RVs with water and electric hookups. Each site has a fire ring and picnic table. Dump stations and pumping services are available. Facilities include a laundry room, recreation hall, and clean restrooms. Firewood and ice are available, and there's a grocery store nearby for supplies. Seasonal campers can get cable TV hookups. There's also on-site RV storage. Leashed pets are permitted.

Reservations, fees: Reservations are recommended. Sites start at $26 a night for two people.

Open: May 1–October 1.

Directions: From Southwick Center, take Highway 10/U.S. 202 south for two miles to the campground entrance on the left.

Contact: Southwick Acres, P.O. Box 984, College Highway, Southwick, MA 01077, 413/569-6339, website: www.southwickacres.com.

Chapter 12

© DEM/KINDRA CLINEFF

Central Massachusetts

Central Massachusetts

Water is everywhere in central Massachusetts, from the Connecticut River chugging through Northampton and Springfield, to the Quabbin Reservoir, which supplies the drinking water for much of Greater Boston, to the hundreds of lakes, ponds, and rivers that make up the central watershed. Not as hilly as the Berkshires but with terrain more varied than the flats of Boston and the shoreline, the middle of the state is a pleasant camping destination for families who like freshwater fun—fishing, swimming, and boating chief among these pursuits.

Most campgrounds take advantage of nature's supply of water. This area of the state is heavily wooded, so campsites are usually tucked into forests. There is an equal mix of state park campgrounds and privately owned parks, so tenters can find wilderness and RVers can find extensive amenities.

Most visitors to the region hit the handful of big attractions: Six Flags New England (Route 159/1623 Main Street, Agawam, MA 01001, 413/786-9300, website: www.sixflags.com/parks/newengland/); The Eastern States Exposition fairgrounds, better known as "The Big E" in West Springfield (1305 Memorial Avenue, 413/737-2443, website: www.thebige.com; the three-week-long annual exposition takes place in September and October); the Basketball Hall of Fame (1000 West Columbus Avenue, Springfield, MA 01105, 413/781-6500 or 877/4HOOPLA, website: www.hoophall.com), sporting a major recent renovation; and Old Sturbridge Village (1 Old Sturbridge Village Road, Sturbridge, MA 01566, 508/347-3362, website: www.osv.org), a living history museum.

For information about Massachusetts State Parks, see the introduction to the Berkshires chapter.

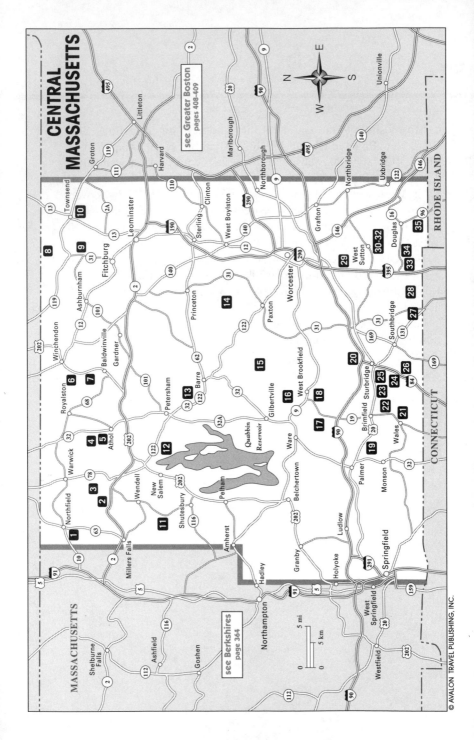

CENTRAL
MASSACHUSETTS

see Greater Boston
pages 408-409

see Berkshires
page 364

© AVALON TRAVEL PUBLISHING, INC.

RHODE ISLAND

CONNECTICUT

MASSACHUSETTS

N
W   E
S

5 mi
0
0   5 km

1 CONNECTICUT RIVER GREENWAY STATE PARK

⚒️ 🏕️ 🎣 🪓 🐕 ⛺

Rating: 10

Along the Connecticut River

The state of Massachusetts is developing formal campsites on a 12-mile stretch of the Connecticut River, one of the state's newest parks. Call to find out which sites have been opened by the state. This stretch of the river offers beautiful vistas of the river and valley—boat camping at its best.

Swim at your own risk and use good judgment; you'll see a number of popular beaches from your canoe. To take fish from the river, you need a Massachusetts license. More than 60 native species live in the river including American shad, striped bass, trout, and the short-nosed sturgeon. The latter is on the federal list of endangered species, and anyone in possession of the fish may be fined up to $20,000. Know your species and check the laws before you throw in a line. Some sections of the river are heavily used by powerboaters, so exercise caution if you are in a smaller vessel. The river is a major migration route for waterfowl, hawks, and songbirds. In summer, you will likely see bald eagles, ospreys, herons, owls, cormorants, and many other birds. Along the shore you may spy deer, fox, muskrat, beaver, woodchucks, and perhaps even a mink or two.

Campsites, facilities: There are no officially designated sites on the Massachusetts section of the river, though the state's Department of Environmental Management is currently working to establish some. Facilities differ from site to site, but most have primitive toilets.

Reservations, fees: Sites are available on a first-come, first-served basis. Modest fees will be charged.

Open: Year-round as weather and river conditions permit.

Directions: The Connecticut River flows south through western Massachusetts from where it forms the New Hampshire–Vermont border

to the Connecticut border, running roughly parallel to I-91.

Contact: Massachusetts Department of Environmental Management, P.O. Box 484, Amherst, MA 01004, 413/586-8706 ext. 12.

2 ERVING STATE FOREST

🚶 🚲 ⚒️ 🎣 🚐 🐕 ♿ ⛺ ⛺

Rating: 6

East of Greenfield

Mountain bikers, you will find 12 miles of prime dirt roads in Erving State Forest that leave right from this campground; just be aware that you are sharing the paths with equestrians and hikers. Sites are spread out along a camp road in a mixed forest of oaks, white pines, and hemlocks. Next to the campground is Laurel Lake, a trout-stocked beauty that's open to motorboating, fishing, and swimming. A boat ramp is situated at one end of the lake, away from the swimming beach.

Campsites, facilities: There are 29 sites for tents and RVs with no hookups or dump station. Piped water, picnic tables, fireplaces, and primitive toilets are provided. Some of the day-use facilities are wheelchair accessible. There's also a boat ramp. Leashed pets are permitted.

Reservations, fees: Reservations are recommended; contact 877/422-6762, website: www.reserveamerica.com. Sites are $6 a night.

Open: May 1–Columbus Day.

Directions: From the town of Erving on Highway 2, travel .5 mile east to Church Street. Turn left and follow signs to the campground.

Contact: Erving State Forest, R.F.D. 1, Highway 2A, Erving, MA 01364, 978/544-7745 in summer months, 978/544-3939 year-round.

3 WAGON WHEEL CAMPING AREA

🚶 🚲 ⚒️ 🐕 🚐 ⛺

Rating: 7

Northwest of Orange near Erving State Forest

Lofty pines and simple, home-style attitudes

make for an agreeable atmosphere at Wagon Wheel, popular with seasonal campers. In summer, the owners regularly book musical acts, comedians, and other performers who entertain in the recreation barn, while swingers young and old enjoy teeing off at the 18-hole miniature golf course on the property. Sites are clean and spacious, and the campground is surrounded by 5,000-acre Erving State Forest, which is traversed with a multiuse trail and road system open to mountain bikers, equestrians, and hikers.

Campsites, facilities: There are 102 sites for tents and RVs, most with full hookups. Each site has a table and fire ring. Dump stations and services are provided. Air conditioner and heater use is allowed. Facilities include a laundry room, sports courts and athletic fields, a store, pool, recreation hall and game room, and RV storage. RV supplies, LP gas, ice, and firewood are available. There's also a traffic control gate. Well-behaved, leashed pets are permitted.

Reservations, fees: Reservations are recommended June 15–Labor Day. Sites start at $20 a night.

Open: May 1–Columbus Day.

Directions: From the junction of Highways 2 and 2A west of Orange, travel .75 mile east on Highway 2A. Turn left and head north on Wendell Road for two miles to the campground entrance.

Contact: Al and Midge Williams, Wagon Wheel Camping Area, 909 Wendell Road, Warwick, MA 01378, 978/544-3425.

4 TULLY LAKE CAMPGROUND

Rating: 8

North of Athol on Tully Lake

A paddler's paradise. Set on Tully Lake, these walk-in tent-only sites include 16 right on the water. Swimming, boating, fishing, and hiking are the usual pursuits here. You can hike around the lake on the 18-mile Tully Lake Trail loop,

ascend Tully Mountain or Jacobs Ridge, or check out the nearby waterfalls: Royalston Falls, Doanes Falls, and Spirit Falls.

Campsites, facilities: There are 35 walk-in tent-only sites (including two wheelchair-accessible sites), each with a picnic table and fireplace with grill. Hot showers, horseshoes, volleyball, and canoe and kayak rentals are available on-site. Leashsed pets are permitted.

Reservations, fees: Sites are $20 a night, $25 a night for waterfront. Campsites can be reserved on a first-come, first-served basis. Before Memorial Day, call 978/248-9455; after Memorial Day, 978/249-4957.

Open: Weekends only May and September, daily June–August.

Directions: From Highway 2, take exit 18 and turn left onto Highway 2A toward Athol. From the intersection of routes 2A and 32 north in Athol, cross the Miller's River Bridge and bear left following the signs on Route 32 north. Proceed about four miles, passing the Tully Dam, then take a right onto Doane Hill Road. Proceed for a mile. The Tully Lake Campground is on the right.

Contact: The Trustees of Reservations, Quabbin Management Unit Office, 100 Main Street, Athol, MA 01331-2222, 978/248-9455; in season, Tully Lake Campground, 25 Doane Hill Road, Royalston, MA 01368, 978/249-4957, website: www.thetrustees.org/pages/30_tully_lake_campground.cfm.

5 LAMB CITY CAMPGROUND

Rating: 7

East of Athol

This is the ultimate RV option for campers who want access to fishing, swimming, and nonmotorized boating on Lake Dennison. Level and shaded sites are either right on or near the lake. You can rent canoes and paddleboats at the campground. Lamb City also coordinates many group activities including live entertainment.

Campsites, facilities: There are 250 sites for tents and RVs, most with hookups. Pull-through sites, seasonal lots, and cable TV are available. Onsite you will find a dump station, free hot showers, restrooms, laundry facilities, a full-service store, LP gas, ice, firewood, three swimming pools, a boat ramp and rentals, sports courts, a recreation hall with game room, playground, and horseshoe pits. Leashed pets are permitted.

Reservations, fees: Reservations are accepted. Sites start at $22 a night per family.

Open: Year-round.

Directions: From Highway 2, take Exit 19 and turn left on Highway 2A. Travel 300 feet and then turn right on Royalston Road. The campground will be .5 mile ahead on the left.

Contact: Lamb City Campground, Royalston Road, Phillipston, MA 01331, 978/249-2049 or 800/292-5262, website: www.lambcity.com.

6 LAKE DENNISON STATE RECREATION AREA

Rating: 7

South of Winchendon

Lakeside sites underneath the pines provide campers with a tranquil setting. Nonmotorized boating, fishing, and swimming are permitted on Lake Dennison, a section of the Army Corps of Engineers Birch Hill Flood Control Project. Multiuse trails leave the campground and access more than 4,000 acres of forest and meadowlands for hiking, horseback riding, and hunting.

Campsites, facilities: There are 150 sites for tents and RVs with a dump station but no hookups. Flush toilets, showers, picnic tables, piped water, and fireplaces are provided. Leashed pets are permitted.

Reservations, fees: Reservations are recommended; contact 877/422-6762, website: www.reserveamerica.com. Sites are $12 a night.

Open: Memorial Day–Columbus Day.

Directions: From Fitchburg, take Highway 12 north to Winchendon and head south on U.S.

202 to the park on the right (west) side of the road.

Contact: Lake Dennison State Recreation Area, c/o Otter River State Forest, Baldwinville, MA 01436, 978/939-8962.

7 OTTER RIVER STATE FOREST

Rating: 8

South of Winchendon

Camping along the Otter River is cool and comfortable even in the dog days of August. Because there are no hookups, this campground is better suited to tenters; RVers will be more comfortable at Lake Dennison State Recreation Area (see previous listing). More than 1,000 state forestland acres are open to hiking, horseback riding, and hunting, while the quiet river waters await your canoe. This was the first area acquired by the State Forest Commission in 1915.

Campsites, facilities: There are 89 sites for tents and RVs with no hookups. Flush toilets, picnic tables, piped water, and fireplaces are provided. Three group sites, open to nonprofit organizations only, can accommodate up to 25 people each. Leashed pets are permitted.

Reservations, fees: Reservations are recommended; contact 877/422-6762, website: www.reserveamerica.com. Sites are $12 a night; group sites are $25 a night.

Open: Memorial Day–Columbus Day.

Directions: From Fitchburg, take Highway 12 north to Winchendon and head south on U.S. 202 to the park on the right (west) side of the road.

Contact: Otter River State Forest, Baldwinville, MA 01436, 978/939-8962.

8 THE PINES

Rating: 7

In Ashby near the New Hampshire border

Old-fashioned country-style camping 'neath tall pines is the order of the day here. There's a stream on the property for fishing and a pool to cool off in on hot summer days. Sites are roomy and shaded and can accommodate all but supersized RVs. Tenters will feel at home in this small-town atmosphere, though RVers do dominate the scene. Just down the road is Townsend State Forest with its easy and moderate hiking trails.

Campsites, facilities: There are 60 sites for tents and RVs, most with full hookups. Each site has a table and fireplace. Facilities include a dump station, camp store, swimming pool, recreation hall, hot showers, and a playground. Firewood is for sale. Sites can be rented seasonally, but there is no on-site RV storage. Leashed pets are permitted.

Reservations, fees: Reservations are recommended. Sites are $25–$30 a night for four people.

Open: May 1–October 15.

Directions: From the junction of Highways 119 and 31 in Ashby, follow Highway 31 north for three miles to Davis Road. Turn right and drive a short distance to the campground entrance.

Contact: The Pines, 39 Davis Road, Ashby, MA 01431, 978/386-7702, website: www. gocampingamerica.com/thepines.

9 PEARL HILL STATE PARK

North of Fitchburg   **Rating: 7**

Campers enjoy the use of a small swimming beach at the park entrance at Pearl Hill Pond, not to mention 1,000 acres of wooded hillsides over which they can stroll. Generous campsites, with ample room in between, are scattered on a hilltop amid an expanse of tall pines. Up the road a piece in Willard Brook State Forest are another 18 miles of hiking trails and a river stocked with trout.

Campsites, facilities: There are 51 sites without hookups; the maximum RV length is 20 feet. Tables, fire rings, and flush toilets are provided. Leashed pets are permitted.

Reservations, fees: Reservations are recommended; contact 877/422-6762, website: www. reserveamerica.com. Sites are $12 a night.

Open: Memorial Day–Labor Day.

Directions: From Highway 2 in Leominster, take Highway 13 north to Townsend. Make a left onto Highway 119, drive west, and look for New Fitchburg Road on the left about 1.5 miles from the turnoff. The signs are faded. Follow the road to Pearl Hill State Park.

Contact: Pearl Hill State Park, c/o Willard Brook State Forest, Highway 119, West Townsend, MA 01474, 978/597-8802.

10 WILLARD BROOK STATE FOREST

North of Fitchburg   **Rating: 8**

Inside the state park you will find a good swimming spot at Damon Pond, brooks for trout fishing, 18 miles of hiking trails that are suitable for horseback riding, and lovely riverside spots where you can sit back and simply relax. The road through the forest winds along parallel to the river and can be crowded in the summer months, but the campground is tucked far enough into the trees to provide peace and quiet. Mountain bikers should head north on Highway 13 and thrash themselves on the trails in Townsend State Forest, located to the west of the road on the New Hampshire border.

Campsites, facilities: There are 21 wooded sites for tents and RVs with a 20-foot maximum length, all without hookups. Grills, tables, and flush toilets are provided. Supplies can be purchased in Townsend. Leashed pets are permitted.

Reservations, fees: Reservations are recommended; contact 877/422-6762, website: www. reserveamerica.com. Sites are $12 a night.

Open: May 1–Columbus Day.

Directions: From Marlborough, take I-495 north to Exit 31 and drive west on Highway 119 toward Ashby. Follow signs to the campground entrance.

Contact: Willard Brook State Forest, Highway 119, West Townsend, MA 01474, 978/597-8802.

11 LAKE WYOLA PARK AND CAMPGROUND

🏃 🏊 🛶 🎣 🚐 ⛺

Rating: 8
Northwest of the Quabbin Reservoir in Lock Village

Stay at this primitive campground in the Quabbin Reservoir district and you will enjoy plentiful fishing and wildlife viewing in a protected watershed. The roomy campsites are set in a pine forest by Lake Wyola. Campers will enjoy the use of a four-acre beach on the lakeshore as well as a boat basin.

Campsites, facilities: There are 48 sites for tents and RVs. No hookups are available, but there is a dump station. Springwater, showers, restrooms, a recreation hall, and laundry facilities are provided. No pets are allowed.

Reservations, fees: Reservations are recommended. Sites start at $18 a night for two people.

Open: May 1–mid-September.

Directions: From U.S. 202 north of Amherst, take the Shutesbury exit heading west. Turn right and continue north at the town junction toward Lock Village and Lake Wyola. Follow signs to the campground.

Contact: Lake Wyola Park and Campground, P.O. Box 83, Montague, MA 01351, 413/367-2627.

12 FEDERATED WOMEN'S CLUB STATE FOREST

🛶 🎿 🎣 🐕 ⛺

Rating: 7
South of Athol on the Quabbin Reservoir

Encompassing more than a thousand acres, this state forest is located in the Quabbin Reservoir watershed. Hunting is permitted in season, and the streams here are stocked with trout. A wildlife sanctuary comprising 140 acres has been set aside in the center of the forest, and a dam on Fever Brook holds back suffi-

cient water to attract migrating and native wild fowl. The southwest section is of particular interest for the forest's chief geological feature, the Gorge.

Campsites, facilities: There are six primitive tent sites with no facilities. Leashed pets are permitted.

Reservations, fees: Reservations are recommended; contact 877/422-6762, website: www.reserveamerica.com. Sites are $6 a night.

Open: April–December, weather permitting.

Directions: From South Athol, drive south on U.S. 202 to Highway 122. Turn left and head east for about three miles to the campground entrance on the right.

Contact: Federated Women's Club State Forest, c/o Otter River State Forest, U.S. 202, Baldwinville, MA 01436, 978/939-8962.

13 COLDBROOK COUNTRY CLUB AND CAMPGROUND

🏃 🚴 🏊 🎣 🐕 🚐 ⛺

Rating: 8
West of the Quabbin Reservoir

Country club camping is the Coldbrook Resort motif. On the site of former farmland, the campground offers spacious grassy and wooded sites atop rolling hills next to a family restaurant, a nine-hole golf course, and a 400-seat banquet facility. Tenters enjoy a separate wilderness area. On the grounds are an Olympic-size swimming pool and wading pool, trout-stocked fishing pond, and multiuse trails that cut through woods and fields. Horseback riding is also offered. The 350-acre resort abuts land controlled by the Massachusetts Water Resources Authority around the Quabbin Reservoir, which is replete with hiking trails.

Campsites, facilities: There are 175 sites for tents and RVs, most with hookups. Each site has a picnic table and fireplace. Restrooms, showers, laundry facilities, a snack bar, picnic grove, poolside lounge, and country store are on the property. You will also find sports courts and fields, two pools, a children's play area, recreation hall, restaurant, and game room. Leashed pets are permitted.

Reservations, fees: Reservations are recommended. Sites are $28–$36 a night per family.

Open: April 15–October 15.

Directions: From Worcester, take Highway 122 north to Barre. In town, turn right on Fruitland Road and then take another right at the stop sign onto Old Coldbrook Road. The campground is 1.2 miles ahead.

Contact: Coldbrook Country Club and Campground, 864 Old Coldbrook Road, Barre, MA 01005, 978/355-2090, website: www.coldbrook country.com.

14 POUT AND TROUT FAMILY CAMPGROUND

Rating: 6

Northwest of Worcester

Most sites at Pout and Trout are occupied by seasonal campers who return each year to participate in a season of group activities such as line dancing, fishing contests, and treasure hunts. A quieter "Adult Leisure Time Area" is tucked away from the activity center. Anglers can fish for trout in the private pond on the property (no state fishing license required) or in a river that runs through here.

Campsites, facilities: There are 156 sites for tents and RVs, 70 with full hookups and 75 with water and electric hookups. Each site has a fireplace and picnic table. Air conditioners are allowed, but heaters are not. A dump station, laundry facilities, a small grocery store, RV storage, LP gas, ice, and free firewood are available on the property. There's also a traffic control gate. You will find a recreation hall, swimming pool, sports courts and fields, and horseshoe pits on-site. Leashed pets are permitted.

Reservations, fees: Reservations are recommended June 15–Labor Day. Sites start at $22 a night per family. Weekly, monthly, and seasonal rates are available.

Open: March 17–Columbus Day.

Directions: From Rutland Center, travel four miles north on Highway 56 to Highway 68. Just north of the junction, turn and continue a mile east on River Road to the campground.

Contact: Pout and Trout Family Campground, 94 River Road, North Rutland, MA 01543, 508/886-6677.

15 PINE ACRES FAMILY CAMPING AREA

Rating: 7

Northwest of Worcester

Set beside 67-acre Lake Dean, these campsites are generally shaded and spacious. Some are right on the water, and there's also a secluded hill for wilderness tent camping. Launch your own boat and dock it by Pine Acres' long, sandy beach for a fee, or rent a boat from the campground. There are three private swimming beaches open to campers. More than a mile in length, Lake Dean is popular with waterskiers, while anglers can appreciate the resident bass and horned pout population. If you're in the mood for socializing, a recreation director plans group activities that range from crafts classes and dances to gambling field trips and tennis tournaments.

Campsites, facilities: There are 350 sites for tents and RVs, nearly 300 of which have water, electric, and sewer hookups. Each site has a picnic table and fire ring. A dump station, LP gas, laundry facilities, a camp store, firewood, a recreation hall and game room, playground, and seasonal storage are available on the property. On-site you will also find tennis courts, sports courts, heated restrooms with showers, horseshoe pits, a lodge, bait shop, and an RV service station. Leashed pets are permitted.

Reservations, fees: Reservations require a 50 percent deposit; to obtain a waterfront site in July and August, reservations must be prepaid in full. Sites start at 22 a night for two people, with waterfront sites priced at $40. There are surcharges for children, guests, pets, air conditioners, heaters, boat launching, and boat-slip use.

Open: Year-round.

Directions: From Worcester, travel north on Highway 122 for approximately 15 miles. Turn left on Highway 148 (North Brookfield Road) and continue for 1.5 miles. Turn left after you pass the lake and then follow signs to the campground entrance.

Contact: Pine Acres Family Camping Area, 203 Bechan Road, Oakham, MA 01068, 508/882-9509, website: www.pineacresresort.com.

16 HIGHVIEW VACATION CAMPGROUND

Rating: 6

West of Worcester in West Brookfield

Most campers at Highview rent sites seasonally, but overnight and short-term visitors are welcome, too. Sites are shaded and cool, set at an elevation of 906 feet on a wooded hillside. There is a pond on-site for fishing, and trails that traverse the surrounding lands are available. With dirt roads and country hospitality, this is an old-fashioned type of campground. It's quiet despite the wide selection of planned activities.

Campsites, facilities: There are 212 sites for tents and RVs, most with full hookups. Each site has a table and fireplace. Facilities include a dump station, hot showers, flush toilets, a laundry room, camp store, and RV storage. There's also a recreation hall, playground, and swimming pool, as well as scheduled activities. Firewood and ice are available. Leashed pets are permitted.

Reservations, fees: Reservations are recommended in summer. Sites start at $27 a night.

Open: April 15–October 15.

Directions: From West Brookfield center on Highway 9, travel two miles north on John Gilbert Road.

Contact: The Frizell Family, Highview Vacation Campground, R.D. Box 173, West Brookfield, MA 01585, 508/867-7800.

17 OLD SAWMILL CAMPGROUND

Rating: 5

West of Worcester in West Brookfield

You might feel a little crowded at Old Sawmill because the sites are typically fewer than 30 feet apart. Most are shaded by trees, but there's not much separating you from your neighbors. Chances are you'll meet them anyway if you're here on a weekend, as Friday, Saturday, and Sunday are loaded with planned activities such as bingo, dancing, cribbage tournaments, and hayrides. From the campground, a nature trail leads to a bubbling brook where you can fish, while other trails explore the wooded hills around the campground. If you're looking for serenity and privacy, this isn't your best bet.

Campsites, facilities: There are 125 sites for tents and RVs, most with hookups. Each site has a table and fire ring. Air conditioners and heaters are not allowed. Facilities include a dump station, laundry room, hot showers, flush toilets, a camp store, recreation hall, and RV storage. Firewood, ice, LP gas, and planned activities are available. A playground, game room, swimming pool, wading pool, and horseshoe pits are provided. Leashed pets are permitted.

Reservations, fees: Reservations are recommended; there are no refunds for cancellations. Sites start at $18 a night. Weekly, monthly, and seasonal rates are available.

Open: May 1–Columbus Day.

Directions: From West Brookfield Center on Highway 9, head south at the traffic light on Central Street to the road's end. Turn right and head south on Front Street, then turn right on Long Hill Road and continue .75 mile to the campground, crossing a railroad bridge on the way.

Contact: Old Sawmill Campground, P.O. Box 377, Long Hill Road, West Brookfield, MA 01585, 508/867-2427, website: www.old-sawmillcampground.com.

18 LAKESIDE RESORT

Rating: 7

West of Worcester in Brookfield

Lakeside Resort is located across the street from Quaboag Lake, a 540-acre freshwater pool open to motorboating, sailing, windsurfing, fishing, and swimming. Boat moorings are available near the resort-owned clubhouse on the shore. In addition, three rivers that are accessible from the lake offer quiet waters for canoeing. The grounds are neatly landscaped, and some of the sites are owned outright—you see travel trailers, motor homes, park models, and even cabins sporting flower beds as well as permanent structures attached to them. Designated areas have been set aside for overnight visitors, so you won't be pitching your tent next to a vacation home. Still, RVers will feel more comfortable here than tenters.

Campsites, facilities: There are 118 sites for tents and RVs, all with hookups. Sites are available on an overnight, seasonal, or for-sale basis, and there are some group sites. Air conditioners are allowed, but heaters are not. Facilities include RV storage, a dump station, hot showers, a hot spa, and laundry room. Tables, fire rings, and a guard service are provided. Ice and firewood are available on-site, and there's a store nearby. Campers can use a dance pavilion, sundeck, clubhouse, sports courts, swimming pool, and horseshoe pits. Leashed pets are permitted.

Reservations, fees: Reservations are recommended in July and August. Sites start at $28 a night.

Open: May 1–Columbus Day.

Directions: From the junction of Highways 9 and 49 in East Brookfield, continue 3.9 miles west on Highway 9 to Quaboag Street and turn left. Follow Quaboag Street for .8 mile to Hobbs Avenue. The campground will be straight ahead.

Contact: Lakeside Resort, 12 Hobbs Avenue, Brookfield, MA 01560, 508/867-2737 or 800/320-2267, website: www.camplakeside.com.

19 SUNSETVIEW FARM CAMPING AREA

Rating: 7

South of Palmer

Seasonal campers dominate the population at Sunsetview. Many return to enjoy the sites by the woods in the shade of an apple orchard and to participate in a host of activities from country line dancing to Monte Carlo weekends. Some sites are available to overnight guests, but be sure to call ahead. A swimming pond and small fishing pond are on the grounds, and a short hiking trail leads through the woods. Hop over to Brimfield State Forest on Monson Road for a day of trout fishing and hiking on 3,250 acres of protected land.

Campsites, facilities: There are 180 sites for tents and RVs, most with hookups. Each site has a fire ring, grill, and picnic table. Air conditioners are allowed, but heaters are not. Dump stations and pumping services are available. Facilities include a laundry room, store, recreation and game rooms, sports courts, athletic fields, and a playground. Firewood, ice, RV supplies, and RV storage are available on-site. There's also a traffic control gate. Leashed pets are permitted.

Reservations, fees: Reservations are recommended Memorial Day–Labor Day. Sites start at $24–30 a night for two people. Seasonal rates are available. There are extra charges for air conditioners, guests, and additional vehicles.

Open: April 15–October 15.

Directions: From the junction of U.S. 20 and Highway 32 in Palmer, travel south on Highway 32 for .75 mile to Fenton Road. Turn left and travel east, turning right on Town Farm Road after .5 mile. Drive 1.5 miles south to the campground entrance.

Contact: Sunsetview Farm Camping Area, 57 Town Farm Road, Monson, MA 01057, 413/267-9269, website: www.sunsetview.com.

20 WELLS STATE PARK

Rating: 7

North of Sturbridge

Wells State Park is a popular 1,400-acre woodland park. A beach on Walker Pond is for use only by registered campers. Fishing and boating are permitted. More than 10 miles of trails cross the property. A popular route leads to the scenic vista at Carpenter Rocks from which the eastern section and Walker Pond can be viewed. Wells is only five miles by car from Old Sturbridge Village, a nationally known living history museum of New England village life in and around 1800. This park is the best option for tenters in the Sturbridge region.

Campsites, facilities: There are 60 sites for tents and RVs, all without hookups. Facilities include flush toilets, showers, picnic tables, a dump station, fireplaces, and piped water. Leashed pets are permitted at the campground.

Reservations, fees: Reservations are recommended; contact 877/422-6762, website: www.reserveamerica.com. Sites are $12 a night.

Open: Mid-May–mid-October.

Directions: From I-84 near the Connecticut border, head north to Exit 3 and then drive a short distance east on U.S. 20 to Highway 49 north. Follow the signs to the park entrance off Highway 49.

Contact: Wells State Park, Highway 49, Sturbridge, MA 01436, 508/347-9257.

21 OAK HAVEN CAMPGROUND

Rating: 7

West of Sturbridge

Many of the Oak Haven sites are rented by seasonal campers who enhance their "second homes" with landscaping, decks, and other permanent fixtures. The park is impeccably clean and neat, bordered with wood fencing, dotted with rustic bridges, and landscaped with perennial gardens. A large swimming pool and recreation area are centrally located to the open and wooded sites set on 90 acres of rolling farmland with a small petting zoo. Five minutes away is the Norcross Wildlife Sanctuary. Located in Wales and Monson, the 3,000-acre preserve is home to rare wildflowers and indigenous wildlife. Two museums and a self-guided nature trail help visitors interpret what they see. The preserve is open year-round, and entrance is free.

Campsites, facilities: There are 90 sites for tents and RVs, most with full hookups. Each site has a table and fire ring. Heaters and air conditioners are allowed. On-site you will find laundry facilities, group sites for tents and RVs, RV storage, LP gas, and RV supplies. Ice and firewood are available. A swimming pool, recreation hall, game room, playground, snack bar, pavilion, and sports fields and courts are provided for use by campers. Leashed pets are permitted.

Reservations, fees: Reservations are recommended Memorial Day–Labor Day. Sites start at $24 a night for two people with water and electric hookups.

Open: May 1–Columbus Day.

Directions: From the junction of Highway 19 and U.S. 20 in West Brimfield, travel south on Highway 19 for 4.5 miles to the campground entrance on the left.

Contact: Alan and Penny Jalbert, Oak Haven Campground, P.O. Box 166/22 Main Street, Wales, MA 01081, 413/245-7148, website: www. oakhavencampground.com.

22 PARTRIDGE HOLLOW

Rating: 7

On Dean Pond in Monson

Camp in the company of young oak and pine trees at Partridge Hollow. The campground has been developed with RVers in mind, but some areas have been set aside for tenters. Summer weekends get a little wild with all the planned events, such as bingo, hayrides, parades, dances, theme dinners, and scavenger hunts. To escape the festivities, head down the road into Brimfield State Forest, where there are multiuse trails for hiking, biking, hunting, and horseback riding. Fast-flowing streams are home to abundant trout populations. And though no boats are permitted on Dean Pond, the largest of several ponds in the forest, swimming is allowed.

Campsites, facilities: There are 240 sites for tents and RVs, all with hookups. Each site has a fire ring, grill, and picnic table. Dump stations and pumping services are available. Air conditioners are allowed, but heaters are not. Facilities include a laundry room, store, recreation and game rooms, sports courts, athletic fields, and a playground. Firewood, ice, RV supplies, and RV storage are available on-site. There's also a traffic control gate. Leashed pets are permitted.

Reservations, fees: Reservations are recommended Memorial Day–Labor Day. Sites start at $21–27 a night for two people.

Open: April 15–October 15.

Directions: From the junction of U.S. 20 and Highway 32 in Palmer, travel 5.4 miles east on U.S. 20 and then head south for .75 mile on Monson Road. At the Brimfield State Park sign turn left on Dean Pond Road and go 2.5 miles southeast to the campground.

Contact: Partridge Hollow, P.O. Box 41, Munn Road, Monson, MA 01057, 413/267-5122.

23 VILLAGE GREEN FAMILY CAMPGROUND

Rating: 6

West of Sturbridge

Set on a small spring-fed pond, Village Green offers campers a chance to enjoy nonmotorized boating, freshwater fishing and swimming, and a family atmosphere. Weekends are studded with group activities, including talent shows, hayrides, beach parties, and cardboard boat races. Walking trails lead through the woods

behind the pond. Sites are mostly spacious and wooded, but they lose some of their natural flavor by being located next to a motel.

Campsites, facilities: There are 130 sites for tents and RVs, most with hookups. Each site has a table and fire ring. There are group sites for both tents and RVs. Air conditioners are allowed, but heaters are not. Facilities include dump stations and service, a laundry room, camp store, playgrounds, recreation hall, LP gas, game room, boat rentals, and RV storage. Firewood and ice are available. Courts for volleyball, basketball, and badminton are on the property, as are horseshoe pits. Leashed pets are permitted.

Reservations, fees: Reservations are recommended in July and August; holiday weekends require a minimum reservation of three days. Sites start at $22 a night for four people.

Open: April 1–October 31.

Directions: From the junction of I-84 and U.S. 20, travel 4.75 miles west on U.S. 20 to the campground entrance. Village Green is operated in conjunction with a motel.

Contact: Village Green Family Campground, 228 Sturbridge Road, Brimfield, MA 01010, 413/245-3504, website: www.villagegreencampground.com.

24 QUINEBAUG COVE CAMPGROUND

Rating: 6

West of Sturbridge

Brimfield Reservoir and Long Pond are the focal points of this lakeside campground in the woods near Old Sturbridge Village. Powerboating and swimming are popular summertime pursuits. Anglers will find perch, northern pike, bass, and pickerel in the several ponds, lakes, and streams that are part of the watershed; licenses are required and are available nearby. The Massachusetts Department of Environmental Management maintains a canoe trail that extends from Quinebaug Cove to the Tolland Pond Recreation Area five miles south—

rent a canoe at the campground. There are hiking trails around the reservoir that hunters use in season. Planned weekend activities include visits from Chippy the Chipmunk and Barney the Dinosaur for the kids, karaoke, live bands, and sports tournaments.

Campsites, facilities: There are 125 sites for tents and RVs, 110 with water and electric hookups and 50 with additional sewer connections. Each site has a table and fire ring. Air conditioners and heaters are allowed. Facilities include dump stations and service, a laundry room, LP gas, a swimming pool, recreation hall, game room, playgrounds, a snack bar, boat rentals, and RV storage. There's also a traffic control gate and boat launch. Courts for basketball, shuffleboard, volleyball, and badminton are located on the property. A camp store carries ice and firewood. Leashed pets are permitted with proof of rabies vaccination, but they must stay off the beach.

Reservations, fees: Reservations are recommended. There's a three-day minimum stay during holiday weekends. Sites start at $25 a night for two people.

Open: Year-round.

Directions: From the intersection of I-84 and U.S. 20, travel three miles west on U.S. 20 to East Brimfield–Holland Road. The campground is .5 mile ahead.

Contact: Quinebaug Cove, 49 East Brimfield–Holland Road, Brimfield, MA 01010, 413/245-9525, website: www.quinebaugcove.com.

25 YOGI BEAR'S STURBRIDGE JELLYSTONE PARK

Rating: 5

Southwest of Sturbridge

Roving costumed characters from the Yogi Bear show are part of the package at this theme park packed with entertainment for the whole family. From fishing in the camp's private pond (no license required), to nightly entertainment by hypnotists and magicians, this is a high-energy

camping experience. Horse-drawn hay wagons and a petting zoo are located on the property, as is an aquacenter, where, for an extra charge, campers can enjoy a water slide and hot tub. This is the closest place to camp near Old Sturbridge Village, a living history museum. It's not for those who want peace, quiet, and privacy.

Campsites, facilities: There are 399 sites for tents and RVs, 350 with water and electric hookups and 60 with additional sewer connections. Each site has a picnic table and fire ring. Facilities include a dump station and service, a laundry room, snack bar, grocery store, RV supplies, LP gas, and a traffic control gate and guard. Recreational facilities include a miniature water park with water slide and hot tub, miniature golf, paddleboats, shuffleboard, movies, horseshoe pits, and sports fields and courts. Ice and firewood are available. Leashed pets are permitted.

Reservations, fees: Reservations are recommended Memorial Day–Labor Day; there are no refunds. Sites start at $43 a night for two people in the summer season.

Open: Year-round.

Directions: From I-84, take Exit 2 and drive west on U.S. 20 toward East Brimfield. Follow signs to the campground.

Contact: Yogi Bear's Sturbridge Jellystone Park, P.O. Box 600, Sturbridge, MA 01566, 508/ 347-9570, website: www.jellystonesturbridge.com.

26 OUTDOOR WORLD— STURBRIDGE CAMPGROUND

Rating: 8

West of Southbridge

This campground is part of a member network. Nonmembers are welcome to try out the facilities, but you'll be encouraged to join up. Families will find no shortage of things to do at this upscale camping resort set on 200 acres of tall pine trees. There are a variety of campsites from private and wooded to wide open.

In the busy summer season, the campground hosts theme dinners and dances, as well as group activities and games for kids. Also on the property is a small lake on which campers can use the resort's paddleboats and canoes free of charge. Old Sturbridge Village, a living history museum recreating 19th-century New England, is one of the area's main attractions. By car, it's less than five minutes away. When you visit, you can talk to costumed interpreters working as blacksmiths, broom makers, shoemakers, and other craftspeople. Even though Outdoor World is just off I-84, the campground is well buffered from the highway noise.

Location: West of Southbridge, see Central Massachusetts map.

Campsites, facilities: There are 92 RV sites, most with hookups. Cabins and trailers are also available for rent. On the grounds are an indoor heated pool and spa, laundry facilities, a camp store, game room, recreation hall, and playground. Boat rentals are available for use on several nearby ponds and rivers. Restrooms are heated, and there is an adult lounge on-site. Pets are not permitted.

Reservations, fees: Reservations are required. Call for pricing.

Open: Year-round.

Directions: From I-84, take Exit 1 and make a right onto Mashapaug Road. The campground is on your right.

Contact: Outdoor World–Sturbridge Campground, 19 Mashapaug Road, Sturbridge, MA 01566, 508/347-7156, website: www.resortsusa.com/ow_sb.php.

27 APPLEWOOD CAMPGROUND

Rating: 8

South of Charlton

Applewood is a great place to bring the family. Extra-large sites in the woods afford maximum privacy, and there's a separate primitive tent area. The playground and group sites are surrounded by forestland that is accessed by stone-bordered pathways. Fewer than 10 miles away is the living history museum of Old Sturbridge Village.

Campsites, facilities: There are 60 sites for tents and RVs, all with water and electric hookups, plus two group safari areas. Each site has a table and fireplace. Facilities include dump stations, a recreation hall, laundry room, metered hot showers in a modern restroom facility, and sports fields. Motorcycles, minibikes, and mopeds are prohibited. Leashed pets weighing less than 35 pounds are permitted.

Reservations, fees: Reservations are recommended in July and August and require a nonrefundable deposit. Group sites must be reserved. Sites start at $21 a night for tents and $20 for trailers.

Open: Mid-May–late September.

Directions: From the junction of U.S. 20 and Highway 31 near Charlton, travel 4.5 miles south on Highway 31 to the Dresser Hill Farm ice-cream stand and turn right. Drive .5 mile downhill to King Road on the left. The campground is just ahead.

Contact: Applewood Campground, 44 King Road, Charlton, MA 01507, 508/248-7017.

28 THE WOODLOT CAMPGROUND

Rating: 6

Near the Massachusetts Turnpike north of Charlton

Beneath a canopy of old oaks and pines, you will find large, wooded sites with plenty of privacy. Pools and sports courts keep everyone busy, and planned events on the weekends only add to the fun. For an excellent family day trip, head six miles west to Old Sturbridge Village, a living history museum designed to re-create an 1830s New England community. Costumed interpreters answer questions, while special events and tours target visitors of every age group.

Campsites, facilities: There are 92 sites for tents

and RVs, most with water and electric hookups. Each site has a table and fire ring. Air conditioners are allowed, but heaters are not. Facilities include dump stations, a laundry room, limited grocery store, RV storage, RV supplies, LP gas, ice, and firewood. A traffic control gate stands at the campground entrance. Courts for basketball, volleyball, and badminton are located on-site, as are a playground, swimming and wading pools, and horseshoe pits. Free movies are included. Leashed pets are permitted.

Reservations, fees: Reservations are recommended in July and August. Sites start at $21 a night for two people. Weekly and monthly rates are available.

Open: May 15–Columbus Day.

Directions: From the Massachusetts Turnpike/I-90, take Exit 9 and follow I-84 south to Exit 3A. Drive east on U.S. 20 for 5.5 miles to Highway 31. Turn left (north) at the traffic light and turn right on Stafford Street after .1 mile. The campground is .25 mile ahead.

Contact: The Woodlot Campground, P.O. Box 968, Charlton, MA 01508, 508/248-5141.

29 SUTTON FALLS CAMPING AREA

Rating: 8

Southeast of Worcester

Aldrich Pond is the centerpiece of this quiet, woodsy campground. Most sites are staked out by seasonal campers, but some are set aside for overnight guests. Electric motors are the only kind allowed on the pond, making this a peaceful place for swimming and fishing. Saturday night movies in the recreation hall are among the many planned activities.

Campsites, facilities: There are 95 sites for tents and RVs, nearly all with water and electric hookups and 80 with additional sewer connections. On-site services include RV storage, boat rentals, and dump stations. Hot showers, a playground, camp store, and an events pavilion are located on the property. You also find group camping areas,

laundry facilities, sports courts, and a lake for swimming. Leashed pets are permitted.

Reservations, fees: Prepaid reservations are a must for holiday weekends. Sites are $21–30 a night for two people. Weekly, monthly, and seasonal rates are available.

Open: Mid-April–Columbus Day.

Directions: From I-395 south of Worcester at Oxford, take Exit 4A to Sutton Avenue. Continue four miles to Manchaug Road on the right. Turn and drive to the campground .8 mile ahead on the right.

Contact: Sutton Falls Camping Area, 90 Manchaug Road, West Sutton, MA 01590, 508/865-3898 in the summer or 508/476-2653 in the winter, website: www.suttonfalls.com.

30 LAKE MANCHAUG CAMPING

Rating: 7

On Lake Manchaug

This campground has a half mile of lake frontage on 350-acre Manchaug Pond. Families come here to swim and water-ski, as well as fish for bass, perch, pickerel, and catfish. The campsites are linked by paved roads, and there's a security gate at the entrance. On holidays like the Fourth of July and Labor Day, there are planned activities such as theme dinners and dances, parades, and games.

Campsites, facilities: There are 192 sites for seasonal and monthly campers, most with full hookups. Dump stations and sewage dumping service are available. Also on the property are a playground and RV storage. Leashed pets are permitted.

Reservations, fees: Reservations are required. Sites start at $30 per night for two people.

Open: May 1–September 15.

Directions: From Highway 146 just north of the Rhode Island border, take the Manchaug exit and continue 2.2 miles to Manchaug Center. Go straight through the stop sign and turn left at the fork. Travel .5 mile, crossing the dam, and then turn left again. Take the first right onto Holt Road and proceed .5 mile to the campground.

Contact: Lake Manchaug Camping, 76 Oak Street, East Douglas, MA 01516, 508/476-2471, website: www.lakemanchaugcamping.com.

31 OLD HOLBROOK PLACE

🏊 🎣 🚤 🐴 🚶 🚐 ⛺

Rating: 8

On Lake Manchaug

Nearly half the campsites are located right on the Lake Manchaug shore, a convenient setup for those who want to swim, powerboat, or fish. Though seasonal rentals are offered, this campground restricts the building of any permanent structure, maintaining a natural appearance throughout the park. The long, sandy beach, boat dock, ramp, and swim raft make this an ideal spot for boaters and young families.

Campsites, facilities: There are 66 sites for tents and RVs up to 28 feet long, each with water and electric hookups and 35 with additional sewer connections. No dump station or service is provided. Available amenities include rowboat rentals, hot showers, a playground, ice, and firewood. Leashed pets are permitted.

Reservations, fees: Reservations are recommended. Sites are $18–25 a night.

Open: Memorial Day–Labor Day.

Directions: From I-395 south of Worcester at Oxford, take Exit 4A to Sutton Avenue. Continue four miles to Manchaug Road on the right, then turn. The campground is a mile ahead on the right, just past the Sutton Falls entrance.

Contact: Old Holbrook Place, 114 Manchaug Road, West Sutton, MA 01590, 508/865-5050.

32 KING'S CAMPGROUND

🏊 🎣 🚤 🚶 🚐 ⛺

Rating: 7

On Lake Manchaug

Wooded and open sites are set either on or near the shore of Lake Manchaug, where campers

can swim, powerboat, and fish. The campground runs a marina on the lake and provides boat rentals. Planned family activities round out the fun. There are lots of seasonal campers here.

Campsites, facilities: There are 90 sites for tents and RVs, most with hookups. Each site has a table and fire ring. A dump station is provided on-site. Also on the property are laundry facilities, metered LP gas, a store, recreation hall, game room, small petting zoo, playground, snack bar, and RV storage. Ice and firewood are available at the camp store. No pets are allowed.

Reservations, fees: Reservations are recommended. Sites start at $35 a night for two people. Seasonal rates available.

Open: Mid-April–mid-October.

Directions: From Highway 146 just north of the Rhode Island border, take the Manchaug exit and continue 2.2 miles to Manchaug Center. Go straight through the stop sign and turn left at the fork. Travel .5 mile, crossing the dam, and then turn left again. Take the first right onto Holt Road to get to the campground.

Contact: Paul Boutiette, King's Campground, P.O. Box 302, Manchaug, MA 01526, 508/476-2534, website: www.kingscampground.com.

33 INDIAN RANCH CAMPGROUND

🏊 🎣 🚤 🐴 🚶 🚐

Rating: 6

Near Webster on Webster Lake

Country music lovers alert! This seasonals-only campground is also the site of a renowned summer series of country music. Enjoy the sounds of such big names as Collin Raye, Tanya Tucker, Charlie Daniels, and Phil Vasser from your lakeside campsite. Webster Lake is surrounded by pine forests and is open to powerboating, fishing, and swimming. The lake is widely known for its native name, Chargoggagoggmanchauggagoggchaubunagungamaugg, the longest geographical name in the United States. Translated, it means "I fish on my side of the lake, you fish on yours, and no one fishes in between."

Campsites, facilities: There are 120 RV sites for use by seasonal campers only, all have full hookups save for 10 sites with just water and electric hookups. Dump stations and services are provided. On-site you will find an outdoor amphitheater, camp store, recreation hall with game room, playground, snack bar, boat rentals, and RV storage. LP gas and laundry facilities are available in Webster. Leashed pets are permitted.

Reservations, fees: Reservations are required. Seasonal rates begin at $2,500.

Open: May 1–October 1.

Directions: From the junction of I-395 and Highway 16 in Webster, travel a mile east on Highway 16 to the campground entrance on the right (south) side of the road.

Contact: Indian Ranch Campground, Highway 16, P.O. Box 1157, Webster, MA 01570, 508/943-3871, website: www.indianranch.com.

34 STURBRIDGE WEBSTER KOA

Rating: 4

East of Webster near Webster Lake

This rural, wooded campground is close to Webster Lake, where visitors can fish, powerboat, and swim in a freshwater setting. Sites are close together—most are about 25 feet wide—so privacy is at a minimum. Tenters have a separate primitive area of their own. Short trails lead through the wooded hillsides.

Campsites, facilities: There are 150 sites for tents and RVs, most with hookups. A dump station is provided. On-site you will find laundry facilities, a limited grocery store, LP gas, a recreation room, playground, sports courts, and horseshoe pits. Leashed pets are permitted.

Reservations, fees: Reservations are recommended in the summer. Sites start at $26–28 a night for two people.

Open: Year-round; fully operational from April 1–December 1.

Directions: From the junction of I-395 and Highway 16 in Webster, travel 2.5 miles east on Highway 16 to the campground entrance.

Contact: Sturbridge Webster KOA, Highway 16, Webster, MA 01570, 508/943-1895 or 800/562-1895.

35 WINDING BROOK FAMILY CAMPGROUND

Rating: 8

North of the Rhode Island border in Douglas

Some 5,000 acres of protected woodlands abut this campground, where the sites are spacious lots shaded by tall pines. Douglas State Forest, a wheelchair-accessible park, offers lake swimming, powerboating, hunting, and miles of maintained multiuse trails for use by hunters, hikers, mountain bikers, and horseback riders.

Campsites, facilities: There are 120 sites for tents and RVs, 25 with full hookups and the rest with water and electric hookups. Each site has a table and fire ring. Air conditioners are allowed, but heaters are not. Facilities include a dump station, new swimming pool, store, recreation hall, game room, playground, snack bar, phone connections, and RV storage. Ice, firewood, and church services are available at the campground. Campers can also use sports courts and fields. Dancing is one of many planned group activities. Leashed pets are permitted.

Reservations, fees: Reservations are recommended July–Labor Day. Sites start at $20 a night per family.

Open: May 15–October 1.

Directions: From the junction of Highways 16 and 96 east of Webster, travel two miles south on Highway 96 to the campground entrance on the right.

Contact: Winding Brook Family Campground, P.O. Box 1011, South Street, Highway 90, East Douglas, MA 01516, 508/476-7549.

Chapter 13

© DEM/KINDRA CLINEFF

Greater Boston

Greater Boston

Bostonians consider their city the Hub of the Universe, and while that might be a lot of fun to debunk, it certainly is the hub of New England. History is foremost on travelers' minds when they take in the city that was home to such Revolutionary notables as Paul Revere and the tea partyers, poets, writers, abolitionists, and inventors. The Freedom Trail literally traces Revolutionary history through the city streets. Other preserved homes and sites interpret America's early years on a smaller scale. The north and south shores of Boston hold just as much history, all of it salted liberally by the sea.

Since the turn of the century, Massachusetts legislators have been consciously saving both the state's history and natural beauty—and nowhere more successfully than around the hub of Boston. Large RV campgrounds are located close to the city and look more like resorts with their asphalt and precise landscaping. However, many public lands exist in this same area and are open to camping. Although these havens tend to have a large number of sites, they are usually set in the woods and are fairly private—a welcome treat being this close to a major urban center.

Perhaps the most amazing public asset of all in this region is Boston Harbor Islands State Park. For just a few bucks, whole families can take a boat ride out to any of several islands and spend the day, or, with planning, camp out for several days. Not only is this a bargain, it's a chance to see the city from the water. For more information about this and other state parks, see the introduction to the Berkshires chapter.

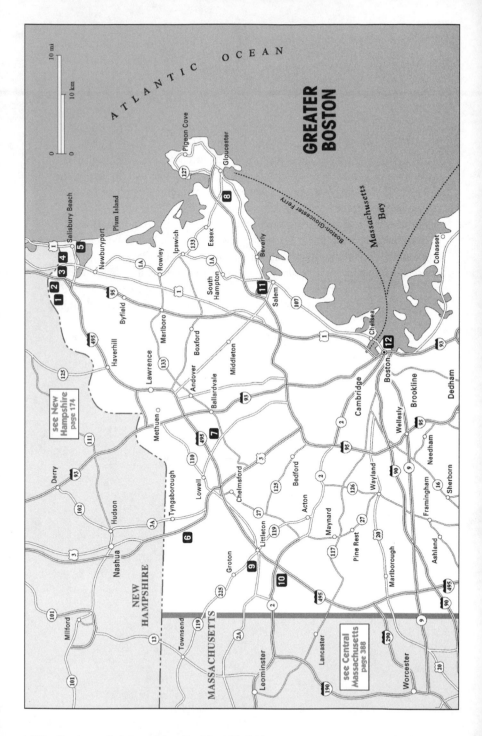

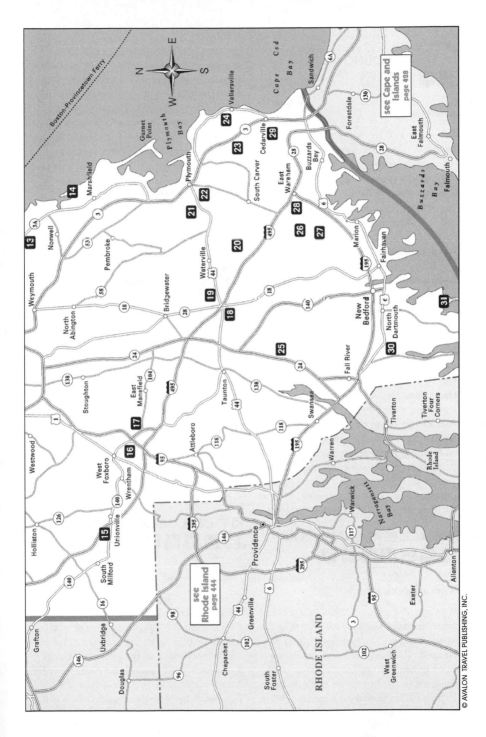

1 POWOW COVE CAMPGROUND

Rating: 6

In Amesbury

Powow Cove offers mostly shaded sites by a small lake. The majority of campers here rent space for the entire season, so call to find out if there is any space available. If you find yourself in the area, the Bartlett Museum in Amesbury features Native American artifacts, natural science collections, and a display of antique carriages.

Campsites, facilities: There are 74 sites for tents and RVs, most with hookups. You will find dump stations, laundry facilities, a camp store, recreation hall, playground, snack bar, boat rentals, and RV storage on the property. Picnic tables, fireplaces, security gate, and restrooms are provided. No pets are allowed.

Reservations, fees: Reservations are recommended. Sites start at $25 a night for two people.

Open: Early May–late September.

Directions: From I-495 east of Haverhill, take Exit 55 and travel north on Highway 150 through the traffic lights. In .5 mile, turn left on Highland Road, proceed to Lions Mouth Road, and bear left. The campground is three miles from Highway 150.

Contact: Powow Cove Campground, 43 Newton Road, Amesbury, MA 01913, 978/388-4022.

2 BLACK BEAR CAMPGROUND

Rating: 5

North of Salisbury Beach

Wooded and open sites at Black Bear are close to the interstate, just three miles north of Salisbury Beach and three miles south of New Hampshire's Hampton Beach. Tenters will enjoy spaces that are roomier than the sardinelike RV sites. Explore the area's tidal bogs on trails leading from the campground. When you tire of surf casting and lying on white-sand beaches, visit the Seacoast Science Center just over the New Hampshire border in Rye. Exhibits, programs, and trails explore Odiorne Point's scenery. Discover how this Native American fishing ground became the site of the first European settlement in New Hampshire. There's also lots of wildlife—snakes, frogs, turtles, crabs, and starfish, to name a few—for kids to handle.

Campsites, facilities: There are 200 sites for tents and RVs, all with water and electric hookups and 175 with additional sewer connections. The campground bills itself as "modem friendly." Facilities include fireplaces, picnic tables, coin-op showers, flush toilets, a dump station, laundry facilities, RV storage, a game room, playground, sports courts, an adult clubhouse, and a pool. Leashed pets are permitted.

Reservations, fees: Reservations are recommended in July and August. Sites start at $30 a night for two people.

Open: May 15–October 1.

Directions: From I-95 north of Newburyport, take Exit 60 and travel east on Highway 286. Turn left at the first set of lights onto Main Street and continue to the campground 200 feet ahead on the left.

Contact: Black Bear Campground, 54 Main Street, Salisbury, MA 01952, 978/462-3183, website: www.blackbearcamping.com.

3 RUSNIK CAMPGROUND

Rating: 7

North of Salisbury Beach

Bring your bathing suit and surf casting rod because the beach is just a stone's throw from this campground. Campsites are large, wooded, and set back far enough from the highway that you aren't bothered by traffic noise. There's a miniature golf course on the property and full-scale courses nearby. Five-mile-long Salisbury Beach lies three miles north of here and is open to the public. Newburyport, just five minutes away, offers numerous "urban" seaside attractions: whale-watching cruises, deep-sea fishing, shopping, summer theater—even greyhound races. When you tire of the ocean, head inland to 480-acre Maudslay State Park in Newburyport where you will find freshwater fishing and trails for hiking, biking, and horseback riding. A two-mile hike along the Merrimack River offers ocean views from Castle Hill.

Campsites, facilities: There are 150 sites for tents and RVs, 140 with water and electric hookups. Facilities include dump stations, fireplaces, picnic tables, hot metered showers, flush toilets, a recreation hall, game room, and laundry facilities. Firewood and ice are available. Leashed pets are permitted.

Reservations, fees: Reservations are recommended. Sites start at $30 a night.

Open: May 15–Columbus Day.

Directions: From I-495 near Amesbury, take Exit 55 and travel 3.5 miles east on Highway 110. Take a left on U.S. 1 and drive one mile north to the campground.

Contact: Rusnik Campground, P.O. Box 5441, Salisbury, MA 01952-0441, 978/462-9551, website: www.rusnik.com.

◢ PINES CAMPING AREA

Rating: 5

South of Salisbury Beach

Self-billed as a "no-frills family campground," Pines offers just the basics, meaning campers must travel to find recreation and amenities. Sites are quiet enough, set among—you guessed it—pine trees. Salisbury Beach is right down the road, and just south of there lies Newburyport, known for Plum Island, a spit of land that's home to the 3,200-acre Parker River Wildlife Refuge. Though boats cannot launch or land on the refuge, it is accessible by car and draws bird-watchers by the thousands. More than 300 species have been sighted in

the area, which is a pit stop for migratory fowl. Hunting and fishing are permitted in designated areas, but swimming can be a bit dangerous: Beware of cold temperatures, rough surf, and aggressive tides. Six miles of barrier shoreline await sunbathers in search of undeveloped beach.

Campsites, facilities: There are 160 open and shaded sites for tents and RVs, 16 with full hookups and 115 with water and electric hookups. Each site has a table and fire ring. Air conditioner and heater use is prohibited. On-site you will find a small playground, horseshoe pits, and a basketball hoop. Group sites for tents and RVs, sewage disposal, firewood, ice, and flush toilets are available. Leashed pets are permitted.

Reservations, fees: Reservations are recommended. Sites start at $20 for tents and $23 for RVs.

Open: Mid-May–Columbus Day.

Directions: From the junction of U.S. 1 and Highway 1A north of Newburyport, travel .5 mile north on Highway 1A, then turn right on Sand Hill Road, and drive .5 mile south.

Contact: Pines Camping Area, Sand Hill Road, Salisbury, MA 01952, 508/465-0013.

◳ SALISBURY BEACH STATE RESERVATION

Rating: 7

On Salisbury Beach

Here's that oceanfront property you've been looking for. Sites at Salisbury Beach—part of a 520-acre state-owned reservation—are on or near the park's 3.8 miles of shoreline. This boat-friendly campground is the perfect spot for sportfishing. A good outing for families with seaworthy craft is the seven-mile boat ride to the Isles of Shoals. Star Island, one member of this rocky string, is home to a hospitable inn and several historic religious structures. It is the largest, most accommodating port in the chain and is also accessible by chartered boats from Salisbury and Hampton, New Hampshire. Another island, Smuttynose, is rumored to harbor pirates' buried treasure. From the campground, a short paddle up the Merrimack River in a canoe will bring you to a good spot to try for striped bass. In the fall, this point where the river meets the sea is prime waterfowl-hunting territory.

Campsites, facilities: There are 483 tent and RV sites, 324 of which have water and electric hookups. The maximum allowable RV length is 31 feet. A boat ramp, grills, tables, a dump station, showers, flush toilets, a recreation pavilion, and playground are located on-site. Leashed pets are permitted.

Reservations, fees: Reservations are recommended; contact 877/422-6762, website: www.reserveamerica.com. Sites are $15 a night.

Open: April–mid-October.

Directions: From I-95 north of Newburyport, take Exit 60 and head east on Highway 286, crossing U.S. 1, to the intersection with Highway 1A. Follow Highway 1A two miles east to the water. The campground will be on your right.

Contact: Salisbury Beach State Reservation, P.O. Box 5303, Salisbury, MA 01952, 978/462-4481.

6 WYMAN'S BEACH

🏊 🎣 🚤 🐕 🚐 ⛺

East of Groton

Rating: 7

RVers predominate at this campground. Shaded sites are packed in close to the waterfront of spring-fed Long Sought-for Pond. With planned activities throughout the summer and a lake open for fishing, swimming, and boating, Wyman's Beach campers have plenty to do on-site. But only seven miles away is Lowell National Historic Park, offering exhibits on waterpower, mill girls, immigrants, and labor history, as well as walking tours. In summertime, a barge and trolley tour the Merrimack

River, famed for its role in New England's early mill history.

Campsites, facilities: There are 210 lakeside sites for tents and RVs, all with water and electric hookups and some with sewer. Fire rings, grills, tables, RV supplies, sewage disposal, LP gas, sports courts, flush toilets, metered hot showers, ice, and firewood are available on the property. There's also a convenience store and recreation hall. Leashed pets are permitted.

Reservations, fees: Reservations are recommended in summer. Sites start at $22 a night for two people.

Open: May–early October.

Directions: From U.S. 3, take Exit 33 to Highway 40. Travel three miles west on Highway 40 and then turn right on Dunstable Road. The campground is a mile ahead.

Contact: Wyman's Beach, 48 Wyman's Beach Road, Westford, MA 01886, 978/692-6287, website: www.wymanscamping.com.

7 HAROLD PARKER STATE FOREST

🥾 🚤 🎣 🐕 🏠 🚐 ⛺

In North Andover

Rating: 7

Set among mixed hardwoods, the sites at Harold Parker are mostly shaded, private, and ideal for tents and tent trailers. The 3,500-acre state forest is crisscrossed with 35 miles of old logging roads, now trails suitable for horseback riding and hiking. Ten ponds keep anglers busy; Berry Pond is stocked with trout, while the rest support populations of bass. Hunting is also permitted in season. An on-site interpreter leads discussions on such topics as native wildlife and celestial events, and there is a nature center just outside the park on Jenkins Road. The campground is only 26 miles from downtown Boston.

Campsites, facilities: There are 90 wooded tent and RV sites without hookups. Fireplaces, picnic tables, flush toilets, showers (no hot water), and a dump station are provided. Leashed pets are permitted.

Reservations, fees: Reservations are recommended; contact 877/422-6762, website: www.reserveamerica.com. Sites are $12 a night.

Open: Mid-April–Columbus Day.

Directions: From Boston, take I-95 north. Get on Highway 114 and drive west for 10 miles. Follow signs to the park.

Contact: Harold Parker State Forest, 1951 Turnpike Road, North Andover, MA 01845, 978/686-3391.

8 CAPE ANN CAMPSITE

Rating: 8

North of Highway 128 on Cape Ann

Campsites are set on 100 woodland acres overlooking saltwater inlets. They are less than a mile from the white sands and dunes of Wingaersheek Beach. Be sure to explore Halibut Point State Park at Cape Ann's northernmost tip. This bluff is an abandoned granite quarry, and on clear days visitors enjoy views all the way to Maine. Just south is the town of Rockport, a veritable artists' colony boasting winding streets lined with galleries and studios.

Campsites, facilities: There are 200 campsites for tents and RVs, about half with hookups. Fire rings, tables, sewage disposal, laundry facilities, RV supplies, flush toilets, showers, a snack bar, and ice are available on the premises. Leashed pets are permitted.

Reservations, fees: Reservations are recommended June–Labor Day. Sites start at $22 a night for two people.

Open: May 1–November 1.

Directions: From I-95 near Peabody, take Highway 128 north to Exit 13. Travel northeast on Concord Street, then turn right on Atlantic Street and continue to the campground.

Contact: Cape Ann Campsite, 80 Atlantic Street, West Gloucester, MA 01930-1699, 978/283-8683, website: www.capeanncampsite.com.

9 MINUTEMAN KOA

Rating: 6

In Littleton

If you're looking for a good place to park the ark and take in the historic sites of Lexington, this is it. Though you're right next to a busy road, sites are wooded and spacious, the grounds are clean, and the services are excellent. An expanded pool and deck area make this a family favorite. Oak Hill and Tophet Chasm offer easy family hiking only three miles away. Anglers will want to seek out nearby Oxbow National Wildlife Refuge. Take Highway 110 west for about seven miles to the small Still River Post Office, turn right at the post office, and continue until you see the refuge sign. You will find level hiking trails, as well as fishing for pickerel and bullhead on the Nashua River, which is also a good choice for canoeing. Just be on the lookout for any metal bomb-type surprises in the woods. This was once a blasting range for the Defense Department.

Campsites, facilities: There are 100 sites for tents and RVs, 26 with full hookups, 62 with water and electric hookups, and 12 with none. Fire rings, hot showers, LP gas, picnic tables, laundry facilities, a dump station, heated pool, and recreation hall are available on the grounds. Groceries, firewood, and ice are sold on-site. Leashed pets are permitted.

Reservations, fees: Reservations are required for group sites. Sites start at $25 a night.

Open: May 1–October.

Directions: From I-495 north of Marlborough, take Exit 30. Travel west on Highway 2A/110 for 2.5 miles. The campground will be on your left.

Contact: Minuteman KOA, P.O. Box 2122, Littleton, MA 01460, 978/772-0042 or 800/562-7606, website: www.minutemancampground.com.

10 CRYSTAL SPRINGS CAMPGROUND

Rating: 5

West of I-495 in Bolton

Sites at Crystal Springs are placed fairly close together underneath tall pines, more suited to RVers, though tenters are technically welcome. There's a small pond on the property as well as a full-sized pool for swimming, with a lifeguard. Campers are entertained every weekend in season by the country sounds of the Goodtime Band. Activities are organized for every age group, so families are the predominant campers. From arts and crafts to bingo, two on-staff recreation directors make sure there's something for everyone to do and ensure that there's never a dull moment.

Campsites, facilities: There are 200 sites for tents and RVs, most with hookups. Available on-site are laundry facilities, a dump station, hot showers, restrooms, a grocery store, RV supplies, LP gas, ice, and firewood. A pool, game room, sports courts, tennis courts, miniature golf, picnic tables, fireplaces, and a snack bar are provided. Leashed pets are permitted.

Reservations, fees: A deposit must accompany reservations. Sites are $17–25 a night for two people.

Open: April 1–late October.

Directions: From the Massachusetts Turnpike/I-90 west of Framingham, take I-495 north. At Exit 27 get on Highway 117 and travel west for two miles. The campground will be on your right.

Contact: Crystal Springs Campground, P.O. Box 279, Bolton, MA 01740, 978/779-2711.

11 WINTER ISLAND PARK

Rating: 8

Near the ocean in Salem

Windsurfers, kayakers, and scuba divers will find Winter Island an ideal place to camp. From here, you can access Salem Harbor as well as a number of coves to the north and south. Right out your front door there are opportunities to swim in the ocean or surf cast on the site of historic Fort Pickering and its lighthouse. Off the water there's even more to do in historic Salem. For a spook, check out the Salem Witch Museum. Literary-minded travelers must pay a visit to the House of the Seven Gables, which inspired Nathaniel Hawthorne's book of the same name. Heritage trails, maritime history tours, museums, and cemeteries are some of the other offerings. Your best bet is to stop first at the Chamber of Commerce in the Old Town Hall in downtown Salem's Derby Square. They can help you narrow down the choices and suggest those which best suit your interests.

Campsites, facilities: There are 41 RV sites, most with hookups. A water shuttle, boat launch, bathhouse, hot showers, grills, picnic tables, and a snack bar are available. The recreation area is open to the public. Leashed pets are permitted.

Reservations, fees: Reservations are recommended. Sites are $20–40 a night. Group and weekly rates are available upon request.

Open: May 1–October 31.

Directions: From the junction of I-95 and Highway 128, take Exit 25 to Gardner Parkway. Travel toward Salem on North Street. At the junction of Fort Avenue and Derby Street in town, take Fort Avenue northeast to Winter Island Road. Follow signs to the park.

Contact: Winter Island Park, 50 Winter Island Road, Salem, MA 01970, 978/745-9430, website: www.salemweb.com/winterisland.

12 BOSTON HARBOR ISLANDS STATE PARK

Rating: 9

In Boston Harbor

Boston Harbor Islands State Park encompasses 34 islands rich in history and natural treasures. Peddocks Island, at 134 acres, is one of the largest and most diverse. Here you can see the remains of Fort Andrews, which was active from 1904–World War II, at East Head; foot trails pass by a salt marsh, pond, and coastal forest; and a visitor center has displays on the island's natural and military history. A new visitor center opened on Spectacle Island in 2004. The island was capped by 3.7 million cubic yards of fill from the Big Dig and now features a marina, café, two beaches, and five miles of trails.

Grape Island used to be cultivated by Native Americans and colonial farmers, and now wild blackberries, bayberries, and rose hips proliferate, attracting many species of birds. Bumpkin Island is lined with slate and shell beaches and dotted with open fields. Fort Warren, a National Historic Landmark, dominates Georges Island (there's no camping, but ferries do stop here daily); this granite fort, constructed between 1833–1869, was used during the Civil War for training Union soldiers and later as a prison for captured Confederates. Sites differ from island to island, but most are partially shaded. No matter where you end up, you will enjoy million-dollar views of Boston.

Campsites, facilities: There are 41 individual tent sites and two group areas for tents only on four of the park's 17 islands: Lovells, Peddocks, Bumpkin, and Grape. Freshwater is not available on any of the islands, but there are toilets. No open fires are allowed in the camping areas, but beach fires are permitted below the tide line. A free water-taxi shuttle runs between the islands. No pets are allowed.

Reservations, fees: Reservations are recommended; contact 877/422-6762, website: www.reserveamerica.com. Sites are $15 a night.

Open: May–Columbus Day.

Directions: Ferries to the islands depart regularly from Long Wharf in downtown Boston. Additional ferries leave from Hingham. Take I-93 south out of Boston and then take Highway 3A along the south shore to Hingham. Follow signs to the ferry.

Contact: Boston Harbor Islands State Park, Lincoln Street, Building 45, Hingham, MA 02043, 617/223-8666, website: www.bostonislands.com.

13 WOMPATUCK STATE PARK

Rating: 8

South of Hingham

Campers can access 12 miles of paved biking trails and many more miles of hiking trails within Wompatuck State Park. Fishing is allowed in Cohasset Reservoir. Don't miss the two-mile interpretive trail that leads through old-growth forest. The Forest Sanctuary Climax Grove harbors large white pine, hemlock, and American beech trees, some nearly 200 years old. If you venture out to the coast just minutes away, you will find the World's End Reservation on the peninsula at the end of Martin's Lane in Hingham; it was landscaped by Frederick Law Olmsted, renowned designer of New York City's Central Park. Seven miles of carriage roads and footpaths traverse the reservation's drumlin—an ancient pile of glacial silt. From atop Planter's Hill, you can look out across Hingham Bay and see the Boston skyline.

Campsites, facilities: There are 262 RV sites, 140 with electric hookups. Facilities include flush toilets, restrooms, showers, picnic tables, piped water, fireplaces, and dump stations. Leashed pets are permitted.

Reservations, fees: Reservations are recommended; contact 877/422-6762, website: www.reserveamerica.com. Sites are $12 a night.

Open: Mid-April–mid-October.

Directions: From Highway 3 south of Boston, take Exit 14. Drive northeast on Highway 228 and follow signs to the park entrance.

Contact: Wompatuck State Park, Union Street, Hingham, MA 02043, 781/749-7160.

14 FOURTH CLIFF RECREATION AREA

Rating: 7

South of Scituate on an ocean spit

The campground overlooks the Atlantic Ocean at the end of the Fourth Cliff peninsula, with the North River on the inside. As part of Hanscom Air Force Base, the facilities are open to active duty, ready reserve, and retired military members. Sites are right on the ocean, so you can surf cast from your front door. An information display booth at the office posts the latest news on local points of interest and entertainment. Discount tickets and season passes for area events are sometimes available.

Campsites, facilities: There are 31 sites for tents and RVs, 11 with RV hookups. The campground is open to military personnel only. Sewage disposal, ice, tables, grills, a recreation hall, and bathhouse are available. Leashed pets are permitted.

Reservations, fees: Reservations are necessary. Sites are $20 a night for RVs with hookups and $10 for tents.

Open: May–October.

Directions: From I-93 south of Boston, take Highway 3 south to Exit 12 and turn right at the bottom of the exit. Travel 1.5 miles to Furnace Street and turn left. When you reach the T intersection, turn left on Ferry Street. Turn right on Sea Street, going over the bridge, and then left on Central Avenue. At the fork, bear left and continue to Fourth Cliff.

Contact: Pat Ames, Fourth Cliff Recreation Area, P.O. Box 479, Humarock, MA 02047, 781/837-9269 or 800/468-9547, website: www.hanscom.af.mil.

15 CIRCLE C. G. FARM CAMPGROUND

🏕 ⛰ 🏊 🎣 🐕 🚐 ⛺

Rating: 5

North of the Rhode Island border in Bellingham

Bring your spurs, for Circle C. G. takes you to the Wild West. Some popular planned activities include country-and-western bands, cowboy breakfasts, wagon rides, and chuck wagon suppers and shows. All summer long, Boston group tours—including visits to the John Hancock Tower and Fanueil Hall—leave and return

directly from the campground. Nearby in Uxbridge, the 1,005-acre Blackstone River National Heritage Corridor offers canoeing, hiking, and hunting in season.

Campsites, facilities: There are 150 wooded sites for tents and RVs, most with hookups. Group safari sites are available. You will find dump stations, tables, fireplaces, ice, firewood, RV supplies, and a grocery store on-site. There are also many sports courts, miniature golf, two swimming pools, and a pond for fishing. Small pets are allowed.

Reservations, fees: Reservations are recommended and are necessary for holiday weekends. Sites start at $30 a night for two people.

Open: Year-round.

Directions: From I-95 southwest of Boston, take I-495 north to Exit 18. From here, travel a mile south on Highway 126 to the campground entrance on the left.

Contact: Circle C. G. Farm Campground, 131 North Main Street, Bellingham, MA 02019, 508/966-1136, website: http://hometown.aol.com/cgfrmcamp.

16 NORMANDY FARMS CAMPGROUND

🏕 ⛰ 🏊 🎣 🐕 ♿ 🚐 ⛺

Rating: 6

North of Foxboro

Offering unrivaled amenities—including four swimming pools, one of which is indoor, developed sites, and wooded sites in rolling terrain—Normandy Farms is an RVer's paradise. There are several safari sites for group camping and a separate tent area by a pond. Multiuse trails leave the campground. Nearby, the F. Gilbert Hills State Forest, also in Foxboro, has nearly 1,000 acres of hiking, cross-country skiing, and horseback riding trails, should you need to get away from the organized recreation philosophy of Normandy Farms. Typical events at the campground include teen pool parties, bingo, dances, and live entertainment.

Campsites, facilities: There are 400 wooded sites for tents and RVs, all with hookups. Each site has a concrete patio, fireplace, and picnic table. Air conditioner and heater use is allowed. Some facilities are wheelchair accessible. Church services, laundry facilities, dump stations, hot showers, four swimming pools, a recreation hall, sports courts, and a traffic control gate are provided. Firewood and ice are available, and there's a store on the property. Leashed pets are permitted.

Reservations, fees: Reservations are recommended during the summer. Sites start at $25 a night.

Open: Year-round.

Directions: From the junction of I-495 and U.S. 1 southwest of Boston, travel one mile north on U.S. 1 and then 1.5 miles east on Thurston and West Streets to the campground.

Contact: Normandy Farms Campground, 72 West Street, Foxboro, MA 02035, 508/543-7600, website: www.normandyfarms.com.

17 CANOE RIVER CAMPGROUND

🚶 🏊 🚣 🎣 🐕 👨‍👩‍👧 ♿ 🚐 ⛰

Rating: 6

East of Mansfield

Geese and ducks call Mill Pond home, and young campers love to keep them well fed. Sites are situated on wooded, flat terrain near the pond, which is open to nonmotorized boating and fishing but not swimming; two heated pools on the property are provided for those who want to take the plunge. Families also appreciate the large playgrounds here. When in Mansfield, you ought to check out the entertainment lineup at the Tweeter Center. Big names in jazz, rock, folk, and classical music are booked at the outdoor theater all summer long.

Campsites, facilities: There are 120 wooded sites for tents and RVs, all with hookups. Flush toilets, hot showers, boat rentals, two pools, ice, firewood, propane, picnic tables, and fireplaces are available. Leashed pets are permitted.

Reservations, fees: Reservations are recommended. Sites are $20–22 a night for two people.

Open: April 15–October 15.

Directions: From I-495, take Exit 10 and head east on Highway 123. Turn left on Newland Street and continue about two miles to the campground.

Contact: Canoe River Campground, 137 Mill Street, East Mansfield, MA 02031, 508/339-6462.

18 MASSASOIT STATE PARK

🚶 🏊 🚣 🚤 🎣 🐕 ♿ 🚐 ⛰

Rating: 7

Southeast of Taunton

Despite its proximity to the urban center of Taunton, Massasoit State Park offers quiet, wooded, natural sites beside a freshwater pond that's open to nonmotorized boating. Hunting, swimming, and fishing are permitted throughout the 1,500-acre park, which includes four lakes (swimming is at Middle Pond). Named for the Wampanoag Indian chief who negotiated a peace treaty with the Pilgrims in 1621, the park displays historic markers telling the story of the first people to inhabit this land.

Campsites, facilities: There are 126 sites for tents and RVs up to 21 feet in length; 24 sites have full hookups and another 81 are equipped with electric hookups. A dump station, boat ramp, piped water, showers, picnic tables, flush toilets, and fireplaces are provided. Leashed pets are permitted.

Reservations, fees: Reservations are recommended; contact 877/422-6762, website: www.reserveamerica.com. Sites are $12 a night.

Open: Mid-April–Columbus Day.

Directions: From I-495 north of Middleboro, take Exit 5 onto Highway 18/105 heading south. Signs will indicate the entrance to the park.

Contact: Massasoit State Park, 1361 Middleboro Avenue, East Taunton, MA 02718, 508/822-7405.

19 PLYMOUTH ROCK KOA

🏃 🏊 🏕 🐕 🚐 ⛺

Rating: 5

North of Middleboro

This campground is designed for RVers, though tenters will find their own separate area nearby, complete with water. Most sites are open, roomy, grassy, and offer some kind of shade. Seventy acres of woods on the premises await hikers. There are organized activities as well as bus tours of all the major Boston and the South Shore attractions. At nearby Massasoit State Park (see previous listing) southeast of Taunton, you will find 1,500 acres of parkland where you can swim, fish, boat, hunt, hike, and canoe.

Campsites, facilities: There are 276 sites for tents and RVs, most with hookups, plus safari areas for groups. Small fire rings, picnic tables, hot showers, modern toilets, sanitary dump stations, laundry facilities, and mail services are provided. You will also find game and recreation rooms, a playground, and off-season RV storage. Leashed pets are permitted.

Reservations, fees: Reservations are recommended. Sites are $23–44 a night for two people.

Open: March 1–November.

Directions: From I-495, take Exit 6 onto U.S. 44. Travel 2.5 miles east to the campground entrance.

Contact: Plymouth Rock KOA, 438 Plymouth Street, P.O. Box 616, Middleboro, MA 02346, 800/562-3046.

20 SHADY ACRES CAMPGROUND

🏃 🏊 🏄 🚐 🏕 🐕 ♿ 🚐 ⛺

Rating: 7

Southwest of Plymouth

Here you find quiet, shady sites on rolling hills beside a pond. Most are fully prepared for RVs, though there's also a less-developed area for tents. Myles Standish State Forest is just down the road from the campground. In winter, miles of trails there are maintained for use by cross-country skiers and snowmobilers. In warmer months, 35 glacial kettle ponds nurture a community of rare and uncommon plants.

Campsites, facilities: There are 200 sites for tents and RVs, most with hookups. Each site has a fire ring and table. Dump stations, laundry facilities, a camp store, recreation hall, playground, flush toilets, free hot showers, and on-site off-season RV storage are provided. LP gas, firewood, and ice are available. Leashed pets are permitted.

Reservations, fees: Reservations are recommended. Sites are $22–26 a night. Seasonal sites are available.

Open: Mid-April–mid-December.

Directions: From I-495 south of Boston, take Exit 6. Travel east on U.S. 44 to Highway 58 and turn right, heading south. In four miles, turn left on Mayflower Road. The Shady Acres entrance is at the end of Mayflower Road on Tremont Street.

Contact: Shady Acres Campground, P.O. Box 128, South Carver, MA 02366, 508/866-4040.

21 PINEWOOD LODGE CAMPGROUND

Rating: 7

West of Plymouth

Tall pines surround campsites overlooking a 50-acre freshwater lake at Pinewood Lodge. Motorized boats are not allowed on the water, so swimming and fishing are the preferred pursuits. The campground also owns a six-acre island on the lake. On weekends, the recreation director plans events with such themes as Western Weekend or Christmas in July. In Plymouth, pay homage to the native American berry at the Cranberry World Visitors Center on the waterfront. It's free, and not only do you learn the history of this native crop, you get to sample the tart treat as well.

Campsites, facilities: There are 250 shaded sites for tents and RVs, most with full hookups. Air conditioner and heater use is allowed. Open fireplaces, breakfast, a restaurant, LP gas, RV service, RV supplies, laundry facilities, a camp store, ice, firewood, rowboat and canoe rentals, dump stations, and a bathhouse are available. On-site you will also find a playground, courts for badminton and volleyball, and horseshoe pits. No pets are allowed.

Reservations, fees: Reservations are recommended in the summer. Sites are $28–38 a night for two people.

Open: May 1–November 1.

Directions: From Boston, follow I-93 south to Highway 3 and continue driving south. Take Exit 6 to U.S. 44 and go three miles west to Pinewood Lodge.

Contact: Pinewood Lodge Campground, 190 Pinewood Road, Plymouth, MA 02360, 508/746-3548, website: www.pinewoodlodge.com.

22 ELLIS HAVEN FAMILY CAMPGROUND

Rating: 6

South of Plymouth

Set in the woods by spring-fed Ellis Pond, Ellis Haven offers campers a place to enjoy a variety of water sports that don't involve motorized boating. Most sites are rented seasonally, but some are available to overnight campers. A trip to Plymouth wouldn't be complete without a visit to Plymouth Rock, the very spot where America's first Pilgrims reportedly landed aboard the Mayflower in 1620. To get a real sense of what life was like for the Pilgrims, stroll around the Plimoth Plantation, a living history museum re-creating village life in 1627. It's also located in Plymouth; for information, call 508/746-1679.

Campsites, facilities: There are 500 open and wooded RV sites, all with hookups. Dump stations, laundry facilities, hot showers, tables, and flush toilets are provided. A camp store sells ice, firewood, and LP gas. Also on-site are boat rentals, sports fields and courts, a playground, miniature golf, a pavilion, and snack bar. Leashed pets are permitted.

Reservations, fees: Reservations are recommended. Rates start at $32 a night. Weekly, monthly, and seasonal rates are available.

Open: May 1–October 1.

Directions: From Boston, follow I-93 south to Highway 3 and continue driving south. Take Exit 6 to U.S. 44 and drive a mile west. Bear left at the lights onto Seven Hills–Federal Furnace Road. Follow signs to the campground entrance on the right.

Contact: Ellis Haven Family Campground, 531 Federal Furnace Road, Plymouth, MA 02360, 508/746-0803, website: www.ellishaven.com.

23 MYLES STANDISH STATE FOREST

Rating: 8

South of Plymouth

Myles Standish is the largest recreation area in Massachusetts and attracts similarly sized crowds, especially in summertime. There are 15 trail miles for bikes, 20 miles for equestrians, and 35 miles for recreational vehicles—and motorcycles are allowed! Thirteen trail miles are devoted to hikers only. You will find bass, perch, and pickerel in several stocked ponds (of the park's 16 ponds), as well as fire towers from which you can get an overview of the entire park. The forest sprawls across more than 14,000 protected acres in Plymouth and Carver, which was once part of the Native American village of Patuxet. Within the park is the Pine Barrens, one of the largest contiguous pitch pine/scrub oak communities north of Long Island. Open seeded fields attract hawks, owls, waterfowl, juncos, and many other winged wonders. In season, hunters can bag pheasants, quail, grouse, and rabbit deer. Snowmobilers and cross-country skiers make their way here in the winter months.

Campsites, facilities: Several campgrounds

within the forest offer a total of 475 RV and tent sites. Some areas have hot showers, and all have restrooms, water, picnic tables, fireplaces, and dump stations. Group sites are available to nonprofit organizations. Leashed pets are permitted.

Reservations, fees: Reservations are recommended; contact 877/422-6762, website: www.reserveamerica.com. Sites are $12 a night; group sites $25 a night.

Open: Mid-April–Columbus Day, but 44 sites are open year-round for self-contained units.

Directions: From Highway 3 south of Plymouth, take Exit 5 and travel west on Long Pond Road. Follow signs to the forest entrance.

Contact: Myles Standish State Forest, P.O. Box 272, Cranberry Road, South Carver, MA 02366, 508/866-2526.

24 INDIANHEAD RESORT

Rating: 5

South of Plymouth near the ocean

Lakeside sites are tucked into the woods at Indianhead Resort. This is a family campground that's serious about its quiet: no hip hop, no rap music. That's the rule. And don't try to bring in firewood; the only thing you can burn in your fire pit is shrink-wrapped hardwood bundles (with fire starters) sold on-site. Campers spend quality time in freshwater Savery Pond, which is open to all types of nonmotorized boating, swimming, and fishing. Paddleboats, rowboats, and canoes may be rented at the campground. Those hankering for the ocean can walk to the beach through tiny Ellisville Harbor State Park (508/866-2580), which is just across the street from the campground entrance. It's less than a mile to the protected stretch of beach where saltwater fishing enthusiasts can cast out a line or spread out a beach blanket.

Campsites, facilities: There are 220 RV sites with water and electric hookups. Each site has a fire ring, grill, and picnic table. Air conditioner and heater use is allowed. Facilities in-

clude metered hot showers, flush toilets, a dump station, insect control, a recreation hall, game room, camp store, sports courts, and a playground. LP gas, firewood, and ice are available on-site. Leashed pets are permitted.

Reservations, fees: Reservations are recommended in the summer. Sites start at $30 a night for two people.

Open: Mid-April–Columbus Day.

Directions: From Highway 3 south of Boston, take Exit 2 and travel two miles north on Highway 3A to the campground entrance on the left.

Contact: Indianhead Resort, 1929 State Road/Highway 3A, Plymouth, MA 02360, 508/888-3688, website: www.indianhead-resort.com.

25 FORGE POND CAMPGROUND

Rating: 6

North of Fall River in Assonet

Large, wooded sites are set on freshwater Forge Pond. This campground is close to the city of Fall River, which boasts many historical sights including the battleship *Massachusetts.* Just down Highway 79 from the campground, Freetown State Forest offers more than 5,000 woodland acres with multiuse trails for biking, hiking, and horseback riding, as well as wheelchair-accessible facilities.

Campsites, facilities: There are 65 sites for tents and RVs with hookups. Dump stations, metered hot showers, a recreation hall, firewood, a game room, and playground are provided. Leashed pets are permitted.

Reservations, fees: Reservations are recommended. Sites start at $22 a night. Seasonal sites are available.

Open: May–mid-October.

Directions: From Fall River, take Highway 24 north to Assonet and then travel northeast on Highway 79 to the railroad crossing. Turn left on Forge Road, go .25 mile west, and turn right at the sign for "A Camper's Campground."

Contact: Forge Pond Campground, 62 Forge Road, Assonet, MA 02702, 508/644-5701.

26 GATEWAY TO CAPE COD CAMPGROUND

Rating: 7

North of Rochester

Gateway is part of the membership campground network, Outdoor World. Nonmembers are welcome to reserve "mini-vacation" visits, but you'll be urged to join. Despite the attractive name, this campground is still a 30-minute drive from Cape Cod. Sites are set under tall pines and are well suited to large RVs. Campers fish, swim, and boat on an on-site pond.

Campsites, facilities: There are 192 sites, most with full hookups. Some trailers are available for rent. Each site has a fire ring and table. You'll find a recreation hall, video games, a pool, mini-golf, a playground, and planned activities. Leashed pets are allowed.

Reservations, fees: Reservations are required. Call for rates.

Open: Mid-April–late October.

Directions: From I-495 north of Wareham, take Exit 2 (Route 58) and head south. This turns into County Road. About four miles from the interstate, take a right and head west on High Street. Stevens Road is 1.25 miles ahead on the left; follow signs to the campground.

Contact: Gateway to Cape Cod Campground, 90 Stevens Road, Rochester, MA 02770; 800-588-2221; website: www.resortsusa.com/ow_cc.php.

27 KNIGHT AND LOOK CAMPGROUND

Rating: 7

In Rochester, south of Wareham and close to Buzzards Bay

Just a stone's throw from Buzzards Bay, this campground is a good choice for people who want access to all that Cape Cod has to offer but don't want to be engulfed by tourist throngs. Campsites at Knight and Look are peaceful and level, and a small pond on the property is stocked with fish. Only nonmotorized boating is allowed. Seafarers can launch their craft, people-powered or motorized, at the public docks in the nearby seaside town of Marion. Buzzards Bay and the Cape Cod Canal offer plenty of protected water for many types of aquatic recreation. The canal makes it a breeze—quite literally for sailors—to access the north shore of the Cape.

Campsites, facilities: There are 135 tent and RV sites among tall pine and oak trees, most with water and electric hookups. Each site has a fire ring and table. Group sites are available. You will find a small grocery store, RV storage, laundry facilities, sewage disposal, hot showers, and flush toilets on the premises. Leashed pets are permitted at the campground.

Reservations, fees: Reservations are recommended in the summer. Sites are $22–27 a night.

Open: Mid-April–October 1.

Directions: From I-195 near Rochester, take Exit 20. Travel about 1.5 miles northwest on Highway 105 to the campground entrance.

Contact: Knight and Look Campground, Highway 105, Rochester, MA 02770, 508/763-2454 or 866/463-2454, website: www.geocities.com/knlcamp.

28 JELLYSTONE CAPE COD AT MAPLE PARK

Rating: 7

North of the Cape Cod Canal in East Wareham

Under new ownership and part of the Jellystone franchise (yes, you will meet Yogi the Bear), this secluded campground overlooks cranberry bogs and borders a freshwater pond where campers can swim. An indoor pool and water park is slated for completion in 2005. Even though the sites are wooded, they are squished together and lack privacy. Between all the towns and villages in the area, there are more than 13,000 acres of cranberry bogs. Depending on what time of year you visit, you get to observe this native plant being fertilized, harvested, or maintained. Be aware that it's illegal to venture onto a bog.

Campsites, facilities: There are 400 wooded RV and tent sites, 300 with full hookups. Dump stations, hot showers, boat rentals, a camp store, horseshoe pits, planned activities, and fireplaces are available. Leashed pets are permitted.

Reservations, fees: Reservations are recommended in the summer, and especially during the Cranberry Harvest Festival on Columbus Day weekend. Sites start at $30 a night.

Open: May 1–October 15.

Directions: From the junction of U.S. 6 and Highway 28 north of the Bourne Bridge, travel two miles north on U.S. 6 to the campground entrance on Glen Charlie Road.

Contact: Maple Park Family Campground, 290 Glen Charlie Road, East Wareham, MA 02538, 508/295-4945, website: www.mapleparkfamily campground.com.

29 SANDY POND CAMPGROUND

Rating: 8

North of the Cape Cod Canal in Plymouth

The campground's 2,000 feet of shoreline lacing freshwater Sandy Pond offer opportunities for fishing and swimming. Sites are surrounded by towering pines, and the grounds are impeccably neat. There are different areas for different tastes, so be sure to ask; for instance, some sites overlook the second hole of the Atlantic Country Club golf course, while remote tent sites provide solitude-seekers with ample privacy. The campground is within easy distance of both Cape Cod and Plymouth. To reflect on our nation's history, amble into Plymouth proper and look for the National Monument to the Forefathers. Perched on a hilltop over-

looking Plymouth Harbor, where the *Mayflower* pulled in more than 375 years ago, this 81-foot structure was built in 1889 to honor the virtues that carried the Pilgrims to the New World: Morality, Law, Education, and Liberty.

Campsites, facilities: There are 200 wooded sites for tents and RVs, most with hookups. Each site has a table and fire ring. A dump station, canoe rentals, hot showers, flush toilets, a camp store, firewood, ice, and playgrounds are available. Leashed pets are permitted; big, aggressive dogs are not allowed during the summer.

Reservations, fees: Reservations are recommended, and sites start at $26 a night.

Open: April 15–September.

Directions: From Boston, take Highway 3 south to Exit 3. Make a right turn at the end of the ramp, drive about 1,000 feet, and then turn left on Long Pond Road. After 1.7 miles, turn right on Halfway Pond Road, and after .7 mile, turn left on Bourne Road. The campground is 5.5 miles ahead on the right.

Contact: Sandy Pond Campground, Bourne Road, South Plymouth, MA 02360, 508/759-9336 in season, or 508/224-3707 off-season, website: www.sandypond.com.

30 WESTPORT CAMPING GROUNDS

Rating: 6

South of Fall River in Westport

This secluded and woodsy campground is the right choice for RVers who want to be close to Horseneck Beach and other waterside locales in the Fall River/New Bedford region but desire more amenities than the state park can offer. Sites are a little close together—each is about 30 feet wide—but natural barriers maintain a measure of privacy. Lovely beaches are a short drive south, including Horseneck Beach State Reservation. If you have an interest in the whaling history of New England, make a trek to the Whaling Museum in New Bedford, where you can board a half-scale replica of a whaling bark. This is the largest museum devoted to America's whaling past.

Campsites, facilities: There are 125 sites for tents and RVs, all with water and electric hookups and 80 with additional sewer connections. Dump stations, fire rings, tables, sports courts, flush toilets, hot showers, and some groceries are available. There's also a game room, recreation hall, billiard room, snack bar, and security gate. No pets are allowed.

Reservations, fees: Reservations are recommended; there are no refunds. Sites start at $25 a night for two people.

Open: April 1–October 31.

Directions: From I-195 east of Fall River, take Exit 10 toward Horseneck Beach. Follow Highway 88 south for three miles and then turn left at the second set of traffic lights. The campground is .25 mile from the intersection on Old County Road.

Contact: Westport Camping Grounds, 346 Old County Road, Box N112, Westport, MA 02790, 508/636-2555.

31 HORSENECK BEACH STATE RESERVATION

Rating: 8

On the ocean in Westport Point

Spread across 600 acres of barrier beach and salt marsh, Horseneck is one of the most popular state parks in the system, and not just for human beings: the estuary habitat attracts birds and those who watch them. If you're more into water than wings, look no further than the park's southwest-facing, two-mile-long beach at the western end of Buzzard's Bay. It's breezy year-round, making it a favorite with windsurfers and campers who want a break from summer heat. If you're a boater, explore the bay, the Elizabeth Islands, or Newport, Rhode Island, from here; there's a boat ramp at the reservation. Anglers surf cast for saltwater species from the campground or head out on the water.

Campsites, facilities: There are 100 sites for tents and RVs without hookups, but a dump station is provided. Facilities include tables, grills, a boat ramp, piped water, hot showers, and fireplaces. Leashed pets are permitted.

Reservations, fees: Reservations are recommended; contact 877/422-6762, website: www.reserveamerica.com. Sites are $15 a night.

Open: Memorial Day weekend–Columbus Day weekend.

Directions: From I-195 east of Fall River, take Exit 10 toward Horseneck Beach. Follow Highway 88 south to the ocean. Signs will direct you to the campground.

Contact: Horseneck Beach State Reservation, Highway 88, P.O. Box 328, Westport, MA 02791, 508/636-8816; campground: 508/636-8817.

Chapter 14

© DEM/KINDRA CLINEFF

Cape and Islands

Cape and Islands

C ape Cod, Martha's Vineyard, and Nantucket Island are some of
the top destinations in not only Massachusetts, but all of New
England. The Cape's mix of long white sand beaches, ocean
views, and freshwater kettle ponds provides perfect family summer
recreation, not to mention the plethora of fried seafood shacks, ice-
cream stands, whale-watching excursions, and mini-golf emporiums.

You will find a wide variety of campgrounds here. Most are set
along or near the shore, but that's where the similarity ends. On the
outer Cape, sites are typically set in the scrub pines on beds of pine
needles with walking trails to the ocean. Campgrounds that cater to

RVs dominate the middle and upper Cape. However, many campground owners recognize the needs of different campers and offer both RV-specific sites and separate wooded sites for tenters. No matter where you camp you're sure to smell the salty sea.

Smack in the middle of the Cape is Nickerson State Park, easily the state's most popular campground. Sites are on and around several freshwater kettle ponds, yet campers are still just a short bike or drive from the Atlantic Ocean. It's the very definition of having the best of both worlds. For more information about this and other state parks, see the introduction to the Berkshires chapter.

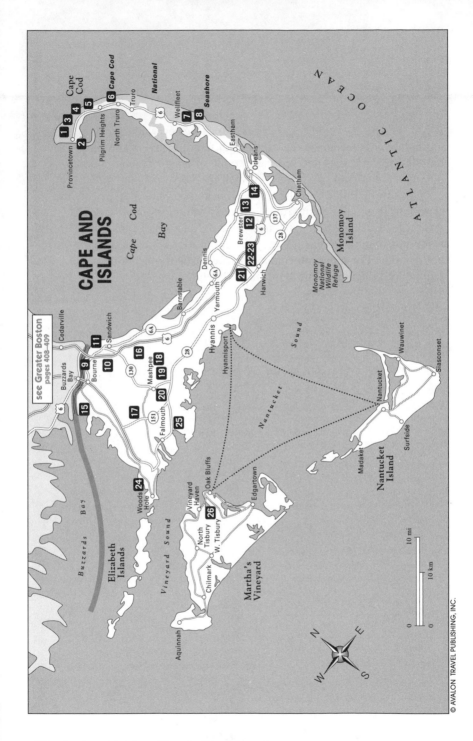

1 DUNES' EDGE CAMPGROUND

🏃 🐕 🚐 ⛺

Rating: 8

At the tip of the Cape, northwest of Provincetown between Race Point Beach and Pilgrim Lake

Quiet and family oriented, Dunes' Edge is a tenter's oasis in the treed dunes of the outer Cape. Most sites afford privacy—they are nestled between the Cape Cod National Seashore and Horses Head, one of the tallest hills on the outer Cape—and once you park your car, you can bike or walk to most of the attractions in Provincetown. In town, you will find some of the best restaurants on the Cape and a slew of quaint galleries and shops. Hiking trails to the national seashore and Race Point Beach leave right from the campground. At nearby Race Point, you can enjoy saltwater fishing and swimming. Just down the road, Beech Forest is a prime birding spot and one of the last remaining stands of the beech trees that once covered the entire Cape. Most of the area was heavily forested until European settlers cleared the land for farming in the mid-1600s. Once the trees were gone, wind and sand collaborated on a successful dune-making enterprise. Race Point Beach is the epitome of Cape Cod, with rolling dunes, an endless ocean expanse, and infinite beachfront.

Campsites, facilities: There are 100 wooded sites, 15 suitable for trailers and the rest for tents. Only 22 sites have hookups, and all have tables. Air conditioner and heater use is prohibited. You will find a dump station, hot showers, laundry facilities, and a limited grocery store that sells ice on the property. Leashed pets are permitted.

Reservations, fees: Reservations are recommended in July and August and require a nonrefundable deposit. Credit cards and personal checks are not accepted. Sites start at $25 a night for two people.

Open: Early May–late September.

Directions: On U.S. 6 heading toward Provincetown, look for the "Entering Provincetown" sign. Travel two miles past the sign and turn right at mile marker 116. The campground will be on your right.

Contact: Dunes' Edge Campground, P.O. Box 875, Highway 6, Provincetown, MA 02657, 508/487-9815, website: www.dunes-edge.com.

2 COASTAL ACRES CAMPING COURT

🏃 🏊 🛶 🚤 🐕 🚐 ⛺

Rating: 7

At the tip of the Cape, west of Provincetown

This is one of the few private outer Cape campgrounds that allows pets during the busy season. There are virtually no amenities at the campground itself, so you have to venture into nearby Provincetown for laundry, showers, and supplies. It is, however, the closest campground to Province Lands Park at the tip of the Cape. Here you'll find a visitor center, foot and bike paths, beaches, a naturalist program, and excellent birding; you are likely to see a number of hawks, cardinals, owls, and kingfishers, to name a handful of the winged locals. This is quintessential Cape Cod, the perfect spot to stake a claim in the sand dunes and read a trashy novel, take a strenuous trek in the soft sand, or pick some wild cranberries.

Campsites, facilities: There are 114 sites for tents and RVs, most with hookups. Each site has a table and concrete patio. Air conditioner and heater use is prohibited. Seasonal sites, RV storage, RV supplies, a grocery store, LP gas, ice, and a dump station are available. Leashed pets are permitted.

Reservations, fees: Reservations are advised in July and August. Sites start at $25 a night for two people.

Open: April 1–November 1.

Directions: Follow U.S. 6 to its end and then turn left at Herring Cove onto Highway 6A. Continue to the Bradford Street extension.

Contact: Coastal Acres Camping Court, P.O.

Box 593, Provincetown, MA 02657, 508/487-1700, website: www.coastalacres.com.

3 NORTH OF HIGHLAND CAMPING AREA

🏊 🛶 🚗 🐕 ⛺

Rating: 7

In North Truro on the east shore of the outer Cape

Surrounded by the Cape Cod National Seashore, this campground with sites set amid scrub pines is designed for beach lovers. Wood fires are permitted on the beach, and just south of here is Highland Light. To better enjoy the shoreline, check in at the National Seashore's Salt Pond Visitors Center in Eastham where you can learn about the 40 miles of sandy beaches and obtain a map of the area's biking and nature trails. Films and exhibits will help you interpret what this 7,000-acre site has to offer.

Campsites, facilities: There are 237 sites for tents and tent trailers with no hookups. Picnic tables, free cold showers, metered hot showers, flush toilets, and a recreation building are available. Pets and wood fires are prohibited.

Reservations, fees: Reservations are encouraged. Sites are $22 a night.

Open: Mid-May–mid-September.

Directions: Take U.S. 6 to North Truro then turn right on Head of Meadow Road. The campground is on the left.

Contact: North of Highland Camping Area, P.O. Box 297, North Truro, MA 02652, 508/487-1191, website: www.capecodcamping.com.

4 NORTH TRURO CAMPING AREA

🚶 🚲 🐕 🚗 ⛺

Rating: 7

In North Truro on the east shore of the outer Cape

Families are the dominant campers at North Truro, where sites are set in native scrub pines. The facility affords easy access to the hiking and biking trails of the 27,000-acre Cape Cod National Seashore to the south, and beaches for sunbathing, swimming, and fishing are just minutes away. One interesting and historical ramble leaves from Truro proper to the south: look for the Pilgrim Heights area. A path leads to the site of a spring where the pilgrims may have first quenched their thirst in New England. The moderate walk is under a mile in length and has some log steps.

Campsites, facilities: There are 350 sites for tents, tent trailers, and RVs, about two-thirds with hookups. Facilities include a store, laundry room, LP gas, a dump station, restrooms, free cable TV, and metered hot showers. Town ordinances prohibit campfires. Dogs are not allowed mid-June–Labor Day and must be leashed at all other times.

Reservations, fees: Reservations require a deposit. No credit cards are accepted. Sites start at $22 a night for two people.

Open: Year-round; fully operational mid-June–Labor Day.

Directions: Follow U.S. 6 east, passing through Truro. Watch for Highland Road (there's also a South Highland Road) and turn right. The campground is a short distance ahead.

Contact: North Truro Camping Area, Highland Road, North Truro, MA 02652, 508/487-1847, website: www.ntcacamping.com.

5 HORTON'S CAMPING RESORT

🚶 🐕 🚣 ♿ 🚗 ⛺

Rating: 8

In North Truro just inland from the Highland Light

Scrub pines and a golf course are all that stand between you and the Atlantic Ocean when you camp at Horton's. Most RV sites are grassy and open, while tenters are nestled into wooded lots. There's also an adults-only area where children aren't welcome. A path from the campground leads to the Highland Golf Links course and down to the Highland Light. Saltwater fishing and swimming are possible at the nearby beaches of Cape Cod National Seashore, where you can hike the coastline to your heart's content.

Campsites, facilities: There are 200 open and wooded sites near the ocean with separate sections for tents and RVs, most with hookups. Each site has a picnic table. A dump station, water faucets, laundry facilities, a camp store, playground, restrooms, metered showers, horseshoe pits, and a volleyball court are provided. Fires are prohibited by town ordinance. No dogs are allowed.

Reservations, fees: Reservations are requested during July and August and require a deposit. Sites are $23–34 a night.

Open: Early May–mid-October.

Directions: From U.S. 6 at North Truro, take South Highland Road east for a mile to the campground.

Contact: Horton's Camping Resort, P.O. Box 308, 71 South Highland Road, North Truro, MA 02652, 508/487-1220 or 800/252-7705, website: www.hortonscampingresort.com.

⑥ PAINE'S CAMPGROUND
🧍 🚲 🛖 🚐 ⛺

Rating: 10

North of Marconi Beach in South Wellfleet

Paine's Campground is a tenter's paradise, with sites divided into sections catering to the different needs of campers. Family sites accommodate multiple tents, vans, and small tent trailers, while the "quiet couples" area is devoid of children. Sites for singles and young couples are more open and thus conducive to meeting neighboring campers. "Lug-in" sites are reached by private, shaded footpaths and are restricted to tents only. A small RV section offers large, deep, shaded sites with water and electric hookups. There are even group sites that are available by reservation only.

Hiking and biking trails lead from the campground to the Cape Cod National Seashore beaches. A mile to the south, scenic sandstone cliffs provide a backdrop to the white sands of Marconi Beach. In South Wellfleet, the Massachusetts Audubon Society operates the Wellfleet Bay Wildlife Sanctuary—800 acres of marsh, pine woods, fields, brooks, and moors laced with five miles of foot trails. Enter the sanctuary on the west side of U.S. 6 just north of the Eastham/Wellfleet town line.

Campsites, facilities: There are 150 sites primarily for tents and tent trailers, with a separate RV area that has 25 sites with water and electric hookups. Ice and a dump station are available. Metered hot showers, approved drinking water, picnic tables, and fire rings are provided. Pets are not allowed in July and August and must be leashed at all other times.

Reservations, fees: Reservations are recommended in July and August. Base rates are $24–30 depending on season.

Open: Mid-May–late September.

Directions: From the junction of U.S. 6 and Old Country Road a mile north of the Marconi Beach access, travel .75 mile east on Old Country Road to the campground.

Contact: Paine's Campground, Box 944, South Wellfleet, MA 02663, 508/349-3007, website: www.campingcapecod.com.

⑦ MAURICE'S CAMPGROUND
🚲 🏊 🎣 🛶 🚐 ⛺

Rating: 6

Near the bay in Wellfleet

This campground is located on the Cape's main access road and thus doesn't offer much natural privacy, though sites are set in a pine grove. Saltwater swimming, fishing, and boating are all possible nearby. A bike trail leads from the campground to the national seashore beaches, so you can bypass the heavy summer traffic.

Campsites, facilities: There are 240 sites for tents, trailers, and RVs, more than half with full hookups. You will find a camp store equipped with a deli on the property. A dump station and LP gas are also available. Pets are not welcome.

Reservations, fees: Reservations are recommended for July and August. Sites start at $28 a night for two people.
Open: Late May–mid-October.
Directions: Follow U.S. 6 past the Orleans rotary heading toward Provincetown. At the Eastham/Wellfleet town line you will see the Wellfleet Drive-In Theater on the left. Maurice's Campground is on the right, 200 yards down the road. Enter at the driveway to Ann's Motor Court/Maurice's Campground.
Contact: Maurice's Campground, 80 Route 6, Unit 1, Wellfleet MA, 02667, 508/349-2029, website: www.mauricescampground.com.

8 ATLANTIC OAKS CAMPGROUND

Rating: 7

North of Eastham

Atlantic Oaks' large, wooded sites are custom tailored to meet the needs of RVers, including cable TV hookups and pull-through sites. Only half a mile south of here, you can enter the outer Cape. The Cape Cod National Seashore encompasses and protects some 40 miles of wind-polished dunes, kettle ponds, scrub forests, marshes, and bogs. And some of the Cape's most serene beaches for strolling are found on this land spit. Windsurfing is allowed in waters outside of the lifeguarded beaches. Don't forget to bring your bike, since the 25-mile-long Cape Cod Rail Trail runs directly behind the campground. Surf, bay, or freshwater swimming and fishing are all possible close by. Several nearby harbors offer boat ramps for public use.

Campsites, facilities: There are 100 sites for RVs with full hookups, as well as a small tenting area. Free hot showers, cable TV, laundry facilities, nightly movies in season, tables, and sewage disposal are available. Campfires are prohibited. Pets are not recommended.
Reservations, fees: Reservations are recommended. Winter season camping is available

by reservation. Sites are $35–49 a night depending on the season.
Open: May 1–November 1.
Directions: From Highway 3 heading south out of Boston, get on the Cape by following U.S. 6. The campground is .5 mile north of the national seashore entrance in Eastham.
Contact: Atlantic Oaks Campground, Highway 6, Eastham, MA 02642, 508/255-1437 or 800/332-CAMP (800/332-2267), website: www.capecamping.com.

9 BOURNE SCENIC PARK CAMPGROUND

Rating: 8

On the west side of the Cape Cod Canal in Bourne

Located on the Cape Cod Canal banks, Bourne Scenic Park offers unique opportunities for boat-watching, as vessels of every kind cruise by between Buzzards Bay and the north shore. Stairways lead down to the canal, and anglers can cast a fishing line from the park into the salty canal waters—without needing a license. Regulations restrict semipermanent campground improvements such as plantings and added structures, so you won't find many seasonal dwellings here.

On the property, there's a 450-foot saltwater swimming pool with a lifeguard; it's located in Area P-X, the only campground section south of the Bourne Bridge. If you're bothered by traffic sounds, consider choosing a site in Area C, the farthest from the busy span. In summer, the bridge is often clogged with traffic, so sometimes the best way to get onto the Cape is by bicycle. On either shore, the canal service road doubles as a 7.2-mile hiking and biking trail. If you are interested in learning about the Cape's first inhabitants, stop in at the Aptucxet Trading Post and Museum on Aptucxet Road in Bourne on the other side of the canal. In addition to a replica of the Pilgrim-Dutch trading post, there are Native American artifacts on display.

Campsites, facilities: There are 476 sites for tents and RVs, all with water and electric hookups except for one area with 39 sites. Each site has a fire ring, grill, and picnic table. Facilities include free hot showers, restrooms, a dump station, recreation hall, pavilion, coin games, a swimming pool, and sports fields and courts. Groceries, firewood, ice, and RV supplies are available. Bikes are welcome but must be on the campsite after dusk. Leashed pets are permitted.

Reservations, fees: Sites are filled on a first-come, first-served basis. Sites start at $24 a night; weekly rates are available.

Open: Late March–late October.

Directions: From Highway 3 south of Boston, take a right turn onto U.S. 6 heading west toward Buzzards Bay. Just before you reach the Bourne Bridge (to the Cape), you will see the park entrance on the left.

Contact: Bourne Scenic Park Campground, 231 Sandwich Road, Bourne, MA 02532-3622, 508/759-7873, website: www.bournerecauth.com/bsp.

🔟 SHAWME CROWELL STATE FOREST
🧍 🚴 ⛹ 🐕 ♿ 🚐 ⛺

Rating: 7
Near the historic town of Sandwich

Shawme Crowell's 742 acres are studded with walking and biking trails. In winter, these same paths become havens for cross-country skiers. Campers can also access the coast; the campground fee includes day-use privileges at Scusset Beach State Reservation (see next listing) on the west side of the canal. The nearby town of Sandwich is definitely worth a visit: Historic homes, the oldest church on the Cape, and the Sandwich Glass Museum are just a few of the attractions. The latter has an interesting exhibit of antique glass made in this town during the mid- to late 1800s.

Campsites, facilities: There are 285 RV and tent sites without hookups, so only self-con-

tained units are allowed. Each site has a table and grill. A dump station and public phone are available. Leashed pets are permitted.

Reservations, fees: Reservations are recommended; contact 877/422-6762, website: www.reserveamerica.com. Sites are $15 a night.

Open: Year-round; fully operational mid-April–mid-October.

Directions: From U.S. 6 near Sagamore, take Exit 1 and turn right at the traffic light onto Highway 6A. Turn right again onto Highway 130 and follow signs to the state forest.

Contact: Shawme Crowell State Forest, P.O. Box 621, Highway 130, Sandwich, MA 02563, 508/888-0351.

🔟🔢 SCUSSET BEACH STATE RESERVATION
🧍 🚴 ⛱ 🎣 🐕 ♿ 🚐 ⛺

Rating: 6
Bordering the Cape Cod Canal in Sandwich, on the northwesternmost portion of the Cape

Anglers can cast a lure into the Cape Cod Canal right from this campground, and they don't need a fishing license to do so. Ocean swimming is another on-site activity, and interpretive programs are presented during the summer months. The campsites are clean, but homogeneous, on this rather flat stretch of land. From here, you can hop on your bike and boat-watch along the canal, or head into Sandwich to check out the Currier & Ives collection at the Heritage Plantation on Pine and Grove Streets. The museum also boasts trails and gardens as well as an antique and classic cars exhibit.

Campsites, facilities: There are 98 open, flat sites for tents and RVs, all with electric hookups and shared water hookups. Each site has a picnic table and fireplace. Flush toilets, showers, and a dump station are available. A group camping area, open to nonprofit organizations only, can accommodate 50 people. Safari camping is available for other groups with self-contained units. Leashed pets are permitted.

Reservations, fees: Reservations are recommended; contact 877/422-6762, website: www.reserveamerica.com. Sites are $15 a night.
Open: Mid-April–mid-October, but self-contained vehicles are permitted year-round.
Directions: Take Highway 3 south from Boston to the Sagamore Bridge traffic circle. Follow signs to the campground.
Contact: Scusset Beach State Reservation, P.O. Box 1292, Buzzards Bay, MA 02532, 508/888-0859.

12 SWEETWATER FOREST

🚶 🚴 🏊 🚣 🚐 🎣 ♿ 🚙 ⛺

Rating: 8

A few miles south of Brewster, just north of Pleasant Lake

Amenities abound at Sweetwater Forest, but this wooded campground manages to remain peaceful. Sites are spacious and well screened by a pine and hardwood forest. Motorboat use is restricted on spring-fed Sweetwater Lake, but at nearby Long Pond you will find a boat ramp and open freshwater ripe for waterskiing. There's also a trail leading from the campground to the Cape Cod Rail Trail, a paved bike and in-line skating path that extends from South Dennis to South Wellfleet.

Campsites, facilities: There are 250 sites for tents and RVs, most with hookups, plus a separate tenting area with water faucets throughout. Each site has a picnic table. Free hot showers, dump stations, a security gate, five playgrounds, horseshoe pits, pony rides, boat and bike rentals, baby-sitting, LP gas, an RV showroom and repair service, video arcade, and adult clubhouse are available on the property. A camp store sells bait, tackle, ice, stamps, and groceries. No open fires are allowed, but charcoal grills and cookstoves are permitted. Leashed pets with rabies vaccination certification are allowed.

Reservations, fees: Reservations are advised in July and August. Sites start at $27 a night for two people.

Open: May–October, but self-contained units are allowed year-round.
Directions: From U.S. 6 south of Brewster, take Exit 10 and head north on Highway 124 for 2.8 miles to the campground entrance on the left.
Contact: Sweetwater Forest, P.O. Box 1797, Brewster, MA 02631, 508/896-3773, website: www.sweetwaterforest.com.

13 SHADY KNOLL CAMPGROUND

🐕 🚐 🚙 ⛺

Rating: 7

North of Brewster near the Cape's north shore

In-town camping is the motif at Shady Knoll. Brewster's ocean beaches are a mile away, and liquor and grocery stores are within walking distance. There's not much in the way of on-site recreation, so most campers tend to make their way to the beach. Boat ramps are available for public use locally at Sesuit and Rock Harbors. To access a bit of wilderness, head west toward Dennis on Highway 6A, turn left at Stony Brook Road (there's a blinking light), and take a second left onto Run Hill Road. You will find a sign and parking for the town-owned Punkhorn Parklands. Once a sheep-grazing area and cranberry farm, the land is now laced with a trail network open for use by mountain bikers, horseback riders, and hikers. Single- and double-track trails crisscross mixed hardwood groves and circle around ponds.

Campsites, facilities: There are 100 sites—some shaded, others open and grassy—for tents and RVs, 49 with full hookups, 31 with water and electric hookups, and 20 with none. Each site has a table and fire grill. Air conditioner and heater use is allowed. You will find free hot showers, restrooms, a dump station, laundry facilities, firewood, ice, and RV supplies available on-site. There's also a game room, basketball hoop, and playground. Pets are not recommended.

Reservations, fees: Reservations are requested. Sites are $35–45 a night for two people depending on season.

Open: May 15–October 15.

Directions: From U.S. 6 south of Brewster, take Exit 11 and follow Highway 137 north to its end. Shady Knoll Campground is directly across Highway 6A.

Contact: Shady Knoll Campground, 1709 Highway 6A, Brewster, MA 02631, 508/896-3002, website: www.capecamping.com.

14 NICKERSON STATE PARK
🥾 🚴 🏊 🛶 🛥 ❄ 🐴 ♿ 🚐 ⛺

Rating: 9

East of Brewster

More than a dozen freshwater kettle ponds, formed some 60,000 years ago by retreating glaciers, are open to swimming, boating, and fishing at Nickerson State Park, and several are even stocked with trout year-round. Trails for hiking, biking, cross-country skiing, and horseback riding traverse the park's 1,955 acres, making this one of the most popular places to camp in all of Massachusetts. Campsites are spacious and natural, and trails lead from them to all the larger ponds. Powerboating is allowed on Cliff Pond, the largest water body in the park. Resident wildlife include red foxes, white-tailed deer, eagles, woodland birds, hawks, and waterfowl. The land was owned until 1934 by the estate of Roland C. Nickerson, who was the largest private owner of forestland on Cape Cod in the 20th century.

Campsites, facilities: There are 420 open, wooded, and shaded sites, split between seven areas, for tents and RVs with no hookups. Each site has a fireplace and picnic table. Dump stations, piped water, hot showers, telephones, recycling bins, and an amphitheater are available throughout the park, and there are boat ramps on the larger ponds. Two group sites, open to nonprofit organizations only, can accommodate up to 30 people each. Leashed pets with rabies vaccination certification are allowed.

Reservations, fees: Reservations are recommended; contact 877/422-6762, website: www.reserveamerica.com. Sites are $15 a night.

Open: Year-round; fully operational mid-April–mid-October.

Directions: From U.S. 6 near Brewster, take Exit 12. Turn left at the bottom of the ramp and travel a mile to the park entrance on the left.

Contact: Nickerson State Park, 3488 Main Street, Brewster, MA 02631-1521, 508/896-3491.

15 BAY VIEW CAMPGROUNDS
🏊 🛶 🛥 🐴 🚣 🚐 ⛺

Rating: 6

In Bourne on Buzzards Bay on the south shore of Cape Cod

Bay View welcomes family campers only, so even though there are more than 400 sites, you don't find too much chaos. What you do find are peaceful campsites on a wooded plateau near the ocean bay, ideal for RVers who want the choice of sampling the fruits of Cape Cod only minutes away, or partaking of the recreational offerings close to home. At Cape Cod Canal and Buzzards Bay, you can enjoy fishing, boating, and ocean beach swimming. While out and about, don't forget to dine on fresh seafood—there's a bounty of take-out restaurants near the Bourne Marina. Recreation and leisure opportunities abound within Bay View, including an ice-cream parlor, organized activities, and entertainment during the summer months. If you decide to take a day trip out on the water, the campground conveniently serves as a ticket agent for local ferryboats.

Campsites, facilities: There are 425 sites for tents and RVs, with an average site width of 40 feet. Full and partial hookups are available. Each site has a picnic table and fire ring. Restrooms, hot showers, laundry facilities, a recreation hall, dump station, tennis courts, three swimming pools, horseshoe courts, and two playgrounds are provided on the grounds. A

camp store sells firewood, ice, gas, and RV supplies. Skateboards, in-line skates, and motorcycles are prohibited. Leashed pets are welcome, but owners are responsible for cleanup.
Reservations, fees: Reservations must be accompanied by a one-night nonrefundable deposit per week, and no personal checks will be accepted upon arrival. Sites start at $43 a night.
Open: May 1–October 15.
Directions: From Boston, follow Highway 3 south to the Sagamore Bridge. After crossing the bridge, take Exit 1. At the traffic light turn left and follow Canal Road to the Bourne Bridge rotary. Follow Highway 28 south for a mile to the campground entrance.
Contact: Bay View Campgrounds, 260 MacArthur Boulevard, Bourne, MA 02532, 508/759-7610, website: www.bayviewcampground. com.

16 LAWRENCE POND VILLAGE

Rating: 7

East of Sandwich on Lawrence Pond

With just 24 sites (compared to most of Cape campgrounds with hundreds), this campground offers privacy on Lawrence Pond. There's great fishing for trout and bass, and boaters are subject to a 10 mph speed limit on the 138-acre lake.
Campsites, facilities: There are 24 spacious sites for RVs, with hookups. A camp store sells groceries as well as lottery tickets and deli meats. Rustic cabins are also available for rent. Leashed pets are permitted.
Reservations, fees: Sites are only offered on a seasonal basis, call for prices. Eight light housekeeping cabins are available for rent on a weekly basis.
Open: May 1–Columbus Day.
Directions: From U.S. 6 in East Sandwich, take Exit 4. Travel two miles south on Chase Road, which turns into Great Hill Road, to the campground on the left.
Contact: Bob and Diane Cotter, Lawrence Pond Village, 45 Great Hill Road, Sandwich, MA 02563, 508/428-6225.

17 CAPE COD CAMPRESORT

Rating: 8

In Falmouth

Nearly half the sites at this campground are rented by seasonal campers who return year after year to swim and fish in the crystal-clear pond on the pine-forested property. Those same folks make you and your family feel at home in the clubhouse and during group events. In addition to the pond, the swimming pool is a favorite watery haunt for kids. The resort is a good jumping-off point for those planning to visit the islands, as the ferries are a short drive away in Falmouth. Some hiking trails lead through the property, but naturalists will want to stop in at the Ashumet Holly and Wildlife Sanctuary on Ashumet Road in East Falmouth to take advantage of self-guided nature walks and a holly trail. The sanctuary also is home to a colony of barn swallows.
Campsites, facilities: There are 200 wooded sites for tents and RVs, most with full hookups. Each site has a picnic table. You will find restrooms, hot showers, a clubhouse, badminton nets, horseshoe pits, a swimming pool, boat rentals, and planned group activities. Ice is available on-site. Fires are allowed only in specially designated fireplaces. Leashed pets are permitted.
Reservations, fees: Reservations are not required. Sites start at $28 a night.
Open: April 15–October 15.
Directions: From the Bourne Bridge, go south on Highway 28A to the exit for Thomas Landers Road. Turn left off the exit; in 2.5 miles you will see the campground entrance.
Contact: Cape Cod Campresort, 176 Thomas Landers Road, East Falmouth, MA 02536, 508/548-1458, website: www.resortcamplands.com.

18 DUNROAMIN' TRAILER PARK

Rating: 6

South of Sandwich on Peters Pond

Quiet, sandy beachfront for swimming and sunning is the main attraction at Dunroamin', which is restricted to family campers. Sites are set in a wooded area of hollies, oaks, and pines beside a 137-acre lake that is stocked with trout and bass and is open to all types of boating.

Campsites, facilities: There are 64 mostly shaded sites for RVs up to 28 feet in length, all with full hookups. Picnic tables are provided at each site, and rubbish containers are centrally located. A private beach, play area, horseshoe pits, and a public pay phone are on the property. Pets are not allowed on the beach and must otherwise be restrained.

Reservations, fees: Reservations are requested. Sites start at $25 a night.

Open: April–October.

Directions: From U.S. 6, take Exit 2, turn right on Highway 130, and drive 1.5 miles. Turn left on Cotuit Road, and after 2.3 miles, make a right onto John Ewer Road. The campground will be on your right.

Contact: Dunroamin' Trailer Park, 5 John Ewer Road, R.R. 3, Sandwich, MA 02563, 508/477-0541.

19 PETERS POND PARK

Rating: 8

In Sandwich on Peters Pond

Boasting a mile-long stretch of sandy beach for swimming and water sports, Peters Pond Park offers campers full access to the 137-acre freshwater lake. Campsites are generous—the most common width is 40 feet—and each is carpeted with wood chips or pine needles and landscaped with split rail fencing and shrubbery. You are sleeping in a pine forest but are still able to smell the salty ocean air. Some campsites are located directly on the lake, which

is stocked with bass and trout. Also on the property is a 20-acre conservation area.

Campsites, facilities: There are 450 sites for tents and RVs, most with hookups. Tent, tepee, cottage, and trailer rentals are available. Restrooms, laundry facilities, metered hot showers, a convenience store, RV supplies, propane, ice, an adult clubhouse, teen recreation hall, playgrounds, playing fields, a security gate, sports courts, and a special events tent are on the property. Group activities include bonfires, fishing derbies, and theme dinners. Campfires are not allowed at sites, but can be lit in a picnic area and are also started nightly by the staff. Pets are not allowed between July 1 and Labor Day except by special arrangement, and all pets must have rabies vaccination certification.

Reservations, fees: Reservations are recommended July 1–Labor Day. Sites start at $30 for four people.

Open: Mid-April–mid-October.

Directions: From the Sagamore Bridge, follow U.S. 6 to Exit 2. Turn right on Highway 130 and travel about three miles, then turn left at the first set of lights onto Quaker Meeting House Road. Turn right at the next set of lights onto Cotuit Road. Peters Pond Park is .5 mile ahead on the right.

Contact: Peters Pond Park, 185 Cotuit Road, P.O. Box 999, Sandwich, MA 02563, 508/477-1775, website: www.campcapecod.com.

20 OTIS TRAILER VILLAGE/JOHN'S POND CAMPGROUND

Rating: 6

South of Mashpee on John's Pond

Campers share space with year-round mobile home residents at Otis Trailer Village. This is a popular place, as the campsites are set in wooded terrain beside one of the Cape's largest natural lakes. At 314 acres, John's Pond can accommodate any kind of boat; there's even a state-run boat ramp right next to the campground. The clear waters are stocked with trout and bass, and the campground owns a long, natural sandy beach. Hikers can explore cranberry bogs and a wildlife sanctuary bordering the facility. About 15 minutes away by car is South Cape Beach State Park, with ocean beaches providing a place to escape and enjoy saltwater swimming, boating, and fishing.

Campsites, facilities: There are 90 open and shaded sites for tents and RVs, most with full hookups. Each site has a picnic table. Fireplaces are not furnished, but you may bring your own grill. Toilets, metered hot showers, laundry facilities, LP gas, and a playground are provided. Supplies are available in Mashpee, about 10 minutes away. Leashed pets are permitted.

Reservations, fees: Reservations require a minimum deposit. Fees start at $25 a night for sites with no hookups and $30 with hookups. There are surcharges for trailered boats and extra vehicles.

Open: April 15–October 15.

Directions: From Bourne, drive south on Highway 28 and take the exit for Highway 151 heading east to North Falmouth. Continue 3.75 miles to Currier Road and turn left. At Hoophole Road turn right and continue straight for two miles to the end of the road. Turn right at the intersection, and you will see Otis Trailer Village.

Contact: The MacDonald Family, P.O. Box 586, Falmouth, MA 02541, 508/477-0444, website: www.johnspondcampground.com.

21 BASS RIVER TRAILER PARK

🏊 🛶 🚣 🐕 🚐

Rating: 4

East of Hyannis in West Yarmouth

Though this may not be the most scenic campground in the area—it's located right off the main drag behind a car wash—it is just a mile from the beach, where campers can while away

the hours swimming, boating, and fishing. Since so many services are available nearby, the only amenity offered at Bass River is a dump station; you must go off-site for all other services, including laundry and firewood. Still, the reasonable prices reflect the spare offerings. JFK buffs will want to pay a visit to the John F. Kennedy Museum in Hyannis, the next town to the west. The collection includes photos and video relating to the president's life on Cape Cod. Also in Hyannis are ferries to Martha's Vineyard and Nantucket, giving campers an abundance of day-trip options.

Campsites, facilities: There are 25 sites for RVs only, with water, electric, and cable TV hookups. Shopping, miniature golf, and restaurants are just half a mile away. Leashed pets are permitted at the campground.

Reservations, fees: Reservations are recommended. Sites start at $24 a night.

Open: May 1–October 15.

Directions: From U.S. 6 south of Yarmouth, take Exit 8. At the bottom of the ramp, turn right and travel two miles through three sets of lights. After the third light, continue a mile to the park on the left side of the road behind the Bass River Car Wash.

Contact: Bass River Trailer Park, Highway 28, Bass River, MA 02664, 508/398-2011.

22 CAMPERS HAVEN

🚲 🛶 🚣 🚐 🐕 🚐

Rating: 6

On Nantucket Sound east of Hyannis in Dennisport

The sites at Campers Haven are a little crowded, as the average width is only 24 feet. It's also an "RV exclusive" spot, meaning there is no tenting and only full-hookup units are accepted. In this light, the campground offers shuttle services to the bustling town of Hyannis for campers who haven't towed along their car. The campground is located across the street from the ocean, but the facility's private beach down the road is available for fishing and swimming in the average 80-degree summer surf. Free shuttles also run to the beach.

You can pick up the Cape Cod Rail Trail a few miles away in South Dennis. This 50-mile round-trip bike path is paved and flat and ends in South Wellfleet to the north. Once the bed of the Penn Central Railroad, the path tends to be crowded in the summer months with amateur in-line skaters, dogs, and families, but it does afford an opportunity to see the non-coastal Cape countryside sans auto. Of course you don't have to go all the way to South Wellfleet; the South Dennis portion provides a short, lovely jaunt through farmland.

Campsites, facilities: There are 262 RV-only sites with full hookups. Each site has a table and fire grill. Facilities include a laundry room, hot showers, exercise equipment, a grocery store, dump station, recreation hall, and sports courts. RV supplies, ice, and planned group activities are also available. Pets are not allowed June 25–Labor Day.

Reservations, fees: Reservations are recommended. Sites start at $45 a night per family.

Open: May–Columbus Day.

Directions: From U.S. 6 south of Dennis, take Exit 9. Keep right and follow Highway 134 south to the stop sign at Lower County Road. Turn left, drive .5 mile, and then turn right onto Old Wharf Road. Continue a mile to the campground on the left.

Contact: Campers Haven, 184 Old Wharf Road, Dennisport, MA 02639, 508/398-2811, website: www.campershaven.com.

23 GRINDELL'S OCEAN VIEW PARK

Rating: 6

On Nantucket Sound, east of Hyannis in Dennisport

You can cast for stripers and bluefish out your front door at Grindell's, where some sites are actually right next to the water, among them T116 b–e and T18–29. And the rest are only a

short walk from the beach. Some strict regulations help keep the peace here, including a town ordinance prohibiting alcohol on the beach and rules specifying where you can hang wet laundry. One rainy day rescue for family campers is the Discovery Days Children's Museum on Main Street in Dennisport, which offers lots of hands-on exhibits and fun activities. For a view across the whole of Cape Cod Bay on a clear day, make the short excursion north to Dennis and climb the Scargo Hill Observation Tower off Highway 6A. From your perch, you see all the way to Provincetown.

Campsites, facilities: There are 160 RV-only sites on sandy knolls by the ocean, all with full hookups. Each site has a concrete patio and space for one car. Air conditioner and heater use is prohibited A small grocery store, RV supplies, LP gas, and ice are available on the property. Many lots are rented for the entire season. No pets are allowed.

Reservations, fees: Reservations are recommended in July and August. Sites start at $34 a night per family. Guests cost $9 a day per car. Weekly and seasonal rates are available.

Open: May 1–September 30.

Directions: From U.S. 6 south of Dennis, take Exit 9. Keep right and follow Highway 134 south to the stop sign at Lower County Road. Turn left and drive .5 mile, then turn right onto Old Wharf Road and continue about 1.4 miles to the campground on the right.

Contact: Clyde and Phyllis Grindell, Grindell's Ocean View Park, 61 Old Wharf Road, Dennisport, MA 02639, 508/398-2671.

24 SIPPEWISSETT CAMPGROUND AND CABINS

Rating: 7

South of West Falmouth and north of Woods Hole, near Buzzards Bay

Shade is plentiful in the terraced and well-groomed sites at Sippewissett. If you like clean facilities, you will find them in fine order here. The campground also offers free shuttle service to the Martha's Vineyard ferries and warm-water public beaches just a mile or two away. If you're interested in Cape Cod sea life, stop in at the National Marine Fisheries Aquarium in Woods Hole. Surf casters should head out to Nobska Point, southeast of Woods Hole proper.

Campsites, facilities: There are 100 sites for tents and RVs, half with hookups. Each site has a fire ring and picnic table. Air conditioner and heater use is prohibited. Facilities include RV storage, dump stations, laundry machines, restrooms, free hot showers, and a traffic control gate. Also on-site are a volleyball court, playground, recreation hall, and video games. Group tent camping is available. No dogs are permitted from Memorial Day–Labor Day.

Reservations, fees: A 50 percent deposit is required for all reservations. Sites start at $33 a night for two people.

Open: Mid-May–mid-October.

Directions: From the Bourne Bridge, take Highway 28 south for 11.2 miles to the Highway 28A/Sippewissett exit. Make an immediate right at the blinking light and continue .5 mile to the campground on the left.

Contact: The Tessier Family, Sippewissett Campground and Cabins, 836 Palmer Avenue, Falmouth, MA 02540, 508/548-2542, website: www.sippewissett.com.

25 WAQUOIT BAY NATIONAL ESTUARINE RESEARCH RESERVE

🏃 🚣 🛶 🚤 ✕ 🐕 ♿ ⛺

Rating: 10

On the coast in Mashpee, south of Waquoit Village

You feel like you've discovered your own private paradise when you camp at the Waquoit Bay National Estuarine Research Reserve. These wilderness campsites can only be accessed by private boat, so you are with like-minded company once you pull up on shore. From the campground, you have access to the reserve's nearly 1,800 acres. Kayaking in the estuary is a spectacular affair, with views of undisturbed land where the river meets the ocean. You can also canoe or kayak across the estuary to Washburn Island State Park. Interpretive programs are conducted at the Waquoit Reserve in season.

Campsites, facilities: Nine beachfront tent sites for families and two group sites are accessible by private boat only. Primitive facilities are provided. Leashed pets are permitted.

Reservations, fees: Permits are required. You can reserve some sites through Reserve Headquarters at 508/457-0495 and others at Camp Massachusetts, 877/I-CAMP-MA (877/422-6762), website: www.reserveamerica.com. Sites are $6 a night.

Open: Mid-April–mid-October.

Directions: From Highway 3 heading south out of Boston, drive onto the Cape via the Sagamore Bridge. Take U.S. 6 south to Exit 2 and travel east on Highway 130 to Great Neck Road, which you then follow to the Mashpee rotary. Get off the rotary on Highway 28 and head west. The park is 3.5 miles ahead to the south. To reach the campsites, you must launch a boat from the park.

Contact: Waquoit Bay National Estuarine Research Reserve, P.O. Box 3092, Waquoit, MA 02541, 508/457-0495, website: waquoitbay reserve.org.

26 MARTHA'S VINEYARD FAMILY CAMPGROUND

🚴 🚣 🛶 🚤 🐕 🎾 🚐 ⛺

Rating: 6

In Vineyard Haven on Martha's Vineyard

Families dominate the scene here, but sites are wooded, so there is some measure of privacy. Campers can access 25 miles of bike paths from the campground, and public ocean beaches for swimming and fishing are just minutes away. Take a few swings at the Farm Neck

Golf Club in Oak Bluffs, or head out on a fishing boat or whale-watch cruise. Families usually swim and sun at State Beach while the single, rowdy set cools off at Katama Beach near Edgartown.

Campsites, facilities: There are 180 sites for tents and RVs, 50 with full hookups and 110 with water and electric hookups. Each site has a picnic table and fire grill. Air conditioner and heater use is allowed. Some sites are rented seasonally. RV storage, sewage disposal, laundry facilities, piped water, restrooms, a grocery store, firewood, ice, a playground, recreation hall, and RV supplies are available on the property. Dogs and motorcycles are prohibited.

Reservations, fees: Prepaid reservations are advised for July and August. Credit cards are accepted; personal checks may be used only for advance reservations. Sites start at $40 a night.

Open: Mid-May mid-October.

Directions: Ferries to the island sail from Woods Hole, Falmouth, Hyannis, and New Bedford.

The Steamship Authority in Woods Hole operates seven days a week and carries campers, cars, and trucks of any size. Advance reservations are recommended and can be obtained by contacting 508/477-8600, website: www.islandferry.com. If you cannot get a reservation, drive to the ferry and take a turn in the standby line. Any driver arriving at either the Woods Hole terminal or the Vineyard Haven terminal on the island before 2 P.M. is guaranteed passage that day. Travel is by reservation only on holiday and busy summer weekends; be sure to inquire. Passengers without vehicles (not including bicycles) do not need reservations.

From Woods Hole on the mainland, take a 45-minute ferry ride to Vineyard Haven. Head out of town on Main Street and turn left on Edgartown Road. Travel a mile to the campground on your right.

Contact: Martha's Vineyard Family Campground, 569 Edgartown Road, P.O. Box 1557, Vineyard Haven, MA 02568, 508/693-3772, website: www.campmvfc.com.

Rhode Island

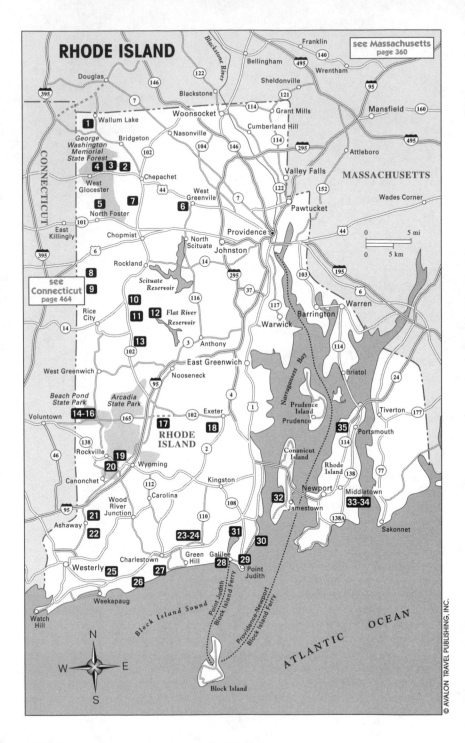

Chapter 15

© RI TOURISM

Rhode Island

Rhode Island

Rhode Island is so small it is frequently used as a measuring stick. People will tell you there are glaciers in Alaska bigger than Rhode Island. Texans will go on about how their ranches are bigger than Rhode Island. Several counties in Maine are much bigger than Rhode Island. The place is small—less than 50 miles from north to south, and under 30 miles from east to west. And yet getting a feel for the true size of this peanut of a state is difficult.

Rhode Island is nicknamed the Ocean State for very good reason—nowhere in the state is more than 25 miles from saltwater, and geographically, emotionally, and commercially, Rhode Islanders have always been oriented to the sea. The United States Navy was born in Newport during the Revolution, and the prestigious America's Cup yachting races were held in Newport from 1851–1983. Even though the coastline of the Ocean State stretches a mere 40 miles, the actual indented shoreline is a complex pattern of bays, estuaries, islands, sounds, and barrier beaches stretching for over 400 miles.

During the Gilded Age at the end of the 19th century, Newport was the exclusive domain of the fabulously wealthy. The Astors, Morgans, and Vanderbilts summered here. They built extravagant palaces with names like The Breakers, Rosecliff, and Chateau-Sur-Mer on expansive grounds overlooking the water. Today, the rest of us can stroll past the well-preserved estates and enjoy the same views over the ocean by hiking the Cliff Walk, a 3.5-mile-long public path skirting the backyards of the Bellevue mansions and overlooking Rhode Island Sound.

There is truly something for everyone in coastal Rhode Island. There is excellent dining, shopping, and waterfront strolling in Newport; fine beaches, exceptional saltwater fishing, and splendid Victorian architecture on Block Island; and great swimming, surfing, sea kayaking, and boating practically everywhere. Summer on the Rhode Island shore is New England at its finest.

Though most people travel to Rhode Island for the sea, there is high-quality outdoor recreation in the interior upland part of the state. Several large publicly owned tracts such as the 13,000-acre Arcadia Management Area and the 3,200-acre George Washington Management Area offer excellent hiking, mountain biking, freshwater fishing, and cross-country skiing. The nearly 3,000-acre Great Swamp is a popular spot for canoeing, freshwater fishing, and birding. Rhode Island may be small, but the state packs in the birds, playing host to over 300 recorded species.

And while you're in the state, be sure to visit the renewed Providence. In the past decade or so, this old city has been revamped, and the place is teeming with activity. The river, which was redirected to allow for the new train station, was cleaned up, and now gondoliers and kayakers paddle through town. Grab a meal in Federal Hill, the Italian part of town where you won't leave hungry. And be sure to stroll along Benefit Street, near Brown University and the Rhode Island School of Design.

1 BUCK HILL FAMILY CAMPGROUND

🏃 🏊 🎣 🍴 🏕 🛶 🚐 ⛰

Rating: 6

West of Pascoag near the Buck Hill
Management Area

Visitors to Buck Hill Family Campground have
access to a lake where they may swim, fish, or
float lazily in a canoe. You'll find the campground near the absolute northwest corner of
Rhode Island, just south of the Buck Hill Management Area, a 2,100-acre upland hardwood
forest that stands on what was once cleared
pastureland. The management area is bordered
to the west by Connecticut and to the north
by Massachusetts, and numerous hiking trails
lead into both states. An attractive part of
Rhode Island, this land consists of rural farming country dotted with small towns and classic Yankee villages—many of which make
interesting day trips.
Campsites, facilities: There are 98 sites for tents
and RVs, 58 with water and electric hookups
and 40 with none. Each site has a picnic table
and fireplace. Flush toilets, hot showers, laundry facilities, a dump station, and a store are
provided. Recreation facilities include canoe
rentals, a recreation room, playground, crafts,
rifle range, and an archery program. Leashed
pets are permitted.
Reservations, fees: Reservations are accepted.
Sites are $20–30 a night.
Open: May 1–October 31.
Directions: From the junction of Highway 100
and Buck Hill Road, drive 1.75 miles west on
Buck Hill Road. Turn left (south) on Croff
Road and continue 1.5 miles to the campground.
Contact: Buck Hill Family Campground, 464
Wakefield Road, Pascoag, RI 02859, 401/568-
0456.

2 ECHO LAKE CAMPGROUND

🏃 🏊 🎣 🚐 🏕 ⛰

Rating: 6

In Pascoag

Echo Lake Campground is located along the
shore of Pascoag Reservoir, the recreational
focal point for campers who enjoy swimming,
boating, waterskiing, and fishing. The park,
which is very popular with seasonal campers,
is set in a rural, scenic part of the state near
the George Washington Management Area
and the Buck Hill Management Area.
Campsites, facilities: There are 150 sites for
tents and RVs with full, partial, and no hookups.
Each site has a picnic table and fireplace. Flush
toilets, hot showers, laundry facilities, a dump
station, and a store are provided. Also on the
grounds are a recreation room, pavilion, volleyball and badminton nets, and horseshoe pits.
No pets are allowed.
Reservations, fees: Reservations are accepted.
Sites are $28 a night.
Open: May 1–September 1.
Directions: From the intersection of Highway
102 and U.S. 44 at Chepachet, drive two miles
west on U.S. 44. Turn right (north) on Jackson Schoolhouse Road, go one mile, then bear
right on Moroney Road, and head northeast
for .5 mile to the campground.
Contact: Echo Lake Campground, Box 4, Moroney Road, Pascoag, RI 02859, 401/568-5000.

3 BOWDISH LAKE CAMPING AREA

🏃 🏊 🎣 🚐 🎿 🏕 🚐 ⛰

Rating: 6

Adjacent to the George Washington
Management Area

A very large campground has been established
on the shores of Bowdish Reservoir some five
miles west of Chepachet, a small New England
village close to the Connecticut border. The
campground lies adjacent to the George Washington Management Area—at 3,200 acres, the

largest public landholding in this part of the state—with its numerous ponds in which visitors can swim and fish. There are hiking loops ranging from two–eight miles in length, and in season, the area is open for deer, grouse, woodcock, waterfowl, and small game hunting. The terrain is wooded, with open forests and many rocky outcrops and ledges.

Campsites, facilities: There are 325 sites for tents and RVs with water and electric hookups. Each site has a picnic table and fireplace. Flush toilets, hot showers, a dump station, and a store are provided. You will also find canoe and rowboat rentals, a recreation room, horseshoe pits, and hiking trails. Leashed pets are permitted.
Reservations, fees: Reservations are accepted. Sites are $25–55 a night.
Open: April 30–October 15.
Directions: From the intersection of Highway 102 and U.S. 44 at Chepachet, drive 5.5 miles west on U.S. 44 to the campground on the right.
Contact: Bowdish Lake Camping Area, P.O. Box 25, Chepachet, RI 02814, 401/568-8890.

4 GEORGE WASHINGTON MANAGEMENT AREA

Rating: 8

West of Chepachet

Just across the border from Connecticut in the northwest corner of Rhode Island is this rather large collection of state-owned lands. George Washington Management Area, along with its well-maintained campground, is nestled in the rolling, hilly terrain that typifies this part of the state. The main draw of the campground is Bowdish Reservoir, a spot where both campers and day visitors retreat to swim, boat, and fish. Powerboating and waterskiing are two popular pursuits. Things get busy here during the summer, as the area is a popular gathering place for local folks. In addition to day visitors to the management area, many private residences line the north and west shores of

the reservoir. Three hiking loops—with distances of two, six, and eight miles—lead throughout the area.

Campsites, facilities: There are 45 sites for tents or self-contained trailers, plus two shelters. Nonflush toilets, picnic tables, fireplaces, and water are provided. Recreational facilities include hiking trails, a swimming beach, and a boat ramp. No pets are allowed.
Reservations, fees: Sites are allocated on a first-come, first-served basis. Fees for regular sites are $12 a night for Rhode Island residents and $15 a night for nonresidents. Shelters are $20 a night.
Open: Mid-April–mid-October.
Directions: From the intersection of Highway 102 and U.S. 44 at Chepachet, drive west on U.S. 44 for five miles. Follow signs to the George Washington Management Area.
Contact: George Washington Management Area, 2185 Putnam Pike, Chepachet, RI 02814, 401/568-2013, website: www.riparks.com.

5 OAK LEAF FAMILY CAMPGROUND

Rating: 6

South of West Glocester

Oak Leaf Family Campground is a pleasant little trailer park set in rural, wooded terrain in western Rhode Island, just shy of the Connecticut border. Several management areas to the near north offer opportunities to spend time hiking, boating, fishing, and swimming. While here, be sure to visit the Brown and Hopkins Country Store to the northeast in Chepachet. Dating back to 1809, it's one of the country's oldest continuously operating general stores and sells such wares as antiques and country furnishings, excellent food, and coffee.

Campsites, facilities: There are 60 sites for tents and RVs with full hookups. Flush toilets, hot showers, picnic tables, fireplaces, and a store are provided. Recreational facilities include a swimming pool, recreation room, playground, volleyball, and horseshoes. Leashed pets are permitted.

Reservations, fees: Reservations are accepted. Sites are $25 a night.

Open: April 15–October 31.

Directions: From the intersection of Highway 94 and Old Snake Hill Road in Glocester, drive .5 mile east on Old Snake Hill Road to the campground.

Contact: Oak Leaf Family Campground, P.O. Box 521, Chepachet, RI 02814, 401/568-4446.

6 HOLIDAY ACRES CAMPGROUND

🚶 ♒ 🎣 🚤 🐕 🚐 ⛺

Rating: 5

West of the town of Harmony

The hilly, wooded countryside west of Providence is where you will find Holiday Acres. This large, full-service campground is situated on a freshwater lake and offers many sites with waterfront and water views. Motorboats are not permitted on the lake, but there are plenty of other opportunities for water-based recreation, including canoeing, swimming, and fishing.

Campsites, facilities: There are 225 sites for tents and RVs, 200 with full hookups and 25 with none. Each site has a picnic table and fireplace. Facilities include flush toilets, hot showers, a laundry room, dump station, and a store. Recreational facilities include a recreation room and pavilion, volleyball, basketball, badminton, miniature golf, horseshoes, and canoe, rowboat, and paddleboat rentals. Leashed pets are permitted.

Reservations, fees: Reservations are accepted. Sites are $25–38 a night.

Open: May 1–October 30.

Directions: From the intersection of U.S. 44 and Highway 116 near Harmony, drive 1.5 miles south on Highway 116, then bear right on Snake Hill Road and continue 2.75 miles west to the campground on the left.

Contact: Holiday Acres Campground, 591 Snake Hill Road, North Scituate, RI 02857, 401/934-0789.

7 CAMP PONAGANSET

🚶 ♒ 🎣 🚤 🐕 ♿ 🚐 ⛺

Rating: 6

West of Providence

Ponaganset is in the northwestern part of the state in high, rolling rural countryside. It's not far from Jerimoth Hill, which at 812 feet is the highest peak in Rhode Island. Also nearby is the Ponaganset Public Fishing Area, where anglers can cast a line for trout in a swift, woodsy stream. The campground specializes in seasonal camping for elderly and retired campers, so if you fit that description, this just might be the place you're looking for.

Campsites, facilities: There are 40 sites for tents and RVs with full or partial hookups. Each site has a picnic table and fireplace. Flush toilets, hot showers, laundry facilities, a dump station, and a store are provided. Recreational facilities include a swimming pool, tennis court, ball field, and recreation room. Leashed pets are permitted.

Reservations, fees: Reservations are accepted. Sites are $20 a night.

Open: April 15–October 15.

Directions: From the intersection of U.S. 44 and Highway 102 in Chepachet, drive four miles south on Highway 102 to the campground on the left (east) side of the road.

Contact: Camp Ponaganset, P.O. Box 399, Chepachet, RI 02814, 401/647-7377.

8 DYER WOODS NUDIST CAMPGROUND

🚶 🐕 🚐

Rating: 6

Near Foster

Looking for a place where you can shed your clothes and your inhibitions? At this campground set in the rolling farm country of northwest Rhode Island, you can join fellow free spirits in an environment that allows you to discover who you really are underneath that external veneer. While you're in Foster, be sure to stop by the Foster Townhouse at 180 Howard Hill Road. Constructed in 1796, the building is the nation's oldest house still used for that New England Yankee tradition, the town meeting.

Campsites, facilities: There are 16 sites for RVs with water and electric hookups. Each site has a picnic table and fireplace. Facilities include flush toilets, hot showers, laundry facilities, a dump station, and a store. Also provided are a hot tub and sauna, heated clubhouse, hiking trails, volleyball and badminton nets, and a bocce court. Leashed pets are permitted.

Reservations, fees: Reservations are accepted. Sites are $15 a night.

Open: May 1–October 1.

Directions: From the junction of U.S. 6 and Boswell Road near the Connecticut border, drive 1.5 miles south on Boswell Road. Turn left, travel .5 mile east on South Killingly Road, then turn right on Johnson Road and go one mile south to the campground.

Contact: Dyer Woods Nudist Campground, 114 Johnson Road, Foster, RI 02825, 401/397-3007, website: www.sunclad.com/dyerwoods.

⑨ GINNY-B FAMILY CAMPGROUND

🚶 🏊 🎣 🚣 🐕 🚐

Rating: 5

Near Foster

The wooded, rolling countryside that characterizes western Rhode Island surrounds Ginny-B Family Campground, which lies not too far from the Connecticut border. Swimmers can take a dip in the pool on the grounds or plunge into a pond, while others cast their fishing lines into the water. For those who want to get in a few rounds of golf, there's a public course conveniently located adjacent to this large, grassy campground.

Campsites, facilities: There are 200 sites for RVs,

50 with full hookups and 150 with water and electric hookups. Each site has a picnic table and fireplace. Flush toilets, hot showers, laundry facilities, a dump station, and a store are on the grounds. Recreational facilities include a swimming pool, canoe rentals, teen and adult recreation rooms, a pond for swimming and fishing, volleyball and basketball courts, and horseshoe pits. Leashed pets are permitted.

Reservations, fees: Reservations are accepted. Sites are $22–27 a night.

Open: May 1–September 30.

Directions: From the intersection of U.S. 6 and Highway 94 near the Connecticut border, drive 3.25 miles west on U.S. 6, then turn left on Cucumber Hill Road and travel another 3.5 miles south. At Harrington Road, turn left and drive .5 mile east to the campground.

Contact: Ginny-B Family Campground, 46 Johnson Road, Foster, RI 02825, 401/397-9477, website: www.ricampgrounds.com/ginny-b.htm.

⑩ WHIPPOORWILL HILL FAMILY CAMPGROUND

🚶 🏊 🎣 🚣 🐕 🚐 ⛺

Rating: 6

West of Scituate Reservoir near the George B. Parker Woodland

Tall pine trees provide shade for the sites at Whippoorwill Hill, a family campground set in the rolling, wooded hills of the state's west-central region. Nearby is the George B. Parker Woodland, a 550-acre preserve owned by the Audubon Society of Rhode Island. The preserve's land was set aside for the study of historical archaeology, and hikers will discover old building foundations, mill ruins, and other points of interest. Hikers enjoy the trails that cut through the woodlands, running up and over some moderately steep slopes and alongside streams that are punctuated with deep pools and waterfalls.

Campsites, facilities: There are 150 sites for tents and RVs, 70 with full hookups, 75 with water and electric hookups, and 10 with none.

Each site has a picnic table and fireplace. Flush toilets, hot showers, laundry facilities, a dump station, and a store are provided. Recreational facilities include a spring-fed pond for swimming, recreation room, playing field, miniature golf, volleyball and badminton nets, and horseshoe pits. Leashed pets are permitted.

Reservations, fees: Reservations are accepted. Sites are $24–28 a night.

Open: April 15–September 30.

Directions: From the southern junction of Highways 14 and 102 in Foster, drive two miles east on Old Plainfield Pike to the campground.

Contact: Whippoorwill Hill Family Campground, 106 Old Plainfield Pike, Foster, RI 02825, 401/539-7011, website: www.ricampgrounds.com/whippoorwill_hill.com.

11 HICKORY RIDGE FAMILY CAMPGROUND
🏕 ⛲ 🎣 🚤 🐕 🚙

Rating: 5

West of Scituate Reservoir near the George B. Parker Woodland

The full-hookup sites at Hickory Ridge are rented primarily by seasonal campers from the area. The campground is located in rolling, rural countryside near the George B. Parker Woodland, a 550-acre state-owned tract where visitors can hike through abandoned farms on miles of trails. These routes wander past old building foundations, mills, and other artifacts of early colonial settlement. A nearby lake is open for fishing and boating.

Campsites, facilities: There are 200 sites for RVs, 60 with full hookups and 140 with water and electric hookups. Each site has a picnic table and fireplace. Facilities include flush toilets, hot showers, laundry machines, a dump station, and a camp store. Recreational facilities include a swimming pool, lake for fishing, recreation room, volleyball and badminton nets, and horseshoe pits. Leashed pets are permitted.

Reservations, fees: Reservations are accepted. Sites are $26 a night.

Open: May 1–October 10.

Directions: From the intersection of Highways 117 and 102 west of Coventry, drive 1.25 miles north on Highway 102/Victory Highway to the campground on the right (east) side of the road.

Contact: Hickory Ridge Family Campground, 584 Victory Highway, Greene, RI 02827, 401/397-7474, website: www.angelfire.com/ma2/hickoryridgecamps.

12 COLWELL'S CAMPGROUND
🏕 ⛲ 🎣 🚤 🐕 🚙 ⛺

Rating: 5

On Flat River Reservoir in Coventry

Campsites for tenters and RVers line the shore of Flat River Reservoir, also known as Johnson's Pond. Set almost smack-dab in the center of the state, this long and sinuous reservoir has a boat ramp and is open for fishing, swimming, and waterskiing. When in Coventry, be sure to visit the home of General Nathanael Greene at 50 Taft Street, George Washington's second-in-command during the American Revolution. Also within the town's boundaries is the George B. Parker Woodland, an Audubon Society of Rhode Island wildlife refuge encompassing 550 acres of woodlands, fields, and streams. The Audubon Society maintains hiking trails, conducts natural history programs and field trips, and offers maps and field guides for self-guided archaeology hikes.

Campsites, facilities: There are 75 sites for tents and RVs with partial hookups. Each site has a picnic table and fireplace. Flush toilets, hot showers, laundry facilities, a dump station, and a store are provided. Leashed pets are permitted.

Reservations, fees: Reservations are accepted. Sites are $17–23 a night.

Open: May 1–September 30.

Directions: From I-95 near Warwick, take Exit 10 and drive west on Highway 117 for 8.5 miles to the campground in Coventry.

Contact: Linda Derocher, Colwell's Campground, 119 Peckham Lane, Coventry, RI 02816, 401/397-4614.

13 WESTWOOD FAMILY CAMPGROUND

Rating: 5

Near the Quidnick Reservoir

Sports lovers will feel at home here. The park is located along the Quidnick Reservoir, which offers ample opportunities to engage in such water sports as swimming, boating, canoeing, windsurfing, sailing, and fishing. And for golf aficionados, there's a golf course just down the road. If that's not enough activity to wear you out, stop in at Lakeview Amusements on Tiogue Avenue in Coventry, where you will find a 19-hole miniature golf course as well as hardball and softball batting cages.

Campsites, facilities: There are 70 sites for tents and RVs, 60 with water and electric hookups and 10 with none. Each site has a picnic table and fireplace. Flush toilets, hot showers, and a dump station are provided. Recreational facilities include a recreation hall, soccer and softball fields, horseshoes, and tennis, volleyball, and basketball courts. Leashed pets are permitted.

Reservations, fees: Reservations are accepted. Sites are $95 a week.

Open: April 15–September 30.

Directions: From Coventry, drive four miles west on Harkney Hill Road to the campground.

Contact: Westwood Family Campground, 2093 Harkney Hill Road, Coventry, RI 02816, 401/397-7779.

14 PINE VALLEY RV CAMPGROUND

Rating: 6

On the Connecticut border near the Arcadia Management Area

The park is located just east of the Connecticut border within a network of public lands that includes the Arcadia Management Area and Beach Pond State Park. This rural region is covered with rolling hills, woods, rocky ledges, and several lakes, three of which are adjacent to the campground—convenient for folks who enjoy fishing, boating, swimming, and canoeing. The surrounding terrain is simply great for hiking, cross-country skiing, and mountain biking.

Campsites, facilities: There are 70 sites for tents and RVs, 20 with water and electric hookups and 50 with none. Each site has a picnic table and fireplace. Flush toilets, hot showers, laundry facilities, sewage dumping service, and a store are provided. Recreational facilities include a swimming pool, tennis court, game field, recreation hall with fireplace, volleyball, and horseshoes on the property, in addition to three nearby lakes. Leashed pets are permitted.

Reservations, fees: Reservations are accepted. Sites are $10 a night.

Open: Year-round.

Directions: From the junction of Highways 3 and 165 in Austin, go 5.25 miles west on Highway 165. Turn right on Bailey Pond Road and continue north to the campground.

Contact: Pine Valley RV Campground, 64 Bailey Pond Road, West Greenwich, RI 02817, 401/397-7972.

15 OAK EMBERS CAMPGROUND

Rating: 7

On the Connecticut border near the Arcadia Management Area

Oak Embers is located just east of the Connecticut border and directly adjacent to the 13,000-acre Arcadia Management Area, the state's largest tract of public wildlands. That puts campers within striking distance of two popular swimming lakes and great freshwater fishing and boating, as well as 40 woodland trails for hiking and mountain biking. This part of the state is absolutely beautiful, featuring rolling, wooded hills and high rocky ledges. Note that the campground is open nearly year-round for those who wish to explore this part of the country during the off-season, maybe by strapping on their cross-country skis.

Campsites, facilities: There are 60 sites for tents and RVs, 37 with water and electric hookups and 23 with none. Each site has a picnic table and fireplace. Flush toilets, hot showers, laundry facilities, a dump station, and a store are provided. Recreational facilities include a swimming pool, recreation room, pavilion, playing field, volleyball, badminton, and horseshoes. Leashed pets are permitted.

Reservations, fees: Reservations are accepted. Sites are $25 a night.

Open: November 1–September 30.

Directions: From the junction of Highways 3 and 165 in Austin, drive 5.25 miles west on Highway 165. Turn right on Escoheag Hill Road and continue 1.5 miles north to the campground.

Contact: Oak Embers Campground, 219 Escoheag Hill Road, West Greenwich, RI 02817, 401/397-4042, website: www.oakembers.com.

16 LEGRAND G. REYNOLDS HORSEMEN'S CAMPING AREA

Rating: 7

On the Connecticut border near the Arcadia Management Area

A one-of-a-kind place, this campground welcomes only people with horses. Riders may practice with their mounts in the show ring or explore the extensive trail system within the campground proper. Or head into the adjacent Arcadia Management Area—Rhode Island's largest public landholding at 13,000 acres—with its 65-mile network of trails. When you or your horse need a break, Beach Pond State Park on the Rhode Island–Connecticut border is a good place for a refreshing swim. In other words, if you want to take an inexpensive vacation with your horse in tow, this might be the answer.

Campsites, facilities: There are 20 tent sites with picnic tables and fireplaces. Nonflush toilets and piped water are provided, as are a show ring and riding trails. Leashed pets are permitted.

Reservations, fees: Sites are available on a first-come, first-served basis, with a maximum stay of four days. The fee is $7 a night, plus $15 a day for use of the show ring.

Open: Year-round.

Directions: From I-95 near Austin, take Exit 5A and follow Highway 102 south. Turn right on Highway 3, travel south to Highway 165, and turn right again. After driving west for several miles, turn right (north) on Escoheag Hill Road and continue to the campground.

Contact: Legrand G. Reynolds Horsemen's Camping Area, 260 Arcadia Road, Hope Valley, RI 02832, 401/539-2356 or 401/277-1157.

17 WAWALOAM CAMPGROUND

Rating: 6

Just east of the Arcadia Management Area

Yet another rather large campground in the west-central part of Rhode Island, Wawaloam is located pretty close to the Arcadia Management Area, the state's largest public landholding. There is good fishing, hiking, boating, and bicycling in the area, and the park is also within easy reach of the state's renowned sandy beaches.

Campsites, facilities: There are 287 sites, 140 with full hookups and 147 with water and electric. Each site has a picnic table and fireplace. Facilities include flush toilets, hot showers, a dump station, laundry room, and a store. Recreational facilities include a swimming pool, recreation room, pavilion, miniature golf, a sports field, volleyball, badminton, and horseshoes. Leashed pets are permitted.

Reservations, fees: Reservations are accepted. Sites are $30–35 a night.

Open: Year-round.

Directions: From I-95 near Austin, take Exit

5A and drive three miles south on Highway 102. Turn right on Town Hall Road, drive .5 mile southwest, and then take Gardiner Road south for two miles to the campground.
Contact: Wawaloam Campground, Exeter, RI 02822, 401/294-3039, website: www.wawaloam.com.

18 PEEPER POND CAMPGROUND

Rating: 5

West of Exeter

Peeper Pond lies hidden away in the woods of central Rhode Island, yet it is still close to the attractions of Providence, the coastal beaches, and the Great Swamp Management Area. While you're here, be sure to check out the Fisherville Brook Wildlife Refuge: miles of hiking trails at the state's newest Audubon Society preserve wind through 700 acres of beautiful forests, ponds, and waterfalls. Also in Exeter is the Tomaquag Indian Memorial Museum, filled with artifacts, information, and exhibits about local tribes.

Campsites, facilities: There are 35 sites for tents and RVs, 29 with water and electric hookups and six with none. Each site has a picnic table and fireplace. Flush toilets, hot showers, a dump station, camp store, volleyball and badminton nets, and horseshoes are provided. Leashed pets are permitted.

Reservations, fees: Reservations are accepted. Sites are $25 a night.

Open: May 1–September 30.

Directions: From the junction of Highways 102 and 2 in Exeter, drive 3.5 miles south on Highway 2 to Mail Road, turn right, and drive 1.5 miles west. Turn right when you reach Liberty Church Road and continue .8 mile north to the campground.

Contact: Peeper Pond Campground, P.O. Box 503, Exeter, RI 02822, 401/294-5540, website: www.ricampgrounds.com/peeper_pond.htm.

19 WHISPERING PINES CAMPGROUND

Rating: 7

Near the Connecticut border in Hope Valley

A 50-acre grove of towering pine trees surrounds this campground. It's located in a rural part of the state, yet is close to many major attractions. Just 20 minutes from Rhode Island's famed ocean beaches, the campground is also within easy reach of the Arcadia Management Area and within 12 miles of the Mashantucket Pequot Indian tribe's Foxwoods Casino, the nation's largest and most lucrative gambling establishment. Campers can fish for trout in a stocked brook, plunk a canoe into the nearby Wood River, or head into the Arcadia preserve or Beach Pond State Park for a few hours of hiking, biking, or swimming.

Campsites, facilities: There are 180 sites for tents and RVs. Each site has a picnic table and fireplace. Flush toilets, hot showers, laundry facilities, a dump station, and a store are provided. Recreational facilities include a sports field, swimming pond, canoe rentals, a recreation room, tennis court, shuffleboard courts, volleyball, basketball, badminton, and horseshoes. Leashed pets are permitted.

Reservations, fees: Reservations are accepted. Sites are $24–32 a night, depending on the season.

Open: March 1–December 31.

Directions: From I-95, take Exit 3B and drive three miles west on Highway 138. Turn right on Sawmill Road and go .5 mile north to the campground.

Contact: Whispering Pines Campground, P.O. Box 425, 41 Sawmill Road, Hope Valley, RI 02832, 401/539-7011, website: www.whisperingpines.com.

20 GREENWOOD HILL CAMPGROUND

Rating: 5

Near the Arcadia Management Area in Hope Valley

This campground is located in the wooded, rolling hills of western Rhode Island, not far from the hiking trails, swimming beaches, and mountain biking routes of the 13,000-acre Arcadia Management Area, Rhode Island's largest public landholding. The management area is a hilly, rocky upland laced with streams and bejeweled with waterfalls. More than 65 miles of hiking trails make it a very popular destination for outdoor recreationalists throughout the year. Anglers will also want to check out the fishing at the Rockville Management Public Fishing Area, with accessible shoreline on both Blue and Ashville Ponds.

Campsites, facilities: There are 50 sites for tents and RVs, 13 with full hookups and 37 with water and electric hookups. Each site has a picnic table and fireplace. Flush toilets, hot showers, a dump station, and a store are provided. Recreational facilities include a swimming pond, playing field, recreation room, volleyball, basketball, badminton, and horseshoes. Leashed pets are permitted.

Reservations, fees: Reservations are accepted. Sites are $24–28 a night.

Open: May 15–October 15.

Directions: From I-95, take Exit 3B and drive 3.5 miles west on Highway 138 to the campground.

Contact: Greenwood Hill Campground, Box 141, 13A Newberry Lane, Hope Valley, RI 02832, 401/539-7154.

21 FRONTIER FAMILY CAMPER PARK

Rating: 3

Northeast of Westerly in southern Rhode Island

Busy I-95 is less than a minute away from Frontier Family Camper Park, making this camp-ground in the southwest corner of Rhode Island near the Connecticut border a good choice for those who just want a convenient place to stop as they travel through the area. Nearby are western Rhode Island's sand beaches, where you can play in the surf or go deep-sea fishing. And just over the state line in Connecticut is the Foxwoods Casino, owned and operated by the Mashantucket Pequot Indians.

Campsites, facilities: There are 218 sites for RVs, 100 with partial hookups and 118 with none. Each site has a picnic table and fireplace. Flush toilets, hot showers, laundry facilities, a dump station, and a store are provided. Recreational facilities include a swimming pool, canoe rentals, a recreation room, volleyball, basketball, badminton, and horseshoes. Leashed pets are permitted.

Reservations, fees: Reservations are accepted. Rates are $20–25 a night.

Open: May 1–October 1.

Directions: From the intersection of I-95 and Highway 3 near the Connecticut border, drive .1 mile south on Highway 3 to Frontier Road. Turn left (east) on Frontier Road and follow signs to the campground.

Contact: Scott and Debbie Thompson, Frontier Family Camper Park, RR 1, P.O. Box 180A, Maxon Hill Road, Ashaway, RI 02804, 401/377-4510.

22 HOLLY TREE CAMPER PARK

Rating: 3

Northeast of Westerly in southern Rhode Island

Set up camp at Holly Tree Camper Park and you'll be just inland from the great swimming, surfing, and fishing beaches of the southern Rhode Island coast. An added attraction for those who enjoy games of chance is the campground's proximity to the Foxwoods Casino, the country's largest, operated by the Mashantucket Pequot Indians just across the state line in Connecticut.

Campsites, facilities: There are 139 sites for

RVs with full, partial, and no hookups. Each site has a picnic table and fireplace. Flush toilets, hot showers, laundry facilities, a dump station, recreation room, and a camp store are provided. Leashed pets are permitted.

Reservations, fees: Reservations are accepted. Sites are $17–22 a night.

Open: May 15–October 1.

Directions: From the intersection of I-95 and Highway 3 near the Connecticut border, drive south on Highway 3 to Ashaway. Turn left on Highway 216 and travel two miles southeast to the campground.

Contact: Anthony and Marie Patrizzo, Holly Tree Camper Park, P.O. Box 61, 109 Ashaway Road, Ashaway, RI 02804, 401/596-2766.

23 CARD'S CAMP

Rating: 7
Just south of the Great Swamp Management Area

Card's Camp is a very large trailer park with no sites for tent campers. Just to the north is the Great Swamp Management Area, a 3,000-acre preserve that includes Worden Pond, the state's largest freshwater lake. Covering some 1,000 acres, the pond is a popular spot for bird-watching, fishing, and canoeing. Several good canoe routes and hiking trails weave their way through the preserve. This is also one of the state's most popular hunting areas for deer, grouse, waterfowl, and small game. A mere 10 minutes away from Card's Camp are the long sandy beaches of Rhode Island's south coast, which attract surfers, anglers, swimmers, and sunbathers alike. Another boon for bird-watchers is that the campground is close to several other federal wildlife refuges and conservation areas situated along the Rhode Island shore.

Campsites, facilities: There are 278 trailer-only sites with water and electric hookups. Each site has a picnic table and fireplace. Flush toilets, hot showers, and a dump station are provided. Leashed pets are permitted.

Reservations, fees: Reservations are accepted. Sites are $26 a night.

Open: May 1–September 30.

Directions: From the intersection of Highway 110 and Worden Pond Road in Tuckertown, drive a short distance west on Worden Pond Road to the campground on the left (south).

Contact: Card's Camp, 1065 Worden Pond Road, Wakefield, RI 02879, 401/783-7158, website: www.cardscamp.com.

24 WORDEN POND FAMILY CAMPGROUND

Rating: 7
In Wakefield, just south of the Great Swamp Management Area

Worden Pond is the state's largest freshwater lake—a thousand-acre gem open to boating, canoeing, fishing, and waterskiing—and this campground is situated near its southern shore. Campers enjoy water access and a sandy beach. Another plus is that the Great Swamp Management Area, a 3,000-acre nature preserve encompassing much of the land abutting the lake's northern end, is nearby waiting to be explored. This is also where the Indian uprising known as King Philip's War came to a bloody end in 1675. The campground is within a 10-minute drive of many of the state's finest ocean beaches and within 20 minutes of the deep-sea fishing and excursion boats based near Point Judith.

Campsites, facilities: There are 200 sites for tents and RVs, 145 with water and electric hookups and 55 with none. Each site has a picnic table and fireplace. Flush toilets, hot showers, a dump station, and a store are provided. Recreational facilities include a lake, recreation room, pavilion, playground, volleyball, badminton, and horseshoes. Leashed pets are permitted.

Reservations, fees: Reservations are accepted. Sites are $22–28 a night.

Open: May 1–October 15.

Directions: From the junction of U.S. 1 and Highway 110 in Perryville, drive two miles north on Highway 110, then turn left on Worden Pond Road and continue one mile west to the campground.

Contact: Worden Pond Family Campground, 416A Worden Pond Road, Wakefield, RI 02879, 401/789-9113.

25 BURLINGAME STATE PARK

🏃 ⛵ 🛶 🎣 🚐 ⛺

Rating: 6

Near the ocean in Charlestown

The biggest of Rhode Island's state parks is 2,100-acre Burlingame State Park. Its centerpiece and main attraction is Watchaug Pond, covering some 600 acres and boasting a sandy swimming beach. Small motorboats and canoes are permitted on the water, and fishing for trout is a popular pursuit. Also within park boundaries is the Kimball Wildlife Refuge, a 29-acre preserve on Watchaug Pond that is overseen by the Audubon Society of Rhode Island. A trail system winds around the area, affording good vantage points for spotting waterfowl and migrating birds. For saltwater swimmers, boaters, and deep-sea fishing enthusiasts, several Atlantic coast beaches are a short drive away. The Ninigret National Wildlife Refuge and Park is also within close driving distance; for more details on activities there, see the next listing for the Ninigret Conservation Area.

Campsites, facilities: There are 755 sites for tents and RVs, all without hookups. Each site has a picnic table and fireplace. Flush toilets, hot showers, a grocery store, and a dump station are provided. Recreational facilities include a recreation room on the grounds, a swimming beach and boat ramp on Watchaug Pond, and hiking trails in the park. No pets are allowed.

Reservations, fees: Sites are available on a first-come, first-served basis, with a two-week maximum stay. Fees are $12 a night for Rhode Island residents and $15 a night for nonresidents.

Open: April 15–October 31.

Directions: From Charlestown, travel southwest on U.S. 1 for four miles. Turn right (north) on Cookestown Road and follow the signs to the park.

Contact: The Rhode Island Division of Parks and Recreation, 2321 Hartford Avenue, Johnston, RI 02919, 401/322-7994 or 401/322-7337, website: www.riparks.com.

26 NINIGRET CONSERVATION AREA

🏃 ⛵ 🛶 🎣 ❌ 🚐

Rating: 9

On the beach near Charlestown

Camping on a spit of sand at the ocean's edge is what people do at the Ninigret Conservation Area. With a campsite bordered on one side by Ninigret Pond (the largest saltwater pond in the state) and on the other side by the Atlantic Ocean, a water lover can't go wrong. The surf casting, swimming, ocean kayaking— and anything else you like to do near the ocean— are all terrific. This place is far from the madding crowds, a real haven.

Campsites, facilities: There are 20 primitive sites for self-contained camping units only. Tenting is not permitted. The campsites are located in two areas accessed by a sand trail requiring a four-wheel-drive vehicle. Pack in your water. No pets are allowed.

Reservations, fees: Sites are available on a first-come, first-served basis. The maximum stay is four days, with a three-day break in between stays. Fees are $12 a night for Rhode Island residents and $15 a night for nonresidents.

Open: Mid-April–October 31.

Directions: From Charlestown, travel south on U.S. 1 for approximately five miles. Turn left on East Beach Road and continue to the end of the road. Access to the camping area is to the left.

Contact: The Rhode Island Division of Parks and Recreation, 2321 Hartford Avenue, Johnston, RI 02919, 401/322-0450, website: www. riparks.com.

27 CHARLESTOWN BREACHWAY

Rating: 8

On the beach near Charlestown

This campground is basically a sand parking lot near the ocean. With vast areas of wetlands, a large saltwater pond, numerous small islands, and Block Island Sound all surrounding the breachway, birders will find plenty of opportunities to observe waterfowl and migrating species. The swimming is terrific on either the pond or the sound side. And for surf casters, this is nothing but paradise. While it would be difficult to imagine why someone would want to leave this spot, plenty of recreational options are available nearby. A hike in the Kimball Wildlife Refuge, a visit to a shoreline community such as Matunuck, and a deep-sea fishing excursion are just three easy day-trip possibilities. The only downside is the plethora of cheap seaside development that you must pass on the drive to the breachway.

Campsites, facilities: There are 75 sites for self-contained camping units only, all without hookups. There are no tent sites. Flush toilets and water are provided. For recreation, there's a swimming beach and a boat ramp. No pets are allowed.

Reservations, fees: Sites are available on a first-come, first-served basis. The maximum stay is one week, with a four-day break in between stays. Fees are $12 a night for Rhode Island residents and $15 a night for nonresidents.

Open: April 15–October 31.

Directions: From Charlestown, travel south on the Charlestown Beach Road. When the road ends, turn right and proceed to the breachway and the campground.

Contact: The Rhode Island Division of Parks and Recreation, 2321 Hartford Avenue, Johnston, RI 02919, 401/364-7000, website: www.riparks.com.

28 WAKAMO PARK RESORT

Rating: 7

South of Wakefield near the ocean

Wakamo Park Resort enjoys a prime location on the water near East Matunuck State Beach, one of the fine stretches of sand and surf that have made Rhode Island a favorite vacation spot for beach lovers. Here you can spend your days clamming, fishing, swimming, or boating. Be sure to visit the Great Swamp Management Area while you're here in South Kingston. One of the state's great public lands, this is where the New England–wide Indian uprising known as King Philip's War came to a bloody end in 1675. The waterways of the preserve offer good canoeing and fine trout fishing.

Campsites, facilities: There are 30 trailer sites with full hookups. A gift store, dock space, paddleboat and canoe rentals, a game room, and planned activities are available. No pets are allowed.

Reservations, fees: Reservations are accepted. Sites are $45 a night.

Open: April 15–October 15.

Directions: From the junction of U.S. 1 and Succotash Road in South Kingston, turn south on Succotash Road and follow signs for East Matunuck State Beach. You will find the campground right next to the beach.

Contact: Wakamo Park Resort, 697 Succotash Road, South Kingston, RI 02879, 401/783-6688.

29 FISHERMEN'S MEMORIAL STATE PARK

Rating: 6

Near the ocean in Narragansett

The well-manicured campground at Fishermen's Memorial State Park has an almost suburban feel, with its tract neighborhoods connected by winding asphalt lanes. From the park, you only have to stroll a short distance to find great swimming spots at Wheeler Memorial Beach or Salty Brine State Beach. If you want to spend a day on Block Island to the south—with its beaches, lighthouse, and national wildlife refuge—head to nearby Galilee, where you can hop a ferry. Or you can explore Point Judith Pond and the Galilee Bird Sanctuary. Fishing enthusiasts might want to take a deep-sea fishing trip or cast from the shore or the state piers. One other site that's well worth a visit is the octagonal brick lighthouse built in 1816 at Point Judith.

Campsites, facilities: There are 182 sites for tents and RVs, 40 with full hookups, 107 with water and electric hookups, and 35 with none. Facilities include flush toilets, hot showers, picnic tables, a dump station, tennis and basketball courts, horseshoe pits, and a children's playground. No pets are allowed.

Reservations, fees: Reservations are available by mail only. You must submit your request on an official form, available at the park, and it must be postmarked no earlier than January 14. Sites are $12–15 a night for Rhode Island residents, and $17–20 a night for nonresidents.

Open: Year-round.

Directions: From the intersection of Highway 108 and U.S. 1 in Narragansett, travel south on Highway 108/Old Point Judith Road to the park.

Contact: The Rhode Island Division of Parks and Recreation, 1011 Old Point Judith Road, Narragansett, RI 02882, 401/789-8374, website: www.riparks.com.

30 BREAKWATER VILLAGE CAMPGROUND

Rating: 7

Near the ocean in Narragansett

Breakwater Village Campground is the place to go if you love surf, sand, and sun. Located on Ocean Road in Narragansett, the campground offers easy access to the town's beach-

es, all five of them. Narragansett is a great summer resort community, one that can satisfy the needs of various beachgoers, from families with kids to surf casters looking for a little solitude. Should you tire of the beach, head to the town's north end to check out Canochet Farm, a 19th-century working farm with a historic cemetery dating back to 1700, a fitness trail, nature trails, picnic areas, and the South County Museum. Also be sure to visit the Point Judith Lighthouse, erected in 1816 on the site of a tower beacon maintained during the American Revolution.

Campsites, facilities: There are 38 sites for RVs with partial hookups. A dump station and a snack bar are provided. Leashed pets are permitted.

Reservations, fees: Reservations are accepted. Sites are $35 a night.

Open: April 15–October 31.

Directions: From the junction of U.S. 1A and Ocean Road in Narragansett, drive approximately four miles south on Ocean Road to the campground.

Contact: Breakwater Village Campground, P.O. Box 563, Narragansett, RI 02882, 401/783-9527.

31 LONG COVE MARINA CAMPSITES

Rating: 6

On a saltwater cove in Narragansett

Long Cove is a saltwater bay fed by the Atlantic Ocean. From this campground, you can launch your boat and be out on the open sea within a matter of minutes. Or stick close to shore if you enjoy surf casting or saltwater swimming. This is a very attractive campground with a sampling of sites in the woods, open fields, and along the water. Many of the sites are either right on the waterfront or at least afford water views. This part of the state is known for its great beaches, interesting villages, and spectacular ocean scenery. Be sure to visit the lighthouse at Point Judith, about four miles south of the campground.

Campsites, facilities: There are 180 sites for tents and RVs. Flush toilets, hot showers, picnic tables, fireplaces, and a dump station are provided. There's also a boat launch, ramp, and docks. Leashed pets are permitted.

Reservations, fees: Reservations are accepted. Sites are $24–26 a night.

Open: May 15–October 15.

Directions: From the intersection of U.S. 1 and Highway 108, drive one mile south on Highway 108/Old Point Judith Road to the campground.

Contact: George And Lillian Kivisto, Long Cove Marina Campsites, 325 Old Point Judith Road, Narragansett, RI 02882, 401/783-4902.

32 FORT GETTY RECREATION AREA

Rating: 7

On Conanicut Island in Jamestown, in Narragansett Bay

Fort Getty Recreation Area is located near the historic town of Jamestown on Conanicut Island in Narragansett Bay. Tall suspension bridges link this tiny island with the mainland to the west and with the city of Newport on the island of Rhode Island to the east. From your campsite at the recreation area, you are able to savor spectacular views of Rhode Island's Atlantic coastline across the water. Equally stunning views are to be had at nearby Beavertail State Park to the south. Water lovers are in their element here, with all the great shoreline access and plentiful swimming and boating opportunities close at hand. Be sure to visit the lighthouse at Beavertail Point at the southern tip of the island.

Campsites, facilities: There are 125 sites for tents and RVs, 100 with water and electric hookups and 25 with none. Each site has a picnic table and fireplace. Flush toilets, hot showers, a dump station, boat ramp, and fishing dock are provided. Leashed pets are permitted.

Reservations, fees: Reservations are not accepted. Sites are $20–25 a night.

Open: May 18–October 1.

Directions: Take either the Jamestown Bridge from the mainland or the Newport Bridge from Newport to Highway 138 and turn south onto North Main Road. Turn west onto Narragansett Avenue and then south onto Southwest Avenue, which merges into Beavertail Road. Continue to Fort Getty Road, turn right, and drive west to the campground.

Contact: Fort Getty Recreation Area, P.O. Box 377, Jamestown, RI 02835, 401/423-7264.

33 MEADOWLARK RV PARK

Rating: 8

In Middletown on Rhode Island

Meadowlark, a mobile home park for RVers only, is situated very close to the attractions of Newport, one of America's best known and perhaps most historic resort communities. From here, you can walk to the famous beaches of Newport, watch a tennis match at the Tennis Hall of Fame, hike the Cliff Walk past the mansions of 19th-century robber barons, peruse the myriad shops and boutiques on Bannister Wharf, and visit the harbor where, on and off for over a century, America's Cup races have been held. There's also a golf course nearby.

Campsites, facilities: There are 40 sites for RVs only, all with full hookups. Flush toilets, hot showers, picnic tables, fireplaces, a dump station, and an RV supply store are provided. Leashed pets are permitted.

Reservations, fees: Reservations are accepted. Sites are $25–30 a night.

Open: April 15–October 30.

Directions: From the Newport Bridge, drive 2.5 miles north on Highway 138, then turn right on Highway 138A and drive two miles south to Prospect Avenue. Continue .5 mile east to the campground on the right side of the road.

Contact: Joe and Mae Rideout, Meadowlark

RV Park, 132 Prospect Avenue, Middletown, RI 02840, 401/846-9455.

34 PARADISE MOBILE HOME PARK

🧍‍♂️ 🏊 🎣 🚣 🍴 🚐

Rating: 8

In Middletown on Rhode Island

This mobile home park offers a great location in the heart of the Newport resort area, within walking distance of beaches, shops, wharves, and turn-of-the-century mansions. For more information about what makes this area so special, see the previous listing for Meadowlark RV Park.

Campsites, facilities: There are 16 sites for RVs with full hookups. Tents are not allowed, and only self-contained units may use this park. Flush toilets, hot showers, and picnic tables are provided. No pets are allowed.

Reservations, fees: Reservations are accepted. Sites are $32 a night.

Open: May 1–October 15.

Directions: From the intersection of Highways 138A and 214 in Middletown, drive .25 mile north on Highway 138A to the campground.

Contact: Paradise Mobile Home Park, 265 Prospect Avenue, Middletown, RI 02842, 401/847-1500.

35 MELVILLE POND CAMPGROUND

🧍‍♂️ 🏊 🎣 🚣 🛖 🐕 🚐 ⛺

Rating: 6

In Portsmouth on Rhode Island

Ⓕ Owned and operated by the city of Portsmouth, Melville Pond is set at the northern end of Rhode Island in Narragansett Bay and offers campers easy water access. There's a nearby lake where you can spend some time swimming, canoeing, or boating with an electric motor (no gas-powered craft are allowed). The campground is pretty close to some interesting historical sites, including Butts Hill Fort, the site of the only major land battle of the American Revolution to be fought in Rhode Island. Look for the Memorial to Black Soldiers, dedicated to the men of the First Rhode Island Regiment, composed mainly of African-American soldiers, who made a heroic stand against British troops during that 1778 battle.

Campsites, facilities: There are 128 sites for tents and RVs. Flush toilets, hot showers, picnic tables, and fireplaces are provided. Recreational facilities include volleyball nets, a playground, a playing field, and hiking trails. Leashed pets are permitted.

Reservations, fees: Reservations are accepted. Sites are $18–30 a night.

Open: April 1–November 1.

Directions: From the Newport Bridge, drive north on Highway 138 to Highway 114 and continue north toward Portsmouth. Turn left on Stringham Road, go .5 mile west, then turn right on Sullivan Road and proceed another .5 mile north to the campground. If you're entering the island from the north, from the junction of Highways 24 and 114 in Portsmouth, drive 1.7 miles south on Highway 114, then turn right on Stringham Road and proceed as above.

Contact: Melville Pond Campground, 181 Bradford Avenue, Portsmouth, RI 02871, 401/849-8212.

Connecticut

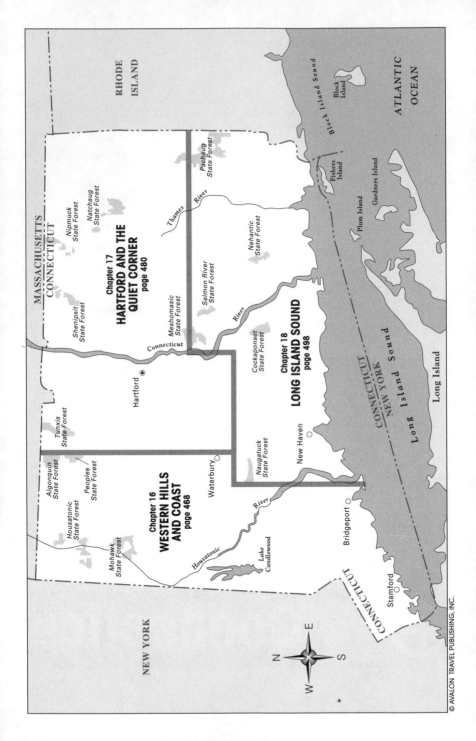

RHODE ISLAND

MASSACHUSETTS
CONNECTICUT

NEW YORK

ATLANTIC OCEAN

Block Island Sound

Block Island

Fishers Island

Gardners Island

Plum Island

Long Island Sound

Long Island

CONNECTICUT
NEW YORK

CONNECTICUT

Pachaug State Forest

Nipmuck State Forest

Natchaug State Forest

Thames River

Nehantic State Forest

Chapter 17
HARTFORD AND THE QUIET CORNER
page 480

Shenipsit State Forest

Salmon River State Forest

Meshomasic State Forest

Connecticut

River

Cockaponset State Forest

Chapter 18
LONG ISLAND SOUND
page 498

Hartford

Tunxis State Forest

Algonquin State Forest

Peoples State Forest

Housatonic State Forest

Mohawk State Forest

Chapter 16
WESTERN HILLS AND COAST
page 468

Waterbury

Naugatuck State Forest

New Haven

Housatonic River

Lake Candlewood

Bridgeport

Stamford

N E S W

© AVALON TRAVEL PUBLISHING, INC.

© ANDREW COLLINS

Western Hills and Coast

Western Hills and Coast

Connecticut is a place of wide contrasts, and this is never more evident than in the western part of the state. To the south, the wealthiest towns in New England are found along what's called the Gold Coast bordering New York City. You won't find much in the way of camping here in the land of multimillion-dollar homes, boutique shops, pricey eateries, and private beach communities.

Amble north toward the Berkshire Hills and you'll discover a Connecticut that feels more like old New England: rolling hills and farms, stone walls, covered bridges, and town greens punctuated by steepled churches. The campgrounds here are a mix of private and state-owned. Many are set beside ponds, lakes, and rivers, so you'll find ample opportunities for fishing, boating, and swimming. This is hill country—the Appalachian Trail passes through the most northwest corner, through state parks and forestlands as wild as any in southern New England. Check out Kent Falls and Macedonia Brook State Parks to experience the region's natural beauty. New Yorkers seeking country airs have discovered this area (among the local residents are Meryl Streep, Whoopi Goldberg, and Dustin Hoffman), but they are here for the quiet and the bucolic landscape, too, and have supported efforts to keep it that way. (As one local recently told me, "We used to milk cows. Now we milk New Yorkers.")

Visitors come mostly in summer and fall when temperatures are in the 70s and 80s and rainy spells only last a day or two. In the fall, the trees amazingly transform into a palette of reds and oranges, and visitors come by the thousands to leaf-peep. Throughout the spring, summer, and fall seasons, travelers can tour numerous well-preserved historic houses, hunt for antiques (the town of Woodbury has more than 50 antiques dealers alone), and find family fun. In Bristol, Lake Compounce Theme Park (822 Lake Avenue, 860/583-3300, website: www.lakecompounce.com), America's first amusement park, is set on a lovely lake and boasts all-new state-of-the-art thrill rides. Nature lovers head for White Memorial Foundation in Litchfield for some of the state's best birding (spring and fall migrations are best) and cozy lakefront campsites, while oenophiles taste of the grape at several of the nine wineries on Connecticut's Wine Trail (860/267-1399, website: www.ctwine.com)—all without ever leaving this corner of the state. From a base camp in the Western Hills, one can explore the culture of the Gold Coast (including several sites on Connecticut's Impressionist Art Trail, website: www.arttrail.org), cast a line in the fabled Housatonic River, or head for Lime Rock Park (479 Lime Rock Road, 860/435-5000, website: www.limerock.com), where Paul Newman and other auto racers hurl vintage cars around a scenic track— the oldest one in the country, in fact.

Connecticut's state parks and forests are open year-round, 8 A.M. to sunset. For site maps, regulations, etc., contact Outdoor Recreation, State Parks Division, Connecticut Department of Environmental Protection, 79 Elm Street, Hartford, CT 06106-5127, 860/424-3200, website www.dep.state.ct.us/stateparks/. For all camping reservations, call 877/688-CAMP (877/688-2267).

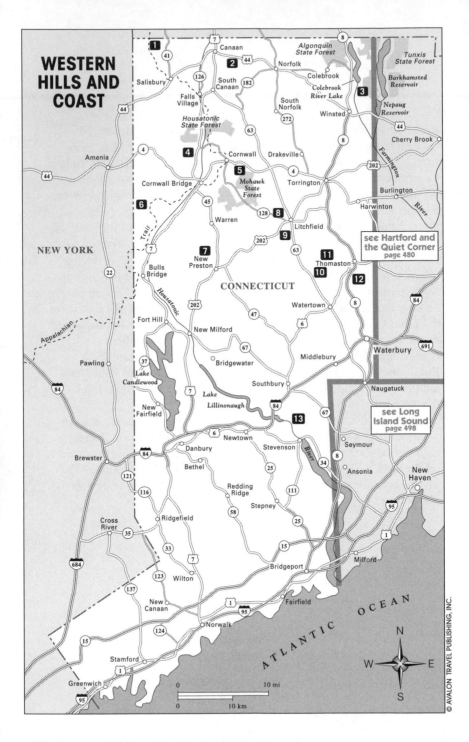

1 APPALACHIAN TRAIL

🏃 🏊 🎣 📷 ⛄ 🐕 ⛺

Rating: 10

In the northwest corner of Connecticut

The 52-mile stretch of the Appalachian Trail (AT) in Connecticut offers some of the best hiking opportunities in the state. Low-slung hills and mountains and rolling, wooded terrain are what you discover as you hike, along with occasional spectacular views of the Litchfield Hills. This area of the AT is noted for an abundance of water. Rivers, brooks, and small clear lakes provide plenty of water, scenic beauty, and good habitat for wildlife. Bald eagles have been spotted near the Housatonic River. In autumn, the colorful mix of hardwood trees (forests of oak and hickory) draw leaf-peepers, especially during peak foliage, usually around Columbus Day.

Campsites, facilities: There are about a dozen lean-tos on the Connecticut stretch of the Appalachian Trail, none of which are more than a moderate day hike apart. Primitive toilets are provided at each site. Current topographic maps show reliable and seasonal water sources. Macedonia Brook, Mohawk Mountain, and Housatonic Meadows State Park are fully staffed campsites along the trail.

Reservations, fees: Lean-to sites are available on a first-come, first-served basis. Sometimes a nominal nightly fee is charged in summer. Check with the Appalachian Trail Conference (see address below) for up-to-date fees and conditions.

Open: Year-round.

Directions: In the northwestern part of Connecticut, the Appalachian Trail extends northward from Kent to Salisbury before crossing into Massachusetts. There are easily accessible trailheads on U.S. 44 just east of Salisbury and on U.S. 7 north of Cornwall.

Contact: Appalachian Trail Conference, P.O. Box 807, Harpers Ferry, WV 25425-0807, 304/535-6331, website: www.appalachiantrail.org. This nonprofit group publishes 10 sectional guides, which are accompanied by topographic maps.

2 LONE OAK CAMPSITES

🏊 🎣 🐕 ♿ 🚐

Rating: 3

In East Canaan

Half of the 500 sites at this self-described destination resort are rented by seasonal campers who set up shop for the summer. All but just over 100 have full hookups, so there is a preponderance of RV campers. This is a busy place; every weekend the recreation director organizes a flurry of events from bingo and kids' arts and crafts to DJ dances, parades, talent shows, and live music. There's even a PA system and a cable access channel to help spread the word on activities. Should you need a respite from all the action, many natural attractions are close by, including the Appalachian Trail to the west off Highway 41, where you can hike a scenic 5.5-mile loop. Campers may want to wet a fishing line in the Blackberry River at the campground, or head north to Campbell Falls State Park, which is open for fishing and picnicking as well as hiking on a winding, wooded trail that leads to Campbell Falls.

Campsites, facilities: There are 500 RV sites in a mix of open and wooded settings. Cabins and trailers can be rented. Recreational facilities include two pools, a hot tub, pub, recreation halls, laundry facilities, an outdoor movie theater, hot showers, a market and deli, arcade, game fields, and sports courts. Also available on-site are dump stations, free cable TV hookups, and a propane filling station. Leashed pets are permitted.

Reservations, fees: Reservations are recommended. Sites with full hookups are $36–55. Weekly and seasonal rates are available. There is a three-night minimum stay during holiday weekends. Cabins and trailers are also available for rent.

Open: April 15–October 15.

Directions: From Highway 8 in Winsted, travel west on U.S. 44 to Norfolk. Continue four miles west to the campground entrance on the south side of the road.

Contact: Lone Oak Campsites, 360 Norfolk Road (U.S. 44), East Canaan, CT 06024, 860/824-7051 or 800/422-2267, website: www.loneoakcampsites.com.

3 WHITE PINES CAMPSITES
🏕️ 🏊 🚣 🎣 🛶 🐕 🚐

Rating: 7

Northeast of Winsted

Named for the tall beauties that shade this 60-acre parcel of land, White Pines is a low-key, attractive campground. Natural-wood buildings and trim lawns set the stage for good, clean fun. Social activities—from fishing derbies to arts and crafts—are geared toward families. Music and movies attract older campers, while sports tournaments are held for campers of all ages. Several large lakes nearby are open for freshwater boating and swimming.

Campsites, facilities: The 209 wooded or open RV sites have fire rings, picnic tables, and full hookups. RV rental units are available. In addition to a stocked fishing pond, the campground offers paddleboat rentals, a pool, sports facilities, and a camp store. RV supplies are sold. Pets are permitted.

Reservations, fees: A 50 percent nonrefundable deposit is required for reservations. Sites are $20–38 a night, with weekly rates available.

Open: April 15–October 15.

Directions: From Winsted, drive a mile west on U.S. 44. Bear right, heading north on Old Highway 8. Turn right (east) on Highway 20 and then take an immediate hard right onto Old North Road. The campground will be a mile ahead on the left.

Contact: White Pines Campsites, 232 Old North Road, Barkhamsted, CT 06098, 860/379-0124 or 800/622-6614, website: www.whitepinescamp.com.

4 HOUSATONIC MEADOWS STATE PARK
🏕️ 🏊 🚣 🎣 ♿ 🚐 ⛰️

Rating: 8

Northwest of Litchfield on the Housatonic River

At this fly fisher's paradise, most campsites are set beneath tall pines just a cast's distance from the mighty Housatonic River, which flows another 132 miles from here to Long Island Sound. Housatonic Meadows State Park is part of a nine-mile trout management area, and the lower half of the protected zone has been set aside for fly-fishing only; check with rangers about boundaries and restrictions. A hydroelectric power station to the north in Falls Village causes the water level of the Housatonic to fluctuate: it rises in mid-morning and doesn't go back down until late afternoon. A white-water outfitter, Clarke Outdoors (Route 7, 860/672-6365, website: www.clarkeoutdoors.com), rents canoes, kayaks, and rafts just up the road from the park entrance. From below Falls Village to the campground, canoeists will find Class I, II, and III white water on a 12-mile stretch of the river.

Campsites, facilities: There are 95 wooded tent and RV sites, all without hookups. Picnic tables and fire rings are provided, as are hot showers, flush toilets, a dump station, and piped water. Maximum RV length is 35 feet. No pets are allowed.

Reservations, fees: Reservations are highly recommended. There's a two-night minimum stay for reservations. Sites are $13 a night.

Open: May–October.

Directions: From New Milford, head north on U.S. 7. Or, follow Highway 4 west from Torrington. The campground is located on U.S. 7 approximately a mile north of the intersection with Highway 4.

Contact: Housatonic Meadows State Park, Cornwall Bridge, CT 06754, 860/672-6772 (campground) or 860/927-3238 (park office), reservations: 877/688-CAMP (877/688-2267).

5 VALLEY IN THE PINES

🥾 ≈ 🛶 🦌 🚐

Rating: 4

West of Torrington

Valley in the Pines is occupied primarily by seasonal campers. Sites are set in thick woodland hills traversed by foot trails. Anglers can try for brown and rainbow trout at the stocked pond on the property. Down the road is Mohawk State Forest, which is crossed by the 35-mile Mattatuck Trail in its northernmost reaches. At the forest headquarters off Highway 4, nature lovers can stroll along a bog trail and boardwalk to view bog flora such as mountain holly and sundew.

Campsites, facilities: The campground holds 35 well-buffered, wooded RV sites, all with hookups. Two-thirds of the sites are rented seasonally by RVers. Facilities include a bathhouse with hot showers and flush toilets, recreation hall, and a swimming pool. Leashed pets are permitted.

Reservations, fees: Reservations are required. Sites are $24 a day, $125 a week. A cabin is available for $10 extra daily. Winter camping is offered seasonally for $350. Seasonal rates for summer are available on request.

Open: Year-round; fully operational April 15–October 15.

Directions: From the intersection of Highways 4 and 63 in Goshen Center, travel west on Highway 4 for approximately two miles. Where Highway 4 makes a sharp right and a camping sign indicates to stay on that road, turn left on Milton Road. The campground is two miles ahead on the right.

Contact: Valley in the Pines, P.O. Box 5, Goshen, CT 06756, 860/491-2032.

6 MACEDONIA BROOK STATE PARK

🥾 🚲 ≈ 🛶 🚐 ⛺

Rating: 10

South of Sharon on the New York border

Macedonia Brook is a serene sound as it tumbles by these wooded campsites.

Birders favor this location for the many woodland species that overnight here during their migrations, and both groups tend to be up at dawn. Be sure to bring your mountain bike, for an extensive dirt road network leads through the park and the surrounding forest. From the park, you can hop on a section of the Appalachian Trail and hike to spectacular viewpoints over the Connecticut countryside. Hit this trail section in late September, and you'll likely meet up with some through-hikers, folks who make a six-month pilgrimage from the trail's origin in Georgia to its terminus atop Mount Katahdin in Maine.

Campsites, facilities: There are 51 rustic sites for tents and RVs in open or wooded settings. Each campsite has a fire ring and a picnic table. Piped water and pit toilets are provided, and there is a group shelter on the grounds. Supplies and laundry facilities are available four miles away in Kent. The maximum RV length is 35 feet. No pets are allowed.

Reservations, fees: Reservations are highly recommended. There's a two-night minimum stay for reservations. Sites are $11 a night.

Open: Mid-April–early October.

Directions: From I-84 north of Danbury, take Exit 7 and follow U.S. 7 north to Kent. Turn left on Highway 341 and continue to Macedonia Brook Road, on the right about three miles ahead. Signs lead directly into the park.

Contact: Macedonia Brook State Park, 159 Macedonia Brook Road, Kent, CT 06757, 860/927-4100 (campground) or 860/927-3238 (park office), reservations: 877/688-CAMP (877/ 688-2267).

7 LAKE WARAMAUG STATE PARK

🚲 ≈ 🛶 🚐 ⛺

Rating: 8

Between Kent and Litchfield

A quiet road is all that separates these campsites from charming Lake Waramaug. Stately homes with sweeping lawns decorate the opposite shoreline, and your property is just as pretty. Sites are fairly open, shaded by tall hardwood trees; sites 65 and above, at the far end of the park, offer the most privacy. Campers can swim or launch a boat from the campground's beach. By bike or foot, you can circumnavigate the lake on eight miles of country roads. Be sure to stop at Hopkins Vineyard a few miles downshore from the state park. It's one of six vineyards that comprise the Connecticut Wine Trail, a tour that loosely strings together the state's nine vineyards. Hopkins offers free wine tasting and informative tours of the facility.

Campsites, facilities: There are 78 sites for tents and RVs. Amenities include picnic tables, concrete fireplaces, hot showers, flush toilets, a sheltered group picnic area, recycling, and a dump station. You may launch your own cartop boat from the campground beach. The maximum RV length is 35 feet. No pets are allowed.

Reservations, fees: Reservations are highly recommended. There's a two-night minimum stay for reservations. Sites are $13 a night.

Open: Mid-May–September 30.

Directions: From Litchfield, take U.S. 202 west to New Preston. Turn left (north) on Highway 45 and drive about a mile until you see the lake. Turn on Lake Waramaug Road, which will be on your left, and drive to the campground. The road circles the lake and reenters Highway 45 to the north.

Contact: Lake Waramaug State Park, 30 Lake Waramaug Road, New Preston, CT 06777, 860/868-0220, park office: 860/868-2592, reservations: 877/688-CAMP (877/688-2267).

8 HEMLOCK HILL CAMP RESORT
🏊 🍴 🐕 🛶 ♿ 🚐 ⛰

Rating: 7

North of Litchfield

Hemlock Hill is a favorite destination for many campers because of its recreation schedule. Every weekend the cooperative campground

organizes family-oriented activities, from Christmas in July and an Italian festival, to bingo bonanzas and pumpkin picking. The spacious, clean sites are on a hillside shaded by towering hemlock trees, and some are available for overnight guests. You can paddle a canoe on the brook that flows through here. The nearby town of Litchfield is full of colonial charm. Driving north along Highway 63, you pass several historic sites, including Harriet Beecher Stowe's birthplace and Sheldon's Tavern, where George Washington lodged for a night in 1781.

Campsites, facilities: There are 125 sites for tents and RVs, most with full hookups. Each has a fire pit and picnic table. This full-service campground has two pools, a hot tub, bocce court, bingo, and laundry facilities. A pavilion, RV storage, sports courts, a playground, and recreation hall are also on-site. Leashed pets are permitted.

Reservations, fees: Sites $22–36 a night, and reservations are recommended. Some sites are cooperatively owned; you can purchase your own campsite and pay annual dues for maintenance. Ownerships are available.

Open: Late April–late October.

Directions: From Highway 8 north of Plymouth, take Exit 42 and follow Highway 118 west to Litchfield Center. Head west on U.S. 202 for a mile. Turn right on Milton Road and follow signs to the campground entrance on the right.

Contact: Jerry and Mary Hughes, Hemlock Hill Camp Resort, P.O. Box 828, 118 Hemlock Hill Road, Litchfield, CT 06759, 860/567-2267, website: www.hemlockhillcamp.com.

9 WHITE MEMORIAL FOUNDATION FAMILY CAMPGROUNDS

Rating: 8

West of Litchfield

The White Memorial Conservation Center owns and operates two family campgrounds along with 4,000 sanctuary land acres on Bantam Lake. Point Folly Campground is set on a peninsula, offering many sites right on the water. Water-skiers will want to reserve lot number 21 there—it has a perfect view of the Bantam Lake Ski Club's ski jump! All sites have some shade but tend to be sloped or bumpy, and many will not accommodate very large RVs; the camp manager makes decisions about allowable vehicle length depending on which sites are open, so owners of large RVs need to call ahead or take their chances.

Eighteen tent-only sites are at Windmill Hill, a peaceful, wooded area with a walking trail to the White Memorial Conservation Center. An additional 35 miles of hiking, horseback riding, and nature trails weave through the preserve. Bird-watchers will delight in the many species that make their home at Bantam Lake, the state's largest natural body of water. The center's Holbrook Bird Observatory overlooks a landscaped area, and 30 sheltered viewing stations are perfectly situated for bird-watchers and photographers.

Campsites, facilities: Between two locations there are 47 sites for tents and RVs and 18 tent-only sites. Pit toilets, fire rings, and a dump station are provided, but there are no showers or hookups. A store and marina are located at the entrance. No pets are allowed.

Reservations, fees: Reservations are recommended; reserve by writing to the address below before Memorial Day or in person at the campground store thereafter. Unreserved sites are available on a first-come, first-served basis. There's a two-day minimum stay—three days on holiday weekends. Sites are $10–15 a night.

Open: Memorial Day–Labor Day.

Directions: From Highway 8 north of Plymouth, take Exit 42 and follow Highway 118 south to U.S. 202 in Litchfield. Continue two miles through town to the entrance for the White Memorial Conservation Center on the left. The entrance to Point Folly Campground is about .25 mile farther down the road, also on the left.

Contact: White Memorial Foundation, P.O. Box 368, Litchfield, CT 06759, 860/567-0857, website: www.whitememorialcc.org.

10 BLACK ROCK STATE PARK

Rating: 6

North of Watertown

Boating, swimming, and fishing on Black Rock Pond are the main attractions at this campground. The mostly grassy, partially shaded sites are perched on a hillside above the water. Across from the park entrance you will find a road leading into Mattatuck State Forest, where multiuse trails provide excellent hiking and mountain biking opportunities. Through these very woods, Indian chief King Philip pursued colonial farmers along a footpath now the 35-mile-long Mattatuck Trail—in an attempt to discourage settlement. The wooded trail also leads past Leatherman's Cave, named for a famed mountain recluse whose former home you are welcome to explore.

Campsites, facilities: The 96 mostly wooded campsites are for tents and RVs. There's a dump station but no hookups. A food concession operates at the beach, and supplies can be obtained in nearby Thomaston or Watertown. Hot showers, picnic tables, fire grills, recycling bins, and a horseshoe pit are provided. A nature center and ball field are on park grounds. Black Rock is a dry campground—alcoholic beverages are not permitted in the park. The maximum RV length is 35 feet. No pets are allowed.

Reservations, fees: Reservations are recommended for Memorial Day–Labor Day. There's a two-night minimum stay for reservations. Sites are $13 a night.

Open: Mid-April–September 30.

Directions: From I-84 in Waterbury, take Exit 20 and drive north on Highway 8. When you reach Exit 38, turn and follow U.S. 6 south. On the last mile, signs will lead you to the state park entrance.

Contact: Black Rock State Park, Highway 6,

Thomaston, CT 06787, 860/283-8088, park office: 860/677-1819, reservations: 877/688-CAMP (877/688-2267).

11 BRANCH BROOK CAMPGROUND

🚶 🚴 🏊 ⛵ 🐕 ♿ 🚐 ⛺

Rating: 5

North of Watertown near Black Rock State Park

Set beside Branch Brook, this campground is popular with seasonal campers, so you will find some permanent structures with a lived-in appearance. The brook offers great fishing from the campground all the way up to Black Rock Dam. Just down the road is Mattatuck State Forest, with its wooded roads and trails that are ideal for mountain biking and nature walks.

Campsites, facilities: There are 68 sites for RVs and tents, most with full hookups. Picnic tables, fire rings, and wheelchair-accessible restrooms are provided. The site has a pool, laundry facilities, a recreation hall, and an RV sales and repair shop. LP gas, ice, and firewood are available. RV rental units are also available. Leashed pets are permitted.

Reservations, fees: Reservations are recommended. There is a three-day minimum stay during holiday weekends. Sites start at $30 a night per family.

Open: April 1–November 1.

Directions: From I-84 in Waterbury, take Exit 20 and head north on Highway 8. When you reach Exit 38, turn and follow U.S. 6 south. Over the last mile, signs will lead you to Black Rock State Park; the campground entrance is directly across the street.

Contact: Branch Brook Campground, 435 Watertown Road, Thomaston, CT 06787, 860/283-8144.

12 GENTILE'S GOLDEN HILL CAMPGROUND

🚶 🏊 ⛵ 🐕 🚐 ⛺

Rating: 3

South of Plymouth

If you don't mind close quarters (these sites are only about 20 feet apart), try Gentile's for a good selection of RV amenities and on-site recreation including tennis courts and a swimming pool. You can set up a tent, but the majority of sites are rented seasonally by RVers; that means you will see many vehicles parked here for good. The campground abuts Mattatuck State Forest, which boasts trout-stocked streams and multiuse trails. For a challenging and rewarding hike, head east to Bristol and strike out on the Tunxis Blue Trail, a 6.5-miler featuring a mile of ledges, beaver lodges, and a scenic lookout over the Bristol Reservoir. To reach the trailhead at the Bristol Nature Center, get on U.S. 6 and follow it east to Highway 69. Travel 2.5 miles north on Highway 69 and then take a right onto Shrub Road.

Campsites, facilities: There are 110 hilly, wooded sites for tents and RVs of any length. Each site has a picnic table and fire ring. Full hookups (including cable TV), a pool, LP gas, a store, and a large recreation hall are provided. The grounds also hold a miniature golf course, bocce court, and a chapel. Leashed pets are permitted.

Reservations, fees: Reservations are required. Rates are $22–32 a night.

Open: April 1–October 1.

Directions: From I-84 in Waterbury, take Exit 20 and head north on Highway 8. When you reach Exit 39, turn on U.S. 6 and drive two miles east. At the light, turn right on Highway 262 and head south for three miles. The campground is on the left; there is a large sign at the front entrance.

Contact: Irene and Ray Gentile, Gentile's Golden Hill Campground, Highway 262/Mount Tobe Road, Plymouth, CT 06782, 860/283-8437.

13 KETTLETOWN STATE PARK

🚶 🚴 🏊 ⛵ 🎣 ♿ 🚐 ⛺

Rating: 8

South of Southbury

At Kettletown State Park, campsites are located in the hills above and directly on Lake Zoar, which is fed by clear, cool Kettletown Brook. There's something here for outdoors lovers of many different persuasions: cast a line in either the stream or the lake—both are stocked with bass—launch a cartop boat at the park. Hikers can head out on the Pomperaug Blue Trail from the trailhead at the park entrance. This four-mile woodland walk offers sweeping ridge-top views of the lake and surrounding hills. Wildlife-viewing opportunities at Kettletown include the endangered wood turtle and the less-innocuous copperhead snake. An extensive network of interpretive nature trails near the campground is perfect for ecology-minded kids. Fresh local honey is sold at a farm just outside the park entrance.

Campsites, facilities: There are 68 open and wooded sites for tents and RVs, all without hookups. Restrooms, hot showers, an outdoor amphitheater, group picnic areas, fire grills, recycling, a dump station, and horseshoe pits are provided. The camp office sells firewood, worms, and ice. The maximum RV length is 26 feet. No pets are allowed.

Reservations, fees: Reservations are highly recommended for Memorial Day–Labor Day. There's a two-night minimum stay for reservations. Sites are $13 a night.

Open: April 19–October 14.

Directions: From I-84 in Southbury, take Exit 15 and drive less than .1 mile east on Highway 67. Following the signs, make an immediate right on Kettletown Road and continue approximately five miles to the park entrance and the campground.

Contact: Kettletown State Park, 175 Quaker Farms Road, Southbury, CT 06488, 203/264-5678, park office: 203/264-5169, reservations: 877/688-CAMP (877/688-2267).

Chapter 17

© CHARLIE BROWN CAMPGROUND

Hartford and the Quiet Corner

Hartford and the Quiet Corner

L urking in the shadow of Boston and Providence, Hartford is probably New England's most underappreciated city. It shouldn't be so. It's ripe with the region's artful past, once home to writers Mark Twain and Harriet Beecher Stowe; visit both of their houses for quick, lively history lessons that even children will enjoy (The Mark Twain House, 351 Farmington Avenue, 860/247-0998, website: www.marktwainhouse.org; Harriet Beecher Stowe Center, Forest Street, 860/522-9258, website: www.harrietbeecherstowecenter.org). The oldest public art museum, the Wadsworth Atheneum Museum of Art (600 Main Street, 860/278-2670, website: www.wadsworthatheneum.org), is located here too with its 5,000 years worth of artifacts—from Hudson River School landscapes to the Amistad Collection celebrating African-American culture. Camping is available at mostly privately owned campgrounds in the Hartford area, and these cater to RVers.

To the north of the city, motorheads should make two pit stops. Stafford Motor Speedway (Route 140, Stafford, 860/684-2783, website: www.staffordmotorspeedway.com) in Stafford Springs hosts NASCAR racing on a half-mile oval. The New England Air Museum (Bradley International Airport, 860/623-3305, website: www.neam.org) in Windsor Locks is a flight of fancy; holdings at the largest air museum in New England include historic balloon baskets, amphibious aircraft, and Hindenburg artifacts. Privately owned campgrounds predominate here and tend to be filled with rowdy race-car fans. Families and folks in search of a more peaceful spot should head northeast.

To the northeast of Hartford lies what's known as the Quiet Corner, a garden-studded landscape of lakes, forest, and small towns. Quiet, however, does not mean drowsy; there are lots of things to do. A good mix of private and public campgrounds takes advantage of the lakes and rivers, and the Pachaug State Forest is the main attraction for outdoor enthusiasts with its miles of hiking, biking, and horseback riding trails.

A sense of history is strong in this corner of the state. Herbalists from around the world make a pilgrimage to Coventry to wander among the 300 herbs planted at Caprilands Herb Farm (534 Silver Street, 860/742-7244, website: www.caprilands.com), a renowned center of study. In Canterbury, visitors learn about Prudence Crandall at a house museum devoted to the history of the first New England school for black women. It became an epicenter of Connecticut's abolitionist movement. To see how the other half lived, mosey to Woodstock's Roseland Cottage, where Presidents Grant, Hayes, Harrison, and McKinley all bowled on a private alley in a Gothic Revival "summer home" owned by merchant and publisher Henry Bowen. And if you want to take home a piece of history, the best place to trawl for treasure is in Putnam at the Antiques Marketplace (109 Main Street, 860/928-0442, website: www.antiquesmarketplace.com), an indoor cooperative with more than 300 dealers.

For details on Connecticut's state parks, see the introduction to the Western Hills and Coast chapter.

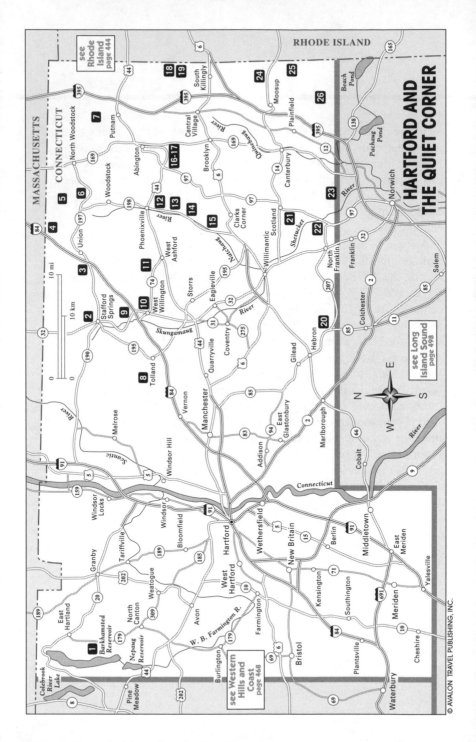

HARTFORD AND THE QUIET CORNER

RHODE ISLAND

see Rhode Island page 444

MASSACHUSETTS

CONNECTICUT

see Long Island Sound page 498

see Western Hills and Coast page 468

© AVALON TRAVEL PUBLISHING, INC.

1 AUSTIN F. HAWES MEMORIAL CAMPGROUND

🚶 🛶 ✕ 🏕 🐐 🚐 ⛺

Rating: 8

Northeast of Winsted in the American Legion State Forest

Campground regulars include anglers and canoeists who are drawn to the Farmington River, which is stocked with several types of trout, perch, bass, and pickerel and is known for its challenging white water. Class I–III rapids dominate the 12-mile stretch from a put-in at Riverton on Highway 20 south to New Hartford. Across the river from the campground is Peoples State Forest. To reach the forest entrance from Pleasant Valley, cross the bridge over the river and take a left heading north on East River Road. From here, the yellow-marked Jessie Gerard Trail starts near the old Native American settlement now known as Barkhamsted Lighthouse. At the fork, the trail to the right goes through the lighthouse site and continues north to the Chaugham Lookouts; the left fork climbs more directly to the overlooks by 299 stone steps.

Campsites, facilities: There are 30 sites for tents and RVs. A dump station, flush toilets, showers, and free firewood are provided. One leashed pet per site is allowed.

Reservations, fees: Reservations are recommended. Sites are $13 a night.

Open: Mid-April–October.

Directions: From Winsted, take U.S. 44 east to the intersection with Highway 318 in Pleasant Valley. Proceed north on West River Road to the campground entrance on the right.

Contact: American Legion State Forest, P.O. Box 161, Pleasant Valley, CT 06063, 860/379-0922; State Forest Headquarters, 860/379-2469; reservations: 877/688-CAMP (877/688-2267).

2 MINERAL SPRINGS FAMILY CAMPGROUND

🚶 🏊 🏕 🛶 ♿ 🚐 ⛺

Rating: 5

North of Stafford

Though rural, this mostly RV campground is not always peaceful; its close proximity to Stafford Motor Speedway (www.staffordmotorspeedway.com) makes it a favorite of NASCAR fans, who can be a little rowdy. The nearby New England States Civilian Conservation Corps Museum, in Stafford Springs on Highway 190, makes for an interesting rainy-day outing. Exhibits at the museum focus on early forestry tools and techniques.

Campsites, facilities: The campground holds 150 sites for tents and RVs in a mix of wooded and open settings. All offer water and electric hookups, picnic tables, and fire rings. Air conditioner and heater use is allowed. Recreational facilities include horseshoe pits, a recreation hall, large playground, and pool. Also available are hot showers, flush toilets, laundry facilities, a group tenting area, and a store selling ice, firewood, and LP gas. Leashed pets are permitted.

Reservations, fees: Reservations are recommended June–September. Sites are $20–25 a night.

Open: May 1–October 15.

Directions: From I-84 northeast of Tolland, take Exit 70 and drive north on Highway 32 to Stafford Springs. At the junction of Highways 32 and 190, head right (east) on Highway 190 for .25 mile and then turn north on Highway 19. In two miles, bear left at the fork and cross a steel bridge onto Leonard Road. The campground is a mile north on the right.

Contact: Mineral Springs Family Campground, 135 Leonard Road, Stafford Springs, CT 06076, 860/684-2993, website: www.mineralspringscampground.com.

❸ ROARING BROOK CAMPGROUND

Rating: 5

Southeast of Stafford

Here's another campground close by Stafford Motor Speedway. The campers at Roaring Brook—predominantly owner-members—tend to stay a while, thanks to the area's abundant recreation and relaxation opportunities. A stocked pond on the grounds offers trout and bass fishing, as well as a white sandy beach for swimming or sunbathing. Nipmuck State Forest is close by for long hikes through the woods. And the Nipmuck Laurel Sanctuary is just off Highway 190—don't miss it when it's in full bloom in late June. The campground also offers group activities ranging from community meals to sporting competitions.

Campsites, facilities: More than 400 RV sites fill this co-op campground. Most are reserved on a seasonal basis by the owner-members, though some overnight spots are available to nonowners. All sites feature full hookups, picnic tables, and fire rings. Facilities include flush toilets, hot showers, a pool, store, and recreation area. Leashed pets are permitted.

Reservations, fees: Reservations are recommended. The minimum stay is one week. Fees start at $545 a week, with monthly, seasonal, and ownership rates available.

Open: Mid-April–October 15.

Directions: From I-84 near the Massachusetts border, take Exit 72 to Highway 89 north. Follow Highway 89 to Highway 190 and turn left (west). The campground is two miles up the road, on the right.

Contact: Roaring Brook Campground, 8 South Road, Highway 190, Stafford Springs, CT 06076, 860/684-7086, website: www.roaringbrook campground.com.

❹ BEAVER PINES CAMPGROUND

Rating: 6

East of Bigelow Hollow State Park

The campground occupies 30 wooded hillside acres punctuated by fields, brooks, and ponds and surrounded by Nipmuck State Forest lands; trails lead into the forest from the campground. Fish, canoe, and kayak in Griggs Pond a short walk away. Annual events include horseshoe and bass-fishing tournaments. At nearby Bigelow Hollow State Park (off Highway 171S/197), Mashapaug Pond offers a public boat ramp and is open for powerboating, fishing, and swimming.

Campsites, facilities: The 30 wooded RV and tent sites are equipped with fire pits and picnic tables. Some sites have water and electric hookups. There is a special area for tenters, plus three remote sites. An additional field is available for group camping, while a conference building has hot showers and heated restrooms. Leashed pets are permitted.

Reservations, fees: Reservations are recommended. Sites are $25–29 a night, with weekly and seasonal rates available.

Open: Mid-April–mid-October.

Directions: From I-84 near the Massachusetts border, take Exit 73. Travel east on Highway 190 for 1.9 miles to Union. Just north of town, turn right on Highway 171S/197. Continue east for 2.2 miles and take a left on Highway 197. Follow Highway 197 to Highway 198 and turn left (north). The campground is 1.7 miles ahead on the left.

Contact: Beaver Pines Campground, 1728 Highway 198, Woodstock, CT 06281, 860/974-0110, website: www.beaverpinescampground.com.

5 SOLAIR RECREATION LEAGUE CAMPGROUND

Rating: 6

Near the Massachusetts border in North Woodstock

Set on Potter Pond, Solair Recreation League—a family-oriented nudist park in operation since 1935—offers boating, fishing, and swimming, as well as a full program of social events and children's activities. The well-established campground draws many returning campers. Worth visiting in nearby Woodstock is Roseland Cottage (circa 1846) on Highway 169. The Gothic Revival summer home was built by merchant and publisher Henry Bowen, who hosted Presidents Grant, Hayes, Harrison, and McKinley at his lavish Fourth of July parties. His barn contains what is believed to be the country's oldest surviving indoor bowling alley.

Campsites, facilities: There are 150 sites for tents and RVs at this nudist park. Recreational facilities include boat rentals, sports fields, and a recreation hall. Among other amenities are a coffee shop, laundry facilities, hot showers, and a dump station. LP gas and firewood are available. Leashed pets are permitted.

Reservations, fees: Reservations are recommended. Sites are $17–22 a night, not including a day-use pass of $25–45 per day.

Open: April–November.

Directions: From I-84, take Exit 73 (Union) and head northeast on Route 190 for 2.1 miles to Route 171. Turn right on Route 171 and go 2.3 miles to Route 197. Turn left onto Route 197 and follow it for 4.4 miles to the intersection of Brickyard Road. Turn left onto Brickyard Road and go three miles to the intersection of English Neighborhood Road. Turn left onto the dirt road and follow it down to the Solair gate.

Contact: Solair Recreation League Campground, 65 Ide Perrin Road, Woodstock, CT 06281, 860/928-9174, website: www.solairrl.com.

6 CHAMBERLAIN LAKE CAMPGROUND

Rating: 5

On Chamberlain Lake in Woodstock

The wooded sites are either on the lakeshore or above it on a slight slope. They're only about 30 feet wide but have plenty of shade and natural buffers. Another plus is that the owners and staff are friendly and accessible. The campground owns 50-acre Chamberlain Lake, so you don't need a fishing license to pull out largemouth bass from the waters. Be aware, however, that all fishing here is catch-and-release, and only electric- or people-powered boats are allowed on the lake. Summertime brings scheduled weekend activities including fishing derbies, horseshoe tournaments, group meals, and entertainment. And there are plenty of dirt roads throughout the campground for mountain bikers. Chamberlain Lake is also a favorite among auto-racing fans, since it's located midway between Stafford Motor Speedway and Thompson International Speedway.

Campsites, facilities: There are 120 RV sites with fire pits and picnic tables. Most have full hookups, and some are right on the lakeshore. A shower house also holds laundry facilities. Other amenities include a snack bar, recreation hall, sports courts, a group camping area, and dump stations. Boat rentals are available, as are ice, firewood, and propane. Leashed pets are permitted.

Reservations, fees: Reservations are recommended. Sites are $38–40 a night.

Open: May 1–October 15.

Directions: From I-84 near the Massachusetts border, take Exit 73. Travel east on Highway 190 for 1.9 miles to Union. Just north of town, turn right on Highway 171S/197. Continue east for 2.2 miles and take a left on Highway 197. The campground is 3.4 miles down the road, on the left.

Contact: Chamberlain Lake Campground, 1397 Highway 197, Woodstock, CT 06281, 860/974-

0567, website: www.gocampingamerica.com/
chamberlain.

7 WEST THOMPSON LAKE CAMPGROUND

🏃‍♀️ 🚣 🚂 🐕 🎣 ♿ 🚐 ⛺

Rating: 8

West of Thompson on West Thompson Lake

Wooded, rustic, and neat as a pin, these spacious campsites next to West Thompson Lake are absolute gems. A short drive past the campground entrance takes you to the lake and a boat ramp. Operated by the U.S. Army Corps of Engineers, West Thompson Lake is a dam-controlled impoundment of the Quinebaug River. The river is stocked with brown, rainbow, and brook trout, while the 200-acre lake supports a healthy population of warm-water species such as bass and perch. Hiking and interpretive trails lace the woods around the dam and lake. Dam tours are given every other weekend in summer and are an attraction in themselves. Also on weekends, nature programs are conducted in the campground amphitheater to discuss the area's flora and fauna. Deer, raccoon, red fox, grouse, and quail are among the critters inhabiting the surrounding forest of eastern white pine, northern red oak, and shagbark hickory. The wetlands area is also a popular stopover for mallards, geese, and black ducks. This is a naturalist's paradise, and the facilities are so well kept even the most fastidious camper will be impressed.

Campsites, facilities: There are 24 wooded sites for tents and RVs, half with hookups, plus two Adirondack-style shelters. Each has a picnic table and fire ring. Facilities include clean showers, flush toilets, and a dump station, as well as a playground and horseshoe pit. Piped water is available, and firewood is for sale.

Reservations, fees: Sites are $2–20 a night. For reservations, contact www.reserveusa.com or 877/444-6777.

Open: The third Friday in May through the second Sunday in September.

Directions: From I-395 near the Massachusetts border, take Exit 99. Follow Highway 200 east to Thompson Center and then make a right onto Highway 193. Follow this road west underneath the interstate and continue straight across Highway 12 at the traffic light. Turn right on Reardon Road after crossing the French River; the campground entrance will be .5 mile ahead on the left.

Contact: West Thompson Lake Campground, R.F.D. 1, North Grosvenor Dale, CT 06255-9801, 203/923-2982, website: www.nae.usace.army.mil/recreati/wtl/wtlhome.htm.

8 DEL-AIRE FAMILY CAMPGROUND

🏃‍♀️ 🚣 🚤 🐕 🎣 ♿ 🚐

Rating: 7

North of Tolland

This tidy, quiet campground enjoys an established seasonal clientele. Most sites are flat, close together, and wooded; a less-developed section is available for tents. Two clear brooks run through the grounds, while nearby Shenipsit Lake offers powerboating, fishing, and swimming. Expect to see many bird species at the lake, including cranes and cormorants. Also nearby, an easy trail up Soapstone Mountain leads to a summit lookout tower and great river-valley views.

Campsites, facilities: Each of the 122 mostly wooded RV sites has a picnic table and stone fireplace; most have hookups. Facilities include metered hot showers, flush toilets, and a small store selling ice, firewood, and limited groceries. A recreation hall, playground, and sports fields are also located on the premises. Leashed pets are permitted.

Reservations, fees: Reservations are recommended July 1–Labor Day. Rates are $19–22 a night; weekly and seasonal rates are available.

Open: May 1–October 15.

Directions: From I-84 east of Vernon, take Exit 67 and travel north on Highway 31 for .25 mile to Highway 30. Make a right at the light and follow Highway 30 for four miles to Brown's Bridge Road. At the intersection with Shenipsit Lake Road (a dirt road) turn right; the campground entrance is on the right.

Contact: Del-Aire Family Campground, Shenipsit Lake Road, Tolland, CT 06084, 860/875-8325.

9 WILDERNESS LAKE CAMPGROUND AND RESORT

Rating: 7

South of Stafford Springs

Wilderness Lake lies in a well-forested region, home to abundant wildlife, including turkey, deer, pheasant, and rabbit. The peaceful, shaded campground sits beside a 30-acre spring-fed lake ringed by white sandy beaches—perfect for long, relaxing afternoons. Only electric- or people-powered boats are allowed on the lake; paddleboat rentals are available. On holiday weekends, the campground hosts special events. Hikers can follow an easy, one-mile trail right from the campground to the top of Beacon Light Hill, where the Carbide Light Tower once stood. When it was erected in 1921, this tower was the country's first air-navigation aid. Race-car enthusiasts will want to check out Stafford Motor Speedway, only three miles away.

Campsites, facilities: There are 72 sites available, some with hookups. A special area for tents lies by the lake. Amenities include picnic tables, fire rings, hot showers, flush toilets, a snack bar, paddleboat rentals, an on-site nine-hole mini-golf course, and a dump station. Several tepees are available for rent. Leashed pets are permitted.

Reservations, fees: Reservations are recommended. Tent sites start at $20 a night, $30 for RVs.

Open: May 1–October 31.

Directions: From I-84 northeast of Tolland, take Exit 70 and travel north on Highway 32 for about 300 feet. Take a right onto Village Hill Road and continue 1.5 miles to the campground.

Contact: Rainbow Acres Campground, 150 Village Hill Road, Willington, CT 06279, 860/684-6352, website: www.wilderness-lake.com.

10 MOOSEMEADOW CAMPING RESORT

Rating: 7

East of Tolland

Grassy meadowlands provide the setting for this full-service RV campground. A pond on the property offers fishing and swimming, and nearby Shenipsit Lake is open to powerboats. A primitive area is available for tenting. Not too far south of West Willington in Coventry is Nutmeg Vineyards Farm Winery, featuring weekend walking tours of the vineyard and samples of European-style wines. The route from the campground to the winery follows quiet country roads, making the excursion ideal for bicyclists.

Campsites, facilities: There are 200 sites for tents and RVs, most with cooking grills. Recreational facilities include horseshoe pits, a miniature golf course, and courts for shuffleboard, basketball, volleyball, and tennis. Hot showers, flush toilets, and laundry facilities are available, as are ice, firewood, and LP gas. Leashed pets are permitted.

Reservations, fees: Reservations are recommended, and a nonrefundable deposit is required. Sites are $27-37 a night.

Open: Mid-April–mid-October.

Directions: From I-84 east of Tolland, take Exit 69, travel four miles east on Highway 74, then turn left on Moosemeadow Road and drive a mile north to the campground entrance.

Contact: Moosemeadow Camping Resort, P.O. Box 38, West Willington, CT 06279, 860/429-7451, website: www.moosemeadow.com.

11 BRIALEE RV AND TENT PARK

Rating: 6

East of Willington

Brialee is surrounded by state forests with three walking trails within the park and stocked trout and bass fishing requiring no license. Swim in the Olympic-size heated pool or catch rays on the campground's 200-foot sandy beach. This full-service RV park is geared toward a seasonal clientele. During the summer months, Brialee features outdoor movies, roller skating, live music, wagon tours through the countryside, and other special events. Look for the Miss Brialee pageant in June. Events also take place on selected weekends in spring and fall. On Easter weekend, for example, campers can learn crafts, attend community dinners, and participate in an Easter egg hunt.

Campsites, facilities: There are 195 grassy or wooded sites for tents and RVs. Most sites have full hookups, including cable TV. All come with fire pits and picnic tables. Recreational facilities include a pool, boat rentals, nature trails, horseshoe pits, and shuffleboard courts. Also on the premises are a store, laundry facilities, hot showers, and flush toilets. There is 24-hour security. Leashed pets are permitted.

Reservations, fees: Reservations are recommended. Sites are $37–46 a night. Group and seasonal rates are available.

Open: April 1–December 1.

Directions: From I-84 east of Tolland, take Exit 69 and head east on Highway 74. After eight miles, take a left onto U.S. 44 east and continue a mile to Highway 89. Turn left (north) on Highway 89, take the first left onto Perry Hill Road, and then the second right onto Laurel Lane. Follow Laurel Lane to the campground entrance.

Contact: Brialee RV and Tent Park, 174 Laurel Lane, P.O. Box 125, Ashford, CT 06278-0125, 860/429-8359 or 800/303-CAMP (800/303-2267), website: www.brialee.net.

12 CHARLIE BROWN CAMPGROUND

Rating: 7

On the Natchaug River in Phoenixville

This full-service RV park in the heart of the Natchaug State Forest lies at the confluence of the Still, Natchaug, and Bigelow Rivers. Brook trout abound in these parts—the state stocks the Natchaug River—and a first-rate swimming hole is right on the grounds. Twenty-five tent sites on an island are slated for opening soon. The state forest borders the campground, beckoning with miles of hiking and mountain biking trails. Charlie Brown also offers a full activities schedule including performances by country bands in the recreation hall every weekend in the summer. Shrubs, fences, and grassy areas separate the campground's shaded, flat sites. Many are rented seasonally or by the week or month.

Campsites, facilities: There are 97 tent and RV sites and another 26 sites in a group camping area. All sites have picnic tables and fire barrels, and most have electric and water hookups. Fourteen sites have sewer hookups. Air conditioner and heater use is allowed. Recreational facilities include a recreation hall, sports courts, and athletic fields. Other amenities include a picnic pavilion, a centrally located bath and laundry facility, dump stations, a camp store, and an RV supply shop. Some facilities are designed for wheelchair access. Leashed pets are permitted.

Reservations, fees: Reservations are recommended. Sites are $26–36 a night.

Open: Mid-April–mid-October.

Directions: From I-84 east of Tolland, take Exit 69 and drive east on Highway 74. Turn left (east) on U.S. 44, drive past Ashford to Highway 198, and turn south on this road. The campground is on the east side of Highway 198, .75 mile south of the turnoff.

Contact: Charlie Brown Campground, Highway 198, Phoenixville, CT 06242, 860/974-0142, website: www.ctcampground.com.

13 PEPPERTREE CAMPING

Rating: 5

On the Natchaug River in Phoenixville

Natchaug means the "land between the rivers," an accurate description of Peppertree's location at the junction of the Bigelow and Still Rivers in Phoenixville. Sites are heavily wooded and private; many are rented seasonally. The 12,500-acre Natchaug State Forest, once part of the hunting grounds of the Wabbaquasset tribe, borders the campground. Multiuse trails web the forest, following riverways, crossing hilly woodlands, and traversing marshes with excellent bird-watching and berry-picking opportunities.

Campsites, facilities: Of the 55 tent and RV sites, 40 offer full hookups and 15 have water and electric hookups. Fire rings and tables are provided, and a small store sells ice, firewood, and LP gas. Amenities include hot showers, laundry facilities, sports courts, and a group picnic site. Leashed pets are permitted.

Reservations, fees: Reservations are recommended. Sites are $21–22 a night.

Open: Mid-April–mid-October.

Directions: From I-84 east of Tolland, take Exit 69 and drive east on Highway 74. Turn left (east) on U.S. 44, drive past Ashford to Highway 198, and turn south on this road. The campground is on the east side of Highway 198, 1.25 miles south of the turnoff.

Contact: Peppertree Camping, Highway 198, Eastford, CT 06242, 860/974-1439, website: www.peppertreecamping.com.

14 SILVERMINE HORSE CAMP

Rating: 9

In the southern half of Natchaug State Forest

Open to equestrians only, Silvermine is a primitive campground reached by dirt roads in the state forest. The grassy, spacious sites are nestled in a private glen. Each has its own hitch-

ing post but little else. The extensive Natchaug horse-trail system begins here and traverses many marshlands. Loops in the trail network permit rides of various lengths. The trails are mostly gravel logging roads without extreme grades.

Campsites, facilities: This wooded 15-site campground is reserved for equestrians only. Facilities include primitive toilets and a central water pump. Leashed pets are permitted.

Reservations, fees: Reservations are required. Sites are free.

Open: Mid-April–Thanksgiving.

Directions: From I-84 east of Tolland, take Exit 69 and drive east on Highway 74. Turn left (east) on U.S. 44, drive past Ashford to Highway 198, and turn south on this road. Follow signs to the state forest entrance on the east side of Highway 198, about three miles south of U.S. 44. Obtain a map at forest headquarters and follow directions to Silvermine; it's several miles into the state forest backcountry.

Contact: Natchaug State Forest, Star Highway Pilfershire Road, Eastford, CT 06242, 860/974-1562, reservations: 877/688-CAMP (877/688-2267).

15 NICKERSON FAMILY CAMPGROUND

Rating: 5

South of Natchaug State Forest on Highway 198

Of the three privately owned campgrounds on this stretch of road, Nickerson is the least expensive and the only one open year-round. Sites are wooded but are spaced close together. The Natchaug River flows through the campground, and nonmotorized boating is permitted. Adjacent Natchaug State Forest is a great place to fish and hunt in season, and Nickerson is an ideal base camp for those activities. In the winter months, miles of roads and trails in the state forest are open for ski-touring.

Campsites, facilities: There are 100 sites, some

just for tents, others with full RV hookups including cable TV and high-speed Internet access. Fire rings and tables are provided, and shower and laundry facilities are centrally located. Other amenities include a full-service RV supply store and a recreation hall. Leashed pets are permitted.

Reservations, fees: Reservations are always recommended and are required on holiday weekends, when a three-day minimum stay requirement is also in effect. Reservations may be made online. Sites are $25–28 a night.

Open: Year-round.

Directions: From I-84 east of Tolland, take Exit 69 and drive east on Highway 74. Turn left (east) on U.S. 44, drive past Ashford to Highway 198, and turn south on this road. Drive 4.5 miles to the campground.

Contact: Nickerson Family Campground, 1036 Phoenixville Road, Highway 198, Chaplin, CT 06235, 860/455-0007, website: www.nickerson park.com.

16 MASHAMOQUET BROOK CAMPGROUND

Rating: 7

East of Abington in Mashamoquet Brook State Park

This is the smaller of two campgrounds at 781-acre Mashamoquet Brook State Park. The other, Wolf's Den (see next listing), is near the park office farther west down U.S. 44. Sites here are set in the woods above meandering, trout-stocked Mashamoquet Brook, but can be noisy due to traffic on the nearby highway. Personal outhouses at each site are a welcome convenience. This parcel was once owned by the Daughters of the American Revolution, which preserved several historic dwellings on the property. At the entrance to the campground stands the Old Red Mill, as well as the flood-damaged remains of an old cider mill, a gristmill, and a wagon shop. The Old Red Mill is maintained by the Pomfret Historical Soci-

ety, whose members provide interpretive programs for visitors. Several good hikes leave from the state park, but if you're looking for a short side trip, try the two-mile hike at the Nature Conservancy's Dennis Farm, off Highway 97 in Pomfret.

Campsites, facilities: The 20 wooded sites accommodate tents and RVs up to 35 feet long. Facilities are primitive: outhouses, concrete fireplaces, piped water, and picnic tables. No pets are allowed.

Reservations, fees: Reservations are highly recommended. There's a two-night minimum stay for reservations. Sites are $11 a night.

Open: May–October.

Directions: From the intersection of U.S. 44 and Highway 198 in Phoenixville, continue east on U.S. 44 through Abington. Signs for the campground will lead you to its entrance on the south side of the road, while state park signs will direct you farther west to the park's main entrance.

Contact: Mashamoquet Brook Campground, Mashamoquet Brook State Park, Pomfret Center, CT 06259, 860/928-6121, reservations: 877/688-CAMP (877/688-2267).

17 WOLF'S DEN CAMPGROUND

Rating: 9

East of Abington in Mashamoquet Brook State Park

Campsites here are open, surrounded by woods, and, unlike Mashamoquet Brook Campground, have modern restrooms. Mashamoquet Brook flows through the park, offering good fishing and some tempting swimming holes. Hiking trails lace the park, winding through scenic hardwood forests crisscrossed by old stone walls. One of the trails leaves from the state park and gradually ascends a hillside to the eponymous Wolf's Den. In 1742, farmer Israel Putnam crept into the den and shot what was believed to be the last wolf in Connecticut. According to the plaque at the site, the animal had been feeding on Putnam's livestock. Nearby are several rock formations including Table Rock and Indian Chair; all three sites can be reached on a four-mile loop from the campground.

Campsites, facilities: This 35-site RV and tent campground offers hot showers, flush toilets, a dump station, and a small camp store selling firewood and ice. Other supplies can be obtained close by in Dayville. The maximum RV length is 35 feet. No pets are allowed.

Reservations, fees: Reservations are highly recommended. There's a two-night minimum stay for reservations. Sites are $11 a night

Open: May–October.

Directions: From the intersection of U.S. 44 and Highway 198 in Phoenixville, continue east on U.S. 44 through Abington. You will see a sign for Mashamoquet Brook Campground, but continue east on U.S. 44 and follow signs for the state park. These signs will lead you a little farther down the road to the main entrance. Take a right on the park road and follow it to the campground.

Contact: Wolf's Den Campground, Mashamoquet Brook State Park, Pomfret Center, CT 06259, 860/928-6121, reservations: 877/688-CAMP (877/688-2267).

18 HIDE-A-WAY COVE FAMILY CAMPGROUND

Rating: 4
Near Killingly Pond State Park on the Rhode Island border

Hide-A-Way is located on Middle Lake, an otherwise undeveloped body of water. Many of the closely spaced sites are permanently occupied by seasonal RV campers. The campground's section of lakeshore offers a sandy beach and a boat ramp; motors up to seven horsepower are allowed on the lake. A smorgasbord of organized activities—a cribbage league, bingo, and crafts classes, to name a few—keeps campers busy.

Campsites, facilities: The 300 RV sites have full hookups, picnic tables, and fire rings. In addition to laundry, restroom, and shower facilities, the campground offers a recreation hall, swimming pool, a camp store, horseshoe pits, and volleyball court. LP gas, ice, and firewood are available. Leashed pets are permitted.

Reservations, fees: Reservations are recommended, and a nonrefundable deposit is required. Sites are $20 a night, with weekly and seasonal rates available.

Open: May 1–mid-October.

Directions: From I-395 at Dayville, take Exit 93 onto Highway 101 and drive 3.5 miles east to North Road. Turn left on North Road just before the blinking light. The campground is ahead on the right.

Contact: Hide-A-Way Cove Family Campground, P.O. Box 129, East Killingly, CT 06234, 860/774-1128.

19 STATELINE CAMPRESORT

Rating: 5
Near Killingly Pond State Park on the Rhode Island border

The campground's owner-members occupy most of the choice, shaded sites beside Killingly Pond, but other sites are usually available; do call ahead, though. A boat ramp allows you to slip your trusty vessel into the pond, but be aware that no motors are allowed. Swimmers can splash about in the lake or the campground pool. Killingly Pond State Park is also on the pond, and hikers will discover several foot trails weaving through the surrounding state-owned woods. For an unbeatable view of Rhode Island, Massachusetts, and Connecticut, stop in at Palazzi Orchard, on North Road in East Killingly. It's open through fall, beginning September 1. The 150-acre hilltop orchard offers hayrides across the property and tours of the cider-making operation.

Campsites, facilities: There are 200 sites for tents and RVs. Most are shaded, and all have fire rings, tables, and water and electric hookups. Recreation facilities include sports courts, playing fields, a recreation hall, and boat rentals. A store sells ice, firewood, and LP gas. Dump stations and laundry facilities are provided. Leashed pets are permitted.

Reservations, fees: Reservations are encouraged. Sites start at $25–32 a night. Most sites are owned through a membership program, but overnight guests are welcome.

Open: April 15–October 15.

Directions: From I-395 at Dayville, take Exit 93 and follow Highway 101 east for five miles to the campground entrance on the north side of the road.

Contact: Stateline Campresort, Highway 101, East Killingly, CT 06234, 860/774-3016, website: www.resortcamplands.com.

20 LAKE WILLIAMS CAMPGROUND

🏊 🚤 🏕 🐕 🚐

Rating: 5

On Williams Pond north of Colchester

Open and shaded sites are available on and near Williams Pond, where campers keep busy fishing for bass, waterskiing, swimming, and boating. Down-home planned events include visits from Santa, barbecues, hayrides, and potluck suppers. When you tire of water sports, check out the historical attractions to the east in Lebanon. On the town green is the Governor Jonathan Trumbell House (circa 1735), home of the only colonial governor to support the Revolutionary War. Nearby on West Town Street stands the Revolutionary War Office, which was built in 1727 and served as the Trumbell family store. Years later, the Council of Safety met in that office to plan the troops' supply lifeline during the war for independence from England.

Campsites, facilities: There are 87 sites for RVs, most with hookups. A few sites are suitable for tents. Tables and fire rings are provided. A store, recreation hall, game room, laundry

facilities, hot showers, ice, firewood, a pavilion, horseshoe pits, and a volleyball court are on-site. Leashed pets are permitted.

Reservations, fees: Reservations are recommended in the summer and are necessary on holiday weekends. Sites start at $28 a night.

Open: April 15–October 10.

Directions: From Highway 2 in Marlborough, take Exit 13 and travel east on Highway 66 to Highway 85. Turn right and continue south on Highway 85 for 1.5 miles. Turn left on Highway 207 and drive 2.4 miles east to the campground entrance on the left.

Contact: Lake Williams Campground, 1742 Exeter Road, Highway 207, Lebanon, CT 06249, 860/642-7761.

21 HIGHLAND CAMPGROUND

🚶 🚤 🏕 🐕 🚐 ⛺

Rating: 5

North of Norwich in Scotland

Camp in Scotland—Scotland, Connecticut, that is. Still, this forested campground has a Scottish flair. Roomy campsites are set on rolling terrain, far back from Toleration Road. A small stream feeds a pond on the grounds where anglers can practice catch-and-release fishing. If you prefer hiking, footpaths lead through the surrounding woodlands. The facilities are modern and clean, and scheduled weekend activities include golf-cart parades, bingo, dancing, and hayrides.

Campsites, facilities: There are 160 wooded sites for tents and RVs, all with water and electric hookups, picnic tables, and fireplaces. Recreational facilities include a swimming pool, sports fields and game courts, a stocked fishing pond, recreation hall, and hiking trails. Also available are free hot showers, laundry facilities, a camp store that sells firewood and ice, a snack bar, adult lounge, and a safari group camping area. Leashed pets are permitted.

Reservations, fees: Reservations are recommended. Sites start at $26 a night.

Open: Year-round; weekends only from November 1–April 3 (reservations required for winter months).

Directions: From I-395 near Plainfield, take Exit 89 and travel west on Highway 14 to Scotland Center. Turn left (south) on Highway 97, drive a mile, and then turn right on Toleration Road. The campground entrance is directly ahead.

Contact: Highland Campground, P.O. Box 305, Scotland, CT 06264, 860/423-5684, website: www.highlandcampground.com.

22 SALT ROCK CAMPGROUND

🏃 🏊 ⛵ 🎣 🐕 🚐 ⛰️

Rating: 6
North of Baltic near Mohegan State Forest

Newly purchased by the state, Salt Rock is the only state-owned campground to offer hookups for RVs and long-term camping options. Perched on a hillside, its wooded sites border the Shetucket River, where campers can float in an inner tube or fish for trout (required permits are sold at the park office). Footpaths lead along the river and throughout Mohegan State Forest just to the north.

Campsites, facilities: There are 71 sites for tents and RVs, most with water and electric hookups. Each has a concrete patio, fire ring, grill, and picnic table. On-site facilities include two swimming pools, dump stations, showers, sports fields, and horseshoe pits. There's also a pavilion for group activities. Ice and firewood are available. Leashed pets are permitted.

Reservations, fees: Reservations are recommended; unreserved sites are first come, first served. Sites are $25–30 a night, $165–200 weekly, and $710 a month for sites with electric, water, and sewer hookups.

Open: April 15–October 15.

Directions: From I-395 northeast of Norwich, take Exit 83 and travel north on Highway 97 to Baltic. The campground is two miles north of town.

Contact: Salt Rock Campground, 120 Scotland Road, Highway 97, Baltic, CT 06330, 860/822-0844.

23 ROSS HILL PARK

🏃 🏊 ⛵ 🚤 🍴 🐕 ♿ 🚐 ⛰️

Rating: 7
North of Jewett City

Neat and friendly, this campground takes full advantage of its location on the Quinebaug River where the Aspinook Dam has created Aspinook Pond. You can rent rowboats, canoes, and paddleboats at the campground, and boats with motors up to five horsepower are welcome. There is a large beach for swimming and sunning, as well as docks and a boat ramp. Every Saturday night, live bands turn up the volume; planned family activities include fishing derbies and theme weekends. Sites are either on the water or on a wooded hillside overlooking the pond.

Campsites, facilities: There are 250 sites for tents and RVs, 100 with full hookups and 105 with water and electric hookups. Each has a fire ring and picnic table. Dump stations, laundry facilities, a grocery store, LP gas, ice, firewood, a recreation hall, boat rentals, a swimming pool, and sports fields and courts are provided. Leashed pets are permitted.

Reservations, fees: Reservations are recommended. Sites start at $30 a night.

Open: Year-round; fully operational April 1–October 31.

Directions: From I-395 at Jewett City, take Exit 84 and travel north on Highway 12 to Highway 138. Turn left, follow Highway 138 west to Ross Hill Road, and then take a right. The campground is 1.5 miles ahead on the right side of the road.

Contact: Ross Hill Park, 170 Ross Hill Road, Lisbon, CT 06531, 860/376-9606 or 800/308-1089, website: www.rosshillpark.com.

24 STERLING PARK CAMPGROUND

Rating: 6

East of Sterling on the Rhode Island border

Peace reigns at this rural 60-acre campground. Sites are mostly grassy and shaded but close together, averaging just 25 feet wide. Weekend events and various recreational facilities, including two large swimming pools and a miniature golf course, make this a good choice for families.

Campsites, facilities: The 150 RV sites have tables, fireplaces, and full hookups including cable TV. Among the extensive recreation facilities are swimming pools, a recreation hall, miniature golf course, horseshoe pits, and sports courts. Laundry facilities are provided, and a small store sells RV supplies as well as ice, firewood, and LP gas. Leashed pets are permitted.

Reservations, fees: Reservations are recommended and require a nonrefundable deposit. Sites are $28–32 a night per family, with seasonal, weekly, and holiday rates available.

Open: May 1–October 15.

Directions: From I-395 north of Plainfield, take Exit 89 and travel east on Highway 14 for approximately six miles. Turn left on Gibson Hill Road; the campground is a mile ahead on the left.

Contact: Sterling Park Campground, 177 Gibson Hill Road, Sterling, CT 06377, 860/564-8777, website: www.sterlingcampground.com.

25 RIVER BEND CAMPGROUND

Rating: 7

South of Oneco

River Bend is a canoeist's paradise. It's located on the gentle Moosup River, which winds its way through a forested landscape. The river is well stocked with fish and flows easy enough for any family member to paddle. The campground rents and sells canoes, but you're welcome to bring your own. Be sure to check out the campground's display of over 40 mounted wildlife. Campers can take archery lessons, pan for gold, and search for fossils, shells, and gems in the Lucky Strike Mine on-site.

Campsites, facilities: The 160 RV sites occupy a mix of wooded, open, and grassy areas. All sites offer picnic tables, fireplaces, and full hookups. Trailer rentals are available. Recreational facilities include boat rentals, sports courts, a miniature golf course, pool, and playgrounds. Other amenities include a camp store, group area, movies, showers, flush toilets, and a riverbank beach. Leashed pets are permitted.

Reservations, fees: Prepaid reservations are recommended. Sites start at $29 a night.

Open: April 19–October 7.

Directions: From I-395 near Plainfield, take Exit 88 and travel 5.5 miles east on Highway 14A to Oneco. Make a right turn at the River Bend sign just before the bridge.

Contact: River Bend Campground, P.O. Box 23, Oneco, CT 06373, 860/564-3440, website: www.riverbendcamp.com.

26 FROG HOLLOW HORSE CAMP

Rating: 7

North of Voluntown in Pachaug State Forest

This secluded campground is reserved for use by campers with horses, as well as those with mountain bikes. Sites are grassy and shaded and are close to a swamp. An extensive equestrian trail system leaves from the campground and explores the mixed pine and hardwood forests of Pachaug. Mountain bikers are allowed on these routes, but they should take care not to startle the horses.

Campsites, facilities: The 18 tent and RV sites have fire pits, picnic tables, and horse tethers, but no hookups. A water pump and primitive toilets are available. One horse and one leashed dog per site are allowed.

Reservations, fees: Reservations are required. Sites are $9 a night.

Open: May–October.

Directions: From I-395 north of Norwich, take Exit 85 and drive east on Highway 138. Past Voluntown, turn left (north) on Highway 49 and follow it to the state park entrance on the left. Follow signs to Mount Misery Campground (see listing in the Long Island Sound chapter), then continue past that campground another 1.5 miles on a dirt road to Frog Hollow.

Contact: Pachaug State Forest, P.O. Box 5, Voluntown, CT 06063, 860/376-4075, reservations: 877/688-CAMP (877/688-2267).

Long Island Sound

Truth be told, most travelers to southwest Connecticut are coming to roll the dice: Foxwoods Casino (Route 2, 800/PLAY-BIG, website: www.foxwoods.com) in Mashantucket is home to the world's largest gaming facility. A few towns away is Mohegan Sun (1 Mohegan Sun Boulevard, Uncasville, 888/226-7711, website: www. mohegansun.com), a smaller, more intimate casino. Your surest bet is paying a visit to the Mashantucket Pequot Museum and Research Center (110 Pequot Trail, 800/411-9671, website: www.pequotmuseum.com). The Pequot Indians built the facility with proceeds from the casino. It tells the 11,000-year history of the tribe in stunning color and interactive exhibits. So come and tango with Lady Chance, but know that it's a mistake to miss out on the coastline. Some of the finest beaches in New England (and some of the warmest water!) are on Long Island Sound.

The town of Mystic is the perfect mix of kitsch and class. Once a busy shipbuilding port, it's now a tourist haunt packed with eateries, shops, and historic properties. Learn all about the history of America and the sea at Mystic Seaport (75 Greenmanville Avenue, 860/572-5315, website: www.mysticseaport.org), with its restored sailing ships and live reenactors. Present-day underwater exploration is more the focus at Mystic Aquarium (55 Coogan Boulevard, 860/572-5955, website: www.mysticaquarium.org), with its live inhabitants like dolphins and killer whales . . . more than 3,500 aquatic sea creatures in all.

To truly experience this part of New England, you must get out on the water. A variety of cruises is offered out of Mystic, from sunset sails on schooners to all-day deep-sea fishing trips. Farther west on the coast, history buffs can see the first nuclear-powered submarine in Groton at the USS Nautilus & Submarine Force Museum (Bridge & Thames Street, 860/399-8666, website: www.ussnautilus.org). Take a trip up the Connecticut River to catch a glimpse of eagles, an antique opera house (it's still running), and a fieldstone castle. It's just as easy to fill yourself to the gills with history here along the coast and river valley as it is to be a beach potato.

Rocky Neck State Park is a half-mile-long crescent of white sand along Long Island Sound with a boardwalk, bath houses, concessions, and a camping area. For more information about state parks in general, see the introduction to the Western Hills and Coast chapter.

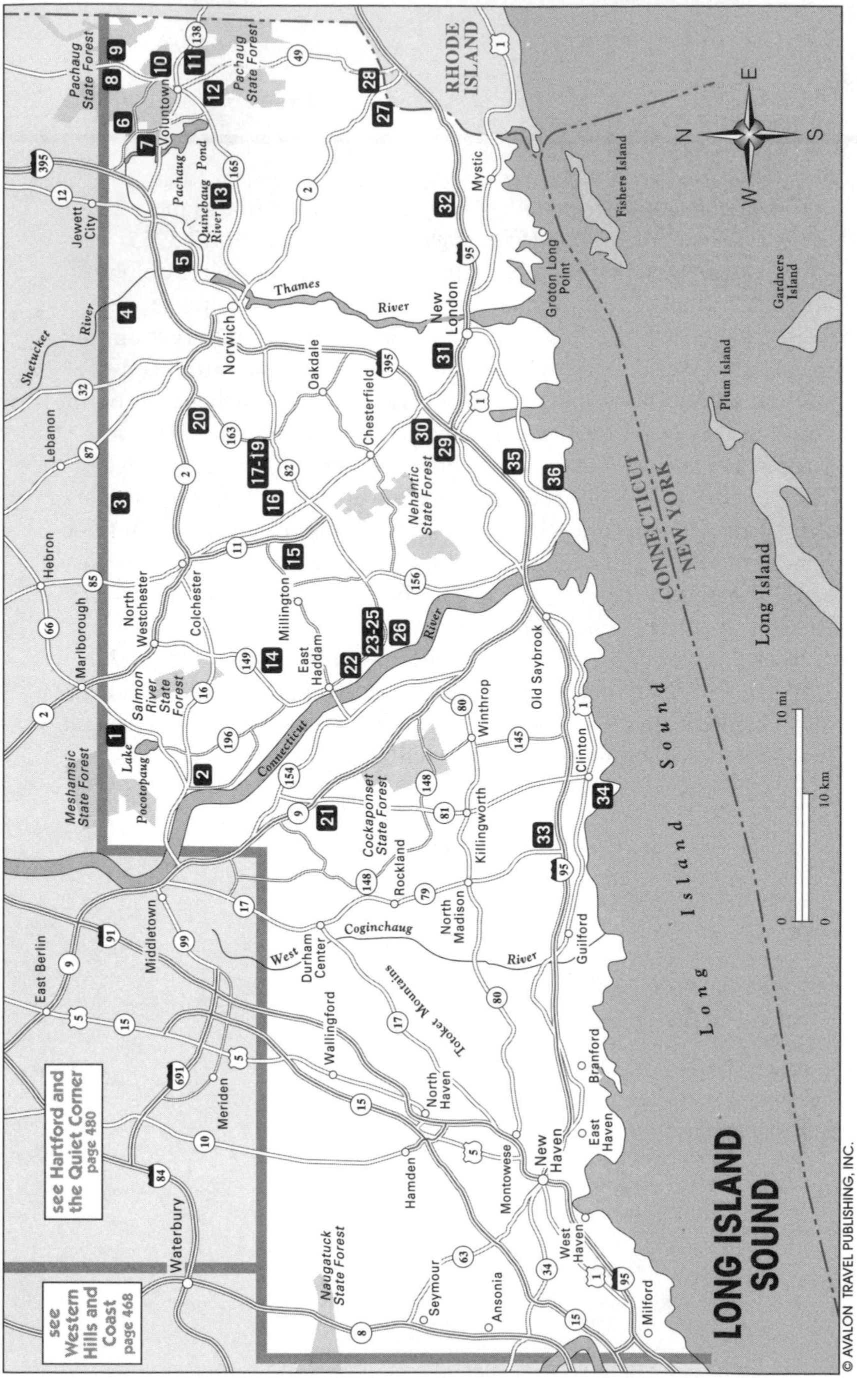
LONG ISLAND SOUND
see Western Hills and Coast page 468
see Hartford and the Quiet Corner page 480
RHODE ISLAND
CONNECTICUT
NEW YORK
Long Island Sound
Long Island
Fishers Island
Plum Island
Gardners Island
Groton Long Point
Mystic
New London
Norwich
Oakdale
Chesterfield
Jewett City
Voluntown
Pachaug State Forest
Pachaug Pond
Quinebaug River
Thames River
Shetucket River
Lebanon
Hebron
Marlborough
North Westchester
Colchester
Millington
East Haddam
Salmon River State Forest
Meshamsic State Forest
Lake Pocotopaug
Connecticut River
Nehantic State Forest
Old Saybrook
Winthrop
Clinton
Killingworth
Cockaponset State Forest
Rockland
North Madison
Durham Center
Middletown
East Berlin
Meriden
Wallingford
North Haven
Totoket Mountains
Coginchaug River
West River
Guilford
Branford
East Haven
New Haven
West Haven
Milford
Hamden
Montowese
Seymour
Ansonia
Naugatuck State Forest
Waterbury
10 mi
10 km
N
E
S
W
© AVALON TRAVEL PUBLISHING, INC.

1 NELSON'S FAMILY CAMPGROUND

🏃 🏊 🛶 🗡 🐴 🚣 🚐 ⛺

Rating: 6

North of East Hampton

While many of the sites here are rented seasonally, grassy, open spaces are available for overnighters. Families will appreciate the accessible pool, playgrounds, and recreation facilities that are always abuzz with organized events. More sedate campers should request a site far from the action if they desire a little peace. One nearby notable is the Comstock Covered Bridge, located off Highway 16. One of the few such bridges left in Connecticut, it crosses the Salmon River and is open to pedestrian traffic only. Another good day trip or evening out is a visit to the Goodspeed Opera House in Haddam, overlooking the Connecticut River.

Campsites, facilities: There are 280 sites for tents and RVs, 255 with water and electric hookups. Each has a picnic table and fireplace. On the grounds are sports courts, a playground, paddleboat rentals, laundry facilities, miniature golf, a dump station, and a pool. Leashed pets are permitted.

Reservations, fees: Reservations are strongly recommended in the summer, especially on weekends. Holiday weekends require a three-day minimum stay. Sites start at $33 a night.

Open: April 15–Columbus Day.

Directions: From the stoplight on Highway 66 in downtown East Hampton, travel two miles north on Main Street to Mott Hill Road. Turn left and continue .5 mile to the campground.

Contact: Nelson's Family Campground, 71 Mott Hill Road, East Hampton, CT 06424, 860/267-5300, website: www.nelsonscampground.com.

2 MARKHAM MEADOWS CAMPGROUND

🏃 🏊 🛶 🚣 🐴 🚐 ⛺

Rating: 5

West of East Hampton near Salmon River State Forest

The sites at this developed family campground are either open and grassy or wooded. A full slate of organized activities is offered every weekend, from the Strawberry Festival in June to the Twilight Family Swim and Bonfire in August. Just down the road is Salmon River State Forest, offering hiking and nature trails, and a chance to fish for trout in the Salmon River. Be sure to check current regulations because some sections are for fly-fishing only. The hatchery at the park entrance turns out salmon that are genetically engineered to go forth to the Atlantic then return to spawn and die.

Campsites, facilities: There are 100 grassy and wooded sites for tents and RVs, most with hookups. Each has a picnic table and fireplace. You will find a recreation hall, group pavilion, laundry facilities, and a bathhouse on-site, as well as sports courts and a library. One dog per site is allowed.

Reservations, fees: Reservations are recommended. Sites are $30 a night, and $125 for holiday weekends.

Open: May–October.

Directions: From Highway 2 at Colchester, take Exit 18 and head west on Highway 16. Travel seven miles to Tartia Road and turn left. The campground entrance is a mile ahead on the left.

Contact: Markham Meadows Campground, 7 Markham Road, East Hampton, CT 06424, 860/267-9738, website: www.markhammeadows.com.

3 WATER'S EDGE FAMILY CAMPGROUND

🚶 🏊 ⛴ ⛴ 🛶 🏕 🐕 ♿ 🚐 ⛺

Rating: 6

North of Colchester

The campground borders a 10-acre spring-fed lake stocked with large bass that are bred here— six- and seven-pounders have been pulled from these waters. Sites are overdeveloped and close together, so there isn't much privacy, but the ultrafriendly staff makes for a comfortable stay. The lake is a major attraction, offering non-motorized boating, swimming, and fishing. Weekends are filled with planned activities such as theme bingo, DJ dancing, visits from Rocky the campground mascot, crafts classes for kids, and special dinners. One nearby historical oddity is the Dr. William Beaumont House on West Town Street on the green in Lebanon. This 18th-century cottage was the birthplace of Dr. Beaumont, known as the Father of Digestion Physiology, and now displays an intriguing collection of early surgical instruments.

Campsites, facilities: There are 170 wooded, lakeview, and safari campsites for tents and RVs, with picnic tables, fire rings, and water and electric hookups; six additional sites have no hookups. Air conditioner and heater use is allowed. Hot showers, laundry facilities, propane, and dump stations are provided. The grounds offer an arcade, store, recreation hall, boat rentals, a playground, sports courts, and athletic fields. Leashed pets are permitted.

Reservations, fees: Reservations are recommended. Sites are $29–34 a night. Reduced fees apply early and late in the season.

Open: April 15–October 15.

Directions: From the junction of Highways 207 and 87 in Lebanon, travel five miles west on Highway 207. Make a left on Leonard Bridge Road and continue to the campground entrance .5 mile ahead.

Contact: Water's Edge Family Campground, 271 Leonard Bridge Road, Lebanon, CT 06249, 860/642-7470, website: www.watersedgecamp ground.com.

4 DEER HAVEN CAMPGROUND

🏊 🛶 ⛴ 🐕 🏕 🚐

Rating: 5

On Williams Pond north of Colchester

This is the camper's alternative to staying at Foxwoods Resort and Casino. You can game all day then retreat to your (affordable) campground at night. Or vice versa, since the casino is open 24 hours a day. This well-kept campground offers a recreation hall with fireplace, on-site laundry facilities, a playground, and scheduled activities.

Campsites, facilities: There are 60 sites, most with hookups for RVs, but a separate area is available for tenters. Tables and fire rings are provided. Hot showers, an arcade, firewood, a dumping station, and convenience store are on-site. Leashed pets are permitted.

Reservations, fees: Reservations are recommended. Sites are $21–29 a night.

Open: May 1–Columbus Day.

Directions: From I-395 north, take Exit 83A, then left onto Highway 169 north. Bear left onto Strand Road (which turns into Kenyon Road). Take a left at the top of the hill to the campground entrance.

Contact: Deer Haven Campground, 15 Kenyon Road, Lisbon, CT 06531, 860/376-1081, website: www.deerhavencampground.net.

5 HIDDEN ACRES FAMILY CAMPGROUND

🚶 🏊 ⛴ ⛴ 🐕 🚐

Rating: 4

Northeast of Norwich

Aptly named, this campground is tucked away in the Preston Woods and borders the Quinebaug River. June is the month to bring your inner tube for a wild ride down the swollen river. This developed campground offers small, level sites under large trees; many are rented seasonally. Sites 5–15, 17 and 18, and 40–50 are right next to the water. Families with boisterous kids dominate the landscape, and planned activities, including Christmas in July and weekend dance parties, create a fun kind of chaos all summer long.

Campsites, facilities: There are 200 sites for RVs, most with hookups. Each has a table and fire ring. Air conditioners are allowed, but heaters are not. Cabins and mobile units are also available for rent. On the grounds are a store, group areas, a snack bar, laundry facilities, RV storage, a recreation hall, petting zoo, metered hot showers, flush toilets, LP gas, and a dump station. Sports facilities include a bocce court. Ice and firewood are available, and there is a traffic control gate. Leashed pets are permitted.

Reservations, fees: Reservations are recommended Memorial Day–Labor Day. Sites are $27–30 a night.

Open: May 1–Columbus Day.

Directions: From I-395 at Jewett City, take Exit 85 and travel south on Highway 164 for a mile. Turn right on George Palmer Road and continue three miles, bearing right at the fork, to the campground.

Contact: Hidden Acres Family Campground, 47 River Road, Preston, CT 06365, 860/887-9633.

❻ HOPEVILLE POND STATE PARK

Rating: 5

East of Jewett City

The campground's flat, wooded sites are on or near Hopeville Pond, which the state stocks with fish. Sandy swimming beaches invite a cooling dip, and a large day-use area with athletic fields might be just the place for a round of Frisbee golf. Nearby Pachaug State Forest, the state's largest, offers 35 multiuse trail miles, seven lakes, many streams, and white cedar swamps. Wildlife is abundant in the area, and the campground showers are an entomologist's dream, infested with insects of every size, shape, and color.

Campsites, facilities: The 82 wooded tent and RV sites have fire rings, grills, and picnic tables but no hookups. A central bathhouse with a dump station, flush toilets, and hot showers is augmented by periphery outhouses. Other amenities include canoe and paddleboat rentals, a boat launch, and group recreation facilities. Ice and firewood are available. The maximum RV length is 35 feet. No pets are allowed.

Reservations, fees: Reservations are highly recommended. There's a two-night minimum stay for reservations. Sites are $13 a night.

Open: Mid-May–mid-October.

Directions: From I-395 at Hopeville, take Exit 86 and travel east on Highway 201. Follow signs to the campground entrance on the south side of the road.

Contact: Hopeville Pond State Park, 193 Roode Road, Jewett City, CT 06351, 860/376-0313 (campground) or 860/376-2920 (park office), reservations: 877/688-CAMP (877/688-2267).

❼ CAMPER'S WORLD

Rating: 3

On the south side of Hopeville Pond near Hopeville

Seasonal campers dominate this park, and despite rules prohibiting permanent structures from being added on to RVs, most are decked out with colorful accoutrements such as screened porches and aging lawn furniture. Sardinelike sites line the waterfront of south Hopeville Pond. Some sites have their own docks, and most have shade trees. Recreation opportunities abound. You can launch your boat from the campground, bask on a petite beach, or go swimming or fishing in the pond.

Campsites, facilities: This adults-only park offers 92 RV-only sites with full hookups. Facilities—some wheelchair accessible—include metered showers, beach access, and, oddly enough, a playground. Leashed pets are permitted.

Reservations, fees: Reservations are recommended. Fees are $20–30 a night or $175 per week.

Open: May–October.

Directions: From I-395 at Hopeville, take Exit 86 and follow Highway 201 east for about .5 mile. Make a right on Edmund Road and a left on Nowakowski Road, following the large signs. The campground is straight ahead.
Contact: Camper's World, P.O. Box 333, Jewett City, CT 06351, 860/376-2340, website: www.campersworld-campground.com.

8 MOUNT MISERY CAMPGROUND

Rating: 7
North of Voluntown in Pachaug State Forest

The Nehantic and Pachaug hiking trails run right through Mount Misery Campground. Horses are permitted at the camp itself and on the multiuse trails, which are also open to mountain bikers and hikers. From the campground, an easy trail leads through stands of cedars and oaks to the rocky Mount Misery summit, an ideal picnic spot. The Pachaug River is open to canoeing; you will find a boat launch at forest headquarters, just a short drive away. Across from the campground is the Rhododendron Sanctuary, an especially colorful treat in early July.
Campsites, facilities: There are 22 wooded sites for tents and RVs. All sites hold picnic tables and fire pits. Piped water and primitive toilets are provided. Leashed pets and one horse per site are permitted.
Reservations, fees: Reservations are not accepted, and the sites are available on a first-come, first-served basis. The fee is $11 a night.
Open: May–October.
Directions: From I-395 north of Norwich, take Exit 85 and drive east on Highway 138. Past Voluntown, turn north on Highway 49 and follow it to the state park entrance on the left. Once in the park, follow signs to Mount Misery Campground.
Contact: Pachaug State Forest, P.O. Box 5, Voluntown, CT 06063, 860/376-4075, reservations: 877/688-CAMP (877/688-2267).

9 CIRCLE C CAMPGROUND

Rating: 4
South of Sterling Hill

Finding this campground can be a challenge, so follow the directions carefully. Sites are either set beneath tall pines or out in the open on grass; some are on the water. Bailey Pond and two other small ponds on the property provide places for fishing and swimming. Bailey Pond is also open to canoeing and power-boating (subject to a 10 mph speed limit). Planned activities, including theme weekends such as Murder Mystery weekend and Las Vegas weekend, parades, water Olympics, luaus, and pizza parties, make this a fun place for the whole family. For an adults-only afternoon of fun, visit the Plainfield Greyhound Park (at Exit 87 off I-395), featuring year-round racing.
Campsites, facilities: There are 118 sites for tents and RVs, some with partial hookups. Each has a picnic table and fire pit. Air conditioner and heater use is allowed. A central bath and laundry facility holds hot showers and flush toilets. Other amenities include a group camping area, recreation hall, adult lounge, playground, arcade, and sports courts. A small camp store sells ice and firewood. Leashed pets are permitted.
Reservations, fees: Reservations are recommended. Sites start at $25 a night per family.
Open: Mid-April–mid-October.
Directions: From I-395 north of Norwich, take Exit 85 and travel east on Highway 138 to the intersection with Highway 49. Turn left and travel 2.25 miles north on Highway 49 and turn right on Brown Road. Travel 2.75 miles northeast on Brown Road and then take a right on Gallop Homestead Road. After one mile, take another right on Bailey Pond Road and continue .75 mile to the campground.
Contact: Circle C Campground, 21 Bailey Pond Road, Voluntown, CT 06384, 800/424-4534.

10 NATURE'S CAMPSITES

Rating: 6

East of Pachaug State Forest

The rustic sites are well shaded by tall pines, though they're somewhat close together (35 feet wide). The campground is located on the state-stocked Pachaug River, which offers excellent bass and trout fishing. A group camping area and a pavilion with a barbecue pit cater to large parties of happy campers. Pachaug State Forest borders the campground, providing on-site access to 23,000 woodland acres linked by hiking, biking, and nature trails leading to seven lakes and numerous streams.

Campsites, facilities: This hilly campground offers 150 wooded or open sites for tents and RVs with full or partial hookups. Each has a picnic table and fire pit. Recreational facilities include a playground, basketball court, volleyball area, two swimming pools, and canoe rentals. A group camping area and a barbecue pit are also available. Other amenities include modern restrooms, a general store, and dump stations. One pet is allowed per site.

Reservations, fees: Reservations are recommended. Sites start at $28 a night.

Open: Mid-April–mid-October.

Directions: From I-395 north of Norwich, take Exit 85 and drive east on Highway 138. Past Voluntown, turn left (north) onto Highway 49. The campground is .5 mile ahead on the right.

Contact: Nature's Campsites, Highway 49 North, Voluntown, CT 06384, 860/376-4203.

11 GREEN FALLS CAMPGROUND

Rating: 8

On Green Falls Pond in Pachaug State Forest, south of Voluntown

Most sites have rocky outcroppings and are well shaded. All are located just across a dirt road from Green Falls Pond. The Narragansett, Pachaug, and Nehantic hiking trails cross through Green Falls Campground, making this a good starting point for backpacking trips on those three state trails. The clear waters of undeveloped Green Falls Pond offer pleasurable swimming, fishing, and nonmotorized boating. All things considered, it's no surprise that this campground fills up fast in good weather.

Campsites, facilities: There are 18 wooded RV and tent sites with primitive toilets and piped water. Each site offers picnic tables and fire rings. Keg beer is prohibited. One pet is allowed per site.

Reservations, fees: Reservations are not accepted. Sites are $13 a night.

Open: Mid-April–mid-October.

Directions: From I-395 north of Norwich, take Exit 85 and drive east on Highway 138. Continue three miles east past Voluntown and follow signs to the park and campground.

Contact: Pachaug State Forest, P.O. Box 5, Voluntown, CT 06063, 860/376-4075, reservations: 877/688-CAMP (877/688-2267).

12 COUNTRYSIDE CAMPGROUND

Rating: 8

In Voluntown near Pachaug State Forest

Natural, wooded campsites surround a spring-fed swimming pond, while trees and understory flora provide maximum privacy. A fishing pond is also on-site. If all the state campgrounds are full, this makes an excellent alternative base camp for Pachaug State Forest recreation.

Campsites, facilities: All 60 wooded tent or RV sites have picnic tables and stone fireplaces. Facilities include flush toilets, a dump station, and hot showers. Firewood is available on the premises. Leashed pets are permitted.

Reservations, fees: Reservations are recommended. Sites start at $35 a night.

Open: May 1–October 15.

Directions: From I-395 north of Norwich, take

Exit 85 and drive east on Highway 138 toward Voluntown. Make a right on Highway 201, travel a mile south, and turn left on Cook Hill Road. The campground will be a short distance ahead on the right.

Contact: Countryside Campground, P.O. Box 80B, Voluntown, CT 06384, 860/376-0029 or 866/247-8316, website: www.countrysidecamp ground.com/home.

13 STRAWBERRY PARK CAMPGROUND

🚶 🚴 🏊 🛶 🐕 ♿ 🚐

Rating: 5

North of the Mashantucket Pequot Reservation

At the 77-acre resort destination of Strawberry Park, campers get the antithesis of a wilderness experience. Over 35 activities are scheduled daily during summer months, from all kinds of sports and athletics, from softball and horseback riding to aerobics and aquacise, to live entertainment, teen dances, and movies. Onsite, three pools, an arcade, and a spa are among the offerings. The Strawberry Grill and Creamery, a full-service restaurant and ice-cream parlor, operates right on the grounds. There's also a cooperative ownership program and an RV sales office. A must-see is the Foxwoods Casino, run by the Mashantucket Pequot tribe fewer than five miles away; in addition to gambling, it offers several restaurants, shopping, lodging, movies, and bingo. Nearby, the tribe has built the Mashantucket Pequot Museum, which tells the tale of the Pequots. It also houses one of the largest Native American libraries and research centers in the country.

Campsites, facilities: There are 440 RV sites with hookups in a mix of settings—open, wooded, grassy, and shaded. Each has a table and fire pit. The campground has three swimming pools, an exercise facility, arcade, store, restaurant, hot showers, flush toilets, laundry facilities, an amphitheater and stage, and a 20,000-square-foot recreation hall. Recreational facilities include a regulation softball diamond, soccer field, horseshoe pits, extensive sports courts, hiking trails, and movies. A cooperative ownership program is available. Leashed pets are permitted.

Reservations, fees: Reservations are necessary during the summer months. On holiday weekends, there is a three-day minimum stay. Sites start at $25 a night for two people.

Open: Year-round.

Directions: From I-395 near Jewett City, take Exit 85 and head south on Highway 164. Drive five miles to the intersection with Highway 165. Turn left and drive east to Pierce Road; you'll see a large red sign for the campground. Follow Pierce Road to the campground entrance on the right.

Contact: Strawberry Park Campground, P.O. Box 830, Norwich, CT 06360, 860/886-1944 or 888/794-7944, website: www.strawberrypark.net.

14 SUNRISE RESORT

🚶 🏊 🎣 🛶 🐕 🚣 🚐 ⛰

Rating: 7

In Moodus north of East Haddam

In addition to the pleasant, grassy sites, campers will enjoy dining on the American Plan (all meals included) at this resort campground. A host of activities—from trail hiking to river or pool swimming to planned events—is available on the grounds. The resort is centrally located to many attractions in the Haddam area, including the Goodspeed Opera House in East Haddam. This historic Victorian facility overlooking the Connecticut River hosts nationally acclaimed musicals. In season, daily opera house tours explain the history of the 1876 structure built by shipping magnate William Goodspeed.

Campsites, facilities: There are 66 sites for tents and RVs with hookups. Each has a picnic table and fire ring. Laundry facilities, a dump station, recreation hall, group pavilion, paddleboat rentals, miniature golf, sports courts, a pool, and a playground are available. Leashed pets are permitted.

Reservations, fees: Reservations are required.

Campsites are $57 a night, with meals and hookups included.
Open: Memorial Day weekend–Labor Day.
Directions: From Highway 9 in Haddam, drive south to Exit 7. Turn left on Highway 82 and go across the East Haddam Bridge, then turn left and continue three miles north on Highway 196. At the intersection with Highway 151, turn left and drive north on Highway 151 for a mile to the resort entrance.
Contact: Sunrise Resort, Highway 151, Moodus, CT 06469, 860/873-8681, website: www.sunrise resort.com.

15 SALEM FARMS CAMPGROUND
🧍🏊🛶🚐🐕🚙🏕️

Rating: 5
South of Colchester near Devil's Hopyard State Park

Kiddie rides on an antique fire engine are among the many special activities at Salem Farms, where both open and shaded sites are offered in a quiet, rural setting. Dances and sporting competitions are frequently held, and costumed characters make appearances in the spirit of family fun. For an outing your whole tribe will enjoy, head to Gardner Lake Park, a privately owned beach at the corner of Highways 82 and 354 in Salem. You can rent wave runners, paddleboats, and bumper boats there, or take a dip in the freshwater. The park also offers inflatable rafts, food, an arcade, and kiddie rides for just a few bucks a head for visitors over the age of six.
Campsites, facilities: There are 185 sites, most with hookups. All have picnic tables and fireplaces, and most come with hookups. Metered hot showers, on-site trailer rentals, dump stations, and a camp store are provided. There are two pools, a petting zoo, sports courts, athletic fields, a large recreation barn with games, and an adult lounge. Leashed pets are permitted.
Reservations, fees: Reservations are recommended. Sites start at $28 a night.
Open: May 1–October 1.

Directions: From Highway 2 in Colchester, head south on Highway 11 via Exit 19. At Exit 5, turn right and drive west on Witch Meadow Road. At the first intersection the road turns into Alexander Road. The campground entrance is ahead on the left.
Contact: Salem Farms Campground, Inc., 39 Alexander Road, Salem, CT 06420, 860/859-2320 or 800/479-9238, website: www.salemfarms campground.com.

16 WITCH MEADOW LAKE FAMILY CAMPGROUND
🧍🏊🛶🚐🐕🚙🏕️

Rating: 4
South of Colchester in Salem

Witch Meadow Lake is a 14-acre pond where campers can spend their days swimming, boating in nonmotorized craft, and taking advantage of great fishing. The campground is situated on the hillsides above the lake. Note that although the sites are in the woods, they are overdeveloped and in no way private. The facility offers boat rentals, a miniature golf course, an on-site restaurant, and theme weekends. From the Great Texas Steakout to Mardi Gras, all events are geared toward families.
Campsites, facilities: There are 280 wooded sites for tents and RVs with full hook-ups. Each has a picnic table and fireplace. A recreation hall, adult lounge, group pavilion, convenience store, laundry facilities, a bathhouse, LP gas, and dump stations are also provided. Pets are allowed, but they must remain on their owner's campsite at all times.
Reservations, fees: Reservations are recommended, and a nonrefundable deposit is required. Sites start at $34 a night.
Open: Early May–late October.
Directions: From Highway 2 in Colchester, take Exit 19 and head south on Highway 11 to Exit 5. Turn left on Witch Meadow Road and travel a short distance east to the campground entrance, which is just ahead on the right after you cross a bridge.

Contact: Witch Meadow Lake Family Campground, 139 Witch Meadow Road, Salem, CT 06420, 860/859-1542, website: www.witchmeadowcampground.com.

17 LAUREL LOCK FAMILY CAMPGROUND

Rating: 8

West of Norwich on Gardner Lake

Occupied mostly by seasonal renters, the sites at Laurel Lock—from open and grassy to wooded and waterfront—are set on a hill above Gardner Lake. The campground boasts 1,000 shoreline feet where all types of water sports can be played. Restrooms are passably clean. The property abuts Hopemead State Park, which has some foot trails. This region of the state is rich in Native American history. To learn more about this heritage, check out the Tantaquidgeon Indian Museum in Uncasville to the south. The facility focuses on the native peoples of the eastern woodlands and contains a unique collection of stone, bone, and wood items.

Campsites, facilities: Most of the 130 sites are for RVs, with cable, water, electric, and sewage hookups. Picnic tables and fireplaces are provided. A safari area is suitable for tents and group camping. A recreation hall, store, laundry facility, flush toilets, metered hot showers, and boat docks are on the property. No pets are allowed.

Reservations, fees: Reservations are recommended. Sites start at $35 a night.

Open: May–early October.

Directions: From Highway 2 at Colchester, head south on Highway 354. Drive five miles to the first caution light and then turn left on Winter Road. At the end of the road, turn right on Lake Road and take the first right onto Cottage Road. The campground is ahead on the left.

Contact: Laurel Lock Family Campground, 15 Cottage Road, Oakdale, CT 06370, 860/859-1424.

18 ACORN ACRES

Rating: 7

Northwest of Norwich near Gardner Lake

Gardner Brook feeds a two-acre pond on the property where you can fish for bass and trout. Primarily occupied by RVs, the naturally landscaped sites here are roomy and attractive, and most have shade trees. With a wide array of recreational facilities—tennis courts, shuffleboard, playgrounds, a pool—and nearby Gardner Lake open to boating and waterskiing, this is a hot spot for families. Land that used to be the Mohegan tribe's hunting grounds surrounds the campground and can be explored on foot trails; not far away is the Mohegan Sun Casino, operated by modern-day tribe members.

Campsites, facilities: There are 200 sites for tents and RVs with full hookups. Each has a table and stone fireplace. On-site, you will find an Olympic-size swimming pool, shuffleboard, bingo, sports courts, and horseshoe pits. Hot showers, a camp store, laundry facilities, and a recreation hall are available. Pets are allowed.

Reservations, fees: Reservations are recommended. Sites are $30–40 a night.

Open: May 1–Columbus Day.

Directions: From Norwich, travel six miles west on Highway 82. Make a right on Highway 163, drive north for a mile, and then turn left on Lake Road. The campground is a mile ahead; follow the signs to the entrance.

Contact: Acorn Acres, 135 Lake Road, Bozrah, CT 06334, 860/859-1020 or 800/772-4691, website: www.acornacrescampground.com.

19 PEQUOT LEDGE CAMPGROUND AND CABINS

Rating: 8

West of Norwich on Gardner Lake

The campground is perched above Gardner Lake in rolling woodlands. Though there are numerous seasonal sites with permanent structures attached, old pine trees help maintain a natural appearance. The lodge owns 900 shoreline feet where campers can swim, fish, and launch a boat. One mile wide and three miles long, spring-fed Gardner Lake provides great fishing for largemouth and smallmouth bass, calico, and trout. Organized activities for children and adults include dances, bingo games, lollipop hunts, and arts and crafts.

Campsites, facilities: There are 92 beachfront and wooded sites for tents and RVs. All sites offer water and electric hookups, picnic tables, and fire rings; most have sewer connections, too. Sixteen furnished cottages near the water are available for rent. A shower house with flush toilets is on the property. There's also a boat launch and docks, dump station, snack bar, two recreation halls with stone fireplaces, and pool tables. Organized events are held for children and adults. Leashed pets are permitted.

Reservations, fees: Reservations are recommended. Sites start at $30 a night; cabins $75–85 a night, $450–510 a week.

Open: April 15–October 15.

Directions: From I-395 south of Norwich, take Exit 80 and drive west on Highway 82. After about five miles (a gas station will be on your left), turn right on Church Road. At the end of Church Road, stay left at the fork. The campground is just ahead on the right.

Contact: Pequot Ledge Campground and Cabins, 157 Doyle Road, Oakdale, CT 06370, 860/859-0682, website: www.pequotledge.com.

20 ODETAH CAMPGROUND

Rating: 7

Northwest of Norwich

Just a few minutes away from Odetah (meaning "home of the deer"), Norwich Navigators minor league baseball team tests future New York Yankees . . . a great, inexpensive diversion for the whole family. Campers have access to a private sandy beach on a 30-acre lake.

Nonmotorized boating is allowed, and rowboats, canoes, and paddleboats can be rented at the campground. Organized activities, including pancake breakfasts, relay contests, pony rides, and live entertainment, keep the place hopping. Formerly the home of E. Judson Miner, a delegate to the Constitutional Convention at the turn of the 19th century, Odetah was most likely a stopover point on the Underground Railroad.

Campsites, facilities: There are 250 wooded sites for tents and RVs, many with full hookups. Each has a fireplace and picnic table. Air conditioner and heater use is allowed. Hot showers, flush toilets, a snack bar, laundry facilities, a grocery store, swimming pool, group area, miniature golf, movies, and sports facilities are located on the property. There's also a guarded traffic control gate. Ice and firewood are available. Leashed pets are permitted.

Reservations, fees: Reservations are recommended. There is a two-day minimum stay on weekends. Sites are $28–38 a night.

Open: April 15–October 15.

Directions: From I-395 north of Norwich, take Exit 81 and drive west on Highway 2. Turn left at Exit 23 on Highway 163 and continue about 1,000 feet to the campground entrance.

Contact: Odetah Campground, P.O. Box 151, 38 Bozrah Street Extension, Bozrah, CT 06334, 860/889-4144 or 800/448-1193, website: www.odetah.com.

21 LITTLE CITY CAMPGROUND

Rating: 5

North of Higganum

This out-of-the-way campground is close to the Connecticut River, which affords boundless fishing and boating opportunities. Spacious, hilly sites and a variety of activities make it popular with seasonal renters, so be sure to call ahead and reserve a spot. The sites are either in open or wooded settings. There's a swimming pond on the property and the area abuts Millers Pond State Park, where you will find hiking trails and ponds and streams that are open to fishing. One nearby spot on the Connecticut River is Haddam Meadows State Park, a short drive south of Higganum Center on Highway 154. This 175-acre meadowland lies in the river floodplain.

Campsites, facilities: There are 50 sites for tents and RVs, most with hookups. Each has a picnic table and fireplace. The campground also has a bathhouse, recreation hall, swimming pond, sports fields and courts, a dump station, and LP gas. Leashed pets are permitted.

Reservations, fees: Reservations are recommended. Rates are available on request.

Open: May 1–October 1.

Directions: From I-91 south of Rocky Hill, take Exit 22 and head south on Highway 9. Follow this road to Exit 10 and then continue south on Highway 154. Just before the light in Higganum, take a sharp right onto Candlewood Hill Road and go 3.4 miles. Turn left on Little City Road and follow signs to the campground.

Contact: Little City Campground, 741 Little City Road, Higganum, CT 06441, 860/345-8469, 860/345-4886.

22 DEVIL'S HOPYARD STATE PARK

Rating: 8

South of Colchester

Spanning a section of the Eight Mile River, the park is named for the pothole formations found in the riverbed rocks. According to folklore, these holes were made by the devil's footpads as he stomped down the river, angry at having gotten his tail wet. From the campground, you can explore the river, which is stocked with brook trout, via the 2.5-mile Vista Trail. In all, about 15 miles of hiking trails are maintained by the state park. The campground is a stone's throw from Chapman Falls, a lovely cascade that tumbles down a 60-foot escarpment. Due to its small size and off-the-beaten-path locale,

the campground is quiet, even in the thick of summer. Sites are flat and shaded by young trees.

Campsites, facilities: There are 21 sites for tents and RVs, all without hookups. Each has a picnic table and concrete fireplace. A central water pump and primitive toilets are provided. The maximum RV length is 35 feet. No pets are allowed.

Reservations, fees: Reservations are highly recommended. There's a two-night minimum stay for reservations. Sites are $11 a night.

Open: Mid-April–early October.

Directions: From Highway 9 south of Haddam, take Exit 7 to Highway 82. Follow Highway 82 across the Connecticut River and through East Haddam to the junction with Highway 151. Continue driving east (Highway 82 veers south here), and the road will eventually enter the park; signs clearly indicate the route to the campground.

Contact: Devil's Hopyard State Park, 366 Hopyard Road, East Haddam, CT 06423, 860/873-8566, reservations: 877/688-CAMP (877/688-2267).

23 WOLF'S DEN FAMILY CAMPGROUND

Rating: 5

South of East Haddam near Gillette Castle State Park

If a private adult lair is what you seek, Wolf's Den is not the answer. Geared toward kids and families, the 35-acre campground features a sizable pool, swimming and fishing pond with a beach, miniature golf, and an overwhelming array of organized activities, including kids' beauty pageants, pig roasts, and auctions. Gillette Castle State Park across the street from the campground features the 24-room fieldstone mansion of William Gillette, a famous stage actor from the early 1900s.

Campsites, facilities: There are 209 mostly grassy sites for tents and RVs with water and electric hookups. Each has a picnic table and fireplace. Campers also have use of a recreation hall, camp store, tennis courts, laundry facilities, flush toilets, and hot showers. On-site, you will find dump stations, two pavilions, and a group camping area. Leashed pets are permitted.

Reservations, fees: Reservations are recommended. Sites are $33 a night with weekly and monthly rates available.

Open: May 1–October 31.

Directions: From I-91 south of Hartford, take Exit 22 and head south on Highway 9. When you reach Exit 7, turn and travel east on Highway 82, driving over the Connecticut River. At the junction with Highway 151, bear right and continue south on Highway 82, looking for signs to Gillette Castle State Park. The entrance to Wolf's Den is on the left, four miles from Highway 9, just before the state park entrance on the right.

Contact: Wolf's Den Family Campground, 256 Town Street, Highway 82, East Haddam, CT 06423, 860/873-9681, website: www.wolfsden-campground.com.

24 HURD STATE PARK
🏃 ≈ 🛶 🗙 🔺

Rating: 8

On the Connecticut River north of Haddam

Located just north of George D. Seymour State Park, the Hurd State Park canoe sites offer access to river woodlands and hiking trails. If you debark before nightfall or rise early enough, make the short hike through the park to Split Rock and on to White Mountain for a great river view.

Campsites, facilities: The riverside tent sites can accommodate as many as 12 campers traveling by canoe. There are fireplaces and pit toilets, but no mooring or docking facilities. Campers must break camp by 9 A.M. No pets are allowed.

Reservations, fees: Reservations are required. The fee is $5 a night per person.

Open: Year-round.

Directions: Accessible by boat only, these sites are on the Connecticut River, 47 miles downstream from the Connecticut/Massachusetts border.

Contact: Supervisor, Gillette Castle State Park, 67 River Road, East Haddam, CT 06423, 860/526-2336, reservations: 877/688-CAMP (877/688-2267).

25 GILLETTE CASTLE STATE PARK
🏃 ≈ 🛶 🗙 🔺

Rating: 9

On the Connecticut River south of East Haddam

Along with Hurd and Selden Neck State Parks, this is one of three camps on the Connecticut River designated for use by canoeists only (see also Hurd State Park, the previous listing, and Selden Neck State Park, the following listing). The surrounding parcel of land was named for the mansion of William Gillette, who won fame as a stage actor by playing Sherlock Holmes and, in 1919, built his 24-room fieldstone home overlooking the river. You can access the castle and the rest of the 184-acre park by following a path from the campground. The park offers castle tours for a fee; use of the walking and nature trails is free.

Campsites, facilities: The riverside tent sites can accommodate as many as 20 campers traveling by canoe. There are fireplaces and pit toilets but no mooring or docking facilities. Campers must break camp by 9 A.M. No pets are allowed.

Reservations, fees: Reservations are required. The fee is $5 a night per person.

Open: Year-round.

Directions: Accessible by boat only, these sites are on the Connecticut River, 56 miles downstream from the Connecticut/Massachusetts border.

Contact: Supervisor, Gillette Castle State Park, 67 River Road, East Haddam, CT 06423, 860/526-2336, reservations: 877/688-CAMP (877/688-2267).

26 SELDEN NECK STATE PARK

Rating: 9

On the Connecticut River east of Chester

These riverside campsites are for the adventurous. A short paddle up Selden Creek takes you to the Observatory Hill trailhead, a great vantage point for expansive views for miles around. One good aspect of the Selden Neck sites is that you don't have to break camp by 9 A.M., as you do at the two other canoe campsites to the north (see prior listings for Hurd State Park and Gillette Castle State Park campgrounds).

Campsites, facilities: Four separate sites are available: Cedars Camp is located on Selden Creek, while Hogback, Springledge, and Quarry Knob are on the Connecticut River. Cedars can accommodate 20 tent campers; Hogback, 6; Springledge, 8; and Quarry Knob, 12. The sites are open to river travelers in any kind of boat. There are fireplaces and pit toilets but no mooring or docking facilities. No pets are allowed.

Reservations, fees: Reservations are required. There's a two-night minimum stay. The fee is $5 a night per person.

Open: May 1–September 30.

Directions: Accessible by boat only, these sites are on the Connecticut River, 58 miles downstream from the Connecticut/Massachusetts border.

Contact: Supervisor, Gillette Castle State Park, 67 River Road, East Haddam, CT 06423, 860/526-2336, reservations: 877/688-CAMP (877/688-2267).

27 MHG RV PARK

Rating: 4

In North Stonington

Rented to seasonal campers only, these sites are coveted for their proximity to ocean beaches. They're partially shaded and grassy, so there is something of a buffer zone from the sound of Highway 184 traffic. This small trailer haven is a good choice for gambling aficionados, as the Foxwoods Casino is only six miles away.

Campsites, facilities: There are five RV sites with hookups. LP gas, laundry facilities, and cable TV and telephone hookups are available. Leashed pets are permitted.

Reservations, fees: Reservations are recommended. Rates are available on request.

Open: Year-round.

Directions: From I-95 north of Pawcatuck, take Exit 93 to Highway 216. Drive a short distance north on Highway 216 and then make a quick left onto Highway 184 heading south. The campground entrance is about five miles ahead on the left.

Contact: MHG RV Park, Highway 184, Box 374, North Stonington, CT 06359, 860/535-0501.

28 HIGHLAND ORCHARDS RESORT PARK

Rating: 6

In North Stonington near the Rhode Island border

Highland Orchards was built on the 250-year-old site of one of Connecticut's first farms, and the landscape includes manicured lawns and century-old maple trees. With a full slate of organized activities (such as line dancing and theme dinners) and a wide assortment of sports and athletic facilities, this full-service RV park caters to families. Campsites are open and grassy, offering little natural buffer between neighbors. Ocean beaches are a short drive to the south. A bonus for campers is free weekend shuttle service to the nearby Foxwoods Casino.

Campsites, facilities: There are 260 mostly pull-through sites for RVs and some secluded and group areas for tent campers; all have picnic tables and fireplaces. Air conditioner and heater use is allowed. Campers have the use of a swimming pool, sports courts, a fishing pond, recreation hall, free hot showers, miniature golf, laundry facilities, dump stations, and a covered pavilion. There is a traffic control gate. On-site RV service and sales are offered, and LP gas, ice, and firewood are available. Leashed pets are permitted.

Reservations, fees: Reservations are recommended Memorial Day–Labor Day. Sites are $36–46 a night.

Open: Year-round.

Directions: From I-95 north of Pawcatuck, take Exit 92 and turn north onto Highway 49. The campground entrance is the first driveway on the right; watch for signs.

Contact: Highland Orchards Resort Park, P.O. Box 222, Highway 49, North Stonington, CT 06359, 860/599-5101 or 800/624-0829, website: www.highlandorchards.com.

29 ISLAND CAMPGROUND AND COTTAGES

Rating: 8

In East Lyme on Lake Pattagansett

This offbeat little island on Lake Pattagansett seems as if it were made for relaxing. Sites either overlook the lake or are just nearby, and all are shaded. When you set up camp in this oasis, the hubbub of the Mystic area to the east is a world away. Just relax on the beach, catch a fish or two, and forget your troubles.

Campsites, facilities: There are 20 sites for tent trailers and RVs, all with water and electric hookups. Each site has a table and is near hot showers and flush toilets. A private beach and play area are on the island. Leashed pets are permitted.

Reservations, fees: Reservations are recommended. Sites start at $20 a night.

Open: May 15–October 15.

Directions: From I-95 in Lyme, take Exit 74 and head north on Highway 161 for a short distance. Turn left, head a mile west on U.S. 1, and then take Islanda Court to the right. The road ends on the island.

Contact: The Island, 20 Islanda Court, East Lyme, CT 06333, 860/739-8316.

30 ACES HIGH RV PARK

Rating: 6

Northwest of New London

Aces High is located on 93 acres of wooded land in East Lyme, Connecticut. There are three ponds on the property—one of which is stocked with large trout. The National Association of RV Parks and Campgrounds (ARVC) awarded the campground its Award of Excellence for Best Small Park in the Country for 2000–2001. The park was built in 1998 and is set in the heart of the Mystic seacoast area, a popular destination with travelers for its proximity to Connecticut's casinos, beaches, and historic villages, such as Stonington and Groton.

Campsites, facilities: There are 43 sites with hookups in a mix of wooded, grassy, and waterfront settings. On-site amenities include laundry facilities, sports courts, hiking trails, a playground, paddle- and surf-boat rentals, and a game room.

Reservations, fees: Reservations are recommended. Sites are $39–42 a night.

Open: April 1–October 31.

Directions: From I-95 outside of New London, take exit 74. Make a left onto Route 161, and the campground will be three miles ahead on the right.

Contact: Aces High RV Park, 301 Chesterfield Road, East Lyme, CT 06333, 860/739-8858, website: www.aceshighrvpark.com.

31 TRAVEL TRAILER HAVEN

Rating: 1

North of Groton

Nothing special, this campground is located on a strip of grass at a motel parking lot's far end. It is, however, near several historic sites in Groton. At Fort Griswold on Fort Street, there's the Ebenezer Avery House, an 18th-century home built by a naval ensign wounded in the 1781 battle of Groton Heights. Fort Griswold Battlefield Park bears a monument to that massacre, in which colonial defenders were bested by British troops under Benedict Arnold's direction. The USS *Nautilus* Memorial and Submarine Force Library and Museum are also in town. Here, the world's first nuclear-powered submarine has been refitted to accept visitors on self-guided tours. The museum provides a visual account of this country's submarine history.

Campsites, facilities: There are 15 sites for self-contained RVs only located in the rear of a Super 8 motel parking lot. Each has a concrete pad, tree, and picnic table, but there are no restrooms. Leashed pets are permitted.

Reservations, fees: Reservations are recommended. Sites are $30 a night, plus $13 for sewer and water hookups.

Open: Year-round.

Directions: From I-95 in Groton, take Exit 86 and drive north on Highway 12 for 100 yards. Pull into the Super 8 motel parking lot. The campground is behind the building.

Contact: Travel Trailer Haven, Highway 12, Groton, CT 06340, 860/445-7791.

32 SEAPORT CAMPGROUND

Rating: 6

North of Mystic

Set in a mostly grassy field with a few shade trees, Seaport Campgrounds' sites are generous and open. There is a separate tenting area. Campers have all the amenities, including a swimming pool and fishing pond on the grounds, as well as access to nearby Mystic. One oft-overlooked attraction is the Pequotsepos Nature Center on Pequotsepos Road in Old Mystic. The 125-acre sanctuary has more than seven miles of hiking trails that weave through four distinct habitats and offers

excellent birding. The Mystic Seaport is a world-famous indoor/outdoor maritime museum that tells America's seaside story. Historic ships, working craftspeople, period homes, and exhibits help to make New England's rich coastal past come alive. The town bustles all summer long with tourists who flock to the museum and other attractions.

Campsites, facilities: There are 130 sites for tents and RVs, most with water and electric hookups. Each site has a picnic table and fire pit. Dump stations and service are provided. Recreational facilities include a full-sized swimming pool, miniature golf course, recreation room, and fishing pond. Also available on the premises are laundry facilities, a store, bathhouse, pavilion, LP gas, firewood, ice, and RV supplies. There is a traffic control gate and a guard. Leashed pets are permitted.

Reservations, fees: Reservations are recommended Memorial Day–Labor Day. Sites start at $33 a night.

Open: Mid-March–late November.

Directions: From I-95 north of Mystic, take Exit 90 and go 1.25 miles north on Highway 27. Turn right and drive .5 mile east on Highway 184. The campground is on the left.

Contact: Seaport Campground, P.O. Box 104, Highway 184, Old Mystic, CT 06372, 860/536-4044, website: www.seaportcampground.com.

33 RIVERDALE FARM CAMPSITE

Rating: 6

North of Clinton near the Hammonasset River

If you are a neatnik, you'll appreciate Riverdale, where the yards are manicured and the facilities are spotless. The campground was built partly on a 100-acre colonial farm. Sites, many of which are rented seasonally, are spacious and flat with natural buffers. A spring-fed pond for swimming and fishing is on the grounds, as is a pool, and the Hammonasset River is close by for fishing. Just three miles away are

Long Island Sound and its beaches. Though tenters are welcome here, more suitable tent camping can be found near the ocean at Hammonasset Beach State Park. In the town of Clinton, the Opera Theater of Connecticut is a popular destination.

Campsites, facilities: There are 250 sites for RVs, 100 with full hookups and 150 with water and electric hookups. Air conditioner and heater use is allowed. Tables and fireplaces are provided at each site. On the grounds are flush toilets, hot showers, laundry facilities, a store, dump stations, and LP gas. There are sports courts, a swimming pool, group pavilion, recreation hall, and planned activities. Leashed pets are permitted.

Reservations, fees: Reservations are recommended. Sites start at $30 a night.

Open: April 15–October 1.

Directions: From I-95 in Clinton, take Exit 62 and drive north to the first road on the right, about 200 feet up. Go .5 mile east on Duck Hole Road, turn left over the bridge, and bear left onto River Road. The camp is 1.5 miles ahead on the left.

Contact: Riverdale Farm Campsite, 245 River Road, Killingworth, CT 06419, 860/669-5388, website: www.riverdalefarmcampsite.com.

34 WILLIAM F. MILLER CAMPGROUND

🧍‍♂️ 🏊 🎣 🐟 🍽️ ♿ 🚐 ⛰️

Rating: 8

In Hammonasset Beach State Park in Clinton

With the most sites of any Connecticut campground, William F. Miller Campground in Hammonasset Beach State Park lacks privacy in the busy season. Still, the camp affords access to all saltwater recreation, and hiking and interpretive trails weave throughout—just watch out for natural preserve areas, which are off-limits. Available on the grounds are a public boat ramp with trailer parking, a nature center, and an amphitheater. Located at the mouth

of the Hammonasset River, the campsites overlook marshlands that are home to herons and various waterfowl species.

Campsites, facilities: There are 558 open sites for tents and RVs, all without hookups. The grounds offer a snack concession, community fireplaces, a dump station, flush toilets, and showers. Piped water and several buildings with electrical outlets are available. No pets are allowed.

Reservations, fees: Reservations are required. There's a two-night minimum stay. Sites are $15 a night.

Open: Mid-May–October 31.

Directions: From I-95 at Clinton, take Exit 62 and follow the turnpike connector south to the park entrance.

Contact: William F. Miller Campground, Hammonasset Beach State Park, Box 271, Madison, CT 06443, 203/245-1817, park office: 203/245-2785, reservations: 877/688-CAMP (877/688-2267).

35 CAMP NIANTIC FAMILY CAMPGROUND

🧍‍♂️ 🏊 🚐 🐕 🚐 ⛰️

Rating: 5

West of Niantic

This RVers' mecca is set on a wooded hillside close to ocean beaches. Home-style hospitality and a creative activity schedule make this a popular park. Bingo, dart tournaments, theme weekends, and cookouts are typical events. Campers can get a free pass to McCook Point Beach, about five minutes from the campground by car. Also nearby is Rocky Neck State Park (see next listing), featuring a half-mile-long crescent-shaped beach open to every form of saltwater recreation.

Campsites, facilities: There are 135 open or slightly wooded sites for tents and RVs. Each has full hookups, a fireplace, and picnic tables. A common bathhouse, recreation hall, sports courts, and hiking trails are provided. Leashed pets are permitted.

Reservations, fees: Reservations are recommended. Sites are $30–33 a night.
Open: April–October.
Directions: From I-95 west of Waterford, take Exit 72 and travel south on the turnpike connector to Highway 156. Turn left and head southeast. The campground is 800 feet ahead on the right.
Contact: Camp Niantic Family Campground, 271 West Main Street, Niantic, CT 06357, 860/739-9308, website: www.campniantic.com.

36 ROCKY NECK STATE PARK

🚴 🛶 🏊 ⛵ 🍴 ♿ 🚐 ⛰

Rating: 8

On the ocean between Waterford and Old Lyme

Ⓕ Ocean fishing and water sports are the main attractions at Rocky Neck State Park, where a half-mile-long crescent-shaped beach offers saltwater recreation at its best. A bike path leads from the campground, which offers sites in a mix of open and wooded settings, to the beach. Niantic is home to the Millstone Information and Science Center, which has exhibits on nuclear and other energy sources. The center also houses an aquarium, multimedia shows, and computer games, making it a good side trip for family campers on a rainy Rocky Neck day.

Campsites, facilities: There are 160 sites for tents and RVs, all without hookups. Each site has a picnic table, but no fireplace; campfires are permitted only in camper-supplied containers or in several community fireplaces. Hot showers and flush toilets are available at centrally located bathhouses. There is a dump station. The maximum RV length is 35 feet. No pets are allowed.

Reservations, fees: Reservations are required. There's a two-night minimum stay. Sites are $15 a night.

Open: Mid-May–mid-October.

Directions: From I-95 west of Waterford, take Exit 72 and travel south on the turnpike connector to Highway 156. Turn left and go east to the park entrance just ahead on the right.

Contact: Rocky Neck State Park, Box 676, Niantic, CT 06357, 860/739-5471, reservations: 877/688-CAMP (877/688-2267).

© CHARLIE BROWN CAMPGROUND

Resource Guide

Maine

Acadia National Park
Bar Harbor, ME 04609
207/288-3338
website: www.nps.gov/acad

Baxter State Park Authority
64 Balsam Drive
Millinocket, ME 04462
207/723-5140
website: www.mainerec.com/baxter1.asp

Maine Appalachian Trail Club
P.O. Box 283
Augusta, ME 04330
website: www.matc.org

Maine Bureau of Parks and Lands
22 State House Station
Augusta, ME 04333
207/287-3821
website: www.state.me.us/doc/parks

Maine Campground Owners Association (MECOA)
655 Main Street
Lewiston, ME 04240
207/782-5874
website: www.campmaine.com

North Maine Woods
P.O. Box 421
Ashland, ME 04732
207/435-6213
website: www.northmainewoods.org

White Mountain National Forest
Evans Notch Ranger District Bethel, ME 04217
207/824-2134
website: www.fs.fed.us/r9/white

New Hampshire

The Appalachian Mountain Club
5 Joy Street
Boston, MA 02108
    For reservations, contact:
    P.O. Box 298
    Gorham, NH 03581
    603/466-2727
    website: www.outdoors.org

New Hampshire Campground Owners' Association
P.O. Box 320
Twin Mountain, NH 03595
603/846-5511
website: www.ucampnh.com

New Hampshire Division of Parks and Recreation
172 Pembroke Road
P.O. Box 1856
Concord, NH 03302-0856
603/271-3254
website: www.nhparks.state.nh.us

New Hampshire Fish and Game Department
Two Hazen Drive
Concord, NH 03301
603/271-3421
website: www.wildlife.state.nh.us

New Hampshire State Parks Camping Reservation Line
603/271-3628
email: nhcampres@dred.state.nh.us

State of New Hampshire Division of Travel and Tourism Development
172 Pembroke Road
P.O. Box 1856, Concord, NH 03302-1856;
800/FUN-IN-NH (800/386-4664)
website: www.visitnh.gov

White Mountain National Forest
P.O. Box 638
Laconia, NH 03274
603/528-8721
website: www.fs.fed.us/r9/white

Vermont

Appalachian Trail Conference
P.O. Box 807
Harpers Ferry, WV 25425
304/535-6331
website: www.atconf.org

Fall Foliage Hot Line
(early September through late October)
800/VERMONT (800/837-6668)

Green Mountain Club
Highway 100, R.R. 1, Box 650 Waterbury, VT
05677
802/244-7037
website: www.greenmountainclub.org

Green Mountain National Forest
231 North Main Street
P.O. Box 519
Rutland, VT 05701
802/747-6700
website: www.fs.fed.us/r9/gmfl

Vermont Campground Association
P.O. Box 443
North Springfield, VT 05150
802/886-3333
website: www.campvermont.com

Vermont Department of Fish and Wildlife
103 South Main Street
Waterbury, VT 05671
802/241-3700
website: www.anr.state.vt.us/fw/fwhome

Vermont Department of Forests, Parks, and Recreation
Division of State Parks
103 South Main Street
Waterbury, VT 05671
802/241-3655
website: www.state.vt.us/anr/fpr/parks

Vermont Department of Travel and Tourism
134 State Street
Montpelier, VT 05602
802/828-3236
website: www.1-800-vermont.com

Massachusetts

Cape Cod National Seashore
99 Marconi Station Site Road
Wellfleet, MA 02667
508/255-3421, 508/487-1256
website: www.nps.gov/caco

Division of Environmental Management
Division of Forests and Parks
251 Causeway St., Suite 600, Boston, MA 02114
617/626-1250
website: www.massparks.org

Fall Foliage Hot Line
(early September through late October),
800/632-8038

Massachusetts Association of Campground Owners
P.O. Box 548
Scituate, MA 02066
617/544-3457
website: www.campmass.com

Massachusetts Division of Fisheries and Wildlife
1 Rabbit Hill Road
Westboro, MA 01581
508/792-7270
website: www.state.ma.us/dfwele/dfw/ dfw_toc.htm

Massachusetts Office of Travel and Tourism

10 Park Plaza, Suite 4510
Boston, MA 02116
800/227-MASS
617/973-8500
website: www.massvacation.com

Rhode Island

Rhode Island Division of Tourism

1 West Exchange Street, Providence, RI 02903
800/556-2484
website: www.visitrhodeisland.com

Connecticut

Connecticut Campground Owners Association Inc.

14 Rumford Street
West Hartford, CT 06107-3761
860/521-4704
website: www.campconn.com

Connecticut Department of Environmental Protection

Bureau of Outdoor Recreation
79 Elm Street
Hartford, CT 06106-5127
860/424-3200
website: dep.state.ct.us/rec/

Connecticut Office of Tourism

505 Hudson Street
Hartford, CT 06106
860/270-8080
website: www.ctbound.org

Acknowledgements

Heartfelt thanks to all of those who work to keep America free.

–C.C.

I am grateful to the sons and daughters of Thoreau who have struggled to keep the wild in New England. Each of us with an interest in this book owes you a large debt.

–S.G.

The chapters on Maine and Rhode Island were written by Stephen Gorman, and those on New Hampshire, Vermont, Massachusetts, and Connecticut were written by Carol Cambo. Both authors contributed to the Camping Tips section.

Index

C

St. Johnsbury: 308
Stadig Campground: 145
Stafford: 481
Stafford Springs: 485
Stateline Campresort: 489
Steep Falls: 106
Stephen Phillips Memorial Preserve: 84
Sterling Hill: 502
Sterling Park Campground: 492
Sterling: 492
Stetson Shores Campground: 73
Stillwater State Park: 312
Stockbridge: 379
Stonington on Deer Isle: 160
Stony Brook Recreation: 90
Stowe: 301, 304, 307
Strawberry Park Campground: 504
Sturbridge Webster KOA: 403
Sturbridge: 397–399
Sugar Ridge RV Village and Campground, Inc.: 308
Sugar River: 229
Sugarhouse Campground: 328
Sugarloaf Campgrounds I and II: 196
Sugarloaf Mtn.: **82**
Sugarloaf Resort: 85
Sullivan: 235
Summit Hill Campground: 375
Sunrise Resort: 504
Sunset Park Campground: 278
Sunset Point Trailer Park: 170
Sunsetview Farm Camping Area: 396
Sunshine Campground: 159
Surry Mountain Camping Area: 235
Surry Mountain Lake: 235
Sutton Falls Camping Area: 401

Swain Brook Campground: 214
Swain Brook: 214
Swains Lake: 268
Swanzey Lake Camping Area: 239
Swanzey Lake: 239
Sweetwater Forest: 434
Swift River: 218

T

Tamarack Trails Camping Park: 231
Tamworth Camping Area: 218
Tarry-Ho Campground and Cottages: 194
Taunton: 417
Telos Management Unit: 47
Tent Village Travel Trailer Park: 74
Terrace Pines Campground: 252
Thames River: **498**
The Beach Camping Area: 208
The Gatherings Family Campground: 157
The Green Gate Camping Area: 274
The Last Resort Campground and Cabins: 62
The Moorings Oceanfront Campground: 114
The Pastures Campground: 213
The Pines: 391
The Seaview: 167
The Woodlot Campground: 400
Thetford Hill State Park: 346
Thomas Point Beach and Campground: 123
Thousand Acres Family Campground: 262
Three Ponds Campground: 272

Ticklenaked Pond: 315
Tidewater Campground: 276
Timberland Camping Area: 186
Toddy Pond: 155
Tolland State Forest: 380
Tolland: 484
Topsfield: 153
Torrington: 471
Town Line Campsites: 120
Townsend: 354
Townshend State Park: 353
Travel Trailer Haven: 511
Traveler's Woods of New England: 367
Tree Farm Campground: 353
Trickey Pond: 101
Tripp Lake: 102
Trout Brook Farm Campground: 48
Tully Lake Campground: 390
Tully Lake: 390
Tunxis State Forest: **468**
Tuxbury Pond Camping Area: 278
Tuxbury Pond: 278
Twin Brooks Camping Area: 105
Twin Mountain KOA Kampground: 191
Twin Mountain Motor Court and RV Park: 193
Twin Mountain: 191–195
Twin River Campground & Cottages: 199
Twin Tamarack Family Camping and RV Resort: 259
Two Lakes Campground: 97
Two Rivers Campground: 72

UV

Umbagog Lake State Park: 181
Umbagog Lake: 181, **82**
Underhill State Park: 303
Valley in the Pines: 471

Notes

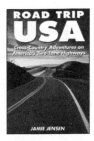

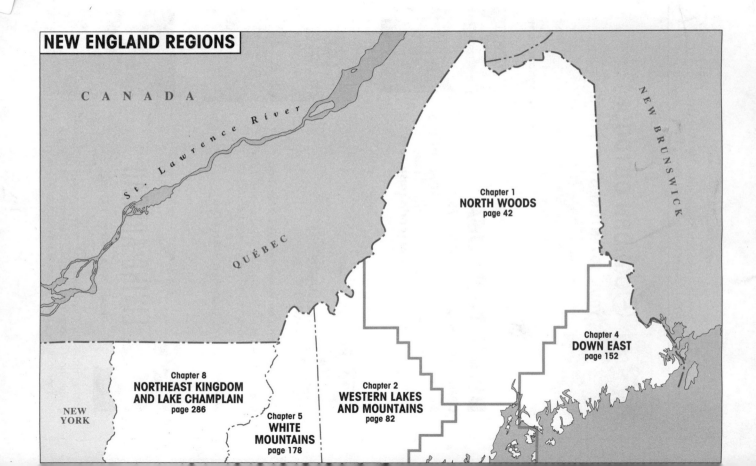

NEW ENGLAND REGIONS

CANADA

St. Lawrence River

QUÉBEC

NEW YORK

NEW BRUNSWICK

Chapter 1
NORTH WOODS
page 42

Chapter 4
DOWN EAST
page 152

Chapter 8
NORTHEAST KINGDOM
AND LAKE CHAMPLAIN
page 286

Chapter 2
WESTERN LAKES
AND MOUNTAINS
page 82

Chapter 5
WHITE
MOUNTAINS
page 178